# Jimmy Carter

BETTY GLAD

# Jimmy Carter

In search of the great

White House

———

W·W·NORTON & COMPANY

NEW YORK·LONDON

**FIRST EDITION**

THE TEXT OF THIS BOOK *is composed in photocomposition Caledonia. The display type used is Americana Bold. Composition and manufacturing are by the Maple-Vail Book Manufacturing Group. Book design is by Marjorie J. Flock.*

*For my mother*
*Edna Geertsen Glad*

Library of Congress Cataloging in Publication Data
Glad, Betty.
   Jimmy Carter, in search of the great White House.
   Includes index.
   1. Carter, Jimmy, 1924–     2. Georgia—
Politics and government—1951–     3. United States—
Politics and government—1977–     4. Presidents—
United States—Bibliography.   I. Title.
E873.G56   1980     973.926'092'4 [B]   80-14744

ISBN 0-393-07527-3

W. W. Norton & Company, Inc. 500 Fifth Avenue, New York, N.Y. 10110
W. W. Norton & Company, Ltd, 25 New Street Square, London, EC4A3-NT
1 2 3 4 5 6 7 8 9 0

# Contents

## I  Early Life

## II  Governorship

## III  Campaign Strategy

## IV  Rhetoric: Love Sweeps the Nation

## V  Presidency

## VI  Interpretations

# Preface

ARLY IN THE COURSE of this inquiry, I discovered that I had undertaken a more formidable task than first anticipated. When I began my research in August of 1976, there were no listings for Jimmy Carter in the Library of Congress card catalogue. Though stories about Carter's past and his character had been flooding the media for the preceding eight months, no independently investigated histories of his life had yet appeared. I quickly discovered that many of the stories circulating about Carter—including some originating with Carter and his family—were factually inaccurate. As a consequence, I have found it necessary to corroborate almost every "fact," either by reference to the public record or by interviews with independent sources.

There are also special methodological problems in writing a biography of any contemporary political figure, particularly a President in office. Direct access to a person holding high office is hard to obtain. Even interviews with associates present problems: close friends and political intimates are apt to be motivated by a desire to assist the leader politically and to protect their own positions in the inner circle. Those who are not constrained by these concerns are apt to be removed from the decision-making center and therefore know less.

The researcher may also have considerable difficulty in distinguishing the public-relations façade from underlying realities. Politicians, as Arnold Rogow states, "are a notoriously secretive lot, and any inkblots they had inadvertently left behind are usually wiped clean by their loyal posterity." The live politician—the presidential candidate or incumbent President—is inevitably on stage, his tastes, political philosophy, and personal style screened by aides and media advisers to assist him in projecting a winning image. Even his own recollections of the past may be screened to coincide with prevailing ideas of how a President's character should be formed.

The problems are not insuperable, however. One way to distinguish the substance from the façade is to check for inconsistencies against the public record and the recollection of others, to seek corroborative testimony, and to look for data in out-of-the-way, unpublicized places. Further, as any psychoanalytically oriented observer is aware, not even a President or a candidate can control all personal projections. Underlying attitudes may be expressed through slips of the tongue, facial expressions, postures, and patterns of speech and behavior. Observers armed with psychoanalytic theory will attend to data the traditionalist may reject or ignore as too private and personal, or simply irrelevant. "Much of this," Rogow says, "may appear to be 'nit picking,' but it is well to keep in mind that it is the nits in psychoanalysis, the seemingly trivial episodes to which, at the time, little importance may be attached, that often supply the principal clues to personality development."

One can also deal with the façade and the access problem, as I have done, by commencing one's research with Jimmy Carter's associates as well as with social and political competitors. (Overall, I have been in touch with over 300 such individuals through interviews, letters, and questionnaires.) To maximize candor, I have used a variety of techniques. Most interview subjects were assured beforehand that they would receive a consent form in which they might provide conditions for use of the material, and most received copies of the interview for correction. Further, I have had information on most persons interviewed before the interview, which helped us to ask questions germane to their relationship with Carter. Where there have been factual contradictions among the accounts of various persons interviewed, I have attempted to corroborate the data against the public record. Where there are differing perceptions or evaluations of Carter's activities or events connected with him, I have attempted to indicate that such differing perceptions exist. The truth about some matters, of course, cannot always be resolved.

My interviewees are listed (with the exception of a few persons who requested anonymity) in the source notes. Most of the earlier interviews were done in person; many of the later ones were done by telephone and were summarized immediately thereafter by the interviewer and the summary sent to the interviewee for corrections. Generally, I have not used data secured through these interviews unless the interviewee agreed that the material could be directly attributed. In a few instances where the data was vital and congruent with other accounts, or the quotation or opinion particularly important, I have used the item without specific citation. It should be noted that all information used here is in my interview file, which, along with the rest of my research material, will be contributed to the University of Illinois Library on terms set by each interviewee.

Aside from the interviews, which cover all periods of Carter's life, I was able to assemble an extensive public record of Carter's life—although the data has been scattered and finding it has necessitated considerable digging. To reconstruct Carter's life in Plains, as both a man and a child, I assembled articles (from 1915 through 1976) from the Americus *Times-Recorder,* which documents the comings and goings, all the social and political events of middle-class families in the region, such as the Carters—people who would have remained virtually unnoticed in a larger urban setting. The details of Carter's family background and his early life in Plains can be reconstructed from birth, marriage, and land records in the Sumter County Courthouse, in the yearbooks and old records of the Plains schools (in the Plains High School library and a materials storage center just south of Plains). Recently published books by Gloria Carter Spann, Ruth Carter Stapleton, and Hugh Carter, Sr., give further data on the Carter clan in the early years. And naturally, Carter's own campaign autobiography, *Why Not the Best?*, served as a first step in beginning much of the research and later analysis. (It is particularly useful as a source of Carter's recollections of the past, if not always factually correct.) Descriptions of the educational settings at Annapolis and Georgia Tech, as well as Carter class standing, are available in published materials covering those institutions. Carter's assignments and duties as a Navy officer and the lists of his fellow crew members during his submarine service have been verified by documents secured from the Department of Defense.

Carter's earlier public life is partially recorded in the Journal of the Georgia Senate, various Sumter County Courthouse records, and several local newspapers: the Americus *Times-Recorder* (the daily newspaper from Carter's own Sumter County), the Columbus *Enquirer*, and the Albany *Herald*.

For Carter's work as governor, I went through his correspondence and interoffice memos in the Georgia Archives, his speeches as published by the state (*Addresses of James Earl Carter, 1971–75*), the Georgia House Journal and the Georgia Senate Journal (which record the governor's official messages and all the various procedural motions and votes in each body), the *Georgia Official and Statistical Register* (which lists state and county government and party officials, giving biographical material on them, official vote counts for all state offices, and other such data); the Atlanta *Journal* and the Atlanta *Constitution*, which provide extensive coverage of his 1970 campaign, his four years as governor, and his early presidential campaign.

For the presidency and the 1976 campaign, I have relied on over 100 interviews with Carter and his associates published in the national press, Carter speeches, statements and position papers (many drawn from three volumes published by the U.S. House of Representatives [*The Presidential Campaign 1976*] and one by Simon and Schuster, 1977). I have also surveyed the New York *Times*, Washington *Post*, *Wall Street Journal*, Chicago *Tribune*, Chicago *Sun-Times*, Boston *Globe* and Los Angeles *Times*, the major periodical press (including *Time* and *Newsweek*), and samples from the ethnic and special-interest press. Further, Wesley Pippert's *The Spiritual Journey of Jimmy Carter* provides a compilation of many of Carter's sermons, prayers, Sunday school lessons, interviews, speeches, and remarks to religious gatherings. The television news coverage of Carter's presidential campaigns and presidency is available on tape at Vanderbilt University in Nashville. Many of Carter's 1976 and some of the 1970 campaign commercials are on deposit at the University of Georgia.

I had the opportunity to observe Carter directly by working with the press corps that covered Carter in August, 1976. On that trip and subsequent visits to Atlanta, Archery, Plains, and other points in south Georgia, I have explored the areas where Jimmy Carter lived and vacationed, the fields where he played, the schools and churches where he was trained, the places he worked, and the homes of friends.

# Acknowledgments

I AM PARTICULARLY INDEBTED in this work to several research assistants. Dennis Rendleman and Sue Osuch-Hatziavramidis served beyond the call of duty—interviewing, gathering and summarizing background materials, making final editorial suggestions, checking footnotes—throughout the course of this work. Gary Reger and Chris Simpson did the same thing for sizable portions of the work. Nancy Carter Dunn patiently dug through Carter's gubernatorial papers in the Georgia State Archives in Atlanta. Nancy DiBello went through the Journals of the Georgia legislature to trace Carter's early senate career. David Crawford helped organize and prepare background materials on the governorship. Margaret Hayes and Mary Kay Buysse prepared background material and typed draft for the 1976 campaign. John Portz went through the Federal Election Commission reports in Washington and with the help of Dr. Herbert Portz checked publications in the library at Annapolis. Dennis Davis read the sections on Carter's religion and made editorial suggestions for some of the earlier chapters. Denise Abbott, Sandra Spring, Catherine Reisner, Pat Stoner, Louise Hubb, and Ronie Johnston and her staff patiently typed the transcripts of interviews and/or the numerous drafts of this manuscript. Jill Blardinelli, Lynn Clark, Christina Dye, Jay Frank, Shirley Furst, Mario Greszes, James Parker, David Piercy, Tony Sullivan, Susan Swearingen, and Barry Borisch helped out for shorter periods of time.

The staff of the newspaper library at the University of Illinois were patient as we monopolized their microfilm reading machines. Sally Wermerantz and her staff were extraordinarily helpful in securing a wide variety and large volume of newspapers and books on interlibrary loan. The Graduate Research Board at the University of Illinois and the Department of Political Science there provided partial funding for travel, photocopying, and manuscript preparation.

Several friends and colleagues have given me the benefits of their expertise. James MacGregor Burns of Williams College, Richard Cottam of the University of Pittsburgh, and Lawrence Levine of the University of California, Berkeley, read the manuscript and gave me the hard but kind criticism one can only expect from friends. Barbara Yates of the University of Illinois patiently listened as I worked out my interpretations of Carter. Virginia Robinson of the Neuro-Psychiatric Institute, University of Illinois Medical Center, gave me good leads on relevant psychoanalytical literature and read my interpretations in the final chapters. Joyce Smith has given me the benefit of her experiences as a Southerner, theology student, and professional psychologist. Harriet Imrey read the section on the presidency, making several useful editorial suggestions. R. Ann Cline and Barbara Shelow came to my aid, typing chapter drafts when I was in a pinch. I am especially indebted to Jeanette Hopkins for her editorial assistance and to Margaret Gates, who put aside her own work to help me meet a publisher's deadline by doing background analysis on Carter's foreign policies and aiding me with the footnotes. Bonnie Donovan was most helpful as copy editor. T. Mc N. Simpson, III kindly sent me his unpublished manuscript *Jimmy Carter: Governor of Georgia.* It provided a good background on the organization of the Georgia government. Ngo Tuan Sit sent me his *Jimmy Carter: A Case Study of the Impact of Christian Beliefs on the Political Leader's "Operational Codes"* (M.A. thesis, University of Canterbury). Both works provided a perspective different from the one given here. I also want to acknowledge Gary Orfield, Marie Golla (O.P.), Thomas Casey (S.J.), Sheila Wiley, and Rozanne Rothman who gave me some help—and Dean Sagar who first suggested I do this book and George Brockway, my editor at W. W. Norton, who saw it through at the end.

The many Carter friends and associates and the other people who have given me material, written letters, consented to interviews, or answered questionnaires are too numerous to mention here—all are identified in the footnotes. Some of them have different interpretations of Jimmy Carter from the one I have presented, but I hope they will understand that the obligations of a scholar overide the feelings of friendship and personal indebtedness.

# In Search of Jimmy Carter

RIVING BACK TO ATLANTA from a dinner party in the suburbs one evening in the early 1960s, Jimmy Carter, then a state senator, looked out at the gilded dome on the Georgia state capitol building, which was bathed in its own spotlights. "It's a beautiful sight," he said softly to his friends in the car. "You know, I thought I would never make it."

That was probably one of Jimmy Carter's most revealing moments. He had a dream to be fulfilled, a treasure to capture. Yet he was less sure of himself than he seemed to be. His sights had always been set higher than the goal just achieved. In rural Plains High School, Carter confided to friends that he would be governor of Georgia one day. At Annapolis he had thought he might become Chief of Naval Operations. And in 1966, with almost no statewide backing, he undertook a campaign to become governor. Profoundly depressed by defeat, he nevertheless immediately began a four-year campaign that would eventually place him in the governor's office—also under that golden dome.

But even before he had secured the governorship, Carter may have had his eye on a more distant prize. One of his closest neighbors had written to a mutual acquaintance in 1966 that the gossip around Sumter County was that Carter was running for President. And Lillian Carter, at the time of his first and unsuccessful bid for the Georgia governorship, confided to friends in her Peace Corps training group that her son would be President one day. Certainly Carter was looking ahead to national office by the summer of 1972, and for the next four years he would concentrate on winning the presidency—an unknown, a genuine dark horse, Jimmy Who?

He sought the prize with single-mindedness and tenacity. The tears he would shed with his supporters in Plains on the night he won the presidency showed how much he had wanted—and needed—that prize.

Yet nothing in Carter's early life—in Archery or Plains or in the Navy— suggested that his ambition was ruled by a passion for justice. His friends do not recall his showing any great interest in political change in his early adult years. As late as 1976 it was not clear why he wanted to be President, what he would do with the presidency when he got it. He did not even seem to have a deep interest in the substance of politics, or special taste for the wheeling and dealing that goes with it—at least in the beginning. While still a young man, he had confided in one friend his scorn for politicians. And in his own political campaigning from 1962 to 1976, he would act as if he was above politics-as-usual.

In other ways Carter has been a puzzling figure. Though he campaigned above politics—he was the ultimate politician in practice. He saw opportunities others missed, and on the campaign trail he knew how to touch the emotions of listeners—employing symbols and projecting himself in ways that encourage hope and trust. In office he used the resources at his disposal to reward old friends and make new ones—and to punish his enemies. The values he pursued, in the state capitol of Georgia and in the White House, were conservative, cautious, hard to oppose, essentially noncontroversial, and he seemed to pursue them with vigor. Yet his genius for winning political office was not matched by a capacity for governing—or for maintaining a broad political following. As governor he moved with verve at first, but his political support soon fell off so badly that the Georgia presidential primary of 1976 had to be scheduled late to allow him time to prove himself up North in order to be sure he would carry his home state. Jimmy Carter pulled off a political miracle in winning the Democratic nomination for President but almost lost the prize in the election campaign. He began his Administration with much good will and high expectations. Eighteen months later he had sunk to a deep low in public approval. He picked up at times of national drama—Sadat and Begin at Camp David, the hostages in Teheran. He fought to hold onto his presidency with hard politics and new symbolic appeals. He used his incumbency to its full campaign advantage. His political malaise he attributed to a national malaise. And out of the crises in Iran and Afghanistan he shaped a unity appeal which boosted his political following. By the spring of 1980 he was winning primary elections in which many of those voting for him had reservations about his leadership skills and disagreed with his policies.

The major goal of this book is to understand Jimmy Carter—who he is, how he became that way, and to understand how all this shaped his political drive and influenced his strategies for winning and exercising political power. Special attention will be paid to the extraordinary process, the rhetorical and psychological appeals by which Jimmy Carter rose out of relative obscurity to capture the presidency of the United States. A full-scale analysis of Carter's presidency is premature at this point, but certain basic stylistic characteristics have been delineated in a section on the presidency. I have tried to re-create in this book my own sense of gradual discovery of Jimmy Carter, reserving major interpretations for the end of the book.

Carter himself has often said that he could be understood in terms of his roots in Plains and the South. That, of course, is a bit too simple. The South has a complex culture, and even in the small town of Plains there is a range of personality types and political commitments. One must also look at Carter's family and its place in regional social structure and culture, as well as Jimmy Carter's interpretations of and adaptations to all these complex forces, realizing that some may be typical of his culture, others idiosyncratic. There may be some wisdom in the observations of Rachael Clark, a black woman who helped care for Jimmy Carter as a boy, to one woman tourist who had come to see Plains, "the town that produced the boy." Mrs. Clark told the lady, "Oh, the town didn't produce him. He was hisself and that was it. He just came from here."

# I

# Early Life

# ONE

# Roots

## *The Carters*

JIMMY CARTER'S paternal ancestors were middle-class farmers, and the men were, on the whole, a sturdy, restless, and sometimes hotheaded lot. Kindred Carter was the first to reach Georgia, moving from Bertie County, North Carolina, to the eastern Georgia frontier, now McDuffie County, in about 1787. With his wife, four children, and ten slaves, Kindred carved out a 307 acre-farm where he grew wheat and cotton and raised livestock. His eldest son, James, gave up his own farm in this part of east Georgia to move to Talbot County in west-central Georgia. He had won large tracts of land in the state land lottery, a device to attract white settlers to lands recently cleared of the Creek Indian nation.

James's eldest son, Wiley, also pulled up stakes, after his five sons and seven daughters were born and his first wife had died, settling in 1849 in Quebec in Sumter County (now in Schley County) eight miles north of modern day Plains. He was a successful farmer, leaving at the time of his death 2,400 acres of land; 30 slaves; and $22,000 to each of his twelve heirs. The Carters of Plains, Richland, and Americus are descended from Wiley and his first wife, Anne Ansely.

Earlier in his life, ten years before his move to Sumter County, Wiley Carter had shot a man named Usry, who was said to have stolen one of his slaves. Wiley had gone to Usry's house with the sheriff to get the slave, and when Usry would not come out, he stationed himself outside the house, exchanging heated words through the night (Usry attacked the virtue of Wiley's wife). At breakfast, when Usry finally emerged, Wiley shot and killed him. He was acquitted of murder in a one-day trial. The sheriff testified that both men had raised their guns and fired simultaneously.

Littlebury Walker Carter, one of Wiley's sons, followed his father to Sumter County in 1860. In 1862, he and two brothers enlisted with Cutt's Sumter County Flying Artillery at Americus; he served through the Civil War as a private in Virginia, but in 1873, at forty-four, came to a violent end—killed by his business partner in a drunken brawl about the profits from their flying Jenny (a kind of handmade merry-go-round). The superior court in Sumter County issued a murder indictment against the partner, who fled to South America before he could be tried. According to a local paper, Walker's wife, Mary Anne Seals, was so torn with grief that she died on the day of the funeral.

In the late 1880s, William Archibald Carter, one of Littlebury Walker Carter's four children, moved from the Quebec area to Arlington, Georgia, fifty miles southwest of what is now Plains. There he farmed, acquired some sawmills, and with his wife, Nina Pratt (who was born in South Carolina), reared five children, one of them—the fourth in line—James Earl, Jimmy Carter's father, was born in 1894.

William Archibald Carter also came to a violent end. In 1903 his business partner, Will Taliaferro, moved out of an office rented from Carter, taking one of Carter's desks with him. The two men began "fussin and fightin," and in the scuffle Taliaferro shot Carter. He died the next day. Taliaferro's three subsequent trials for manslaughter ended in mistrials.

The second oldest son, Alton, then fifteen, who had witnessed the shooting, tried to take his father's place at home, looking after his mother and the three younger children: Earl and two sisters. He was strictly Bible Belt, frowning on smoking, drinking, and swearing. He moved the family close to Americus so they could call on relatives in times of need. They were the first Carters to settle in Plains.

Plains, originally located in Magnolia Springs, had been moved a few miles south to its present site in 1888 when the Americus, Preston, and Lumpkin Railroad (later part of the Seaboard Airline Railway) was built. Incorporated in 1896, Plains was a thriving town when the Carters arrived. There were several businesses on the block-long Main Street: the McDonald Department Store, the F. F. Timmerman Store, a bank building, the Plains Cotton Warehouse, a hospital staffed by three doctors named Wise, a drugstore, and a consolidated public school for whites.

Alton Carter, Jimmy's uncle, obtained a job at the McDonald Department Store for sixty dollars a month and by 1909 had started his own general store on Main Street. His younger brother, Earl, attended the old Plains school for a short while, then went on to the Riverside Academy (a military school) in Gainsville, Georgia. He finished the tenth grade—the most advanced education of any Carter man since the clan had moved to Georgia 125 years earlier. At seventeen, he left Plains for two years—going to Texas to work as a cowboy. On his return to Plains, he sank his meager savings into an ice house, then a laundry and cleaning establishment.

Despite Jimmy Carter's later recollections before the American Legion, the evidence suggests that Earl never served as a first lieutenant in World War I. He was drafted into the new national army in 1917 as a result of the lottery, according to the Americus *Times-Recorder*. About three weeks later, after a period of physical training, he claimed exception from the draft because his mother was widowed. On October 1, the *Times-Recorder* noted that Carter was leaving Plains for Camp Gordon in Atlanta. But subsequent issues of the newspaper, which carried regular stories of the boys from home and their promotions, carried no stories on Earl's military career. American Legion records that picture the men from the area who served in World War I do not show Earl Carter. The man known locally as "Mr. American Legion," a café owner in Americus, recalls that Earl Carter was not a member of the Legion during the long period for which he kept the local records.

By the early twenties Plains was on the verge of a ten-year boom. There were two banks, two drugstores, a funeral home, and several other shops and warehouses. The new Wise Hospital—a "little Mayo Clinic" for that part of the country—had been completed in 1920, with a section for colored people in the rear. On the corner across Logan Park from Main Street, where Billy Carter's gas station now stands, Dr. Thaddeus Wise built a two-story hotel. The three white churches—the Plains Baptist, the Plains Methodist and St. Andrews Evangelical Lutheran—had been built by this time. So had the Negro school. By 1923 a school bond had been floated for the Plains High School and the colored Rosenwald School had been expanded to include junior-high-school students.

In Plains, Earl invested in farm and timberland, brokered peanuts, and dabbled in a variety of businesses. Everything he touched, according to his brother, Alton, turned to gold. Like the other young men around he dated some of the young women living in town, and one was Lillian Gordy, a free-spirited young woman (about twenty-three when they met) who had come to Plains from Richlands to train in nursing at the Wise Hospital. She had been dating another boy but Dr. Sam Wise took Lillian aside. "I'll tell you who I would like you to go with. It's Earl Carter. He's a boy that has more ambition than anybody in this town, and he's going to be worth a lot some day."

On their first date they went to Americus to see a production of Shakespeare's *The Merchant of Venice*. Over the months they "kind of drifted together and grew to love one another." After about a year they were engaged. Lillian considered Earl "a fine catch. . . . He had a grocery store, a dry-cleaning place, and a farm. . . . I wanted to forget about nursing entirely and just get married," she said. But Earl, as she recalls, urged her to finish her work—which would require her attendance in Atlanta for six months. (Actually, Lillian was probably there for a shorter time. The Grady Hospital has no records of her attendance, but they did have an arrangement with the Wise Hospital to collaborate in the training of nurses, and Lillian could have completed her work over the summer months without appearing on the record as a Grady student.)

Lillian, twenty-five, and Earl, twenty-nine, were married on September 26, 1923. Lillian's family was Methodist, but the simple wedding took place in the pastorate at the Baptist Church in Plains on a Thursday evening. The reception afterward was an informal gathering of friends and relatives at Earl

Carter's home. The Americus *Times-Recorder*, noted at the time: "Mr. Carter is regarded as one of the representative young businessmen of Plains, and has hundreds of friends who are congratulating him upon his happiness."

## The Gordys

Alton Carter described Lillian Carter as the politician in the family—the one from whom Jimmy inherited his skills. And in *Why Not the Best?* Jimmy notes that Lillian's grandfather, Jim Jack Gordy, had managed to retain the postmaster position at Richland through four different Presidents because of his "nimble political footwork."

Actually, Jimmy Carter inherited his political skills from both sides of his family, but it was from the Gordys that he received his Irish and Scottish blood, and perhaps their gift of dramatization and a tendency to exaggerate.

The Gordys had come to America from Scotland, settling at first in Delaware. A grandson of one of the early immigrants, Peter Gordy was the first of his family to settle in Georgia, and his son, Wilson, was one of the pioneer settlers of the Chattahoochee County in west-central Georgia. He married Mary Scott in 1825, settling on the Cusetta-Columbus road in a location known today as Gordy's Lane. One of their sons, James Thomas Gordy, worked a farm near his father's, married Harriett Emily Helms in 1854, served as a wagon-master for the Confederacy (enlisting as a private in 1864), and was for a time a tax collector.

James Jackson Gordy—called "Jim Jack"—one of their nine children, married Mary Ida Nicholson in Chattahoochee County in 1888, moved to Richland, where he served as postmaster for thirty-three years, and dabbled in local politics. Their daughter, Bessie Lillian Gordy, was born in 1898—the fourth of their eight children. (Two adopted children and a grandmother at their home brought the family size to thirteen. "With thirteen of us around the table for supper," Lillian recalls, "we had to learn that we couldn't always have an extra slice of bread just because we wanted it." It also meant that Lillian had responsibilities toward the younger children. She used to tell her younger sister that her uneven gait was due to the fact that she had carried her [the sister] around on her hip when she was a child.)

Lillian's mother, Mary Ida, was from a respected family (her uncle was a physician), and she was a typical housewife and mother—a "very fine, quiet lady," as one of her daughters-in-law recalls. But Lillian was closer to her father, admitting in one interview that she loved him best. Jim Jack seems to have been a big man physically, and Lillian clearly idealized him, portraying him as a man of political and moral stature. "People from all over the county came to consult him," she says. She also recalls: "He was the best, biggest politician in this part of the world. He kept up with politics so closely that he could tell you—almost within five votes—what the people who were running would get in the next election. And so he was very popular." It may also have been from Lillian that Jimmy Carter obtained the idea (which he later included in his official gubernatorial biography) that Jim Jack Gordy had suggested to the great Georgian populist, Tom Watson, the idea for his single greatest achievement as a Congressman, the Rural Free Delivery System.

Lillian remembers Jim Jack also as a compassionate man. She says he taught her not to judge people by their skin color; he was "kind to people, black as well as white." Bishop William D. Johnson of the African Methodist Episcopal (AME) Church (who ran the Home Industrial College in Archery, near Plains) was a regular visitor to their home. The two men—both Methodists—would talk together about the Bible and "the living Christ," and then raise their voices in disharmony and sing.

Lillian has painted her father with a golden brush. The evidence suggests that he was not particularly close to Tom Watson—and certainly did not give him the idea for the RFD. Nor does Gordy seem to have been particularly influential in his part of the country. Neither he nor his family is mentioned as holding important political office in the major history of Stewart County. He was postmaster of Richland for several years. And as an Internal Revenue agent in the 1920s, he was responsible for locating stills in the countryside—a function not apt to make him popular in that rough world of southwest Georgia. Nor is there any external evidence that his brand of populism included any special concern about the racial system of the day. Gordy's son, Tom Watson Gordy, was born and named in 1903, after his namesake had become a virulent racist. Jim Jack was a supporter of Gene Talmadge, whose appeal to rural constituents of the Georgia Black Belt was based equally on a commitment to white superiority and verbal attacks on big business. Indeed, Jim Jack's main political plum was not his appointment as a doorkeep of the state senate, as Alton Carter has suggested, but his position as a guard, after his retirement, at the mansion of the late Governor Gene Talmadge.

Jimmy Carter's ancestors, in short, put down their roots in the Georgia land in the late eighteenth and early nineteenth centuries. His paternal antecedents were farmers moving about the southwest Georgia frontier until his father, Earl, came as a boy to Plains, in 1904. His maternal antecedents were mainly small officeholders—tax collectors and civil servants. It was a good, solid, respectable background, but there was nothing in it to suggest that Jimmy Carter was destined for great accomplishment.

## Archery

Lillian and Earl Carter's first child, James Earl, Jr., was born nearly a year after their marriage at about 7:00A.M. on October 1, 1924, at the Wise Hospital in Plains. They brought him home to a rented apartment in a house in town.

Earl and Lillian Carter managed to save out of the 100 dollars a month he made in these early years of their marriage and acquired—on credit—some farmland in Webster County, one of the few times in Earl's life when he ever bought anything except with cash. When Jimmy was four (two years after the second child, Gloria, was born), the family moved to the farm in Archery, a small, unincorporated community about two miles west of Plains and a mere flag stop on the old Seaboard Railroad. The farm was on the old Preston Road, a dirt trail paralleling the railroad that connected Columbus to Americus and to the ocean at Augusta. It was beautiful country, the orange clay earth contrasting with the greens of the pines, the oaks, and the young pecans in the orchard near the house. The summers were hot, the winters mild (Archery was only about 130 miles from the Gulf of Mexico), and on a warm, pleasant afternoon in the fields one could hear the meadowlarks and catch the heavy, sweet scent of the pines.

Only one other permanent white family—the Watsons—lived in Archery. (He was the railroad foreman.) A mile away on the Preston Road toward Plains lived three other white farm families. Some poor, transient whites lived across the fields east of Archery, along with twenty-five black families scattered in shacks about the countryside. The one prominent black was Bishop William Johnson of the African Methodist Episcopal Church. His large two-story home, the Industrial College for blacks across the road from the Watsons (which attracted blacks from throughout the South) and the AME church in the center of Archery must have been the most imposing buildings in the area.

The Carter house was a modest clapboard cottage without indoor conveniences, power, or sewage lines, as was common in rural areas at the time. Cooking was done on a wood-burning stove in the kitchen, and when the mornings were chilly, fires were built in the fireplaces in each room. The Carter household workday began at 4:00 A.M. when a large farm bell clanged, calling all the hands to the barn. By lantern light, the workers loaded their supplies on the wagon, harnessed the mules, and headed out to the fields. (In those days, Earl Carter raised mainly cotton, corn, and peanuts, and also watermelons, sweet potatoes, Irish potatoes, and other household vegetables.) The land was difficult to work—the clay was exceptionally hard—and farming methods were still quite primitive—planting and cultivation were done by hand.

Jimmy would help in some of these chores—swabbing cotton with a mixture of sorghum oil, soap, and water to kill the boll weevils (for which he was paid). But his studies "always came first," as he recalled, and the more difficult tasks on the farm and in the house were performed by local blacks (which fact he later glossed over). At one time, according to Lillian Carter, 200 blacks, men and women, were working for Earl Carter in the fields from sunup to sundown. And some of the black women helped Lillian in the house.

The farmhouse was a kind of social center for whites and blacks alike. Across the yard was a commissary for the black workers, open in the evenings on paydays and weekends, or whenever a customer came "for a nickel's worth of snuff or kerosene." And Earl Carter had provided playthings for Jimmy, Gloria, Ruth, and later Billy. There was a tree house for Jimmy in an elm beside the house, a tire for everyone to swing on, and a playhouse for Gloria, Ruth, and their friend Ruby Watson. The children had a Shetland pony named Lady and, when they were older, bicycles. Earl Carter built a tennis court in the yard and children were permitted to use the cement floor of the commissary for roller skating. There was a pond to swim in on the other side of the railroad tracks and softball games in the field. When the children reached their teens, Earl built the first Pond House and furnished it with a pool table, ping-pong table, and juke box stocked with the latest records of Tommy Dorsey, Glenn Miller, and the other big bands.

On Saturday afternoons, after the oldest Watson boy turned sixteen and could drive, the white children would pile into his car and go to a show in Americus. And sometimes the Watson and Carter families would pack into the old Watson pickup truck for hunting or fishing in the nearby Kitchnoohee.

Reading was a favorite recreation for Lillian and the children. Often they would bring their books to the dinner table and read and eat in silence. Whenever school was in session the children would gather in the dining room, where a fire was kept blazing throughout the cooler months, to sit around the large walnut table, their books and papers stacked high, reading or writing by the light of the kerosene lamps. Jimmy Carter, in short, grew up neither a culturally nor an economically deprived child.

He also had interesting, competent parental models with which he could identify. Earl Carter was a matter-of-fact person, all business when he did his rounds of the farms, and fairly quiet at home. According to the recollections of people other than Jimmy, he very seldom joined in the softball or tennis games at the house. And he easily met the patriarchal values of his culture—he could handle authority and he was a good disciplinarian at home. When his wife needed some control, (as one family friend notes, "she did"), he would exercise it. Indeed, as Lillian says: "My husband was the strong one in the family. He was the boss. He was the head of the family and I never did anything that he didn't want me to do. If I did, I had to apologize—or I was in trouble." And with Jimmy, at least, he had a kind of natural authority—the boy mostly obeyed him. But when the occasion called for it, Earl could use the whip.

He was also a hard worker. In his early years on the farm he would get up at the crack of dawn, to lead the workers into the fields. In later years he was to recall, with some regrets, how he used to get up at four in the morning, leaving some bawling kids and a "fussin" wife, to travel around to oversee his scattered properties, talking to the sharecroppers and handling problems that would arise, sometimes not returning until 9:00 P.M.

Even during the bad times—with the Georgia banks failing because of some wild land speculation in the late twenties, and the subsequent stock market crash of 1929 and Depression causing some of the local people to lose their farms—Earl pushed ahead. While others lost land and property, he acquired new interests. He had cash, and that made the difference. Moreover, in 1934 he acquired a farm fire insurance and mortgage firm from a Mr. Thomas, who wished to retire which gave him additional opportunities to pick up land cheaply. Lillian said, "He'd buy one piece of property and sell it, and he would help people who wanted to buy a farm [through loans]. . . . But when he died he left considerable property for us. That was from the time Jimmy was seven [about 1931] until Earl died in 1953."

And though his friends remember him as strongly opposed to FDR, he took advantage of some of the New Deal programs. According to one of his friends, he once made a killing on a federal program that provided subsidies for those who enclosed their meadowlands. He bought land others were forced to sell at about thirteen dollars an acre—and then ran a piece of barbed wire around these new lands so he could receive the ten dollars per acre the federal government was giving anyone who could enclose their land. And when the rural electrification program was first announced, he was appointed to the local board and used his influence to get a line laid out as far as his house in Archery. (Only later did it reach the Watsons.)

He was shrewd in other ways. When Jimmy first was in school, the children on the old Preston Road had to rely on the elder Watson boy to drive them to school. But when the Watson boys entered high school, Mr. Earl figured out a way to obtain bus service out there. Ruby Watson recalls: ". . . Mr. Earl came down to our house one night and said the only way we can get a bus . . . to get everybody to go to school—is to tell them you're going to Webster County school if we don't get a bus out here. . . . So they sent a little old bus. We called it a cracker box."

And Earl could be tough even with the poor white farmers in the town. Once one of the small farmers borrowed for seed money in the spring, putting up some farm equipment as security. When the note became due in the middle of the summer, he asked for an extension until fall, when his crops would be harvested and he could pay off the loan. Earl at first refused, insisting that he would take the collateral as agreed. Only when a more influential neighbor intervened on behalf of the poor farmer did he back down.

Yet Earl had a softer side. He was especially generous to his friends. Once, a close friend, Frank Timmerman, was flat on his back with tuberculosis; Earl sent him twenty-five dollars, saying God had blessed him (Carter) and he wanted to do something for his best friend. He continued to send the money until Frank died a few months later. On another occasion he bought a car of coal from a local dealer and asked the dealer to deliver it to a widow in town without identifying its source, instructing him, "You watch and whenever she needs coal you take it to her." He asked Ida Lee Timmerman to take a poor girl in the high school to Americus to buy a graduation outfit. (The young woman, pushing her luck, proceeded to one of the best stores in Americus and ordered one of the most expensive dresses, but Earl paid the bill.) And he remembered those who helped him. In his will he left his insurance business to Nellie Walters, who had managed it for him for several years.

Earl Carter, however, was not all work and civic duty. He was a part of the male culture in Plains, hunting quail and doves with neighboring farmers, fishing the streams and the lake nearby. By the 1930s Earl had damned a stream that ran through his property, and next to the pond he built a three bedroom house—a place to have his friends over for fish fries, some drinking, talking, cards, and a bit of dancing. Sometimes he and Lillian (and Ruth, when Lillian was busy) would go to the dances at the Elks Club in Americus.

Lillian Carter's personality provides a contrast to that of her husband. She was perceived by most of her friends and neighbors as a vibrant, dynamic woman who liked to have a good time; she was fun to be around. One friend of Earl Carter's recalls her as a "swinger," and one of Jimmy's childhood friends from Plains who would sometimes stay overnight at the house, found her "interesting" and "quite a character." She was also a bit of a maverick, though she never stretched her eccentricities beyond tolerable bounds. After her marriage to Earl she converted to the Baptist church, but when the children were young, she seldom went to church. She had a bit of bourbon now and then and was unusually direct and vivid in her speech, and sometimes witty. She dressed and acted pretty much as she pleased.

In some ways she provided a kind of counterweight to her husband. She was generous; he was "tight as a tick" with his money. Once when Gloria bought a purse for $2.98, she colluded with her daughter to hide the extravagence from Earl. Another time, Lillian tried to get a close friend to side with her in an argument over Earl's frugality. When the friend conceded to her that Earl couldn't take his money with him, she responded: "Well, if Earl ever discovers that, he isn't going."

Like the other women in the area, she helped friends in need. When the elder Watson boy was critically ill, she would come every four hours to give him shots. She attended the births of her friend, Ida Lee Timmerman, at the Wise Hospital and would take no money for it until pressured to do so. When Edgar Smith, the town bus driver and father of Ruth's close friend, Rosalynn, was dying of leukemia, she helped out, as did Earl and the other townspeople.

Still, Lillian Carter held herself apart. Most of the people in town liked her. She was socially accepted, attending the many barbecues and card parties (rook and bridge were popular, as were decorations of myrtle and fern) in Plains in the twenties, belonging to a missionary circle and the local Stitch and Chat Club. Nevertheless, she said, "I never had close friends. . . . I was never one to be running in and out of people's homes. Small-town people can sometimes be afraid of independent minds."

There are other indications from her later speech and behavior that suggest she tends to see herself in perfectionist terms. During the 1976 campaign she described herself as giving and receiving a perfect love. In an interview with her daughter Gloria, Lillian said, "I would like to be remembered as a person who loves everybody and everything." When Gloria asked, "Do you?" Lillian responded: "Yes. I want to kill some people, but I love them. What I mean by everybody is every single person—regardless of race, color, creed or anything. Yes, and every living thing." In another interview she told Henry Allen, "I'm sure I'm not even bragging when I say that I never had anybody work for me who didn't love me. . . . Nowadays, I am supposed to be, and I think I am, the most liberal woman in the county, maybe the state." And when Allen told her that not one of her old friends "has spoken a bad word about her," Lillian replied, "No, you can't find 'em. They admire me for what I am." (Yet when Allen mentioned one person he had seen—a man at Billy's gas station—Lillian knotted her face "in exasperation" and sighed: "I can't stand that man. Who told you to see him?") In other interviews she portrayed herself as the lone proponent of virtue in her town. She alone among her white women friends attended the funeral of the black school principal, Annie B. Floyd. She and Jimmy were the only ones who stood up on matters of race in Plains. (She does admit that her contemporary, Ida Lee Timmerman "would be just like I am if she'd come along a few years later.")

She brooks no questioning of that self-portrait. When someone asked if Jimmy could question her, she responded in amazement: "Criticize his Momma?" In her interview with Henry Allen she shows her concern about criticism: "This one reporter, he went into Ernest Turner's store, and a woman in there was saying I wasn't sincere about civil rights. I can't find out who it is. Ernest doesn't know anybody like that. All the blacks, they say, Miss Lillian, I don't know who in the world has said a thing like that about you. I'd give anything if I knew who it was in there. It must have been a complete stranger." When pressed, she shows a biting, sophisticated, put-down humor. Once a woman journalist asked her to explain what she meant by saying that Jimmy told "white lies," she gave her an example of one: "When you came here and I said how pretty you are—that was a 'white lie.' "

Jimmy Carter's later behavior suggests that he picked up characteristics from both of his parents. But perhaps more important than their function as role models was the nature of the demands they placed upon him and the quality of the nurturance given.

Lillian, according to her own recollections, was tense with her first child. Everything with Jimmy was very strictly handled—his bottle had to be exactly so, and given on a precise schedule. Whether cause or effect, Jimmy was often sick and showed signs of tension. He was colicky and cried often; he developed pneumonia and at age two almost died from bleeding colitis. Lillian, who was in the last months of her pregnancy with Gloria at this time had to minister to him constantly. With the help of Dr. Logan, with whom she had worked during her nurse's training, she developed a regimen that helped him pass the crisis.

As a baby Jimmy could be very demanding. On one occasion, as his Aunt Sissy recounts it, he bit through his pacifier then screamed and yelled so that she walked to town and persuaded the pharmacist to open up the drugstore so she could buy another pacifier. When he was hospitalized for colitis, he cried for a goat—a common pet in the rural South—until Miss Abrams, the head nurse at the Wise Hospital and a friend of Lillian, brought the first kid she could find and put it in a small box beside his bed.

When Jimmy was a bit older, his mother returned to her nursing. She was out of the house much of the time—working twelve to twenty hours a day, Jimmy said. Annie Mae Holley, a black who lived in a ramshackle house just up the road, recalls that "Miz Lillian, she nursed day and night. She was just like a doctor. If anyone got sick on the place, she'd be right there. . . . She'd leave in the evening and she wouldn't be back until the next morning. She'd come in and she'd have to go to bed and go to sleep." Annie Mae, who worked for Lillian Carter for several years, filled in whenever Lillian needed her, beginning when Jimmy was about five: "I did practically everything 'cause she would be on night duty." She had to cook, feed the children, get them off to school in the morning. "I was right there every day." Rachael Clark, Annie May Harvey, and Annie Mae Kitchens were other black women who did domestic work for the Carters.

Working within the caste system of the time, these black mother substitutes disciplined the children when they were in charge. Rachael Clark spanked them on occasion with "some branches from a peach tree . . . or an oak tree— whatever was nearby and necessary to do the job." Annie Mae Harvey could always discipline Jimmy by hollering that she would tell his daddy about any misbehavior—and "he'd hush me up and I wouldn't tell anybody." Jimmy "was crazy about his Daddy." Annie Mae Holley employed scare tactics. As Gloria tells it, "There was a boogie man who lived about a hundred yards from the house. So there never was any thought of running away from home at night. There was also an old bloody ghost that walked the railroad tracks right in front of our house. So we never went on the railroad tracks." (Proud that the Carter children never called her "nigger," Annie Mae Holley says that when they were angry at her they would say, "I don't like you—you go home." Then, after a short time they'd come and hug her.)

Annie Mae Harvey's recollections of Jimmy are revealing of the playful interaction that existed between them—and of a teasing streak in him. "He used to chase me with worms, saying he was going to put them on me. . . . Of course he never would, but it used to scare me so." She continued: "Then I'd drop something else I was doing to take him down to the pond and he'd pretend he was drowning and scare me to death."

Lillian Carter was not the main authority figure for her son. Her husband forbade the children to speak back to her (an order Gloria, at least, did not always obey). But Lillian seldom, if ever, spanked the children. Rachael Clark and some of Jimmy's playmates see her as kind of a softening influence over Earl's harsher discipline. As Lillian herself recalls, the children knew of one sure way to get around her: ". . . all my children read all the time, and they took advantage of me about that. When I would say, 'Jimmy, what are you doing?'—I wanted him to do a chore for me—and he would say, 'I'm just reading, what do you want, mama?' And I'd say, 'go ahead.' "

Jimmy Carter, in his recollections of the past, does not really deal with the feminine influences in his life. He does not even mention his black nursemaids.

Although he describes his mother as an "extrovert, very dynamic," and designates her as his compassionate parent, his recollections of her compassion are either abstract or related to others—local blacks or the poor in India. In *Why Not the Best?* Carter describes only one instance of his interactions with her. Like other boys, he had a slingshot and used to scour the railroad track by the house for stones the right size for his weapon. On one occasion, after arduously filling his pockets and hands with "the most perfectly shaped rocks of proper size," his mother came out onto the front porch: " 'Honey,' she asked, 'would you like some cookies?' " Carter vividly remembers standing there "about fifteen or twenty seconds, in honest doubt about whether I should drop those worthless rocks and take the cookies which Mother offered me with a heart full of love." Though he uses the story as a parable about dropping the invaluable in favor of the more valuable, Carter never says whether he gave up his ammunition (power?) for the cookies (love?).

The recollections of some neighbors and friends suggest that Earl Carter was the more nurturing parent—the one who was most interested in the children, paying attention to their studies, their interests. He also showed his care in the recreations he provided for them. And from him young Jimmy received extra instruction in how to hunt and fish. Certainly Jimmy Carter gives his father much more attention in *Why Not the Best?* and assigns to him the more important role in the development of his character. As he states in his autobiography, his father was a "firm but understanding director of my life and habits. . . . Also, he was always my best friend." His idealization of Earl is apparent in the portrait he paints of him—as a model of masculine virtue and, not incidentally, close to Carter's own projected self-image. To Jimmy, Earl was an "unusually hard worker," an "extremely competent farmer and businessman" with a wide range of interests in public affairs. He was "scrupulously fair with all those who dealt with him," "very aggressive and innovative in selling," "extremely intelligent," and was "well read about current events, always probing for innovative business techniques or enterprises." His father was, in addition, civic-minded, a popular community leader. "He laughed a lot and almost everybody liked him." And he was a good athlete. Jimmy could not beat him in sports, especially tennis. "He had a wicked sliced ball which barely bounced at all on the relatively soft dirt court."

It is interesting to note Carter's specific—and seemingly admiring—recollections of how his father controlled his behavior. Jimmy was not rewarded for good behavior—his father simply expected him to be "the best." And when he misbehaved, he was punished severely. Jimmy recalls each punishment, in some detail. "From the time I was four years old until I was fifteen years old he whipped me six times and I've never forgotten any of those impressive experiences. The punishment was administered with a small, long, flexible peach tree switch." One whipping was for taking some money that should have been in the collection plate at church. And the story shows the small boy presenting his daddy with the evidence of his misdeed—as if he may have been wishing to get caught.

I had been to my Sunday School class, and as was his custom Daddy had given me a penny for the offering. When we got back home, I took off my Sunday clothes and put the contents of my pocket on a dresser. There were two pennies lying there. Daddy thus discovered that when they passed the collection plate I had taken out an extra penny, instead of putting mine in for the offering. That was the last money I ever stole.

On another occasion, when Earl and Lillian were holding a noisy party while he was trying to sleep, Jimmy took a blanket and retreated to his tree house, spent the night, and refused to answer his father's calls, for which he was whipped when he came down the next morning. Thus Jimmy learned honesty and obedience to authority.

One story Carter recalls is particularly revealing—showing an emotionally wide-open boy still being held to a strict standard. When young Jimmy shot his first quail, he was so proud and happy he dropped his rifle and ran to find his father. Earl's response, according to Carter's recollection was not to rejoice with him, but to ask him where his gun was.

There are some problems in these accounts. Earl Carter, according to others, was indeed, a strong disciplinarian. In this and other ways he seems to have been a typical, moderately successful Southern businessman—no better or worse than his peers in Plains. But in describing his daddy as exuberant and athletic Jimmy saw something his neighbors did not. And in focusing on Earl's role as a community leader, he misses the shrewder and tougher side many of Earl's colleagues noted. Indeed, Jimmy's portrait blurs at one point. He states that his brother Billy reminds him of his father more than of anyone else. But the Billy Carter of contemporary Plains is quite clearly different from the father Jimmy has recalled. He is a likable, beer-drinking, down-to-earth fellow who gets along with the other men in Plains—and in that respect he may indeed resemble Earl. But as Billy's black nursemaid, who virtually raised him, recalls, "Billy is more like his mom." Except for a physical likeness to his father, and his anchoring in the local male culture, Billy does seem more like Lillian—volatile, impulsive, and talkative.

## In the Mold

Following in his father's steps, Jimmy developed a capacity for hard work and entrepreneurship. In *Why Not the Best?* he gives an appealing picture of a little six-year-old boy taking his wagon full of peanuts to Plains to sell on the street. Though few outside the family recall this particular enterprise, various townspeople do recall that Carter as a fourteen- or fifteen-year-old went to town on Saturdays with his cousin Hugh to sell peanuts, hot dogs, and ice cream in front of the old bank. (Carter also remembers saving and selling cotton and buying some houses with the proceeds. They must have been shacks for the blacks given the price he recalls paying for them.)

Almost everyone remembers Jimmy as "a good boy," doing what was expected of him. His friends recall no "cussing," or smoking or fighting with the other boys (though he could be a tease). Others say that he was determined to be "the best" from a very early age. As black childhood friend A. D. Davis put it, "Jimmy doesn't like to lose, but he always loved to be up front." His mother remembers, that when he played ball, he wanted to hit a home run every time. When he was on the debating team, he wanted to win there, too.

The other Carter children made somewhat different adaptations to their environment. Two years younger than Jimmy, Gloria was the rebel, the nonconformist. A "tomboy," she climbed trees and slid down the pigeon roost with her friend Ruby Watson at the house in Archery. Her parents did not try to constrain her, but she had some open conflicts with her mother. As one friend recalls, Gloria decided once to get even with Miss Lillian, with whom she had had an argument. When Lillian went to town, Gloria cut down the shrubbery in the yard. Another time, she became so angry that she left for the Watsons' house and stayed several days—despite her mother's repeated pleas to return home.

As one might expect, there was some competition between the two oldest children. Jimmy teased his sister. Once he paid Gloria a nickel to pick peanuts for him, then got her to plant the nickel in a flowerbed—telling her that it would become a "money tree" (He then dug up the nickel, himself). On the other hand, at least two of his whippings were set up by Gloria. "I remember once she threw a wrench and hit me, and I retaliated by shooting her in the rear end with a B.B. gun. For several hours, she re-burst into tears every time the sound of a car was heard. When Daddy finally drove into our yard, she was apparently sobbing uncontrollably, and after a brief explanation by her of what had occurred, Daddy whipped me without further comment." Lillian Carter recalls another situation: "Gloria came running into the house one afternoon and asked her Daddy for some matches. Earl wanted to know what for, and she said in little-girl talk, that Jimmy wanted to burn down the barn."

Ruth, born three years after Gloria, was for several years the baby of the family and indulged in ways the two older children were not. In some ways she was her father's favorite. As Lillian says, "He [Earl] thought Ruth was the most beautiful thing on earth and he told her that every day." Ruth agrees: "I was led to believe that I was the most talented, the most gifted of persons. I grew up thinking I was queen of the universe." Unlike Jimmy and Gloria, Ruth was protected from any experience that would cause suffering or pain—she never attended the funerals of relatives or observed the birth of animals on the farm. She was made to feel that she was the best without having to prove herself. However, Ruth was like Jimmy her brother in idealizing her father. As a young woman she saw him "as the most wonderful, the most beautiful man I had ever known in my life . . . in fact, the only perfect human being."

As a consequence of her training, Ruth was put in a bind. She expected to be recognized as exceptional, but she had not been taught to win recognition through her own efforts. As she was later to remember: "When I went away to college and later when I married, I was shocked to discover an inability to cope normally with life. I was not the best, the most beautiful, the most loved of all. I didn't have all the answers, and I was almost totally unable to make decisions.

. . . To fall short of 'number one' in any area of life registers as unbearable failure."

Jimmy escaped this particular dilemma. Perhaps because he was the eldest male (the only one during his formative years—Billy was born when Jimmy was thirteen), he was put through a discipline that developed the traits that would enable him to secure success in the world outside Archery or Plains. His father required him to do chores, taught him to swim and hunt, and expected him to perform well in whatever he did. (The training was not always tender. When Jimmy was only three he threw him into a pond saying, "Swim, son, swim."). Even Lillian seemed to expect more from him than her other children. She saved all of Jimmy's schoolwork, for example, but not Ruth's or Gloria's. "A mother's premonition" she has since called it—but a sign, nonetheless, of her expectations that he would make his mark on the world.

## Plains

Carter's life as a young boy centered around the farm in Archery. Nearby Plains, as he later recalled, was the big and somewhat awesome outside world.

Although the hustle and bustle of Plains in the booming twenties had been replaced by the stagnation of the depressed thirties (the Plains population had declined from about 600, when Jimmy was born, to about 300 in the mid-1930s), the block of stores and offices on Main Street still had business. Farmers from the outlying areas came in to sell their crops and buy their seed and supplies. (The hotel had closed, however, and the Wise clinic burned down in the mid-thirties—which meant Plains was no longer a medical center.) On school days white children came from as far as Archery, Smithfield, Botsfield, and other housing clusters on the roads radiating from the town to attend the Plains school. On Saturday everyone, black and white, from the outlying areas converged on the town for shopping and socializing. On Sundays and some weekday evenings families would ride or walk to town to attend church. On special occasions there were tent shows or religious revivals in Logan Park, and every so often, a political rally. (Because the rural counties had disproportionate weight in statewide elections, Georgia's politicians would work the rural parts of the state; consulting the "big men" there—men like Earl Carter.)

Though the Carters were known and respected in town, the community life of Plains did not center around them as it had in Archery. Earl Carter had his insurance office downtown; his processing business had expanded as he became an agent for McClouskey Mills in Americus, buying peanuts for their peanut oil manufacturing. He served for many years on the county school board (as Jimmy did after him). And in 1937, when Jimmy was about thirteen, Earl became one of the first directors of the local Rural Electrification Association (REA), which brought electricity to the Carter's Archery home. Earl's brother, Alton, was mayor of Plains off and on between 1918 and 1954 and was a county commissioner at one time.

Yet the Carters did not run the town. Indeed, there was no one leading family. The McDonalds and the Bradleys were the richest folks around, and the Wises and the Chappells probably the most prestigious, with their social and professional ties to nearby Americus. Several other business and farm families were on par with the Carters. The Williamses had a warehouse operation; the Godwins owned and operated a drugstore; and the Walterses had a general store. Thaddeus Jones was developing an automatic sprinkler system that would be marketed nationally and make him wealthy. The Murrays, the Ratliffs, and the Sutherlands had acreage to the south and the Youngs to the north. For the white males who headed these families and dominated the town's politics and economy, Plains was a rural democracy in which they could all play a role.

Jimmy would experience no cultural shock in this town, though he remembers himself as shy on his initial forays into Plains. The dominant whites in Plains were homogeneous. Primarily English, Irish, or Scottish, they had intermarried—almost everyone had at least a second cousin in one or more of the major town families. And they were all Protestants. Though there were some differences in the theologies of the churches around which the social life of the town revolved, they all ascribed to the same practical Protestant ethic. They lived by a standard of hard work, charity, and helping one's neighbors. In each family the father was the boss and corporal punishment was the usual way of dealing with challenges to his authority. None of the churches questioned the system of racial segregation.

The Carter children also attended the Plains school from the first through eleventh grade. (Jimmy's education will be dealt with in the next chapter.) The Carters belonged to the Plains Baptist Church, which Jimmy later recalled as the biggest and most prestigious church in town, its membership about 300 and its regular attendance around 150. (The other white churches, however, had equally prestigious members in their congregations.) The Carters were not especially pious, however. Lillian stayed home most Sunday mornings; Earl did not "take much part in church affairs," and did not care for sermons. And he never showed any desire to be a deacon—because he liked to take a drink or two, and deacons should not do that. But he did pack the children in the car each week and take them to Sunday school. He usually attended the men's Bible class, then skipped the church service to talk with his friends at the drugstore, then collected the children from church and took them home to dinner. Occasionally the children were allowed to sit in the car and watch Earl at the drugstore rather than go to church, a big occasion.

## Social Setting

The social and political climate in which Jimmy Carter matured reinforced the ideas, values, and self-conceptions he learned at home.

Earl Carter could appear powerful to his children in part because of this broader political and social setting. (Ruth, as late as the 1976 presidential campaign, saw him as a kind of "rural royalty.") Webster County, where he lived, and Sumter County, where he later had his office, both had small populations, and half the people were black and excluded from politics. Almost any middle-class white male, especially if he headed a family and had his own farm or business, could find a role to play in town and county politics if he was so inclined.

Further, Georgia's county unit system of voting, which gave each county from one to six electoral votes with the whole bloc in each county going to the candidate who won the largest number of popular votes, was heavily weighted in favor of the smaller counties. (In 1930, for example, the combined electoral votes of Webster County—population 5,032—and Sumter County—population 26,800—were equivalent to the vote of Fulton County, where Atlanta is—population 380,587.) This gave local leaders like Earl Carter who could influence the votes of others disproportionate influence on state politics.

As a consequence, the "big men" in the county were astute politicians. As Gene Talmadge's biographer, William Anderson, described their operations: "Members of the courthouse gang represented the needs of their county as a lobby of sorts to the legislature, and would wheel and deal with great majesty, offering to 'give' their county or 'deliver' it to the politician who promised to serve the local needs." And because various factions competed to perform these roles, their members were often adept at political intrigue. "While serving in a useful political capacity, they also appeared to expend great energies in maneuverings and intrigue designed to maintain their cohesion and membership," according to Anderson. "These struggles appeared insignificant and ego-serving to an outside world, but to the gang and its aspirants, they were gargantuan battles for power, influence, and often money."

Earl Carter, as farmer, businessman, and holder of various public offices at times, would clearly have had his hand in the politicking of the counties where he worked and lived. And as the brother of Alton Carter, who served several times as mayor of Plains, and as a member of the Sumter County Commission he was certainly one of the people "in the know." Politics, in short, was in the air that Jimmy breathed as a child.

In Archery, moreover, the Carter family was the hub of a predominantly black community over which they had clear economic, social, and political superiority. Most of the blacks in the area (as in the rural South generally) relied on white families for their livelihood, working as day laborers or sharecroppers. Nor did the blacks participate in any way in local politics. As late as the 1950s no blacks were registered to vote in Webster County. There was strict racial segregation in the churches, schools, even the cemeteries, and the white facilities were usually better. Thus, the "colored" children, when they went to school, attended local one-room schoolhouses, while the white children went off to Plains to a larger, better equipped school.

Underlying this racial system in southwest Georgia was the law, and sometimes the mob, to keep in line blacks who might seriously challenge the order. Labor recruiters from the North who came to the area were viewed as seducers, holding up pie in the sky to local blacks. The Americus *Times-Recorder*, on April 24, 1923, ran a story "White Man Caught Deporting Negro at Oglethorpe Depot." It told of how Negroes were being promised "work with a fence around it" and were being shipped to Atlanta and then to the North. Said one area farmer: "I firmly believe the Negro is happier here in this section than anywhere else on the globe."

The *Times-Recorder* carried stories of occasional lynchings throughout the 1920s and early thirties. In 1920 a Negro who had purportedly shot and paralyzed a white man was found dead in a gully with three bullets in his head. In 1922 a black man from Sandersville who confessed to an assault on a white woman was taken from the sheriff by a mob. His body was discovered riddled with 200 bullets. In 1933 a mob, incensed by a Negro's attack on a white policeman who tried to arrest him for molesting a ten-year-old black girl, took the Negro from a jail in Richland. He was shot and beaten, his body left in a wooded section outside town. He died in jail. In all, between 1882 and 1930 there were 508 lynchings in Georgia, an average of 10.3 per year. Between 1931 and 1945 there were 19.

Blacks and whites, however, did maintain friendly relations. In the country they worked together in the fields, and the children would hunt, fish, and play games together. Until they were about fourteen or fifteen years of age, the Carter, Watson, and other white children played with black children. They were "not friends in the sense that he and I, Jimmy, were friends," Billy Wise, who lived near Archery in the thirties, explained. "But we played with them; you'd normally play as you got to about fifteen. . . . In fact the first chewing tobacco I ever got was from one of them." Blacks were his only friends as a child in the country, Carter says in *Why Not the Best?* "We . . . rode mules and horses through the woods, jumped out of the barn loft into huge piles of oat straw, wrestled and fought, fished and swam. Their mothers had complete authority over me when I was in their homes (I don't remember that their fathers did)."

Lillian was friendly with blacks. She was affectionate and kind with her household help and looked after the blacks who worked for Earl on the farm: "It shames me now to talk about it, but they made practically no money, so they couldn't pay for any medical expenses. Well, I would go to the homes and nurse them and deliver their babies." And when one of their Negro workers died, Lillian said, "We would attend the funeral. He [Jimmy] always—he would always want to go with me. He did that just because he was so compassionate."

Earl, according to Lillian, didn't "talk friendly" about blacks and he didn't go into their homes or to their funerals. But Lillian always had her husband's full support: "He paid the expenses of anything I did for the blacks. He was just as kind as I was." Actually, Earl did mix with the blacks. He often went out in the fields with his daily workers, taking the lead row himself. In later years, when he toured his scattered properties to check up on the black sharecroppers who worked much of his land, he would also stop at the farms of neighboring black tenant farmers, talking about crops and the weather.

In Archery at Christmas, blacks would come to the houses of friendly whites, caroling them with their own special music and receiving gifts in return. The Carters and the Watsons sometimes shared in the festivities at the annual AME missionary gathering at the church in Archery—eating from the large tables heaped with fried chicken and crusty fruit pies and enjoying the singing and the praying of their hosts. Once when the AME church was damaged by fire, some white churches in Plains undertook a money-raising campaign to help them rebuild.

Yet in all their social contacts, a strict etiquette was followed—a recognition by both races of the superior position of the whites. In polite exchange, older whites were called "Miss" Lillian or "Mr." Earl, whereas older blacks were called "Aunt" Annie Mae or "Uncle" William. White children were permitted to go in and out of blacks' homes, but black children did not visit whites homes. When blacks had business with the whites, they would ordinarily go to the back door of the white homes. (Bishop William Johnson of the AME Church, when he came to see the Carters, would not go to the back door—but neither would he try the front door; the Carters would talk to him at the car.)

This etiquette even influenced the children's games. Blacks had to lose. As Ruth recalls, "At home I played with the black children on the farm. I never knew until I became an adult that there had been an unwritten law spawned by centuries of prejudice, that the white children must be allowed to win all the time. So every game I ever played throughout my childhood, I won. I was best at kick-the-can, fastest in any race, and I always caught my friends immediately at hide-and-seek."

On rare occasions, whenever the etiquette was breached, there would be a certain tension. Carter says that Alvin Johnson, the Boston-educated son of Bishop Johnson, was the one black man "who habitually came to our front door. . . . My daddy would leave and pretend it wasn't happening while my mother received Alvin in the front living room to discuss his educational progress and his experiences in New England." Actually, Alvin was never as bold as that. Alvin came to the house only once—to give Lillian a box of candy for an earlier favor (she had fetched his mother for a long-distance call). "My husband shook hands with him and went to the back of the house in our bedroom where we also had a phone, presumably to read the paper. I just stood there and talked to Alvin for a while and that is the only time he ever did come to my house." Years later Alvin Johnson, in Lillian's living room, told a reporter who asked him about Carter's account of his visits to their home: "That was all true. But I never did go sit down and talk to Miss Lillian."

Actually, the contacts between the Carters and the blacks in Archery were typical of broader social patterns throughout rural Georgia and the South as a whole. As John Dollard notes, this "tolerant poised affection" for Negroes is an upper-class mark. "If a Negro gets sick, a white person will get him a doctor; if he is hungry, he is given food; if he is in trouble, his white patron will intercede for him." Lillian and Jimmy, then, were not really challenging the caste system. Motivated by warmth and affection, as they seem to have been, they were at the same time being "genteel." And whatever the long-term effects of the entire racial experience on Jimmy, the overall social structure put the Carters in a central and superior position in Archery—Earl ruled the roost and Lillian was the benevolent lady of the house and the Carter children certainly could not have missed this fact.

# TWO

# Education

I N HIS EIGHTH-GRADE SCRAPBOOK Jimmy Carter listed six good mental habits:

> If you think in the right way, you'll develop: 1) the habit of expecting to accomplish what you attempt, 2) the habit of expecting to like other people and to have them like you, and 3) the habit of deciding quickly what you'd like to do and doing it, 4) the habit of sticking to it, 5) the habit of welcoming fearfully all wholesome ideas and experiences. 6) A person who wants to build good mental habits should avoid the idle daydream; should give up worry and anger; hatred and envy; should neither fear nor be ashamed of anything that is honest or purposeful.

A few years later, along with some other boys in his class, he built a small replica of the White House. His education for the presidency had begun early.

## Country School

At the age of six, in 1930, Jimmy Carter began his formal education at the white school in Plains. It was in many ways a typical country school. There was no kindergarten and the last grade was the eleventh. The grammar and high schools were in one building, and through the seventh grade, one teacher taught all subjects for each grade. The first and second grades were together; one class recited while the other studied. The school day usually began with a general assembly. The principal would read a prayer and conduct a general program, then the students would march to class in a military formation and take their assigned seats. Their teachers—there were ten to fifteen on the staff—were mainly local people who knew the families of their charges. They expected their students to behave, and those who did not were sent to the principal's office, where they were shamed, scolded, or whipped as the occasion demanded.

At the time the Sumter County public schools lagged behind the Georgia average in their students' achievement scores. A state report on all Sumter County schools in 1929 concluded that "the greatest deficiency is reading."

Moreover, for a "rural community the scores in nature studies are much too low. Over-emphasis has been placed on arithmetic as compared with other subjects."

But in some respects, at least, the schooling was vigorous. The dominant force in the school was Miss Julia Coleman, the principal and high-school English teacher. The daughter of a Plains Baptist minister and a graduate of Bessie Tift College in Forsyth, Georgia, she devoted herself completely to the Plains school and made it a cultural center for the town. Although she was crippled and her eyesight was bad, she had authority over the students and knew how to exercise it. "Miss Julia," one of Jimmy's schoolmates recalled, "she'd get you in there and she'd tell you how she'd taught your mother and how could you be out on the campus fighting. 'Your mother was such a nice person.' . . . She'd make you feel about this high."

She also used corporal punishment. On one occasion a group of boys caught smoking in the boiler room were taken to her office (Jimmy Carter was not one of them). Miss Julia said, "Okay, boys, I can't take care of you all by myself, so Mr. Y. T. Sheffield [the math teacher and school coach] will whip half of you and I will take care of the other half." One boy who lined up on Miss Julia's side because he thought she would be lenient discovered his mistake when Mr. Sheffield administered a slight tap to those assigned to him and Miss Julia laid on the paddle.

But most important, she was a fine teacher. Students would try to get her off the subject matter to hear her talk, because they found her fascinating. Once she kept the students in rapt attention simply by describing the things she saw and felt and heard on her walk to school that morning from her house on the outskirts of town. She created special projects to capture the students' interests. They would present a program of "living pictures" for their parents, or perform in the plays she had written. The high-school students kept special notebooks for her with lists of such items as their ten favorite authors or ten favorite Georgia poets. One year she obtained some money from the Works Progress Administration to keep the library open during the summer. She organized round-table discussions on literature for the townspeople in the evenings.

At the beginning of his schooling there, Jimmy Carter was embarrassed by his country background, or so one would gather from a comment of his sister Gloria: "The day I started school, he asked me not to tell anybody I was his sister because I didn't talk right; I had been raised out there in the country around the black children and I talked like they did. And he was grown then, see, third grade, and I was still a baby."

In addition to his father's high expectations, Jimmy felt the pressure of living up to the reputations of older neighbors and relatives. The Watson boys were natural athletes who led the Plains team to a championship, and his cousins Donnel (Don Earl) and Hugh Carter (Alton's sons) were top academically, personally popular, and class officers. (A cousin in another family, however, was mentally retarded and inclined to make a nuisance of himself—hanging around the center of town from time to time taunting others.)

Jimmy met the challenge. He was one of the smart ones in his class (along with Teeny Ratliff, Grace Wiggins, Billy Wise, and Bobby Logan). He was also likable—ingratiating with teachers and students alike. On one occasion—in the first or second grade—he even offered one of his mother's diamond rings to his first-grade teacher. When she wondered how his mother would like that, he confidently remarked that his father could always buy her another! And one of his contemporaries recalled that he was popular with his classmates: "When you're short, red-haired, and freckled, all you can do is grin," she said.

Sometimes Jimmy would go home with "townie" Bobby Logan for lunch, or hitch a ride on Thomas Lowery's bicycle to Aunt Ethel's home. (Lillian paid her ten cents a day to feed the Carter children.) After school he might stay in town to play dodgeball or stickball, and occasionally spend the night in town with Bobby Logan, Rembert Forrest, or Richard Salter. Or his friends would come out to Archery to go skinny-dipping in a stream in the woods or fishing in the backwaters of the dam at Cordelia.

When he was thirteen, Jimmy had his first date with Teeny (Eloise) Ratliff, calling for her in the family pickup truck. (She lived next to his grandmother's house in Plains.) She thought Jimmy Carter was a bit tight with his money, according to one friend, and sometimes told her sister to say she was not home if he came calling. (In high school she went "steady" with Lonnie Taylor, a boy from Tennessee, whom she later married. The entire family was later killed in a plane crash.) As a college man Jimmy pursued Marguerite Wise, Dr. Bowman Wise's daughter, and Betty Timmerman, both of them younger than he, leading town beauties, and sought out by the other men in town.

There were few places to take a girl. They could stop off at the Godwin Drugstore for a soda after school or go to school dances or church socials, or to summer "prom parties" at each other's houses, or occasionally drive to the movies in Americus or to Magnolia Springs for dancing and swimming. Once Jimmy picked up Betty Timmerman in a horse and buggy and took her to a nearby Negro church for services. Except on very special occasions, all the teen-agers in Plains were home by 9:30 or 10:00 P.M. Their parents, who usually went to bed at dark, would be waiting for them on the porch. Some of the Americus "city" boys, who drove sports cars and were beginning to drink, thought that their country acquaintances were somewhat "square."

Jimmy also participated in extracurricular activities. Though small for his age and no scrapper, he played forward on the high-school basketball team. He was not a star, but he did try: as one friend recalls, he was fast on the court and moved around a lot. He also joined the Book Lovers Club, whose motto was "Readers Make Leaders." (During the 1939–40 school year, for example, they read Gayles's *Mythology*, *King Lear*, *Ben Hur*, *The Hunchback of Notre Dame*, *Return of the Native*, and John Muir's *Story of My Boyhood and Youth*.) In the eighth grade he joined the debating team; on Friday afternoons it would meet to discuss such contemporary social issues as whether the United States should send aid to the allies in Europe, the boys debating the girls.

Generally Jimmy kept out of trouble, but he did meet the paddle once. One day in the ninth grade Jimmy and Al Seckinger received three whacks from Y. T. Sheffield for being noisy during the chapel assembly. And just before graduation several boys in the senior class, deciding to take advantage of their last chance at mischief before leaving school, jumped into a stripped-down Model A Ford and, clutching each other and anything else they could, tore down the road to Americus at a hair-raising speed of forty miles an hour. They saw a detective movie, toured the Coke plant, and had a soda. When they returned to Plains, their parents insisted that Sheffield punish them. He offered them three choices: make up the missed school time, write a 5,000-word theme, or get a whipping. Jimmy's friends do not agree on the punishment he chose. The story circulated in 1976 was probably untrue—that his punishment was to have points shaved off from his grade, keeping him from becoming valedictorian of his class. (Actually there seems to have been no official record of class rankings, and some classmates recall Teeny Ratliff and Grace Wiggins as the best students in class. Richard Salter confesses that Jimmy and he used to be especially exasperated by Grace Wiggins. She had few of their advantages— she came from a large family that lived in a very small house in the country— yet she outstripped them all in her ability to get to the center of things.)

Whatever their punishments, the "class of '41" did not lose its special celebrations. In the middle of May the entire senior class took off in the school bus for a weekend trip to Jacksonville Beach, St. Augustine, and other points of interest in Florida, chaperoned by Y. T. Sheffield. And just before graduation Jimmy's parents gave a party "in his honor" (as the local paper noted) for the graduating class, their guests, and the school faculty. They ate a chicken dinner from long tables and talked and danced and promenaded throughout the night.

Graduation was June 2, 1941. The four members of the class who were on the debating team—Jimmy Carter, Billy Wise, Doris Cosby, and Richard Salter—were chosen by Miss Julia to speak. Miss Coleman wrote their addresses; Jimmy's was entitled "The Building of a Community," an elaboration on the general theme, "Building for Today and Tomorrow." And as the Americus *Times-Recorder* noted, the school took pleasure in their choice of such a constructive theme.

In short, Jimmy lived the life of a "typical country boy," and there was nothing on the surface that marked him for future greatness. But underneath that nice grin there was a strong competitive streak, an ambition to get ahead. The next step was college—an ambition not quite so unusual in Plains as Carter suggests in *Why Not the Best?*. Alton's boys had already gone to college by this time, as did many of Jimmy's friends. But Carter's ambition did not stop there. He had already confided to a few close friends that he was going to be governor of Georgia one day.

## Higher Education

As a child Jimmy had been fascinated by post cards he received from varied and distant ports sent by his uncle, Tom Watson Gordy, a Navy enlisted man. At age six, he says, he decided he wanted to go to Annapolis and while still in grade school he sent away to the Naval Academy for catalogues, which he studied with great intensity. He was worried he might not qualify on physical grounds. The Annapolis catalogue of the time listed all the imaginable diseases and conditions a midshipman must not have—from underweight, color blindness, malocclusion of teeth, and poor posture, to an abnormally large head or loss of a limb. Carter was concerned that his teeth did not meet and wondered if he might have some problem with urine retention. He also needed political support to win admission, and at the proper time Earl Carter went to work to induce the local Congressman, Stephen Pace, to name Jimmy as one of his appointees. The appointment was not immediately forthcoming on Jimmy's graduation from high school—there may have been some problem about Jimmy's high-school degree, for the science curriculum at Plains High School was weak (for example, chemistry was not taught).

As a temporary expedient, Jimmy enrolled at Georgia Southwestern, a junior college in Americus. It was a natural choice for Plains residents; cousins Hugh and Donnel had gone there for their first two years of college and shone in everything they did. Further, tuition at the time was only $204.00 per year and Jimmy could live at home while attending. Along with Teeny Ratliff, Virginia Harris, and some other friends from Plains, he commuted by auto each day.

In 1941–42 the campus consisted of one administrative-classroom building, two dormitories, and a gymnasium. The student body was small (the yearbook records about 200 students) and predominantly female as a result of the draft. Course offerings were limited: no social science, chemistry through quantitative analysis, English composition, two world literature survey courses, mathematics through college algebra, and introductory physics. In 1941 journalism, aviation, and ballroom dancing were added.

Carter was an apt pupil, taking his first courses in chemistry and engineering, and working as a laboratory assistant his second semester. He played some intramural basketball and made the freshman "all-star" team.

But he was evidently socially shy—in this setting at least. One friend from Plains recalls that as country boys they had been taught to listen and not be seen. And the students from Americus tended to view themselves as rather more sophisticated than the students from Plains. Further, most of the students lived in the dormitories or in Americus, and Carter, as an out-of-town commuter, was even more of an outsider.

But Carter did try to enhance his social life. Occasionally he would stay overnight at the dormitory with his old friend Bobby Logan. He was one of the Investors, a club, that sponsored a big school dance in the fall. He joined the

IFT fraternity ("Ingenuity, Fidelity, and Trustworthiness") and went along with some harmless hazing. On one occasion the boys were driven out into the country in their pajamas and abandoned to find their way back as best they could. Another time each initiate was given a couple of pennies and told to knock on certain farmhouse doors and beg for lunch, leaving the two small coins as a tip. (They did not know that the people they begged from were in on the game.)

And after his initiation, on a Saturday in February, 1942, Carter was host at a fraternity picnic at the Pond House. The event was covered by the campus paper, which noted that the "beautiful" lake and surrounding forest afforded an ideal setting.

In a playful moment Carter and three of his friends wrote their names in wet cement on a campus walk. Yet Carter did not make a big impression otherwise at Georgia Southwestern. One of his fraternity brothers does not even remember him. He was not elected to any class office or chosen "the most likely to" do anything. (Garland Byrd, who was to run against Carter in the gubernatorial primary of 1966, was noted in the yearbook as the "most attractive" male student.)

"Jimmie" (as he was called in the yearbook) did not seem seriously concerned by his lack of prominence—as he explained to Bobby Logan, the class leaders were politicans who knew how to butter up the administration. Georgia Southwestern, moreover, was but a way station. He did not discuss politics very much, or show any great interest in it, but he told his friend B. T. Wishard, from the Plains area, who was attending Gordon Military College, that one day he was going to be governor of Georgia.

Whether his goal was the governorship or a high position in the Navy, Carter had his eyes set on Annapolis, as the next step up the ladder. The Academy could provide several opportunities. Not only did most of the top military officers come from the Academy, but its graduates also gained prestige, especially in rural areas of the South—opening doors in finance, law, or politics.

By the end of the year Carter spent at Georgia Southwestern, the Selective Service Act of 1940 was extended (requiring all males eighteen to sixty-five years of age to register with local draft boards); that year Pearl Harbor had been attacked and the United States had entered World War II. Carter's appointment to Annapolis had not yet come through, so he went to Georgia Tech the next year, where he was in the Navy ROTC. His life there was regimented—good preparation for Annapolis. Freshmen were required to stay in the dormitories, and Carter roomed for a while with Bob Ormsby (later president of Lockheed of Georgia). On an ordinary weekday a student would arise at 6:00 A.M., go to the field for fifteen or twenty minutes of calisthenics, and return for a quick breakfast in the central dining hall. Classes began at 7:30 or 8:00 A.M. Physical training was interspersed throughout the day, including a form of survival training in which the men were thrown into a pool with first their hands, then their legs, and finally both hands and legs firmly tied.

Carter was listed in the school bulletin as a student in general engineering. Like all students in the naval ROTC he took classes in seamanship, navigation, and other military sciences (no social science courses were offered, and only two in the humanities). He made the top 10 percent of his class and the honor roll. He joined no fraternity, and from the pages of *The Blue Print*, the Tech yearbook, he seems to have participated in no extracurricular activities though he did attend the football games. He did, however, work to improve his chances for Annapolis by eating bananas to gain weight and trying to improve his posture. He was finally accepted for the Academy—on certificate without examinations.

In June, 1943, at the age of nineteen, Carter made his way to the Naval Academy. During the war the regular four-year program was condensed into three years. Thus, Carter was considered a member of the class of 1947 although he actually graduated in 1946.

He was assigned to the 13th Company, one of the four companies in the 4th Battalion. (In his third year Carter and other seniors in the 13th would be reassigned to the 15th Company.) The company—usually composed of approximately 100 men equally divided among plebes, youngsters (second year), and seniors (third year)—served as the basic administrative and social unit. The men lived in the same wing of Bancroft Hall, ate their meals together at the same tables, took their recreational activities together, sat together in general gatherings, and marched together in sections to classes.

That first semester Carter and the other plebes learned to live under a harsh set of rules, designed both to promote uniformity and to impress plebes with their insignificance. They marched wherever they went under the command of seniors and were told what to do. Their clothes and all personal belongings were assigned in order to efface any connection the men may have had with home. And their social life was severely restricted. They could receive guests only on weekend afternoons—and then only their families (except for a few "hops"). They were now naval men, and their loyalty was no longer to parents or hometown, but to the Navy and its traditions.

The men were also subjected to a great deal of hazing to test their stamina, their ability to act under stress, and their commitment to their new career. As a classmate explained, the class had a "rough plebe year under the then-existing customs, and Carter got his share of the harassment along with the rest of us. There were capricious assignments of extra duties, physical endurance tests, infamous 'cruise box' races, occasional beatings with swords, and other inhumane treatments that went on occasionally for a full year." The plebe was expected to keep himself well informed on Mary Haworth's lovelorn column in the Washington *Post* (if he could not recite that day's column, he might be required to eat by "shoving out," i.e., eat at the table without a chair, or he might be required to do forty-seven pushups, the number determined by the year of his graduation). Other torments were designed to test one's regional sensitivities. A student might be required to quote a long speech given by one of his state's senators. Carter was ordered to sing "Marching Through Georgia"; when he politely refused to conform to this order, he was assigned punishment—to "shove out" and eat a "square meal" (i.e., make a square with each forkful of food).

Outwardly at least, Carter took all this as a joke, as most successful plebes do. As he later recalled, ". . . I refused to take the abuse seriously and treated it as a game." He even became the cruise box racing champion of his company. This was a contest in which midshipmen were required to don dress blues, leap into the boxes used to store personal belongings, shut the lids, change into their work whites, leap out, salute, leap back into the box, change back to dress blues, and jump out again.

Whatever the external appearance, the system did build some tension in Carter. A diary he kept at this time shows some of his tactics for avoiding those excesses:

On Thursday night I cut my hand on a broken cup at the table and had to have two stitches taken in it. I got on the excused squad because I couldn't wear a glove, and it wasn't so bad. . . . Wynne had me calling cadence and beat me with a klak. Not too bad. Been having three speeches per meal in Bull, and I'm really tired of them. I cut my gums this morning at table and as it was bleeding I didn't have to speak. I think it was worth it.

An institutional outlet was available for venting the bottled-up aggression hazing could cause. One hundred nights before graduation, from the evening meal until taps, the plebes and upperclassmen reversed position. Carter evidently fully enjoyed this occasion. One classmate recalls hearing of Carter's relish at paddling the posteriors of some of the more obnoxious members of the class of '45 with an aluminum bread tray.

Although the pressures were the most severe in the plebe year, a midshipman was subject to strict discipline throughout his stay at Annapolis. A naval officer had to learn how to meet routine tasks without dallying, to perform under pressure, and to conform gracefully to the orders of his superiors and the goals of his organization. Thus, all of Carter's three years at the Academy were strictly regulated. The midshipmen arose at 6:15 A.M. to reveille; everyone had to be out of his bed with the door of his room opened within forty seconds. From that time until "lights out" at 10:00 P.M. every moment of his day was accounted for—the midshipman was not even permitted to lie down on his bed while studying or relaxing.

The men marched to their classes under their section leaders and sat in assigned seats. Instructors were rotated every four weeks to prevent one section from suffering a poor teacher throughout an entire term. (Indeed, classes were so structured that the only way the midshipmen could make personal contact with the faculty was through extracurricular activities.) The curriculum was equally structured. Except for the language selection there were no electives. The curriculum was designed to train a man in naval engineering and the few

offerings in the social sciences and humanities were combined into one department of English, history, and government, which offered only one course each
term.

Carter's classes were mainly in engineering, mathematics, and other technical matters. Spanish was his language elective—he studied it for three years.
His only social science or humanities courses were a literature class his first
year, American government in his second summer, and modern European history and U.S. foreign policy in his second year. In Carter's last year almost
every course was devoted to some aspect of naval engineering: naval correspondence, navigation, strategy and tactics, gunnery, military law, ballistics,
thermodynamics, and alternating current.

In his senior year he signed up for ballroom dancing and received formal instruction in after-dinner speaking. (A naval officer was expected to be not only
an officer but a gentleman.) Like all the others, once or twice a month he would
join a group of midshipmen, officers, and the head of the department of English
in a small dining room of the main hall for a full banquet, with ginger ale in the
wineglasses. Several midshipmen would be called on to give short speeches on
behalf of the guest of honor following a "Hints on After Dinner Speaking" pamphlet from the English department. Through his stay at Annapolis, Carter, like
the other midshipmen, made "social calls," in which he left his calling card and
learned the etiquette that would train him in the proper behavior for high society. Even the proms, held bimonthly, served this end. The settings for the
dances were always elegant, and the midshipmen were expected to follow the
prescribed etiquette and act with grace—the officer should know how to perform with some chivalry toward the ladies.

The Annapolis regimen recognized the need for recreation. After drills and
just before dinner, the midshipmen had a free period, which most of them
devoted to sports. Carter turned out for cross-country track during his plebe
year. His coach, Captain Ellery Clark, has observed that this sport attracts a
unique breed—usually thin and introverted, intelligent, friendly, dedicated to
self-improvement, and willing to work very hard for the team. Indeed, Carter
and seven teammates tied for first place in one meet against Baltimore City
College, crossing the finish line abreast to demonstrate solidarity and loyalty.
But they were no stars. In the final meet, against Mercersburg Academy of
Pennsylvania, Carter placed seventh.

Aside from cross-country running, which he only did during his first year, in
his spare time Carter read periodicals such as *Look, Time,* and *Life,* and listened to records. After his plebe year he was fortunate to room with Robert
Scott, who owned a good collection of classical music. Though one classmate
does recall hearing Carter shout, "Shut that goddamned phonograph off," he
did acquire a taste for classical music.

In choosing his friends Carter turned to a kind of natural fraternity—the
men of the class of '47 in his company. He was not atypical. The social life at the
Academy was confined almost entirely to one's own classmates in one's own

company. Fraternizing with lowerclassmen was frowned upon for disciplinary reasons. And Bancroft Hall was so large, (the largest dormitory in the world with its forty acres of deck space), one did not meet others outside one's own living section. Except through sports and extracurricular activities, the mid-shipman did not get to know many classmates outside his own company.

In Carter's group there were about twenty-eight men who stayed together all three years. His closest friends were his rommates; D. J. Yuengling during his plebe year; and later, Blu Middleton, Louis Larcombe, and Bob Scott. In his senior year Carter asked Al Rusher to move in after the tragic death of Rusher's roommate, who killed himself by jumping from one of the towers in Bancroft Hall. The man who died was to have led the company spring semester. One of his classmates remembers, him as "exceptionally well liked, a top student, handsome, engaged to a beautiful girl, a good athlete, and seemed to have everything going for him. . . . He gave no hint of what he planned to do, or why. Speculation was that a football injury was causing occasional blackouts and that he felt his health was failing." The Academy dealt with this death by confronting it directly. "There was an impressive military funeral at the Academy, attended by the full brigade." Carter was also friendly with Francis Hertzog, Ralph Rodney Huston, Ralph Kinser, and John Thornton. As with other midshipmen, Carter's friendships were often based on geography—he tended to mainly "run with Southerners."

Carter's classmates saw him as the ever smiling "nice guy"—a brain without being a "slash" (i.e., he got good academic grades easily and naturally, not as a result of unseemly efforts at the expense of his classmates). As his yearbook entry read: "Studies never bothered Jimmy. In fact, the only times he opened his books were when classmates desired help on problems. This lack of study did not, however, prevent him from standing in the upper part of his class. Jimmy's many friends will remember him for his cheerful disposition and his ability to see the humorous side of any situation." He was not a womanizer, nor did he drink, tell dirty stories, use rough language, or make waves. Like most of the men he "blended in with the woodwork." His academic success is evident in his class standings. In his first year he scored 96.00 (out of a possible 110.00), placing him thirty-second in his class. At graduation he stood sixtieth (not fifty-ninth as he has reported) in his class.

His overall conduct score, however, suggests that he had a rebellious streak. (The score is computed on the basis of permissible demerits a midshipman may accumulate during a semester, the number of which decreases each year.) At the end of his plebe year he was ranked 398 in a class of 877. In his second year he was marked 564 on conduct (out of a class of 849); and his senior year score was 556 (out of a class of 822). His aptitude grades (assigned by the faculty and the company commander on the basis of their personal evaluations of the midshipman's potential as officer material) were somewhat higher. In his second year he was graded 345 out of a class of 849; and in his senior year he received a score of 99 out of 822.

But Carter did not win prominence as a class leader. Midshipmen became known outside the company through excellence in sports, dramatics, and other extracurricular activities, or through a position as a brigade or battalion officer. Carter never attained prominence in any of these ways. "A big man on campus," as one classmate recalls, "he was not."

Even in his company he did not really stand out. Though he performed at one time as the executive officer in charge of the hall formations, he never won command of his company. The selections were made by the officers from the first class men (i.e., seniors) based on their academic standing, athletic participation, personality, and general leadership skills, and the sets were changed each trimester to allow as many men as possible to gain the "command experience." The best officers were usually chosen for spring term as they officiated at graduation exercises.

No one seemed to consider Jimmy Carter as the man most likely to succeed. He was capable, but not marked for greatness. One classmate recalls that he seemed to be more of a follower than a leader: "He didn't show any signs of greatness, and I don't recall that he held any strong political or religious views. . . . I think we were all amazed when he became governor of Georgia, and positively astounded when he ran effectively for President. I still can't get over it."

It was Stansfield Turner of whom the class expected great things. As one old classmate recalls: "Stan . . . was extremely prominent at the Academy. He was a major athlete, very active in student affairs, and was brigade commander our last spring term, presiding over June week and graduation ceremonies. At the time it seemed quite likely that Stan would someday be an admiral, and probably Chief of Naval Operations. Unlike Carter and most of the rest of us, he had the appearance of 'greatness,' even at age twenty and twenty-one." He received a letter of commendation during senior year. In Carter's company, Don Whitmire had the mark of a man who would go to the top. He was an all-American football star and the informal company leader; he was the only one to win command outside the company (he was the spring striper, the commander of the 4th Battalion) and the only company member to win special recognition at graduation.

Yet Annapolis did help Carter gain social polish and the confidence that comes from survival in a highly competitive situation. Some social insecurity, derived from being a country boy, not of the upper class, may still have been there beneath the surface, to emerge when he entered politics as defender of the little guy against the "big shots." But he had made his way in the outside world. He would go home to Plains, Georgia, again but then it would be a base for power in the larger world.

Carter's graduation was June, 1946. On a Wednesday morning at eleven, the class of '47 and their guests gathered in Dahlgren Hall for the short graduation exercises—a fitting end to an emotionally rich and colorful six days. The men received their diplomas and their commissions, and the climax came when the men tossed their midshipmen's caps high in the air. They then dashed to their rooms for the last time, grabbing their traveling bags, officers caps, and shoulder boards, and then joined their guests by the Japanese bell, where their best womenfolk pinned on their shoulder boards. Lillian Carter and Rosalynn Smith did the honors for Jimmy Carter.

## Courtship

The Annapolis humor magazine, *The Log*, once printed a chart describing the different types of girls the midshipmen might date: the regal girl, the coquette, the childish girl, the athletic girl, the personality girl, and the natural girl. Only the latter two would do as naval wives. Rosalynn Smith would have been the model of the natural girl.

| | |
|---|---|
| *How She Looks:* | Brown hair, innocent-looking features, bright teeth. |
| *Why Do We Hate Her:* | She's hard to get next to . . . ! |
| *Why Do We Like Her:* | She's naive—truthful—modest, sincere—and straightforward. |
| *By These Words Ye Shall Know Her:* | "I don't love you, John, but can't we still be friends?" |
| *Is She Worth the Time and Trouble:* | Nice work if you can get it! |
| *The Successful Wooer Will:* | Be natural—gay—truthful and candid—and own a sense of humor. |
| *And This Is How It Will End:* | It will end like all marriages should—IN HEAVEN! |

From a respectable family with roots in southwest Georgia, Rosalynn Smith shared Jimmy's background and values. Her mother, Allie Murray Smith, had been reared on the family farm at Botsford, south of Plains, by a strict Baptist father, "Captain Murray," and a Lutheran mother, Rosa Wise. After a period studying home economics at the Georgia State College for Women in Milledgeville (a favorite college of the women of Plains), Allie Murray married Edgar Smith, whom she had known since ninth grade when he drove her school bus. After their marriage he clerked in a store to support his family, then became the town mechanic. A respected member of the community, he was at one time elected to the city council.

Their first child, Rosalynn, was born about a year after the marriage, on August 18, 1927. "She was meek and shy," and even as a child could go a whole day in a white dress and keep it clean, her mother says. She seldom disobeyed her parents. Allie was to say later, when asked if she could recall any naughtiness by Rosalynn:

Well, I can't think of anything. She used to run away. Well, I don't mean really run away, she would just go off and not tell me. Then one day her daddy came home . . . and he asked where she was and I said I guessed she was over there (at a little boy's house across the street) because I couldn't find her. He went over and got her and switched her little legs all the way home. Used to tell me I didn't switch 'em quite enough and I used to tell him he switched 'em too much.

They had no specific ambitions for her. "I just wanted her to live a good life and be a good person," Allie recalls.

In 1940, when Rosalynn was in high school, her father developed leukemia. Lillian Carter was one of the neighbors who helped out, often coming to give him the shots the doctor prescribed. One Sunday morning he called his children into the bedroom and told them his working days were over. "I want you, all of you, to go to college. . . . I want you to have a better position in life." When he died, on October 22, Earl Carter was one of the pallbearers. In his will he left a small fund for his children's college education. Allie went to work "taking in the town's sewing" (she would later remember with a smile), then as a clerk assisting the town postmaster until she retired at seventy. When Allie's mother, Rosa, died in September 1941, "Captain Murray" came to live with the Smiths in Plains and to work their farms until he no longer could; then he sold his half of the land to Jimmy Carter and willed the half he owned to Allie.

Edgar Smith's death, of course, had an impact on the thirteen-year-old Rosalynn. She had "worshiped" her father, as she recalled, though she remembers chiefly that he drove a school bus and drank hot, hot coffee and thought the worst thing that a woman could do was to smoke in public. Rosalynn helped her mother with the younger children. "Looking back on it," Rosalynn says, "I didn't do nearly enough to help my mother." And her brother Murray remembers "Those long afternoons, we were by ourselves at home . . . Sister—that's Rosalynn—was old enough to know right from wrong and she kept us kids pretty straight." But her obligations were not that onerous. The house on South Bond Street was larger and somewhat nicer than the old Carter home in Archery, and was paid up at the time of Edgar's death. The farm property Allie inherited from her husband brought some rental money and Allie also inherited some money from her mother.

Certainly Rosalynn never had to help support the family. As a teen-ager she did get some extra spending money by working in Ann Dodson's Beauty Parlor, over the drugstore downtown. But "she just washed hair and did things like that," according to Allie.

She was subjected to a strict discipline. Alcohol was not permitted in the home; she had to go to Sunday school and church and study the Bible regularly. When she began to date, Allie impressed upon her, as she did the other children, a moral obligation to do what is right to show that she had not failed as a mother.

Rosalynn studied hard and did well in school. "She was an excellent student," her mother remembers, "read a lot and rarely needed help with her homework. Social studies was her hardest subject; and she'd ask me to wake her at five o'clock in the morning so she could go over her lessons two or three times before getting on the school bus." After graduating from Plains High School, Rosalynn enrolled at Georgia Southwestern, where she took the general curriculum. (The tuition was low and Rosalynn could live at home and commute to school on the bus each day. As Allie says, "She didn't pay a penny of her education.") But if she had any special amibitions or dreams, she didn't share them with her mother. Although her father had expressed a desire that she become a nurse, she showed no inclination toward that profession. She just wanted to do her best in school.

As a good friend of Ruth Carter, Rosalynn had seen Jimmy off and on at the Carter home in Archery and at the Pond House, and they ran into each other at school, in the drugstore, or on picnics or outings at Magnolia Springs. Apparently he didn't interest her especially—until one summer when he came home on leave from the Academy in his snappy white uniform. She developed a "crush" overnight. Two days before he was to return to Annapolis in the summer of 1945, she and Ruth Carter volunteered to help him clean the Pond House. "We just slaved all day and then I went to the Methodist Youth Fellowship at the church. . . . After supper Ruth and her date came by [the church] and Jimmy was sitting in the rumble seat [of their car]. He got out of the car and asked me if I'd go to a movie with them. I was so excited. It was wonderful."

Jimmy's recollection of that first date is similar. He also says that he paid little attention to Rosalynn, but that after that first date, he decided he wanted to marry her: "I returned home later that night and told my mother that Rosalynn had gone to the movies with me. Mother asked if I liked her, and I was already sure of my answer when I replied, 'She's the girl I want to marry.' Rosalynn has never had any competition for my love."

Lillian was less sure of Rosalynn. When he told her in passing that he had another date with Rosalynn the next night, Lillian said: "Jimmy, she's just a little girl. She's Ruth's friend." What Lillian was actually thinking, as she told Gail Sheehy later, was: "My Jimmy is so much more sophisticated than she is. . . . this little girl Rosalynn is naive."

During his Christmas vacation in 1945, Jimmy asked Rosalynn if she would marry him. She said, "No," but she did accept his invitation to visit Annapolis in February, and there she said, "Yes." They were married on Sunday, July 7, 1946, Rosalynn in a navy and white suit bought for the occasion and a "shoulder corsage of purple throated orchids." The society news of the Americus *Times-Recorder* wrote of the wedding:

Tall flower baskets filled with soft ferns and daisies were placed on either side of the pulpit stand. . . .

Preceding the wedding, Mrs. J. E. Hall played "Evening Star", Wagner's "Tannhauser" and Nevin's "Venetian Love Song," Miss Gene Hall sang "I Love You Truly" and "Because."

Mrs. Hall played softly McDowell's "To a Wild Rose" while the vows were said . . .

After the wedding the couple headed for a short honeymoon in the mountains at Chimney Rock, North Carolina, where they stayed in the home of an Annapolis friend.

With his Navy commission and a wife who would give him the emotional and physical support he would need, Jimmy was ready to start working toward the realization of his dreams—whether to become Chief of Naval Operations as he later stated, or governor of Georgia as he had told some of his friends in Plains while in school there.

# THREE

# Naval Career

J IMMY CARTER reported to his first naval post at Norfolk, Virginia, on August 8, 1946—the beginning of a seven-year, four-month career in the Navy. His initial assignment was to the USS *Wyoming*—his fourth choice in the lottery held at Annapolis. (He was one of the last to draw.)

The *Wyoming*, an old battleship used to test new weapons and methods of fire control, had been launched in 1911 and was declared unsafe during Carter's tour of duty.

Carter's billet on the ship was as a deck officer, a radar officer, and an Information Center officer. When the ship was decommissioned and scrapped, the crew was shifted to the USS *Mississippi*, where Carter served for another year, this time as training officer. (With the *Wyoming*'s retirement, the *Mississippi* served as the gunnery development ship of the Atlantic Fleet.)

Carter's service on these two ships must have been quite tedious. In the Navy the ships were known as the "Chesapeake Raiders," because their operation was limited to the Navy's gunnery practice ranges in Chesapeake Bay. As Carter recalled the *Wyoming*, "The work was interesting, but the duty was terrible. We were at sea most of the time with only about two-thirds of a normal crew." As the training officer on the *Mississippi*, he was confined to an office deep in the ship, and thus missed more varied activities on the ship's deck.

His duty created problems for his personal life. Rosalynn and he had rented an apartment in Norfolk, but Jimmy was at sea all week, as well as every third weekend. Nor did the young couple have much money. (Carter made only $300 per month.) And about one year after arriving in Norfolk, John William Carter, called "Jack," was born in the Portsmouth Naval Hospital on July 3, 1947. The young couple did have old friends to socialize with, however; Albert Rusher, Carter's former Annapolis roommate was there with his bride, and the couples often got together in each other's homes.

While on the USS *Mississippi*, Carter applied for a Rhodes Scholarship. He did not discuss his application with his friends at any length, but some did know about it and were impressed that he should be considered for such an honor. Carter, did not get the scholarship, nor did he even secure a nomination for it from Georgia, nor make the national finals (contrary to what he was to imply in later interviews). Although his associates do not remember that he was particularly upset by the failure, he stated later that it did send him into a depression. His 1975 description of the man who beat him in the Rhodes competition (probably the Georgia nominee) is especially interesting:

I got to the final screening board and there was another fellow in there with me. He was a tall gangly fellow, real peculiar-looking guy. We were the last two. He studied Elizabethan poetry, and the interviewing board asked him something about current events, and he said he wasn't interested in anything that happened after Queen Elizabeth died. . . . They asked me every question they could think of. I answered them all. Current events. Philosophy. Music. Nuclear physics. But the other kid got the Rhodes scholarship. I didn't even feel bitter about it. But, as a matter of fact, he went over there from Georgia and he had a nervous breakdown.

If Carter did indeed suffer depression as a result of this rejection it was over a disappointment he should have anticipated. While he had been a good student at Annapolis, he had not been a star. He had not led his class academically, nor could he claim either class leadership or special athletic ability compared to stars like Stansfield Turner and Don Whitmire—qualities particularly important in Rhodes competition.

When his two years of compulsory surface-craft sea duty were over, "Jim" (as he was then called) chose submarines as "the best opportunity for purposeful service." It was a prestigious and highly prized service because it could lead to an early command position. Carter was accepted into the six-month training school and, in the summer of 1948, the family moved to New London, Connecticut.

Carter's training class included about sixty junior officers, all coming from two to five years of sea duty. Competition was intense and about 15 percent of the class failed to graduate in December. Aside from the classroom work there was practical training on locally based submarines. As a classmate recalls: "We went to sea frequently, on a daily basis, getting under way from the submarine base in the early morning hours, diving and firing torpedoes in the nearby waters of Long Island and Block Island Sounds, and returning to post at nightfall." The pay was very low—about $282 a month—and for entertainment many of the couples settled for playing bridge in their homes, going to an occasional base movie, and drinking a little "grocery store beer." The Carters did not often join in these "informal entertainments." "Jim" and Rosalynn seemed shy and hard to get to know. He seemed to study more often and appeared "somewhat more conscientious" than many. He graduated near the top of the group of forty-four survivors of the program.

In December of 1948 Carter received his first assignment of submarine duty—as the electronics officer on the USS *Pomfret*, a conventionally powered, submarine of World War II vintage. It was a small boat, carrying a crew of seventy-five men and only five or six officers. Carter flew to Hawaii to join the crew, and shortly after his arrival the *Pomfret* left for a trip to the Far East. Carter recalls experiencing one of the worst storms in Pacific Ocean history. He was seasick for five straight days. As Warren Colegrove, the engineering officer of the *Pomfret*, reports: "He had one helluva time. But I will say this. He never refused to take his watch. He'd take his bucket right up on the bridge. He was a gutsy guy."

Carter later told of being washed overboard and almost losing his life:

In the middle of one night—during a heavy storm—we were on the surface and I was on the submarine bridge about fifteen feet above the level of the ocean itself, holding on as tightly as I could to an iron pipe hand rail inside the bridge shield.

An enormous wave rose around us to a level of about six feet or so above my head. I lost my grip as the force of the wave tore my hand from the hand rail, and I found myself swimming literally within the huge wave, completely separated from the submarine itself.

After I swam for a good while—it seemed forever—the wave receded, and I landed on top of the five-inch gun located about thirty feet aft of where I had been standing. I clung desperately to the gun barrel, and finally was able to lower myself to the deck and return to my watch station. Had the currents been even slightly broadside instead of from forward to aft, I never would have landed on the ship as the wave receded, and would undoubtedly have been lost at sea in the dark storm.

Being washed overboard was not an uncommon experience, and the men, usually tied themselves to the deck with a lifeline as a precaution. It is not clear from Carter's retelling, whether he had on that lifeline or not.

Usual social distinctions between officers and enlisted men were maintained on the *Pomfret*. Despite its small size, there was a separate officers' quarters/ship office just behind the forward torpedo room; and at dinner the officers were served by Filipino stewards on service of good silver and china. Roy Smallwood, the commander, says the officers were a "clique." Yet the constant threat of danger forced all the men to learn their duties and work in close cooperation with each other. In one officer's words: "In a very real sense, each crew member controlled the lives of every other crew member on board." Carter later stated: "There was . . . a closeness just among men which I liked."

Most members of the *Pomfret* crew remember Carter as a competent, hard-working, soft-spoken person who smiled a lot and was easy to get along with. He even tutored some of his shipmates. But some of his colleagues viewed him as a person apart. When the other officers lingered over their after-dinner coffee each night in the tiny wardroom, or settled in for a long game of cribbage, bridge, or poker, Carter would simply watch—or retire to read or work some sonar problems. Nor did he participate in the long, soul-revealing talks that occupied some of the men at sea.

The *Pomfret* returned to Hawaii in the spring of 1949, and Rosalynn, who had driven their first car to San Diego, arrived about a week later. (As Carter later says, his married life with Rosalynn was one of "constant separations interspersed with ecstatic reunions and the melding of ourselves over the years into a closer relationship of love, understanding, and mutual respect.") They settled in a two-bedroom apartment in a complex for married officers on the island of Oahu.

Their best friends were "Hap" and "Rebel" Trottier, a young couple who lived in the same complex. "Hap" was on the *Pomfret*, and "Rebel" and Rosalynn often got together while their husbands were at sea. When the men were home, the two couples would go to the beach, to the movies, or dine together or take the children to the zoo or sight-seeing. There was no money for nightclubs but they did have parties in their homes or, Saturdays, at the officers' club.

Rosalynn, was quiet, not very outgoing. One friend saw her as a "Southern belle"—seemingly helpless. But as the Trottiers remember, she was "delightful once you got to know her." Rosalynn was pregnant with her second child at the time. Jimmy wanted a girl, but they had a boy—James Earl Carter III—born on April 12, 1950, in Tripler Hospital on the island of Oahu. The nurses called him "Chip," a name he carried thereafter.

With the beginning of the Korean War in June, 1950, the *Pomfret* was ordered back to San Diego. The seaport was so crowded with military personnel that the only place the Carters could find to live was in a neighborhood of Mexican immigrants. In these alien surroundings, and with Jimmy often at sea, Rosalynn felt lonely and isolated.

Shortly after settling there Carter received orders to proceed to Groton, Connecticut to help prepare for service the USS *K-1* a small diesel-powered attack submarine and sonar platform. For a short time Carter was the only Navy person on the submarine, which had not yet been commissioned. But when the *K-1* was launched, more senior officers were assigned to the boat. Carter served as a junior officer in charge of the engineering division from November, 1951, to October, 1952. Later, recalling his tour on the *K-1*, he said he had been "intrigued with the innovative and experimental nature of this work." And the *K-1* itself "contributed a great deal to the knowledge of undersea sound transmission and an analysis of enemy ship movements by monitoring various noises at long range."

While on the *K-1*, Carter qualified for command of submarines of the conventional kind. His command thesis (suggested to him by his superior officer) dealt with a new method of establishing underwater distances using only passive listening devices. On June 1, 1952, in accord with the usual three-year schedule, he was promoted to full lieutenant. He did not gain sufficient seniority, however, to win command of his own submarine.

He was an effective officer, as other men on both the *Pomfret* and the *K-1* were later to testify. Most remember his extreme self-confidence, his complete self-control, his capacity for hard work, his desire for new fields to conquer, and his ability to work with others. He was able to trust his subordinates, according to Captain Smallwood of the *Pomfret;* and Warren Colegrove says he was not afraid to take stands in the wardroom with senior officers—a man who could say, "Captain, you're wrong." A sailor on the *K-1* also found him to be a helpful officer:

There were several sailors, including myself, who had been trying to make chief petty officer. . . . Of course I'd just completed a test that I'd failed because the basics of studying I didn't have. Thus when he started talking to me about "are you going to stay in the Navy?" I told him I had planned to. He said, "I imagine you'd like to go as high as you can go." I said, "I certainly would." So he said, "Okey, I'm going to start teaching you some mathematics. Maybe you'd like to learn to use a slide rule." I told him I would.

Yet while on the *K-1*, Carter exhibited that trait of personal elusiveness earlier shipmates had noticed. When off duty, he usually rushed home to his wife and growing family (their third son, Jeff Donnell, was born on August 16, 1952), and his fellow officers never really got to know him. Captain Charles E. Woods, who shared a stateroom with him, says that he probably was as close to Carter as anyone on the *K-1*, but the relationship was not a "close friendship." Roy Cowdrey, the ship's executive officer, when showed photographs of the crew by a newspaper reporter, could remember satires of the peccadilloes, and scrapes of many of the men but not one about Carter: "It's hard to believe about anybody in the Navy . . . but there are no sea stories about Jimmy Carter."

William Lalor, who first met Carter on the *K-1*, remembers that while Jimmy did not play jokes on people, he could laugh at funny situations and the jokes of others. "I can remember him being in a really precarious situation a couple of times . . . the ship would be sitting almost vertical. He'd just laugh and scratch his head and say, 'You know there's something wrong. We shouldn't be this way.' "

There is conflicting testimony about Carter's political concerns at this period. Carter himself says he was the only officer in the submarine school to favor Truman openly in the 1948 election. And an officer from the *Pomfret* says:

He was interested in politics, he liked to discuss them. He would talk about the '48 election, which had only been a year or so previously. He was also interested in social areas. Very, very concerned about the plight of the black man in his home state. He had grown up and played with black boys. He couldn't understand that at a certain point in time, they went their way and he went his way. It always concerned him. There was a nagging concern about this. I have no trouble believing his real interest in social welfare areas.

Smallwood and Lowell Fitch from the *Pomfret*, however, say that Carter had no real political affiliations at the time (an attitude encouraged in the professional Navy, where the ideal is the officer who remains above partisan politics), and Frank Andrews, Carter's commander on the *K-1* notes: "I was with him two years. I can't recall any discussion about politics. He wasn't forever running up on the base, organizing people. He was down on the ship, working his backside off."

## Rickover's Nuclear Submarines

While on the *K-1*, Carter applied for an assignment to what he thought the "finest Navy billet available to any officer of my rank"—the atomic submarine division of the Bureau of Ships headed by Admiral Hyman Rickover. Earlier, Rickover had won support for the development and construction of the first atomic submarine. Now the Navy was going to build two prototypal atomic-powered submarines: the *Nautilus* and the *Sea Wolf*. Rickover, who was in charge of all these programs, personally interviewed all officers who applied for duty under him. In his interviews Rickover always gave stress tests to the candidates, and his screening of Carter was typical. As Carter remembers it:

It was the first time I met Admiral Rickover, and we sat in a large room by ourselves for more than two hours, and he let me choose any subjects I wished to discuss. Very carefully, I chose those about which I knew most at the time—current events, seamanship, music, literature, naval tactics, electronics, gunnery—and he began to ask me a series of questions of increasing difficulty. In each instance, he soon proved that I knew relatively little about the subject I had chosen.

He always looked right into my eyes, and he never smiled. I was saturated with cold sweat.

Finally, he asked me a question and I thought I could redeem myself. He said, "How did you stand in your class at the Naval Academy?" Since I had completed my sophomore year at Georgia Tech before entering Annapolis as a plebe, I had done very well, and I swelled my chest with pride and answered, "Sir, I stood fifty-ninth in a class of 820!" I sat back to wait for the congratulations—which never came. Instead, the question: "Did you do your best?" I started to say, "Yes, sir," but I remembered who this was, and recalled several of the many times at the Academy when I could have learned more about our allies, our enemies, weapons, strategy, and so forth. I was just human. I finally gulped and said, "No, sir, I didn't *always* do my best."

He looked at me for a long time, and then turned his chair around to end the interview. He asked one final question, which I have never been able to forget—or to answer. He said, "Why not?" I sat there for a while, shaken, and then slowly left the room.

Carter was accepted into the program and at first had temporary duty with the Atomic Energy Commission in Washington, D.C. (from November 3, 1952 to March 3, 1953), then returned to Schenectady to train himself and the prospective crew of the USS *Sea Wolf*. There, with Lieutenant Charles Carlisle, he participated in two different noncredit programs offered by the Extension Division of Union College: one-semester graduate-level courses in reactor technology and nuclear physics. (Carter recalls: "I'll never forget the difficulty of those assignments nor the rapidity with which I was taught nuclear physics and mathematics.")

He and Carlisle were in charge of the noncommissioned officers, who came in groups of thirty or forty to study nuclear physics for about twenty weeks. (The course was given by Professor Way of the physics department, the text was White's *College Physics*, and laboratory facilities were available at the nearby Knolls Atomic Power Laboratory at the Navy installation in West Milston, and in a mock nuclear submarine, complete with console, at Schenec-tady.) Their job was to help the men in these study sessions—the activity Carter was evidently referring to in *Why Not the Best?* when he mentioned tak-ing the enlisted men "from simple fractions through differential equations within a year."

In addition to his class obligations, Carter was a trouble-shooter. On one oc-casion he helped disassemble a damaged nuclear reactor core at Chalk River, Canada, dangerous work, as Carter describes it, that left anxiety in its wake. As he has written: "For several months afterward, we saved our feces and urine to have them monitored for radioactivity. We had absorbed a year's maximum al-lowance of radiation in 1 minute and 29 seconds. There were no apparent after-effects from this exposure—just a lot of doubtful jokes among ourselves about death versus sterility."

Though Carter was to later call himself a nuclear scientist, it is apparent that his formal training in that field was limited; he had had no training in nuclear physics at Annapolis and his subsequent graduate work at Union College con-sisted of a noncredit, one-semester course. One professor who taught the course says that "No one who took that program could be classed as a nuclear engineer—it was at quite an elementary level." Yet Carter did pick up a great deal of practical experience. (Joel Snow, an official with the National Science Foundation, who served as an instructor in the nuclear power program that Carter attended, reports that "The officers in that program participated very di-rectly in the construction process [of the reactor] and they certainly functioned on board as engineers.")

Perhaps the most significant aspect of his eleven months in the nuclear sub-marine program was the impact Rickover had on him. The young lieutenant formed an extravagant admiration for the detached and driving admiral, so much so that Carter was to testify later that Rickover had a "profound effect on my life—perhaps more than anyone except my own parents."

One can discover a great deal about a person through the heroes he chooses as well as the traits he admires. For Carter, Rickover was "probably the most competent and innovative naval engineer of all time, . . . unbelievably hard-working, . . ." and he exacted the last drop of performance from both himself and others: "He always insisted that we know our jobs in the most minute de-tail, which is really a necessary basic characteristic of good submariners."

He also admired Rickover's way of relating to subordinates: the absence of comment was a compliment and criticism was severe if the job did not meet his perfectionist standards.

Whenever the admiral would come around to inspect my work, if I had done a perfect job, which wasn't too often, but every now and then I did, he never said a word—never once did he say, "Good job, Jimmy" or "Well done, Carter." If he found no fault, he sim-ply looked, turned around, and walked away.

However, if I made the slightest mistake, in one of the loudest and most obnoxious, voices I ever heard, he would turn around and tell the other people in the area what a horrible disgrace I was to the Navy, and that I ought to be back in the oldest and slowest and smallest submarine from which I had come.

Rickover had some other traits that Carter does not mention. An unorthodox naval officer, he was often arrogant with his fellow officers and inclined to bypass normal channels. Expert at bureaucratic infighting, by February, 1949, he had secured two offices for himself—heading both the Navy and the Atomic Energy Commission branches of the same projects, a straddle that became invaluable later as work on the atomic submarines proceeded: Rickover could write himself letters, to which he would immediately dictate a reply, obtaining in a moment complete AEC approval for what he wanted to do.* In 1952, passed over for promotion to rear admiral a second time, which ordinarily required one to retire from the Navy, he showed both "propriety" in his handling of the press and political skill in dealing with his Congressional supporters, who spearheaded a campaign that ultimately led to an unprecedented reversal of the earlier decisions of the selection boards—and Rickover's own promotion to rear admiral.

It is interesting to note the similarities in Carter's descriptions of the two authorities whom he sees as the most influential in shaping his character: his father, Earl Carter, and Rickover. Both were viewed as extraordinarily competent, hard-working, and demanding of those who worked under them. Both expected conformity from their subordinates; good work was not applauded and failure was noticed and punished. It is also interesting to note that the two men had some qualities in common that Jimmy Carter does not discuss—both have been described by associates as political men who looked after their own, shrewd, manipulative, and tough.

The act of conforming to such exacting figures is apt to become onerous. To relieve such pressure, some subordinates find ways to get around the situation. One of Carter's associates at Schenectady gives an example of such adaptation: "[Rickover] had us all write reports to him each week and we weren't supposed to show each other the reports. So we figured out amongst ourselves that we'd better compare notes on these reports or otherwise we'd cause ourselves some unnecessary problems. We had enough things to get fixed anyhow." Carter, however, identified with the heroic figure—Rickover's demands were perceived as a force for his own betterment.

Nonetheless, Carter was to admit later, in passing, that "deep within I had an adverse reaction, I felt like he was pushing me too hard, because I had been a pretty good officer when I got there." And while at Schenectady, Carter did a

---

* According to one of Rickover's critics, Admiral Elmo Zumwalt, he was also a harsh administrator, running his department like a "totalitarian mini-state," often violating Navy regulations himself while severely punishing subordinates who might violate his rules. Zumwalt also views Rickover as a martinet, drawing a portrait of members of his AEC inspection team walking around, "clipboard in hand, making notes on who was smoking and drinking a soda or talking to friends." And Zumwalt thought him vindictive, claiming that he ruined the career of at least one man because he opposed a Rickover management plan.

landscape painting that suggests an inner bleakness his verbal recollections deny. A historian who saw the picture describes it and his reaction to it: "My God—what utter despair—such a bare, windswept painting. Four trees stood out, three of them almost levelled by the wind, one straight, with a bit of water and a boat, a mountain, and an overwhelming greyness."

There are also some indications that Carter may have escaped the demands of his father by a certain emotional detachment from him. In 1976 he was to state that he had not seen his father from the age of seventeen until his return to Plains in 1953. That may have been an indication of a certain emotional separation, rather than a physical one—for Earl did visit Jimmy at Annapolis quite often, as well as at his base in San Diego, and Jimmy made the usual vacation trips home both as a midshipman and a young naval officer. (Later, on his trip home to Plains over the Memorial Day weekend in 1977, Jimmy did not decorate his father's grave, though he is buried on a road leading to the Pond House; most of the other townspeople did put flowers on the graves of their relatives.)

Another way of dealing with an authority toward whom one feels ambivalence is to assume the superior's role oneself. There is a fascinating symbolic role reversal in Carter's recollection of his part in saving his hero's career. In an interview for the Richard Russell Oral History Project, Carter recounts his talks with the Senator about Rickover's situation when he was passed over for promotion to Admiral, and how Russell played a key role in changing the law so Rickover could stay in the Navy. Carter also joked about Rickover having only a few people on his side—Senator Russell, President Truman, Congressman Vinson, and with a grin, "Lt. J. G. Carter." (The occasion was a meeting with Vinson on the courthouse steps at Milledgeville just before the general election in 1970.) In these recollections Carter suggests (though he does not explicitly claim) a role in saving his hero's career. Actually he seems not to have been that close to Russell, and Senator Henry Jackson and Congressman Sidney Yates were the prime movers in the campaign to keep Rickover in active service, though Russell undoubtedly supported them.

In his father's case, Carter could take over his role literally. When Earl Carter became ill sometime in 1952, Jimmy started talking to his commander on the *K-1*, Frank Andrews, "about the plantation in Georgia—he used that word—and all the people who worked on it. . . . I remember that clearly, because it was just about the only time he wasn't talking about the ship or the Navy." In the summer of 1953, when word came that his father had cancer, he obtained a leave and went back to Plains. There father and son "talked about old times together and about those intervening eleven years when we had rarely seen each other." Jimmy was impressed by the friends his father had. Exaggerating a bit, he remembered "hundreds of people came by to speak to Daddy or to bring him a choice morsel of food or some fresh flowers." And after Earl's death, on July 22, 1953, Jimmy began to compare his own life, with its relatively detached and transient relationships, to his father's solid anchoring in a community. "When my father died," Gloria remembers, people came that we didn't know at all—the whites, the blacks, from all walks of life. Later, I heard Jimmy talking about it when he was trying to decide whether to come out of the Navy or not. He said, 'If I died, nobody would care. Not really care.' Not that he wasn't doing the important things in life, but in that atmosphere [Navy life] there was no place to make the kind of friends who really would stand and cry.

Carter has since described his feelings: "I began to think about the relative significance of his life and mine," he said. "He was an integral part of the community, and had a wide range of varied but interrelated interests and responsibilities. He was his own boss, and his life was stabilized by the slow and evolutionary change in the local societal structure."

Back in Schenectady Carter discussed his own future with his friend Bill Lalor. He made it sound as if it was his moral duty to return to Plains to save the farm and all those who depended on it.

. . . he'd come from this little town in Plains, Georgia, and it was almost like a medieval idea. One man, his father, was responsible for all the souls in Plains, Georgia. Without his father, those 1,500 people were not going to have any means to live. . . . As I recall, there was nobody at the right age in his family to take over this business. He was just torn over that obligation to those people and the idea that he was picked to be chief engineer of the *Sea Wolf*.

This idea struck Lalor as odd, since he came from a big city where no one family was as vital as Carter perceived his to be.

Whatever the psychological pull of Plains, Jimmy had certain conflicts with Rosalynn over this future course. She liked the cosmopolitan life of a Navy wife and had no desire to exchange it for what Jimmy described as "the restrictive life of our home in Plains, where our families lived and where our married freedom might be cramped or partially dominated by relatives, particularly her mother and my mother." And as she says, "We were just having a good time, kind of independent of the family. I was afraid my mother and Jimmy's mother would all be telling me what to do."

Carter had to sort out his career plans. As he suggested to Bill Moyers, later, it was a hard choice. "Did I want to be the Chief of Naval Operations . . . or did I want to go back and build a more diverse life . . ." There were drawbacks to remaining in the Navy—though Carter does not mention them in his later accounts. The Navy did not provide much room for the luxuries of life. And as a fellow officer at Schenectady noted, the outlook for the future was not particularly good. One of Carter's Annapolis classmates, who also left the service after eight years, recalls:

At this time, the pay was low. . . . promotions were exceedingly slow. . . . During the war promotions had been automatic after eighteen months or less, with no examination. Even though most of us made full lieutenant during the Korean War (the war opened up promotions briefly), a bulge had developed in the ranks ahead of us, and the next jump [to lieutenant commander] appeared far away.

The alumni class secretary, describing the situation in a similar vein, writes; "The national economy was starting to boom with lots of opportunity for those who left the service. Many [Navy officers] decided they wanted to become doctors or lawyers or ministers or businessmen. . . ." Indeed, of the 760 of Carter's classmates who were alive thirty years later, only forty-three were still on active duty.

If Carter ever wished to achieve his earlier goal, to become governor of Georgia, he would have to return home. His father's death provided the opportunity to step into an already successful peanut-processing and -farming enterprise. But he had to act now: Billy was still in high school and too young to take control of his father's business; Lillian was too depressed by the death of her husband; Gloria was locked into the traditional role of farm wife; and Ruth was living in North Carolina, raising her young children.

Whatever the complexity of his motives, Carter finally applied for a release from the Navy. It was approved in October, 1953.

# FOUR

# Return to Plains

BACK IN PLAINS, Jimmy Carter quickly stepped into his daddy's footsteps. As executor of the estate, he first had to deal with the division of his father's property. In his will Earl had provided funds for the education of his two youngest children, given the house and his town lots to Lillian, and requested that his other property be sold and divided equally among his wife and children. Jimmy merged his own share of the estate with Lillian's and Billy's, and bought out Gloria and Ruth—forming a corporation with himself as manager.

Earl Carter had already planted that year's peanut crop. He had died as the harvest peanut season approached—so Jimmy and Rosalynn drove back and forth between Schenectady and Plains that summer to process the crops. Back home for good, they had the problem of collecting the outstanding accounts from the feed and seed business. Earl had made the usual loans (about $90,000) to local farmers for their seed in the spring of 1953, with payment due after the fall harvest. But 1953 was a bad drought year and Carter had difficulty collecting. He netted less than $200 during his first year home. The debts were not written off; they were simply extended to the next year.

With the drought continuing into the summer of 1954, bringing most farm operations to a standstill, Jimmy took an active civic role, as Earl had done before him. He and Rosalynn joined the Plains Baptist Church to which he had belonged as a boy, and became active in its organizations. Their eldest son, six-year-old Jack, was sent to the Plains school (Miss Julia Coleman still taught high-school English, though Y. T. Sheffield had taken over her position as principal.) They became involved in the Plains Parent-Teachers Association. Jimmy was elected a vice-president of the Plains Lions Club and pushed their drive to build a community (but segregated) swimming pool. Along with other town leaders he planned a political rally and barbecue in August, 1954, bringing him into contact with gubernatorial candidates M. E. Thompson and Marvin Griffin, and other political leaders.

At first Jimmy and Rosalynn lived with Lillian. But "there is no house big enough for two women to live together," as Lillian Carter later said. So Jimmy and Rosalynn moved out of her house into an apartment in a red brick public housing project on Olive Street, a block away. A few months later they rented the old Montgomery house, and in 1956, they moved to Dr. Thad Wise's house on Old Preston Road near the Carter family home in Archery where Jimmy had been reared. (It was as drafty as the old Carter house had been. The boys had to sleep under electric blankets, causing Lillian to confide to her friends at the Stitch and Chat Club her fears that they might be electrocuted.)

Carter took over his father's office in the business district of Plains, still but a block long on Main Street. But unlike Earl, Jimmy made Rosalynn a working partner in the business. (As Lillian has said somewhat wistfully, "My husband owned the business and I was just his wife. But when they came home, Jimmy and I bought the business from the other children and her name was not on the deed as a partner, but immediately she was just a co-partner.") As business picked up, Rosalynn came to work full time at the warehouse, keeping the books, doing the taxes, and performing general office chores. During the harvest season she weighed the farmers' trucks and wrote their checks—sometimes in the thousands of dollars, representing the farmer's whole year of toil. She took a correspondence course in accounting and mastered the subject. ("I was sure I could have even passed the test for CPA . . . And I *loved* it. To make all those books balance? I liked it better than anything I've ever done.")

Jimmy sought her advice, and she gave it: "He came to me on all the decisions about the business, and I could advise him, because I kept all the books, I studied the tax laws, I knew everything that was going on—and it was always exciting." Later she managed the business for the three months a year that Carter was away in the state legislature. "And I felt very, very important, because he couldn't have done it all if I hadn't managed the business."*

Jimmy and Rosalynn's return did require some adjustment by the rest of the family. Billy, only eight when Jimmy first left home, did not know his brother well. An impulsive and forthright youngster, he did not respond well to authority or discipline. Further, he had been very close to Earl, whose death occurred at a time when a boy normally needs his father to provide direction and discipline. In the fall of 1953, Billy became a student at the nearby Gordon Military Academy, but he returned to Plains High School and graduated from there in June of 1955. He was near the bottom of his class academically, the only member of his class not to submit a picture for the school yearbook. His rebellious tendencies were even noted in the ironic testament attributed to him in the yearbook: "I, Billy Carter, do hereby will my ability to stay out of arguments to Jimmy Jones." Right after graduation he enlisted as a private in

* In assuming business responsibilities, Rosalynn was showing the same energy that characterized many wives in Plains. The women frequently worked as nurses, teachers, bank tellers—or as business partners with their husbands. The Carters' major competitors in peanut processing were the Williamses, and in that operation Virginia Harris Williams was a full partner and bookkeeper. When Billy took over the Carter warehouse later, his wife, Sybil, would do the same.

the Marines and that same summer married Sybil Spires, a fifteen-year-old junior at Plains High School, in a formal wedding in the Plains Baptist Church. Despite her youth, Sybil was a fortunate choice for Billy—intelligent, popular, attractive, and a talented pianist. More important, she was to provide the stability and support that Billy sorely needed.

After assignments in Illinois, California, Japan, and North Carolina, Billy left the Marines in 1959. He returned home for about two years, but evidently did not take to his brother's authority in the business and departed again for Emory University. According to his own accounts he flunked out after three years, knocked about the country a bit with his wife and small children (selling paint for a while in Macon), drank too much, got into a few fights, and occasionally landed in jail for minor offenses.

Lillian Carter also had some adjustments to make. Her husband's death had put her into one of her "black moods." Although she was a partner in the Carter Farms and Warehouse, she decided to leave the active management to Jimmy and Rosalynn. She was soon restless: "I couldn't fish all the time; I couldn't play bridge all the time."

So when her sister, Emily Dolvin, a fraternity housemother at Auburn University in Alabama, told her of an opening at the Kappa Alpha fraternity, she applied and was accepted. Jimmy, concerned that people might think she was working because she had to, bought her a new white Cadillac; Lillian kept it on the road between Auburn and Plains on weekends and vacations and on occasion lent it to her boys in the fraternity. After five and a half years in this position (Lillian says eight), with her responsibilities as a housemother wearing on her nerves, she resigned and returned to Plains in the summer of 1961.

A year later Lillian asked her friend Pete Godwin for a job managing a nursing home in Blakely. ("I'll go for nothing 'cause I'm miserable," she said. "I'm bored to death.") She held that job for two years until she noticed that the residents she was caring for were younger than she. During these years she went off to a number of family visits and prayer retreats, and in 1960 journeyed to New York City with Gloria, Ruth, and her sister, Susie French—where Gloria appeared on a quiz show, "The Price Is Right." (She didn't win). In the summer of 1963 she took the Goodwill Tour to Europe, sponsored by the State Department.

Jimmy also had some readjustments to make to his new role as farmer and businessman. Whatever he might have learned about farming as a child, advances in farming techniques made most of his knowledge obsolete by the 1950s. Following World War II, Sumter County experienced a significant shift from cotton to peanut production, and the latter was a more difficult crop to produce, requiring complex, expensive machinery and a more scientific approach. Moreover, the land surrounding Plains required special attention; with a high percentage of clay, the soil was unusually difficult to cultivate. He enrolled in a crash course in scientific agriculture at the University of Georgia Experimental Station in Tifton and became involved in the operations of the local Agricultural Extension Center just outside of Plains, which his father had helped to establish in 1952, shortly before his death.

Carter showed enthusiasm for trying out new machinery and techniques. In the late fifties he rigged a peanut-drying system that helped increase yields, installed a modern seed peanut–shelling plant, purchased three acres in Plains for peanut storage, and expanded the business to include the sale of Southern Nitrogen fertilizer. In 1961 he constructed a new warehouse on the corner of Main and Bond streets, and in 1962 installed the first cotton gin in Sumter County in twelve years—an ultramodern $300,000 machine with fingertip controls. (In August the Carter Warehouse ginned a bale that received the highest grade possible. But the investment was less profitable than expected because of poor cotton conditions in the county and low prices.)

In addition to building their business—and perhaps as an aid to it—Jimmy and Rosalynn were active in various clubs. Rosalynn attended some of the meetings of the Women's Missionary Society of the Plains Baptist Church, the Plains PTA, and the Plains Garden Club. Jimmy was so active in civic affairs that in January of 1956 he was considered for selection as Sumter County's "Outstanding Young Man of 1955" by the Americus Jaycees. (Though he lost to Fox Stephens, vice-president of McCleskey Mills and a member of the Americus Jaycees, he was the only non-Americus resident named on the Distinguished Service Award list.) By that time he had served as a member of the Sumter County Board of Education, scoutmaster of a Plains Boy Scout troop, vice-president of the Plains Lions Club and chairman of its community development committee, counselor for the Baptist Church's Royal Ambassadors, junior boys' Sunday school teacher, co-chairman of the Better Hometown Contest project, member and director of the Americus and Sumter County Chamber of Commerce, chairman of the Friendship Campsite committee, commodity chairman of the Friendship Association for Children's Homes, and lieutenant in the U.S. Naval Reserve program. He was elected president of the Georgia Central Seed Association in 1962.

As a businessman and civic leader, Jimmy Carter was performing much as his father had before him. And like his father he was strict with his three boys. Jack, the eldest, was winning more honors than Jimmy had at the same age. In 1964 he had been chosen to attend the Governor's Honors Program for the summer at Wesleyan College in Macon. (These plans were almost tragically interrupted when a small pistol he and his friend Murray Walters had been playing with at the Walters home accidentally discharged and hit Jack in the neck. It was a minor wound, fortunately.) In September he was named as a finalist in the National Merit Scholarship competition, and in 1965 was the first runner-up in the Third District "Star Student Competition."

More than Earl, however, Jimmy was involved in "self-improvement." He and Rosalynn took courses at Georgia Southwestern—one on "great issues" and another on the "great books" (the instructor has forgotten the Carters). In the "great issues" class, Jimmy and Rosalynn alternated attendance so one of them could be at home. Jimmy took a speed-reading course and joined in literary discussions at the library in Americus.

Beyond family, business, community, and self-improvement, the young couple maintained an active recreational life. "The Carters," Mary Anne Thomas, wife of a Carter business acquaintance, Russell Thomas, says, "were probably the most social of the Plains people." They belonged to two overlapping social circles. In Plains there were L. C. "Pete" Godwin and his wife, Dorothy ("Dot"); cousin Hugh Carter and his wife, Ruth; Gloria Carter and her husband, Walter Spann; and Carter's old high-school friends, B. T. and Gloria Wishard and Joel and Barbara Thomas, who farmed in nearby Smithville. On Saturdays Carter would sometimes close the office and go fishing with Wishard and Thomas. On Saturday night they would sometimes meet at the Pond House for a fish fry and a few drinks and conversation.

In Americus the Carters went with a young "society crowd"—John and Margaret Pope (and after her death, his second wife, Betty), Billy and Irene Horne, Russell and Mary Anne Thomas, and later Billy Blair and his wife. (Rosalynn had known Irene Horne from their Georgia Southwestern days, though they had not been close friends.) They usually met at each other's homes for card playing, but at times they would meet at one of the few restaurants in town or attend a movie or go bowling. Some Saturdays they went to the country club, a pleasant building with brick tile floors, for a smorgasbord and dance, the women often dressing in long, elegant gowns. For a time, the Carters and their friends took ballroom dancing lessons at the club and square dancing sponsored by the Sumter County Recreation Department. (Class rules required, as one townsperson recalled with a grimace, that one should use a deodorant and not eat onions beforehand.) Open to almost any white who could pay the moderate dues, the country club was a good place to meet people. (Here Carter was introduced to Griffin Bell, an Americus boy from a poor family, who was also on the rise; and to James Deriso, vice-president with the Winn-Dixie Container Corporation and later one of Carter's chief financial backers in southwest Georgia.)

On weekends the couples took trips to Atlanta for the stock car races or games of the Atlanta Braves, or to Florida for the Daytona stock car races. (On one of these trips they had no hotel room and wound up staying in a private home, an experience Carter was to duplicate later in his political campaign.) Sometimes they took vacations with the Thomases or the Wishards or the Hornes.

Despite all this activity, Rosalynn and Jimmy kept an emotional distance from their friends. Rosalynn explained to Kandy Stroud, "I've never had time for friends . . . I've always worked too hard. Besides, I never was one for coffee klatches." Jimmy was similarly elusive. One Americus friend later remembered Carter as

. . . a very seductive personality. He very quickly embraces and takes you in, very readily. But you reach a point with Jimmy where you suddenly found you hit wall . . . and you're totally not expecting it. The feeling seems to be that you one day find that you seem to be dancing a tune—with him playing the fiddle—and you're the only one doing the dance.

Yet both Carters were admired by their friends. They saw Rosalynn as a pleasant person—a kind of peacemaker when little triangular situations would crop up. And Jimmy was admired as the intellectual in the crowd and later, as someone who was going places in the world.

The people in this circle didn't usually discuss politics, religion, or other weighty matters when they got together. Irene Horne, however, a devout Methodist, did discuss religion with Jimmy—though about the only topic she can recall was Carter's idea that a drunkard might have a greater chance of entering heaven than the most respectable individual! Mary Anne Thomas used to catch Jimmy for a discussion of a book she had just read. "I remember that's one of the reasons I liked him—because he read a lot of books. And I liked to go on binges of reading and talk about all these books. And I don't know how profound Jimmy is. My feeling was probably no more profound than I was." She remembers reading some very complex theological and philosophical works: "My feeling is that Jimmy read those books like I did, somehow you just stumble from one to the other and you would enjoy them but there was nobody here that could really discuss them with you."

Except for the Thomases, most of their friends were politically conservative. But they found that they could disagree with Jimmy without fearing a heated political discussion that would harm their relationships.

On the whole their friends were financially successful: Billy Blair's family owned the Americus *Times-Recorder;* John Pope and Billy Horne were successful building contractors; Russell Thomas was a leading Americus banker and farmer; and B. T. Wishard (with Jimmy's help) was to become regional sales manager for International Mineral and Chemical Corporation. They all owned large, tastefully furnished homes, and the women were all attractive and slender: Irene Horne, a demure, blue-eyed blonde; Mary Anne Thomas, a lively, outspoken, and sophisticated woman who would have been at home in a salon in Atlanta, New York, or Paris.

The Carters were at a slight social disadvantage—outsiders, to some extent. Neither of their families was prominent in Georgia or the region as a whole (as distinct from Plains). Further, there was a tendency for the society people in Americus to set themselves apart from country folk from Plains. Thus, Jimmy never belonged, as one friend recalls, "to the in-town Americus civic clubs, the power-structure civic clubs." (That is, the Kiwanis, Rotary, or Jaycees. The Elks Club and the American Legion were more for "just plain folks.") And Rosalynn, despite the efforts of some of her women friends in Americus, was not asked to join the most prestigious women's club, the Junior Women's Welfare League (the counterpart of the national Junior League). Nor was her mother, Allie Smith, invited to join the Americus chapter of the Daughters of the Confederacy, for which she was eligible.*

Yet they made their way up the social ladder. When the prominent people of Americus wanted representatives from the outlying country towns on their boards, they would think of the Carters as presentable, and willing, candidates. Rosalynn joined the board of the Sumter Players in the early 1960s (along with Mary Anne Thomas). She worked for the Red Cross Blood Bank in Americus in 1962 and was on the Board of the Golden Age Club.

The Carters, in the twelve years after their return to Plains, had built a prosperous business and created a pleasant and attractive home in town. They had friends their own age and were in a position to enjoy the good life as it was defined in that part of the world. They did not rule their little section of the world, but they had won a respected position for themselves in the community of Americus as well as in Plains. In general, their life was indistinguishable from that of upper-middle-class couples in suburbs and small towns throughout America. It was a placid, easygoing life—on the surface, at least. In this respect the Carters were fortunate, for there were others in their town and region who had to face personal tragedy and social privation. Even some of their acquaintances were to be personally embroiled—on one side or the other—in the racial and political storms that were rolling over southwest Georgia during the 1950s and 1960s.

## Black and White

Plains is not an all-white town. Coexisting with the whites were the blacks—about half the total population, with different social patterns and a somewhat separate culture.

They were also rooted in the community—their histories intertwined with the white families'. Their ancestors had served as slaves, and many of them in the fifties and sixties served whites as tenant farmers, domestics, and hourly wage workers. The Reverend Holley, for example, an itinerant preacher and a sharecrop farmer, was descended from an old slave family. His daughter, Annie Mae Holley, had worked for the Carters. Aurelia Jackson, born of slave parents in 1874 in Webster County, served both the Murrays and the Smiths (Rosalynn's grandparents and parents) throughout much of her life, while raising nine children of her own.

In the fifties and sixties the blacks had difficulty finding work. The shift from cotton to peanut farming after World War II had caused a shift from human to mechanical labor and the advent of new and better machines for cultivation and harvesting undercut the need for a large number of black field hands. Many

---

* Rosalynn Carter was asked to join the Junior Women's Welfare League after her husband was elected governor (she accepted), and her mother was asked to join the Daughters of the Confederacy (she did not accept).

blacks had left the rural areas for the larger cities of the North; most who stayed performed the traditional agricultural and service roles for daily wages and very cheap or free shelter in the shacks that dotted the countryside. According to the 1970 census, 68 percent of the black population in Webster County, which includes Archery, had a per capita income of only $875 a year, making it one of the poorest counties in the nation. In the area covered by the Middle Flint Regional Commission, which included Sumter County, per capita income was $1,037 in 1959. The blacks on Carter's land in the 1960s farmed as sharecroppers. One, the Wright family, did much better than these averages suggest. The Wrights earned a family income of about $10,000 in 1969.

Responsible white leaders—like Jimmy Carter and his friends—were aware of these problems and sought to bring in industries that would alleviate the situation. Yet through the fifties and into the sixties the social and political interactions of blacks and whites remained much as they had been when Jimmy was a boy. In Plains the blacks lived in their own section of town, mainly south of the railroad tracks down South Hudson Street, where the shacks of the poor stand close to the neat brick cottages of the middle class. The separate black primary school system still survived. To attend high school, blacks had to commute to Americus. There were still separate churches—in Plains black social life revolved around the Lebanon Baptist Church and St. John's African Methodist Episcopal (AME). When their activities were recorded in the local Americus paper, which was seldom, they were identified as "Negro" or "colored." Blacks were required to use separate hospital facilities in Americus—a separate Negro hospital before 1953 and a separate wing of the Sumter County hospital after that; when they died, they were buried in one of the separate black cemeteries out on the old Preston Road. There were even separate black-owned businesses in Plains for black customers, clustered on Hudson Street, just south of Main: a mercantile company, a shoe shop, a barbershop, a cotton gin, grocery stores. A restaurant was later bought by a black, Charles Hicks, a retired Navy man, and remodeled and opened as the Skylight Club, the only bar, black or white, in Plains. (Blacks could shop in white stores, however, and vice versa.) And the few blacks who voted in Sumter County (none were registered in Webster County) stood in separate voting lines. They even had their own Negro county agricultural agent—as was the practice throughout the South at that time.

No blacks held office in Plains until 1972. But their own organizations did provide a cohesiveness to their community and an opportunity for some black leaders to arise. When Jimmy was a boy, Bishop William D. Johnson and his wife, Winnie—founders and operators of the Johnson Home Industrial College in Archery—had been among the most influential leaders in the area. In the fifties black ministers, businessmen, and educators were leaders of their own people and contact points with white leaders. Annie B. Floyd, for example, a daughter of Aurelia Jackson, was principal of the Rosenwald Elementary School in the 1950s, a leader of the New Lebanon Baptist Church, and the owner of a small business. She graduated from high school in Forsyth, Georgia, earned her B.S. from the black Albany State College in 1949, her M.A. from Columbia University in 1955, and was working on her Ph.D. at Atlanta University at the time of her death in 1972.

Blacks' and whites' relationships with each other in Plains tended to follow the same pattern that existed when Jimmy was growing up. There were blacks in the back of the Plains church at Earl Carter's funeral. And the Carters reciprocated. As Lillian explained:

We've always gone to the funerals of our hands. Once the superintendent of the black schools [Annie Floyd] was sick in the hospital. She was dying terminally with cancer. So Jimmy and I went out to the black hospital. And he leaned down and she said, "Oh, Mr. Jimmy, Governor, will you do my eulogy. I know I'm going to die." And he said, "If I'm anywhere in this country, I'll be happy to do it." And when he started to leave he kissed her on the cheek.

And later I was in Atlanta to see about my eye. . . . A woman said, "Miss Lillian, Annie Bee is dying, and Mr. Jimmy has gone to South America . . ."

So Lillian postponed her eye surgery and in Jimmy's place gave a eulogy at Annie B. Jackson Floyd's funeral.

Such contacts were permitted, but the interactions were asymmetrical. Blacks could attend the funerals of the whites they worked for, but they had to sit in the back of the church, or they were permitted to attend only the graveside service. Whites, on the other hand, were honored guests in black churches they visited.

Responsible whites were expected to show concern for blacks with whom they had a special relationship or the black leaders with whom they had business dealings. Some local blacks who do not remember Lillian's eulogy recall that J. T. Sewell, one of the strongest segregationists in Plains, attended Annie B. Floyd's funeral. ("He was all right," one black said, "once you got to understand him.") "Better-class" whites always helped their blacks when they were in trouble. On Monday mornings white employers lined up around the Sumter County Courthouse, come to bail out "darkies who had gotten drunk or into a fight and landed in jail over the weekend." If there was an illness or death among the black domestics, some employers would bring soup or medicine. One local black, John Lundy, who moved to Plains in 1950, recalls being aided by those members of the Carter clan who were not particularly noted for liberal racial attitudes. Earl Carter and Alton Carter provided a loan for his car insurance and Alton Carter gave him groceries over the years "when I was down and out."

But the system itself—the racial segregation and the political, social, and economic subordination of the blacks—was not challenged by these acts of concern. Such affection for individual blacks, the psychologist John Dollard suggests, was a defense "used to allay the anxiety which inevitably arises over the invidious distinction maintained against Negroes as a caste." In acting as a kind of "social parent," the white reinforces black dependency in a feudal pattern of giving or withholding support. Indeed, it is almost a sign of being from the better classes, this caring about blacks. "But the Negroes have to be the right kind, the 'old timy' ones who draw out this friendliness in the class to which they were once related as slaves. Still, in all cases the upper-class attitude toward Negroes seems mild and there is no sense of being challenged or threatened by them."

Through the fifties and the sixties Carter simply accepted the racial pattern of his town. As a member of the Americus and Sumter County Hospital Board (1959–61) and the Carnegie Library Board (1959–62), he went along with the segregationist policies of the time. And as a member of the Sumter County Board of Education from 1956 to 1962, and as its chairman in 1962, he did the same.

In *Why Not the Best?* Carter explains his votes on the Sumter County Board of Education during these crucial years as a kind of naive unawareness: "It seems hard to believe now, but I was actually a member of the county school board for several months before it dawned on me that white children rode buses to their schools and black students still walked to theirs." The Sumter County School Board minutes show, however, that at a board meeting on September 24, 1956, Carter moved to delay construction of a new Leslie-DeSoto Elementary Negro School when parents complained that the black and white children would have to travel the same roads to their respective schools. Only after studies showed that moving the building site would be too expensive did Carter change his mind.

While there were several instances when Carter initiated purchase of materials for white schools, he was tightfisted with similar purchases for the "equal" black schools. Thus, at one meeting he supported acquiring new typewriters for the white schools and giving the used ones to the black schools. And in January, 1958, he voted against an appropriation for new window blinds for the black schools—he felt the cost was too great. However, he did support the construction of a new, larger black elementary school in Plains—the Westside School, built in 1957 to replace several inferior buildings in the district.

Carter did take some controversial stands on local educational issues, but none that involved integration. As chairman of the Sumter County Board of Education in 1961, he led a move to consolidate the county and Americus school systems: to combine the two school boards and replace the three white high schools (in Americus, Plains, and Leslie) with a single countywide white high school in Americus. The one black high school would be left unchanged, and elementary schools already in existence in the small towns would continue operating. There was considerable support for the measure in Americus; the Americus *Times-Recorder* pointed out the advantages of consolidation for educational expansion in mathematics and other areas. Carter, in a speech before the Jaycees, emphasized the heavy financial burden facing both systems, saying that consolidation might be the last chance for a "superlative system for all our children."

But in Plains there was considerably less enthusiasm. Carter's cousin Hugh and his former teacher and principal of Plains High, Y. T. Sheffield, led the opposition to the referendum. The proposal carried in Americus but was defeated in the county by 84 votes. In Plains the vote was 33 in favor to 201 opposed.

Carter was to recall in *Why Not the Best?* that this "first venture into election politics" was a "stinging disappointment." And though he noted that Plains would have lost "one of its schools," he suggested that the opposition in Plains was based on a suspicion that the plan would eventually lead to school integration. The primary concern of the people of Plains, however, seemed to be that Americus would dominate the Plains school system. Further, removal of the Plains High School would have destroyed the institution in which the community of Plains was rooted. The basketball games, and student shows were central events in that small town.

In the spring of 1964, Carter, by then a state senator, again supported a consolidation attempt—combined this time with a proposed bond issue of $900,000 for upgrading the schools. In a one-third-page advertisement in the Americus *Times-Recorder* he called attention to the courage of his stand: "As a State Senator and a politician I have been advised against taking a public stand on the school bond issue. But as the parent of three sons in school, as a former chairman of the Sumter County School Board, and as a legislator who is vitally interested in improving education . . . I feel compelled as a matter of duty to express my deep feelings on this subject." He explained that his support of the referendum was based on his concern that Sumter County schools were falling behind those in larger schools. "Plains and Union are good schools with able and dedicated staffs, but the small enrollments and few teachers do not permit a full high school curriculum offering." The proposal was defeated by a vote of 938 to 910. Carter backed one final consolidation attempt that November this time with a proposed bond of only $394,000; this bond attempt was also defeated.

While Carter was fighting these battles, challenges to the caste system were coming from other quarters. The U.S. Supreme Court, the U.S. Department of Justice, and such civil rights organizations as the National Association for the Advancement of Colored People and the Southern Christian Leadership Conference raising fundamental questions about key aspects of the legal and social order—the very existence of a dual system of schools and hospitals and other public facilities, as well as the almost systematic exclusion of blacks from the voting rolls. In the process deep resistance in the white communities of southwest Georgia and the South developed, while some white leaders would try to mediate and adapt to these new forces. The Carters were not among them. Not until his governorship, after his election in 1970, did Jimmy Carter move from the old pattern of paternalism to support for a new pattern of racial justice.

## Challenge and Response

On May 17, 1954, during Jimmy Carter's first year back in Plains after his Navy career, the Supreme Court removed the key legal prop from the system of segregation in the South when it declared, in *Brown* v. *Board of Education,* that racially segregated educational systems are inherently unequal.

In Georgia there was almost unanimous opposition to the decision. Herman Talmadge of Georgia was the first governor to declare that his state would not abide by it. And the Georgia legislature, like others in the South, embarked on a course of massive resistance. Among other things the General Assembly declared *Brown* v. *Board of Education* "null and void," passed a law to require the closing of all public schools should one school in the state be forced to desegregate, and made the use of state funds to finance desegregated schools a felony.

At the grass roots, the Ku Klux Klan, dormant for several years, was reactivated. A Georgia chapter organized in 1955, and by 1957 there was a Sumter County chapter. The "respectable" resistance to integration was to come from another organization, the States Rights Council, organized by Herman Talmadge and his associates (as a Georgia counterpart to the White Citizens Council) in 1955. An Americus chapter was organized by some of its leading citizens in 1956.

In Jimmy's part of the county there were some early troubles centering around the Christian interracial community of Koininia, just south of Plains. In the summer of 1956 nightriders shot up the community welcome sign, and farm buildings were scarred by fire bombs and shotgun blasts. Community members were also subjected to a variety of legal harassments and to an economic boycott by the merchants in Plains, Americus, and other neighboring towns that would last for several years. They could not sell their own farm products locally, nor could they purchase seed or other supplies to keep the community farm going. Their insurance was canceled.

Even merchants or residents who were sympathetic to them were punished. Herbert Birdsey, a white Macon businessman, had his Americus supply store dynamited less than a week after it sold seed to Koininia residents. Jack Singletary, a farmer south of Plains who had lived at Koininia for a while and had some contacts with them, was threatened by nightriders, his produce was boycotted, and his informal queries about possible membership in the Plains Baptist Church were met by the response that his family would not be welcomed.

The resistance worked—at first. Despite the U.S. Supreme Court's school integration decisions of 1954 and 1955, there was no discernible implementation in southwest Georgia until the 1960s. The first breakthrough came in voting rights and the integration of public facilities, as elsewhere in the South. In 1961 in Albany, the old slave-trading center of southwest Georgia just forty miles south of Plains, the Albany Movement was born. That November, two

Student Nonviolent Coordinating Committee organizers made a well-publicized Freedom Ride from Atlanta to Albany, the first in a long series of legal tests of segregation in public facilities. On December 12 they were joined by Dr. Martin Luther King, Jr., who told over 1,000 people packed into Albany's Shiloh Baptist Church: "Don't stop now. Don't get weary. We will wear them down with our capacity to suffer." The following evening Dr. King, and several hundred men, women, and children marched toward the county courthouse singing hymns; scores were arrested for parading without a permit. The jails were so full that the prisoners were farmed out to surrounding counties and Dr. King was sent to the Americus jail.

The Albany Movement included a voter registration drive in the city and countryside. Between 1961 and 1962 more than 500 blacks were registered in Albany alone. In response, black churches in the country were burned to the ground—the Shady Grove Church near Leesburg, the Mount Olive Church in Terrell County, and four other churches in Sasser. Nightriders roamed the back roads, shooting into black homes where registration workers were assembled. In Dawson, a Vermont civil rights worker who was sitting in the house of a local black was wounded by gunfire.

These events were occurring in towns ten to twenty miles from Americus and Plains, and civil rights demonstrators were sitting in county jails in Americus and other towns throughout the area. But Americus itself did not become a storm center until the summer of 1963. One warm August night eleven black youths went to the "white" window of the Martin Theater on Forsythe Street to purchase tickets. The police arrived and ordered the blacks to disperse; when they refused, they were arrested for blocking a sidewalk. A few days later, on August 8, about 200 blacks gathered at the Friendship Baptist Church to protest the segregation of public facilities and marched to a nearby café. The police fired shots in the air to disperse the crowd and, in the altercation that followed, seven policemen were injured and five blacks arrested. The following night about 200 blacks met and marched to protest the arrests of the previous night. This time forty-seven blacks were arrested and police closed several black businesses "to prevent further disorder." (The city council requested all news media "not to print or broadcast news of racial disturbances without the council's prior approval.") A week later a Congress of Racial Equality worker from Minnesota was arrested and charged with encouraging blacks to march without a permit and urging black bystanders to ignore a police order to halt the march. And a month later, after a secret hearing before a local justice of the peace, this man and three associates were charged with attempts to incite an insurrection—a capital offense in Georgia. (However, a three-person federal panel met in Americus in November and found the penalty unconstitutional.)

Throughout these racial confrontations several white civic leaders in Americus—conservatives and moderates—worked behind the scenes to get people off the streets and defuse the explosive situation. In the subsequent months they were to integrate public facilities—such as the Sumter County hospital and the Carnegie Library—in a quiet way that would cause little public notice.

In May, 1965, the political climate heated up once again in Americus. Roberta Freeman, a senior at the first integrated high school and the daughter of a local black minister and civil rights leader, was arrested in "Lover's Lane." Though it was just before final exams and graduation, she was not permitted to leave the jail. The county officials seemed determined to place her in reform school. This was too much for Warren Fortson, member of a prominent Georgia political family, the county attorney, and a friend of Jimmy Carter. With Dr. Lloyd Moll, the head of Georgia Southwestern College, he came to the defense of the young woman—despite disapproval from many of their friends in Americus.

In July and August there were new racial confrontations in Americus. The problems started when four black women were arrested for trying to integrate a white voting line. Dr. Martin Luther King, Jr., sent in workers from the SCLC to aid the movement there. One night a large group of blacks arrived at the Sumter County Courthouse for an all-night vigil; a group of whites gathered nearby. Shortly before midnight a man in a speeding auto fired shots into the white crowd, killing Andy Whatley, a white Marine recruit. Two Americus blacks were arrested.

With this murder all hell broke loose. There was a boom in gun sales in Americus. About 500 people attended the Whatley funeral on Saturday, July 31, at the First Baptist Church in Americus. Afterward both white and black demonstrators marched to the courthouse. State troopers (100 men had been ordered there by Governor Carl Sanders) escorted both groups. Governor Sanders urged outsiders to stay away from Americus. "We don't need outside influences at Americus either white or Negro. Responsible Georgians can solve their own problems." The next day two small groups of white and black civil rights workers tried to enter the Sunday services at two white churches—in Americus. They were denied entrance at both and the police arrested them.

The protestors were at this time demanding the establishment of a biracial committee to work on plans to secure integration on the several fronts where they had been attacking—the voting lines, public facilities, private firms selling to the general public. Many communities in the South had established such committees. After some resistance to this proposal, the Americus City Council met with leaders of the Sumter County Movement (a coalition of various civil rights groups) the night of August 12. Although they failed to establish a special biracial committee, they did agree that delegates of the movement could meet with the council from time to time to discuss problems. A special community relations committee was formed, though the members were all white. With this, the blacks discontinued their marches.

Despite all these confrontations there had been practically no integration in the public schools up to this time. But the passage of the Civil Rights Act in the spring of 1964 changed this, by shifting the burden of implementing the *Brown* decision from black individuals to the federal government. The law's primary provision was Title VI, which prohibited discrimination in programs partially funded with federal money and established administrative procedures for withholding funds from schools and programs denying blacks equal access.

Most school boards in Georgia began bowing to the inevitable—including those in Sumter County. The Americus Board of Education moved first with its "freedom-of-choice" plan in early 1964. That summer the requests of four black children were honored and they were transferred to a previously all-white school. The following year eighty-seven Americus blacks asked to transfer to the white schools in the city system, and as the local paper indicated, most transfers were expected to be granted.

The Sumter County Board of Education was slower in its initial adaptation. By May, 1965, the board had signed a certificate of compliance, but it remained one of the two Georgia boards that had not filed a desegregation plan. Further, there were no immediate requests from blacks for transfer to previously all-white schools in the county school system. As the chairman of Sumter County Board of Education explained: "There are six or eight paid agitators in the city day in and day out working at it. They don't get out in the county much."

In the fall of 1966 the Sumter County board, with its own freedom-of-choice plan, enrolled thirty-seven blacks in the previously all-white schools in Plains and Leslie. This first integration attempt in the countryside did not work well. Although most local residents are hesitant to discuss that troubled period, the *Buffalo*, the Plains High School yearbook, gives some indirect evidence that the few blacks who entered that school were not accepted by their classmates. In the 1967–68 yearbook no blacks were pictured as participants in any of the extracurricular activities. Nor were any blacks given any of the accolades— "best" of this or that—so typical of the yearbook. The yearbooks for the next two school years included no black faces at all—they had evidently dropped out of school rather than face such a difficult situation.

Neither the Americus nor the Sumter County integration plan fully met federal guidelines. In early 1966 the United States Department of Health, Education and Welfare decreed that both school systems would lose federal funding unless they complied with these guidelines. And by July, 1966, after both systems declined to comply, federal funds were being withheld.

There were further legal and political challenges by both sides in the next three years. Late in 1969 the U.S. District Court in Atlanta directed all public school systems in Georgia to submit plans for compliance with HEW directives abolishing dual school systems by September 1, 1970. With this sanction over their heads, the Americus and Sumter County boards of education, on January 15, announced completion of their plans: both systems would follow the federal court orders to bring about total integration.

Though the residents of Americus and Sumter County generally reacted strongly against these decisions (Hugh Carter addressed a protest assembly of nearly 2,000 persons at the Sumter County Fairgrounds in January, 1969), the fight was basically over. By May, 1970, despite some vacillation, the two boards finally provided desegregation plans that were accepted by the State Superintendent of Schools. The Americus plan called for pupils in grades one through five to be "paired" and pupils in grades six through twelve to attend the same school.

## Avoiding the Issue of Race

Throughout these troubled years most Georgia political figures—especially statewide leaders and those in southwest Georgia—had to take a stand on racial integration, either because of their leadership positions or their own personal inclinations.

Somehow, Jimmy Carter kept out of most of this turmoil. He did refuse to join the States Rights Council in the mid-fifties. He states that two members of the local States Rights Council, the Baptist minister and the manager of the train depot, visited his business in an attempt to convince him to join. He refused their solicitation with considerable indignation. And as a consequence, he says, he was punished by a brief boycott of his business. Townspeople do not recall it. And he and his family stood almost alone in 1965 against a move in the Plains Baptist Church to bar all blacks from church attendance at all times.

On at least two other occasions Carter tried to soften the more extreme reactions of his community against white acquaintances ostracized for their civil rights stands. Jimmy Carter never offered to aide Koininia himself, but he induced the merchants of Plains to ease their boycott against Singletary so that he could use the phone of a local grocer to obtain medicine for his son. When the boy died of leukemia, Rosalynn Carter asked the local Baptist minister to perform a graveside service for the child. (It was not necessary—there were ministers at Koininia.) At another time, when 1,000 citizens petitioned for the resignation as county attorney of Warren Fortson, Carter's lawyer, friend, and political supporter, Carter attended the meeting before the Sumter County Board of Commissioners to speak on Fortson's behalf. (He did this despite Fortson's pleas that he stay away.)

Except for these episodes, however, Carter was essentially uninvolved. Koininia had never conducted business with Carter and did not seek his help—so he did not have to face an explicit decision to honor or break the boycott against them. (Carter later said that from time to time he had visited the farm to offer moral encouragement to Clarence Jordan, Koininia's founder. Jordan's wife, Florence, does not recall any Carter visits and says that he was no friend to them. Certainly he never offered to trade with them, as Herbert Birdsey had when he heard of their plight.) He does not seem ever to have taken a public stand for or against compliance with federal integration guidelines in the schools or other public facilities. Nor did he provide the behind-the-scenes leadership that others attempted in one way or another.

Carter was able to avoid taking stands on racial policies in the fifties and early sixties because he never held office at a time or in a place where he was forced to do so. Thus, he was on the Sumter County Board of Education, the Americus and Sumter County Hospital Board, and the board of the Americus Carnegie Library Association just before the first major civil rights push in Sumter County in 1963. He would enter the state senate in 1963, just after the General Assembly had decided to end its policies of massive resistance to federal demands for integration in the schools and other public institutions. And he lived in Plains, where there was only one demonstration, not in Americus, where the many racial confrontations between 1962 and 1965 forced most city leaders to take sides.

But to avoid these conflicts to the extent that he did, he had to define his responsibilities as a leader and citizen in restrictive, even passive, terms. Serving on the education committee of the Georgia Senate at the time when the school boards in Sumter County were being forced to establish integration plans, he confined his commitments to less controversial objectives, such as upgrading the educational facilities in the state and shifting the tax burden away from local school districts. And though two of his children attended the Plains schools most of the time between 1966 and 1970 (Jeff went to a private school one year) when the Sumter County Board of Education was being forced to integrate, he was able to avoid this divisive issue by concentrating his civic efforts on the promotion of multicounty planning for economic development.

As a community and political leader, of course, Carter could have assumed more active leadership on racial issues. Several of his friends in Americus did just that—though they ran the risk of social ostracism. But as one Americus man, one who did run this risk, has pointed out, one cannot expect any human being to run such risks. It was a difficult situation, and each person had to pick and choose when and where he or she would take a stand. Had Carter been pulled into these conflicts, it would have created serious problems for his political future. If he had been active in the integration effort, he would have undermined his base in southwest Georgia, and probably in the state as a whole. If he had stood with some of his other friends against integration, he would have undermined his potential as a political leader for the entire state, and eventually for the nation.

# FIVE

# Entry into Politics

IN HIS EARLIER DAYS Jimmy Carter had not shown any great passion for the substance of politics. He attended political rallies in his youth, but more because they were social events than from any strong political interests. High-school friends do not remember Carter talking specifically about political issues. Bobby Logan says that he "never figured him for a politician." During his years in the Navy, as Carter himself says, his political contacts were "transient and superficial." One Navy colleague recalled Carter discussing the 1948 Truman-Dewey election and pegged him as a traditional, conservative Democrat. But generally the other officers do not remember Carter as having any great enthusiasm for political affairs.

His lack of interest was not due to lack of exposure. Grandfather Jim Jack Gordy had served as a local postmaster and toward the end of his life became a guard at the governor's mansion, when Eugene Talmadge was there. Uncle Alton Carter served as a mayor of Plains off and on when Jimmy was a boy and was on the Sumter County Board of Commissioners as well. And his teacher, Miss Julia Coleman, served on Eleanor Roosevelt's commission to choose school textbooks and conveyed her enthusiasm for the New Deal to her students.

Earl Carter also had a great interest in politics. He took Jimmy to various political rallies. And aside from his position on the Sumter County School Board and the district Rural Electrification Administration, he liked to talk politics with his neighbors. Like Old Gene Talmadge, whom he personally supported, Earl was vocal in his opposition to Roosevelt and the New Deal. Joe Bacon, who owned the farm down the road from the Carter's Archery home, recalls arguing about the New Deal with Earl in the early thirties (Bacon supported Roosevelt then, but has since come to the conclusion that Earl was right in opposing him). Another farmer friend, who calls himself a "conservative," says that Earl was so conservative in those days that he "gave conservatives a bad name."

After Old Gene died, Earl transferred his loyalties to Herman Talmadge. In his successful campaign for the state legislature in 1952, for example, he ran as a Herman Talmadge supporter. His opponent, Frank Meyers, a young Americus attorney, a World War II Navy veteran, and a native of Plains, ran as an anti-Talmadgite. The campaign really evolved into a contest of political and personal styles. Neither candidate made speeches on the stump; they simply went around the county talking to friends. Though Meyers seemed to be winning by a small margin on election night, the Plains district, which was the last to report, gave Earl such a large edge he won the election 2,177 to 1,936. As late as June 2, 1953, at a time when Earl was suffering from the cancer that would kill him a few weeks later, the Carters entertained the governor at their home.

After Earl's death the House seat was offered to Lillian Carter, and when she refused, to a friend of Earl's, Sherrard Horne, who accepted it. Jimmy Carter recalls that he considered running for the position several times in the succeeding years. But he decided that it would be best to concentrate on building a successful business and confine his civic activities to his work for the Sumter County Board of Education, the Americus hospital and library boards, the Certified Seed Organization, and Lions International.

Sometime in the early sixties his friends in Americus—Charles Smith, who ran the local radio station, and Warren Fortson—made a trip to Plains to ask Jimmy Carter if he would consider running for office. They saw Carter as progressive, clean-cut, businesslike, professional, and intelligent; and his record as an Annapolis man and the son of an old-style politician was no handicap. On this occasion Carter turned them down. But by the fall of 1962 he had changed his mind; on September 30, 1962, he announced his candidacy for the state senate and he formally qualified for that race on October 8, 1962.

His motives for this decision may have been mixed. Lillian suggests that he may have become bored with life in Plains: "He came home and had to get books to learn to farm." But after he learned all that he wanted to try new things. "I think he got bored just having to sit down and think about peanuts and things like that." His Americus friend Mary Anne Thomas put the situation somewhat more dramatically: "What else is there to do—except drink liquor and chase women? Once you reach forty, some men—attractive, bright men—really go down the drain in a small town."

Further, if he retained his earlier ambition to become governor someday, this was a good time to enter the field. The family business was now in good shape and Rosalynn could take care of it in his absence. There was also a group of potential supporters in Americus, about twelve of them, centered in the Chamber of Commerce and the Jaycees, who were oriented toward good government, scientific management, and a rationalistic approach to politics and economic development. They also wished to put the issue of race behind them as best they could, so that the people in Americus could concentrate on economic development and the building of what they considered a more rational political system. Further, as one of them later recalled: "We were somewhat upset with the very conservative bend of all of the politics in that area." And when Kennedy came in—with federal funds for local programs—a few of them tried to find out about the new programs and how to implement them.

But perhaps the most important consideration for Carter's decision to enter politics at this particular moment was that the rules of the game in Georgia had just been changed. After the U.S. Supreme Court decision in *Baker* v. *Carr*, which declared that the courts could look into whether or not legislative districts were rationally and equitably drawn, an Atlanta federal court in May, 1962, had declared the county unit system unconstitutional. Electoral decisions now would have to be by a majority vote from more equal districts. The senate was then reorganized—the districts enlarged to cover more counties, the seats made permanent, rather than being rotated between the counties within a district, as had been the case. This made the prize more attractive and the possibility of wresting it from the "old boys" more likely.

One election under the old electoral system had been held earlier that spring and Homer Moore of Richland had been elected. A new election was called for in the new and larger 14th District, now composed of seven counties. The campaign that followed was a prototypic battle between an old-line politician, Homer Moore, and the new, young, good government people backing Carter. Carter himself avoided the controversial issue of race that was tearing southwest Georgia apart at the time, concentrating in his campaign on his own personal qualities as a well-educated Annapolis man, local farmer, businessman, club and civic leader, good family and church man, "and an officer in the U.S. Navy submarine force for seven years."

He secured endorsements where he could—Billy Blair, whose father owned the Americus *Times-Recorder*, had a role in his endorsement by that paper (which usually supported Sumter County candidates anyway). And he took to the hustings with his family and friends, conducting an "amateurish and whirlwind" campaign through the seven counties of his district in an attempt to win the Democratic primary then tantamount to election.

On election day, Tuesday, October 16, Carter saw his potential victory slip away in Georgetown, a small community by the Chattahoochee River on the Alabama border, where Joe Hurst, the Quitman County boss, was managing the local election. Hurst had been a member of the Georgia House of Representatives since 1949. A charming, ruthless man, he usually got what he wanted, and in 1962 he wanted Homer Moore. Voting was supposed to take place in the county courthouse, but on the day of the primary the Georgetown officials arbitrarily moved the voting to the ordinary's office. "Collapsible voting booths were available, but during this particular election, they didn't even set them up; voting was across an open desk." The man who was in charge of the election would lay the ballot flat on the open desk, while another said: "Scratch out Jimmy Carter's name." On several occasions, according to Carter, Hurst, who was standing by, "reached into the box and extracted a few ballots to be examined."

That morning John Pope, the Americus building contractor with whom Carter was friendly, received a call from Ralph Balkcom, who belonged to a rival political clique in the county. Pope traveled the fifty miles to Georgetown to poll-watch for Carter. He said he saw Hurst adding extra ballots. (When the box was opened, and the ballots examined, it became apparent that 126 individuals had managed to vote in alphabetical order, and ballots were found in bunches of four to eight, folded together before being put into the box.) Pope challenged Hurst: "I stated again that I didn't think it at all fair for an election officer to try to influence the voters." Hurst replied: "I'll run my county like I always have for twenty-seven years and nobody's gonna come in and tell me how to run it." And he reminded Pope that "he had put three men in the river for doing less than I had been doing that day. But he would meet the voters at the front door and speak to them . . . and sort of love 'em up."

Carter arrived in Georgetown a little after noon. "It was unreal," he says. "I talked to that official [Hurst] myself on that election day, and he told me much the same thing: that he had voted for my opponent and would tell all the voters he saw to do likewise." Carter went to a café and telephoned one of the nearby Columbus newspapers, which promised to send a reporter. When he returned a couple of hours later, after a visit to another county, Hurst and the reporter from Columbus were chatting on the steps of the courthouse. It was obvious that they were old friends, and the reporter was not interested in writing any story critical of election procedures in Quitman County.

That night Carter and his group received the election results by telephone in the Carter Warehouse in Plains. He had lost the primary by 139 votes: 3,063 to 2,924. Moore carried Quitman County by 224 votes—360 to 136 for Carter.

Carter decided to do battle. He was to put an extraordinary amount of effort into something others might consider not worth the investment. In maneuvers during the twenty days remaining before the general election, he showed a tenacity and an ability to pull the right political levers that were to mark his future political career.

On Wednesday Carter announced that he was asking for a recount in Quitman County and that he might contest the election. He already had done some of his homework. John Pope had documented the iregularities he saw at the polling station. And immediately after the election Carter contacted Warren Fortson and they began to obtain statements from Georgetown residents about "the illegal voting procedures that had long been part of the community's political life." At the time, Carter told a reporter that people in Georgetown were eager to give him affidavits and he obtained some the first day. However, he would say later, "At first the people were quite timid and reluctant to talk. Our opponents were tough," he said, "and in the subsequent weeks our lives were threatened several times. Each time I drove into Georgetown to collect evidence or to obtain affidavits, at least one or two men would silently follow me at a distance of not more than ten feet. They listened to all my conversations, and made frequent notes in order to intimidate me and the person I was visiting."

Right after the election Carter and Pope also tried to appeal to the State

Democratic Convention in Macon, where candidates were formally seated. Neither gubernatorial candidate Sanders nor party chairman J. B. Fuqua were interested in his case. The convention declared Moore the official Democratic nominee for the senate. Nor was he making much headway in other quarters. As he later recalled, ". . . the nearby Columbus newspapers pictured me as a politically naive sorehead and a poor loser. . . . The local judge and attorney had strong ties in the county. Eventually we realized that for years the Quitman County votes had been delivered to state and local candidates in an arbitrary but politically important way."

Stymied, Carter gathered a group of supporters at cousin Hugh Carter's house. Hugh suggested that they call his brother, who had been working in Atlanta for *The Wall Street Journal*, and the brother suggested they call John Pennington, a young investigative reporter for the Atlanta *Journal*.

Pennington was interested in the story. He made several trips to Georgetown to get affidavits; and, through a series of articles in the Atlanta *Journal*, focused statewide attention on Carter's election challenge. Carter states in *Why Not the Best?*: "After his publication of the list of voters, dozens of people from around the nation called or wrote to tell us that they had not voted, even though their names were listed." Fortson also gained top-flight assistance: Griffin Bell, an Americus native, asked Charles Kirbo, partner in one of Atlanta's most prestigious law firms, King and Spaulding, to help present Carter's case.

In the meantime Carter proceeded with his formal appeals. On the Thursday after the election, (October 18) he formally demanded a recount in all the counties in his district. Two days later the Quitman County Democratic Executive Committee was served with copies of the call for either a recount or an invalidation of the whole Georgetown ballot box. Several days later, on Monday, October 29, the Quitman committee heard attorneys for both Carter and Moore—and dismissed the case on a technicality. (Fortson, who left the room briefly, returned to hear the decision being announced by the committee's chairman, Joe Hurst.) The next day, Tuesday, Fortson appealed to the State Democratic Committee in Atlanta. On Wednesday they appointed a subcommittee to hear Carter's case. On Thursday, a recount committee headed by Judge Crow of the Albany Circuit and including a Carter and a Moore representative opened its hearings in Georgetown.

Like most judges, Crow was not inclined to invalidate any election results. But the influential Charles Kirbo was arguing Carter's case before him and the evidence supported Carter. When the ballot box was opened in the courtroom, the voters list and the numbered ballot stubs from which they voted had disappeared. "Of course," Carter later recalled, "the officials seemed mystified about who could have done such a thing." The Quitman County election managers testified that they couldn't remember how many people voted, how many ballots were used, or how many names were on the list. Hurst said that the box was sealed when he got it, and he couldn't remember who the election workers were. On the other hand, Tom Gray of Georgetown testified that he saw Hurst start out of the courthouse with the ballot stubs right after the poll closed. "I made this statement to him. 'Those stubs are supposed to go in the box, if I'm not mistaken.' "

On Friday, November 2, the day after the hearing and five days before the general election, the recount committee ruled in Carter's favor. Crow, speaking for the committee, claimed that "it was impossible to determine the legality of the ballots so we just took out the whole precint." With the entire Quitman County vote thrown out, Carter was the winner by sixty-five votes.

But he still needed to be certified as the official Democratic nominee. He was unable to contact the party secretary. (In *Why Not the Best?* Carter says they later found out that the party secretary had gone on "a long weekend vacation trip with my opponent's campaign manager!") But Charles Kirbo was able to reach J. B. Fuqua, chairman of the State Democratic Executive Committee, and on Saturday Fuqua came back from a hunting trip near Canada for a meeting of the State Democratic Executive Committee. Ben Fortson, the Secretary of State (and Warren Fortson's brother), was called; that same day he wired all the county ordinaries to put Jimmy Carter's name on the ballot. Thus, on the Saturday night before the general election Carter was certified.

Carter's ability to motivate his friends now became important. On Sunday, John Pope, Rosalynn, and three or four others found the ordinaries of the seven counties and got them to open up the courthouses. With Magic Markers and rubber stamps they placed Jimmy Carter's name in place of Moore's on every single ballot in seven counties.

But the battle was not yet won. Moore and his attorneys (Jesse Bowles and George Busbee) had discovered another provision in the law that permitted them to appeal to Hurst's Quitman County Democratic Executive Committee. On Saturday morning that committee served notice on Carter that the decision of the recount committee headed by Judge Crow would be held in abeyance until a hearing could be conducted. But this hearing would have to be on Monday, the day before the election, and would inevitably mean that no definitive action could be taken until after the voting had taken place, leaving, as a consequence, Moore's name on the ballots.

Carter countered on Sunday night, November 4, filling an injunction petition with Judge Tom Marshall of the Superior Court in the adjoining Southwestern Judicial Circuit (Marshall had just a year earlier gone through a similar recount victory of his own, guided by attorney Charles Kirbo). Marshall signed the injunction against the Quitman County Democratic Committee, and a hearing was set in his court in nearby Leesburg for the next day. On Monday, Moore's attorney countered with a cross-action suit, asking Marshall to throw out the vote of the entire senatorial district. After hearing arguments from both sides Marshall called the ordinaries of the seven counties into his chamber to see if they could take the names of both candidates off the ballot. All but one (Robert Ellis of Quitman) indicated that the job of removing Carter's name from the ballot was physically impossible. Yet that night at 12:01 A.M., Marshall ordered the ordinaries to strike all names from the ballot and set up a complete new write-in election. And in five of the seven counties the ordinaries went to work scratching Carter's name off the ballot, working far into the night. The Sumter County ordinary, Guntherad Hawkins, refused to strike Carter's name off the ballot, saying Ben Fortson had ruled the opposite of Marshall and he would rather be in contempt of a local court than in contempt of the state. In Quitman County, Robert Ellis (who originally had had to vacate his office so Hearst could use it as a polling place) also kept Jimmy Carter's name on the Quitman County ballot.

The election took place as scheduled on Tuesday, but it was unclear to voters who the official candidate was. Each candidate tried to explain to the voters, through handbills, newspaper ads, and radio spots, how to vote for him in this confusion. In the Tuesday Americus *Times-Recorder,* for example, an advertisement appeared instructing voters to mark an "X" at the top of the Democratic column and, if Carter's name did not appear on the ballot, to write it in.

Carter, as it turned out, led Moore 3,013 to 2,182, the winner by 831 votes. He carried four counties, including Sumter and Quitman—in the latter by a vote of 448 to 23, an interesting statistic given the earlier primary results there, which had Moore winning 360 to 136. He was no doubt aided in these two counties by the refusal of the two ordinaries to comply with the court order, thus leaving Carter's name the only one on the ballot.

But the legal situation was not clear. The Atlanta *Journal* noted: "The fact that Mr. Carter's name remained on the ballots in Sumter and possibly other of the seven counties further confused the picture. The judge's injunction was against leaving Mr. Carter's name on the ballot and apparently could not be construed as an injunction against counting votes for him if the name remained on."

Judge Marshall decided not to take action against those who had left Carter's name on the ballot, stating, "Any further action will have to come from one of the parties involved in the suit." And Moore, after some vacillation, finally conceded the election. Thus Carter finally secured his victory—as the senator from the 14th District of Georgia.

In this struggle Carter exhibited many of the qualities that would help him in his later political quests. He pursued this senate seat with an intensity and a single-mindedness that seemed disproportionate to the end he would obtain. He saw the importance of favorable press coverage. He portrayed himself as an innocent, surprised by the evil he found and showed an ability to dramatize the righteousness of his own cause, while at the same time pulling the political levers that would promote that cause. By retaining a representative from one of the most influential law firms in the state to argue his case in court and take his appeal to the head of the state party organization, he maximimized his chances of receiving a favorable hearing. And while fighting a corrupt local boss, he showed his political acumen in accepting the support of a rival political clique in that boss's territory—even accepting a legally ambiguous action that violated a court order. He demonstrated his ability to develop an enthusiastic and dedicated following; without Warren Fortson, John Pope, Charles Kirbo, and John Pennington he could not have won his appeal.

This election was significant in other ways. Two follow-up actions were a direct result of the waves Carter made in Quitman County. When Carter first realized he had lost the primary because of illegalities in Georgetown, he investigated the whole town's history. He found evidence of Hurst's moonshine business, previous vote frauds, and land thefts, and turned the information over to the FBI. As John Pope recalls, they "wanted to get Joe Hurst!"

Not only did Carter remember Hurst after that campaign, he also supported a political friend. Ralph Balkcom, who in 1962 had summoned John Pope to Georgetown, wished to run against Hurst for a seat in the Georgia House of Representatives in 1964, but he had filed after the filing deadline (forty-five days before the election) so his name was not going to be on the ballot. This time Hurst had committed no great wrong. Carter intervened to get Balkcom on the ballot, saying that he had become involved "only at the request of concerned voters" in Quitman County. He promised he would not back down in his efforts to obtain a fair election—even if it meant going all the way to the Supreme Court. And again, Carter and Fortson, after failing to obtain a favorable decision at the county level, secured the intervention of state Democratic chairman, J. B. Fuqua—this time without difficulty. Fuqua, who was on a fishing trip in Louisiana, immediately returned to Atlanta, the state committee again overruled the decision of the Quitman County committee, and Balkcom's name was placed on the ballot.

### State Senate

The new General Assembly met in January, 1963, under the golden dome of the state capitol in Atlanta. The newly elected governor, Carl Sanders, a former member of the state senate, had won on a progressive and racially moderate platform. On Wednesday, January 16, 1963, he outlined a series of reform measures, including a major constitutional revision and a plan for reorganizing the state government, as well as plans for increasing the budget to upgrade educational and mental health programs in the state. He also proposed a bill for highway reform "to take the highway department out of politics," a new fair election code, and a war on crime with more effective rehabilitation procedures. (All these were the kinds of proposals that Carter would forward when he obtained the governorship.)

Not only was the new governor cast in a progressive mold, the senate had also attracted many new, well-educated members. The General Assembly as a whole had a total of eighty-nine new legislators—and there was a feeling that Georgia politics was moving into a "new era." The senate had its first black member since Reconstruction, Senator Leroy Johnson of Atlanta. The new members struck Reg Murphy, who covered the Georgia State House for the Atlanta *Constitution*, as "sensible executives."

Carter was to find several friends and associates from this "progressive" group—Robert Rowan from Enigma, Robert Smalley from Griffin, and after 1964, Senator Paul Broun of Athens; he worked closely with Ford Spinks and Lamar Plunkett. But he perhaps was closest to Senator Brooks Pennington (who first served in the House in 1962 and the Senate from 1963 to 1970), with whom he cosponsored several bills aimed at helping Georgia agriculture. (Carter had first met Pennington through their mutual work in seed business.) And he had some Americus friends in the house. Billy Blair, whose father owned the Americus *Times-Recorder,* had won a seat in the state legislature in 1962. Carter was particularly close to Blair—a relationship fostered, Blair explains, by Blair's desire to support young, idealistic, Kennedylike men to get into politics. Janet Merritt, a distant relative of Rosalynn's and an Americus resident, was elected the next term.

The legislative sessions were short—about forty days—and most of the legislators were in town from Monday through Thursday, staying at hotels in the vincity of the capitol building and working wherever they could.

Carter and Blair first stayed at the Henry Grady Hotel, later moving to the quieter Piedmont—"with its polished brass doorknobs and other appurtenances that bespoke an earlier, courtlier, age." They would wake up early every morning, take their breakfast at a café a couple blocks from the hotel, and then walk to the capitol. Carter became quite a worker. A friend remembers, "Jimmy would sometimes stay up all night studying, and the next day would go over and talk to a department head to find out how that department functioned." He would often stay over into Fridays, he later said, after most legislators had gone home, so that he could get more work done and oppose "special-interest" legislation (private bills came up on Friday). As Carter later remembered, he had made an "unfortunate pledge" to read every bill he voted on. "Although the promise was made originally only to myself, I told several people about it, and for four years I read them all! I would estimate that in the State Senate we voted on 800 to 1,000 bills during each legislative session. Some are quite brief, yet a few are several hundred pages in length. It was a time-consuming chore, but I took a rapid reading course, and indeed became an expert on many unimportant subjects."

He did not, however, play an active role in the senate during his first term. His activities were hardly noted in the Americus *Times-Recorder,* the Atlanta papers, or the Senate *Journal.* He did sponsor (with Pennington) a bill "to regulate the registration, labeling, analysis and sale, and application of agricultural limestone." Yet, generally, he was quiet and voted with the majority—which was endorsing most of the good government programs Sanders had set forth.

In assuming this low profile, Carter was simply going along. The lieutenant governor made the committee appointments, ran daily matters with a firm hand, and for the most part, what Governor Sanders wanted, Governor Sanders obtained. As one reporter noted, all the governor had to do was to let it be known that he wanted something and the Senators "would fall over themselves getting it done." Indeed, most of the bills passed in the senate during this session were by very large margins or unanimously.

In 1964 Carter began to play more of a leadership role when Sanders appointed him to the Governor's Commission to Improve Education in Georgia (he was one of the two legislators on the thirty-two-member Commission; he also chaired the subcommittee on higher education of the Educational Matters Committee in the Senate.) For Carter the appointment opened a whole realm of possibilities: of becoming "somebody" in the state and legislature, and of making a trip or two to Washington for conferences with the important people there.

Along with Senators Pennington, J. B. Fuqua, and others he introduced the commission's recommendations, incorporated in Senate Bill 180 (also called the Minimum Foundation Program for Education). It increased state spending and provided for an overall upgrading of educational programs in Georgia. And it recommended the establishment of Georgia Southwestern as a four-year college—which won him points in his home district. Eventually the whole education package would pass the General Assembly with only minor revisions. As Reg Murphy wrote in the *Constitution:* "Everybody can support enough of it enough of the time for it to pass, and oppose often enough [in terms of the distribution of the tax burden] to get elected."

Carter himself would later hedge on certain educational matters. Generally he supported the upgrading of education, but he also raised questions about the allocation of the tax burden and services between the larger urban school districts and the small rural ones. His argument was that educational opportunities should be equal throughout the state, but that the rural and smaller school systems should not be overburdened by the tax load. During the special session of the legislature in 1964, for example, Carter said he would propose an amendment to the education bill which would give local school board members some say in selecting members of the State Board of Education (though nothing seems to have ever come of this). In February, 1965, he put forth (with Senator Roy Foster of Wedley) a plan to place large schools on a sliding scale for state funding. (He saw the blanket allocation of state funds for professional personnel on a strict ratio of one professional for each 200 students as unfair to the small schools.)

Carter was the recipient of certain favors from Governor Sanders. In January, 1965, the governor approved an $8,750 grant to the regional planning commission, which Carter had helped found and was heading at the time (the grant was followed with matching funds from Washington). In February, 1965, Sanders agreed to support a Carter proposal for reallocating personnel funds in a way that would aid the smaller schools. In March, Sanders wrote Carter and others that the Board of Regents would upgrade Georgia Southwestern to a four-year college. Sanders also appointed Carter (and Milton Carlton of Swainsboro) to represent the state in meetings with HEW officials in Washington to clarify details for the administration of the new Higher Education Act in Georgia.

Although he specialized on educational matters, Carter avoided the issue of school integration—as did most of the other state legislators at the time. He did take two stands on matters of principle, both during the General Assembly's special session in 1964, which was called to deal with the proposed Fair Election Act and the revision of the state constitution. He recalls that his maiden speech in the senate as a representative of "the most conservative district in Georgia," was to support the abolition of the infamous "thirty questions"—a "subterfuge to keep black citizens from voting."

I spoke in that chamber, fearful of the news media reporting it back home, but overwhelmed with a commitment to the abolition of that artificial barrier to the rights of an American citizen. I remember the thing that I used in my speech, that a black pencil salesman on the outer door of the Sumter County Courthouse could make a better judgment about who ought to be a sheriff than two highly educated professors at Georgia Southwestern College.

That speech was not recorded in the Atlanta or Americus newspapers or the Senate Journal (recording was done only upon the speaker's request and few such requests were made, at least not during the special session in 1964 when the matter came up for consideration), so one cannot independently corroborate what he said at the time. The summer of 1964, however, was late for a maiden speech by Carter, so he might have made it earlier. It is clear that the senate, after some revisions, retained the "questions" in its election bill, that there was an eventual compromise between the senate and house versions, and that the final Election Act contained some revised "questions." In the end Carter did not oppose the bill.

While the senate was working on the Election Act, the house was revising the constitution. When their proposals came to the senate, Carter objected to one section of the proposed bill of rights that read: "Every man has the natural and inalienable right to worship God according to the dictates of his own conscience." He viewed this as a requirement that "God be worshipped" and so presented to the Senate a substitution drawn from the U.S. Bill of Rights: "No Law shall be passed respecting an establishment of religion or prohibiting the free exercise thereof." His amendment was at first approved by the senate, but about twenty senators opposed it, and the senate approved the house's version. There were only four votes against this final action, and Carter's was one of them.

In the general election of 1964 Carter ran unopposed for reelection to the senate. But for someone with larger political ambitions, the Democrats' presidential slate that year presented a problem. The Civil Rights Act of 1964, on top of the many civil rights confrontations in Albany and Americus in 1963 and 1964, had created a backlash against the national Democratic Party—allowing the Republicans to sweep both southwest Georgia and the state in that fall's election. (Indeed, Goldwater won the presidential race by a substantial margin in both Sumter County and the state, and Howard "Bo" Callaway, the Republican candidate for Congress from Carter's 3rd District won his race by 11,812 votes—the first Republican to win a congressional seat from Georgia since 1874.)

Carter finessed the situation as best he could. Running on the Democratic ticket, he urged his constitutents to vote the entire Democratic slate. His mother, Lillian, as an alternate to the Democratic convention, had supported Lyndon Johnson, and in the fall campaign she cochaired, with Gloria Spann's aid, the Democratic headquarters in Americus—which was supporting Johnson. In late October, Carter introduced Orville Freeman, who was campaigning for Johnson in Americus, at a rally at the local ballpark, while Goldwater supporters marched around with placards and handbills questioning Johnson's farm program.

Carter's major effort, however, was on behalf of Garland Byrd, a conservative Democrat who was seeking a seat in the U.S. House from the 3rd Congressional District. Byrd, a former classmate of Carter's at Georgia Southwestern, had served as lieutenant governor of Georgia. More important, he was a conservative Democrat and Carter ran no political risk in giving him active and visible support throughout that campaign.

The campaign also gave Carter a chance to test some populist rhetoric against Bo Callaway, whom he viewed as his own rival—and to do so without running the real risk of losing. Thus, the week after Byrd's nomination, Carter charged that Callaway had used his influence as a state regent to prevent the elevation of Georgia Southwestern to a four-year school, while praising Byrd for his efforts on behalf of the project. This "rich young Republican from Harris County," he charged, "had asked every single regent just before the decisive vote not to approve our college, but to consider other locations such as Albany, Georgia." Callaway countered by calling Carter's presentation "false and misleading." Carter reaffirmed his charges—the college had been needed because many couldn't afford to send their children to the University of Georgia or Auburn, let alone Harvard or Yale.

Byrd lost to Callaway by a large margin. Shortly afterward Carter decided he would challenge Callaway, two years later—though he naturally kept his plans quiet for a time.

His plans may have been on his mind during the next two sessions of the state legislature. Carter showed concern for saving money in the state, keeping a balanced budget, and promoting good organizational principles in the administration of state affairs. Along with Bobby Rowan, he opposed the proposed construction of a $6 million office building, suggesting that the funds be used at the Milledgeville State Hospital or for a facility for female prisoners. He questioned the necessity for a high-priced prison system consultant, opposed a Sanders-sponsored wage increase for state judges, the appropriation of $210,000 to add a dental school to the state medical college, and the allocation of funds to create a statewide driver's training program at all high schools. To maintain revenue, he voted against constitutional amendments to give property tax relief to persons over sixty-five and homestead exemptions to disabled persons on fixed incomes.

Carter was energetic in promoting economic development in his part of Georgia—an activity not directly related to his role as a senator, but one that brought him a lot of publicity and no doubt helped prepare the groundwork for future political campaigns. He chaired the first organizational meeting of the West Central Georgia Area Planning and Development Committee (WCGAPDC) at the Americus country club in January, 1964, then served as the temporary chairman of the group, and (along with Jack Gant of Americus) prepared a charter and set of bylaws for the commission. He gave speeches to drum up support for the project and in late May was elected permanent chairman of the group.

The commission's projects included plans to develop the Andersonville National Cemetery-Prison Park as a tourist attraction, the restoration of an antebellum plantation and an old Indian village, sponsorship (for a short time) of the Office of Economic Opportunity's Neighborhood Youth Corps and Head Start programs, the development of nearby Lake Blackshear as a recreational area and of the Columbus-to-Brunswick South Georgia Limited Access Highway. Carter also appointed a steering committee to study the development of the Flint River Valley and served as the agent for the application for a charter for a national bank in Americus.

In all these activities—shifting the tax burden away from the local school districts, urging more efficient government and a balanced state budget, and promoting the economic development of southwest Georgia—Carter was clearly supporting interests that none of his constituents could fault. At the same time he was avoiding the highly controversial issues of school integration and/or equalization of services between black and white schools in the rural districts.

As a senator, Carter was highly visible in his district. He spoke before many different groups, emphasizing his commitment to the matters discussed above. He also spoke on such general topics as the principles of representative government, issued mild warnings about the shift of power away from the legislative to the executive branch of government, and exhorted individuals to get politically involved. On one occasion he even discussed the "sheer impossibility" of any legislator's reading all the bills coming up before the senate. "Since so many bills and resolutions are introduced—1,290 at the last session—the members do not have time to study and do research on many of them, and as a result must depend upon the information given them by those interested in or opposed to the measures, to a large extent." He kept the people back home informed, through letters to the newspaper as well as his speeches, of what the legislature was up to and where he stood on various issues.

Carter generally used the press effectively, but he sometimes got into trouble. In justifying his opposition to state funding for the driver's education program, he said, "My little community doesn't have advanced math, foreign languages, and a lot of other absolutely mandatory courses." Y. T. Sheffield, his former coach, was so irritated at this that he wrote an open letter to the Americus *Times-Recorder* pointing out that the Plains school offered Latin II, Spanish II, and the same math courses that most Georgia schools offered, as well as driver's education: "We commend you on your effort to secure funds for the maintenance and operation of our schools and hope you are successful. However, we would appreciate you not using Plains High School as an example unless you are sure of the facts." Carter wired Sheffield back, saying he had been "misquoted," that he had been referring to schools in his district in general: "I intended no criticism of our own school which is doing an excellent job under a limited allotment of funds and teachers. You may use this statement as you see fit to correct the newspaper report."

His concern over his image sometimes made him overly sensitive to his press coverage. Reg Murphy recalls the first time he met Carter:

> He had just been elected to the state senate for the first time and he met me in a hall of the capitol building waving a copy of the [Atlanta] *Constitution*, explaining to me how a story we had in the paper was wrong and how we rarely get things right in reporting on the state senate. I think he believes there's a conspiracy in the newspaper business to get things wrong. You just dreaded to see Carter coming down the hallway in the legislative session because you never could talk about substantive issues for him wanting to point out little picayune comma faults in stories. My first reaction to Jimmy Carter was that there is a man who I never will get along with and who will never be human enough to overlook the faults of anybody else.

Overall, Carter did perform well as a new-breed legislator and made a good record for himself. He worked hard, cooperated with the governor's programs, committed himself to progressive reforms in the area of education, and secured favors in return. He looked after the interests of his constituents, avoided the controversial race issues that were tearing his home territory apart, and secured a good press at home. Indeed, as the Americus *Times-Recorder* reported early in 1965, he had been selected (though whether by a poll of the press or his fellow legislators is not clear) as one of the eleven most influential legislators in the state.

### First Gubernatorial Race

On March 3, 1966, shortly after the General Assembly had adjourned, Jimmy Carter officially announced his candidacy for the United States Congress from Georgia's 3rd Congressional District. Three months later, on June 12, just four days before the filing deadline, he announced that he was running for governorship of Georgia instead.

His shift took some of his friends by surprise. Four or five of them had paid his entrance fee for the congressional race—and he was a "shoo-in" for that. As one friend says ". . . he turned around and called us and said come out and meet him in Albany—at the Holiday Inn or something. We went down there. . . . I've never seen Rosalynn that zonked from liquor. And he told us that he was going to run for governor. We sat and had a few drinks. We couldn't believe it." And John Pope, one of the friends who had given Carter a contribution for the congressional race, was already committed to the candidacy of Bo

Callaway, the leading contender for the Republican nomination for governor.

Carter was to suggest later that his shift resulted from a late decision by Callaway to enter the governor's race as the Republican candidate, and that he may have been motivated by a personal rivalry with him.

He had graduated from West Point just about the same time I completed my work at Annapolis. When I was a state senator, one of my major projects was to secure a four-year college in Southwest Georgia. As a member of the University System Board of Regents, Callaway tried unsuccessfully to block the college. He was leader of the Young Republicans and in some ways I had become a leader of Georgia's Young Democrats. When we were around each other, both of us were somewhat tense.

(Callaway was also from a very wealthy family from the Columbus area, which had made its money in the textile mills.)

The only constraint on Carter's entering the race, he recalls, was whether or not he had the necessary backing—and that constraint was lifted when a telephone call from Atlanta assured him of the support of certain influential friends there.

An analysis of the political scene at the time suggests another possible explanation for his decision. As early as September, 1965, former governors Ellis Arnall and Ernest Vandiver were being touted as the leading contenders for the Democratic gubernatorial nomination, while Bo Callaway, who could give the Democratic nominee a real battle, was being discussed for the Republican nomination. But on May 18, 1966, Vandiver announced that a heart condition made it impossible for him to seek the nomination, and the Democratic field opened up for candidates from the center to the right. (Vandiver was a strong conservative, but main line in terms of his Georgia political support.)

For a short period after Vandiver's announcement, U.S. Senator Herman Talmadge considered entering the gubernatorial race. This shook the entire Georgia political world and temporarily forced the withdrawal of one announced candidate and shattered the hopes of several others. On May 23, after Talmadge announced his decision to stay in the Senate, the field was again wide open, and the scramble began.

Two strong conservatives—James Gray, an Amherst graduate and the editor of the Albany *Herald*, and Garland Byrd, Carter's classmate at Georgia Southwestern and his candidate for Congress in 1964—decided to make the race. Lester Maddox, infamous for his recent ax-handle stand at the door of his Pickrick Restaurant, who had already entered the competition, now became a serious contender. And farmer-businessman Hoke O'Kelley, a perennial candidate, would enter the competition shortly thereafter. The Democratic battle seemed to be shaping up into a contest between Arnall, the most liberal of those still in the race, and four conservatives fighting it out at the other end of the political spectrum.

There was room in this crowded field for a candidate who could appeal to the centrists of the party and possibly gain votes from both right and left. One "top Democrat" was quoted as saying that the Democrats' only hope of beating Bo Callaway in the general election was to come up with a "youthful and vigorous" candidate unattached to any political camp, including Talmadge. A few days later Carter's name surfaced as a possible candidate, though he stated that he was still concentrating on the congressional race. But shortly thereafter he announced that he would accept a draft. And two days later the Macon *News* noted that a draft Carter movement had begun—headed by Carter's Senate friends Bob Smalley, Brooks Pennington, Ford Spinks, and Paul Broun.

When Carter announced his candidacy on June 12, he made it clear that he would attempt to fill the void at the center of the Democratic Party. He identified himself with the major forces in Georgia politics, referring favorably to the significant progress under the Vandiver and Sanders administrations, both considered moderate in Georgia politics, and promising to continue that progress. And though earlier that spring, while still a congressional candidate, he had identified himself as a "Russell conservative," he now refused political categorization as a conservative, moderate, liberal, or anything else. He distrusted political labels: "I believe I'm a more complicated person than that." But he did make a carefully hedged pitch to the Arnall followers, saying that while he might tend to be conservative or moderate on various issues, he would not attack the federal government (though he would not let it usurp "our own government"). Each level of government has its place, and "nobody believes greater in the place of local government than I. I am a Georgian, and a Southerner, and I am an American." Both tactics—hedging, avoiding labels—were to become features of his later campaigns.

Yet Carter was virtually unknown statewide, and he had only three months to campaign before the primary. Moreover, he had lost some hometown support because of his earlier identification with Sumter County school bond and consolidation projects. Even his cousin Hugh Carter, who had led the opposition to these issues and was running for Jimmy's senate seat, kept his distance from Jimmy in the campaign—emphasizing in his advertisements that he had always been a conservative, which suggested that some others were only recent converts. Carter's old friend John Pope would oppose him in his campaign; having moved over to the Republican Party in 1964 during the Goldwater campaign, he was now the manager of Callaway's effort in the district. And Warren Fortson, who had handled Carter's legal appeal against Moore in 1962, had become such a controversial figure by 1966, as a result of his stands for moderation in the racial conflict in Americus, that his aid would have been detrimental. As he explains, "In more conservative circles, at the time, I was like a dose of poison."

Yet Carter was able to secure a broad cross section of local support—another tactic he was to employ in later campaigns. His Sumter County campaign committee was cochaired by two conservatives, W. E. (Billy) Smith, an Americus attorney who had been secretary of the Americus States Rights Council in 1956, and Frank Chappell, Jr., from Plains, who was influential in county politics. His friend, the "liberal" Russell Thomas, Jr., owner of the Old Citizen's Bank in Americus, served as his finance chairman and donated the office space for Carter's Americus headquarters; Mary Anne Thomas, his wife, helped by passing out handbills from time to time. Frank Myers, the mayor of Americus (in 1960–61), Earl Carter's opponent in the 1952 Georgia house race, a Johnson delegate to the Democratic convention in 1964, the treasurer of his state senatorial campaign, and an attorney for Carter's warehouse, supported him with both time and money. And another Americus influential and distant relative, Jimmy Deriso, offered to underwrite the cost of paid personnel for the initial week the offices were open.

From his senate contacts Carter drew other support. Senator Brooks Pennington agreed to act as manager of his campaign. Voter strategy and polling was done by the Voters Research Institute, an organization operated by Pennington and another senate colleague, Ford Spinks. Later in the campaign, when extra funds were needed, Pennington, Senator Bill Gunter, and others signed a note for him so he could borrow the money.

Through Charles Kirbo and Bill Gunter, Carter was introduced to influential people in Atlanta. Eventually his supporters included Bob Lipshutz, a prominent Jewish lawyer, and Bert Lance, the president of the First National Bank of Calhoun and two other small-town banks, who had been "instantly impressed." Carter also met Phil Alston, a wealthy attorney and Annapolis graduate, who was looking for an alternative to both the less-than-respectable Maddox and Ellis Arnall, whom he considered "old hat." David Grambrell, son of a major Eastern Airlines stockholder, was also a supporter, as were Alston's daughter, Elke Cushman, and Anne Chambers Cox, the daughter of the owner of the Atlanta Newspaper Corporation, which publishes the *Constitution* and the *Journal*.

Carter also put together a politically useful staff. He tapped as aides two "moderates with good political connections": Mrs. James Meachum headed the women's division of his campaign (she had served in a similar capacity with Vandiver before his withdrawal); and Bob Short, former speech writer for Carl Sanders, served as the campaign's public-relations director. He gained the assistance of another young man who would be important in Carter's future political career. Hamilton Jordan, a native of Albany, Georgia, first heard Carter speak at a meeting of the Albany Elks in the summer of 1966—and he went to work for Carter two weeks later. Though some of Carter's friends did not like Jordan—they found him arrogant—he was willing to serve as Carter's factotum in the campaign, and ultimately he would prove to be smart, tough, and through his strategy skills, a major factor in Jimmy Carter's future political successes.

Though Carter had won some significant support, the two leading figures in Georgia politics at that time, Senators Richard Russell and Herman Talmadge, made no commitments to him—or any other candidate. But during the campaign, there was some "gray" propaganda distributed—cards implying that

Carter was supported by associates of these two men. If Ellis Arnall should win, one postcard message read, the Georgia Democratic Party would be molded in the image of the national Democratic Party. Jimmy Carter, it said, was the only man certain to beat Arnall, though there were other acceptable candidates. "Call at least ten of our friends, have them spread the word. Defeat Arnall with Carter." And it was signed "Concerned friends of Senator Richard B. Russell and Senator Herman Talmadge." Just before the election another post card soliciting support for Carter was mysteriously mailed, this time under the signature "concerned friends of Jim Gillis." Gillis, who for a long time had controlled the state highway system, angrily denied having any knowledge of it.

One of Carter's key strengths, as this campaign was to show, was his ability to charm and attract certain members of the press. Back in November, 1965, the Columbus *Ledger-Enquirer* magazine featured a story on Carter's attractive qualities—former submariner, farmer, warehouser, businessman, family and religious small town man, and man of the world—and noted his possible candidacy for the Congress or the lieutenant governorship. In accompanying photos he was shown playing football in the back yard with his family—"just like another public figure, the late president John F. Kennedy." During Carter's brief congressional campaign, Jim Wynn of the Columbus *Ledger-Enquirer* said, "Carter radiates an unmistakable aura of confidence." And shortly after his gubernatorial announcement, the resemblance to Kennedy was noted again. Bruce Galphin wrote: "he does strongly resemble Jack Kennedy, even to emphasizing points with jabs of an open hand." Galphin went on:

Here was a breed of politician new to Georgia's big contest: subdued, frank even about his deficiencies, refusing to torture the traditional whipping boys. When he got to talking about Milledgeville State Hospital, he said the plight of the patients there made him choke up, and indeed his voice faltered and his face reddened a shade.

Carter made his personal integrity a salient theme in this campaign—as in later ones. On July 14, 1966, for example, he told a group of about fifteen teen-age campaign workers in Hall County: "If I ever let you down in my actions, I want you to let me know about it and I'll correct it. I promise never to betray your confidence in me." And in his campaign brochures, personal qualities were the focal point. Carter was portrayed as a civic leader, a good and religious man, a family man, and an Annapolis graduate. Later in the campaign Carter showed his instinct for the memorable. When children wrote requesting information from him, Carter would send them a story about his childhood and his pony, Lady. One can hear the children reporting this to their classes—a contrast to the more prosaic statements on issues that his competitors might use. On one occasion he staged a wade-in. Campaigning at Savannah Beach, Carter rolled up his pants and waded out to shake hands with some bathers. He and Rosalynn spent the entire day in the beach area—talking to fishermen, sunbathers, and shoppers at nearby stores. And another time, after Rosalynn

caused a traffic jam on a highway where she was passing out campaign literature, he said with a slight smile:

I've investigated this charge thoroughly and it's false and misleading. My wife and my
son were standing beside the road on the grass holding a Carter-for-Governor poster and
waving at cars as they passed. She did not stop any cars, give out any pamphlets or delay
any traffic. Although my wife is very pretty. I don't think her beauty would stop Macon
traffic at rush-hour—at least for 30 minutes as reported.

Carter showed his capacity, in this campaign, for turning a weakness into a
strength, for making a virtue out of necessity. Without much money or a large
popular following, he worked out a campaign style that would not cost too much
or expose him to situations where he looked weak. "No longer can votes in
Georgia be bought by plates of barbecue," Carter said in announcing that he
had vetoed the idea for a campaign kick-off barbecue. And after that he avoided
large rallies of any kind. As one reporter speculated, he may have wished to
avoid the embarrassment of planning even a small rally and having only a handful of persons show up. And he put in long hours, pressing the flesh across the
state. He noted late in the summer: "I've shaken more hands than any other
man in Georgia in the past two and a half months." By the September 14
primary, he and his wife hoped to shake 250,000 hands. His reason, he explained, was, "To let people know I'm interested in them and their problems."
And after a Labor Day weekend of shaking hands at the main shopping center
at Jekyll Island, he remarked, "The handshaking is paying off very well."

Though he resisted political labels, Carter did take stands on specific "good
government" issues throughout the campaign. On July 23 he released a campaign platform in which he called for an increase in teacher pay (to bring it up to
the national average), a study of urban problems, measures to guarantee freedom from political interference at state colleges and universities, an immediate
increase in aid to the state mental hospital at Milledgeville, and aid to the cities
for parks, rapid transit, and prevention of crime and juvenile delinquency.
Speaking to the Georgia Sheriffs' Association one week later, Carter praised his
audience and affirmed his confidence in the ability of state and local officials to
control crime and lawlessness. He proposed a new criminal code to permit the
legal use of confessions in the arrest and prosecution of accused criminals. Later
in the campaign he emphasized his commitment to economic development in
Georgia, the importance of the autonomy of local governments, the possible advantages of reducing the size of the Georgia House of Representatives (then
under a federal court order to reapportion its districts), and his support of popular election of delegates to the national nominating convention of the Democratic Party.

The controversial race issues of the day he mostly avoided, although on a
few occasions his comments showed him to be a moderate on the subject. On
July 22 Carter took exception to James Gray's plan to establish "home guards"
in Georgia communities to prevent riots and killings, saying, "The full force of

the state law enforcement officials will always be available to enforce law and order in Georgia where the law enforcement officials request such assistance." In August he stated: "Many responsible Negro educators and churchmen are openly supporting me because of my long time interest in education. In my campaign, I speak to white people and Negroes." Later he accused some of his opponents of "rebel rousing" and hoping for racial trouble to get themselves elected (apparently referring to Gray, Maddox, and Byrd). He made a plea for responsible local leadership to meet integration and consolidation problems in Georgia schools. But after the arrest of Stokely Carmichael of SNCC in September, he commented: "I think he should have been arrested. Anyone who incites a riot should be." And he criticized the federal government for making it almost impossible for local school officials to meet the demands of frequently changing desegregation guidelines. Local school boards could handle their own problems.

Midway through the race, it was clear that Carter had a major problem. In a poll conducted by Gerald Rafshoon for Comptroller James Bentley, Carter received only 4.2 percent of the votes, beating only Garland Byrd and Hoke O'Kelley. Callaway led with 37.1 percent, followed by Arnall with 20.1 percent, James Gray with 7 percent, and Lester Maddox with 4.7 percent.

Up to this point Carter had engaged in few personal attacks.

After the poll mentioned above was released, he came out swinging at all his opponents. Before a group of supporters in Marietta, he accused Arnall of "gross favoritism" to his home county in road building during his term as governor. He charged that Arnall had alienated large segments of the Democratic Party and argued that his extreme positions would prevent a united Democratic front in November. Two weeks later Carter accused Arnall of staging a "power grab" disguised as government reorganization. A few days later he charged Arnall with corruption and immorality. On another occasion he suggested that Arnall was old hat—he had "been removed from the political scene for nearly a quarter of a century." (Arnall had not been active in state politics for eighteen years.)

Commenting on the other candidates near the end of August, Carter said: "I am finding everywhere that the people are embarrassed and nauseated over the frivolity and clownish stunts that Mr. Arnall and Mr. Maddox continually inject into the campaign." (One incident that Carter was referring to was Arnall's signing of a Callaway for Governor petition.) In one day he took shots at Gray, O'Kelly, and Callaway, as well as Arnall and Maddox. In a speech to the Tucker Jaycees, he accused Gray of refusing "every opportunity to appear before the people by declining to participate in public forums with other candidates." Before the Atlanta Jaycees he stated that although Georgia had "faced many problems in recent years," Maddox, O'Kelly, and Gray (referred to as "these men") had not "stepped forward when their help was needed." And when an Atlanta Jaycee asked Carter about the difference between Callaway and himself, Carter replied: "So far Mr. Callaway has been running only on a platform of country, God and Motherhood. I served in the Navy longer than he did in the Army. I go to church every Sunday and also teach Sunday school class, and I love my mother just as much as Callaway loves his." (Carter may have learned something from Callaway, however, as his '76 presidential campaign emphasized similar themes.)

Throughout the campaign Carter had the assistance of his whole family. Though Rosalynn Carter's prior public-speaking experience had been confined to the missionary society of her church in Plains, she toured the state giving talks and interviews on radio and television shows, usually accompanied by two or three of her sons. Jimmy's sister Ruth came to Atlanta that summer to work in the campaign, returning to her home in North Carolina on weekends only. In Plains, Gloria managed the local campaign headquarters, while Billy attended to the family farm and business. Even Carter's mother traveled widely on his behalf.

Lillian, however, dropped out of the campaign in late August, shortly before the election. She had considered joining the Peace Corps for some time, and one night, after watching an advertisement on the Jack Paar show, she decided to apply. In early September she left for the University of Chicago to undertake her training program. She slipped out of Plains without public notice, however, for in this campaign the Carters feared that Lillian's endeavor might arouse the conservatives in the state. (Though she left in the middle of his campaign, Lillian told some of her new friends in the Peace Corps training program that not only would Jimmy be governor of Georgia, he would someday be President of the United States: "My boy gets what he wants.")

But he did not get what he wanted this time. He placed third in the Democratic primary, trailing Arnall by 67,000 votes and Maddox by 21,000.

Carter decided to support neither Arnall nor Maddox in the run-off, it was said at the time, because his supporters thought his endorsement would have little impact. Yet the race between Arnall and Maddox would be close and Carter, as a "moderate," might have influenced some of his supporters to move to Arnall. His decision was more likely based on a concern for his own political future. In his home district Carter had drawn support from many conservative voters, most of whom would shift to Maddox in the run-off. To avoid alienating those friends in his home territory, and to maintain as wide a following as possible, it would certainly be smart for him to avoid any unnecessary commitment to one side or the other in this campaign.

Maddox was victorious in the run-off and, as Carter himself later concluded, he may have won because of a Republican crossover aimed at keeping Arnall from winning the Democratic nomination. In the subsequent general election Arnall ran as an independent—pulling enough votes to deprive any candidate of a clear majority. As a result the election was thrown into the state legislature, which as a Democratic-controlled body, chose Maddox over Callaway as the new governor (though Callaway had received a plurality of the general election votes).

Carter had lost money, time, and had not even gotten into the run-off. Yet the campaign had not been a complete loss for him. He had come from nowhere to a close third in the primary, gained visibility, made new political friends, built a press following, shown his skills and charms as a campaigner, and developed an ecumenical political style. All were to prove useful to him in his subsequent campaigns. A number of the themes that would resound in his candidacy for the presidency were now emerging: refusal to accept ideological labels; avoidance of controversy; emphasis on personality, morality, and integrity; preference for concrete proposals over broad political issues; ability to corral a network of talented and energetic supporters as well as a disciplined, effective staff; and willingness to go for the jugular of his opponents when the circumstances seemed to demand it.

# SIX

---

# Born Again

CARTER'S DEFEAT IN 1966 propelled him into a classic mild depression. The entire experience, as he says in *Why Not the Best?* was ". . . extremely disappointing. . . . I was deeply in debt, had lost twenty-two pounds (down to 130), and wound up with Lester Maddox as governor of Georgia." As he later explained his state of mind: "I was going through a stage in my life then that was a very difficult one. I had run for governor and lost. Everything I did was not gratifying. When I succeeded in something, it was a horrible experience for me."*

Shortly afterward Carter went through a series of emotional experiences he was to later identify as being "born again." The first seems to have occurred in late 1966 while walking through the pine woods near his Webster County peanut farm with Ruth. As she recalls their exchange, he turned to her to learn the secret of her newfound peace: " 'You and I are both Baptists, but what is it that you have that I haven't got?' I said, 'Jimmy, through my hurt and pain I finally got so bad off I had to forget everything I was. What it amounts to in religious terms is total commitment. I belong to Jesus, everything I am.' He said, 'Ruth, that's what I want.' "

The two remember the incident differently. She says that he cried; he does not recall any such reaction. But he does share her memory of their talk about sacrifice. "Ruth asked me if I would give up anything for Christ, if I would give up my life and my possessions—everything. I said I would. Then she asked me if I would be willing to give up politics. I thought for a long time and had to admit that I would not." From that time on, he experienced a "more intimate relationship with Christ" and developed an inner peace and inner conviction and assurance that transformed his life for the better. But he would not give up his political ambition.

*Such reactions are often the consequence of a loss of self-esteem. Like the Rhodes scholarship, Carter evidently had made a major emotional investment in his campaign. He thought he should win, and expected he would. When he did not, his self-estimation was undermined. This will be discussed at great length in the final section of this book.

In *Why Not the Best?* Carter tells of two other episodes that brought him new awareness. One day he went to hear a sermon titled "If You Were Arrested for Being a Christian, Would There Be Any Evidence to Convict You?" While listening, he realized: "My answer by the time the sermon was over was 'no.' I never had really committed myself totally to God. My Christian beliefs were superficial." Later he was asked to speak on "Christian Witnessing" at the Baptist church in Preston, ten miles from Plains. He was proud at first: "I thought immediately that they had undoubtedly heard about the wonderful work I was doing in my own church. . . . While I was congratulating myself, suddenly I remembered the 1966 governor's election . . . I left everything I cared for—my farm, my family, my bird dogs—and my wife and I spent 16 to 18 hours a day trying to reach as many Georgia voters as possible." He continues, "The comparison struck me—300,000 visits for myself in three months, and 140 visits for God in fourteen years!"

As a result of this experience, Carter says, he "began to read the Bible with a new interest" and realized that he had been a "Pharisee." He then expanded his "personal service in the church," doing personal witnessing in states outside Georgia with non-English-speaking people.

In the fall of 1967 Carter and Hoyt Robinson (a former Plains resident) attended a layman's retreat at the Toccoa [Georgia] Baptist Camp. Though the conference was defined as a husband-wife conference, Rosalynn did not accompany Carter. For three days about 100 laymen from the state met. Carter was one of those who addressed the group, speaking about his personal commitment to Christ. And early in 1968 Carter and Robinson attended a second retreat at Toccoa (planned by the Baptist Brotherhood Commission of Atlanta). The gathering was to promote Project 500, an outreach program designed to establish 500 churches and missions, and was attended by about 25–30 men.

The first trip Carter undertook with this program was a two-week mission in Lock Haven, Pennsylvania. On the morning of May 18, 1968, Jimmy Carter met Hoyt Robinson at the Marriot Hotel in Atlanta for their trip north. The timing was bad: Robinson had qualified the day before as a candidate for the state senate (he was now from Dahlonega, Georgia), and Carter had to make two or three speeches that day. Robinson wound up driving the car to Williamsburg, while Carter flew from Atlanta a couple of days later. At an orientation meeting in Williamsburg, Carter suggested that he and Robinson, who were new to missionary work, be assigned to partners with more experience. The project director agreed and paired them with Milo Pennington of Elkhart, Texas, and Claude Perry of Plainview, Texas.

That evening the four of them drove to Lock Haven, where they stayed at the Fallon Hotel. Carter and Robinson shared a room and later that night Carter told Pennington that the day had been the greatest day in his life.

Each morning the four men would have breakfast in the hotel café and divide their prospect cards on local families, which had been prepared beforehand by a preacher working with the mission and the local congregation. By

8:30 or 9:00 A.M. they would start their rounds, concentrating on those with no religion as well as Baptists. When they stopped at a house, Carter and Pennington would often pray together before getting out of the car. Carter would then knock on the door and say, "Hi! I'm Jimmy Carter, a peanut farmer. Do you accept Jesus Christ as your personal savior?" If people showed an interest, Carter and Pennington would go into their homes, talk of the Lord, quote the scripture. At noon they would stop for lunch—and drop by a local bookstore to replenish the supply of Bibles they gave to those who had none—splitting the costs. The two men worked the field until past sundown; during the evening there were other meetings to attend and a worship service conducted by a pastor from Miami, in a room at the YMCA.

Even after this long day, as Hoyt Robinson recalls, Carter always took the time before going to bed to write the notes of the day on a yellow legal pad. He recorded people's names and addresses, he told Robinson, just in case he should visit the area again.

To his coworker Pennington, Carter seemed truly dedicated. The first person he talked to was a man at home alone. The man accepted Christ as his savior that very day and attended that evening's Baptist service at the YMCA. On another occasion they visited a non-Christian family who lived about three quarters of a mile down the river. It had rained the previous night and the road to the house was impassable. Rather than giving up, as Pennington thinks most people would have done, at Carter's suggestion they parked the car and walked a distance down the railroad tracks to make their visit.

During the two weeks that Carter and Pennington were in Lock Haven, Pennington says, twelve to fourteen people made their professions of faith. (Mazlish says fifteen to twenty families.) And as Carter was to confide later to Bruce Mazlish, he was impressed by Pennington's power to convert people and reach them emotionally—though Carter evidently saw him as an unimpressive man in other ways. Carter said: "Milo Pennington was not well-educated. He happens to be a peanut farmer—there aren't very many of them in Texas—and he did the work and talking. It seemed to me he was the most inept person I had ever known in expressing himself. He fumbled and didn't know what to say and I thought, 'Oh, I could do much better . . .' But he had done it before and he was a deeply committed person." (For some reason Mazlish and Diamond also picked up the idea that he was in his seventies at the time.)

Actually, Milo Pennington, fiftyish at the time, was the owner of a small cattle ranch, articulate, and responsible for much of their success. Once inside a house, Pennington would sit down at the kitchen table in a relaxed manner to promote informality. When he was ready to press his point, he would knock on the table as if it were a door and say, "Jesus is knocking at the door of your heart and only you can open it. You have to decide whether you're going to reject him or accept him, keep him out or let him in. He loves you, but only you can let him in. All he wants is for you to love him back." This approach was very effective: simple, straightforward, and honest.

Carter, however, did impress Robert and Thelma Farewell the Lock Haven residents who had asked for the missionaries. Although Carter did not tell them of his background and political interests, the Farewells knew by his clothes, carriage, and manner that he was a distinguished man. His love of Christ, according to Mrs. Farewell, shone on his countenance. And she remembers two incidents that were, to her, indications of his compassion. Once when she had Carter over for dinner, he walked into the kitchen and affectionately kissed her on the cheek. On another occasion when the Farewells' child was sick in bed, Carter asked to visit her. Mrs. Farewell went into the child's room to ask her if she wanted a visitor, and she said, "No." Carter, his hand on the doorknob, was still ready to walk in, insisting that he knew all about sickness because his mother was a nurse. Mrs. Farewell explained that she had to abide by the wishes of her child, and Carter relented.

This period in Lock Haven, according to Carter, was "almost a miracle to me." His call to Rosalynn one night shows that enthusiasm. She said: "Jimmy, you don't sound like the same person. You sound almost like you're intoxicated." Carter retorted: "Well, in a way I am." What he had discovered, he said later, was a sense of release, an assurance, and a better ability to relate to people. "I felt then and ever since that when I meet each individual person, they are important to me."

Carter may have also seen the political potential for such ways of relating. Certainly on the drive back to Atlanta he and Robinson discussed the political implications of his recent religious experience. Carter said he saw his role in politics as an implementation of his religious beliefs—doing what he believed was right to fulfill human needs. Later he wrote the Farewells: "Lock Haven will always have a special place in my heart because your community was where I have been closest to Christ and first experienced in a personal and intense way the presence of the Holy Spirit in my life."

Six months later, just before Thanksgiving, 1968, Carter and Hoyt Robinson were on their way to do missionary work in Springfield, Massachusetts. John Simmons, pastor of the Plains Baptist Church; Jerome Ethredge, who worked at the Agricultural Experimental Station outside Plains; and Ed Timmerman, a former Plains resident, went with them. They stayed at a YMCA in downtown Springfield. Carter, who knew some Spanish, was teamed with José Reyes, and they worked the Puerto Rican section of town. It was a great success—they had forty to fifty conversions.

Or at least it was a success until Thanksgiving Day. They had all received invitations to dinner from various members of the local Baptist congregation, but they had nothing to do that morning. So Carter, Robinson, Simmons, and Ethredge went door to door in a suburb of Springfield. Carter, teamed with Ethredge, took one side of the street, Simmons and Robinson on the other. They gave out several copies of the New Testament but had little success; some people even slammed the door in their faces. A squad car pulled up and the officers jumped out of the car: "Who are you? Don't you know it is illegal to solicit without a license?" Simmons tried to explain that what they were giving was free, that, in fact, it couldn't be bought or sold. The police, suspicious, told the men to follow them to the police station to fill out an application for a license to solicit. At the station, their identification as Baptist lay missionaries clarified, to the policemen's embarrassment, Carter and company wasted no opportunity: they left behind a New Testament and some tracts, just in case.

The men were in Springfield for eight to ten days. Carter suggests that the high point of his experience occurred in a meeting with a young man whose wife had just died "after a freak accident at a dentist's office." The man was so distraught he had tried to kill his baby and then retreated to his room. Eloy Cruz, a minister from Brooklyn, persuaded the man to open his door to them. "Later, inside the apartment we had one of the most moving religious experiences of my life."

Carter explained what had gone on in that apartment. Eloy Cruz told the young man that despite his sorrow and loneliness, "Christ was [to him] available with all his love and all his protection and all his guidance and all his forgiveness . . ."

Back on the street, Carter recalls, he had tears running down his cheeks. He decided to ask Cruz his secret. As Carter wrote in *Why Not the Best?*:

> I asked him how a tough and rugged man like him could be so sensitive, kind, and filled with love. He was embarrassed by my question, but finally fumbled out an answer:
> "Señor Jaime, Nuestro Salvador tiene los manos que son muy suaves, y El no puede hacer mucho con un hombre que es dura." [Our Saviour has hands which are very gentle, and he cannot do much with a man who is hard.]

Carter later told Jim Newton that at Springfield he had become "uniquely aware of the Holy Spirit as an integral part of my life. I learned that I cannot depend on myself for every need and to solve every problem."

Shortly after his return from Springfield, Carter chaired a week-long Billy Graham Film Crusade in Americus, sponsored by fifty-eight area churches, representing most denominations. More than 3,059 persons viewed the film, *The Restless Ones*, during its seventeen showings at a local theater. As Carter reported at the time: "Of this number, 515 made decisions for Christ, including 168 for the first time." Of the latter number, he said, 134 were white and 34 Negro. Carter said that about 17 percent of all those seeing the film had expressed salvation experiences. "This is twice as high as the national average and resulted because of the great effort made by so many individuals. . . . The result far exceeded our expectations." He called the crusade "the most dynamic and moving Christian experience ever for those of us who took part in it."

Carter, in short, had several religious experiences between late 1966 and December of 1968, which he was to describe later as being "born again."

## Church Christian

Prior to these experiences, Carter had been only a "church Christian," he says. As a child he attended church with his dad—as all the children were expected to do. (The first preacher he heard was Jesse Eugene Hall, a graduate of Louisville seminary, schooled in Greek.) At eleven he was baptized in the Plains Baptist Church by Royall Callaway, a member of a family that claims over thirty Baptist preachers. (A premillennialist, Callaway preached that the Jews would return to Palestine soon, and that Christ would return and "rapture" his church away from the evil world.) And when he was an adolescent, his social life centered around the church: the boys were members of the Young Ambassadors and attended the Sunday night socials where they met the girls. Later, at Annapolis, in addition to his required attendance at chapel, Carter taught a Sunday school class for the officers' dependents. And as a submarine officer he sometimes conducted services.

On his return to Plains, Carter rejoined the church of his youth. Tommie Jones, who was the pastor from 1951 to 1955, assigned him a Sunday school class of boys aged nine to twelve. In 1962 Carter was elected deacon. (His name had been presented before, but he had not secured enough votes—possibly because he had opposed the minister who followed Jones, Robert Harris, in Harris's successful fight to keep Sumter County dry.)

None of his pastors discouraged his interest in public life. Harris even promoted the Peace Corps among his parishioners, and during Carter's 1966 gubernatorial campaign he sent letters of recommendation on Carter's behalf to every Baptist preacher in Georgia. Indeed, the Baptist preacher in Georgetown, Comer Williamson, did the spadework for Carter's victory in Georgetown in his 1962 senatorial campaign. He preached and got local people upset about the situation there. Later he kidded Carter about winning his first election for him. Even Allen Comish, the "visiting minister" from Columbus, Georgia, who, Carter says in *Why Not the Best?*, tried to dissuade him from entering politics, abetted his political career. Comish does recall discussing Carter's decision to run for the state senate, but he did not try to dissuade him from it. In the 1966 campaign he wrote letters to ministers and laypeople on Carter's behalf.

Though most of the time Carter blended into the local culture, on two occasions he took stands against the views of his neighbors, though his principles in both cases were in accord with the area's basic traditions. As a state senator, he argued against a proposed section of the new Georgia Constitution that could establish a state religion (which Baptists have always opposed). And in 1965 Carter and his family opposed a motion of the Board of Deacons of the Plains Baptist Church first to bar all "Negroes and other civil rights agitators" from the services.

There had been no direct pressure to integrate the Plains church, but the deacons were reacting to the attempts to integrate two churches in Americus. As is the custom in the Baptist church, a conference was called to approve the deacons' decision. Carter was in Atlanta for a social weekend when this occurred. But when someone telephoned him of this development, he dropped everything and headed back home.

At the meeting, according to Lillian's recollection, he stood up and said, "Before we vote I've got to tell you how I feel. This is God's house, not ours. How can we stand in the doorway and tell God's people they cannot come into His house?" Only his immediate family and one other person voted with Jimmy, though many members of the congregation abstained.

The Carters had not taken a radical stance. As Billy Wise later recalled: "The way I saw it, maybe other people too, was that blacks had always been allowed to go to the funerals. All Miss Lillian and Jimmy were doing was trying to preserve that. And you have to remember that they kept it inside their own church." The Williamses, who opposed him on the issue, had a similar understanding.

## Family Healing

In his new religious interests Carter was not alone. His sisters and mother had all been "born again" before him. Their religious experiences provide a basis for contrasting Jimmy's experience with theirs, as well as a glimpse into the culture of the Carter family.

Ruth was the first in the family to turn to religion as a way of resolving her personal conflicts. She had dropped out of college at age nineteen to marry an Americus boy, Bobby Stapleton, but soon found her marriage in trouble; she had developed a habit of running home to her parents (only nine miles away) at any sign of trouble. To save her marraige, she and her husband moved to North Carolina. But in 1959, when her fourth and last child was born, she was possessed by a sense of "hopeless failure—as a wife, as a mother, as a person." A series of troubles followed. She was in an auto accident that almost killed her. With the help of a friend, she realized that the accident was related to her depression—her conflicts had made her suicidal. Sometime thereafter (between 1959 and 1969, according to her own accounts), she tried group therapy (which lasted three years), returned to college (where she studied psychology), and turned to Christ and developed her "Inner Healing" therapy.

Although the sequence of these emotional traumas and her religious experiences is not at all clear from her various reports, it is evident that in 1974 she had a profound and emotionally moving religious experience. As she described it to Myra MacPherson: "I woke up in my sleep and there was this light, this glow in my room. Something inside of me said I was moving into a place of 'unconditional love.' My total healing took place when I fully realized God was a God of Love, not one who punished." In *Inner Healing*, she is apparently describing this moment as a witnessing of the kingdom of God. "In that blessed radiance, every painful memory is washed clean; we are revealed in our wholeness to others and to ourselves. And we discover that our wills are no longer ours. They have become his will, and there is no separateness. We are whole; we are *alive* at last!"

Gloria's religious experiences also had their roots in personal distress. She had married a local war hero, First Lieutenant William Everett Hardy, back in July, 1945. From a poor family in Americus (he had worked as a counterboy at Walgreen's in town, something the "better families" did not have their children do) he had been shot down over Italy, spent some time as a war prisoner in Germany, and received the Presidential Citation, the Air Medal, the Purple Heart and four Bronze Stars. They were divorced in 1949, and Gloria married Walter G. Spann, a local farmer in 1950. He adopted William, her son from the first marriage.

By 1959 William, who was then fourteen, had been expelled by both the public and private schools in the area. His behavior problems were troubling Gloria, as she later recounts:

> William's nocturnal wanderings were becoming more frequent, and occasionally he would disappear for several days at a time. I was becoming more and more frantic with each of his escapades. My time was spent either searching for my son or writing to various schools all over the country in an attempt to find one that would accept him.

In her distress, sometime in late 1959, Gloria fled to North Carolina to visit Ruth "just to get away from home." She ignored Ruth's suggestions of a prayer retreat, insisting, "I don't want to hear about Jesus—or God—or prayer—or anything else pertaining to religion." She shut herself up in Ruth's mountain cabin to get a good night's sleep, but there was nothing there to read but religious works. Eventually she picked up a book of Gertrude Keehn's transcribed radio tapes and began to read, "expecting to be bored to sleep instantly." On the fourth page of the book, Gloria came across a sentence that made her stop: "If you have a real problem, and you become a physical and emotional wreck worrying about it, how do you expect to solve it?" The answer was: "Give your problem to God for sixty seconds, and rest your mind." Gloria tried it.

> Suddenly I looked around, and the whole world seemed different. The moon was shining, the forest of pine needles before me were almost iridescent. For the first time in two years, beauty came into my mind. Since that moment I have never doubted the existence of God. And hope for my son has been renewed every day.

Gloria went to a prayer retreat some weeks later where she "cried . . . and cried . . . and cried . . ." But no one pushed God on her. "Everyone truly loved me," she felt. The experience, as she recalls, filled her with love for Jesus Christ and relaxed her so "an earthquake wouldn't have shaken me." In the next few years she also found she had the strength to deal with her son.

Through this period Gloria attended retreats at least twice a year—leaving her husband at home. But then at a prayer retreat in 1969, she sensed something was wrong. She said: "Lord, I'm willing to give up anything for you, even my husband. What can I do?" And then she heard, "How about giving up prayer retreats?" She concluded it might be better to put God in her everyday life—as a housewife. She rushed home to Walter, for whom she now felt "homesick." Upon seeing him, she said on impulse, "Walter, if you'll get a motorcycle, I'll learn to ride it." He laughed and said, "Gloria, welcome home!"

Lillian's commitment to Christ took place at a Tennessee meeting when she was sixty-seven years old. A Methodist evangelist offered an altar call: "If there is anyone here," he declared, "who would be willing to commit their life completely to Christ—if you're willing to give up home, friends, family, material possessions, comfort, everything for God—I'm going to ask you to come and lay your life at the altar." There was a moment of quiet. Lillian turned to her daughter, Ruth, and said, "Let's go." Ruth thought her mother wanted to leave. "You go on out if you want to," Ruth said, "but I want to stay for the rest of this." Whereupon Lillian Carter rose and strode to the altar. According to Ruth, she gave her life to Christ.

The meaning of these salvation experiences cannot be second-guessed in religious terms. As Glenn Spivey of the Preston, Georgia, church explains: "No one can judge the quality or meaning or depth of another's commitment to Christ, and therefore the confession itself, if freely given, is considered sufficient." Brooks Hays, a Southern liberal and a former head of the Southern Baptist Convention, puts it another way—respect for another's confession is a kind of "consideration of the other person, preserving [his/her] privacy."

But one can attempt a description of the experience from the reports of theologians and of those who have been through it. All Southern Baptists see the salvation experience, and the accompanying sacrament of baptism, as a condition of church membership. Though most Baptists are received into church membership sometime between the ages of nine and eleven, this often is followed in adulthood by other deeper and emotionally moving experiences. Being born again is simply spiritual rebirth arising from the experience of God's grace. It does not represent any new revelation from God, for that would diminish the authority of the Bible. And it is ultimately offered "to all who patiently wait for his inevitable knock at the heart's door." It comes through a conviction at hearing the word preached—rather than as a reward for good work. And the experience can never be undone. As one commentator points out: " 'falling out' is impossible if the experience was a true one: for who could reject Christ having truly seen him? The person is permanently changed."

There are, however, from the reports of those who have been through it, different types of born again experiences. For many Christians there is no one moment when one can be called "born again." Rather, there is a kind of growing into the Christian commitment. As Brooks Hays has said: ". . . the Christian experience should be termed in the plural—it should be Christian 'experiences,' which lead to growth and grace and a . . . moral life, and religious life."

There are other Baptists who describe the born again experience as one dramatic moment—a vivid emotional experience when one truly accepts Christ as his or her savior. The Reverend Fred Collins, minister of Carter's church in Plains from 1972 to 1974, explains that being "born again" "is an instantaneous experience. A persons past life, temperament, age, and etc. all has a bearing.

. . . legitimate conversion to me is a definite experience that comes to those persons who are convicted by the Holy Spirit and respond in repentance toward God and faith in our Lord Jesus Christ." And Reverend Spivey provides a yet another perspective:

Being born again means only confessing one's faith in Christ openly and publicly before the congregation. Although there can be only one true born again experience, for the acceptance of Christ is a totality which must happen in full at once or not at all, the believer may and usually does have further experiences which deepen the meaning of Christ in his life.

However they might explain the process, traditional Baptists North and South do not see the results of the experience as manifesting itself in special signs or lifting the individual above temptation. But for some Christians— mainly those in the older Pentecostal churches and the contemporary charismatic movement—there is another possibility. It is usually perceived as a third birth, a kind of baptism by fire, in which the individual is united with the Holy Ghost, cleansed of guilt, and transformed. "Sanctification," as it is called, is often accompanied by a kind of ecstasy and manifestations of "gifts of the spirit" such as speaking in tongues and the ability to effect, through the Holy Spirit, miraculous cures. "Sanctification" is different from "justification," which assumes only repentance, conversion, and forgiveness of individual transgression. Derived from John Wesley, the distinction is explained by M. Pearlman:

But in the merely justified person, there remains a corrupt principle, an evil tree, a root of bitterness, which continuously provokes to sin. If the believer obeys this impulse and willfully sins, he ceases to be justified. Therefore the desirability of its removal so that the likelihood of backsliding be therefore lessened. *The eradication of sinful root is sanctification.*

Against this background, it appears that the various Carters had different kinds of salvation experiences. Ruth and Gloria, and to some extent Lillian, have been influenced by the charismatic movement. From the reports of their friends, all have been interested in "signs of the spirit," such as speaking in tongues. Ruth, in her book *Inner Healing*, is open to the possibility of exorcism (with its implication that one can be literally possessed by the devil) as a technique one might resort to should her own process of inner healing fail to bring peace to a sick or troubled soul. None of them has strong ties to any specific denomination.

And while they have not publicly used the word "sanctification," Ruth Carter Stapleton and Gloria Carter Spann report dramatic experiences that could be interpreted as "baptisms by fire." Certainly Ruth and Gloria act in ways that suggest they have collapsed the tension between the ideal and real that traditionalists see as a permanent feature of this world. Ruth, for example, suggests that one should strive to love the important human beings in one's life unconditionally, as God has loved her. In her article, "The Message of Easter," for example, she holds up as an ideal a woman who helped her husband defeat his alcoholism through an unfailing gentleness, an "unconditional love," during his drunken stupors. Gloria has embraced a philosophy of equanimity. All the various people around her should be accepted as is—her husband, her brother, her son—despite their differences and various failings. God is manifest, she says, in the variety of people and things that exist in the world—and there is good in each.

Lillian Carter, on the other hand, has a more earthy view of the consequences of her own religious commitment. She said that she was perplexed and puzzled about it. "I don't know how to give up my family or my friends or how to give up everything I own, to give up all my possessions." Further, she doesn't like to be considered a "square" and admits to an occasional cigarette, an ounce of bourbon at bedtime, and playing bridge ("for money" she says in a mock whisper). But she does believe in the power of prayer. "While I'm not as deeply religious as Jimmy is, the very thought of anything else other than God never enters my mind. . . . To take care of Jimmy, and make him able to say the right thing at the right time."

Jimmy Carter's experiences are clearly different from those of his sisters. Though he has shown a passing interest in the charismatic movement, he gives no detailed, poetic account of one dramatic moment in which he became whole with God. He seems to have had the "born again" experiences of the traditional Christian—growing in his faith through a series of experiences.

Psychologically, he says he has become less prideful, more aware of his dependence on God, achieved an inner peace. "Because I am a Christian, I feel my limitations more intensely. I used to deny my limitations and conceal them. Now I am much easier in my relations with other people and with God." And he does not see himself as having been removed from ordinary human temptations. As he told a United Methodist Conference in Atlanta in 1974, his religious experiences are related to a continuing "search in my own heart for a corrective attitude toward my natural inclinations." Through them he "initiated a process of personal growth designed to impose control over such passions as anger, lust, pride, and fear, and to elicit the more positive virtues of love and compassion." As he told Bill Moyers in 1976, "I feel at ease with myself. And it doesn't mean that I'm better, but I'm better off myself."

Whatever the changes in his relationship to God and in his own inner feelings, Carter's religious experiences seem to have worked no dramatic alteration of the external man. His charm, his apparent sincerity before audiences, his ability to relate one-on-one had been noted by personal friends and reporters during his 1966 campaign. His increase in self-confidence during that campaign could well be the natural outcome of practice in public speaking and greater exposure to others. Nor did his experience of conversion change his political ambitions. His commitment to God did not rule out politics. As he was to later report, "I also have a conviction that whatever talent God gave me should be used to the maximum degree. I believe God wants me to be the best politician I can possibly be."

If anything, Carter's political drive was stronger after his born again experiences. After losing his first campaign for governor, he resolved to run again—and the next time he would make it. As he states in *Why Not the Best?*, "You show me a good loser and I will show you a loser." And in his next campaign for the governorship, his tenacity, determination, and political flexibility demonstrated his commitment to that philosophy.

# II

# Governorship

# SEVEN

# Winning

RIGHT AFTER HIS DEFEAT in the 1966 primary, Carter met with some of his closest supporters to discuss the campaign and plan for the future. The decision to run in 1970 was made at that meeting, though it seems to have been assumed rather than explicitly stated.

At a subsequent Jimmy Carter Appreciation Dinner on November 4, more than 500 people poured into an Atlanta ballroom, each paying fifty dollars for a ticket to retire the Carter campaign debt. The mood was jubilant. As a local reporter noted—from Carter's behavior "you'd have thought he'd won." And the crowd was "given to frequent applause, much laughter and occasional bantering and they perhaps cheered loudest when Senator Brooks Pennington, Senator Carter's erstwhile campaign manager, declared they really hadn't lost because now: 'They don't say Jimmy Who, they say Jimmy When—1968 or 1970?' "

The 1966 campaign had put Carter in a good political position. As Charles Kirbo was to say, "It gave him prestige all over the state, and developed an organization. He gained experience and maturity." Now he began to expand further his contacts in the state. He describes a typical day during this period:

I would go to the warehouse or farm early, and perform my extracurricular duties, along with my regular business work until late in the afternoon. Then I would drive somewhere in Georgia to make a speech, and return home late at night. Names, information about the community, and speech notes for later use were all dictated into a small tape recorder in the automobile. The next day Rosalynn wrote thank-you notes on an automatic typewriter which also recorded names and addresses and code descriptions of the persons I had met.

He worked through his contacts in farm organizations such as the state seed association, and in business groups, including local chambers of commerce and Lions Clubs. Building on his work in the Middle Flint Regional Planning Association, he helped found a statewide planning association, and served as its first president. He was chosen state chairman of the March of Dimes and was elected district governor of Lions International, and then chairman of the six regional district governors of Lions International in Georgia. And his church work gave him another kind of access to an important segment of the downstate population—the Baptists and the broader groups of evangelical Christians who dominate religious life in Georgia.

His skill in capturing the attention of the press was evident from the beginning. Lillian Carter's departure for India in December, 1966, was one of the first human interest stories about the Carters to appear in the Atlanta press. On October 25, 1967, there was a story in the Atlanta *Constitution* entitled "Plains Somehow Seems Too Small for Jimmy Carter," noting his heavy speaking schedule, his youthful good looks, his interest in books, and his unpretentious house near Main Street in Plains with its Chinese-red front door. On November 5, 1968, a story in the *Constitution* interpreted a poll of the state board members of the Junior Chamber of Commerce as a sign that Carter might be "the man to beat" in 1970. On November 19, 1968, the paper ran another story entitled "Carter Displays Same Old Candor," and on November 21 John Pennington did a feature story entitled "Visit with Jimmy Carter."

Politically, Carter took no public stands that might lose him support in the state. He refused to be a delegate to the Democratic convention in 1968, though he later criticized those who abandoned the party that year. In 1969 he declared his support of Nixon's handling of the Vietnam war. He assailed Georgia's "mediocrity syndrome," saying Georgia could not blame its problems on the Civil War, the Supreme Court, the federal government, or the government in Atlanta. The state could not sit back and let the federal government solve problems by default. He criticized the dumping of nuclear waste in Georgia and urged that political considerations be eliminated in the selection of judges. And at this time he was willing to identify himself with the conservative label. The state should act—conservatively. "Conservative leadership resides with bankers, businessmen and state legislators," he said. "We resent the equalization of conservative with racist or with hard-heartedness, or with an unawareness of problems that prevail in our state."

He was also making inroads into a very important political network. Charles Pou, the political editor, wrote in the *Constitution* of Carter's appearance before the annual convention of the Association of Georgia County Commissioners in 1969: "The commissioners appear to like Carter, a surprise entry in the 1966 rhubarb. There was even one little rumor going around, though it really got no further than the notions shop in the lobby, that he might be named 'Man of the Year' by the organization." (He did win that title in 1970.)

By 1969 Carter had put together a top-notch campaign staff and hired some professional advisers. Hamilton Jordan was back. (After the 1966 campaign and his graduation from college, he had been deferred from the draft and gone to South Vietnam with the International Volunteer Services.) Carter had also won over Jody Powell, a young graduate student in political science at Emory University and a former Air Force cadet (who had been forced to leave the Academy in 1964 because he had cheated on a history examination). Powell, who had been writing a graduate paper on Southern populism, sent Carter a description of his work, and Carter invited him to Plains. As a result, Powell was signed on as a general handyman—driver, leaflet distributor, press contact man, and all-around helper. Hotheaded, free-wheeling, cynical in many respects, he nevertheless devoted himself to the Carter cause. Powell was later to say that he had been attracted to Carter by his "sincerity," the fact that they were both from southwest Georgia (Powell hailed from Vienna, former Senator Walter George's hometown), and by his special qualities as a politician. As the campaign developed, Powell became noted for the ferocity with which he defended his boss against all criticism. It was said he even carried a roll of dimes—so he could place a call instantly to anyone on radio or television who criticized Carter.

Carter also secured the assistance of Bill Hamilton, a professional political pollster based in Washington, D.C., and of Gerald Rafshoon, who had recently returned to Atlanta to head his own public-relations firm after three years in New York as national advertising manager for Twentieth Century–Fox. With the help of young volunteers, Carter had put together the voting results of all counties in Georgia since 1952, "showing how the people there had voted in state and local elections for all different kinds of candidates, emphasizing all kinds of issues." But he needed to know where people stood in their political attitudes at that time, and a professional pollster like Hamilton was to be crucial in the final phases of the campaign. Rafshoon would aid him in shaping a self-presentation.

Carter also retained the support of a number of Georgia influentials. Robert Lipshutz, who had backed him to a limited degree in 1966, gradually became more active. David Gambrell, Carter's campaign treasurer in 1966, was to continue as the treasurer in 1970, accepting contributions at the First National Bank in Atlanta. Philip Alston, the Atlanta-based realtor, stayed with Carter. So did Bill Gunter and J. D. Deriso (an old family friend who had lent Carter his plane for campaigning in 1966). In the latter phases of the 1970 campaign, these men of the "inner circle" would meet every Sunday in Atlanta to discuss campaign strategy. The meetings were sometimes attended by two women—Elke Cushman, the daughter of Phil Alston, and Dot Padgett, wife of David Padgett, an Atlanta banker.

There was some change in the political cast—not unusual in Georgia politics. Pennington, who had managed Carter's campaign in 1966, worked for Sanders in 1970 (he later explained it in terms of a political obligation to Sanders, rather than any falling out with Carter). J. Frank Myers, who had cochaired Carter's 1966 campaign in Sumter County, also switched to Sanders in 1970—Sanders had appointed him district attorney and placed him on the State Board of Health. But John Pope, who had directed Callaway's effort in the county in 1966, was back in the Carter camp. (He once donated all his leftover travelers checks to Carter's campaign, and Rosalynn said it was the first money they received.) Perhaps even more significant for the tone of the campaign, Carter had brought cousin Hugh back into the fold, naming him campaign chairman. An old-style politician with solid conservative credentials, Hugh was to play an important role in reassuring conservatives in the state that Jimmy Carter was a safe man.

By 1969 Carter had stepped up his pace—meeting people in factory lines, at restaurants, barber shops, shopping centers, and football games. He visited towns so small they were usually bypassed by other politicians seeking state office. His son Chip, a sophomore at Georgia Southwestern, took a year off from school to drive for his father; later Rosalynn or Jody Powell accompanied him on most of his trips. Lillian, after her return from India in early 1969, traveled on her own throughout the state, speaking of her experiences and drawing attention to her son.

On most of his visits Carter was assisted by local supporters who had been won over by his earlier work in the various associations he belonged to or through the speeches he had given at their clubs. When Carter was in Dahlonega, for example, Hoyt Robinson, with whom Carter had done missionary work, would travel with him. In Macon, Joe Andrews did the same. Andrews had first met Carter when he gave a speech before the Rotary Club in Milledgeville in 1969. Carter's story of Rickover's influence in his life had moved Andrews and in a later Carter appearance at Macon, Andrews was completely won over. Carter seemed so clean, so open, so good that Andrews volunteered to help him in whatever way he could. (When Andrews was later asked to explain Carter's attraction to people, he replied by saying it was just one of those things: "How do you explain falling in love?")

Carter and Powell came to Macon to campaign, Andrews, with his dog, would go to a local motel so Carter and Powell could have his bachelor apartment for the night, a means of cutting down on expenses. Early in the morning the three of them would meet and hit the street—Carter moving ahead, Jody following with campaign literature. Carter moved fast, shaking as many hands as possible with the same litany: "Hello, I'm Jimmy Carter and I'm running for governor. I hope you will vote for me." There was no discussion of the issues— he just moved and touched and charmed. The smile was there and Carter's eyes didn't slide over their faces as political candidates' are apt to do—he looked people in the eye, which made them feel they had personal contact with him.

From the beginning of the campaign it was clear to Carter that his main opponent in the 1970 election would be former Governor Carl Sanders. And despite the work he had done, it would be a tough race. Carter's September, 1969, polls showed he was considerably behind Sanders 53 percent to 21 percent.

But Carter had a plan for closing that distance. The shape of the forthcoming encounter had already surfaced in a piece published in the Columbus

*Ledger-Enquirer* in 1968. A local reporter published a memo he said Carter had scribbled on a yellow legal pad:

Some images to be projected regarding Carl Sanders . . . more liberal . . . has close connections with Ivan Allen [then Atlanta mayor] and Atlanta Establishment . . . refuses to let Georgia Democrats have a voice in the Democratic party . . . pretty boy . . . ignored prison reform opportunities . . . nouveau riche . . . refused to assist local school boards in school financing . . . excluded George Wallace from the state . . .

You can see some of these are conflicting but right now we just need to collect all these rough ideas we can. Later we can start driving a wedge between me and him.

### Primary Battle: the Low Road

On Friday, April 3, 1970, Jimmy Carter strode into the supreme court room at the Georgia state capitol, carrying two-year-old Amy in his arms. His first words to a crowd of 250 supporters were: "I am a candidate for Governor of Georgia.

"I'm convinced that the best man did not win in 1966," he said. "But the best man will win this year. . . . I will win the Democratic nomination and the election." He once again refused political labels, but promised to speak to the issues. And he outlined his stand on several matters—showing himself a moderate, good-government man. He wanted to help restore the confidence of people in their government. He was for conservation of the environment, but with "freedom, opportunity and equal treatment." He called for obeying school desegregation laws and for building a school system "for the benefit only of the children." He pledged to veto any attempt to raise the sales tax unless accompanied by legislation for equalizing or eliminating tax inequalities. And he favored the development of a broader tax base for cities and counties.

More important, he introduced the subject that would become one of his main campaign themes. "Georgians," he said, "never again want a governor who will use the tremendous power and prestige of the office for his own personal wealth." They "want a governor who will speak up for Georgia and not spend time seeking favor with the Washington crowd just to make himself look important."

Now that he had a stronger following he lost his distaste for rallies and barbecues. The next day he came home for an affair much like a festive country fair, with music from the Americus High School Band and a free barbecue at noon. Reverend John Simmons, pastor of the Plains Baptist Church, gave the invocation. Cousin Hugh Carter introduced the candidate. Jimmy Carter greeted the gathering with a broad grin and said: "I've spent many days in Plains, but this is the greatest day of all." He covered some of the same issues he had discussed the previous day in Atlanta. He accepted in the formal ceremony a check for $2,125 (his filing fee) from Jimmy Deriso, his campaign chairman in Sumter County. The Plains Methodist pastor gave the benediction, and the crowd was now free to go the tables for their food.

Carter also knew how to make his campaign credible with the people who really count. Soon after the rally, in the Carter Warehouse office, Carter mapped out his strategy for Steve Ball, the political editor of the Atlanta *Journal*. There were seven other persons seeking the Democratic gubernational nominations—among them J. B. Stoner, an avowed white supremacist; an osteopathic physician; a local socialist; and a civil rights lawyer, C. B. King, the first black to run for statewide office since Reconstruction. The strongest candidate was former governor Carl B. Sanders.

Carter told Ball how he planned to beat Sanders. He would conduct a "populist" campaign aimed at winning over a broad range of Georgians in the middle and low income brackets, the downright poor (black and white), young and old moderates, and the conservative Georgian supporters of Lester Maddox and George Wallace. From his travels across the state the past three and a half years he knew what the voters wanted. And he had taken polls. One, conducted the previous October, showed that concern over unfair taxes, not school integration, was the major issue among whites. "Both the rich and the poor white people thought they got taken in taxes." There was an underlying suspicion that they had no voice in the government. Carter rather eloquently elaborated on this theme:

They want to have rights which I believe in as deeply as they do. They are average working people, what they want is someone in the governor's office who understands their problems, who has worked with his hands, who knows what it means to be left out, who knows what it means to be fearful of the system of justice, to have cold chills go up and down their spines when a patrolman stops 'em. These [Wallace] people are for me . . . I've talked to 'em, I've wooed 'em. They don't ask me for any commitment that's racist in nature or that would discriminate against anybody. They want some rights.

Sanders had the advantage, Carter granted. A February poll indicated that Sanders was ahead of him 60 to 40 percent, and winning 91 to 92 percent of the black vote. But Carter thought that C. B. King would draw a big chunk of the Sanders vote, that he could draw a good percentage himself because of the resentment against Sanders. Moreover, Carter was campaigning among blacks: "I've been to see 'em in their filling stations, in their churches. I've been to see 'em in their drugstores and their homes."

He intended to attack Sanders on several counts: his wealth, his ties to the National Democratic Party, his refusal to allow Wallace to speak in Georgia, his purported use of "secret" state government information for private purposes, and his failure to deliver on some of his earlier promises while governor. Carter's object was to attract Wallace supporters who held Sanders's support of Lyndon Johnson and Hubert Humphrey against him. At the same time he had to avoid alienating the young people and those who believed in the national party. One way to do this, he explained, would be to charge that Sanders's support of the national ticket in 1964 had been based not on party loyalty but on a desire for personal gain from Washington. The whole strategy, he admitted, would require him to take both sides of an issue—a rather tricky business. But he expected to narrow the race down to a two-man competition and possibly avoid a run-off primary with Sanders. It is a safe bet, Ball said, that "Sanders will know he has been in a fight before the summer is over."

In a television program on May 8, Carter began to implement his strategy. He charged Sanders with: (1) using his control of the Georgia Democratic party to gain favor from the national Administration to influence the granting of TV station licenses; (2) receiving large retainer fees from big businesses after his first term as governor; (3) buying property with advance knowledge that programs like highway construction would appreciate its value. Carter dared Sanders to release a complete financial statement and pledged to release his own financial statements in a few days—to do so once again after his term as governor.

Ten days later, at a meeting of the Atlanta Press Club on Thursday, June 18, Carter released his financial statement. He said his assets totaled $455,000 at market value and $366,000 after deduction of certain liabilities. Again he hit Sanders, this time without mentioning his name.

Abuse of power or misconduct in office can be subtle . . . and in this form it is most dangerous and difficult to detect. The question is not whether an act is legal or illegal, but whether it is right or wrong when judged by the rules of life, which simple, ordinary people can understand . . .

At a meeting of the Georgia Press Association at Jekyll Island on June 28, Carter charged that Sanders was more interested in winning the ailing Richard Russell's Senate seat than in being elected governor. A member of his staff had discovered that the registration number of Sanders's airplane—6272 Victor— was out of the normal sequence of plane registration numbers. Carter interpreted the number as a symptom of Sanders's Senate ambitions. "1962 was the year he [Sanders] was elected governor and 1972 is the year Senator Russell's term expires."

Sanders, who was at this meeting, denounced this attack as "smear tactics" and countered that the numbers were already on the plane when he leased it. (Indeed, this was true. The manufacturer had requested the number and it had been assigned before the plane was sold to the leasing corporation that rented it to Sanders.) Nevertheless, the charge received press coverage, drawing attention to Sanders's affluence and reminding Russell's supporters that Sanders had considered running against Russell in 1968.

Carter, a few days later, explained the bitterness of his attacks by blaming his 1966 defeat on Sander's interference in the campaign. He said Sanders and the then state chairman J. B. Fuqua in June, 1966 had asked him not to run because they were already committed to former Governor Arnall. "If they had supported me, or even if they had stayed out of it, I would have been elected."

Sanders refuted this charge:

I told him if he's running for governor that was fine. But I was not going to get involved. I would support the nominee. It's becoming more and more difficult to understand what Carter means or to believe what he says. In his last race he was known as Jimmy Who?

This time he is becoming known as Jimmy the Fabricator. He had absolutely no credibility as a responsible candidate. . . . He can blame anyone he wants to for this [the 1966 defeat]. He seems to be blaming everyone but himself.

Whatever the validity of Carter's charge, it linked Sanders to the liberal Arnall, exaggerated the strength of his own earlier candidacy, and suggested that such opposition was somehow wrong, rather than politics as usual.

On July 15, a letter from Carter to his county campaign chairman found its way into the press. It suggested a pro-Sanders cabal:

Things are not going too smoothly in the Sanders camp. On Monday, July 13, a group from the huge Atlanta financial establishment met in the afternoon in a private club in Atlanta to plot the Sanders campaign. . . . As you probably know by now, Carl Sanders is launching the biggest political advertising campaign ever to hit the State of Georgia. It is, in fact, a million-dollar brainwashing campaign to convince voters that they owe Sanders the governor's chair again.

Sanders's advertising campaign seemed to buttress the charge. He opened his media blitz in July with a Sunday newspaper supplement, then a TV campaign, billboards by the hundreds, and finally radio spots. His overall expense for TV time (the air time only) was $290,207, compared to Carter's $170,238.

Though Carter may have had less money, he had the more powerful theme. In television spots prepared by Gerald Rafshoon, Carter was depicted as the representative of the common people. One advertisement, showed a man wearing a hard hat coming out of a manhole to greet a smiling Jimmy Carter with his outstretched hand. Carter wanted to know what he could do to help the working man—because he was a workingman, too. Another spot, reported by Bill Shipp at the time (Rafshoon later denied its existence) showed Sanders boarding a Lear jet, followed by a shot of two men—one wearing big cufflinks (a Sanders trademark)—passing a bundle of money from one to the other.

Carter also took after Sanders for his anti-Wallace stance during his earlier term as governor:

I was a member of the Georgia Seedmen's Association. We rented a National Guard Armory and asked Governor Wallace to address us. At the last minute, Governor Sanders sent us word that he would not allow Governor Wallace to speak on Georgia state property. I don't think it is right for Governor Sanders to try to please a group of ultra-liberals, particularly those in Washington, when it means stifling communications with another state.

Carter said that he would invite Wallace to Georgia and would attempt to form a number of interstate compacts with Alabama, including the equalization of certain college fees and cooperation on crime prevention and pollution control.

For more than four and a half months Carter attacked Sanders. Not until August 26, only days before the election, did Carter finally present his "proof package"—containing photostats of documents that purportedly backed up his charges. In the package were copies of the minutes of a board of directors' meeting of the Willingham Finance Company on June 15, 1964, which showed that Sanders had been present at a meeting at which the president of the company, J. B. Fuqua, had been authorized to purchase the assets and license of WROZ Radio Station in Evansville, Indiana. There were also copies of subsequent papers filed by Fuqua with the FCC, which listed Sanders as secretary of the firm, giving his occupation as governor of Georgia and his address as the governor's mansion. It also contained statements that Jones and Fellers, Augusta architects, (identified as "political cronies" of Carl Sanders) had received $1,282,853 in fees from the state in 1966—"a major percentage of all fees by the state to architects." Other documents purported to show that at the beginning of the Sanders administration the state had shifted deposits to the Georgia Railroad Bank—which Carter claimed was a favored bank because it made loans to Fuqua during Sanders's term as governor. Also Carter called on Sanders to disclose all the special retainers he received as a private citizen from 1967–70, while campaigning for his second term, including a purported $100,000 contribution from Delta Airlines. As Carter summarized his case: "These documented facts show a consistent pattern of combining political and business interests on behalf of Mr. Sanders."

Carter had raised some sticky questions about possible conflicts of interest between a person's public roles and his private interests. But he did not claim that any of Sanders's acts had been contrary to the law. Nor did he apply equally strict standards to himself. In response to a press inquiry about his own finances, Carter said he would not identify any of the large contributors to his own 1970 campaign, and he indicated that he would not dispose of his own private holdings should he be elected governor. Instead he simply promised to show no favoritism toward any large financial contributors—and the check on this would be his own subsequent financial statements. In effect, the public was asked to trust him.

Sanders responded to Carter's charges, labeling them a political ploy, and calling Carter "the penny-antiest politician I've ever come across."

I've really been massacred in this expose. The only thing I'm worried about is that here's a man who has been kicking my name and reputation around in a fashion no reasonable human being would do. After four or five months, this is what he's released. He also makes no accusation that I've done anything illegal or unlawful.

Carter turned Sanders's words to his own advantage. At a meeting in Macon he reported: "I've been accused by the rich candidate of running a penny-ante campaign. . . . I have to plead guilty because I'm running a relatively low budget campaign and I've tried to reach the poor people who, like myself, have to make ends meet."

Carter ran not only against Sanders, but the Atlanta newspapers, as well. In a speech at the Atlanta Press Club he described "one of the strangest editorial flip-flops I've ever seen in a newspaper." The Atlanta *Journal*, he said, had run one editorial endorsing financial disclosures by candidates, but the next day knocked the idea, referring to candidates who had made such statements as in effect saying "What a good boy am I." "For such editorial fence-jumping, the Atlanta *Journal* can't be beat. . . . I wonder who pulled the chain on the Atlanta newspaper editors." On June 27 he wrote the editors of the Atlanta *Constitution*, charging them with a pro-Sanders bias, implying that the bias was due to Jack Tarver Jr.'s partnership in Sanders's law firm (Jack Tarver was the president of Atlanta Newspapers, Inc.). He told another audience on August 16: "You won't read much about my campaign in the Atlanta papers because they just won't report it." And on September 2, just before the election, he said that the Atlanta newspapers have "projected me as an ultra-conservative racist, which I am not."

In actuality the Carter campaign was extensively covered in both Atlanta papers, and on the whole the coverage was matter-of-fact in tone. They had not portrayed him as a racist—though there was one suggestion that Carter once used the word "nigger" in a joke. Two writers for the *Constitution*, Bill Shipp and Reg Murphy (the editor), did write critical articles about Carter under their own bylines, and Reg Murphy was close to Sanders. (On a vacation at the Doral Hotel in Miami, Murphy had let a Sanders aide pay some of his greens fees. Carter, according to Murphy, secured copies of the American Express receipts showing Murphy's indebtedness and threatened Murphy with "exposure" if he did not receive better treatment at his hands. Murphy states that Carter only dropped the threat when Murphy made it clear that he "didn't give a damn about the receipts.")

Further, Carter himself had a close relationship with Anne Cox Chambers, chairman of Atlanta Newspapers, Inc., which owned both the *Journal* and the *Constitution*. She was the largest single contributor to Carter's campaign ($26,000), and she and her husband later helped Carter to cover his remaining debts, which may have been an addition to the above figure.

In addition to attacking Sanders and the Atlanta establishment, Carter made many policy statements—each finely honed to attract the widest possible following. Many politicians avoid controversial issues totally or escape into meaningless abstractions. But Carter tried a different approach. He took specific stands—many of them. Indeed, his seventeen-page platform, released in late July, contained promises on everything from battling marijuana use to preserving historical sites. But he did not aggregate issues in accord with any discernible philosophy, thereby avoiding identification with any one part of the conventional political spectrum. Possibly controversial stands were followed by qualifications, which, when carefully read, undercut the thrust of the original statements. In short, Carter sent out mixed messages, and various groups could interpret the statements to fit their own predispositions and discount the inconsistent parts as just political noise.

On the campaign trail Carter appealed to many groups. For conservatives he said: "I will not hesitate to call in the National Guard" in case of riots or campus uprisings. He said after the Kent State shootings, "If I send the guards-men, they will be armed. The rioters must know that the guard means busi-ness." He opposed the decriminalization of marijuana, and he told college students that he would crack down on drug abuse on Georgia campuses.

For "progressives" he promised to upgrade the Georgia educationa system, expand the vocational training program and educational programs for retarded children, and support salary increases for teachers. He emphasized the need for decent housing; a central state agency to deposit state funds equitably in banks throughout the state; the development of "predictable, fair and equita-ble" formulas for spending highway money; the development of a four-lane highway between Columbus and Atlanta; a small increase in the sales tax to help develop local rapid transit systems; an upgrading of police training pro-grams, including salary increases to officers who earned college credit; the de-velopment of a state salary scale for county sheriffs; a study of a possible depart-ment of youth to deal with problems of juvenile delinquency; and provisions to separate first offenders from hardened criminals in prisons. The proposals were concrete good government ones, that would not trigger ideological protest.

His "hedges" were evident in his call for enforcement of antipollution laws. He stood barefoot one August day on the banks of the South River and refused photographers' requests to wade in the "muck" which contained raw sewage and soapsuds. But when asked how long he would take to clean up the south River if he were elected, he replied: "I didn't say I was going to clean up the river. That's up to all those different governments. I can enforce the law, but I can't cut down a sewer plant which is polluting the river."

In the troublesome area of racial integration, he took stands people could read in various ways. In many speeches he quietly and quickly stated that each man should have equal opportunity before the law. But the burning issue was school integration and at the time of the election many Georgians were putting their children in private schools. Carter said he was opposed to the use of state funds for private schools and suggested that certain minimum standards be es-tablished for them by the state legislature. But he also called the private schools a safety valve in areas where blacks outnumbered whites. And on August 27, 1970, in a "rafter-ringing" address to approximately 400 supporters at a bar-becue-rally, Carter strongly endorsed the private school system in Georgia: "Don't let anybody, including the Atlanta newspapers, mislead you into crit-izing private education. They need your support. There is a legitimate and nec-essary place for both private and public education in Georgia."

Carter also taped a radio commercial in which he said he did not want to be beholden to any "block" vote, slurring over the crucial word so one could hear it as "black." (Actually the "block" vote is usually used to refer to blacks in Georgia, so the slurring was not really necessary.) With this appeal Carter was paralleling some of Wallace's earlier winning rhetoric.

At the same time Carter promised to appoint black leaders to policy-making positions—but not the "so-called black leaders who had in the past taken money to deliver the black vote." He did not commit himself to appoint blacks to specific positions.*

Though Carter stressed his status as an outsider, he asked for the endorsements of leading Georgian politicians. He arranged a visit with Senator Richard Russell and, according to a former aide, was politely and warmly received. A few weeks later Carter told Beau Cutts, a reporter from the Marietta *Journal* that Russell had said he would vote for Carter in the election and that other members of the Russell family would support him. But Russell denied it: "I have never endorsed any candidate seeking nomination to any office in a Georgia Democratic primary nor even suggested to any member of my family their support of any candidate. Any statement to the contrary is of whole cloth." Carter initially denied that he had made the statement, saying he was "misquoted." Later he admitted that he had said it "off the record."

Carter did receive an important endorsement from former Governor Ernest Vandiver, husband of Senator Russell's niece and a noted political conservative. And former Governor Marvin Griffin, who had been defeated by Sanders in 1962, announced, "I do not agree with all the political philosophy of the peanut farmer from Plains, but we have not tried him yet, so I shall cast my vote for him."

There was a murky aspect to the campaign. Newspaper photos showing two black members of the Atlanta Hawks professional basketball team (in which Sanders had a financial interest) pouring champagne over Sanders's head at a victory celebration were mailed to white barber shops and country churches across the state. Another brochure widely circulated in the black districts linked Sanders to the death of a black prison inmate, whose body had been found floating in a duck pond. About two weeks before the election several radio spots plugging C. B. King (the black candidate) were broadcast. King, who had been bankrolling his campaign out of his own personal funds, did not buy the time and knew nothing about the spots or who financed them. His strength, however, was in the black community and any increase in his vote would presumably pull votes from Sanders, the only white candidate with pull in the black districts.

Carter and his staff have denied responsibility for any of these tactics. Yet, former associates of the Gerald Rafshoon Advertising Agency have suggested

* Sanders also tried to escape labeling. After the two men had released their campaign platforms in late July, a writer for the Macon Telegraph noted: "It's hard to tell who is more liberal or conservative than whom." Sanders outlined a plan for eliminating many of of the county-operated public work camps where abuses to inmates (who were mostly black) had often been pointed out. (This stand was more controversial than any Carter took, threatening certain interests in the counties.) He favored a revision of drug laws to provide for graduated penalties to fit the crimes, proposed the creation of a state housing corporation to carry out a guaranteed loan program for low and middle income housing, and pledged to take welfare recipients off welfare rolls through self-help and job training programs. He also promised to stop campus disorders, calling out the National Guard if necessary—though, unlike Carter, he would not put himself personally in charge of the scene.

that some Carter supporters were responsible for them. Bill Abernathy, a former vice-president of the agency, says that the leaflet showing Sanders being showered with champagne was prepared by Bill Pope, then Carter's press secretary. Dorothy Wood, another former Rafshoon vice-president, corroborated Abernathy's claims, saying she saw the leaflet being boxed "in groups of several hundred or so in the office." And she recalls talking "about it with Gerry [Rafshoon] over a beer." Bill Shipp of the Atlanta *Constitution* says he saw Bill Pope distributing the handbills at a Ku Klux Klan rally. Carl Pederson, an artist with the Rafshoon agency in 1970, says he drew the cartoons for the pamphlet that linked Sanders to the death of the black prison inmate—on orders from his superiors at the agency.

C. B. King's radio ads, according to Abernathy, were personally prepared by him, on a request from Rafshoon. "And I helped channel money to the company Rafshoon used to pay for them." Dorothy Wood has also stated that "the C. B. King ads were laundered out of the Carter campaign. It was common knowledge in the agency." (Carter's campaign staff acknowledges that Abernathy worked on the King radio spots, but insists that the ads were not paid for by the Carter campaign and were done by Abernathy on a "freelance basis.")

There never has been any testimony linking Carter, personally, with any of these activities. But he did set the tone for a low-level campaign with the kinds of attacks he made against Sanders. What journalist Steve Ball saw as his "deviations" from his strategy of placing himself with "just plain folks," slightly to the right of Sanders, were an integral part of his campaign strategy all along, and they worked.

As election day drew near, the polls showed a narrowing gap between Carter and Sanders. As the returns came in on election night, September 9, Carter appeared close to winning a clear majority, thus avoiding the almost traditional run-off. At 11:15 he appeared at his campaign headquarters, made a "V" sign with his fingers, and said he would not come back until it was clear that a run-off was not necessary.

The next morning Steve Ball, the Atlanta *Journal* political editor, described Carter's victory as the most "stunning political upset in years." Carter had expected to do well downstate and in rural areas. In fact, he carried 135 counties to Sanders's 23 and King's 1, and finished no worse than second in any county. He led in almost every voting category. But despite these results, he failed to secure clear majority—so the nomination would hinge on the run-off with Sanders.

Carter interpreted his showing as a victory over the establishment. He had never seen a campaign where the power structures were so solidly in opposition, he said. "Almost all the banks, newspapers, and politicians were against me, but the few who were for me will always be close to my heart." And he noted that, though it would be easy to repay debts to "a powerful few," it would be difficult to pay a debt to 4.5 million people. He promised to spend the next four years in that attempt.

*Run-off: the High Road*

In the run-off campaign, Carter and Sanders reversed roles. Angered by Carter's smear campaign, Sanders had vowed: "I can take it; and I'm not going to forget it either. . . . I've got a memory like an elephant." So he now took the offensive—releasing data that purported to show that Carter was a liar (he claimed to have authored legislation as a senator which he had not), a hypocrite (he was not a workingman), an oppressor of tenant farmers, and an ultraliberal who had once worked to delete the word "God" from the Georgia constitution. In addition, Carter had "sided with organized crime" (by voting as state senator for the lottery). Sanders also accused Carter of paying for ads for C. B. King and inducing Hosea Williams, a black activist, to attend a Sanders fundraiser to create the impression that Williams backed Sanders—and create a backlash vote.

With Sanders counterattacking, Carter now took the high road. He accused Sanders of conducting a smear campaign, denied charges about King and Hosea Williams and invited the press to his farm near Plains, so they could see exactly how he treated his black workers. (He pointed out that two of the black families working his property had averaged $10,000 in annual income over the past ten years.) The Atlanta *Journal* did dispatch a team to the Carter farm. So did Sanders. "Bill" Carter (as he was called) joked with the visitors: "You want to see the tenants we keep penned up, or the ones we let out to pick the peanuts?" The *Journal* portrayed the Carters as reasonably fair, though not extraordinarily benevolent, landlords and bosses. The reporters also noted, ironically, that the Sanders people came to do their investigation in sleek limousines.

As for Carter, his final response to these accusations was as follows: "I'm a Christian, I love God. I do not love Hosea Williams. I do not hate old folks. I'm not a land baron. I do not have slaves on my farm in Plains, and I did not inherit 2,000 acres."

Carter also rejected Sanders's challenge to a statewide debate. Although he often arrived at a place fifteen minutes before or after Sanders, he always offered plausible reasons why he could not engage in a direct exchange. He said he didn't have much time available. Having provoked Sanders into personal attacks, Carter used these attacks to suggest there was something wrong with Sanders. Once he said that Sanders "has apparently become very bitter and has changed his whole campaign style. I don't think in his present frame of mind, it would be right to engage in a personal name-calling exercise on television." When Sanders said that if Carter would debate, he would personally hand him his financial statement, Carter responded: "I'm not the one interested in seeing Carl Sanders's financial statement. The people of Georgia are the ones who have wanted to see it."

After hearing one radio commercial describing him as a "land baron," he said of Sanders: "He is a sick man." Here, Carter had become a bit too explicit. When questioned about it he explained that he had been referring to Sanders's approach to advertising, not to him personally. "I certainly don't think he is a sick man."

Supporters of both candidates engaged in competitive leafleting—each trying to identify the other, in certain white areas, with unpopular black leaders. At one stop, where children were distributing a handout that pictured Carter with Hosea Williams, Carter workers whisked out a bundle of leaflets containing reprints of a newspaper article in which Sanders paid tribute to Martin Luther King, Jr.

As the front runner, Carter also tried to build on that advantage and suggest that there was a momentum to his campaign that would make his election inevitable. Carter outlined to House Speaker George L. Smith a "buddy system" for the forthcoming general election: legislators who were unopposed in their own districts would work for Carter in exchange for his helping other Democrats who did have Republican opponents. He secured political endorsements from diverse "establishment" groups—newspapers like the Atlanta *Journal* and the Columbus *Enquirer*, and labor unions such as the aircraft machinists at the Lockheed plant in Marietta, the largest union local in Georgia. He wooed away from Sanders' political bosses Ralph Dawson of Long County and Sheriff Tom Poppel of McIntosh County, both counties notorious for gambling and speed-traps.

In the run-off election, on September 23, Carter captured 60 percent of the vote. Two hours after the polls closed Sanders went to Carter and offered to help in the fall campaign. And Carter, also gracious, told Sanders he was a "great guy and a worthy opponent." Lester Maddox, who had refused to endorse Sanders or Carter, announced now that Carter's victory was a triumph over the establishment—they had better "shape up or ship out."

## General Election

Carter's opponent in the upcoming general election was a television news broadcaster, Republican Hal Suit. Carter now had time for a debate, telegraphing Suit his offer to meet on television. In their subsequent exchange, they mainly fenced over charges Suit had picked up from Sanders—that Carter had made a deal with Long County boss Ralph Dawson and with Hosea Williams. There were virtually no policy differences between them (though in one later interview Suit qualified his support for capital punishment, while Carter said he favored it).

As the nominee of the Democratic Party, Carter gained additional support from the establishment he had attacked. Jim Gillis, the state road commissioner and a Sanders ally whom Carter had often targeted in the primaries as the kind of politician he would eliminate, showed up at the state party convention wearing a Carter button. Contrary to reports that Carter wanted him out of office, he said, he expected to remain there as long as his health permitted. J. B. Fuqua now pledged Carter his wholehearted support and contributed to the campaign. Delta Airlines made a contribution to the Carter campaign, as did other members of the Atlanta establishment, like Coca-Cola, Southern Power, and Anne Cox Chambers.

But Carter, taking no chances, continued to appeal to conservatives. When asked if he would vote for Andrew Young, then running for the 5th District congressional seat, Carter declined to offer him any specific support, saying that he would leave the matter to the local voters (he did not live in Young's district). But he did urge all Democrats to vote a straight party ticket. He projected himself on several occasions as a close friend of Maddox: once he said that Maddox had brought a "high standard of forthright expression and personal honesty to the governor's office"; he declared that the division between them was a figment of the Atlanta newspapers; he attended a Maddox appreciation dinner, saying, "Despite reports you have heard, there had never been any differences between us in the primary."

He also conferred privately with Roy Harris, the head of the white supremacist States Rights Council on September 14. They discussed "politics in general and the election," Carter noted afterward. And though they made no deals, Harris reasoned at the time that Carter was a conservative, a friend—and that therefore there was no need to bargain with him. After that meeting Harris announced that he had voted for Carter in the primary and planned to do the same in the general election.

One month later, however, Carter told a heckling and hostile crowd of students at the University of Georgia that he had no "intention of reappointing Mr. Harris to the Board of Regents." The boos turned into cheers. The next day, so Harris reports, an upset and apologetic Jimmy Carter called him and expressed a desire to retract his statement of the previous evening. Indeed, within the week Carter was publicly defending Roy Harris. On October 22, he told a stony-faced, predominantly black audience at the Atlanta Hungry Club that Harris had been a good member of the Board of Regents, that he had been long interested in education, initiating the first statewide minimum foundations programs, and that he was "articulate and hard-working." When Carter met with the press after that meeting, he told reporters that he had not ruled out reappointing Harris to the Board. On October 25 Carter again said he had not made up his mind about Harris, adding that Harris had four more years on his term, "so it's a moot question." (He went out of his way to make his point, choosing to answer a question about Harris from a pile of written questions.)

Though he might flirt with Maddox or Harris, Carter now wanted to be identified as a mainline politician. On October 31 he stood on the steps of the Milledgeville courthouse with former Representative Carl Vinson by his side. Carter said he had three heroes; the eighty-six-year-old Vinson, Senator Richard Russell, and Admiral Hyman Rickover.

His attitude toward the press remained ambivalent: "Radio and television have been great," he said, and most of the papers had been "fair." But the Atlanta *Constitution* and the Valdosta *Times* were "grossly unfair." He described one news story by Bill Shipp of the *Constitution*, which said that Carter had indirectly criticized Senator Russell for appearing on a television documentary with Suit, as a "deliberate and erroneous inference." Carter said he had made it clear to Shipp that he believed Russell had no knowledge of Suit's plans to run for governor when he made the documentary. "I wouldn't criticize Senator Russell any more than I would criticize my own mother or father."

Carter's win over Suit was large—630,419 to 424,983. He had taken 59.35 percent of the vote, carrying all but a handful of Georgia's 150 counties. (Much of the Sanders run-off support appears to have gone to Suit, and several other Democrats on the state ticket did even better—Lester Maddox won 73.59 percent of the vote for lieutenant governor, and Ben Fortson, who was running for reelection as secretary of state, won 81.7 percent of the total vote.)

Carter had run a careful and, in some respects, unique campaign. He had avoided all political labels, except for his own characterization of the campaign as "populistic," an ambiguous term in Georgia. Certainly his campaign had little in common with the Populist movement of the 1890s. Unlike Tom Watson, he raised no basic questions about the prominence of banks and the large corporations in the political and economic life of the country—and proposed no programs for changing the economic and social structure. Actually Carter embraced what his pollster, Bill Hamilton, was later to call "stylistic" populism. It was more an attempt to articulate the deeper feelings and frustrations of the small people—their suspicions of the urban centers, the rich, the big interests—than a fundamental challenge to the established centers of power. Carter welcomed establishment support whenever it came to him.

In one respect his populism was reminiscent of the latter-day populism of old Gene Talmadge, who had played such a powerful role in the politics of rural Georgia when Jimmy Carter was growing up. The rhetoric that the little people were being forgotten was unaccompanied by programs for increasing their power. Yet it was an updated, urbane version of that rustic Talmadge style. It contained no embarrassing racist rhetoric, though his attacks on the Atlanta establishment and on the national leaders of the Democratic Party were doubtless interpreted by some as echoing their own frustration with outsiders who were forcing racial change upon them. The old resentments were now being expressed by this smooth, middle-class man in a period when the old rustic style was becoming anachronistic. Lester Maddox, who still talked in the old idiom and played the country bumpkin, embarrassed even those who embraced his values. Maddox's vivid prose, his puritanism, his emotionalism, his widely publicized antics (once, at the governor's mansion, Maddox rode his bicycle backward and ran into some of his audience) made him faintly ridiculous. Carter made the old-time values respectable. He was proud of being rural, committed to family, church, and all the conservative social values. And he wasn't eccentric.

It was a complex and subtle approach, and it enabled Carter to appeal to a wider variety of social groups than Talmadge or Watson or Maddox ever could.

Some of the old "rustics" could identify with Carter because he expressed their resentments. Moderates could approve of his disarming and sophisticated manner. And business leaders in Atlanta could embrace Carter as a progressive but safe politician who would cause them no anxieties. Indeed, he might help bring the old-time conservatives into the political system in such a way that the one stumbling block to economic progress—racial discrimination—could finally be removed.

Few politicians could make this kind of appeal. Never having had major political responsibilities, he had been spared the need to come down on one side or the other on the troubling issues of the day. Most other political leaders in the state had taken stands. Sanders was a "liberal," as was Arnall. Vandiver was a "conservative," though progressive. Maddox was a segregationist and proud to admit it.

The ambiguity in Carter's positions in the 1970 gubernatorial campaign was later to be justified by his admirers as political expediency that would be justified by his accomplishments as governor. As governor, he would have to define himself more explicitly than he had as a candidate. Would he set a course fundamentally different from Carl Sanders's—who after all had shown himself to be a moderate, progressive administrator? Would he now champion the little man? Or would he do as had Old Gene, who "in the showdown turned upon the side of the fellow who did the forgetting"?

# EIGHT

# The Compleat Politician

T HIS IS the first REAL inauguration we've ever had," one of the planners of Carter's gubernatorial inauguration remarked with satisfaction. The new governor was greeted with a nineteen-gun salute; a plane circled overhead with a banner reading "Welcome Aboard, Governor Carter"; a band from the Naval Academy performed military numbers and show tunes; and the all-black choir from Morris Brown College sang "The Battle Hymn of the Republic." And as one Atlanta reporter noted, a visitor from New York asked, "But is it customary to sing 'Battle Hymn of the Republic' in the South?"

State officials and former governors had been invited to sit on the podium as a show of harmony and support, though there were three conspicuously empty seats bearing the names of three former governors—M. E. Thompson, Marvin Griffin, and Carl Sanders. On the stage behind the speaker's podium was a grand (eight-by-four-foot) portrait of Carter, woven of over 2,000 camelias by women from Colquitt County. As one reporter remarked, it was "Camelot—all over again."

. . . More than one person saw a similarity Tuesday between the charisma of the young Carters of Plains, Ga., and the young Kennedys of Hyannis Port. The 46-year-old Governor with his reddish hair and white toothy smile bore a certain resemblance. His wife Rosalynn, slim and dark-haired in a trim green coat with a white fur beret, and their four children, Jack, Chip, Jeff, and Amy, looked young and beautiful and eminently photogenic.

The whole affair, according to one journalist, constituted "some of the most elaborate inaugural ceremonies in history." Perhaps more important, in his inaugural address Carter made it clear that he aspired to more than representing the narrow interests of those who had been his most active supporters during his campaign. He came up with a ringing declaration in favor of racial equality: "The time for racial discrimination is over. No poor rural white or black person should ever have to bear the additional burden of being deprived of the opportunity of an education, a job, or simple justice."

Later that afternoon, in response to Carter's open invitation to all Georgians, thousands of people visited the governor's mansion. There were four big tents on the front lawn where the Hopeville High Marching Band and Valdosta High School Band played. And the afternoon sky—blue and bright— was streaked with white from jets flying in formation overhead. As late as 5:30 there was still a long human chain from the Sears lot, where the visitors parked, winding up West Ferry Paces Road and driveways to the mansion. The mood of the day was expressed by the Atlanta *Journal*'s society editor, Yolande Gwinn: "Governor and Mrs. Carter received, standing at the right of the doorway in a bright spotlight, courtesy of Mother Nature, who sent a strong ray of sunshine directly on them." In the evening there were four inaugural dances with 30,000 invited guests.

## *Supports*

The festivities over, personal housekeeping matters had to be taken care of. Carter moved his family—Rosalynn, and the four children—into the recently constructed and very elegant governor's mansion on an eight-and-one-half-acre estate in Atlanta's most fashionable district. Carter quietly ordered the construction of a swimming pool and tennis courts—a fact disclosed by Atlanta columnist Bill Shipp after an anonymous telephone call one night. Carter, who usually tried to avoid the appearance of profligacy, justified the additional luxuries with some irony: "I need some place where I can relax. And actually I can think better at the bottom of a swimming pool than I can at some other places."

Rosalynn Carter quickly adapted to her new role as First Lady of Georgia. Amy was cared for by a black woman (a parolee convicted for manslaughter in the death of her boyfriend) and, after 1973, attended a school in a well-to-do area outside the neighborhood school district. Rosalynn was then free to be an active first lady. She took an interest in mental health, as other governor's wives had before her, was available for interviews, and overcoming the shyness she had shown during the campaign, made confident speeches. She was one of her husband's closest political confidantes. Relishing politics, she came to play a gate-keeper role—screening Carter's associates for their loyalty to him, warning Jimmy about whom he could and could not trust.

The Carter boys helped out. Jack, twenty-three, a student at Georgia Tech (graduating in 1972) did liaison work with the General Assembly, counting noses on important issues. When he finished his first year of law school at the University of Georgia, Supreme Court Justice Bill Gunter got him a job as a summer intern in the Fulton County district attorney's office. Chip, twenty-one, having dropped out of Georgia Southwestern after his first year, worked in the governor's office. So did Jeff, eighteen, who had graduated in 1970 from the Woodward Academy, a private high school in College Park, Georgia.

Except for some moderate coverage of the weddings of the two eldest sons (Jack married Judy Langford, the daughter of family friend State Senator Beverly Langford, and Chip married Caron Griffin, an intern at the state capitol), the boys got far less press attention than their sister, Amy, who was three when her father first came into office. Amy often accompanied the governor on his state tours and on ceremonial occasions. As a reporter wrote of the governor's appearance at the Sixth Annual Atlanta Hunt Club and Steeple Chase, the "living doll," as she was described, "was stealing the spotlight and camera angles from the governor . . ." But Carter also made personal time for Amy. One Halloween he accompanied her trick-or-treating along West Ferry Paces Road. Another day Amy and Jimmy and Irene Horne and her son David were discovered in Amy's secret retreat—a large closet—sitting on the floor playing Henny-Penny.

Carter was assisted by an able and devoted staff. Among them were a few "old hands" who could help him find his way around the capitol. Mary Beazley, Carter's receptionist–appointments secretary, who had held similar positions with Governor Ernest Vandiver, Lieutenant Governor Peter Zack and Governor Lester Maddox, knew the people who counted in the state. William Harper, executive counsel, had been with the State Department of Law since 1961. Carter's confidential secretary, Sarah Hurst Lee, also had an impressive resume; a law school graduate, she had served with the Army, the Terrell County Superior Court, and the U.S. State Department.

But Carter came to rely mainly on those young men who had served him in his political campaigns in 1966 and 1970. Hamilton Jordan, only twenty-six at the time, became his executive secretary, acting as chief of staff for the thirty to thirty-five people who worked in the office. He supervised the distribution of rewards and handled relations with the General Assembly, at least for a time. He was willing to serve also as Carter's political buffer. As early as May, 1971, he was named in the press as the person who said "no" to political requests in the governor's office. Jordan also gave advice on administrative and legislative strategies. The grandson of Hamilton McWhorter (a former president of the Georgia Senate and a close friend of Senator Richard Russell), Jordan proved to be adept as a political strategist—advising Carter on how to surmount the various political and legal blocks in his way.

Jody Powell was Carter's press secretary, replacing Bill Pope, who had served in that role during the campaign. He assisted the legal office, helped draft legislation and write speeches, lobbied with the General Assembly, helped with the governor's appointments—and generally performed as a trouble-shooter. It was Jody Powell to whom Carter seems to have been closest among his aides. Powell in turn was perhaps the most intensely loyal of them all. Whenever Carter was criticized, he would strike back—almost instinctively. (On one occasion he borrowed from a letter mentioned by Ted Sorensen in his book on Kennedy. To a constituent who had called Carter a "gutless peanut brain," and a user of "communist tactics," he wrote: "Among the many burdens that fall upon a governor, one of the most exasperating is having to read barely legible letters from morons like you. I am very happy that I can at least

spare the governor from having to respond. I respectfully suggest that you take
two running jumps and go straight to hell." Asked if his reply was in keeping
with the dignity of the governor's office, Powell replied: "The governor didn't
write that letter—I did. I am just a functionary in the governor's office, and I
never have claimed to be a particularly dignified functionary.")

Jody felt free to joke with Carter. On one draft of a Carter speech, he commented: "Jerry and Stu think this may be too strong. I like it 'cause I wrote it."
And in another place he noted that he was outvoted on a phrase by Jerry
Rafshoon and Stu Eizenstat, ironically saying: "Those people who control all
the newspapers and financial institutions won." He also felt free to criticize the
boss, though taking care to do it as inoffensively as possible. Writing about one
Carter speech, he said: "There were still numerous places where transitions
were rough or nonexistent and a few places where you seemed to be fumbling
around for a way to get into the next subject." He pointed out that "in every
instance but one the applause came in response to your delivery of a 'prepared'
line or statement." But he tempered his criticism with compliments and closed
the memo saying:

I hope that you have not misinterpreted my comments on your speeches. I hate to
bug you about anything because I know you have enough to worry about anyway. Even
your worst speeches are generally pretty good, but since we are moving into the big
leagues now and I feel that it is my responsibility to do what I can to make sure that you
always leave the best possible impression with the people you talk to. Certainly, you do
not need to be reassured of the great respect, admiration and affection that I and all of us
who work for you have for you—as an individual and as a governor.

Frank Moore, a young man who had first worked with Carter as executive
director of the Middle Flint Area Planning and Development Commission,
took over Jordan's duties in the spring of 1973, when Jordan went to work for
the Democratic National Committee in Washington. Duane Riner, a reporter
with the Atlanta *Constitution,* was given a job in the office as special assistant
midway through Carter's term. Frank Sutton, a lawyer from Tifton, joined the
staff in late 1971 to take over some of the legislative liaison duties that Jordan
had been handling. After about a year, he retired to wage his own successful
campaign for the state senate.

Despite their relative youth and inexperience, Carter's key political aides—
Jordan, Powell, and Moore—were all supremely confident men with a taste for
political maneuvering. Powell was to become a popular figure around the state
capitol, winning over newsmen with his down-home humor and free-wheeling
ways.

Carter also contracted for the services of two independent professionals who
had worked with him earlier. From the beginning of his term as governor, Bill
Hamilton prepared polls for him. As early as February, 1971, Hamilton tacked
some political questions onto a poll he did for the Metropolitan Atlanta
Regional Transportation Authority, testing Carter's personal popularity against

that of other state leaders, including former governors Sanders, Maddox, and Vandiver, and measuring his support among various categories of voters, including persons who had voted for Hal Suit. (As Hamilton wrote after that poll, "It looks as if the Atlanta bigwigs have begun to appreciate you more than they did before the election.") Carter took his suggestion that he conduct other periodic, statewide checks on Carter's popularity and issue positions during his term in office.

While Hamilton was gauging public opinion, Gerald Rafshoon was selling Carter and his programs to the people—as he had done during the 1966 and 1970 gubernatorial campaigns. During Carter's reorganization struggle a Rafshoon memo outlined several suggestions for Carter's forthcoming tour of Georgia. He produced a film of Carter's "Operation Feedback Tour" around the state. By late 1974 he was making suggestions about some of Carter's speeches. He also did some work, on contract, for the Georgia Crime Commission, which included a commercial featuring Carter standing under a streetlight at night reminding Georgians that November was Crime Prevention Month. In 1973 the State Department of Industry and Trade awarded the Rafshoon agency a $750,000 contract (which included Rafshoon's own $108,000 fee).

In addition to his office aides and hired professionals, Carter was assisted by his own kitchen cabinet—a small group of influential attorneys who had been supporters since 1966 and now served as Carter's policy advisers and as links to the higher echelons of the business and legal community in Atlanta.

Most visible was Charles Kirbo, who was given his own office at the capitol building. As honorary chief of staff and State Democratic Party Chairman, he helped Carter on personal matters, negotiated staff conflicts, and advised him on strategy. William Gunter, at least before his appointment to the Georgia Supreme Court in 1972, was equally important in his work for Carter. A native of Gainesville and a former state representative, Gunter and his law firm represented the Ralston Purina Company and Georgia poultry producers. Besides introducing Carter to attorneys Robert Lipshutz and Philip Alston, other key advisers, Gunter acquainted Carter with the writings of Reinhold Niebuhr, which Carter was to quote with some regularity later in his career.

Alston (whose law firm sometimes represented Chrysler Corporation, American Oil Co., Eastman Kodak, and E. I. du Pont de Nemours & Co., and the Citizens and Southern Bank of Atlanta) was originally attracted by Carter's credentials—particularly since they were both Navy men. He had been important in selling Carter to the banking and business establishment in Atlanta, serving as financial chairman of the 1970 campaign; now he would sell Carter to the national elites. Alston also took a position in state government when Carter appointed him member-at-large on the University of Georgia Board of Regents. Robert Lipshutz, who had also joined forces with Carter in 1966 and 1970, provided a link to the Atlanta Jewish community. Carter was to appoint him to the new Board of Human Resources in the position of vice-chairman, and he remained a close advisor on political matters.

In contrast to Carter's young staff, this older group was more established with influentials in the state. They helped smooth the road for Carter in circles in which he did not have deep support. Overall, they provided a mature perspective and depth in their advice, which could not be found in a young office staff.

### Routine

Carter's working routine was disciplined and orderly. Generally arriving at his office between 7:00 and 7:30 A.M., he usually met first with Sarah Hurst Lee, his confidential secretary, and Mary Beazley, his receptionist–appointments secretary, who would outline his schedule for the day. At 8:00 or 8:30 Carter began meetings with visitors, ordinarily scheduled in ten- to fifteen-minute segments throughout the day. Some blocks of time were reserved for Carter himself to study issues, read, and handle his mail. Routine correspondence was handled by a secretary. Responses to important items were drafted and placed on Carter's desk for signature or amendment. (On average, he saw 15 percent of his mail. After 1973, at the suggestion of Betty Rainwater, then a secretary, a tally sheet noting the names, locales, and concerns of his correspondents was prepared. Carter would then make a check next to the letters he wished to see.)

Sometimes an aide would advise him to write a handwritten letter, which had become a trademark after a widely circulated newspaper article on them. For example, Jordan suggested that he send one of his "famous handwritten notes" to Dean Swift, recently elected president of Sears Roebuck's national organization, "a very powerful position." Again on the advice of Jordan, Carter jotted a brief message to former President Lyndon Johnson, complimenting him on an address at the University of Texas symposium, expressing admiration for him "personally" and appreciation for his "unprecedented achievements as President." The handwritten notes were sent, according to Carter, when "I want someone to know I wrote it personally."

At noon, Carter customarily ordered his lunch from the cafeteria and ate it at a marble coffee table, where he read and worked. About once a week he went out for lunch, often with Charles Kirbo or Hamilton Jordan. Afternoons there might be appointments or study, or a speech or ceremonial task, such as throwing out the first ball of the season for the Atlanta Braves. On Thursdays he would hold a press conference. On the second Wednesday of each month anybody who wished to see the governor could come to the office between 1:00 and 3:00. (Governor Lester Maddox had started this practice, calling it "Little Peoples Day"; Carter changed the name to "Speak Up Day." While Maddox had greeted people in a line, Carter took each individual aside for a private chat.) At 5:00 or 5:30 Carter would leave the office and the state capitol. He usually took along a briefcase full of memos to work on after dinner. Some nights he might deliver a speech at a convention or, with Rosalynn, attend a gala, theater opening, or charity event.

On Saturdays he usually did not go to the office. His calendars often show a large block of time put aside for Hamilton Jordan or some other political adviser. He would frequently put in an appearance at some local event—to crown a beauty queen or present the cup at a steeplechase. On Sundays the Carters attended the Northside Drive Baptist Church in Atlanta where from time to time Jimmy taught a Sunday school class. Sunday afternoons the mansion was open for visitors, and Sunday evenings were reserved for social relaxation with family or friends. Later in his term a Sunday night group of advisers would meet at the mansion. Originally the group consisted of his closest political advisers—Jordan, Powell, Rafshoon, and Kirbo—with the occasional addition of David Gambrell, Bill Gunter, Robert Lipshutz, Philip Alston, and a few other members of the Atlanta establishment. Later this core group was extended to include Dr. Peter Bourne, Landon Butler, John Pope, Dot Padgett, and others.

This routine was frequently interrupted by travel. Aside from his several "people-to-people" tours of the state, there were several out-of-state trips: twenty-four in 1971; fourteen in 1972; forty in 1973; and more than twenty in 1974. His overseas travel consisted of a trip to Brazil in 1972 and one to Europe and the Middle East in 1973.

Carter took his family and friends on many of these trips, combining business and pleasure. Over Thanksgiving, 1972, Jimmy, Rosalynn, Amy, Jeff, Chip and his future wife, Caron Griffin, and a number of aides went to Cabin Bluff Lodge on the Georgia coast at the invitation of officials of Brunswick Pulp and Paper Company. Carter was prepared to do some hunting—he was outfitted for the trip with "adequate bird-hunting clothes" by persons in the Department of Natural Resources. In the spring of 1973, Carter and a number of other state officials spent a day or two at Palmetto Bluff, a Sourh Carolina hunting lodge. And in July, Carter, his aides, and twenty state employees returned to Cabin Bluff; Brunswick Pulp and Paper provided free food, lodging facilities, and a boat trip to Cumberland Island.

In some respects Carter was a strict boss. A hard worker himself, he expected an equal effort from his staff. When meeting with an aide, he expected the homework to be done. And he was stern. As one staffer said: "He doesn't spend any time telling you you've done a good job." He preferred working from memos rather than oral reports. Yet he was not the severe taskmaster his later public relations suggested. His staff had access to him. He was open to suggestions for improvements in routine (as when Betty Rainwater's suggestion on handling the mail was adopted). There is no evidence from his letters and memos that he obsessively corrected the grammar of his aides as they later suggested. In his own words, he was "rather lax" in terms of the attire of his staff. He even complimented people who worked with him.

Further, Carter trusted the people on his staff and delegated authority to them. Mary Beazley handled his appointments—Carter often relying on her good judgment as to whom he should see and where he should speak. Betty Rainwater routed his mail. Hamilton Jordan, and later Frank Moore, managed the staff operations, and they had the authority to make important organizational decisions, sometimes in the governor's absence. In November, 1971, for example, while Carter was in New York City for a meeting with key people in the bond market, Jordan presided over a meeting in which staff changes were spelled out—including a decision to relegate the role of "chief arm twister" to Highway Director Bert Lance for the upcoming reorganization fight.

## Spoils

Carter proved to be a traditional politician in many respects. He would note during his last year as governor: "I've used the absolute, full resources of the governor's office to win arguments or win legislative approval, or to win points at issue that relate to state government, when I felt the purpose was worthwhile." And on another occasion he proudly noted that he had built one of the best political organizations the state had seen.

His organization, however, differed from the more traditional political cliques in Georgia. As long as the old county unit system of government had survived, the state organizations had been loose and shifting coalitions of statewide leaders and county politicians—the latter generally rural folk who liked to protect their political clout and show themselves as people who knew how to wheel and deal. Carter, on the other hand, appealed to well-educated men and women, many of them tied to the educational, corporate, and financial elites of Georgia—and most of them publicly committed to the principles of clean and efficient government. During his gubernatorial campaign Carter had promised to make his appointments on the basis of merit. With this kind of following, Carter now could select the "better people" for office and make many decisions on the basis of good management principles while still rewarding his friends and supporters and winning over new ones.

One of Carter's first moves was to place his friends in key positions in the Democratic Party, making room for them by elbowing aside the incumbents. When Carter called a meeting of party officials shortly after the 1970 election to discuss ways of "democratizing" the party, he did not invite Georgia's two Democratic National Committee members, Marjorie Thurman or William Trottier, both Sanders supporters. And a few days later, according to Mrs. Thurman, a Carter associate called saying that Carter wanted her to resign so he could make his own appointment to the position. While Thurman insisted she would not quit, Trottier yielded, resigning on January 24, 1971. He was replaced by Bill Gunter. For his cooperation Trottier was evidently kept on the large (approximately two hundred members) State Democratic Executive Committee. Mrs. Thurman, however, was not even named to this group.

To head the Georgia Democratic Party, Carter first named David Gambrell, a Harvard Law School graduate, who had been treasurer of and one of the largest private contributors to his 1970 campaign. When Senator Richard Russell died on January 22, 1971, Carter chose Gambrell to serve out the remainder of Russell's term (after Charles Kirbo turned it down). Carter then asked his cousin Hugh (who wanted the Senate appointment) to head the party. When he declined, Charles Kirbo unenthusiastically accepted the job—and ran it from his law office on the twenty-fifth floor of Atlanta's Trust Company Tower. Later, when Kirbo decided to leave the job, Joe Andrews of Milledgeville, one of Carter's most fervent admirers, filled in for him while Carter sought a replacement.

For the position of State Democratic Treasurer, Carter chose Jimmy Deriso, one of his chief fundraisers in southwest Georgia. In July of 1972 Deriso sent Carter a $6,000 check the remnants of Carter's 1970 campaign fund, rather than turning it over to the state party as some of the Atlanta people had been asking him to do. Carter used the funds to help pay his personal campaign debts. Other party offices were filled with Carter friends, while most of Carter's opponents in the 1970 election were squeezed out. Former Governor Lester Maddox, however, remained on the executive committee.

The more influential appointments were in the government and here Carter had an advantage over his immediate predecessors. In addition to the usual department heads and commission members, the 1972 reorganization of government created new departments and boards, and thus new offices to fill. Further, it discreetly removed an entire administrative level—the division directors of any agency created by the transfer of functions—from the control of the state merit system.

Sometimes Carter appointed his man downright casually. A month before the election, Carter told Hoyt Robinson, an old friend and full-time volunteer for the 1970 campaign, that he wanted him to help "run the state." After the election, on a ride to the airport, Carter inquired what kind of job Robinson wanted, if he had anything in mind? Robinson said, "No." Had Robinson been to college? "Yes." Did he know anything about accounting? "No." "How about purchasing?" "Yes." Carter told Robinson to go to the head of the purchasing department and tell him that he was being replaced.

Overall, Carter put political allies in positions where they might help him, and he rewarded friends. Robert Lipshutz and Jack Watson were appointed to the Board of Human Resources. Former Governor Ernest Vandiver was named head of the Georgia Department of Defense. Ray Pope, police chief of Waycross, Georgia, campaign adviser on law and order, and brother of John Pope of Americus, was named State Public Service Director. Bill Gunter was named an associate justice of the Georgia Supreme Court. (Of the five men the governor named to the Board of Regents, four had been 1970 campaign contributors: Alston—$6,276—Lamar Plunkett—$2,160—Charles Harris—$200—and David H. Singer—$345. One career state patrolman, J. Herman Cofer, who had contributed $325 to the campaign, was plucked from the ranks to head the Georgia State Patrol.)

Carter also remembered his friends from southwest Georgia. Mary Anne Thomas, Carter's friend and supporter since 1966, was appointed to the Governor's Commission on Human Relations; Dr. John H. "Bud" Robinson of Americus, the Carter family physician, joined the state Board of Regents; P. J. Wise, a former neighbor and Carter ally in the Sumter County school consolidation fights, was named to the newly created State Board of Electrical Contractors; Frank Easterlin, Jr., an Americus native and Annapolis schoolmate, went to the Board of Corrections.

In these appointments, Carter was aided by Charles Kirbo, an adviser sensitive to the needs of various Carter supporters. For example, on April 8, 1971, Kirbo wrote to Bruce Kirbo of Bainbridge (an attorney who had contributed to the Carter campaign), urging him to submit the names and addresses "of those persons whom you wish to receive appointments. . . . It is expected that you will be liberal in making your recommendations so as to include all of the key Carter supporters who assisted in the campaign and who contributed time, money, advertisements, etc." Kirbo anticipated further requests to "correct oversights or errors." Hugh Carter played a similar role. In one memo to Carter he listed fourteen job seekers, all of them campaign contributors. The shopping list included: John Pope ("Wants job. Prefers corrections or something similar."); Frank Sutton ("Wants responsible job. No. 1 or 2 spot. Lives in Tifton. Lawyer."); and Charles Hill ("Union County. Wants to be considered for Game and Fish Commission. Great worker for Jimmy. Also a good contributor. County Chairperson.").

Carter used the little perks of his office for symbolic purposes to stroke and win over friends. These were the special favors: baseball and football tickets for Hugh Carter and Bob Smalley; special tickets for Lillian to attend Atlanta Braves baseball games. "Don't worry!" she said in one letter. "I don't want much. Just please have it arranged for me to go to ball games (Dodger especially) while you are away . . . tell someone reliable (like Hamilton or Mary or Sarah) so there will be *no* slip up—or you know *me*—how sensitive I can be—."

## Symbols

Perhaps more important than the concrete favors were the intangible rewards. Carter was aware of how hungry people are for a little glamour in their lives, for being touched and seen, known and heard by those who are attractive and powerful. And so he let them share his life. Earlier he had opened and closed his campaigns with free barbecues or rallies for his neighbors, friends, and workers. As governor, he made effective use of the mansion (Rosalynn later called it even more luxurious than the White House), opening it to the public and entertaining special groups on a variety of occasions. He was host for reunions of old friends and distant relatives—his thirtieth Plains High School class reunion, the Carter, Gordy, and Wise family reunions. He made new and diverse friends with the help of invitations to formal dinners, informal weekends, or personal conversations. In April, 1971, for example, he fulfilled a campaign promise and invited the stock car drivers in the Atlanta 500 to an elegant dinner the night before the race. He chatted at length with A. J. Foyt and Richard Petty and told them: "You two have been my heroes for more than ten years. This is the greatest honor I have had since I got into politics." The men in turn were equally impressed. As one driver reflected: "You sat there in the elaborate dining room and reflected how far stock car racing has progressed. A few years ago you'd never have convinced the NASCAR old guard that drivers would eat in the governor's mansion for two hours listening to a duet sing Lawrence Welk tunes."

Carter brought in stars from the world of rock music—the Marshall Tucker Band and Gregg Allman and Dickie Betts of the Allman Brothers Band—and a 1960s star, Bob Dylan, whom he was to describe as one of his sources of "understanding about what's right and wrong in this society." Carter would later "recall" his meeting with Otis Redding, who had played with bands in Albany—though the conversation that evening was probably not too lively, as Redding had died in 1967.

He showed his ties to the people in many visible ways. Aside from his "Speak Up Days" at the mansion, he took the government, symbolically, to the people. During his first year in office, for example, Carter held three "State Capitol for a Day" events to give the public "the honest feeling that this is their government." In the summer he "moved" the state capital to Savannah; in the fall he "moved" it to Dalton; and in the winter to Moultrie. He would take several state officials with him and set up shop in some local offices to listen to people's problems. (The sites were carefully chosen for their publicity value. For Carter's trip to southwest Georgia in December, Jody Powell recommended Moultrie over Albany because there would be better TV coverage—from both Albany and Thomasville, and noted: "We could use a little 'small town' publicity.") In addition to these moves, he traveled with his "Goals for Georgia" project in 1971 to solicit support for his reorganization project.

Carter was aware of the importance of symbols in winning the political allegiance of various groups. His most sensitive dealings along these lines were with certain black leaders. Though he had little black support in 1970, with a few key appointments, some friendly words, and symbolic acts that recognized blacks' importance in Georgia life, he was able to win them over.

At his first press conference after taking office, Carter repeated his inaugural pledge to end discrimination and said he was directing all departments under his control to follow a nondiscriminating policy toward employees. And shortly thereafter he appointed a black—Dr. Thomas Jenkins, vice-president of Georgia State University—to a position on the parole board. On June 12, 1971, Carter accepted an honorary degree from the predominantly black Morris Brown College of Atlanta, explaining at the ceremony that as a boy he had gone with his father to a local church for concerts featuring that college's choir. And that same month he conferred with a coalition of statewide black leaders led by Hosea Williams—even though Williams had recently called him a "racist" because he refused to suspend a sheriff over an incident in a county jail where a black man was found hanged in his cell. Carter told the blacks that he had requested state investigators to probe the incident: "I'm your governor. I guarantee you I'll do what's right." Later that same month, Carter, on his own initiative, met with 300 black maintenance workers striking against the State Building Authority. And he relayed their grievances to other state officials. Further, Carter endorsed Andrew Young in his 1972 campaign for Congress and appeared with him on one tour of his district. The Atlanta papers, in February 1974, carried stories of Carter and Young in a well-to-do white area of North Atlanta, wading in mud and jumping over ditches after a heavy rain, emphasizing their mutual commitment to programs that would prevent such flooding in the future.

But Carter's most important symbolic act was to arrange for the hanging of Dr. Martin Luther King, Jr.'s portrait in the Georgia State Capitol—an honor previously reserved to whites. Rita Jackson Samuels, a black on the governor's staff, first proposed that portraits of noted black Georgians be hung in the capitol. (She noted that Tennessee had already hung a portrait of a black man, W. C. Handy, in its capitol.) Carter responded by appointing a special committee composed of four blacks and four whites to select nominees for this honor.

There was some opposition to the project in its early stages. Lester Maddox refused to release money from the state building fund to pay for the project (at one point he promised to pull down the portrait if he were elected governor in 1974). But Carter got around this, asking three black universities to send representatives to the committee meetings at their own expense (for which he promised to reimburse them later through the State Board of Regents). And Secretary of State Ben Fortson, who was on the selection committee, explained the situation to his son-in-law, portrait painter George Mandus, who offered to do the portrait for free. (After receiving several threatening notes while painting the portrait, Mandus hid the canvas at night on the canopy above his bed.)

The committee eventually submitted five names to Carter and from these he selected Dr. Martin Luther King and two others.

There remained, however, potential for too much public linkage with King. Coretta King, his widow, had asked Carter to serve as the honorary chairman at the annual Martin Luther King birthday celebration. Carter aides suggested that the unveiling of the King portrait be advanced to coincide with the birthday celebration during the third week in January—which would permit Carter to participate in both events on the same day. (They feared that if he took part in too many separate events honoring the slain civil rights leader, some people would classify him as a "King Lover.")

The dedication, it turned out, was delayed to February 17, 1974. In a solemn ceremony in the rotunda of the Georgia State Capitol, Mrs. Coretta King unveiled the portrait of her late husband—shown standing before the memorial statue of Abraham Lincoln—while Governor Jimmy Carter, a few steps from her side, looked on. As the ceremony came to a close, Secretary of State Ben

Fortson, from his wheel chair, invited the crowded gathering to join in singing "We Shall Overcome." The moment was, Mrs. King said, a milestone, and "perhaps one link in that long chain of freedom that the people of this world dream [of]." Actually, the portrait would not be hung until later, but by participating in the unveiling of it, Carter showed his awareness of the deep emotional importance this acceptance of the slain leader had for blacks.

## Self-Presentation

Carter also showed considerable skill in presenting himself as a personality. Even when discussing technical matters he might make a personal remark—by recalling his boyhood on the farm in Plains, or his encounters with Hyman Rickover as a young Navy officer, or how he had built up his business from the $184 he had earned from it his first year back from the Navy, or how as a school board member he did not realize for two whole months that white children rode buses to schools while the blacks walked, or how he had apprehensively spoken out against Georgia's "thirty questions" while a state senator. Occasionally, he mentioned his religion, though he seems not to have discussed his born again experiences, except possibly before religious groups.

His speeches were sprinkled with superlatives—Georgia was the best or the worst, the first or the last in the nation, depending on the issue. His own accomplishments as governor, as we shall see, were presented in glowing terms. He made jokes, quoted Reinhold Niebuhr, spoke of his tastes in poetry and music.

More than that, he told his audiences what he was like. Neither he nor Rosalynn was a social climber. He could make a lot of money from his position, but he wanted nothing selfish from it.

He was committed to excellence, but compassionate as well. His feelings for the mentally retarded, he suggested, may have been rooted in family experience, for he had two cousins who were so afflicted. Legitimate self-criticism did not bother him. Two examples of the latter themes give some feeling of the tone of these statements:

. . . Criticism had never bothered me if it was unwarranted or personal in nature. The time when it does bother me is when some politician, simply to derive political benefit for himself, attacks programs that are important to the people I care for.

It is a powerful weapon for a governor to criticize personally someone else in the state. I feel a strong responsibility to defend programs that I consider to be important. On occasion I do—I hope accurately—describe the motivations of the people who are attacking those programs. I reserve the right to reply. I have always tried not to make the replies personal in nature.

On another occasion he said:

My nature—as a member of the Sumter County School Board and Chairman, as an active participant in Georgia School Boards Association before I was elected Governor, as a Senator for four years, as a candidate for four years, as governor now for a little over three years—has always been to avoid self-congratulations and to dwell on the unfulfilled needs that I could discern as an active participant in the preparation of Georgia's future life. Sometimes we can brag on ourselves and thereby lull our own circle of friends and those who participate with us into a sense of false security.

At times these self-revelations carried tacit messages that went against the manifest content. The following explicitly shows his vulnerability before an authority out of his past, while at the same time showing his importance as the object of attention of powerful national figures:

. . . I still am heavily influenced by the man for who I used to work. Every now and then the President calls me and the other governors on the phone. The Vice-President calls quite frequently about some proposals of the President to Congress, with which he wants help from the governors; and I can accept this with complete equanimity, but when the operator says "Governor, Admiral Rickover is on the phone," I break out in a cold sweat; because he still watches very closely what I do and some days he is proud of me and on some days he says he is ashamed. So you have got a governor in office who has a very severe taskmaster over him as well as 4½ million people.

He also put himself into situations that were bound to bring him good publicity. He panned for gold and fished Georgia's fresh water streams. Dramatizing his interest in the environment, he shot the dangerous Bull Sluice rapids in the Chattooga River, made famous in the movie *Deliverance*. (His guide, an accomplished canoeist who doubled for Burt Reynolds in the film's rapids scenes, did the steering; Carter, at the bow, properly attired in crash helmet and well-padded life jacket, paddled and looked out for rocks.

In 1973 he and fifty-five other state officials—including four judges, four state senators, and eleven representatives—made plans for an overnight stay at the Jackson Prison, for a firsthand look at life inside a prison and a chance to "rap" with the prisoners. The visit had to be postponed because of an uprising at the Reidsville Prison, which required Ellis MacDougall's full attention. Carter, however, indicated that the group still wanted to go ahead with the visit. He said he was looking forward to being fingerprinted, donning the uniform of an inmate, and spending the night in a cell.

## Business Connections

Carter proved to be as friendly to business interests in the state as "Old Gene" Talmadge had been. He held up big business as a model for his major political task—the reorganization of state government. He told a group of businessmen on one occasion that he had done the best he could to "institute the same kind of business management practices in the State Government of Georgia that I see exemplified in Delta Airlines or the Coca-Cola Company or Sears or IBM or General Motors, or as you exemplify in your own business." He told a group of exporters that "the strength of relationships between business leaders in this country and other nations will in large part determine the degree of political and economic stability in the future." He compared government officials to "the icing on a cake or the froth on a glass of beer. . . . Presidents and governors come and go . . . Permanent relationships with foreign economic leaders must be maintained by business leaders in order to insure continuity and understanding between countries."

As governor, one of his major undertakings was the promotion of business interests in his state. When the U.S. Congress was considering a $250 million, government-guaranteed loan to Lockheed of Georgia in 1971, Carter helped rally support by declaring Dan Haughton Day in Georgia. (Haughton was the chairman of the board of Lockheed.) Carter's trip to Brazil in 1972 was tied in with Lockheed's promotion in Latin America of its Jet Star and C-130 Hercules (Lockheed had planned a promotional tour for the middle of the year, but moved the tour ahead to coincide with Carter's trip). After that trip Carter wrote Lockheed vice-president Bob Roche that the trip was "one of the finest experiences of my life" and had increased his appreciation for Lockheed's C-130 Hercules. "I have carried this message of admiration to our own national leaders in the State Department, Defense Department, and the Congress, and will continue to do so."

The official purpose of his tour to Europe and the Middle East in May, 1973, was to promote Georgia business. On this occasion there seems to have been inadequate advance planning. On the flight from London to Cologne, Carter happened upon an article in a London financial newspaper that mentioned Georgia as the sole site under consideration for a Volkswagen plant in America—the first Carter had heard of it. He and his aides arranged impromptu meetings with VW officials after they landed in Cologne. In Brussels, he met with a Belgian tractor firm, and in Paris he tried to convince the French Foreign Affairs Ministry to establish a consulate in Atlanta. (When told the French government was inclined to close consulates rather than open them, Carter replied, "You should abandon other places in favor of Atlanta.") He sought to have a French bank open an Atlanta office and tried to rent some shop space to other French companies. In Israel he met with the Minister of Commerce and Industry to discuss the possibility of Israel's importing prefabricated and mobile homes from Georgia, and he met with former Prime Minister Golda Meir to discuss foreign relations.

The following spring Carter and Congressman John Flynt went to great lengths to persuade Anwar Sadat of Egypt to visit Georgia at the request of a substantial segment of the business community in Atlanta. Coca-Cola seemed particularly interested (a consequence, perhaps, of Pepsi's success in Arab countries and the Arab blacklisting of Coca-Cola because of its bottling plant in Israel).

Carter promoted movie making in Georgia. In late 1972, he flew to California in the private plane of Rankin Smith (owner of the Atlanta Falcons) to meet with influentials in the film industry. He offered Georgia as a location to Jake

Wells of Mark VII Limited Productions for the filming of the "Hec Ramsey" television series. He stimulated the state's cooperation with Robert Aldrich, Burt Reynolds, and the company of *The Longest Yard*—arranging for a plane to fly Reynolds and the cast to Atlanta to see a Falcons-Rams game.

Carter assisted established businesses in Georgia, backing legislation that would aid the pulp and paper, rug, peanut, airline, banking, motel, convalescent home, and mobile home industries. After meeting Phil Walden, President of Capricorn Records, for example, he supported a tape-pirating bill in the Georgia legislature. When the Federal peanut support program was revised so that rotten peanuts could no longer be purchased by the government (the government held that rot was caused by poor handling and improper storage), Carter introduced legislation to allow Georgia to buy them instead. He appointed Dan Hodgson (a partner with Philip Alston in a law firm representing the Citizens and Southern Bank) to head a commission to draw up a new consumer credit code—their proposals were so favorable to big banks that the measure was defeated in the General Assembly.

He also did favors for campaign supporters. When Carter's widely heralded policy of automatically rotating of the state's bank deposits among various banks (rather than depositing the funds in politically favored institutions) threatened to create a problem for a 1970 Carter campaign contributor, a prudent exception was made. Julius B. Dodd learned in April, 1971, that the account of the Battery Hospital was to be transferred from his Rome Bank and Trust Company. He wrote Hamilton Jordan: "I am *very* much surprised in view of the fact that the governor assured me (in your presence) that the account would remain at my bank . . . during his term—I would appreciate your efforts in *blocking* this transfer." With Jordan's help the transfer was blocked. Dodd wrote a thank-you note: "I assure you that your and the Governor's efforts in our behalf are greatly appreciated."

In return for his support, Carter expected business to adapt to his concerns for the environment, reasonable utility rates, and conservation of energy. In the spring of 1971, after the defeat of an administration-backed environmental protection bill, for example, he lashed out at Georgia Power. And shortly thereafter Georgia Power began to woo the new governor. Less than five months later Carter was commending the company for their establishment of 100-foot-wide green belts along the Chattahoochie River. By May of 1972 the company had donated 157 acres to form the first major park along the river.

Carter had one subsequent dispute with Georgia Power over a rate increase and the cavalier dismissal of the need to conserve energy by one of the company's vice-presidents. Most of the time, however, Carter enjoyed good relations with the major economic institutions of Georgia. Aside from contributions to his reorganization and park-building efforts, they aided him in his own special projects. Several companies contributed money to the Georgia Narcotics Treatment Program, headed by Dr. Peter Bourne. Sears Roebuck, Delta Airlines, the Jeanette Lafayette Montgomery Foundation (administered by Coca-

Cola), the First National Bank of Atlanta and the Calhoun National Bank all contributed to the program. J. Paul Austin, president of Coca-Cola, took a personal interest in another of Carter's projects, a citizens exchange program in which Georgians would befriend people of their "sister state," Pernambuco, Brazil, whose people would do likewise with Georgians.

Carter also accepted contributions of a more personal nature. The top officers of Coca-Cola had contributed a total of $6,200 to his campaign; a Southern Bell Telephone Company vice-president gave $1,000, while Delta Airlines made a company contribution of $4,995. And, as noted earlier, Anne Cox Chambers (owner of the Atlanta Newspaper Company) and her husband, Robert, helped pay off the Carter campaign debt.

Carter seems to have had a close friendship with Erwin David Rabhan, who built an unstable business empire of forty assorted corporations that ran nursing homes and day care centers in four states, all under the name Rabhan Associates of Savannah. Rabhan and Carter had met in 1968 while Carter was campaigning for the 1970 gubernatorial nomination. Rabhan put his small plane and skill as a pilot at Carter's disposal, flying him throughout the state. And in approximately thirty-one separate donations from February, 1969, to November, 1970, Rabhan Associates contributed a total of $8,600 to the campaign, making it the largest corporate contributor. After the campaign Rabhan took an interest in Jeff Carter, giving him a job with one of his companies in Seattle. In 1974, when he was having financial problems, he stayed in a basement room at the mansion for two or three weeks and used Carter as a personal reference. (When Rabhan became the object of investigation by several federal agencies for questionable business dealings, he left the country—possibly for Iran.)

As governor, Carter received other kinds of donations from companies as well—most of which he seemed to assume were proper supports of his gubernatorial role. Just as Lockheed had provided the free Jet Star for his Brazilian trip in 1972, so Coca-Cola, Georgia's "built in state department," as Carter later called it, provided him with introductions to leaders of the nations he visited in Europe in 1973.

Insofar as these were promotional tours, made on behalf of Georgia's industry, Carter felt justified in accepting the generosity of the companies. But he accepted other modest gifts that could not be justified in this way. Lockheed provided a plane for Carter and David Gambrell to fly to Washington, D.C., in February, 1971, and for him and his party to meet David Rockefeller in New York on November 23, 1971. Coca-Cola provided the company airplane for Carter and his entourage to fly to several southern governors' conferences, and on one occasion gave him limousine service from the airport in New York. On three other occasions, as noted earlier, Carter took work-vacation trips to lodges owned by lumbering interests—twice to Brunswick Paper and Pulp's Cabin Bluff Lodge, and once to a resort paid for by the Union Camp Company.

These campaign contributions and gifts were all perfectly legal. The Georgia law prohibiting state officers from accepting private gifts specifically exempted the governor and high political officers. And prior to 1974 the law did not even require campaign contributor lists. Aside from the fact that Carter had attacked Sanders for accepting funds from and being close to the Atlanta establishment, he had done nothing out of the ordinary in terms of Georgia politics.

## Alliances

Carter's early career had given indications of an ability to shift political alignments as circumstances changed—a rather common political attribute, especially in the South, where competition typically has been between rival personal coalitions rather than parties. In his 1966 gubernatorial campaign Carter was supported by several men with whom he had worked in the state senate, including his old business acquaintance, Brooks Pennington. Generally, his campaign had run down the ideological center, opposing "rebel rousing" on one hand, while focusing his attacks on the liberal candidate, Ellis Arnall, on the other. (In the primary run-off, he refused to be drawn into any coalition against Maddox, Arnall's competitor.) In the 1970 campaign Carter shifted to a "populist" style, hitting hard at Sanders (who had aided Carter in his senate days, giving him a certain political visibility) and J. B. Fuqua (who had helped in his 1962 election appeal) as representatives of the Atlanta establishment. His 1966 campaign manager, Brooks Pennington, was replaced in 1970 by Hugh Carter, a "conservative," who had maintained a discreet distance from Jimmy Carter in 1966. Carter accepted the endorsements of former governors Maddox, Griffin, and Vandiver, as well as of Roy B. Harris of the States Rights Council—men noted for their opposition, in varying degrees of intensity, to racial integration.

Once elected, Carter moved away from these racial conservatives. Cousin Hugh, who had contributed money, energy, and his own clout with conservatives, was rewarded with attention to needs in his district and to his recommendations for political appointments (more on this later)—but he did not receive the U.S. Senate appointment he had desired. Former Governor Vandiver, the most moderate of the conservatives who had backed Carter, was the only person of that group to receive an appointment or any other token of political friendship—and that relationship was quickly ruptured. In a meeting with Carter in the summer of 1971, Vandiver apparently refused to go through an exercise, based on zero-based budgeting, in which he would have shown what he would do if his budget was reduced 15 percent. There were some heated words. Shortly thereafter Carter complained about the operations of the civil defense office (he had tried to reach someone there for over two hours without luck) and said he would transfer it to his own office, out of Vandiver's jurisdiction. Vandiver left the Carter administration after this incident (though the civil defense office remained in Vandiver's old department).

Throughout most of his governorship, nevertheless, Carter did maintain the support of those senate friends who were among his first backers in the 1966 campaign. By 1971 several were in positions that made it possible to help him in the senate. In the house, where he lacked such ties, he would forge a new working relationship with the established leaders—Speaker George Smith, Majority Leader George Busbee, and Minority Leader Mike Egan—a relationship that would falter after he had secured passage of his reorganization proposals.

Carter sometimes hedged his support for the ambitions of his political friends when it portended political trouble. In the 1972 U.S. Senate race, he refused to endorse David Gambrell, who was running for a full term but showing himself weak in the polls against his main competitor, Representative Sam Nunn (who had been a district manager for Carter's 1970 campaign and supported his reorganization program in the house). Relations between Carter and Nunn soured briefly in the late summer of 1972, when Nunn charged that Gambrell had bought his 1971 Senate seat from Carter with large 1970 campaign donations. Carter fired off a terse response to Nunn: "I've never been so surprised and disappointed in anyone before—I just don't understand you." But the rift was temporary. After Nunn defeated Gambrell in the run-off primary, Carter said he would "support him [Nunn] to any extent he wants me to." And after Nunn had taken his seat in the Senate, Carter wrote, noting Nunn's hard work and saying, "I am very proud of you."

There was one man, however, who seemed to be a permanent political friend—Bert Lance. Carter supported him in the 1974 gubernatorial primaries despite the presence in the race of several former Carter supporters, David Gambrell, Robert (Bobby) Rowan, and George Busbee, among them. Carter made no public commitment to Lance, but political insiders were aware that he was backing him privately. A "piggyback poll" he helped set up in the fall of 1973, for example, was clearly designed to test Lance's popularity in addition to Carter's own. And a tour of Georgia in the summer of 1974 that included at least one joint appearance with Lance (at Lake Blackshear) was interpreted by some observers as a campaign trip for Lance.

Carter's support of Lance's ambitions was based partly on common political interests. Lance had backed Carter politically and financially since 1966; he had come to his first public office in the state, highway director, as a result of that relationship. In this position he helped Carter with a few specific road requests, as well as with some arm twisting on behalf of his reorganization plan. In 1976 Lance would aid Carter substantially through various loans (more on this later). But the tie between them appears to have been cemented by mutual admiration. As Lance wrote Carter in July 1972:

I meant what I said about 6 years ago being a red letter day for Bert Lance because of meeting Jimmy Carter. I also thought the words of John Dietrich really sum up what you have really done as Governor, so I will repeat them again, "The highest and best thing that man can conceive is a human life nobly and beautifully lived. Therefore his loyalties and energies should be devoted to the arrangement of conditions which make this possible. The sole issue is how to make the world a place conducive to the living of a noble human life and then to help people in every way possible to live such lives."

Jimmy Carter has given and is giving many people including Bert Lance such an opportunity.

And Carter returned the praise. In March, 1973, just before Lance's retirement as highway director, he wrote:

I have a deep feeling of admiration and appreciation for what you've done. I doubt that anyone has ever come into state government and in such a short time had so beneficial an effect on the reputation and effectiveness of a major department. You've brought daylight where there was dark, humor instead of gloom, and fairness rather than political favoritism. . . .

I thank you, and pray believe that our people will soon share my belief that the state needs you in its top office. I'll be eager to turn the keys over to you. I'm really proud to have you as my friend.

For the most part, the relationship with Lance aside, Carter adapted his political alliances as his political circumstances changed. He showed a genius at capitalizing on the particular position he held at any one time. As a relative unknown, he had run against Atlanta and its establishment—emphasizing his own qualities as an outsider, as one of the people, as six years later he would do in his campaign for the White House. But having won office as governor, he then became an insider, utilizing the resources of his own tentative relationships with the "establishment" to advance his programs. He effectively used the symbols and backdrops of office to enhance his personal authority and public support, and took advantage of his multiple roles to gain politically important information and make contact with other influentials outside of the state. He was a politician plying his trade.

# NINE

# Making a Record

THE REORGANIZATION of the Georgia state government was Carter's top priority as governor. Here he would accomplish some important reforms—though somewhat more modest than his later statements would suggest. More interesting than his substantive accomplishments, perhaps, was the process—which proved to be predictive of his later political style. He combined political acumen and an ability to maneuver with a combative style and some puzzling blind spots.

Reorganization was not a radical program—no one in the state opposed it on principle. Carter was going with the mainstream of reform politics in Georgia and the nation as a whole. Back in 1930, Governor Richard B. Russell had cut the number of state agencies from 197 to 18 in a major overhaul. Piecemeal efforts toward reorganization had been initiated by Carl Sanders when he appointed the Governor's Commission for Efficiency and Improvement in Government (The Bowdoin Commission); and his successor, Lester Maddox, had carried out some of its recommendations. Civic groups such as the Chamber of Commerce and the League of Women Voters had supported reorganization throughout the sixties. And in the 1970 election both state party platforms and both candidates committed themselves to the cause. Throughout the nation other states were traveling the same path. To encourage such reforms the federal government provided planning grants, and at the time Carter was to draw up his reorganization program, twelve other states had completed similar plans. By 1976 a total of twenty states had undertaken comprehensive reorganization, with another twenty completing partial reforms.

Carter decided to undertake reorganization at the very beginning of his term, and to do it all at once. In 1971, HB 1—the number traditionally given to the governor's most important legislative initiative—provided for a planning group to draw up a comprehensive reorganization plan. And it carried an important provision for a reverse veto: the final reorganization packet would be automatically approved fifteen days after the beginning of the 1972 legislative session unless specific provisions were vetoed by a majority of both houses of the General Assembly. Thus the burden of winning a majority vote was placed on the opponents of the measure rather than on the proponents. As a concession to department heads who had some reservations about enabling legislation, the bill also provided that constitutionally based elected officials could veto changes directly affecting their offices. The governor then could introduce the vetoed provision to the General Assembly through the normal affirmative lawmaking processes.

In the house, where Carter had the cooperation of both Speaker George Smith and Majority Leader George Busbee, the reorganization planning authorization passed 166 to 8. It was stalled, however, for a time in the senate (where there were questions about the constitutionality of the reverse veto provision), but it eventually was passed 53 to 3.

Carter then appointed more than 100 persons to various study teams to develop recommendations for reorganization. Some of them were state employees, others faculty members from the University of Georgia system. Almost half of them came on loan from private enterprise, their salaries underwritten by private employers—Coca-Cola, Sears, Delta Airlines, the Georgia Power Company. Arthur Andersen and Company, a national management accounting and consulting firm, lent one of its senior advisers (he had worked on its Wisconsin reorganization plan) to the group and paid the salary of a young accountant, Richard Harden, to work full time on the project. Even registered business lobbyists were appointed to aid in one capacity or another: Peter Bland of the Atlanta Gas and Light Company, Clifford Clarke of the Georgia Business and Industry Association, and Earl T. Leonard, Jr., of Coca-Cola. Carter was to say later that business participation was one of the "gratifying aspects of the administration"; and "none of them ever asked for any special favor or privileged treatment in return."

At the beginning Jim Moore, the registered lobbyist of the state AFL-CIO, complained about the complete absence of labor representatives on the various panels. Carter, hearkening to a theme he would use often as governor, justified this imbalance by pointing to the tax savings that the business donations made possible: "This involvement of private industry makes possible the use of top-notch personnel at no cost to the taxpayer—a savings in excess of $300,000." But he also asked Moore to give him some names and subsequently did appoint labor representatives.

These individual planners were initially divided into eight different groups, with business and government people on each. Their recommendations were sifted by screening groups. Eventually the recommendations were reviewed by an executive committee composed of Carter and six others. With the exception of State Auditor Ernest Davis and Representative George Busbee, all were close associates of Carter, or politically indebted to him. Senator Lamar Plunkett had supported Carter politically since the 1966 campaign. Clifford Clarke had headed the committee that, back in 1970, had named Carter Georgia's Business Man of the Year. Tom Linder received his appointment as head of the

State Bureau of Planning and Community Affairs from Carter, and J. Battle Hall, originally a Maddox appointee, had been reappointed by Carter to his position as state budget director.

Carter was able to keep his finger on the whole planning process—to help frame the recommendations that came to him. He met with the executive committee as a whole at least three times—suggesting, rejecting, modifying recommendations as they evolved. With James McIntyre (commissioner of revenue) he drafted the final legislation. As one key member of that group put it: "The important thing is that he was right there with us, working just as hard, digging just as deep into every little problem. It was his program and he worked on it as hard as anybody and the final product was distinctly his."

Nor did he lose sight of the importance of public opinion. In his original planning budget, $15,000 was set aside for Bell and Stanton, a public-relations firm, to help sell the idea to the public (disbursement made more palatable by the accompanying statement that their fee was 50 percent less than usual). And he sought additional exposure on state public television. Early in 1971 Gerald Rafshoon outlined a soft-sell educational campaign. The goal, Rafshoon wrote the governor, was to make the average Georgian feel that the government was responsive to his needs:

We think it is necessary to involve some average Georgia citizens in the reorganization process. A factory worker. A farmer. A small businessman. A teacher. A welfare mother. Let them have their say. Get their opinions. FILM THIS. . . . [his capitals]

It actually gives the little man a voice in government (we've certainly talked about this a lot) and gets away from the big business, establishment-oriented program that could be easily used against reorganization: ("Of course, the big companies donated men, they run the government and the governor anyway.")

. . . The most you want to get out of it is for the viewer, either on TV or at a civic club, to come away with a warm, favorable feeling toward the reorganization concept. Let him see this and then the next time he sees his legislator, he'll say, "Man, I really like Carter's plan to save money, give more services."

In accord with Rafshoon's suggestion, Carter announced on May 29 that an eight-minute film, costing $14,000, would be produced. For those who might be concerned about using state moneys for public relations, Carter explained that a public utility company might pay for it and that Rafshoon would not charge for his services as director.

At Rafshoon's suggestion, Carter hit the road that summer, traveling off and on from the end of June to almost the middle of August. More than 13,000 persons were interviewed in approximately sixty regional meetings across the state. Ostensibly he was on the road in connection with his Goals for Georgia program—to seek public guidance on the goals his administration should follow. As Carter later described the results: "We spelled out in writing what he hoped to accomplish at the end of two, five, or even twenty years . . . Our people were encouraged to express their criticisms and suggestions, and to describe how their most important needs could be met."

This effort, according to newspaper accounts at the time, evoked little popular enthusiasm. So near the end of November, Carter approved a plan proposed by Philip Alston and relayed to him through legal adviser Bill Harper, for a "spontaneous reaction on the part of many citizens in support of Reorganization"—to be arranged by Bennett A. Brown, assistant president of Citizens and Southern National Bank. And as one would expect from such choreographed spontaneity, there was some concern about keeping the plan secret. As Bill Harper wrote: "Philip [Alston] said to be sure that this was strictly treated as confidential at this time." By December, Carter had rallied his 1970 campaign staff behind this new public-relations effort. Redubbed "The Citizens Committee for Reorganization," the group included Lipshutz, Gunter (only weeks before appointed by Carter to the Georgia Supreme Court), a dozen of Carter's county campaign chairmen, and several of the largest 1970 contributers. They mailed out more than 50,000 handbills outlining the governor's plan and depicting the situation in a cartoon as a fight between the clean-cut and the courageous Carter as Saint George preparing to do battle and the four-headed monster of "Waste, Inefficiency, Special Interests, and Petty Politics."

Carter took steps to blunt the potentially negative reaction of department heads to reorganization. Initially Carter had tried to quiet their apprehensions with the veto provisions in the enabling legislation and assurances that there would be no wide-scale firings as a part of the reorganization plan. Yet Carter had told his study groups on several occasions that they should not let the potential disapproval of department heads deter them from recommending changes. And his planners did as suggested. When the preliminary reorganization plan was revealed on July 29, it was clear that some territories had been invaded.

There were strong negative reactions from four state department heads—Secretary of State Ben Fortson (who would lose all the regulatory commissions under his control), State Superintendent of Schools Jack Nix (who would lose vocational education and rehabilitation), Labor Commissioner Sam Caldwell (who would lose the Workmen's Compensation Board and the Safety Inspection Division), and Comptroller General Johnnie Caldwell (who would lose control of the fire marshals and the state insurance commissioner).

These men still had the right to veto portions of the reorganization plan—or so they thought. Later, when the final version of the reorganization plan was released, they, along with other department heads, submitted forty-five vetoes within the period permitted. But Carter had an ace up his sleeve. After reviewing the vetoes, he characterized the majority of them as "frivolous" and said that he was the one who would make that determination—a discretionary power never mentioned in the original legislation. He allowed only seven of the forty-five vetoes—declaring that the others went beyond the scope of the official authority to veto.

Carter's rejection of these vetoes was to result in a legal challenge by Labor Commissioner Sam Caldwell and two other state officials. First, they asked for an opinion from Attorney General Arthur Bolton. Bolton refused, whereupon the three filed separate suits asking the court to declare both the Carter reorganization plan and the enabling legislation unconstitutional. They also asked that an injunction be issued to prevent reorganization from being written into law while the challenge was being heard—though this would not prevent the General Assembly from considering or acting upon the proposal in the meantime.

Judge Charles Wofford agreed to hear the suits, but not until January 26, 1972—one day after the fifteen-day period during which the General Assembly could veto the reorganization plan or any part of it. In winning this postponement, Carter had promised the court that the state would not implement any plan passed in this form until the court disposed of the case. As his aide Bill Harper suggested, the arrangement worked to Carter's advantage. It permitted the General Assembly to proceed without any worry about the constitutionality of the plan—leaving the issue to the court.

For all his skills in finessing these problems, it was clear that Carter was going to have trouble with the senate. Neither President Pro Tem Hugh Gillis nor Majority Leader R. Eugene Holley (Carl Sanders's law partner) was very friendly to Carter. And the Senate Committee on Economy, Reorganization and Efficiency in Government (EREG), which would initially deal with reorganization, had been stacked by Lieutenant Governor Maddox and the chairman, Senator Stanley Smith.

The EREG Committee began its hearings on December 13, 1971—and several department heads ripped the reorganization proposals to shreds. Ben Fortson, the highly respected and popular secretary of state (who had served in that capacity for almost thirty years) caught the attention of the press when he rolled his wheel chair into the senate chamber and thundered into the hand-held microphone that he intended to veto a provision of the reorganization bill that would take the Georgia Historical Commission from his department and place it in the new Department of Natural Resources. "I've known Jimmy Carter all my life. Don't you pay any attention to that smile. That don't mean a thing." And the committee laughed when Fortson said Carter reminded him of "a south Georgia turtle. He doesn't go around a log. He just sticks his head in the middle and pushes and pushes until the log gives way."

Fortunately for his program, Carter still had the support in the house of Speaker George Smith and Majority Leader George Busbee (who had been on the executive committee). Both were committed to the idea of reorganization. Skilled and smooth negotiators, they were able to secure concessions from Carter and his enemies in the house—eventually producing a package palatable to both.

Shortly before the General Assembly convened, Carter met with the House Democratic Policy Committee and in a three-hour session agreed to revise and clarify one section of his plan. Such basic functions as hiring and firing of personnel would not be shifted out of individual departments and into the new Department of Administrative Services. After the opening sessions of the General Assembly were gaveled to order, the house Democratic leadership again met with Carter to insure that he would stand by these compromises. The house GOP caucus shortly thereafter announced its qualified support for the plan. So did Carter's 1970 Republican opponent, Hal Suit.

At this Lester Maddox registered his distress. "It looks like the Senate's going to have to be the stabilizing force in state government." And it appeared that the senate might create serious impediments to the plan's passage. Aside from the stacked EREG Committee, Senator Holley of the Senate Policy Committee was now intimating that his group would push to sustain all forty-five vetoes by the departmental heads.

The next day Carter met with Holley and his committee and ironed out several of their differences. After the meeting Holley emerged to announce: "I'd say this is definitely the best meeting we have had with the governor." Carter, in a complaisant mood, had evidently agreed to accept additional vetoes in return for pledges of support for treating several of them as simple legislative measures. Carter himself was smiling as he emerged from the first week of the 1972 session of the General Assembly. His conciliatory stands were winning him needed legislative support.

The following week, however, the senate vetoed a section of the bill that would have transferred the Georgia Forestry Commission to the new Department of Natural Resources. A scowling Carter condemned Hugh Gillis for having "betrayed" the interests of the state's forestry industry solely out of political motivations. Shortly after that a pro-Carter house committee and an anti-Carter senate committee voted to strip the governor of any further authority to reorganize the government through the use of the reverse veto. (Carter managed to stall passage of this measure, however, by assuring the senate that he would never use the reverse veto procedure again.) Then several senators questioned the administration's attempt to centralize computer and printing services. On Thursday, February 3, Carter was pulled into a shouting match with both Lester Maddox and George Smith over their support of a measure that would enable a department head to prevent the removal of computer or printing operations from his department. The senate further blocked Carter's plans when they approved a bill that would keep the state Occupational Safety and Health Administration in Sam Caldwell's Labor Department, rather than transfer it to the Workmen's Compensation Board.

As the clock began to run out on the session, the Carter forces introduced an omnibus bill to provide a positive legislative vote on every aspect of reorganization already approved. This shift in strategy left the way open for Maddox, Smith, and others in the senate to make a last ditch effort to halt the Carter blitz through parliamentary delays—and they did just that during the final meeting of the session. But the Carter people were able to muster their forces for a final vote and approval of the omnibus bill. And on April 6, 1972, as the midnight deadline approached, Carter signed the reorganization measure into law.

Through the whole reorganization battle Carter had projected himself as a tough leader—determined and willing to see a few heads roll to achieve his ends if need be. Concerning the original enabling legislation, he said in the spring of 1971, "I had to browbeat people and twist arms to get the bill through, and I'll do the same thing this time to get the plan passed." The summer of 1971 he warned that objections by constitutional officers to reorganization proposals would not be definitive. He would entertain their objections, "but if we can't agree on something, I intend to fight it out before the legislature." He even labeled Labor Commissioner Caldwell's objection to the plan "ridiculous" and suggested that opposition to the plan was based on selfishness. The fate of reorganization would determine if "the people or some special interests will control government." When he unveiled the final fifty-seven-page reorganization report early in December, he said: "I'm gonna get it [because it's right] . . . If I don't get all I want this year, I'll introduce revisions next year and keep trying."* As Duane Riner explained, Carter had "removed his nice guy cloak . . . and revealed beneath it a seldom-seen bareknuckled style that apparently portends a hotter-than-expected fight in January." He took on his Senate opponents at a Macon press conference on December 16, challenging the EREG Committee to "live up to its name and not use its position to play back-door politics." On December 30 he again hit that committee as "inquisitorial" in its approach.

Actually Carter was more shrewd than punishing—he outmaneuvered his potential opponents at several points. He had shown considerable savvy in securing the original planning legislation—which shifted the burden of mustering a majority in a limited time to his opponents. And in other ways he kept his opponents off base until he could present them with a fait accompli. To win the initial compliance of the constitutionally based department heads to the "reverse veto," he had conceded them the right of veto—though he did not tell them until later that he would decide whether or not their vetoes were frivolous. In securing a delay of the court ruling on the constitutionality of the process, he avoided the possibility that a legal clinker might be thrown into the works while the General Assembly was debating his package. Then, after the entire package had been hammered together, he eliminated the possibility of legal challenges by presenting an omnibus bill to the General Assembly—which, by forcing the members to accept all or reject all of reorganization, assured him a positive vote.

Further, Carter's bluster was really less significant in his final success than the help he received from certain important backers. He could have accomplished nothing without the support of strong and effective leaders in the house—men like George Busbee, George Smith, and Minority Leader Mike Egan, who went along with him because they, too, were committed to the reorganization of state government.

Moreover, Carter relied more on persuasion and rewards than his rhetoric

* In *Why Not the Best?* Carter took a similar view of his opposition: "There was intense opposition from the bureaucrats who thrived on confusion, from special interests who preferred to work in the dark, and from a few legislative leaders who did not want to see their fiefdoms endangered. But the people insisted on the changes, and they were made."

suggested. Throughout the reorganization battle Carter entertained prospective supporters with breakfast and lunch in his office or dinner and drinks at the mansion. After gaining the resignation of George Bagby as director of the State Department of Game and Fish, Carter quickly gave Bagby another position as head of State Department of Parks (House Speaker George Smith intervened on his behalf). And at a crucial point in the senate debate, Carter told that body that he would see what he could do to get the members more office space (ultimately nothing was done about this). Carter also used his emergency fund, consisting of approximately $2 million a year, to reward his friends in the General Assembly—allotting funds for politically important and visible projects in their home districts (for more details on this, see Chapter 11).

Nor was Carter uncompromising, as his rhetoric indicates. Despite the rhetorical bloodletting, he compromised at various phases of the legislative process to win some final general package of state reorganization. He canceled the proposed shift of securities regulation from Secretary of State Fortson's office and retreated from a battle with Labor Commissioner Caldwell by withdrawing a proposal to remove two units from his department. He attempted to soothe physicians angered by the abolition of the State Board of Health by agreeing to include five physicians on the board of the Department of Human Resources. Under pressure from both friends and foes, he backed off from his proposal for a constitutional amendment to permit the governor to appoint a majority of the members of the state Board of Education, settling instead for the existing selection by popular vote. When his plans to centralize the state's computer and printing operations ran into trouble in the senate, he agreed to exempt the university system, the Board of Regents, and the Labor Department's Employment Security Agency from the proposed centralization. And he had no choice but to swallow his biggest loss of all—the refusal of the General Assembly to incorporate the State Forestry Commission in the Department of Natural Resources.

The various concessions led several Georgian politicians to suggest later that Carter made many more compromises along the way than he admitted. Robert Shaw, chairman of the Georgia Republican Party at the time suggests that "Carter gave way on practically every issue just so he could get a bill passed that was titled 'Reorganization.' " Carl Sanders thought "it was more show than substance." Tom Murphy, who would succeed Smith as speaker of the Georgia house upon Smith's death in December, 1973, was to call the plan "a cosmetic rearrangement of the furniture."

Carter and his aides, however, put the best face on the final outcome. When the final bill was passed, he proudly announced that he had secured 90 to 95 percent of what he wanted. Jody Powell was to say later that the "dozens of agencies, boards and bureaus were simply and completely abolished." In his autobiography Carter suggests that he made major cuts. "I had run on a platform promising reorganization of the state government, stating that there were 146 agencies in all. Our later analysis revealed 300, and we abolished 278 of them!"

### Proving Ground

The Department of Human Resources (DHR), Hamilton Jordan noted in the spring of 1972, would be the most crucial test of all. "This is where the critics are looking for us not to succeed," he said. "We've got to make this one go."

On paper, the new agency combined in one superdepartment (of approximately 17,000 employees), two of the state's largest departments—health and welfare—and smaller agencies. The policy for the DHR would be set by the Board of Human Resources, to be appointed by the governor with the consent of the General Assembly. The top administrative officer, the commissioner, would be appointed by the Board of Human Resources with the approval of the governor.

For the next two and a half years much of Carter's energy and attention would be devoted to this project—and he would have some rough going along the way.

First, there was a battle over the make-up of the board, particularly over the right of the Medical Association of Georgia to choose half the membership of the nominating committee that would select it. The MAG members felt that they were being steam-rollered by the governor's people and walked out of the first meeting. As the MAG president-elect William Dowda, a member of the nominating committee, explained, "All we want is one-half of the input naming the 25 individuals, and as soon as the governor's appointees are willing to give us that, we will sit down with them and go to work."

Hamilton Jordan was so exasperated that he sought ways of getting around the medical members. He suggested that Carter seek an opinion from the attorney general that would, in essence, allow the nominating committee to meet without the medical members and possibly to make the top appointments. He wrote Carter: "It would be my strong recommendation that we proceed to appoint the Board, elect the Chairman, and select the Commissioner without the medical members."

Jimmy Carter took Jordan's advice. By Thursday, April 6, 1972, he was able to announce eight of his fifteen scheduled appointments to the board—a quorum composed of personal allies or supporters (including his seventy-three-year-old mother, Lillian Carter, Robert Lipshutz, and Hugh Gaston).

After an intricate formula had been worked out between the MAG and Carter factions to select the other seven, Carter named three of the five medical nominees to the board—all of them candidates from the Carter faction's original list. Carter then moved to appoint the two remaining nonmedical members of the board—one of them Jack Watson, another Carter political intimate and a young attorney with Charles Kirbo's firm of King and Spaulding. With his friends solidly in control, the Board named Robert Lipshutz chairman and Jack Watson vice-chairman. (Later these positions would be reversed.)

Finding a commissioner was also a problem. Carter would have liked state Welfare Director Jim Parham as his commissioner, but he had enemies in the

General Assembly and they had exacted a concession from Carter—that no stage agency head would serve as the new commissioner of the DHR for at least three years—as the price of their approval of the department.

Carter had a way around this constraint. In early April, 1972, Carter named State Budget Director J. Battle Hall as acting director and his personal representative at the meetings to plan the mergers that would form the DHR. Hall, in turn, chose Jim Parham as his "special temporary assistant" to deal with such matters" and named him as the head of the department's implementation task force, which was to come up with a blueprint for the new Department of Human Resources. In his memo appointing Parham, Hall directed the division directors and other unit heads within the department to look to Parham for "leadership in this area." Parham, in short, became the de facto commissioner of DHR—the central figure in putting the new department together.

Meanwhile, Carter had a problem in securing a permanent head of the giant agency. Critics say top professionals turned him down because of the overcomplexity of the department. So in October, 1972, he turned to Richard M. Harden, the twenty-eight-year-old accountant on loan from the Arthur Andersen firm, and son of Delton Harden, head of the GFA Peanut Association, and a member of the national peanut advisory commission during Carter's administration in Georgia. He was young, had a very late start in the organization, and was not even close to being the first choice. Further, the DHR, from its inception, was the subject of intense criticism by several powerful members of the General Assembly and Lieutenant Governor Lester Maddox.

In his first major move, Harden announced on October 24, 1972, the formation of a new staff unit called the Division of Community Services—to coordinate and strengthen the "last mile" delivery of assistance to people at local levels. But though Harden could provide for integration at the top, he was to have a more difficult time integrating services at the bottom. An administration-backed bill providing for the consolidation of boards of health and welfare in each county into a single Board of Human Resources passed the house, but died in the senate committee. An alternative plan was devised: the state would be divided into twenty-three "service areas," each to be headed by an area network director.

Funding for this proposal was another matter. The General Assembly slashed from the department's budget $3.2 million that was to pay the salaries for the new area network directors. Harden, however, decided to divert other funds he had on hand to pay for the program. This prompted angry responses from several legislators, including Representative James H. "Sloppy" Floyd, Chairman of the House Appropriations Committee, and Speaker Pro Tem Murphy. Representative George Busbee threatened to line-item DHR (rather than simply giving the department a total budget that its director would use as he saw fit to assure that legislative intent would be met.)

Harden's problems were not only with the state legislature, but with the department itself. Internal organizational and morale problems were as serious as the external bickering between the administration and the legislature. For one thing, there were problems in bringing the various professionals together. Public health workers were protective of their domain, and social workers felt threatened by the greater prestige of their "medical" colleagues. Social workers (mostly female) were thrown together with vocational rehabilitation counselors (mostly male) and comparison of the respective pay scales showed that the social workers were relatively underpaid. In the attempt to demonstrate that reorganization was indeed saving money, the administration had demanded an unreasonably small number of replacement positions. Money was saved—but at the cost of a further reduction in morale.

Further, the policies of Dr. Gary Miller, who had been named director of the Mental Health Division in August, 1972 (there were two Public Health divisions—Physical and Mental) before Harden took the helm, got him into problems with Harden and Watson—and attracted some flack from at least one powerful member of the General Assembly.

Miller had held top positions in the New York and Texas mental health programs and in these positions had promoted several innovative changes. For Georgia he initiated and won formal support in the department for a single delivery system in which welfare and all health programs would be coordinated at the local level. Miller also had a plan for decentralizing Georgia's mental health care facilities. Rather than shipping all mental patients to Central State Hospital in Milledgeville, his goal was to make the regional health care centers more responsive to clients in their geographic sector. And as part of this regional care concept he pushed intermediate care (also called "day hospitalization") as an alternative to full-time hospitalization of the mentally disabled. Further, at Central State, Miller introduced an open hospital policy—most of the patients were freed from the locked wards. Taking a personal interest in this reform, he came into conflict with the administrator of the facility.

Other problems flowed from his convictions, shared by others in DHR, that human resources workers at the local level need not necessarily be trained professionals and that professionals at the top—including superintendents of regional mental health centers—did not have to be licensed physicians. One segment of the Georgia Psychiatric Association gave tacit approval to such moves, but some leaders in the medical profession regarded such action as an infringement of their domain.

In challenging what some physicians in the mental health field consider their prerogatives Miller was bound to run into trouble. And in making his reforms at Central State Hospital at Milledgeville, Miller had entered Senator Culver Kidd's domain—the hospital was in his district and he was used to having a hand in what went on there.

In September, 1973, Kidd took the offensive, leading a group of Georgia legislators on a fact-finding visit to Texas—ostensibly to study that state's mental health institutions. Their real purpose was to gather dirt on Dr. Gary Miller. During the trip Kidd reported that Miller had been fired from his Texas post because he "alienated doctors and professional people in the state." He told reporters that Miller was prone to "taking off on tangents and refusing to accept directions." Kidd, however, did not present an accurate story on Miller. Later, Mrs. H. E. Butt, a member of the Texas Board of Mental Health and Retardation, wrote Carter that she had met with Senator Kidd and "his comrades" during their visit to Texas. She recalled telling them of the many gains in Texas's mental health program during Miller's tenure and said he had been "the most valuable deputy commissioner the department has had during my eighteen years on the Board." Mrs. Butt added: "It is unfortunate that the Georgia delegation chose to ignore that statement . . ." She also listed a wide range of professional groups that supported Dr. Miller and noted her indebtededness to Carter for "the courageous leadership you are giving in a cause important to us all."

When his Texas expedition failed, Kidd took another tack, claiming that the "open door policy" at Central State was responsible for the rape of a female patient and other sexual misconduct. Carter, in this instance, came to Miller's aid. For the rape incident he blamed the hospital administrator for not applying proper procedures. And in October, 1973, Carter expressed his "complete, unadulterated backing" for Miller and hinted that selfish economic interests might be behind the resistance to Miller's reforms at Central State.

But Miller's relationship with Harden had cooled to the point at which they no longer worked closely together. (Beverly Long, head of the Georgia Mental Health Association, had told Carter earlier that Harden and Miller were victims of inexperience and responding to political and other pressures that old hands would ignore. She urged Carter to take action to stem the problems between the two, adding: "They seem to be partly channeling all the outside problems into criticism of each other.")

The DHR as a whole was having difficulties with the legislature. In late March, 1974, a special committee was established by the new house speaker, Thomas B. Murphy, to work with the board "to alleviate some of their problems with the General Assembly." Murphy wrote Lieutenant Governor Maddox, with a carbon copy to Carter, who sent it to Jack Watson with an added message: "Do not get your department [of Human Resources] in a more vulnerable position—Be careful! JC."

The first week in April, Miller, Harden, and Watson attended the annual meeting of the Division of Mental Health on Jekyll Island. It was a good meeting at a pleasant setting, and when it ended, Miller thought he might stay over for a short vacation. But he learned from Harden that there was to be a staff meeting the next morning, so he returned to Atlanta. The next day, a Friday, Board Chairman Jack Watson told Miller that a letter of resignation had been prepared for him. He had discussed it with Harden and others. The resignation would be effective Monday morning. Miller refused to resign. But he learned from the evening news that a replacement had already been hired.

Miller immediately called Carter. (Though not a member of the governor's inner political circle, Miller had been on very friendly terms with the Carters; he had stayed in the mansion for a while, and traveled with Rosalynn Carter, studying mental health matters throughout the state.) Carter invited Miller to the mansion for breakfast the next morning. There he offered Miller his support saying, "I'll talk to Jack, I'll back you up."

Carter was concerned about the peremptory firing. He sent Jack Watson a handwritten note: "Gary tells me that no one in the past year has expressed any criticism of his work nor consulted with him about any modification of his policies or attitudes without immediate and harmonious results." He continued, "Also, it is obviously not right to peremptorily dismiss him without pay. I can't agree with this kind of punitive action."

Watson responded in a "Personal and Confidential" memo to be hand-delivered to the mansion, giving his views on the firing. And he claimed that Miller had been offered an "arrangement whereby he would, in effect, consult with the Department at full salary for a period of approximately two months." But Miller had "indicated that the only way he would leave his position was to be dismissed." Watson claimed several examples of "situations in which Gary's insensitive handling of people and policy changes were called to his attention."

Carter backed down. When he informed Miller, in their next meeting, of his decision to uphold Watson's action, the ordinarily sharp blue-eyed gaze was cast conspicuously downward—away from the disbelieving and disappointed Gary Miller.

According to Miller, he had been fired to placate Kidd. The press interpreted Miller's firing as a trade-off for legislative support for the area network system, which the General Assembly had been fighting against for two years. But the governor denied that politics had anything to do with the decision. As he wrote Beverly Long, president of the Georgia Mental Health Association: "So far as I know, no outside political or professional forces were instrumental in the department decision to appoint a new director." He assured Senator Julian Bond and others who had supported much of Miller's work that "there would be no retrogression in mental health progress."

In a press conference on April 8, 1974, Carter called Miller "one of the finest public health officials in the United States," but said his "unlimited courage and tenacity" worked "against the harmonious development" of mental health programs. His firing had been "discussed for at least a year."

Gary Miller (three days after meeting with Watson) had filed a suit in federal district court, contending that the summary dismissal violated his rights to due process and that statements by public officials damaged his ability to earn a living. Miller claimed that Carter had given him assurances that he, Miller, would have the position until at least the end of 1974. Carter, in a sworn deposition, denied ever making such assurances. In early May the court refused to issue a temporary restraining order. Later it denied a defendant's motion to dismiss the case. Finally, after a ruling favorable to Miller regarding discovery, an out-of-court settlement was reached, which included the publication and widespread dissemination of Miller's achievement as director of the Georgia mental health programs.

Actually, Miller's firing came at a time when it appeared that his problems were being resolved. Open conflict with Harden seems to have been muted, as he cleared most of what he did through Jim Parham, who acted as a kind of intermediary. And he was successful in securing legislative support for many of the programs in which he was interested. He might well have been the "sacrificial lamb," as some observers suggested, thrown out in an attempt to appease those who were angry at Carter himself (for the diminished power of the medical profession in the state health bureaucracy, as well as his public attacks on the medical profession) or at Harden and the DHR concept.

The DHR as a whole remained an object of controversy. While there were advances (its family planning services were given credit for an 11.9 percent decrease in Georgia's pregnancy rate; and thirty-four new drug addiction treatment centers opened around the state), the department as a whole was in a great deal of trouble. The organizational drift, as well as the lack of an adroit administrative hand at the top, had created such an accounting mess that the books could not be properly audited. State Auditor Ernest B. Davis said early in 1974 that the department had created such a "colossal muddle" of its bookkeeping and accounting that he could not certify the accuracy of an audit of its books. Several weeks later another audit suggested that the Medicaid nursing home program was not operating in an efficient, effective, or economical manner. (The state auditors, visiting fifty-three nursing homes, reported that cost statements for sixteen of the homes could not be verified and that thirty-five of the remaining thirty-seven contained bogus expenses. They noted that it was as difficult getting information from the DHR as from the nursing homes.) The auditors had discovered a decrease in activity of the state cancer program: only 28 percent of those eligible for services were receiving it, and the number of patients participating in the program had decreased by 37 percent since 1968—though there had been no corresponding decrease in the incidence of cancer. The area network system in practice simply set up another bureaucratic layer, mixed up lines of authority, and seemed to be oriented more toward extending state control over local agencies than integrating the delivery of services to clients.

Thus, near the end of Carter's term, his favorite department was still the source of continuing controversy. In January, 1974, in an effort to stem the disagreement, Carter had met with top leaders of the Georgia House in a secret session at the governor's mansion, where they discussed the state budget and the area network system. Hoping to avert a special budgetary session, Carter and the house leadership hammered out a deal. One "insider" told a reporter that Carter agreed to take the political heat for vetoing a property tax rebate, while the house would comply with the senate version of the budget. Carter told the group that he intended to continue the area network arrangement and asked their cooperation in working out a compromise in the system. His request was reportedly met with a "tacit" acceptance. It was more of a "gentleman's agreement" than a political deal.

Throughout most of Human Resources' first two years, Jimmy Carter supported the department's leaders. Richard Harden says that he saw Carter as often as necessary, usually once a week. Nor did Carter stint on his praise, as subsequent reports would suggest was his style. In a handwritten note of July, 1973, Carter told Harden and Jack Watson, "I'm very proud of the recent reports on the administrative progress being made in your department. . . . Any time you need me, just let me know." As late as May, 1974, Carter was still sending complimentary notes to Harden, noting the "outstanding progress" made by DHR and offering his assistance "whenever I can be of service to you or to the fine and dedicated personnel of the Department of Human Resources." Indeed, at the height of the area network controversy, Carter publicly supported Harden's action on several occasions, and accused the legislature of attempting to usurp the authority of the executive branch.

But then, after almost two years of promoting and defending Richard Harden, Carter shifted. In July, 1974, he sent Harden a seething memo that found its way into the press. In it he demanded an explanation from Harden for the failure of DHR to win contracts for construction of two needed "sheltered workshops" for the mentally retarded before the end of fiscal 1974. And he rejected Harden's attempts to blame the delay on Lieutenant Governor Maddox's failure to attend a meeting of the State Properties Commission, which resulted in the lack of a quorum and no action on the projects. The failure to meet, Carter countered, played only a "minor role in the failure of the state to complete the transaction." The fiery memo was prompted, in part, by the DHR's loss of funds through "lapsing" in previous years.

On September 18, 1974, Harden, noting that the department was "beginning to have a diminishing value in regard to my professional development as an accountant," announced that he would resign "some time between now and the end of Governor Carter's term."

Shortly before Harden's departure, Jim Parham outlined the basic problems of the DHR. The coordination of services at the district and county level was nonexistent. The area network system had survived only because of Carter's tenacious commitment to it. Conflicts with the legislature and lack of administrative ability were major impediments. Indeed, the whole future of the department was in doubt.

The controversial concept of coordinating human services at the regional level did not survive the Carter administration. One of George Busbee's first acts as the next governor of Georgia was to eliminate the area network system. He took steps to return administrative control directly to the head of Central State Hospital. And in an effort to get a rein on the unwieldy department, he pared it down by transferring the health and welfare benefits unit out of it. Slowly but surely the bookkeeping and other administrative problems were worked out. As a consequence, there has been a marked improvement in the relations of the department with the General Assembly.

In short, the major organizational goals of the DHR never were accomplished. Though the department remains as an umbrella agency and some improvements occurred in medical and social services, the most innovative aspects of the plan were dropped as soon as the pressure was off.

### Reorganization: the Results

Overall, the restructuring of the state government had an impact on power relationships within the government. It was Carter's position that reorganization would permit people to have more control over state government. "As it is fragmented now," he said, "it is very subject to the control of special interest groups who have very highly paid lawyers, lobbyists or legislators who are friendly to them and can take care of their needs often to the detriment of the people."

Yet if one looks at the changes that Carter proposed, and to some degree achieved, reorganization would result—for better or worse—in the centralization of political authority in the hands of the chief executive.

Carter was successful in extending the governor's control over several important agencies—with his power to appoint the heads of the Office of Planning and Budget, Department of Banking and Finance, the Department of Revenue, the Department of Defense. But the governor's most far-reaching power came with the establishment of the Department of Administrative Services (DOAS), which took over the functions previously performed by the old state treasurer's office (previously headed by an elected official) and seventeen other formerly separate agencies—dealing with purchasing, data processing, printing, personnel management, and space allocation. The head of DOAS was appointed by the governor, and through him the governor would be able to influence both elected and appointed department heads by controlling what they could and could not have in resources and services. Further, the governor's control over purchasing, Culver Kidd was to charge, was such that Carter was able to "substantially abandon" the legal requirement of preparing "adequate specifications, securing bids and awarding the contract to the low bidder." And the extension of executive control over the State Depository Board, a previously bipartisan group that supervised the handling of the state's cash, could be misused by governors who were so inclined.*

Reorganization also removed an entire administrative level from the State Merit System. In most agencies, prior to reorganization, only the hiring and firing of the department head and perhaps his deputy were in the hands of the

---

* Carter did not achieve *all* the centralization he desired, failing to place control over the state's education system in the governor's office and to put the reins on the hiring and firing of all state personnel in the hands of the new Department of Administrative Services.

governor or the departmental governing board. But reorganization quietly removed the middle-level division directors and agency heads it created from the
protection of the State Merit System—thus greatly increasing the number of
jobs, patronage or otherwise, to be filled at the governor's discretion.

Political considerations aside, reorganization certainly did create a neater
and more readable organization chart, putting units together in larger departments. And the centralization of certain administrative services, such as printing and computer processing, was a means of avoiding duplication between
agencies and possibly of reducing administrative expenses.

Carter did not, however, trim the state bureaucracy as much as he later suggested. The big reductions were in the advisory, nonbudgeted agencies, cut
from a paper strength of 200 to a post reorganization total of 9. (These units had
cost the state little or no money and many had been defunct for some time.
Moreover, Carter himself created new boards and commissions—though most
did not show up on the organizational chart because they were placed in the
new departments "for administrative purposes.") The more important
budgeted state agencies were reduced from an original sixty-five to twenty-two.
But aside from the deletion of state treasurer's office, most of the older units
were retained and combined into three new larger units, the Department of
Human Resources, the Department of Natural Resources, and the Department
of Administrative Services.

Further, the elimination of duplication in activities between departments is
not always cost efficient. Centralization is economical when the economies of
scale outweigh the possible loss in employee time caused by the inconvenience
of going through a larger apparatus. Those department heads who checked the
administration's attempt to centralize all printing and data processing may
have saved the state from great inefficiencies. Sam Caldwell, for example,
would argue later that if the State Employment Security Agency had been
moved from the Labor Department to the DHR, unemployment checks would
have been funneled through the centralized computer and data processing
operations of DOAS; when the 1974 recession brought a rise in state unemployment checks from 15,000 to 100,000 a week, an intolerable crisis caused by
DOAS red tape would have resulted.

But maybe there were savings due to reorganization. Carter had attempted
to sell Georgians on his plan by saying there would be some. In fact, the overall
budget of the state increased about 55 percent from 1971 to 1974. What he had
promised, Carter explained in June, 1973, was not a cut in the overall state
budget, but a *percentage reduction* (italics mine) in administrative costs. ("During the last fiscal year before I took office the cost of administering state government consumed 9.6 percent of the state's budget . . . During my first budget-
year the figure was 7.9 percent. This present year saw a further reduction to 5.4
percent.")

Accounting problems, which inevitably accompany any major reorganization, make it difficult to assess these claims. The allocation for "administrative

services" between 1973 and 1974 did drop from $14 million to $8 million, but that figure does not cover administrative costs in the various departments or the expenses associated with the new data processing systems. Hidden capital costs may also have obscured the figures. For example, the reorganized motor pool was run on the basis of a cost per mile estimate of 4.7 cents, an estimate which Culver Kidd pointed out "omitted capital costs, spare parts costs, loss of income costs, depreciation costs, excessive trade-in estimates and exaggerated length of use estimates." Further, the total budget for administrative services in 1974 was less than one half of 1 percent of the state's total budget—which would make any savings minuscule. Auditor Ernest Davis said, "I have personally not been able to identify any savings that resulted from reorganization per se."

The number of state employees rose from 49,125 to 60,937 during Carter's term in office. The 2,100 unnecessary state jobs Carter would later say he had eliminated existed only on paper. Indeed, as Carter explained in 1972, when he spoke of reducing the number of state employees, he referred only to the reduction in the *rate of increase* in the hiring of state employees. Thus: "in the four years prior to this administration, the number of people on the state payroll increased by almost 56 percent—an average annual increase of over 14 percent. By contrast, in the last two fiscal years, due to the effects of reorganization and zero-base budgeting—we were able to cut this rate by over half to only 5.8 percent . . ."

But what about the surplus of $116 million he left in the state treasury? There had been a $103 million surplus when he entered office, and the state's outstanding debt increased during his administration from $892 million to $1.097 billion. Thus, the statistics are less clear and maybe less promising than they at first appear.

Yet, when all is said and done, the original purpose of reorganization as pronounced in the study group's final report in 1971 was somewhat different from the efficiency claims that Carter would emphasize. The central purpose, as stated there, was the creation of a "structure of the Executive Branch of State Government which is responsive to the needs of the People of this state and sufficiently flexible to meet changing conditions . . ." It attempted to design a new structure in which closely related functions could be grouped in the same agencies and placed under one responsible authority. Programs could be coordinated and the responsibility for various programs pinpointed. By this standard, reorganization moved toward its goal. Responsibility for diverse services was more centralized—which made it easier to locate and place authority—in the hands of the Governor and his appointed department heads. And some of the new entities, as we shall see, found a political clout that enabled them to advance programmatic reforms.

## Zero-Based Budgeting

Carter saw "zero-based budgeting" as an integral part of the reorganization process. Shortly after drawing up his original reorganization proposal, Carter had invited Peter Phyrr, who introduced zero-based budgeting at Texas Instruments, to Georgia to develop the concept for the state government. In January, 1972, Carter introduced the new system to the General Assembly in his State of the State Address, stating that this "unique zero-based budgeting procedure" was "almost certain to be copied throughout the nation." In zero-based budgeting, he explained, each governmental unit constructs a "decision package" which is then reviewed at each succeeding administrative level. Each agency, in turn, assigns a priority to each of its decision packages and funds are allocated on the basis of that ordering. Ideally, zero-based budgeting encourages "the search for more efficient ways to do the job." Moreover, it makes it possible to evaluate the performance of an agency in relation to budget by demanding "clear descriptions of the results to be expected from every dollar spent." Further, as Carter said in 1974, "Zero-base budgeting in itself has given me an extremely valuable method by which I can understand what happens deep in a department."

The zero-based process soon proved to be unwieldy. For one thing, the governor could not personally review all of the 11,000 decision packages. (One management specialist has calculated that even if Carter set aside four hours every day for two months, he could only have spent about a minute on each decision package, hardly enough time to read it, let alone determine its merits.) Carter only reviewed policy questions, new programs and capital expenditure, and major increases and decreases in existing programs, while sampling a few specific packages. In fact, a decision was made, even before the end of the first budget cycle, to give a core 80 percent of the state's level of spending "only a cursory examination and that attention would be focused on the increment." Thus, like all his predecessors, Carter spent most of his time simply reviewing changes in the budget, as well as attending to a few problem areas.

Nor was Carter able to accept the rank order of the programs that various administrators gave him, adjusting them as the funds available for state programs fluctuated. Administrators preparing the priority rankings, chose their own maximizing strategies. As Ernest Davis described it: when the governor asked a department head to assign priorities, the administrator "would put a low priority on things he knew had so much public support they couldn't be done away with, and assign top priority to things he's close to but which may not have much support. That's exactly what every state agency did." Thus, in fiscal year 1974, when there was an increase in available funds in Georgia, Carter had to request new decision packages from department heads, rather than shifting the cutoff line downward in order to include more of the original packages. And for fiscal year 1975, when there was a decrease in available funds, the cutoff line was not simply shifted upward. The department once again had to construct new decision packages based on the more limited funding. In short, for all the rhetoric, the governor fell back on an old process that went against one of the fundamental principles of the zero-based system.

The result: zero-based budgeting caused few or no shifts in spending despite fluctuations in the budget. In fact, only two of thirteen Georgia department heads responding to one survey would go so far as to say that zero-based budgeting "may have led" to a reallocation of resources.

Moreover, there was a cost to the whole process. The extensive self-evaluation and the paper work required by annual zero-based budgeting may increase administrative costs because of the time and effort lost in preparing the budget. According to one report, this was a major reason for widespread discontent with the process among many department heads and employees in Georgia.

Zero-based budgeting, in short, was an attractive and simple concept that seemed to promise efficiency throughout the bureaucracy and control at the center. But like many simple concepts, it did not work so well in practice, giving way to older ways of doing things under the stress of competing organizational interests and the practical necessity of getting things done. Its value as a political symbol, however, was considerable. A chief executive seemed to have discovered a technique whereby one could impartially and rationally control and evaluate all the major operations in a bureaucracy. And Carter was to make political capital out of this innovation. He had been the first chief executive to try out the new system in a major political entity and his experiences with that system, he would later suggest, would be one of the contributions he could make to rationalizing the federal bureaucracy.

## Protecting the Environment

Carter did achieve considerable success with what he described as his second greatest interest as governor—protection of the environment. He recalls in *Why Not the Best?* that, outside of reorganization, he spent "more time [on] preserving our natural resources than any other one issue." The new Department of Natural Resources was perhaps the most successful of the reorganized state departments. It gave the environmentalists more political clout and a larger share of the state budget. (Spending on all natural resources rose from $55 million a year to $70 million.) Indeed, Carter and his aides steered legislation through the General Assembly to strengthen enforcement procedures and provide civil penalties for violations of air, water, and surface mining protection laws. And he took a hard line with some he considered violators. By the end of Carter's term, all but 5 of the 2,300 industrial air polluters, and all but 1 of the 450 industrial water polluters in Georgia had met federal and state pollution control regulations.

A strong advocate of state land use planning and regulation, Carter also proposed several measures for the protection of sand dunes, the prevention of excessive erosion and sedimentation, the regulation of flood hazard areas. He sometimes checked the attempts of commercial interests or developers to move into areas without taking proper steps for the maintenance of environmental values. Thus, in an attempt to protect a stretch of the Chattahoochee River north of Atlanta, he withheld rezoning permits, blocked a contract for a new bridge, forbade new highway construction, and warned developers that the state could withhold permission to build sewers along the river if they did not abide by all environmental regulations. He was also interested in the preservation of historical sites, and in 1972 he established, by executive order, the Georgia Heritage Trust Commission, a high-profile and popular project.

Carter showed a tendency to duck, however, when caught between strong competing forces. His handling of the controversial Interstate 485, a part of the Atlanta expressway system, pleased neither supporters or opponents. Highway Director Bert Lance was eager to proceed but a federal judge ordered the project halted until an environmental impact study could be completed. When several Atlanta citizens' groups and aldermen asked Carter to halt construction to prevent environmental destruction and traffic congestion, he accused the aldermen of "yielding to political pressure." Blocking the expressway, he said, would dry up downtown Atlanta and cost the state millions in federal highway funds. But then he called a meeting of the opposing forces—with representatives of the state highway agencies, downtown civic organizations, MARTA, the Atlanta Chamber of Commerce, and other groups on one side, and several state legislators, city aldermen, residents along the route, and environmentalists on the other. Carter presided. Despite the fiery clash between the two sides, and the indeterminate outcome of the session, Carter said that he was pleased with the meeting.

Afterward Carter announced he had put the fate of I-485 in the hands of professional pollsters. The Atlanta *Journal* editorialized that this decision "would be astounding if it weren't so ridiculous. . . . A politician who doesn't know his own mind, who can't face a tough decision, would be better to leave politicking to those who can and return to the simple life of a peanut farmer." (As it turned out, the results of the poll were such that he had no clear mandate: 38 percent favored the expressway, 19 percent opposed, and 43 percent were undecided.)

Carter was equally indecisive on the completion of Interstate 75. Construction of the final section, which would pass through a wilderness area above Lake Allatoona, had been halted by environmentalists. On the other side, certain politically powerful investors who had procured choice sites along the route managed to block any alternate routing. As a result of these contending forces, all building was halted on the Allatoona route. In the end Carter avoided making any decision: "Decision's in hands of Secretary of Transportation. Whatever decision is made, my responsibility will be to minimize adverse effect on environment."

## System of Justice

Carter made a beginning in his effort to reform Georgia's penal system. To aid him in this endeavor he brought in a man with an outstanding reputation as a reformer, Ellis MacDougall, from the Connecticut prison system, to head the board of corrections and reorganize the Department of Offender Rehabilitation. MacDougall proceeded to set up, in each of the state's major cities, new classification centers where prisoners would be assigned to specialized institutions, depending on the nature of their crimes and their individual character. (This permitted five or six prison branches to be phased out of existence.) He expanded the prisoner early release program, which had been introduced by Lester Maddox.

But Carter stopped short of other fundamental changes required in the crowded and antiquated system. He was unwilling to ask for additional funds for construction of new prisons. Instead, he wrote Georgia's superior court judges asking them to use probation in lieu of imprisonment whenever possible. Some judges said this would be improper, and Fulton County Superior Court Chief Judge Claude Shaw responded that it would be better for the state to expand prison facilities than for judges to strain their consciences by extending probation. By the fall of 1974 Carter was warning state officials he eventually might have to refuse to accept any more inmates—the state's facilities could hold only 800 more people.

Carter also tried his hand at some needed reforms in the Georgia Bureau of Investigation in an attempt to bring up its professional standards. Early in his term he appointed a ten-member group headed by Ted King, a former FBI man and then head of security for Southern Telephone and Telegraph, to study the matter. Eventually, in line with its recommendations, the GBI came under the Division of Investigation in the Department of Public Safety and provisions were made for more extensive training, higher employment standards, higher pay, and pay incentives for special educational courses. He ran into more difficulty in his attempts to give the GBI investigatory and arrest powers throughout the state without first obtaining the permission of local sheriffs. Such proposals stirred up the Georgia Sheriffs Association and some members raised the specter of a repressive statewide police force. There were even rumors that the Division of Investigation had already investigated local cops. In the fall of 1974 Carter was still calling for statewide arrest powers for the GBI.

One particularly interesting innovation of the Carter administration was the biracial Civil Disorders Unit, created in late 1971 within the Department of Public Safety. Three to four people, dressed in civilian garb, would slip quietly into a community at the first sign of trouble, identify leaders, and try to reduce tensions so local officials could deal with the problem. In the first three and one half years of operation, the CDU was called into fifty-five counties. State troopers had to be called in only twice.

On more specific law and order issues, Carter appealed at different times to liberals and to conservatives. On the "conservative" side, he took tough law and order positions opponents would regard as anti–civil libertarian. Early in his term he expressed the view that prison administrators should deal with prison riots by avoiding protracted, highly publicized negotiations with prisoners—freeing hostages by force if necessary. He supported a measure to extend the use of electronic surveillance equipment by law enforcement officers for the crimes of theft and extortion, permitting the data secured to be entered as evidence in court trials. He signed legislation restoring the death penalty in Georgia—for hijacking and treason in all cases, and for murder, rape, armed robbery, and kidnaping in many instances. (As a part of his anticrime campaign, an advertisement by Gerald Rafshoon was run with the caption "If you get raped, maybe it's your fault." When this advertisement aroused what Jody Powell called "a dozen or so" complaints from "extremely vocal" women, Carter asked the media not to use it.) In 1974, he undertook a major campaign to sell an anti–organized crime package that would allow the courts to compel testimony from witnesses in exchange for granting immunity from prosecution. It would also increase the penalties for loan-sharking and commercial gambling, and give the Law Department the power to revoke the charter of any corporation operated or controlled by organized crime.

On the "liberal" side, he backed a task force recommendation urging a system of state licensing and registration of handguns—and to require such licenses and registrations for the sale of ammunition. He signed a 1971 law giving judges the power to grant conditional discharges to first-time drug offenders, rather than penalizing them under Georgia's tough drug laws. And in 1973 he approved a law reducing the possession of an ounce or less of marijuana to a misdemeanor.

The Carter administration undertook some reforms within the judiciary. To recommend persons for vacancies on the bench, Carter reestablished by executive order the Judicial Nominating Commission, originally appointed by Governor Sanders. Following the procedures recommended by the American Judicature Association, the commission publicized vacancies and held open hearings followed by closed interviews with those under consideration. Five names would then be confidentially submitted to the governor, from which he would make each selection. To consider other changes he appointed a commission on judicial processes, headed by Appellate Court Judge Robert H. Hall, who had been campaigning for reform of the judicial structure since 1962. Throughout the deliberations of the commission, as well as their meetings with members of the General Assembly, Hall was in close contact with Carter's legal adviser, Bill Harper (a former student of Hall's at Emory University Law School). Though Carter was not personally involved in the details of the commission's work, he did lend his assistance when opposition to the commission's reforms surfaced in the General Assembly. Eventually, two major judicial reforms were approved by the General Assembly and the voters in the form of constitutional amendments: the first established the Judicial Qualifications Commission on Discipline and Removal, which provided professional guidelines and disciplinary rules for judges; the second created a unified judicial system headed by the Judicial Council of Georgia. To administer the new system, the General Assembly approved the creation of the Administrative Office of the Court.

## Affirmative and Nonaffirmative Action

Carter had a mixed record in the promotion of the rights of women and blacks. Formally, he supported the Equal Rights Amendment. But his statements on the subject exemplify a technique he often used of diffusing the anger his positions might arouse by adding qualifications or pointing out that some people close to him didn't agree with him. Thus, in January, 1972, Carter told an anti-ERA contingent in his office: "I have to tell you in complete honesty that I favor the passage of the amendment." However, "I might say that my wife disagrees with me on this." When a minister in the group read Carter a section from the Bible wherein the Apostle Paul maintained that wives should remain subject to husbands, Carter responded that, as a Sunday school teacher, he was not inclined to argue with Saint Paul, but he believed Paul was addressing himself more to domestic arrangements than to business and politics.

The national media reported the following day that three irate women were demonstrating in Carter's office. One of them was identified as Rosalynn Carter, a resident in the governor's mansion. She was sporting a large red, white, and blue banner—"ERA YES." The amendment, she said, "talks about rights, equal rights and I am for that. Jimmy was just mistaken, that's all." Carter responded: "I thought I knew what Rosalynn thought. But I was wrong." A few days later he spoke in favor of the ERA to the Georgia Legislative Forum. When the house defeated the ERA, he said he was "very disappointed" and blamed "major employers in Georgia and the John Birch Society for the defeat."

In the area of racial integration, the Carter administration also played an ambiguous role. In a series of public actions from May, 1971, through February, 1972, he opposed compulsory busing of students (as well as faculty transfers) to achieve integration in the classroom. Later he claimed to have worked hard on an Atlanta voluntary busing plan, which he regarded as a model for the nation. However, the NAACP did not share his enthusiasm for the plan, expelling the Atlanta chapter for supporting it. Some blacks saw the plan as a deal in which school integration was traded away for black representation on the Atlanta School Board—an unnecessary trade since blacks would have won new seats in the forthcoming election, anyway.

There was limited progress during Carter's term in fair housing legislation. Georgia's antiblockbusting law had been passed by the General Assembly in 1970 before Carter entered office. But Andrew Young, chairman of the Atlanta Community Relations Commission, wrote Carter in 1971 that the Real Estate Commission was apparently not enforcing it. He suggested that the Real Estate

Commission be urged to enforce the law and that its chairman (against whom Attorney General John Mitchell had filed a civil suit charging him and his firm with discriminating against blacks in the purchase and sale of homes) step down until his guilt or innocence had been determined in the federal courts. Carter appointed a committee to study the situation and asked the commission chairman to step down—but to no avail. Carter had no legal right to remove him and his term and his term did not expire until 1973.

Hamilton Jordan, in a May, 1971, memo, had suggested that the responsibility for enforcing the 1970 measure lay wih the state, but Carter's legal adviser, William Harper, did not agree. An enforcement bill, which went before the house in 1972, reflected Harper's position. It would have increased penalties for violating the law, while empowering the Georgia Real Estate Commission (not the state) to guarantee enforcement. In 1973 the General Assembly gave the Real Estate Commission power to pursue violators and originate complaints, and the commission drew up more detailed regulation to guarantee open housing and end blockbusting.

By 1973 the make-up of the Real Estate Commission had radically changed because of legislation that increased its membership from three to five and the replacement of members who left. Instead of a Maddox-appointed majority of two to one, it had Carter-appointed majority of five to one. The future looked bright.

But practically nothing changed. By September, 1974, the commission had only two full-time inspectors, though the legislature had authorized the hiring of eight new ones. The Atlanta Community Relations Commission blasted the Georgia Real Estate Commission for inactivity and "damn near zero credibility in the black community" as enforcers of state fair housing regulations.

The employment record of the state was equally mixed. In October, 1973, the president of the statewide chapter of the NAACP, Reverend J. C. Hope, said he was "disappointed" with the progress made in hiring blacks. He was particularly concerned about the Highway Patrol Department, where only 7 of Georgia's 677 state troopers were black. "We had a commitment from Governor Carter and [State Patrol Commander] Ray Pope to hire twenty-five blacks before the end of 1972." He added: "the Governor has ignored a telegram requesting a follow-up on the commitment. If necessary, the NAACP will take action in court." Shortly after that a black state trooper was assigned to the governor's security staff.

Carter did appoint some blacks and women at the top. As he wrote the leaders of the Southern Christian Leadership Conference in 1974, he had appointed blacks to a number of policy-making boards and there were more "black people in top administrative positions than ever before."

An analysis of the state employment record undertaken by the Governor's Commission on Human Relations was less sanguine. No departments, it claimed had initiated "really effective affirmative action plans." And the figures were there to support their claims. Eighty-four percent of the higher level positions in the eighteen departments and commissions reviewed were held by white males. No blacks (male or female) participated in employment decisions in ten departments, including the new Office of Planning and Budget. There was not one white female above grade eighteen on the twenty-four–grade pay scale; 91.6 percent of female state employees were at grade eleven or below. Further, of the forty-four blacks on the twenty-four major boards, councils, committees, and commissions listed in the report, six were on the Governor's Council on Human Relations—a group with no legal power; three were on the forty-five–member Commission on the Status of Women.

Carter responded to these figures by sending a tough, handwritten memo to department heads. Some had made "fine progress," but others were in "an indefensible situation regarding discrimination in hiring practices." He asked for a confidential outline of plans to correct these disparities.

But Richard Harden of Human Resources took these instructions too far. He asked an employee, who happened to be Jewish, to waive his number-two spot on the regional administrator merit system list so that the number-nine person, a black, could be appointed. The employee responded with an angry telegram to the governor. Four days later Carter issued a directive on hiring practices, saying: "We have not and will not establish quotas or pass over better qualified individuals just to be able to say that we are meeting a certain goal."

Despite the fits and starts, Carter did make some progress on the integration front. By the time his term came to an end, the number of black appointees on state boards and agencies were fifty-three (compared to a starting base of three). The number of black state employees had increased from 4,840 to 6,684. Further, his personal relationships with many black leaders were so good that he received very little public criticism. (Andrew Young, for example, would later say that under the Carter administration he felt comfortable, for the first time, at the state capitol.)

Yet some of the governor's own staff felt that progress had been very slow. John Martin and David Fox, who were preparing a booklet outlining Carter accomplishments as governor of Georgia, wrote him in 1974: "It will be difficult to talk about initiatives in the area of minority employment under the 'Executive/Legislative Action' heading. The 'Results' section would actually contain the present status of minority employment, which is not very good. The 'Unmet Needs' section would be full."

As this record of Carter's governorship suggests, he was certainly no populist—at least not as the term was understood by the young Tom Watson and those other American radicals who had pushed controversial reforms at the turn of the century. Pollster Bill Hamilton may have been more accurate in characterizing him as a "stylistic populist." In the programs he embraced, Carter had shown himself to be a conventional good-government man, pushing mainstream reforms favored by good-government people in his and other states. The net result of his reorganization program, which he had made the hallmark of his administration, however, was less impressive than his later claims were to suggest. His other accomplishments were in the areas of natural resources development and protection of the environment, judicial reform, improvement in the treatment of the retarded and mentally ill, and certain modest changes in the prison system. In the promotion of sexual and racial equality he had a mixed record. When judged on a scale other than his own, Carter had proved to be a good, but not extraordinary, governor.

But Jimmy Carter had tried for more than that. In his inaugural address in 1971, he had outlined what he wanted to do: ". . . I am determined that at the end of this administration we shall be able to stand up anywhere in the world—in New York, California, or Florida and say 'I'm a Georgian'—and be proud of it." And along the way, in his discussions of zero-based budgeting, Carter suggested that Georgia had been establishing a model for the nation to follow. John Crown of the Atlanta *Journal* wrote in January, 1973: "I believe that Jimmy Carter is the best governor that Georgia has had in my memory." The controversial piggyback poll, which he had run in late 1973, was less sanguine. To the statement "Jimmy Carter has been one of the best governors we've had in Georgia for a long time," 34 percent agreed; 43 percent disagreed, and the rest did not know.

# TEN

# Legislative Front

REFLECTING ON HIS GOVERNORSHIP, Carter wrote in 1975: "I enjoyed my four years in this office, in spite of it being a highly controversial, aggressive, and combative administration." And Hamilton Jordan has suggested that these combative relations with the General Assembly were due to Carter's refusal to engage in politics as usual. In November, 1971, the following story—frequently to be repeated during the 1976 presidential campaign—first appeared. It seemed that Carter badly needed votes in the state senate on some matter, and one senator said he would vote with the governor if the senator's father was promoted one step up the bureaucratic ladder, to an open position for which he was qualified. Carter, however, refused to deal in this manner, and thus lost the vote and the bill. In a later version of the story, Jordan reported that Carter had said that ". . . he didn't spend four years of his life running for governor to promote some guy's father-in-law [or father]. He wouldn't do it—and here we were, idealistic young kids, urging *him* to be more political."

Another explanation of Carter's embattled relationship with the General Assembly was suggested in 1971 by reporter Duane Riner (who would later join Carter's staff). He quoted one unnamed house leader who thought Carter would get most of his reorganization plan through that body—but only on its merits. "Jimmy's his own worst enemy as far as getting something done is concerned. . . . He feels he's right and he's got a lot of integrity, but he just doesn't communicate."

Actually, Carter's troubles with the General Assembly in Georgia cannot be attributed to some special political innocence on his part or any reluctance to engage in power politics. In his dealings with the state legislature he used all the techniques and resources at his command.

Even before he was inaugurated, Carter followed Georgia tradition, trying to put his own friends in leadership positions in the General Assembly. During the 1970 campaign he had told his friend Senator Robert Smalley that he wanted him to be president pro tem of the Georgia Senate. And right after the polls had closed, he had several senate friends sound out their associates to see if Smalley could win. They told Carter that he could, but only if he and his cousin Hugh did some calling to line up support for Smalley.

At this, Lester Maddox, the newly elected lieutenant governor, hit the roof. He thought he had exacted a pledge from Carter during the campaign that Carter would not interfere in the senate's selection of its leaders. When Carter visited him the day after the election, Maddox let Carter know that he considered this activity an encroachment on the lieutenant governor's traditional prerogatives: "He's really mad," Carter told his senate supporters after the meeting.

With that, as one reporter noted with astonishment, Carter backed off from the whole affair. "He did not ask Smalley to get out, did not suggest a compromise candidate, and he did not call those senators he still might have influenced." Shortly thereafter Smalley was beaten (27 to 17) by a group composed of supporters of Lester Maddox, Carl Sanders, Jim Gillis, and a coalition of blacks—all of whom rallied behind Jim Gillis's son, Hugh.

Carter may have backed off because he realized, after his first moves, that he could not win. He had incensed Sanders's supporters with the tone of the campaign; he had enraged Lester Maddox by moving into an area Maddox considered his political domain; he had lost other old-time politicians by hinting throughout the campaign that he would oust Jim Gillis, one of the most powerful men in the state, as chairman of the State Highway Board; and the blacks were no particular friends of his, given the campaign he had waged. And now he was openly challenging Hugh Gillis for a leadership spot in the senate. In essence, Carter had moved too hard and too fast against four power centers, and he must have realized he could not carry it off.

With this incident Carter intensified the political problems he would have with the senate. Maddox, of course, having just been governor, with ambitions to return to that office in the future, had ample reason to oppose Carter. But Carter made matters worse by challenging him. In addition, Maddox claims that Carter told him in January 1971 that ". . . if I crossed him on any issue he would work to destroy me with the full resources at his command." If Carter uttered such words, he made a mistake. In a man as proud and volatile as Maddox, they would raise the fighting spirit, rather than quenching it.

As lieutenant governor, Maddox had the power to appoint committee chairmen. He quickly chose his friend Stanley E. Smith to head the Senate Committee on Economy, Reorganization, and Efficiency in Government (EREG), which initially dealt with Carter's reorganization proposals. Only two of the eleven committee members, Bob Smalley and Albert Holloway, were from the Carter camp. The remaining seats were held by Maddox, Sanders, and Gillis supporters. Still, Maddox, whose own relations with the General Assembly had been tumultuous, could not have blocked Carter if Carter had had wide support in the senate. But his campaign against Sanders and the Gillises turned other leaders against him, and his quick and unusual rise to power meant he had no in-depth support among the membership. As Carter's friend Representative Sidney Marcus noted: "Most people have a long and ongoing political career. They make alliances and friends, and at the end of 10 or 12 years become a statewide public official. He came to this from a different situation. He was not active in the General Assembly when he ran for governor, and didn't have all those relationships."

To compound their problems, the governor and his staff were insensitive in some early dealings with the legislators. One senator, who had considered himself a Carter supporter, spent fifty dollars of his own money to fly to Atlanta shortly after the election to meet Carter. He was greatly upset when a state trooper abruptly ended the meeting after only five minutes. And shortly after Carter took office, the parking area alongside the capitol suddenly blossomed with new signs—nineteen parking spaces marked "reserved for Governor's staff." When Representative Dewey Rush of Glennville was asked by a guard to remove his car from one of these spaces, he refused and promptly introduced a bill to reduce the governor's parking allocation to three spaces while the legislature was in session.

Eventually Carter did evolve a modus vivendi with the General Assembly. In early 1971 he decided to work through the elected party leaders, with an informal coterie of personal friends advising him on floor strategy. In the senate he had nine key supporters: Lamar Plunkett, Hugh Carter, Al Holloway, Cy Chapman, Jack Henderson, Robert H. Smalley, Julian Webb, Paul Broun, and Bill Fincher. In the house he had even fewer supporters: Sidney Marcus and Peyton Hawes, Jr., Al Burruss, Sam Nunn, Carl Drury, and Bob Farrar. But as the story of his reorganization efforts has shown, he was fortunate to have the support of the leadership—Speaker George Smith and Majority Leader George Busbee. With these legislative friends Carter was in close communication. "They came to see me almost every day to help assess the situation in the General Assembly," he said. And he tried to make the best of his need to rely on a small group of followers: ". . . it gives me the backing of a wider group of people and at the same time I have the benefit of advice from a heterogeneous group."

More important, Carter signaled that he was willing to make legislative trades. During the last week of the 1971 session, for example, one senator asked the governor for aid on a piece of local legislation. Carter responded by asking the senator if he thought the gas tax, a measure Carter favored, would pass. When assured it would, Carter agreed to support the sentor's bill. As reporter Bill Shipp observed, "The Senator got the message."

In his various media blitzes and tours of the state, which started with the Goals for Georgia program in the summer of 1971 and ended in 1974 with his Operation Feedback tour, Carter tried to strengthen his hand in another way. If Carter could demonstrate that he was well liked, his programs popular, his prestige and influence over the legislature would be enhanced. In 1971 Carter suggested he might appeal to the public in yet another way. As his reorganization plan was being unveiled in December of that year, he told the press that he might go into the legislative districts in the next election; and though he wouldn't go so far as to tell the people how to vote, he thought it quite legitimate to tell the voters how the candidates stood on the issue of reorganization.

Carter used the carrot as well as the stick. In the fall of 1971 he threw a party for legislators at Jekyll Island. Though Carter had given standing orders against accepting gratuities, his staff let the Revenue Department know that they had difficulty providing liquor for the occasion. The Liquors Wholesale Trade Association came to the rescue, providing the necessary refreshments. By early 1972 Carter was wooing the legislators with breakfasts and dinners at the mansion. (On one occasion, the invitation to a series of legislative dinners requested "black tie"—an obvious reaction to criticism of an earlier affair at which the meal was served on paper plates. When one south Georgia legislator explained that he had not attended the first night's dinner—he was not going to put on one of "them monkey suits"—a quick assurance was forthcoming. Dark suits would be perfectly acceptable.)

At the beginning of 1972 session of the General Assembly, Carter backed at least one measure designed to increase his popularity with that body. On January 11, 1972, the second day of the new session, Carter's senate floor leaders, Al Holloway and Hugh Carter, introduced a resolution to propose to the Congress of the United States a constitutional amendment to prevent busing as a means of achieving racial integration in public schools. It read in part: "No student shall be assigned to nor compelled to attend any particular public school on account of race, religion, color, or national origin." (The idea for the amendment seems to have come from a letter Carter received in October, 1971, from a Michigan state senator. Jody Powell, on the routing sheet forwarding the letter to Carter, noted that such an amendment would be "most popular." He added: "I think we will need to do something like this next session.") On January 31 the resolution passed the Georgia Senate, 46 to 0, with ten senators not voting.* In February Carter urged the General Assembly to approve the resolution. On February 22 the resolution sailed through the House by a vote of 163 to 14.

Before the 1972 session opened, Carter had also made certain staff changes that he hoped would soothe his troubled relationship with the General Assembly. Frank Sutton was brought in to perform the legislative liaison duties that Jordan had handled. He talked to legislators daily. "The record," he said, "was when I talked to 15 one morning before 8 o'clock."

Carter used all the rewards Georgia governors traditionally have employed to woo legislators, including highway funds, administered by his friend Bert

---

* Among those not voting was Senator Leroy Johnson, who following the roll call vote on the resolution recorded an impassioned statement in the Senate *Journal*. "To oppose busing suggests a continuation of segregated schools. Our society can never again return to segregated education . . . this resolution is not deserving of the strides that we are attempting to make in Georgia."

Lance. In a May 26, 1972, "Personal and Confidential" memo, he asked Lance to see about the resurfacing of a road in Hugh Carter's district. "The portion of the road in Lee County is what Hugh is particularly interested in as that is where Hugh's opponent is living." Lance responded, in a note to Jordan: "Like Delta, ready when Hugh is. I will call him and discuss timing etc. Bert." Hugh Carter received some other help, too. In October, 1972, he announced that the governor had approved an emergency fund request for $42,691 to help pave an expanded parking area at the Americus and Sumter County Hospital. During that election year, $410,212 was spent in Sumter County, compared to $118,749 in preelection 1971, and the amount fell back to $101,964.50 in post-election 1973. And by 1974 funds were up again to $230,000.

The Governor's emergency fund provided $2 million annually to be used at his discretion. Once, when someone from a community college asked for funds to finance a chorus trip to Israel, Carter wrote: "The Governor's Emergency Fund is to be used as described for 'emergency situations' and it is necessary that we keep a sufficient sum available in the fund for emergencies such as civil disorders and disasters."

The definition of civil disorders and disasters apparently included favorite projects of legislators. Carter used the emergency fund mainly to build support for his legislative programs. He instructed his staff that emergency fund requests should be originated by state legislators. On such requests, Carter would note "ok;" "no;" or "np" (not possible). Even request for genuine emergencies were handled this way. Thus, Carter wrote a note on one staff memo recommending a grant to Berrien County (in supporter Bobby Rowan's district) where a school had been burned down, "Let him ask me." And as a rule, Carter wanted credit for these awards. After one transfer of $16,000 to the Department of Agriculture for the Georgia Agriculture Development Authority, Jordan wrote Ford Spinks and Duane Riner, indicating that the governor would like to have the award handled "for full political advantage for both him and Ford Spinks, particularly in the Tifton area."

On occasion the fund was offered without solicitation to help supporters who needed a political boost and to keep them in the Carter fold. In a memorandum of September 12, 1972, Hamilton Jordan recommended doing something for Bert Hamilton of Macon, who had to run for reelection in a recently reapportioned district. "As you know, Bert voted with us on everything during the last session and has never asked for anything. Al Holloway and Bobby Rowan are concerned as they understand Culver Kidd is trying to get close to Bert and is trying to help Bert in order to obligate him on the critical battles in the Senate." In an obvious attempt to beat Kidd to the draw, Jordan said, "I called Bert about a week ago and told him that we were anxious to have him back in the Senate and wanted to help him in his bid for reelection. In response to my call, Bert has mentioned several things that have merit and would be of help to him in his new district." Jordan recommended that $8,600 be transferred from the emergency fund for these projects. Carter gave his "ok."

One can get a feeling for the extent and the utility of this fund by looking at a short list of awards made from it in fiscal 1973. A few Carter opponents received grants, but the following amounts went into friends' districts:

| | | |
|---|---|---|
| Frank Eldridge | 7th District | $11,600 |
| Bobby Rowan | 8th District | $46,000 |
| Julian Webb | 11th District | $51,250 |
| Al Holloway | 12th District | $ 9,000 |
| Hugh Carter | 14th District | $28,245 |
| Bert Hamilton | 26th District | $33,600 |
| Jimmy Parker | 31st District | $50,000 |
| Max Cleveland | 55th District | $ 8,000 |
| Frank Sutton | 9th District | $22,532 |

Carter also used his appointive powers to win over General Assembly members. At the same time he recommended emergency monies for Senator Bert Hamilton, Jordan recommended that he be appointed to the State Crime Commission. Carter "ok'd" that suggestion. In 1974 Carter appointed several friends (and campaign contributors) to the General Assembly Fiscal Affairs Sub-Committee (Terrell Starr, Beverly Langford, Pierre Howard, Jr., Hugh Carter, and Ed Garrard). Ford Spinks, who had resigned from the senate in March, 1971, was appointed to the Public Service Commission (and was elected to the post in 1972). Lamar Plunkett was appointed to the Southern Regional Education Board of Control for 1973 and then in 1974 was placed on the State Board of Regents. And Julian Webb was appointed to the Court of Appeals in 1974.

But Carter also applied the stick to those who opposed him. When Hugh Gillis blocked one of Carter's appointments in the senate, Carter retaliated by not reappointing his brother, Jim Gillis, Jr., to the State Soil and Water Conservation Board. On another occasion, when Carter learned that Senator Roscoe Dean of Jessup would invoke "senatorial courtesy" to prevent senate approval of Carter's choice for the State Board of Regents (a resident of Jessup's district), Carter responded with a veiled threat: "I think he [Dean] is making a mistake, and I think any senator who supports him in this frivolous kind of opposition is making a mistake. Senator Dean is trying to prevent his own district's people from having long-awaited representation on the Board of Regents." And a few months later Carter criticized George Bagby, director of the Department of Natural Resources for praising Dean, who was then facing a tough legislative fight.

By the middle of his term Carter had evidently decided that the informal system of working through party leaders and his small coterie of supporters in each house was not working well. In November, 1972, he tried again to put his supporters in leadership positions in the senate. The battle was fought in the strategically powerful Senate Democratic Caucus. Twenty-one pro-Carter senators resigned from it, including chairman Bobby Rowan, reducing the caucus to twenty-seven members—two short of twenty-nine which constituted a majority of the senate. In Rowan's view this meant that the caucus could no longer exercise influence over senate Democrats. The senators who remained in the caucus decided, in a counter move, that they would continue to act as a majority caucus. (This test of strength was not simply between the Carter and Maddox forces. As Senator Leroy Johnson, who remained in the caucus, said, he was, "not Lester Maddox's man, not Jimmy Carter's man—the only man I am is Cleopatra Johnson's man, and she's my wife.")

When this move failed, several pro-Carter senators next made an abortive attempt to "reorganize" the senate and take away Maddox's power to assign senators to committees. At the opening of the 1973 session, Bobby Rowan and Frank Eldridge introduced a resolution that called for striking the existing rule on standing committees, substituting in its place a rule specifically designating senate officers and members of the standing committees. The proposed chairmen named in the substitute resolution read like a list of key Carter supporters. But in a 27 to 29 vote the resolution was voted down.

Carter also lost important support in the House. By the beginning of 1973 Carter's previously cordial relationship with Speaker Smith and Majority Leader Busbee had degenerated into open conflict. Smith, hearkening back to the budgetary powers the house had enjoyed under Governor Maddox, introduced his own appropriations bill. Smith's measure included a proposal to relieve local governments of two thirds of the cost of education, which would give county officials an opportunity to reduce property taxes. Carter had proposed a more complicated measure toward a similar end.

Whatever the relative merits of the two plans, Carter was not to take a loss without a fight. He revised his annual budget address to attack the house measure. The beneficiaries of the plan, he charged, would be "a few farm and timber magnates, corporations and ultilities, and landlords . . ." The reaction to the speech was "distinctively cool"—the legislators interrupted Carter with applause only once, and when he finished, the applause was "spiritless." When the house and senate began wrangling over their separate appropriations measures Carter threatened simply to veto the tax relief measure. In the end, a compromise was passed, which Carter signed.

Carter also failed to secure passage of the two consumer protection measures he placed before the General Assembly in 1973. One measure would criminalize deceptive practices and charge the state attorney general's office with the enforcement of the measure. The other proposal, referred to as the "credit code" law, would provide new rules on sales, leases, and loans, and provide for remedial action by the consumer against creditors.

The latter was introduced in the house, where it ran afoul of unenthusiastic legislators and the banking and merchants associations, who were joined in their lobbying efforts by Legal Aid attorneys from the other end of the political spectrum, who felt the maximum interest rates permitted would be too high for their clients. The bill fell two votes short of passing because its proponents were unable to rally all their supporters for the roll call vote. Eventually the house approved an amendment-ridden Unfair Trade Practices Act that required a consumer to prove willful intent to deceive or engage in unfair practices. In the senate the bill was tabled in committee.

During the regular 1974 session of the General Assembly, the tension at the state capitol reached a point where David Nordan of the Atlanta *Journal* saw the possibility of the worst rupture between the General Assembly and the governor in recent state history. As in 1973, the battle centered on the budget. Carter's proposed a decrease in expenditures for fiscal year 1975, based on his view that the energy crisis would cut consumer and industrial spending, and thus state revenues. Starting early, he warned the General Assembly against tampering with the budget, against promises of cost-of-living pay raises for state employees, and against further "tax relief."

But the General Assembly, with somewhat more optimistic revenue estimates proceeded to give state employees cost-of-living increases and approve a tax relief plan. Even more upsetting to Carter, the legislature had line-itemized almost the entire budget (appropriating money for a specific purpose rather than giving block allocations that would permit administrators to allocate funds within their departments as they saw fit). This was in retaliation for Richard Harden's use of block allocations to the Department of Human Resources to establish the area network system after appropriations for that system had been specifically struck by the General Assembly the previous year.

Carter had earlier tried to mend fences by saying that the members of the General Assembly were too often "maligned" by the press and "not given adequate credit" for what they did, but now he reacted vehemently to the line-item budget. A few legislative leaders are attempting to usurp the authority of the executive branch, he said. "I consider this to be a crucial question and I do not intent to yield . . ." In fact, he threatened the legislature with "an expensive and disruptive lawsuit" or an "equally expensive and distracting special session in the midst of an election year, or possibly both." Members of the legislature, however, were not overly concerned, and before the season was over, Carter had backed down. He finally conceded that he was willing to "make every effort and personal sacrifice to draw us back from this abyss." Shortly thereafter he met with House Speaker Murphy and Appropriations Committee Chairman "Sloppy" Floyd to work out a compromise. After that meeting Carter revised his revenue estimates upward, announced his support for a "well deserved" cost-of-living increase for state employees, including schoolteachers, university system employees, and the state patrol. Carter also vetoed the tax relief plan, taking the political flack away from the legislature. He signed the budget finally approved by the General Assembly, though with several amendatory vetoes. Though the funds were not as specifically appropriated as in the initial version, the 1975 budget had more line-item restrictions than ever before.

Carter had problems in other areas besides the budget. At the beginning of the session he had predicted major action on seven bills dealing with no-fault insurance, consumer protection, judicial reform, the energy crisis, and political ethics. While the legislature did enact proposals in several of these areas, only the judicial reform proposals—supported by the judiciary and the bar association as well as Carter—passed in much the form proposed.

The administration's consumer protection legislation failed to pass the General Assembly—Carter's greatest disappointment as governor, he was to later say. Carter would later explain his failure by saying his efforts had come too late in his term. Actually, it was more complicated than that. Carter had pushed and failed to secure legislation along these lines in 1972 and 1973. In January, 1974, he announced that he would submit another, more "refined" consumer protection bill to the legislature. The proposal had been drawn up by a special credit code commission appointed by Carter and headed by an attorney whose firm represented the Citizens and Southern Bank. Though the group worked closely with Carter's legal staff, its proposals had fatal weaknesses. They would have allowed small finance companies to set finance charges as high as 36 percent—a figure almost everybody found unpalatable. More important, the bill substantially raised the interest rates large banks could legally charge. The numbers were just too high—so the bill died in a senate committee. (A House bill was eventually passed but did nothing more, as Howell Raines noted, than create "another money-gobbling, patronage-producing state bureaucracy" that did "nothing to disturb the status quo.")

Carter also failed to get his ethics bill through the General Assembly. Drafted in cooperation with Attorney General Arthur Bolton, the bill would have required elected and appointed officials to reveal relationships with business and legal clients, listing any gifts or contributions of $25 or more. (Contributions exceeding $499 received within thirty days of a primary or general election were to be reported immediately by telegram to a five-member commission.) The bill also contained requirements for listing contributions in cumulative totals. (Thus, if a contributor gave three $24 contributions to get around the law, the candidate would have to report the contributions as a donation of $72.) The goal, Carter said, was to clamp down on state officials who frequently accepted "wining and dining" favors. Lester Maddox sentenced this and another tougher ethics bill (introduced by Bobby Rowan) to death by sending them to the Maddox-dominated EREG Committee. Then Maddox's forces pushed their own ethics bill through the senate—a loophole-ridden measure that Carter promptly labeled a "farce."

Meanwhile, House Majority Leader George Busbee, a master at legislative maneuvering, resurrected his own ethics bill, which had previously died in the EREG Committee. Invoking a seldom-used procedural rule, Busbee pushed his own bill through the House—which meant it would go directly to the senate floor for debate. Rowan and Carter, having little alternative, agreed to rally behind the Busbee bill. In one final effort to block it, however, Maddox's people amended the bill, hoping to make it unacceptable to its supporters in the house. (One of their amendments provided for a five-man ethics commission, giving it broad and ill-defined powers. Another extended the bill's coverage to county and city officials—the assumption being that house members would not wish to regulate hometown office holders.) Just before the gavel fell to end the session, however, the house passed the ethics bill, with these Maddox amendments, 102 to 0.

Carter put the best face he could on the measure. "There are no major defects in this bill," he said at the signing ceremony on March 5, 1974. "As far as the campaign this year, it will be as far-reaching a disclosure bill as exists anywhere in the nation."

It is true that the law did set a higher, more realistic figure for reported contributions than Carter had proposed. But the bill had serious defects, both in comparison to the 1974 national law and Carter's own proposals. It failed to provide a mechanism for the prompt reporting of large contributions received after the last preelection reporting date. It did not require contributors to list any information other than their name and mailing address, making it difficult to identify special-interest contributions. Even more important (here it did not differ from Carter's original bill) was the absence of a provision for tracking campaign loans and contributions made after the election—an old Georgia practice whereby an officeholder could square campaign debts or pay off loans without disclosing the source of the funds used. Even the constitutionality of the new law was in doubt. Eventually the Georgia Supreme Court, on June 29, 1974, struck down the provision for establishing a state ethics commission, saying its powers were too vaguely described in the bill, and exempted county and city officials from the law. The court did not, however, declare the entire act unconstitutional.

In addition to these defeats the General Assembly overrode Carter's vetoes of an act allowing nonprofit organizations to sponsor bingo and of a measure to provide tax relief for the elderly in some counties (a measure Carter said was unconstitutional, because it lacked uniform statewide application).

Nearing the end of the session, Carter almost lost on another matter of considerable concern to him. Early in his term Carter had supported building a dam on the Flint River at Spewrell Bluff. By 1973 it had been approved and signed by the President. But by 1973 Carter says he had been convinced that the Army Corps of Engineers had exaggerated the benefits and underestimated the cost of the project. He vetoed the project. (Tourist facilities at other nearby lakes, including one federally financed lake just twenty-six miles from the Spewrell Bluff site, were "going bankrupt" because of inadequate usage, he said. State surveys showed that free-flowing streams, not more lakes, would best meet recreational needs.) When proponents of the dam took the matter before the General Assembly, Carter called out the troops. He had various groups help him in his lobbying efforts in the General Assembly and personally researched and prepared a comprehensive statement criticizing the U.S. Army Corps of Engineers.

But he almost blew it. At a press conference on February 14, he blasted the legislative leaders: "Because of poor leadership, including some of which is my own responsibility, this will probably go down in history as the most non-productive of all General Assembly sessions." These remarks set off a reaction in both chambers, infuriating even Carter's own house floor leader, Denmark Groover: "I indeed am revolted by the statement. . . . To the extent that I may be associated with the executive branch, I apologize to the membership for the criticism in any respect that it might imply lack of leadership and of lack of ability in the House."

There was an immediate reaction on the house floor. The house debate on the resolution urging the construction of the Spewrell Bluff dam had opened with some good-natured antics—bird calls filled the chamber as some representatives ribbed the environmentalists who had been fighting the project. Representative Claude Bray quipped that Meriwether County, where the reservoir created by the dam would be located, was so economically depressed that "with $500.00 you could start a period of inflation." But the debate became acrimonious, Celestine Sibley noted in the Atlanta *Constitution,* "as speakers began to mention the man on the second floor [the governor]." The final vote, passing the resolution 96 to 43, was a "quick retaliatory gesture" motivated by Carter's blast on the General Assembly.

Both sides now mobilized their forces for the senate fight. On February 26, the resolution was defeated—by only two votes. In the showdown, Carter's own floor leader and long-time political ally, Al Holloway, voted for the resolution—as did three other long-time supporters: Bob Smalley, Bobby Rowan, and Frank Sutton. (The break with Holloway was never fully mended. He was to recall the episode during the 1976 spring primaries, sharply noting Carter's political style, how Carter would often tell some people he would do something for them and never would, and how he told others he would do something to them and never did.)

Carter, on March 3, 1974, blamed the adverse vote in the house on the lobbyists and claimed that his victory in the senate came "in spite of intense lobbying efforts by some elected officials, military and Defense Department officers and administrators, land developers and other pressure groups . . ."

Despite his problems, Carter projected himself as a successful legislative leader. He told some reporters in early 1974 that he had had almost a 100 percent rate of success with the General Assembly: "Look at the record. Look at the proposals we've made. Look at my campaign platform. And look at the results obtained from the legislature. In every instance the legislature has carried out what I promised the Georgia people. I've been vigorous and very determined to bring about very controversial changes in the state's government and the legislature has approved them."

As this account suggests, Carter used the traditional weapons of power—patronage appointments, dispersal of discretionary funds, attempts to maneuver his supporters into key legislative posts.

His problems were more subtle. Carter tended to move out strongly on projects without having first explored the political terrain to assess the opposition. And when he discovered that he did not have the necessary support, he would be compelled to back down in public, with a consequent loss of personal and public prestige. His compromises came late in the game after damage had been done to his own political reputation and his relationship with politically powerful others. Moreover, Carter let himself get pulled into several ego-bruising exchanges with those who opposed him—even those on whom he would have to depend in the future. He seemed to experience opposition as a personal affront and as a consequence responded to it with attacks on the integrity of those who blocked his projects. He showed a tendency (which will become even clearer as other facets of his career are explored) to equate his political goals with the just and the right and to view his opponents as representative of some selfish or immoral interest.

## Other Battles

Carter's fights with legislative leaders extended beyond the halls of the General Assembly. There was the "parole mill" controversy, for example, which won considerable press attention off and on during 1972 and 1973. Carter had charged that certain "unscrupulous attorneys" in a dozen or so firms in the Atlanta area were charging prison inmates exorbitant fees to represent them before the Parole and Pardons Board. When the Georgia Bureau of Investigation subsequently zeroed in on two Atlanta attorneys, one an associate of Senator Leroy Johnson, Johnson exploded. The entire parole investigation is a political hatchet job, he said—Carter was after him because he had supported Sam Nunn instead of Carter's man for the U.S. Senate. Carter, however, persisted. There was a good chance that disbarment and possibly criminal prosecution would result from the investigation, he said, and many attorneys have been scrambling to obtain supportive affidavits from prisoners they had represented. The general counsel for the state bar of Georgia, however, a former superior court judge, Omer Franklin, said that the investigation was still in the early phases and most of the evidence so far was hearsay.

The next summer Carter said he had reports that Culver Kidd had "interceded on behalf of several prisoners who are prospective parolees and I don't know what his motivations are. He isn't an attorney certainly." Two months later, when House Speaker Tom Murphy charged that the parole board was not granting paroles to eligible inmates (ostensibly for fear of an attack by Carter), Carter took out after Murphy. Murphy, he said, had a history of going before the board with statements that were inflammatory, ill advised, and inaccurate, and had used the power of his office to pressure the board to release at least one prisoner. Murphy called Carter a "liar." Georgia would be in better shape if "the governor would spend more time working here looking after the state instead of running all over the country" in pursuit of support for his presidential ambitions. After the exchange with Murphy, the controversy simmered down and nothing more came of it.

Carter also went after Lester Maddox in the summer of 1973, informing the press that Maddox had used state aircraft seventy-eight times in a recent ninety-day period. As governor, Carter said, he wanted to limit the overuse of state aircraft by state officials for personal precampaign politicking. Maddox admitted that the figures released by Carter might be correct, but he called Carter "a liar and a hypocrite." And he leveled some charges of his own, saying that Carter had flown "his family and friends all over the state," and had even sent a plane to Jekyll Island to pick up a set of golf clubs. (A Carter spokesman gave assurances the latter charge was untrue.) Later that month Carter released a memo that announced a crackdown on use of state-owned aircraft. The "wing clipping" was interpreted by Prentice Palmer in the Atlanta *Journal* as a veiled attack on Maddox.

Not only with old-style politicians did Carter get into these kinds of exchanges, but also with leaders of various professional or other interest groups in the state who questioned or opposed him. In May, 1972, Dean Mary Louise McBee of the University of Georgia, having failed in her private efforts to get the governor to appoint or reappoint the members of the Commission of the Status on Women (established by Governor Sanders in 1966), publicly raised some questions about the governor's failure. Carter countered that the group's inactivity was their fault. The commission was an "honorary thing," he said. "One hundred and twenty-five women had a certificate they could hang on the wall." Having a commission on the status of women is "like having a commission on the status of men or on the status of blacks or the status of Jews." But, he added, "I'd like to see it activated perhaps to the point where it would look for and report instances of discrimination. . . . Any woman who points out to any actions or lack of action in my administration, I'll take care of that immediately."

When some members took exception to these remarks, pointing out the commission's efforts on legislation, Carter retorted that he was not looking for a verbal battle with the group. But he insisted the commission after the "first flush of enthusiasm" had become "ineffective," and contrasted it with "54 other women's groups in the state," which had aided him in appointing an "unprecedented" number of women to state boards and agencies. (Carter shortly thereafter did reactivate the commission, though he reduced its size.

Carter's handling of criticism from the Georgia Association of Educators (GAE) was similar. In early 1973 the annual convention of the Georgia Association of Classroom Teachers (a GAE affiliate) unanimously called for a proposed 5.5 percent pay increase, which Carter was then opposing (because of a national freeze on salaries). Then the Georgia Association of Educators charged that Carter had forgotten Georgia education in the proposed budget—ignoring the need for salary increases, lower student-teacher ratios, sick leave, and medical insurance.

At a hastily called press conference, Carter said: "I feel this should be the year for the school child, and apparently the GAE feels this should be another year for the teacher." He had never known the GAE to "come to the state capitol to see me or anyone else and ask for improved programs for children." At the end of March, Carter voiced similar views at a GAE conference, to a cool response from the convention and a more volatile reaction from Mrs. Reba Lucy: "He's giving us a good ---- and everyone is sitting there like a bunch of dummies. I went to school with him and I swear, he's a bigger S.O.B. than I thought he was." Still Carter did not let up. In a subsequent speech at a national education conference, he noted that the education system was turning American children into "little more than educational anemics. They sit at the educational tables and eat everything that is on their plates, but they still end up hungry for the knowledge needed to prepare them for productive and happy lives." In his 1975 budget, as we have seen, Carter had no provision for a salary increase for teachers (or any other state officials), but later in the year, under pressure from the house leader, he backed away and came out for an increase.

Though Carter generally kept the initiative in these exchanges, and at least appeared to be on the right side, he did find his own conduct questioned on occasion. For example, Bobby Pafford, elected to the Public Service Commission in 1970 (described by Neal Pierce as a "stormy south Georgia politician," and a champion of consumers over the utilities), charged in 1971 that David Gambrell had bought his appointment to the Senate and called on Carter to reveal the amount of a 1970 bank loan purportedly cosigned by Gambrell. When Carter asked Pafford to let him know "in writing, what accusations you actually made against me," Pafford responded that the newspaper accounts of his charges were accurate: "What I tried to share with the people of this state was my concern with people of extraordinary wealth attempting through their sons to dominate our political system . . . I further stated that regardless of who became governor—you or former Governor Carl Sanders—that Georgia was destined to have the son of a millionaire in the United States Senate."*

Late in 1973 Carter experienced a more serious assault—this time over his "piggybacking" of political questions on a poll about the proposed Interstate 485. Anticipating the blowup, Carter said that every poll he had ever been associated with in his political life has been piggybacked. He had learned that Charles Kirbo was planning a political poll after he, Carter, had decided to conduct one on I-485. The joint poll had saved the state $4,500. It would be improper for him to reveal the exact political questions asked, however—the political questions had been paid for by the party.

On December 5 the political part of the poll was published in the Atlanta

---

* In October 1971, Carter suggested that Pafford was using his office for his own political advantage: "I think it is apparent that Bobby is running for some sort of office. He is making speeches around the state that don't relate to his own job. I think it is a little bit early for him to do that having just been elected and to be running for another job." Any public official, he said, "major or minor," should resign before waging a campaign for the Senate. Pafford retorted that he would not be "gagged" by Jimmy Carter: "I bitterly resent Governor Carter's suggestion that I should limit the topics about which I make statements or else resign my office as public service commissioner."

*Journal.* There were nineteen questions relating to I-485 and thirty-four political questions, some clearly designed to test Carter's popularity. "Now, how would you rate the job that Jimmy Carter is doing as governor: excellent, good, not so good or poor?" Other political questions were designed to determine Bert Lance's popularity *vis-à-vis* other announced and potential gubernatorial candidates.

Reacting to this, House Majority Leader George Busbee, who was a gubernatorial candidate, said he was "utterly shocked and dismayed to learn that Governor Carter had authorized $5,500 for an I-485 poll and then turned around and piggybacked it and spent $3,000 of the Democratic Party's money—all in secret." State Republican Chairman Bob Shaw charged that the governor had "cheated the people of Georgia for his political advantage" and he wrote the presiding officers of the senate and house, asking for a joint investigation. Carter would eventually admit that this poll was "obviously a political mistake."

Given such contretemps, Carter's political base in the state had deteriorated by 1974 to the point that most statewide politicians preferred not to be closely associated with him. In the scramble for the governorship that year, the candidates, rather than vying for his endorsement, tried to avoid any identification with him. When a newspaper editor in Fitzgerald asked candidate David Gambrell if he was being supported by Governor Carter, Gambrell smiled and said, "No, he's supporting another candidate." George T. Smith, another gubernatorial hopeful, charged that fellow candidate Bert Lance would "simply hold the governor's office for Carter while Carter seeks national office." Candidate George Busbee, too, hit hard on the Carter-Lance connection. On July 3, 1974, the day after Carter announced that he would undertake a feedback tour of the state, Busbee blasted the governor in public: "You don't have to have tea leaves to read or peanut shells to see that Carter is trying to Jimmy his way into the governor's office for the next four years." In a private letter to Carter he wrote: "That choice of a successor is still reserved to the people of Georgia just as it was four years ago when you were elected." Reminding Carter of a conversation they had had earlier that year, when Carter had pledged he would not use his office to help Lance, Busbee continued: "I regret to say that I review your announced tour as a breach of that personal commitment." Indeed, as David Nordan reflected on the primary campaign: "Saddest of all is former State Highway Commissioner Bert Lance of Calhoun, who had hoped in his bid for the governor's office to convince Georgians that he was not allied with Carter."

Though he ran a strong third in the subsequent Democratic primary, behind Lester Maddox and George Busbee, Bert Lance failed to make the runoff. His defeat was attributed to several factors, including his personal wealth ($3.1 million) and his close ties to Carter.

Carter, in short, was very much a politician. Though he had gained office as an outsider, he quickly capitalized on his advantages as an insider, using all the traditional rewards and punishments at his disposal. And though he had run as a populist, and occasionally resorted to populist themes while in office, he enjoyed a close relationship with most of the major financial and industrial interests in the state. Further, he had a facility for shaping and reshaping alliances to fit each phase of his political career.

But Carter differed from many politicians in other ways. The "above politics" rhetoric covered his political side—hiding his maneuvering as well as his skills. He did not always do his political homework before taking public stands. He had fragile relationships with many powerful politicians in the state. His very flexibility was a handicap at times—when he went against certain tacit rules that govern the relationships among politicians. He may have switched friendships and positions a little too fast, been a bit too facile in accepting the support of persons he would quickly forget. In attacking competitors whose behavior was not noticeably different from his own and in questioning the integrity of those who opposed his plans, he created enmity that could rise to haunt him later. Potential problems would be contained, however, as long as he won new political victories. And with his skills at using symbols, Carter would obtain one of the great triumphs in American electoral history.

# ELEVEN

---

# Aiming High

I‍T IS NOT QUITE CLEAR WHEN Jimmy Carter began thinking of running for President of the United States. When Charles Kirbo saw Carter campaigning in 1966, he "began to wonder" about Carter's presidential potential. And shortly after the 1970 election Frank Moore drafted a congratulatory message suggesting that Carter's sights would soon expand from Georgia to the South and beyond. Shortly after the 1970 inaugural his pollster, Bill Hamilton, sensing his interest in acting as a broker in national politics, suggested periodic statewide political polls: "A side effect of any survey would give you data on the presidential contest. I know you are playing a role in this whole selection process of a candidate. Data from a Georgia survey could provide you with some leverage with the Democratic hopefuls in terms of what they must do in order to win the South."

When presidential aspirants visited the governor's mansion in 1971 and 1972, Carter's family measured him against the others. As Rosalynn Carter said: "We—my boys and I—decided that Jimmy knew a lot more about a lot of things than did these men who were running for president." Carter, too, began to feel he could measure up: "Before becoming governor I had never met a president, although I once saw Harry Truman at a distance . . ." (A friend recalls that he also saw Lyndon Johnson in a parade in Atlanta one time.) "Then during 1971 and 1972 I met Richard Nixon, Spiro Agnew, George McGovern, Henry Jackson, Hubert Humphrey, Ed Muskie, George Wallace, Ronald Reagan, Nelson Rockefeller, and other presidential hopefuls, and I lost my feeling of awe about presidents." Carter recalls that he came to the "slow realization . . . that I was equal to them—not better than anybody else—but equal to them."

## New South

Carter had attracted considerable national attention with his call for racial justice in his inaugural address. The Washington *Post* and *Life* saw him as a representative of the "New South." His face was on the cover of *Time* magazine in May 1971—a Confederate flag behind him and a caption "Dixie Whistles a Different Tune." His appointment of David Gambrell to fill the unexpired Senate term of Richard Russell less than a month after his inauguration was hailed by *Newsweek* as another sign that "a new day" had arrived in Georgia.

Actually Carter's New South was and has been exaggerated in national accounts—perhaps a reflection of the Northern caricature of the South and a tendency to focus on the more colorful demagogue, forgetting the many moderate, responsible political leaders from that region. Several governors of similar stripe to Carter's had been elected in the South in 1970—Linwood Holton of Virginia, John West of South Carolina, Reubin Askew of Florida, and Dale Bumpers of Arkansas. Even earlier, in 1966, Senator Herman Talmadge, called a "bellwether for Southern politicians" by a friend, had told a group at the predominantly black Hungry Club of Atlanta that he would appoint blacks to high office if he were governor again. He said that "in future races, all candidates are going to solicit the votes of all Georgia citizens." Carter himself did not risk alienating traditionalists by pushing too hard on the New South theme.

Shortly after his inauguration, when Lieutenant William Calley, a Georgia native, had been convicted of violating the Army Rules of Land Warfare, several conservative groups in Georgia, including the VFW, urged Carter to declare a William Calley Day. Carter hedged. At an April 4 press conference he said that Calley had been made a "scapegoat," that his conviction put every young man sent to Vietnam "in a very doubtful position," and predicted that it would "seriously demoralize our troops." But he did not declare a William Calley Day, proclaiming instead an "American Fighting Men's Day," and asking all Georgians to fly the flag and drive with their headlights on. He could later say, without contradicting his earlier statements: "I never thought Calley was anything but guilty. I never felt any attitude toward Calley except abhorrence. And I thought he should be punished and still do. I never expressed any contrary opinion."

Nor did he take exposed positions on matters of race. Early in his term, according to the Atlanta *Constitution*, Carter told a Muskie aide that Muskie should not join other liberal Democratic Senators in backing a campaign fundraising dinner for Charles Evers, the black mayor of Fayette, Mississippi. Carter purportedly said: "If he joins sponsors of that dinner he can forget about Georgia." Carter also took an early and highly visible lead in the antibusing movement. In May, 1971, after the Supreme Court upheld the constitutionality of busing for the purpose of school integration, Carter resorted to an old theme: "I'm tired of being singled out, just because I'm a Southerner, for special rulings by the Supreme Court and federal courts, and special laws passed by Congress and special directives of the present attorney general. I think it's time for Georgia people to be treated on an equal basis with all other Americans." At the National Governors' Conference in Puerto Rico in September, 1971, Carter and Governor Winfield Dunn, Republican of Tennessee, presented an antibusing resolution that caught even Governor Wallace by surprise. And a few weeks later at the Southern Governors' Conference in Atlanta, Carter pushed another antibusing resolution—while speaking of the South as an "equal partner" with other regions of the country. Most important, in February, 1972, he urged the General Assembly of Georgia to pass a resolution calling for a constitutional convention to consider an antibusing amendment. And if this was not forthcoming, he said he would support a one-day statewide school boycott in protest (though he withdrew his support when he learned that the boycott would require an additional day of school to meet state legal requirements). Later that month he tried to form a coalition of Southern governors whose aim would be to force potential national candidates into antibusing stands; no candidate, he stated, would stand a chance of being elected in 1972 unless he opposed busing.

Among those governors Carter contacted on behalf of the proposed coalition was George Wallace of Alabama, with whom Carter had been building a friendship since his 1970 gubernatorial race. At his first meeting with Southern Democratic governors in Dothan, Alabama, in May, 1971, Carter hailed Wallace as "an internationally known figure," and noted that he and Wallace "share leadership of the same kinds of people." (As he wrote one constituent: "I have never had anything but the highest praise for Governor Wallace . . . I think you will find that . . . George Wallace and I are in agreement on most issues.") In August, 1971, Carter suggested that the best way to defeat Nixon in 1972 would be for Wallace to enter the presidential race (though he hedged—offering him no specific "encouragement" to run, as Carter would later point out). He would be interested in any candidate who would pledge that the South "will not be discriminated against." And a few weeks after Wallace was shot at a Maryland shopping center, at an "appreciation" day for him at Red Level, Alabama, Carter recognized Wallace "as an important figure in the national Democratic party." As the 1972 Democratic convention drew near, Carter expressed the opinion that McGovern and Humphrey were premature in their refusal to accept the Alabama governor as a running mate. A ticket that included a liberal like Humphrey and Wallace would win in the South, he said, and possibly across the country as well.

Yet Carter stopped short of full and direct support for Wallace, either as a presidential or vice-presidential candidate. Indeed, in the fall of 1971 he noted that any one of the new breed of Southern governors—Reubin Askew, John West, Dale Bumpers, or Jimmy Carter—could head off Wallace on the one hand, the GOP on the other, and restore the South to a strong position in the Democratic Party. The leading presidential candidates in the South, he said, were Senators Jackson and Muskie—though Muskie would have to stop attacking FBI Director J. Edgar Hoover and going out on the road to meet antiwar demonstrators. He responded sharply to a report in the Sunday Atlanta *Journal-Constitution* in January, 1972, that a "high official" of the Democratic National Committee thought that "Georgia may be taking herself too seriously as a state ripe for Democratic pickings, . . ." that the battle in the Deep South in 1972, at least, would have to be left to Wallace and Nixon. In a sharp letter to Lawrence O'Brien, chairman of the Democratic National Committee, Carter said: "If you feel this way, you have certainly misled me in my assurances of bringing the deep south states and their people back into the Democratic voting ranks." (O'Brien responded that he was appalled by the suggestion that he had misled Carter. He was interested in being the chairman of a truly national party, in which the South has a rightful place.)

The one candidate Carter clearly did not support was George McGovern. After an Atlanta meeting with McGovern in March, 1971, Carter had found McGovern a little too "dovish" for the average Georgian. And at the Democratic Governors' Conference in Omaha in June, 1971, he offered a resolution that opposed making the Vietnam war a campaign issue. (He obtained unanimous support for a watered down version of it.) Early in 1972, as McGovern emerged as the front runner, Carter joined in a stop-McGovern movement, though the leadership was in the hands of Senator "Scoop" Jackson, labor leaders, and certain Northern politicians. Carter wrote several of the other Southern governors to enlist them in the cause. News of Carter's involvement in the ABM (Anyone But McGovern) movement was leaked to the press. And in June the Atlanta *Constitution* quoted him as saying he feared McGovern and Humphrey would ignore the South in the forthcoming presidential campaign, and that McGovern was a radical on some issues.

At the National Democratic Governors' Conference in Houston, which met just before the Democratic National Convention, Carter received some private assurances from governors he had written to, but little open support for the stop-McGovern movement. So he backed off to a "unity" position. He served as chair of a four-man committee whose objective was to persuade various Democrats to withdraw the flood of challenges to delegates not allied with McGovern. He met with McGovern and secured what he thought was a commitment to oppose any special requirements or enforcements of the Voting Rights Act of 1965 that would single out the South. And on June 9 he appeared before the Democratic Platform Committee to suggest that the four leading contenders for the nomination—Muskie, Humphrey, McGovern, and Wallace—"combine their efforts and seek out a common platform on which each of the four and all four could stand with a maximum degree of compatibility."

## . . . And Beyond

Despite his endeavors, Carter was not yet a political mover and shaker. Lacking strong established ties with the national leaders and the unions, he was not a central leader of the ABM movement (Theodore White does not mention Carter in his discussion of the movement in his book on the 1972 campaign). At the convention, Carter could not "deliver" the Georgia delegation,* in fact, he himself barely made it to the convention—narrowly defeating two college stu-

* As governor, Carter had secured passage of a law in Georgia requiring convention delegates to be chosen in district party conventions rather than by the governor.

dents and a candidate committed to Wallace in the district party conventions. Given the independence of several members of the Georgia delegation, he decided not to act as its head—though he portrayed his decision as a preference to free himself of responsibilities at the convention so he could work on other things. He did gain some leverage, however, by remaining uncommitted until the convention opened. To do this, he had to detach himself from Wallace's candidacy and, according to Wallace, from a commitment he had made earlier that spring. (Wallace said he had agreed not to run delegates in opposition to Carter delegates in the Georgia conventions in exchange for Carter's promise to support Wallace if Wallace came to the convention with 300 or more committed delegates. Carter denies this.) What is clear is that Wallace, on June 21, sent Carter a wire asking him to "urge the uncommitted delegates in your delegation to unite with us." And Carter responded on June 26 that he intended to remain uncommitted.

By the time the Democratic convention opened in Miami in July, Humphrey and Muskie had dropped out of the race. Only Wallace and Jackson (who had earlier dropped out of the primary contests) remained in the field as alternatives to McGovern. On July 11 Carter joined the Jackson camp—saying he wanted to support a candidate who would be a unifying force. The next evening at approximately 10:00 P.M., Carter went to the podium to make the nominating speech. He was clearly nervous, licking his lips, his face tight as the delegates ignored his presentation.

The text, linking "Scoop" Jackson to John Kennedy—and to Jimmy Carter—suggests Carter might have had other things in mind. The first third of the speech dealt with the plight of the country in 1960 and how the Democratic Party had earned the trust of the American people. It ended with a reference to Carter's mother. "Inspired by this leadership and challenge, for instance, my own mother joined the Peace Corps a few years later. Returning from her service in India to this country at the age of 70. We earned the trust and the confidence of the American people in 1960 by nominating a man of compassion and courage. That man was John Fitzgerald Kennedy."

Carter then turned to Jackson.

I come tonight to nominate a man for president who shared the responsibilities and the glory of that victorious year and of those next 1000 days. I first met this good friend Senator Henry Jackson when I served under Admiral Rickover as a nuclear submarine officer. As a young congressman, Senator Jackson shared my belief that there was a more noble purpose for atomic power than a bomb to kill people. He wanted to generate electricity, to propel ships and to prevent a nuclear war. . . .

Carter spoke of Jackson's commitment to social justice, his commitment to a strong government, controlled by the people themselves, and his commitment to "provide whatever resources are required to keep our nation the strongest in the world." Carter concluded with another strong and long recollection of John Kennedy.

protect state and local Democratic candidates in the face of strong opposition to the McGovern ticket (shortly thereafter, at the Southern Governors' Conference at Hilton Head Island, South Carolina, Carter nominated Wallace to be vice-chairman of the conference, which would automatically place him in line for chairmanship at the next annual meeting). The attitude of Carter and his people is evident in their response to Eleanor McGovern's telegram to Rosalynn Carter asking her to submit a family photo as a part of a campaign effort called "First Families for McGovern." The letter was turned over to Carter's office for handling. Jody Powell scribbled a notation: "I think we are out of family pictures. I can get some of Lester and Virginia [Maddox] though."

By the end of November, Jordan had written a long confidential memorandum that was to provide the outline for Carter's activities in the next four years. Jordan made his own suggestions, incorporated materials from Bourne's earlier memo, took some ideas from a paper in which Rafshoon had shown how Carter's "negatives could be turned into positives"—and came up with a brilliant plan of battle. Armed with this plan, Jordan went to see the governor, who was vacationing (at the Cabin Bluff Lodge) on the Georgia coast for Thanksgiving. The blueprint prescribed a course of study for Carter: he was to read the major national newspapers every day, bone up on foreign affairs, defense, and economic matters, and study previous presidential elections. Task forces would be assembled to advise him on various issues. He was to expand his contacts in Washington and cultivate the "fat cats" and the "Eastern Establishment" press (eighteen journalists were named). Strategies for dealing with Wallace, Jackson, and Ted Kennedy were outlined. An electoral strategy was set forth: running in only selected state primaries; emphasizing a good early showing in New Hampshire and Florida. There were other suggestions about style and rhetoric. Carter was to "cultivate his Kennedy smile" and emphasize his personal qualities—his competence, honesty—and his "anti-establishment ties." Generally, he was advised to run against Washington.

It was considered important that Carter not tip his hand for some time. To cover his many activities, Jordan suggested that he pretend to be running for the Senate (after first reassuring Georgia Senators Talmadge and Nunn that he was not). This would enable him to comment on governmental and domestic issues without frightening people who would think him crazy to try for the presidency. He should also seek a position from the chairman of the Democratic National Committee (DNC) so that he could travel around the country without his own political intent surfacing.

By December, 1972, the battle plan was set and Carter had told his staff, his immediate family, and a small group of long-time political confidants and supporters that he would make the run. With his political allies, those who traditionally met for Sunday night suppers at the mansion, he began to explore the means. Initially the group included Philip Alston, Charles Kirbo, William Gunter, and Robert Lipshutz. By 1974 these meetings had become regular strategy sessions and had expanded in membership to include Elke Cushman (Alston's daughter), Jack Watson, Barbara Blum, Dot and Dave Padgett, Landon Butler, Greg Schneider, and John Pope—as well as Jordan, Powell, and Rafshoon.

Carter began to prepare himself for the campaign, following in most respects the guidelines laid down in the Jordan memo. He read books on national and international issues and the presidency, paying special attention to David Barber's *The Presidential Character*, which Bert Lance had called to his attention. (As his sister Ruth was to recall, he studied the book and tried to improve himself by developing the "positive-active" traits that the good Presidents had shown.) He also studied geography—the family bought a jigsaw puzzle of the United States so they would know where each state was.

In March, 1973, he also obtained the position he desired with the Democratic National Committee. (The recently installed chairman, Robert Strauss, on a visit to Atlanta, was invited to the governor's mansion. There, with Kirbo in attendance, Carter told Strauss that he was interested in helping the party with the 1974 elections. Carter had strongly supported Strauss in his recent effort to replace Jean Westwood as head of the party. So even though Strauss had already hired Terry Sanford, the former governor of North Carolina, to head the 1974 congressional and gubernatorial campaigns, he agreed to make Carter cochairman of the Committee to Elect Democrats in 1974, and to put Hamilton Jordan on the DNC payroll.) Shortly thereafter Jordan went to Washington to assume a position as executive director of the campaign division (where he worked with Robert Keefe, who had been a key figure in the Anybody But McGovern movement at Miami). In that job Jordan traveled around the country holding campaign workshops for Democratic candidates and meeting potential Carter campaign workers. Bill Hamilton was to conduct polls for the DNC and even Jody Powell traveled to help various campaigns.

Carter himself "took off as if he were being chased," according to Jody Powell. By August, 1973, as he wrote Senator Walter Mondale, he had met with Democratic leaders in thirty-nine states. And he tried to keep his potential opponents off the trail. As he wrote Mondale: "Most of these meetings have produced the hope that major leaders of our party like you, Kennedy, Jackson, etc., will help me to concentrate effort and attention on 1974, and forego to the maximum extent possible any preoccupation with 1976 until November of next year [1974]." Yet Carter himself met with the leaders of numerous groups normally affiliated with the Democratic Party—"labor unions, farmers, Spanish-Americans, teachers, environmentalists, women, local officials, retired persons, government workers, blacks and the House and Senate campaign committees." He even campaigned for a non-Democrat, Henry Howell, who had bolted from the Virginia Democratic Party to run for governor as an independent. (Carter's staff was extremely discreet about Virginia—the schedule given reporters omitted mention of his two visits there in November of 1973.)

Carter had already been pursuing the "fat cats" and "Eastern Establishment," as Jordan called them. Shortly after coming into office in 1971 he had initiated contacts with David Rockefeller, calling him to say that Georgia sold a lot of bonds in the Northeast, and he would like to meet with him and other bankers in New York sometime. In November, 1971, he flew to New York City with several other Georgians to meet with Rockefeller and other financial leaders. Phil Alston also went to work for him, writing Carter in January, 1974, that he had "plowed some ground in New York and it looks as though you will have the opportunity to meet some interesting people there. Why not give me several dates which might involve going up to the Big City a night before, having lunch and dinner with two separate groups, and perhaps staying a second night if this can be done to advantage."

While Jordan, Powell, and Carter were making contact with political and economic elites, three other people were laying the groundwork for Carter in liberal circles. Andrew Young, who had become a member of Carter's inner circle by 1973, began putting in a good word for Carter in his many speeches to black groups and other religious, civil rights, and liberal organizations throughout the nation. In Washington, Peter Bourne (who had in September, 1972, joined the Nixon White House as assistant director of the Special Action Office for Drug Abuse Prevention) and his new wife, Mary King (who had her own advertising agency), were key figures. An attractive and poised couple, Bourne and King had good connections and liberal credentials (he helped organize the Vietnam Veterans Against the War after serving with the Green Berets in Vietnam as a psychiatrist, while she had been an antiwar activist). They were in a good position to sell Carter to the Georgetown set and various liberals around town.

### Speaking Out

To make himself a viable candidate for the presidency, Carter had to win a reputation as a recognized spokesman on major national issues. In February, 1973, Jody Powell had suggested a possible approach: "We have spent so much time and effort fighting our often superfluous intramural ideological battles that we forgot the real purpose of a political party—putting together a winning coalition." To this end he suggested that Carter shift his emphasis from social programs, which might get him into trouble, to less controversial subjects such as fiscal responsibility. Carter should also find something new: "We need an issue on which you can speak with some authority and from a position of personal knowledge and concern, I believe the Democratic Party and its future fits the bill almost perfectly." Powell concluded by pointing out the advantage of joining this approach with "good populist" issues. "We can use this theme as a platform to take off on general comments about crime, drugs, busing, tax reform, welfare reform and governmental waste—and can get away for a while with merely pointing out that these problems are real and worthy of consideration without having to propose any specific solutions."

To a great extent Carter followed this advice in his subsequent campaign. His first pitch as a Democratic leader was against President Nixon. In January,

1973, shortly before departing from Georgia to attend Richard Nixon's second inauguration, Carter called Nixon the "poorest President" in United States history. In February he made a special trip to the nation's capital and, in remarks before the National Press Club, accused the President of perpetrating a "cruel hoax" on the American people with his revenue-sharing plan. He accused him of running a government by "crisis and surprise." Final decisions, he added, were made by "the Ehrlichmans, the Haldemans, and the Ashes. I don't know them and I have no access to them."

After this trip Carter complained at an Atlanta press conference that he had sought an appointment with John Ehrlichman and never even received a response from his aides. A Georgia Republican then arranged a meeting for him with Kenneth Cole, the new head of Nixon's Domestic Council. In a subsequent trip to Washington, Carter went to Cole's office, where he was greeted not by Cole, but by one of his five deputies. It was not until he was halfway through the half-hour meeting that Carter realized the man was not Cole.

Carter returned the snub when Nixon invited the nation's governors (in Washington for a National Governors' Conference) to attend a briefing with his aides on the new fiscal policy. Carter was the only governor absent from that meeting, sending Hamilton Jordan as his personal representative. (He explained later that key legislation in the General Assembly had required his presence in Georgia.) The White House refused to grant Jordan clearance and after the meeting, Ron Ziegler, White House press secretary, swiped at Carter's complaints of White House inaccessibility: "those who say that the loudest do not avail themselves of the opportunity." Despite all this, Carter invited Nixon to attend the Atlanta 500. When a letter from Nixon's special assistant declining the invitation arrived, Jody Powell noted in the margin: "If we keep joining in all the invites to Nixon to visit Georgia we may be able to keep the S.O.B. out of state for the next two years." Throughout the summer Carter continued to blast Nixon's domestic policies, calling the results of the food price freeze "chaos and disaster" and the phase four economic control program a "slapstick approach" to curing inflation. And he derided the Nixon Administration for its peanut programs.

Despite his contretemps with Nixon, Carter moved slowly on the Watergate scandal. In early 1973, shortly after the first five members of Nixon's staff had resigned, Carter warned Democrats not to manipulate the Watergate scandal "in an overly partisan manner." And when Governor Patrick Lucey of Wisconsin (at the June 1973 National Governors' Conference) called on the President to resign, Carter demurred—there was not yet sufficient information on Watergate, and a resignation would have an adverse impact on the nation. In August, speaking to an American Bar Association panel, Carter declared that no national Democratic candidate "worth his salt" would base his campaign on the Watergate scandal. This is no time for "accusations and recriminations," he said. "The tone of a campaign is always set by the candidate himself, and the responsibility of the candidate is, of course, to win, but to win fairly." Later that month, after a Nixon press conference in which the President answered several blunt, probing questions about the affair, Carter noted that the President had taken "a very fine step in the right direction. He needs to hold more of them and let every question be asked about Watergate."

A few days after these last remarks, John Crown wrote in the Atlanta *Journal* that Carter's conciliatory stance "was so unusual that I'm still trying to fathom whether there is some dark and diabolical ploy behind it." He speculated about Carter's motives: "one would be that Democrat Carter no longer views Republican Nixon as any sort of political threat and so there is no need to further castigate him. Another would be that the governor is planning to really tear into President Nixon in the near future and the effect of such an attack would be enhanced by cooing soothing words about him now."

In any event, by talking about not talking about Watergate, Carter was talking about Watergate. Further, in a July, 1973, speech to some Legionnaires in Alabama, Carter ignored his own advice. He described himself as "shocked and heartbroken" to read (in the newspaper accounts in Europe on his recent visit there) that the White House press secretary had announced that "burglaries, briberies, and perjury of Watergate were a normal part of American political life." He invoked the statement of personal honor presented to each new cadet at the U.S. Air Force Academy, "We will not lie, cheat, steal, nor tolerate among us those who do." That call to duty and honor, he said, "needs to be handed to a lot of people in the White House, the executive offices, and the Congress in Washington."

That same summer, as a cloud of scandal began to envelop Vice-President Spiro Agnew (over an earlier misuse of funds while he was governor of Maryland), Carter launched a somewhat puzzling defense of the man. He knew Agnew well, he said, and he thought the Vice-President not guilty. "I don't have any inside information. That's just my feeling." In a September, 1973, press conference, Carter speculated that Richard Nixon might have withdrawn his support from Agnew because of his own Watergate troubles. Carter had called the Vice-President, he revealed, and had told him that he had been "abused" and was not receiving the proper support from the President. He even advised Agnew to remain in office and not resign under pressure. After Agnew's resignation, following pleas of *nolo contendere* to bribery charges, Carter did not seem embarrassed by his support. He was surprised and sorry, he said, and "very much afraid and convinced the present administration, as a result of the Watergate revelations, has already seriously damaged confidence in government." He thought that Agnew's replacement should have no ambitions for 1976, and suggested Barry Goldwater as a possibility.

Carter had not said much about Watergate after Nixon's Watergate press conference in August, and his support of the Vice-President may have been an oblique attack on the embattled President. But then, after that "Saturday night massacre," October 20, 1973, when Attorney General Elliot Richardson resigned rather than carry out a presidential order to fire Watergate Special Prosecutor Archibald Cox and Deputy Attorney General William Ruckelshaus was fired when he refused to carry out Nixon's directive, Carter called an unusual Sunday press conference. He said the President had committed impeachable offenses, that "no rational man would have done what Nixon has done." Calling Nixon "paranoic," he went on to say that "he has deliberately withdrawn himself from contacts with reality. He has cut himself off from normal contacts with members of congress and become a recluse, an isolated person." Nixon feared, Carter continued, "the whole of the outside world, the Congress, the People, the Courts, and the forces of the law."

Carter drew fire with these remarks. "Who is this guy to be making a decision about the effectiveness of anybody's administration when he's had the most ineffective administration in memory?" queried Georgia's Republican Party chairman. "He's only engaged in a grandstand play to gain national recognition. He can't get elected to anything in Georgia again. He's got to try somewhere on the national ticket where he's not known." And George Bush, GOP national party chairman, who was in Georgia to address a Republican fund-raiser, said: "I was deeply offended that the Governor of the great state of Georgia made allegations about the mental condition of the President. . . ." A month later, on November 20, Carter belatedly admitted that his use of the word "paranoic" to describe Nixon's behavior was "unfortunate."

After Nixon's resignation on August 9, 1974, Carter described President Ford as "a good man" and noted that he "had the confidence of the American people. He certainly has mine." But following Ford's pardon of Nixon, Carter termed the pardon a mistake and attacked the new President's domestic policy. "There's no way to tell what's going to happen five weeks from now in any policy area. There's just no real direction." And the cure he recommended was two or three years of a strong Democratic Administration that "would turn inflation around" through "the establishment of national planning of clearly established goals and stabilization of national policy, such as export tax policies which really don't exist now."

### The Credibility Problem

When Carter had made one of his blasts on the Nixon revenue-sharing plans in October, 1973, the Washington *Post* ran the story and a photo of him—but identified him as Governor Jimmy *Collins*. And though the *Post* got his name correct in another story shortly thereafter, it spelled his first name "Jimmie." As the mystery guest on *What's My Line?* in December, 1973, he stumped the panelists—who were without the blindfolds used when well-known guests appeared. When Gene Shalit finally determined, through his questions, that the mystery guest was a governor, the host, Larry Blyden, cut off the futile guessing by saying, "Yes, he's Governor of Georgia."

To correct this problem at home, Carter talked of the important people he had met as governor. On one occasion in 1974 he listed the following: Oral

Roberts, Billy Graham, Astronaut Walter Schirra (a classmate of Carter's at Annapolis), Van Cliburn, Bob Dylan, Ted Kennedy, Scoop Jackson. "We've had ambassadors and foreign ministers [stay at the mansion]" Carter said. "Three secretaries of state—Dean Rusk, William P. Rogers, Henry Kissinger —spent hours telling me about foreign affairs." In a speech in November, 1974, Carter talked of his foreign contacts (based on two trips abroad), suggesting close relationships with foreign heads of state and other such leaders: "Since I have been in office, I have visited ten nations, and in each instance I've gone as the personal guest of the governments involved. I have met with the Presidents, Prime Ministers, Foreign Trade Officers, Cultural Exchange Officers, or others, and I have received treatment I think equivalent to that of the head of a nation."

In another effort to correct his relative anonymity, Carter had begun to woo the national press. Even before the Miami Democratic convention he had invited journalist Garry Wills, a fellow Georgian, to accompany him on a trip to a meeting with south Georgia sheriffs. Later, visiting journalists were invited to the governor's mansion for one reason or another. By 1974 he had won a feature story in *Reader's Digest*, which highlighted his brave stand against the Army Corps of Engineers on the Spewrell Bluff dam project. The same year Carter met with the publishers of several major newspapers. He went to New York City to meet with Arthur Ochs Sulzberger, publisher of *The New York Times*, and later in the year had lunch with Warren Phillips, president of *The Wall Street Journal*. And one journalist, who had told an obviously moved Carter about his daughter who was suffering from leukemia received some arrowheads for her. Carter had collected them in the fields.

To become a credible candidate Carter would have to overcome his lack of expertise in the foreign policy arena. As an Annapolis graduate he had mainly a technical education, and as a naval officer he attained neither a command position nor the rank that could have opened up a year or so of study on broader strategic and foreign policy issues at one of the war colleges. To make up for such deficiencies, Carter worked with the Southern Council on International and Public Affairs (headed by Dean Rusk) and through that organization met foreign leaders and ambassadors. Frequently an ambassador would spend the night at the mansion, and Carter would discuss foreign policy issues with him in more depth. On his trips—to Europe and the Middle East in 1973 and to Latin America in 1974—Carter tried to meet other foreign statesmen. (Here he had not been all that successful. Phil Alston's attempts to arrange a meeting with the British Prime Minister through a prominent solicitor evidently did not take, and Carter wound up meeting only two prominent foreign leaders: Helmut Schmidt of Germany, the number-two man in the Socialist-Democratic Party, and former Israeli head of government Golda Meir.)

He also sought advice of his former boss, Admiral Hyman Rickover, still in Washington with the Atomic Energy Administration. He wrote him one rather cryptic and formal note in 1973, asking for additional information on defense and national affairs, "which you think I may use in preparing for 1974 and 1976—as it becomes available." (Carter and Rickover do not appear to have been on particularly close terms, to judge by their limited correspondence and its formality.)

But his most important connections in the foreign policy area were to come through the Trilateral Commission, a prestigious organization formed by David Rockefeller to promote the concept of a "community of developed nations." When the commission was established in the spring of 1973, Carter was one of the sixty North American members. In joining this group Carter had access to the elites Jordan had urged him to cultivate. (Members of the commission included such notables as Hedley Donovan, the editor in chief of *Time*, who was to join his White House staff later; Arthur Taylor, president of CBS; and several individuals from government and business who were later to serve in his Administration: Zbigniew Brzezinski, W. Michael Blumenthal, Harold Brown, Walter F. Mondale, Cyrus R. Vance, Paul Warnke, and Leonard Woodcock.) In Brzezinski, the executive director of Trilateral Commission, Carter found a willing mentor. As the only governor on the commission, Carter gained a certain authority among his peers as a foreign policy spokesman, which he employed when he agreed to present the Trilateral concept at the National Governors' Conference in 1974. He suggested later that he would be able to distribute literature regarding the commission to the Democratic candidates he was aiding in the 1974 election.

While laying down his national base and positioning himself as a spokesman on national issues, Carter had to define his relationship to other national Democratic leaders who might seek the presidency in 1976. Hamilton Jordan had warned him to be wary of some leaders of the "New South"—Governors Reubin Askew of Florida and Dale Bumpers of Arkansas might also have presidential ambitions. Nor should Carter draw too close to Senator Henry Jackson. (Jordan suggested that Carter had been using his name too frequently. "Although you're compatible on most issues, don't promote him or you will sound like you're touting him for 1976.") With respect to George Wallace, Carter should try to repair relations that had been strained at the 1972 convention. (Jordan guessed that Wallace "resents you a little, as we used him effectively and beneficially in our campaign. . . ." Carter should court Wallace and gain his "friendship and trust. . . . I would hope that you might gain his support if he saw in your candidacy an extension and continuation of his earlier efforts.")

Carter did not follow this advice on Wallace, for by 1974 it was clear that Carter would have to present himself as the moderate alternative to Wallace, a candidate liberals could back in the primaries in Florida and other key states of the South regardless of whom they might ultimately support.

Carter had already set about improving his relatively weak record on blacks. His participation, in 1974 in the hanging of Martin Luther King, Jr.'s portrait in the state capitol brought him once again into the limelight as a representative of the New South and a progressive on race issues. And on March 7 he openly broke with Wallace, declaring on a television talk show that Wallace could no longer "deliver the votes that were loyal to him two years ago." Any candidate with "populist issues" could use the Wallace image to his own advantage, but Wallace's racist image, unfortunately, was a lingering factor that could not be overcome. On June 2 Carter completed the break, saying that Wallace was "wasting his time" trying to thrust himself into a national role by dangling votes in front of Democratic presidential candidates such as Senator Edward Kennedy: "Part of his [Wallace's] support is based on his past positions on race. That vote can't be transferred."

In his dealings with Ted Kennedy, Carter also departed from the Jordan scenario. Jordan had recommended that Carter meet with Kennedy at an early date and inform him of his intention of playing an active role in the 1976 election—the assumption being that they had some common interests, at least in the early phases of the campaigning. (Kennedy, Jordan wrote, "knows that he cannot depend on the Southern states for any initial support for the nomination and would rather have someone like yourself to deal with than with George Wallace. He would have hopes of encompassing your candidacy and effort by putting you on the ticket or involving you in his administration, but he could not risk doing this with Wallace.") Yet Carter's meeting with Kennedy did not occur until May, 1974. And on that occasion, rather than attempting to woo Kennedy, Carter upstaged him.

Kennedy had been asked to speak at the Law Day ceremony at the University of Georgia at Athens, at which time a portrait of Dean Rusk was to be unveiled. The plans were for Kennedy to fly to Atlanta, spend the night at the governor's mansion, and then fly to Athens the next morning on the governor's airplane. On the drive from the airport to the mansion, Kennedy told David Nordan, political writer for the Atlanta *Journal-Constitution,* that the nation was ready to accept a Southerner on a national political ticket, and when pressed for a name he said that Governor Carter would be one of several well-qualified Southern possibilities.

The next morning, Kennedy's attitude might have changed when, at the last minute, according to Hunter Thompson, Carter informed the Senator that a sudden change in plans made it impossible to provide a plane for the sixty-mile trip to Athens. Kennedy's aide Jim King quickly got on the phone to have two cars brought to the mansion immediately so the Kennedy party could get to Athens in time for the unveiling. When Hunter Thompson entered the dining room where Carter and Kennedy were eating breakfast, he noticed that Kennedy was sitting there "looking stiff and vaguely uncomfortable in his dark blue suit and black shoes." Jimmy King was off in a corner yelling into a telephone. "There were about 15 other people in the room, most of them laughing and talking, and it took me a while to notice that nobody was talking to Kennedy— which is a very rare thing to see, particularly in any situation involving other politicians or even politically conscious people." An hour or so later a tense Kennedy party was speeding down the highway to Athens.

After the unveiling a group of selected Georgia alumni went to a school cafeteria for a luncheon, at which Kennedy was to speak. Carter stepped to the podium for what the Kennedy party, at least, assumed would be a few introductory remarks. He began with a self-deprecating joke about people feeling honored to pay ten or twelve dollars to hear Kennedy speak, whereas he could only get people to listen to him when a free lunch was offered. As Thompson recalls the scene: "The audience laughed politely, but after he'd been talking for about 15 minutes I noticed a general uneasiness in the atmosphere of the room, and nobody was laughing anymore." Soon after beginning, Carter was talking about himself:

I'm not qualified to talk to you about law, because in addition to being a peanut farmer, I'm an engineer and nuclear physicist, not a lawyer. . . . But I read a lot and I listen a lot. One of the sources for my understanding about the proper application of criminal justice and the system of equities is from Reinhold Niebuhr. The other source of my understanding about what's right and wrong in this society is from a friend of mine, a poet named Bob Dylan. Listening to his records about "The Lonesome Death of Hattie Carroll" and "Like a Rolling Stone" and "The Times They Are A-Changing," I've learned to appreciate the dynamism of change in a modern society.

After some references to Watergate, Attorney General John Mitchell, and a joke or two, Carter was warmed up and ". . . for the next 20 or 30 minutes his voice was the only sound in the room." Kennedy, according to Thompson, never changed ". . . the thoughtful expression on his face as Carter railed and bitched about a system of criminal justice that allows the rich and the privileged to escape punishment for their crimes and sends poor people to prison because they can't afford to bribe the judge."

Carter's speech not only discomforted Ted Kennedy—it overwhelmed Hunter Thompson. As Thompson recalls, he asked Carter for a copy of the speech:

"There is no transcript [Carter replies]." I smiled, thinking he [Carter] was putting me on. The speech had sounded like a product of five or six tortured drafts. . . . But he showed a page and a half of scrawled notes in his legal pad and said that was all he had. "Jesus Christ," I said. "That was one of the damnedest things I've ever heard. You mean you just winged it all the way through?" He shrugged and smiled faintly. "Well," he said, "I had a pretty good idea what I was going to say, before I came up here—but I guess I was a little surprised at how it came out."

It is hard to understand Carter's audacity in this affair. He had acted against Jordan's practical advice and, except for winning over Gonzo journalist Hunter Thompson, he gained no concrete political advantage in upstaging the powerful Kennedy. In this instance his motivation might best be understood in terms of the competitiveness that had led him to take on Bo Callaway in 1966. Kennedy, like Callaway, was young, attractive, socially favored, and a more powerful male with whom Carter identified. Given the opportunity, Carter evidently could not resist competing with the favored man and outdoing him in some way.

Later in 1974, when Carter heard that Kennedy had decided not to be a presidential candidate in 1976, Carter wrote him expressing his regret over the "tragedies which have made it necessary for you to withdraw from consideration for the Presidency in 1976." But a touch of grandiosity—given Carter's relative obscurity at the time—crept into his letter: "Let me say quite frankly that as one who has considered becoming a candidate myself, I've always viewed you as a formidable opponent . . . and I certainly take no pleasure from your withdrawal."

## Mending Fences at Home

Meanwhile Carter's public support at home was slipping. Columnists in the Atlanta papers began to discuss his sinking popularity. Back home in southwestern Georgia there were some rumblings: Carter didn't answer his mail, he had not been home for some time, he was ignoring the people in the districts who gave him his start in state politics. David Nordan, after a listening tour of his own in the spring of 1973, postulated that Carter's popularity had dipped in south Georgia because he turned out to be much less conservative than people there had thought. Ex-Governor Marvin Griffin told him: "A lot of people down here who voted for Jimmy are just disgusted with his political philosophy." Others, Nordan reported, said such things as: " 'He's not what I thought he was . . . he's 'two-faced:' '. . . He comes down here and tells us one thing then goes back to Atlanta and says something else.' "

Beginning in 1973, Carter took some steps to repair home relations. He allotted $200,000 from his emergency fund to help clear the stumps out of Lake Blackshear, on the border of Sumter and Lee counties, so the lake would be safe for boaters. Funding for roads in Sumter County once again increased, up to $230,000 by August 1, 1974. Among the projects authorized were funds to drain, grade, and surface the road to James Earl Carter Library at Georgia Southwestern. Other improvements were made in Plains—West Main Street (the site of Hugh's store and the later presidential campaign headquarters), Woodland Drive (on which only Jimmy Carter's home is located), and Paschall Street (which runs from Woodland Drive to the Plains Baptist Church). Total cost: $29,025.26. He also allocated $10,000 out of his emergency fund to help finance a public swimming pool in Plains, which would give the blacks a place to go given the customary constraint on their using the private Lions Club pool in town. (Frank Moore, on December 4, recommended that Carter allocate $12,000 to nearby Ellaville, making explicit the complex motivation in situations such as this. One would probably never see the same set of circumstances again, he wrote, where the city, the county, and the American Legion were each willing to put up $12,000 "to build a beautiful recreation center in the black area. Of course the motive is to keep the blacks out of the Lions Club pool but it would still be a chance to do something for the black community in Schley County.")

The summer of 1973, returning to past successes, Carter undertook one of his most dramatic people-to-people tours. Starting in the north Georgia town of Rome, Jimmy, Rosalynn, and five-year-old Amy criss crossed 1,550 miles down the middle of the state, visiting mostly towns removed from the major highways of Georgia. Unlike his pregubernatorial campaign trips when he slipped into an area unnoticed, Carter now had the trappings that went with his office. Traveling in a Lincoln Continental provided by the state, he was accompanied by an entourage of three uniformed state troopers (including the black recently appointed to guard the governor), aides, several statewide reporters, and a camera crew from the state-owned educational television network. The Governor and First Lady of Georgia would hit one of those small rural towns, Rosalynn would jump out to work one side of the street, and Jimmy would hop out and work the other. Shaking hands, exchanging pleasantries, Carter would ask, "Is there anything I can do to help you?" And when there was a request he could not meet on the spot, he would promise to have the matter checked out when he got back to Atlanta. After he had worked a stretch, the big car would catch up, the governor and Mrs. Carter would leap back in and "the whole caravan went screaming down the road to the next town."

The Carters visited cotton and tobacco warehouses, schools, prisons, institutions for juveniles and the retarded. And most evenings they spent the night in some private residence in one small town or another, shoring up their personal contacts throughout the state. In Rome, Carter spoke to down-and-outers in a shabby room over a store, offering encouragement and affection. In Newman he empathized with juvenile delinquents. At Ellaville, just north of Plains, the Carter retinue visited the office of the Middle Flint Area Planning and Development Commission, which Carter had helped establish, and a new center for the mentally retarded. A few miles out of Ellaville, as they neared Plains, the cortege stopped beside a stretch of wood and Carter led the newsmen in a short walk up to a small cemetery where his great-great grandfather, Wiley Carter, some of his descendants, and at least two slaves were buried. Carter told the journalists that his family had only recently discovered the graves, that they had partially restored them in 1967, that on an earlier visit he had almost been bitten by a rattlesnake. In Plains he met with Hugh Carter and other relatives and friends. With the newsmen listening in, Jimmy bantered with cousin Hugh about turning one of the town buildings into a museum for Carter memorabilia. "Why not?" Hugh said. "We're going to make a tourist town out of this."

That evening about 100 people from the area, with few politicians other than Bert Lance in attendance, gathered at the Veteran's Memorial State Park near Cordele, for a free fish fry. The affair, as the Albany *Herald* noted, "resembled a political campaign. . . . Rosalynn wandered through the crowd shaking almost everyone's hand, while her husband chatted with the home folk covering everything from grits to Watergate."

Carter had said the purpose of his trip was to obtain feedback on his reorganization plan, to "expose" department heads who had not been honest in their assessment of the new programs, and to establish an "inner relationship" with the people. But it is clear that the trip had an important public-relations purpose as well. Gerald Rafshoon had used the tour to produce film—as Carter himself ordered—showing him "moving through the state, visiting and listening to the people." Not only did Carter star in the film, he told Rafshoon how to edit it afterward. "My participation is inherently adequate—focus should be on the people. They seem to be basically happy and glad to have a governor visit them." For one scene he told Rafshoon that he wanted "shots of hands shaking. Warm Springs, and others where sound is bad with a lot of overalls and pickup trucks in the background." Carter concluded: "I don't want two separate films—what we compose should be adequate for commercial TV & ETV."

The tour won considerable press attention. Carter still had that old magic. As David Nordan, who traveled with him, observed, an excited citizen meeting him would often promise a vote to the governor and Carter would reply, "I'm not running for anything." The feedback on this tour was so good that Carter took several other such trips during his remaining eighteen months in office.*

### Surfacing

This was a lot of activity for a governor who could not succeed himself, and questions were bound to arise about what he was up to. Carter followed the suggestion in Jordan's memo of November, 1972, that he project himself as a possible aspirant for Talmadge's seat in the Senate. Thus, in February, 1973, in a speech before the National Press Club in Washington, D.C., Carter said that Senator Talmadge knew "that times change, and someone might emerge who could give him a good run for his money." And in an address before the Yale Political Union in April, he said that he would decide in the next two or three months "whether to go back to Plains to be a peanut farmer, join a business and make some money for a change, or run against Herman Talmadge for the U.S. Senate."

His political opponents took the feint as his real political objective. When Bob Shaw, the state Republican leader, criticized Carter's piggyback poll of November 1973, he charged that Carter was gauging his chances of opposing Talmadge in the forthcoming Senate race. And George Busbee, who would be seeking the Democratic nomination for governor in 1974, failed to see the poll as a test of Carter's own popularity—rather, he was "shocked and dismayed" that the governor would use his emergency fund in conjunction with a poll

---

*In September, 1973, he went on a three-day tour of east Georgia, starting in Augusta where he appeared on a radio call-in show in the afternoon and spoke in the evening at the Kiokee Baptist Church near Appling, the oldest Baptist church in the state. (There he described himself as a "conservative businessman," explaining his more liberal programs in terms of "Christ's ministry to the suffering.") In March, 1974, he undertook another short tour with major stops at Macon, Columbus, Camilla, Augusta, Thomasville and Savannah. (As on his September tour, he appeared on television and radio shows.) In July, 1974, Carter took an extended tour of the state—this time, as he put it, to discuss the issues that would face the state in the next four years. Starting in Warm Springs, he visited eight towns and cities in northeast and coastal Georgia in five days: Gainesville, Toccoa, Savannah, Brunswick, Waycross, Moultrie, and Jekyll Island.

disguised to aid his own political favorites. Further, when Busbee heard that Carter was undertaking a "listening tour" around the state in July, 1974, a few weeks before the gubernatorial primary, he interpreted it as a tour for Bert Lance. In a public statement he said: "The announced tour is the final Carter contribution to the Lance campaign. One of the early donations of the Carter organization was when the governor authorized a piggy back poll which purported to sample public opinion about highways, but was in reality designed to sample the highway director's chances to be governor."

Actually, Carter appears to have done something even more subtle than what Jordan had suggested. Even while denying his national aspirations and providing an alternative interpretation for his politicking, he implanted the idea that he was a man of presidential timbre. At a meeting of the Georgia Press Association in June, 1973, for example, Carter admitted that national issues were "very much on my mind" and that he would announce his future political plans in about thirty days. He said, "I feel it is time to let the people know what I intend to do." Less than a month later Carter said that he would not be a candidate for elective office in 1974 nor would he actively seek the vice-presidential slot in 1976. "I want to be a full-time governor," he declared. He added that he would probably be a candidate for elective office at a later time.

In March, 1974, Carter and Charles Kirbo engaged in a little exchange in which Kirbo floated out the tantalizing possibility that Carter might be the presidential choice in 1976. While Carter was in Albany on one of his listening tours, Kirbo, in Atlanta, warned that the party standard-bearer should not be one of the old regulars—Humphrey, Kennedy or McGovern. Jackson was his choice and Carter's. But he considered Florida's Askew, Ohio's Gilligan, Arkansas's Bumpers, and Georgia's Carter real possibilities. When asked about Kirbo's statement, Carter said that he would accept the nomination if handed to him "on a silver platter," but dismissed his chances as "extremely remote." Kirbo, he said, "didn't consult me before making that ridiculous statement. . . . But I think it is very complimentarty as far as Mr. Kirbo is concerned. There are always a few people who think their governor ought to be Vice President or some other high office and I am glad that Mr. Kirbo thinks that I am one who should be considered."

Touring New Hampshire in late March, Carter told a questioner that he didn't know what he would do in 1976. "I'm not interested in running for Congress or the Senate. I might pick a candidate I like for President and work with him. Or else I might strive for a place on the 1976 ticket myself."

"I'm the same kind of person you are, I'm not a fulltime politician," he said on another occasion, "I don't want to stay in politics." Three months later on his last downstate tour he continued:

I'm not running for any office as you know. I'm going out of office. But I see some things that touch my heart and I see some things that concern me deeply. But the message I want to leave with you . . . is that we do have the ability among our people to demand and receive a standard of service and a commitment in government that will meet the highest level of excellence and achievement that the people of this state and Nation so richly deserve.

Picking up on these and similar cues, Atlanta journalists such as Bill Shipp, David Nordan, and John Crown had speculated off and on since 1971 that Carter's activities suggested national ambition. They seemed to think of him as a vice-presidential candidate or a Cabinet member or a Senate nominee. But John Crown, noting Carter's travels for the national party in Septembert 1973, queried: "Who knows where lightning will strike at the national convention in 1976?"

In the summer of 1974 Carter aides began to leak items to the Atlanta press about the forthcoming campaign. The *Constitution* reported that Carter was being urged to enter the New Hampshire primary, quoting one Carter supporter to the effect that he was avoiding the spotlight to "avoid making too many enemies too early." In October "undisclosed sources" revealed to the *Constitution* that Carter had already made an "irrevocable decision" to seek the 1976 Democratic presidential nomination, that he had already developed a sophisticated fundraising plan, relying on mailing lists and lists of recent Carter contacts. One of Carter's supporters had even printed "Carter for President" buttons. In November the *Journal* reported that Hamilton Jordan had resigned as executive of the Democratic National Congressional Ca˘ ˙aign Committee to set up the "Committee for Jimmy Carter" office in Atlanta.

Carter himself gradually moved toward an announcement of candidacy. In early October he told reporters he could not be ruled out as a presidential candidate. In late October he admitted that he was a presidential possibility though he portrayed himself as an underdog who was being "mentioned along with twenty to twenty-five others, and I might say frankly that I put myself near the bottom of the list." At the Democratic miniconvention in Kansas City in early December, the campaign was clearly under way. A ten-page brochure heralding "Jimmy Carter: Georgia's Governor for a New Political Season" was circulated to the delegates. It included a long laudatory article and more than thirty photographs of Carter—making speeches, shoveling peanuts, rocking in a rocking chair, consulting with a laborer near an uncovered manhole, consoling a tornado victim, hurling a Frisbee, and working at his capitol desk. Carter spent much of his time making informal speaking appearances before state delegations. And he received substantial attention at the convention by piggybacking at the cocktail parties of the other presidential hopefuls.

On December 12, 1974, one month before his term as governor ended, Carter formally announced his candidacy. At the National Press Club in Washington in an address entitled "For America's Third Century Why Not the Best?" Carter outlined the themes upon which he would base his subsequent campaign. (The Atlanta *Constitution* reported that many of the journalists present complained that Carter's remarks were "long, dull and boring.") He returned to Atlanta to make his formal announcement in the hot, stuffy lobby of the Atlanta Civic Center. But the well-dressed, mainly middle-aged crowd was happy, and the candidate was confident. As Carter left the jammed Civic Center, an anxious staffer grabbed for his hand and yelled, "We're going to win, Governor." Carter, moving through the crowd, looked back, grinned, and responded, "I know."

As governor, Carter still had a few matters to attend to in his final days of office. He helped make way for his successor Goerge Busbee. The press carried a story, attributed to an aide, that Carter had turned down hundreds of requests for funds from the governor's emergency fund in order to keep a promise to leave $1 million dollars of the $2 million fund for the governor-elect. (However, he did withdraw $20,000 from the fund to cover cost overruns for the publication of his speeches by the state archives.)

The day before he left office, Carter sent his aides out to deliver certificates—inscribed, sealed, and suitable for framing—to many members of the Atlanta press corps, appointing them: "Lieutenant Colonel, aide-de-camp, . . . For the defense of the state and for repelling every hostile invasion thereof to take rank thereof from the date of this commission and to hold such office during the term and under the conditions prescribed by law." As his final legacy, he left a handwritten note on Governor Busbee's desk—"May God's richest blessings be upon you." Busbee, when he picked up the note, purportedly said, "Now what do I do with this?" He wrote on it, "Jimmy, May God bless you too. George"—and sent it back to Carter.

# III

# Campaign Strategy

# TWELVE

# Early Primaries

### Beating the Bushes

RISING EARLY ON Monday, January 20, 1975, Jimmy Carter drove the 150 miles from his home in Plains to the Atlanta airport. It was less than a week after he had left office as governor of Georgia. Now an open and avowed candidate for the presidency, he was starting on the first lap of a grueling run that would take him into approximately twenty-five states in the next few months.

On this first trip out, Carter did not look like a full-blown presidential candidate. His entourage was small and he was covered by only two national newsmen: Tom Ottenad of the St. Louis *Post-Dispatch* and Jack Germond of the Washington *Star*. Both were along because they had been intrigued by Carter at earlier national governors' conferences. Carter was just a peanut farmer from Plains, Germond noted, his only credentials a single term as governor and his being a Southerner. "When he passes through town he is regarded by the local news media as so much more fodder for the television interview programs and a brief story on page 6." Ottenad observed that Carter was forced to take whatever invitations might come his way—often finding an audience in groups meeting for some other purpose. Sometimes he met in small rooms with an embarrassingly small number of people. It looked as though Carter was "back home in Georgia running for sheriff." Usually, Ottenad continued, "the political community would dismiss a long-shot campaign like his as a joke." But Carter possessed qualities that made his ambition less funny. "Even in a trade where egos are unbounded, Carter's self-confidence is dazzling." Germond wrote: In the face of "self-assurance that would shame Mohammad Ali," Carter made his handicap seem almost irrelevant. While other candidates were still modest about their plans, "Carter gives the impression that the only decisions still to be made are those about his running mate and his cabinet."

In Santa Fe, New Mexico, for example, Carter told a group at Governor

Jerry Apodaca's annual prayer breakfast, "I intend to be elected." He identified himself as one of the four major candidates for the nomination. He was already presenting his campaign slogan, "For the American Third Century, Why Not Our Best?"—and the best meant Jimmy Carter.

In moving out early and projecting himself with such self-confidence, Carter was not acting naively. He was making the best of what was clearly a vulnerable situation. Peter Bourne had suggested to him in an October 24, 1973, memo that McGovern had shown the advantages of early campaigning to the relative unknown. "The key to his success which seemed so bizarre at the time was his early declaration. It is only someone without major name recognition who can grab control of the activist people of the country and hold them. The ability to do this in 1976 will be just as important next time as it was in '72." Equally important, "McGovern never wavered in his belief that he would win. If he had any private doubts, he kept them very well hidden. I think that attitude was crucial in allowing his staff to live for two years facing insurmountable odds. A candidate has to really believe that his success is preordained. If he does not, it gets transmitted in many non-verbal ways to those around him."

Carter went beyond just projecting self-confidence. He showed he could win people over and that he had a viable plan to help him win the nomination. His strategy, which he laid out on "Meet the Press" three days after his formal announcement, was to run in every one of the state primaries, through which 70 percent of the convention delegates would be chosen. And he showed Ottenad on this first tour that he had the drive and the scientific know-how to implement the strategy. In the forthcoming year he would spend 250 days on the campaign trail, devoting his time to the various states in accordance with a formula that seemed "almost mathematical." It assigned weights to each state based on the delegate votes at stake, the media impact of the campaign, and the relative appeal of his opponents in each contest. On the basis of these assessments Carter would spend seventeen days in New Hampshire, fifteen in Florida, eight in Illinois, and fifteen in California. (Sparsely populated New Mexico rated only a few hours' stopover on his way to somewhere else.)

Carter's stance toward his Democratic opponents figured significantly in his overall strategy. For liberals and Northerners, he was the moderate Southern alternative to Wallace—the man who could defeat the Alabaman on his own turf and remove him as a factor in national politics. For others Carter was the Southerner who could win and carry out some of the good things Wallace stood for, such as reforming the government in Washington, making it more responsive to the people.

In his appearance before the Louisiana legislature on his first campaign swing, Carter made the latter appeal. Wallace, he suggested, understood "the yearnings and frustrations of the American people." (A poll splashed across the front page of the local press on the day of his speech, indicating that Wallace was the favored Democratic candidate in Louisiana, showed the problems he would have were he too critical.) But Carter said "he was not content to send a message to Washington." Contrasting himself with Wallace, he emphasized that he would be slated in all of the Democratic primaries. He had secured Martin Luther King, Sr.'s endorsement, and would amass support from other black leaders as well.

In New York City in May, 1975, Carter argued that only a good Southerner like himself could take the vote away from Wallace. Liberals who travel to "Wallace Country" to be seen with the governor, he said, seriously underestimate the intelligence of the Southern electorate. Wallace votes cannot be "transferred to more liberal candidates."

In his fundraising letters he even told liberals that he would accept a kind of conditional commitment, through Florida. After that they were free to transfer their efforts to other candidates, should they be so inclined: "I can understand that you may not be ready to commit yourself to a candidate at this time, but if you agree with me that George Wallace should not be the next Democratic presidential nominee, help me defeat him in Florida."

What Carter had figured out and many liberals had not was that if Carter should succeed in knocking Wallace out in Florida, it might be too late to go elsewhere. Carter would have a free run in several of the Southern states, racking up delegates without much effort—as such, he would be the man to beat.

Though Carter had publicly announced a run-everywhere strategy, his efforts in 1975 would be focused on the early primary and caucus states. New Hampshire was given top priority, Florida second, Illinois third—Iowa, which turned out to be the first caucus state, rated behind the others. In his 1974 memo, Jordan had delineated the reason for these priorities:

The press shows an exaggerated interest in the early primaries as they represent the first confrontation between candidates, their contrasting strategies and styles, which the press has been writing and speculating about for two years. We would do well to understand the very special and powerful role the press plays in interpreting the primary results for the rest of the nation. What is actually accomplished in the New Hampshire primary is less important than how the press interprets it for the nation. Handled properly, a defeat can be interpreted as a holding action and a mediocre showing as a victory. . . .

Carter and his aides made a conscious decision to downplay their effort in New Hampshire, however, focusing attention on Florida instead. It heightened the possibility of a "strong surprise in New Hampshire." And as a proving ground for Carter, Florida made good sense. With eighty-one delegates, it was an important state. It would provide a real competition. Florida had been Wallace country back in 1972, when Wallace, riding the antibusing crest, captured 42 percent of the vote and every congressional district in the state. If Carter could now beat him there—and he told almost everyone he met in 1975 that he would—Carter would be in a good position to win the rest of the South and, with good showings in the North, the Democratic nomination.

Florida was a good state for Carter to work. Former Georgia residents and their relatives lived in the Florida panhandle, where Wallace had his strongest base of support. Carter could call on the ties of regional affinity to build a solid political base there. Florida is geographically proximate to Georgia—Tallahassee is as close to Plains as Atlanta. Thus, Carter and his friends could easily slip out of Plains for a few days of campaigning in Florida.

Carter was able to persuade the liberal presidential contestants to stay out of Florida. And with no other place to go, blacks and liberals and labor leaders lent a hand to Carter's endeavor. Andrew Young campaigned vigorously for him. Even Julian Bond supported Carter in Florida, although he later switched to Udall. The United Auto Workers pulled out all the stops for Carter in a move to undercut Wallace's strength in Michigan. On January 12, 1976, reporters learned that the Florida council of the Citizens Action Program (CAP)—the UAW's political arm—endorsed Carter in that state only. For blacks and labor he was "the only game in town."

In his campaign tactics as in his strategy, Carter showed an ability to turn necessity into virtue and potential weaknesses into assets. As an unemployed politician, he would have trouble gaining national exposure. At the same time he would be free of any other responsibilities, so he could devote all of his energies in 1975 to the campaign effort. Carter spent most of the year traveling, building contacts with people and laying down the roots of the organization that would deliver for him in 1976 (thus earning James Reston's label, "Mayor Daley in the binding of a hymn book").

Initially Carter pursued every possible contact. He and his staff worked over the lists of names he had acquired while working for the Democratic National Committee on the 1973 and 1974 congressional campaigns and called in the IOUs. An invitation from Jerry Apodaca led to Carter's stop at Santa Fe on his first trip following his formal announcement. There, Carter first encountered Tim Kraft, who would eventually join the Carter campaign. In New York City, Midge Costanza, whom he had aided in her congressional attempt, was to become his upstate coordinator. His early workers in Ohio were people who had originally been contacted by staff aides when they had come through earlier on congressional campaigns.

Carter pursued other leads that more established candidates would have ignored. His first trip to Iowa, for example, was in response to an invitation to attend a retirement party in Le Mars for Marie Jahn, an official of Plymouth County. (All seven of the Democratic presidential candidates had been invited, but the others either declined or ignored it.) At the Amber Inn, where he stayed, the owner later confessed she did not know who Carter was when he checked in. Carter, however, "made a very good impression even with all of my Republican friends there," said Marie Jahn. "He comes from a small town, and being small town people, we just felt we had something in common with him." Flattered that a candidate for the top public office would bother to attend such a small event, she and several of her friends committed themselves to his campaign almost at once. During the Nebraska and Wisconsin primaries, Marie

Jahn accompanied a busload of Iowa women to campaign for Carter door-to-door. And John Devereaux, who had driven Carter and Powell to Le Mars, became Iowa state director for the Carter campaign during the fall.

Carter's staff turned his heavy travel schedule into a public-relations advantage, periodically issuing numerical summaries of his efforts that demonstrated his unfailing commitment and stamina. By June, 1975, according to his staff's calculations, he had traveled more than 50,000 miles, visited 37 states, delivered over 200 speeches, appeared on 93 radio and TV interview shows, attended 26 editorial board meetings, and established an in-house mailing list of 25,000 potential supporters (in addition to the purchased direct mailing lists). His pace, his staff noted, was "almost brutal." By December 12, 1975, Carter claimed to have traveled to 43 states and established 16 campaign offices in addition to his headquarters in Atlanta.

His need to run an economy campaign was one source of his intimate style. Rather than hiring a large, salaried campaign staff, Carter initially relied on himself and his family to do his advance work. They flew on commercial airlines and traveled separately to maximize their exposure. To limit expenses, as well as to establish personal ties with their supporters, they stayed in friends' homes wherever they could. More than one hostess would recall pleasant conversations with Carter over a sandwich and milk at night and be impressed that the candidate did not consider himself too important to make his own bed the next morning. And for each potential supporter who did not meet him personally, there were several others who felt they had a line to him through encounters with Rosalynn, Chip, Caron, or Lillian's sister Emily Dolvin, called Sissy.

Despite everything, Carter remained barely visible throughout the spring of 1975. Not until April was he even mentioned in the Gallup Polls—with approximately 1 percent of the vote of Democrats and independents. One episode is illustrative of his problems. After six months of active campaigning Jimmy and Rosalynn Carter went to the Grand Ole Opry in Nashville to see seven-year-old Amy dance with the Lil' General Cloggers, a gingham and denim–clad group from Kennesaw, Georgia. Before the show Carter made a special point to go backstage and meet Roy Acuff, the "king of country music" and a friend of George Wallace and Richard Nixon. Acuff was pleasant, but during the show he introduced Carter, not by name, but as the "former Governor of Georgia," with no mention of his presidential aspirations and no invitation to stand up. What there was of an audience reaction came from the section reserved for relatives of the Cloggers. As the reporter covering this event pointed out: "Carter can stroll through the giant Opryland Park adjoining the Grand Ole Opry or walk into a McDonald's and order a hamburger without causing a ripple."

The problem was that aside from the initial media flurry at the time of his announcement Carter was not getting any national publicity. The Atlanta Con-stitution noted in February: ". . . the hurdle remains that what Carter says in Chicago is not news in Kansas City."

Carter and his aides suggested that they could make up for this with good local publicity. There is no way to attempt an independent assessment of how successful his strategy was. But Carter's appearance at the dinner for Marie Jahn was buried by the local *Sentinel* in its story covering the dinner, and Kraft's announcement about the composition of Carter's Iowa steering committee appeared deep inside the Des Moines *Register.* Carter was to complain later, in October, 1975, "I've gotten more coverage from *The New York Times* than I have from the Atlanta newspapers."

Publicity was not the only problem in these early months. Carter and his aides had serious financial problems throughout 1975. Carter was able to attract money to his campaign in the first part of the year (starting with $40,000 in January, and running it up to over $400,000 by early fall), but most of that money came from Georgia. Having to raise $5,000 in each of twenty states in order to qualify for federal matching funds presented the greatest challenge. Not until August 14, after Jackson, Lloyd Bentsen, Wallace, and Udall had all qualified for federal funds, was Carter able to claim the same. Even after this the Carter campaign suffered a setback. On August 28 the FEC ruled that candidates must deduct the cost of fundraising events before reporting the events' incomes. Carter said it was "a contradiction of what we assumed all along." The FEC ruling could force Jimmy Carter to fall below the federal matching requirements. Moreover, as his popularity rating continued to hover around the 1 percent mark, he was finding no new sources of money. By the fall the campaign was operating on a deficit. Some of Carter's inner circle—Frank Moore, Jody Powell, and Hamilton Jordan—even agreed to work the rest of the year without pay so their salaries could be spent in other areas of the campaign. According to the FEC report for 1975, the campaign had taken in $504,587 and spent $506,518.

The situation seemed so desperate that at one point the future of the campaign was in doubt. Carter himself finally got on the phone and told Phil Walden, the founder and president of Capricorn Records, that unless they could raise $50,000 in a hurry, he might have to stop running for President. (Carter had been cultivating Walden since 1973, when he had dropped in on Capricorn Records in Macon during one of his tours of the state.) Walden convinced the Allman Brothers, Marshall Tucker, Charlie Daniels and the Outlaws—all on contract with Capricorn—to do benefit concerts for Carter. On October 31, 1975, the Marshall Tucker Band performed at a Carter fundraiser at the Fox Theater in Atlanta, and the Allman Brothers played a concert in Providence, Rhode Island on November 25, 1975. The two events brought in nearly $100,000 for Carter.

By September, however, Carter had met the initial "qualifying test." (He was then offered Secret Service protection, which he accepted with alacrity.) With this, Carter had crossed one hurdle that divided the serious from the non-serious candidates. The national media, looking for some break, some sign of a trend or development that could make sense out of the crowded presidential race, had earlier decided that qualification for federal funds would be a marker.

There was now a thaw in Carter's publicity freeze. On September 22 *U.S. News and World Report* gave Carter a two-page spread and outlined his strategy, though it ended with a realistic note that ". . . like many other Democratic aspirants, Mr. Carter suffers from a popularity and identification problem." *Time*, on October 13, 1975, ran a page-and-a-half profile of Carter—the third piece in *Time*'s series on the candidates. Entitled "Carter: Swimming Upstream," the first page of the article carried the striking photograph of Carter in a pose reminiscent of John Kennedy, sitting reflectively in a rocking chair on the porch of the governor's mansion.

Then in late October, 1975, a minor event in Iowa was treated as a sign of some national trend. On October 25 the state Democratic party of Iowa held its annual Jefferson-Jackson Day fundraising dinner in Ames, to which all the presidential candidates were invited. Tim Kraft, learning that the Des Moines *Register* and *Tribune* were planning to conduct a poll at the dinner, guessed correctly that the dinner guests would be asked to identify their favorites in the forthcoming presidential sweepstakes. So he got to work to get Carter people out and voting. Of the 4,000 attending the dinner, only 1,000 voted in the poll. Carter came in first with 23.6 percent of the total (or about 250 votes). Humphrey received 12.4 percent, Birch Bayh 10.4 percent, Sargent Shriver 8.5 percent, Udall 7.1 percent, Fred Harris 5.6 percent, and Jackson 5.2 percent (with Wallace, Milton Shapp, and Bentsen all claiming less than 1 percent).

R. W. "Johnny" Apple of *The New York Times* took this as a break in the campaign. Carter "appears to have taken a surprising but solid lead" in Iowa's delegate race. "Whether he can maintain his early lead here when the contest switches from opinion leaders to rank-and-file voters is unclear," he went on, but "what is evident is that Mr. Carter, working from Atlanta rather than Washington, has made dramatic progress while attention was focused on the scramble for liberal primacy" among Udall, Bayh, Harris, and Shriver. Others followed Apple's lead. Peter Goldman of *Newsweek* later recalled that his magazine decided to give much greater attention to reporting the Iowa caucuses upon reading Apple's story and an equivalent piece by Jules Witcover in the Washington *Post*. Dick Duncan of *Time* recalled that Apple's story in *The Times*, coming "out of the blue, ordaining a new phenomenon . . . [was] the most important single event in the relationship between the media and Jimmy Carter." Shortly thereafter Tom Wicker noted that the press and the politicians have "underestimated the new boys, just as they did in 1968 and 1972."

In the meantime, Phil Wise, Carter's state coordinator in Florida, had prepared for a similar coup there. When Wise learned that there would be a presidential preference poll at the Florida Democratic state convention in mid-November, he got his people organized. The result: in the straw poll, held on November 16, Carter won a "whopping" 67 percent (697 of the 1,035 votes). Milton Shapp, the only candidate who attended the convention besides Carter, came in second with 60 votes, while Wallace received 57, Jackson 46, Bayh 32, Shriver 15, Udall 8, and Harris 1. Contacted by UPI after the straw vote, Carter said, "This vote in Florida was the first major test of strength in the South . . . a good indication of what's going to happen in 1976."

Suddenly, Carter was someone to watch. On December 1, 1975, *Time* ran a two-column story titled "Suddenly he is no longer Jimmy *Who?*" *Newsweek*, in its page-and-a-half story (part of a series on all the candidates), said: "Carter has succeeded in making Democrats who once dismissed him as a regional non-starter look twice." Major newspapers and syndicated columnists began to take him seriously. Marquis Childs, in his December 16, 1975 column, said: "Visionary as it seems, I believe Carter at the present moment has a better chance than any of the others to win the nomination." Frank Starr of the Chicago *Tribune* noted with amazement that suddenly Carter was plausible: "He knew foreign policy. His being a non-Washington non-lawyer was suddenly not a debt but a credit. The media blitz flashed—two major news magazines, three networks, *People, Rolling Stone*, and major newspapers were noticing him."

In early December, shortly before the Iowa caucuses, *The New York Times* ran a feature story on Jimmy Carter, the second in a seven-article series on presidential candidates. The author, Patrick Anderson, had been asked by the *Times* to prepare a piece on one of the candidates. At first he was thinking about doing someone else. Then after hearing about Jimmy Carter at a cocktail party at Peter Bourne's Washington home and making a trip to Plains, he decided to profile Carter. (Anderson would later join his campaign as a speechwriter.) After recounting biographical material of the sort presented in *Why Not the Best?*, Anderson went on to describe Carter's special qualities as a campaigner—how he could win people over, or stand up to them if need be. After Carter refused to back off from a confrontation in one Florida bar, Anderson noted, "Good—stubborn—stuck to his guns." Jimmy Carter, he concluded, "may or may not become President, but he is certainly one of the more interesting men to seek that office in recent times. Carter is a soft-spoken, thoughtful, likable man, an instrospective man who enjoys the songs of Bob Dylan, the poems of Dylan Thomas, the writings of James Agee, William Faulkner, John McPhee, and Reinhold Niebuhr."

Despite the growing and glowing press coverage, these pro-Carter sentiments were not reflected in the polls of the general public or elites. In a general Gallup Poll taken in November, Carter was the first choice of only 2.5 percent of the Democrats polled when Kennedy was included in the poll. In a poll of independent voters, with Kennedy excluded from the list, Carter was the choice of only 4 percent. In the general Gallup Polls during December, 1975, Carter ranked only in the "All others" category among Democratic votes, which accounted for 8 percent of those polled (this list included Kennedy's name). Carter's name only surfaced in the poll of independent voters, where he received 4 percent of the vote, equaling Muskie, Bayh, Shriver, Udall, and Harris.

There were indications that he was not all that strong with Democratic Party activists. Earlier polls of regional Democratic gatherings in the Northeast and the Middle West showed Carter with practically no support there. In the Midwest poll, taken in Minneapolis, Carter was not even mentioned. (Udall, Harris, and Bayh led, in that order.) In a similar poll of the Northeast Democratic Conference in Springfield, Massachusetts, conducted by and reported in the Washington *Post* in late September, Carter secured one vote. Even in Iowa, where Carter had done well at the Democratic dinner in Des Moines, a subsequent poll raised some questions about those earlier results. A survey of 1,000 Democrats at a Waterloo "First Choices—76" rally had different results. Bayh led this group by 38 percent, Harris came in second with 20 percent, and Carter came in third with 13 percent.

These three polls—like the surveys of opinion at the Iowa dinner and the Florida Democratic convention where Carter had done well—were informal at best. But a Gallup Poll, published on December 8, which did follow more rigorous sampling techniques, suggested that Carter was not that popular with broader elites throughout the nation. Opinion leaders across the nation in the fields of business, government, education, science, law, and the arts were asked if they thought each Democratic hopeful would or would not make a good President. Only 17 percent believed Carter would make a good President. (Hubert Humphrey received a 69 percent positive reaction, Muskie 50 percent, Jackson 36 percent, Udall 35 percent, Kennedy 32 percent.) Eleven percent thought Wallace would make a good President.

Yet for all this, Carter had some room for maneuver. He had a relatively low "negative" rating. Only 31 percent in the Gallup Poll thought Carter would *not* make a good President. Except for Hubert Humphrey, whose negative rating tied Carter's, the other better known candidates had considerably higher negative reactions: Wallace (83 percent), McGovern (74 percent), Shriver (60 percent), Jackson (51 percent), Muskie (40 percent), Harris (38 percent), Bayh and Udall (33 percent). From another perspective, a majority of those polled, 52 percent, "knew too little to judge" whether or not Carter would make a good President. Only Bentsen, Terry Sanford, and Shapp were less known than he. There was an opportunity here. If Carter could do well in the early caucuses and primaries and secure a good press build-up, he might be able to win over those "don't knows." Maybe that is why Jimmy the Greek was giving odds of 8 to 1 that Carter would become the Democratic nominee for President.

### Moving Out Front

With the opening of the 1976 campaign season, Apple, of *The New York Times*, gave a rundown on the potential of the various starters in the race. "A kind of rough standing among the candidates has suddenly started to emerge in the minds of political professionals around the country," Apple wrote. "In the group from which the nominee is believed most likely to be selected are Senator Henry M. Jackson of Washington, Senator Birch Bayh of Indiana, former Governor Jimmy Carter of Georgia and Senator Hubert Humphrey of Minnesota." A second group—those with a "conceivable chance" of being nominated—included Shriver, Harris, and Udall. Those having only a remote chance for the nomination were Bentsen, Shapp, Sanford, Frank Church, Wallace, and Robert Byrd. But, as Apple concluded, "such early calculations are highly speculative . . ."

Spurred by what Udall had called "that silly poll in Iowa," the press descended on that state shortly after New Year's to cover the opening event of the season. NBC and CBS set up their Tabulation Center at the Hilton Inn just outside of Des Moines, preparing for the major spectacle on January 19 when the first returns of the season would come in. With stars such as Roger Mudd on hand, the state chairman, Tom Whitney, was able to sell admissions to citizens who wanted to watch the reporting.

Some presidential entries were not at the starting line, but Carter, Bayh, Udall, and Shriver were there, enough to make it a race. And the press was determined to correct a mistake made back in 1972 when they had let McGovern's early showing there go relatively unnoticed. (Theodore White had not even mentioned the Iowa caucuses in his book on the 1972 campaign.) In a field with so many unknowns, something like that might happen again. On the other hand, there was a potential for publicity overkill in this event. Iowa, after all, would choose only 47 out of 3,008 possible delegates to the national convention in July; moreover, in the caucuses on January 19, Iowa Democrats were taking the first in what was a series of steps leading to the selection of the state's delegation. Precinct delegates were being chosen; later they would go to the county convention, which would select delegates to the six congressional districts' convention, which in turn, would choose delegates to the state convention.)

The Carter people had been working the state for almost a year: Carter himself had been in Iowa a total of seventeen days and his campaign organization was the only one listed in the Des Moines yellow pages. Both Bayh and Udall, viewed as Carter's strongest competitors in the state, had to husband their time because of congressional duties and entered late. Each had been competing for the endorsements of liberal groups in New York and Massachusetts and preparing to seize the liberal banner from the other in New Hampshire, traditionally the first contest of the campaign. Each entered Iowa at the last minute only to keep the other from gaining a publicity harvest that could lead to an edge in New Hampshire.

The television press had set guidelines for choosing "winners" in each of those early ordeals by poll—whichever candidate received the largest plurality would be declared the victor, regardless of other considerations (such as how large his plurality was relative to the rest of the field). Only 10 percent of Iowa's Democrats turned out for these neighborhood caucuses. When the returns trickled in, it was apparent the "uncommitted" delegates, with 37.1 percent, had received the largest plurality. Of those who did designate a favorite, 27.6

percent marked Carter as their choice, more than double the votes of second place Birch Bayh, with 13.1 percent. The press could not sit with this amorphous result. They had to have a "winner," and the uncommitted delegates would not do. They declared Carter the victor.

Carter had been spending the night at a friend's apartment in Manhattan. At 2:00 A.M. the phone rang. It was Powell, telling him he was winning. Carter thanked him and went back to sleep. By 6:00 A.M. he was up and on his way through the empty streets of New York for a series of TV and radio interviews for CBS's "Morning News," NBC's "Today" show, and ABC's "Good Morning America." The next day when he moved to New Hampshire, a press retinue accompanied him. The Miami *Herald* described Jimmy Carter as "the Man to Beat." Apple in *The New York Times* said that the Iowa result had made Carter a "major contender" for the Democratic nomination. He also developed a theme that was to continue throughout the campaign: "He [Carter] scored heavily among farmers as well as urban folk, among Roman Catholics as well as Protestants, among blue-collar as well as white-collar workers, even among Iowa's few blacks." And the consensus among Iowa and Washington analysts, he continued, was that Carter had put on an "A" campaign.

Carter was unable to parlay the publicity he received from the Iowa win into a victory in the Mississippi caucuses the next week. Wallace smashed Carter and all his other opponents, taking 44.5 percent of the vote to Carter's 13 percent, Shriver's 12 percent, and Bentsen's 1.6 percent, and the rest uncommitted. (Carter had not been expecting a defeat of this dimension. On the day of the Mississippi caucuses, he told some members of the press who were traveling with him in Vermont that he would surprise Wallace.) Two weeks later, in Oklahoma, Carter did better. As in Iowa, he again ran behind an uncommitted slate—which was led by Governor David Boren. But again the press concentrated on the committed delegates and here he eventually tied Fred Harris in his home state. The Oklahoma results were most significant for Carter, however, in that they eliminated the final moderate Southern alternative to Wallace—Senator Lloyd Bentsen of Texas—from the race. (Terry Sanford, the former governor of North Carolina and the president of Duke University, had never been able to get his campaign off the ground and had withdrawn from the race the day after the Mississippi caucuses.)

The New Hampshire primary, which followed Oklahoma by two weeks, was to be the testing ground in the early campaign. Here Carter had a real advantage. Wallace and Jackson had both decided to bypass the state, leaving the conservative field open to Carter. He proceeded to fill it. In his radio and television advertising, Carter appealed to conservative values, emphasizing the work ethic, the need for welfare reform and reorganizing the government. (The Manchester *Union Leader*, published by the arch-conservative William Loeb, even took its eyes off its first interest, Ronald Reagan's campaign, to run an editorial on December 10, entitled "Carter Vs. Chiselers." His proposal to remove persons who could work from the welfare rolls "makes sense," it said. "If Jimmy

Carter were Barry Goldwater, against whom the liberal news media can justify any slur, he could anticipate seeing his welfare proposals caricatured in a *Concord Monitor* headline: 'Carter to Kill Welfare.' ") In late January, at a dinner billed "New Hampshire Dines with the Next President"—Udall, Bayh, and Harris also attended—Carter staked out the territory to the right of his liberal opponents. He did it in a way that showed his mastery of political ambiguity. He opposed socialized medicine, for example, praising the strength of the American system, but favored mandatory comprehensive federal health insurance, and promised a government that was "good, honest, decent, truthful, fair, idealistic, compassionate and filled with love."

Carter's strategy, as Powell later noted, was to create the "one candidate opposition—us against everybody else—by painting Congressman Udall and Senator Bayh as being all of one piece." And as Bayh people found out, when they began to campaign actively in the state in early January, Carter had already captured the field from the center of the right in the Democratic Party. This meant that all the other candidates had to share the liberal votes—and that included Shriver and Harris in addition to Udall and Bayh.

Carter, by this time, had built a good organization. Jean Wallin, a former national committeewoman (who had signed on with Carter after the Kansas City miniconvention) helped lay down an organization for the state. But Carter did not attract the party activists the way Udall or Bayh did, so he had to supplement his organizational activity with other kinds of help. His aides compiled a 50,000-card file with a list of potential Carter voters and the campaign hired National Telephone Advertisers of New York, paying them $18,000, to conduct a phone canvass of these supporters. Volunteers from Georgia helped out. Bert Lance and Philip Lance and Philip Alston came up from Atlanta for a few days of campaigning. In early January a planeload of Georgians—ninety of them— flew to New Hampshire to canvass for him. The members of this Peanut Brigade each paid $150 to charter a jet from Atlanta and ranged in age from eighteen to eighty.

The group was broken up and assigned to various regions in Manchester and Nashua, where 80 percent of the New Hampshire Democrats were located. At a brief orientation meeting they were given cards with the names of Democrats on them, a quick lesson in pronouncing the most common French names in the area and how to use their scoring system. Then they hit the streets in subzero weather to approach those houses in which registered Democrats lived. Roy Ingram, a sixty-two-year-old dean of South Georgia College, showed the kind of devotion these people had. He trudged through the near-zero weather against a brisk thirty-mile-per-hour wind in one of the worst sections of Manchester. A reporter who followed him watched as he approached a row of rusty, unlabeled doorbells and proceeded to ring them all. Nobody answered. He knocked on the glass. Finally, he pulled out his voter card, made the appropriate notation on it, and eased down the treacherous steps to the sidewalk.

Then he remembered he'd forgotten something. Once again he renegotiated the stairs, took out a green pamphlet from his pocket, and scrawled a personal note across the front. "Sorry I missed you. R. D. Ingram, Fairburn, GA."

John Pope, an old family friend who joined the Peanut Brigade, tells of their efforts:

The Peanut Brigade was Jimmy's idea. He thought of it; and it derived from another idea of his when he was running for governor, when he asked Sumter County people to go over the state and he called it "Hi! Neighbor, Day" . . .

We went to New Hampshire. These people were so disgusted with form letters in the mail all the time. You know there were 7–8, candidates running at that time, filling a box full of mail—computer letters, but nobody was getting out there. All of them tried just a little bit. They'd hire a few students to go, but the students would go to the beer hall and have a good time and never made the calls. We would start working every morning, at least by 10:00 and work until 9:00 at night, which was 4 or 5 hours after dark. And call on every house whatever, every Democratic house. . . .

[At the] motel that night, we rated them . . . 1, 2, 3, 4, 5. And all of the ones with "3's," or better, we'd sit down and write them a handwritten personal note, and we spoke of something that happened while talking to them, during the day: "Enjoyed meeting your child, Rachel," or something like that. Trying to be real personal with them. And this went over with a bang; they were so impressed that someone would take the time to write them a personal letter instead of sending them a computer letter. And this, I think, did more for Carter than anything else, those letters.

All the candidates had their canvassers. (There were more than 1,000 volunteers in New Hampshire on the two weekends before the primary.) They all had a system of targeting their potential supporters, and Udall also had personal follow-ups similar to Carter's. What was most special about the Carter brigade was their maturity. As John Pope's wife, Betty, noted: "They were used to meeting college kids . . . but with us, they were meeting mature people of all ages . . . and all walks of life who were not giddy and silly, but serious people who cared enough to talk to the waitresses and the garbage men as well as the executives."

On election day, February 24, 80,000 Democrats trudged to the polls. Twenty-one thousand of them voted for Carter—30 percent of the vote. Udall took 24 percent; Bayh 16 percent; Harris 11 percent; Shriver 9 percent; Humphrey 6 percent. The liberal field took more than two thirds of the total vote but it was split among five candidates. As a CBS–*New York Times* poll showed, Carter had drawn mainly from conservative Democrats, although he had help from liberals, moderates, blue-collar workers, and those not educated beyond high school.

Later that night, after a celebration with his staff and family, Carter, happy and smiling, appeared before a cheering crowd at a Manchester hotel ballroom—to claim his New Hampshire victory. More than that, he said, he was going to win the Democratic nomination on the first ballot. "I remember when we couldn't even find a microphone," he told them, speaking of his early campaign days in the state. But that was all over now: ". . . Being from the South is not a handicap. . . ."*

One week after the New Hampshire vote, in the Massachusetts primary, Carter would face all the announced candidates: Wallace (who had made the decision to run in Massachusetts over the objections of his campaign manager), Jackson, Udall, Bayh, Harris, and Shriver.

Carter's earliest strategy had been to skip Massachusetts and focus on winning the Florida primary, which was scheduled for two weeks after New Hampshire. But the night of the New Hampshire primary, Carter and his strategist met in Manchester's Carpenter Hotel to reconsider their decision. They decided to escalate the effort in Massachusetts but to keep the operation as low-profile as possible. (Jody Powell told the press that no extra effort was being made in Massachusetts as a result of Carter's New Hampshire victory.)

In Massachusetts, Carter had to face an increasing barrage of criticism from the other candidates. The night before the New Hampshire primary, Carter and some of the other candidates had gone down to Boston for a League of Women Voters Presidential Forum, and Carter, in response to a question, had indicated that his proposal for income tax reform might include the elimination of deductions for interest payments on home mortgages. The following day, Boston *Globe* reporter Robert L. Turner began calling the other candidates for their reactions. Birch Bayh accused Carter of sounding too much like a Republican. "We don't need a Democrat running around the country peddling Republican principles," he said. Jackson insisted that Carter was "threatening the destruction of the working and middle-class American family."

On a trip back to Massachusetts, Carter aides decided that "it was best for Jimmy to go up there and take the high road. It was our on-going tactic to emphasize that the country did not want bickering and divisiveness." Carter took this tack in his address at Faneuil Hall in Boston. He branded as a gross distortion, the criticism of his proposal to abolish income tax deductions for mortgage interest payments. What he would do, he said, would "seriously consider abolishing all exemptions" except those related to job expenses. This should enable the government to "cut the tax rate by 40 to 50 percent." He then identified himself with the public interest: "I don't believe that the nation appreciates personal animosities and attacks among candidates hoping to be President of the United States." And he continued:

. . . [the attacks] won't hurt me, but I'm afraid it might hurt the country . . . one of the things that concerns the people . . . is the bickering, squabbling, hatred, and animosities, and blame handed back and forth in our great nation's capital in Washington. This is not good for our country. I want to be the next President. But that doesn't mean that I have to take my political success from personal hatred and attacks on the

* Carter's plurality was similar to Muskie's in 1972—which had then been interpreted as a loss. But Carter, unlike Muskie, was not perceived as an established candidate, and so the expectations for him were lower.

character or ability of my opponents . . . the people have got enough judgement, enough common sense, and know me well enough so that these attacks will hurt the ones who make the attacks.

Carter then took off for a visit to Salem, where he blitzed the Parker Brothers games factory. As a *Harvard Crimson* reporter described it, "Beginning at 2:47 a.m., the Nuclear Peanut blurred through all levels of the three-story factory like an overheated molecule going into the terminal phases of Brownian motion."

On the bus back to Logan Airport, Powell traded quips with the press. Referring to Carter's tax deduction proposals, Powell laughingly told them: "See. You bastards tell us to get specific. And when we do, we burn our ass on 'em. Kinda like spitting to windward." Then somebody mentioned Jackson and why he had bothered to attack Carter in Massachusetts. Powell said: "There's one candidate who can never use 'I'll never tell a lie.' " "Never has," Apple interjected. In fact, said Apple with a straight face, Jackson once got up and said, "I reserve the right to lie in the defense of freedom."

Carter's showing in Massachusetts was poor. Jackson took 23 percent of the vote; Udall 18 percent; Wallace 17 percent—Carter 14 percent.

Jackson had run an old-style Democratic campaign. He had stressed employment in a state with high unemployment. He poured money into television and press advertisements. He had the old pros working for him—labor alone supplied him with about 2,500 workers. On election day, when a heavy snow threatened to keep people from voting, his people sent cars to the neighborhoods to drive his voters to the polls. Elated by his win, Jackson crowed that he had put together the "grand coalition that elected Franklin D. Roosevelt, Harry Truman, John F. Kennedy and Lyndon Johnson." (Actually he shared the blue-collar vote with Wallace, who took Boston, and the black vote with Carter, who carried Roxbury.)

But the press was unimpressed. One magazine interpreted his victory as a "triumph of will, cash and organization." Ben J. Wattenburg, a Jackson adviser, later noted:

After the Massachusetts primary, Jackson, unlike Carter, was not on the cover of *Time;* he was not on the cover of *Newsweek;* we did not get articles about his cousin who has a worm farm. And that was the story of the Jackson campaign for the next six weeks, and that was what I think killed that campaign. Jackson had won a totally unanticipated victory, beyond what the press had expected, in a state with ten times as many delegates as New Hampshire, and the effect was barely visible. We were dismayed.

Carter seemed shaken by the loss. The night before the voting, when Caddell and Rafshoon had warned Carter that Jackson might win, Carter serenely replied: "I can't believe that. That defies everything I know about politics." But as the Massachusetts returns came in at a television election center in Orlando, Florida, Carter was stunned. "That's too bad, that's too bad," he stuttered to reporters. He placed a call to Caddell. "What happened?" he asked in "icy rage." Caddell explained that the weather had worked against them—Carter's support was soft and the election day snowstorm had kept a large number of people away from the polls. "The forty-eight hours after Massachusetts were just horrendous," Caddell admitted. "We were off base, our candidate was off stride, and we were facing the crisis of our lives."

The Massachusetts results were a serious matter. Proving Carter up North had been a central part of their strategy for winning Florida. And Florida was widely perceived as the testing ground of their campaign. Ever since January, everybody else had been seeing it that way. As Lou Harris noted in January: "The common presumption is that if Carter can defeat Wallace in Florida, the Georgian will become a real possibility for the Democratic nomination and if Wallace defeats Carter, the Georgian will be finished."

Suddenly Carter's credibility as a winner had been undermined. The Miami *Herald,* the day after the Massachusetts debacle, ran a piece in which they noted that most of the people they interviewed thought Carter would "definitely run second" to Wallace. Mike Abrams, Carter's Dade County campaign manager, said: ". . . it has to cut our chances of beating Wallace." Former State Representative Talbot D'Alemberte, a liberal Miami Democrat, said of other liberals: "If they can't put an anti-Wallace vote where they think it will really count they may just go off and vote for somebody they really like."

The Massachusetts results also fired up the Jackson people in Florida. They had never really put together a statewide organization. But they did undertake a media blitz. Jackson himself came into the state for one final concentrated tour in which he put the Georgian under sustained fire for the first time in the campaign. At one stop he said, "We're trying to offer more than just a smile." Taking off on Carter's earlier remarks before the League of Women Voters, Jackson charged that Carter's proposal would "cost American homeowners $6 billion more in taxes." At a pep talk for local campaign workers at a Biscayne cafeteria, Jackson said: "The Carter proposal would destroy the homebuilding industry in America . . . there would be no incentive to buy a home." He later cautioned: "He'd better do some homework before he comes up with fuzzy ideas." At a press conference in Titusville, he accused Carter of "saying one thing in the snow and another thing in the sunshine."

Carter, working his way down the middle of the state on a Greyhound bus, took out similarly after Jackson. At an Orlando press conference the day after the Massachusetts vote, he charged that Jackson had won his first primary by exploiting the busing issue, running advertisements that were "divisive, emotional, [with] connotations of racism." (Pat Caddell, at first, was not sure why Carter did this. Later he realized that Carter was appealing to the black vote, which the campaign staff had just learned Carter had won in Massachusetts.) Speaking before the Tallahassee's Tiger Bay Club, Carter said of Jackson: "I can't sit back and let one of my opponents deliberately and consistently make false statements. He has been in Congress 35 years. He's not a dishonest man, he's not a bad man, but he wants to be president so bad that he's departed from his normal truthfulness."

Meanwhile, Wallace headed off in his own direction—picking up on the condominium and abortion issues in an attempt to extend his appeal. There was, however, a silent issue stalking him. In the past Wallace had been the embodiment of male vitality and power to his followers. Now, in 1976, he was campaigning in his wheelchair, hauled off planes by aides and Secret Service men, speaking from behind bullet-proof lecterns cut low to suit his wheelchair. Wallace said of the voters: "All they see is the spokes on my wheelchair. The television catches every one. . . . And you got a man in a wheelchair, all humped over, saying the same thing. It's hard to beat."

On March 9 the Florida voter turnout was heavier than expected. Carter captured 34.3 percent to Wallace's 30.6 percent and Jackson's 23.9 percent. Shapp received 2 percent. Carter carried the new suburbs in the geographical center of the state as well as southwest Dade County and increasingly Liberal Leon and Alachua counties. He even cut into Wallace's strength in the rural areas in the north and north-central part of the state. He took Florida's black vote, Carter running ahead of Jackson about 2 to 1 in the precincts of Florida's central cities. The young, like the liberals and blacks, were left with little choice but to pull for Carter. Jackson, a Vietnam hawk and vocal opponent to the decriminalization of marijuana, was not a real alternative to Wallace.

For many Florida voters, however, Carter was a second choice. An NBC election poll showed that many persons voted for Carter because they were concerned about Wallace's health. Over 50 percent of the voters interviewed said their philosophy agreed with Wallace's, but he took only 30.6 percent of the vote.

With Bentsen and Sanford eliminated from the race and Wallace weakened by his Florida defeat, Carter was now in a good position to pick up, almost without competition, all the votes in the Southern primaries and caucuses.

Carter, however, had potential organization problems. His family and friends had focused their full attention on the early contests. As Joel McCleary, Carter's national finance director, said: "We had no structure after Florida; we had planned only for the short haul." Yet that would not really matter. "After Florida, it was all NBC, CBS, and the *New York Times*." As Caddell later noted, "After Florida, there was one serious candidacy—Carter's—and everybody else, because the media had made it that way."

The week after Florida, Carter would again face Wallace—along with Shriver and Harris—in Illinois. Mayor Daley, whose delegation had been unseated at the 1972 convention, was fielding a slate of delegates nominally pledged to the favorite son candidacy of Adlai Stevenson. Daley was engaged in a bitter struggle for influence over the Democratic Party in the state and determined to head the Illinois delegation and play the broker's role at the convention. It was a complex political field laden with potential booby traps. Jackson, Bayh, and Udall backed away from Illinois altogether.

Carter had been courting Daley since 1972—supporting the Daley delegates in their credentials fight at the convention in 1972, offering him a place to stay at Sea Island, Georgia, after his stroke in 1974, voting with him on some key issues at Kansas City in 1974. His policy of entering every state meant that his running in Illinois could not be interpreted as an anti-Daley maneuver. Further, in deference to Daley, none of his delegates were running in the major central Chicago districts. And though the head of Carter's state campaign was Jim Wall, who led the McGovern slate that had challenged Daley in 1972, Wall now assured the Daley organization that Carter's delegates would vote for him to head the Illinois delegation at the 1976 convention. Indeed, Carter had handled Daley with sufficient delicacy that the Cook County delegates put out sample ballots without the name of Stevenson or any other presidential contenders at the top of their slate. People in Chicago could vote for Daley in the delegate race and still state their preference for Carter in the separate, non-binding presidential popularity poll.

On election day Carter led the popularity poll with 48 percent, compared to Wallace's 28 percent, Shriver's 16 percent and Harris's 8 percent. In downstate Illinois he won 53 percent of the vote. Carter's finish in the delegate race in Illinois surprised many. He won more than double the twenty to twenty-five he had predicted, taking fifty-five delegates. As Daley said after the results were in: "It's something you have to pay respect to." And Democratic National Committee Chairman Robert Strauss called Carter "the obvious frontrunner," adding: "It is a fact of life that a Southerner is no longer a regional candidate."

Yet Carter's support was less solid than it seemed. Some of his workers were on board because they wanted a winner. (Wall had given that as one of his own motives.) Many of the voters would have preferred to vote for someone not on the ballot (as a CBS–*New York Times* poll revealed). One third of those who backed Carter would have supported Udall or Jackson had either been on the Illinois ballot, while 50 percent would have backed Humphrey. Humphrey would have obtained 43 percent of the Democratic vote had he run. One national pollster noted: "People aren't voting for Carter on the issues. They're voting for him because he comes across as the nicest personality in an unexciting field."

Harris and Shriver both withdrew from active campaigning after Illinois but Wallace would face Carter again in a one-on-one race in North Carolina the next Tuesday. This was to be Wallace's last hurrah. His advertisements emphasized his physical stamina. He took out after Carter personally, something he had done only sporadically in his earlier campaign, calling him a "warmed over McGovern." (He dropped that when it seemed to backfire.) He accused him of being "wishy-washy" on the issues and of duplicity in his claims that he had never supported Wallace. In a speech at Winston-Salem, he waved around an old copy of a 1970 article in the Atlanta *Journal*, in which Carter was quoted as saying he would support a national ticket of Humphrey and Wallace.

Carter took all these shots coolly—reassured, no doubt, by a North Carolina newspaper poll published a week before the election that showed him with a ten-point lead over Wallace. In Raleigh he responded to Wallace's charges that Carter had once backed him by saying that he vaguely remembered telling reporters that a Humphrey-Wallace ticket would be popular in the South. He

added: "I have never supported Wallace, and I never will." Wallace's three terms as governor of Alabama, he claimed, had not been all that good for the "little man" Wallace professed to represent. On another occasion he told reporters that he might not run against Wallace in Alabama because he did not "want to rub his nose in it any further."

Carter won 53.6 percent of the vote in North Carolina. Wallace pulled in 34.7 percent.

Up to this point in the campaign, there had been only six primaries, and Carter had never had a head-on race with a major contender who could equal him in effort and money. Now, as Jordan had noted immediately after Florida, the Carter organization would have to start picking and choosing which primaries to emphasize. The major goals would be to pick off Udall in Wisconsin and Jackson in Pennsylvania. Caddell agreed: "I don't think there is any question that we must win Wisconsin, avoid embarrassment in New York, and beat Jackson in Pennsylvania, and then in Indiana to effect a quick kill in the primaries . . . My position is, unless we can put together a first-ballot victory or damn close to it, this party will deny us the nomination. Popular with the elites, we are not . . ."

There was real potential for embarrassment in New York. Carter did not enjoy wide appeal among Catholics, Jews, and liberals, who are so important in New York. He also had little support from the political establishment there. Indeed, Jackson claimed most of the recognizable political names as his delegates—and this was important because of the way the ballot was set up. The presidential candidates would not be listed on the ballots, only the delegates. Also, Jackson had invested in palm cards listing the delegates committed to him, which voters could take with them into the booths. (Three weeks before the primary, however, the New York legislature changed the rules and permitted the names of the candidates to whom the delegates were pledged to appear on the ballot.)

Carter's showing in New York was disastrous. Jackson took 38 percent of the vote and 104 delegates; Udall (who at last had picked up support from former Bayh supporters and won the endorsement of Americans for Democratic Action) 25.5 percent and 70 delegates; Carter 12.8 percent and 35 delegates; 23 percent and 65 of the delegates were uncommitted.

The press could have raised some questions about the viability of Carter candidacy. This was the second major industrial state in the North where Carter had met real competition—and been overwhelmed. Jackson's 38 percent might have been taken as a sign of victory. It was not. Ben Wattenberg who was working for the Jackson campaign, later recalled the press response after the election: "I woke up the next morning in a hotel, and I think it was the Today Show that they said, 'Well, it's now a showdown between Carter and Humphrey.' I literally fell off the bed. Instead of it finally being a head to head clash between Jackson and Carter, it was still Carter versus the pack, and pack then was Udall and Jackson, symbolized by Humphrey."

Indeed, the morning after the New York and Wisconsin primaries, Ca

had the positive headlines and attracted the television interviews. Viewing New York as a foregone conclusion, the media had shifted its attention to Wisconsin. NBC and CBS had established their election night headquarters there instead of New York. Television stations and the print media the next morning carried a shot of a triumphant Carter, in a Harry Truman–like pose, looking at a copy of a Wisconsin paper that earlier in the evening had proclaimed Udall the winner.

As that photo suggested, Wisconsin was a close one, with Carter winning by less than 5,000 votes. In the final tallies Carter obtained 271,220 votes (37%), Udall 263,771 (36%).

Wisconsin just about closed the door on Morris Udall's candidacy and Pennsylvania did the same for Henry Jackson. Patrick Caddell had called Pennsylvania the " 'O.K. Corral' of the campaign between Jackson and us . . . In this state, we must effectively find a way to cut Jackson's blue-collar employment issues . . ."

On Carter's side there was momentum. With victories in Illinois, North Carolina, and Wisconsin, he was the man to beat. Further, he altered his schedule and canceled a rest weekend in Plains to allow himself ten days in Pennsylvania instead of three. His Pennsylvania organization was patterned after the successful organization of earlier states. Tim Kraft, who by this time had emerged as the maestro of "grass-roots" campaigning, was dispatched to Philadelphia in mid-March to set the Carter organization in motion. There would eventually be twenty-two offices throughout the state. Kraft hired a professional telephone service and installed 100-phone banks in Pittsburgh and Philadelphia. Nearly 300,000 phone calls were made to potential voters from these stations. The Peanut Brigade came in again—more than 100 Georgians and Floridians combed the state, staying with Carter delegates each night after canvassing. Carter was also able to gather limited support from Pennsylvania's political establishment. Pittsburgh Mayor Peter Flaherty flew to upstate New York to meet Carter and endorsed him publicly afterward. Even Philadelphia Mayor Frank Rizzo's support of Jackson indirectly played into Carter's hands. Since Rizzo was unpopular with the city's black population (34.4 percent), his endorsement helped push the black vote into Carter's corner.

Carter also had the money for a media blitz in the state—all the while he was also overwhelming his opponents with an abundance of free television and newspaper coverage. One day when Carter, Jackson, and Udall were all in Philadelphia, the Philadelphia *Bulletin* ran two front-page stories on Carter and printed his picture twice in the paper's first four pages. The others were covered in brief paragraphs.

On the surface Jackson appeared to have several factors working for him. The polls in early March showed him leading Carter in Pennsylvania by a small margin. Governor Milton Shapp, who had hoped to take most of the state's 171 delegates to the convention, abandoned his bid in mid-March, releasing his delegates with the suggestion that they support Jackson. Humphrey supporters

in the Democratic organization were backing Jackson for the duration, with the intention of swinging their support to Humphrey when, as expected, he became a candidate. Organized labor, including Ed Toohey, president of the state AFL-CIO and the leader of organized labor in Pennsylvania, were working with them.

Yet Jackson had his problems. The "Anyone But Carter" message was complex. "Despite the unquestioned political clout of these forces," one *Wall Street Journal* reporter noted, "this strategy may prove difficult to put into effect. 'This requires a tough message: First, Humphrey is a great guy; secondly, Carter is a jerk, so therefore you have to vote for Jackson,' says one public opinion expert. That's an awfully complicated set of ideas to get around; . . ." More important, the Pennsylvania political establishment played their own brand of "wait and see." Shapp went to Germany on a trade-promoting trip. Sample ballots distributed by Philadelphia's Democratic machine in some areas of the city did not include Jackson's name. Organized labor gave Jackson half-hearted support at best. The Sunday before the primary Ed Toohey offered: "It's going to be very difficult" to get the labor vote out for Jackson. Calling the rank and file "cynical and fed-up," Toohey felt that getting them to vote at all could be counted as a major victory. Other labor leaders made statements that indicated that while their hearts were with Humphrey or Jackson, their minds were on Carter. As one AFL-CIO official noted, "It's not particularly constructive to start attacking someone you might end up embracing."

As dusk settled over Pennsylvania on April 27, it became clear that the voters were not much interested in any of the candidates. Only one third of the registered voters went to the polls. Of those who voted, many had to settle for their second choice. Forty-six percent of them (according to a Washington *Post* exit poll) would have cast their vote for Humphrey had he been a declared candidate. "By that test, the Minnesota senator would have beaten Carter by a two-to-one margin."

Once again Carter failed to secure a majority. In the game of the campaign, however, he came out on top with 37 percent of the vote to Jackson's 25 percent, Udall's 19 percent, and Wallace's 11 percent. Once again Carter showed his "broad appeal"—he carried sixty-six of the state's sixty-seven counties, winning the votes of white- and blue-collar workers, the elderly and the young, and Catholics and Protestants (though Jackson could lay claim to the Jewish bloc). Essentially, the "O.K. Corral" worked just the way the Carter people had hoped it would.

# THIRTEEN

# Bandwagon

## Outsider

FROM THE BEGINNING OF his campaign, Carter ran on the same kind of "outsider" theme he had used in his 1970 campaign in Georgia, though Washington, not Atlanta, was now the "inside" he was "outside" of. One of his mailings read: "We will not see the kind of change we need in Washington by moving from Congress to the White House." At a rally in Berlin, New Hampshire, Carter told a crowd: "It's time for someone like myself to make a drastic change in Washington. The insiders have had their chance and they have not delivered." An advertisement read: "The candidates from Congress running for President are telling the people . . . about the evils of Washington bureaucracy, when they have been a part of that bureaucracy all along."

His anti-Washington stance provoked the reaction one might expect. In New Hampshire, Birch Bayh said he was proud of his service in Congress and that he didn't know how "experience in peanut farming qualified someone to be president." Morris Udall said it was about time the Georgian be asked about his own record as well as his stand on issues. Even non-Washingtonian Terry Sanford, when he withdrew from the race in January, made the pointed remark that Jackson, not Carter, would be the best man to beat George Wallace in North Carolina. In late January, journalist Elizabeth Drew was finding a certain uneasiness among the other politicians in Washington. "Politicians here are troubled by the substance of what he is saying. They are also bothered by the fact that, a loner, he does not seem to need them."

As the anti-Washington candidate, Carter would thrive on opposition from the "insiders." In a telephone interview with an Atlanta reporter immediately after his Iowa win, he said: "The Iowa caucus does separate me at least temporarily from the pack . . . they have already taken pot shots at me." Just before the New Hampshire primary, he hinted at the existence of some kind of cabal opposed to him: "It's obvious that many of the other candidates look on me now as an obstacle on the way to the White House." At a fish fry in Tampa, Carter said: "A lot of the insiders in Washington are saying that Jimmy Carter has to be stopped, but I want to tell you, there's no way to stop me." While campaigning in Illinois, he saw the situation in New York as one "contrived to suit the political bosses of the state," and said he would not deal "with the backroom boys in New York for delegates. I deal in the open." (At about the same time Carter noted that he had been asking Chicago's Mayor Daley about his plans for endorsing political candidates.)

Later in the campaign Carter would seize upon any criticism from the Washington crowd (or their cohorts, the "bosses" in the states), any sign of a possible move to oppose him, as an indication that there was indeed a cabal against him. When Hubert Humphrey, in late March, suggested that the "anti-Washington" campaign theme showed some signs of "racism" (from which charge he excluded Carter), Carter said he resented the implications that "an attempt to make the government more effective is an attack on Washington or an attack on the poor or racist." He then proceeded: "I think Senator Humphrey perhaps is concerned because some of the things that he was influential in passing 15 or 20 or 25 years ago are challenged as being not too perfect . . . And I think he's also concerned by the fact that some of us don't believe that Washington is the repository of all national wisdom." There was a "stop Carter" strategy, he said. It was "devious"—though they had the right to do it. During the Pennsylvania campaign, he claimed to have discovered certain "machinations" by Humphrey operatives ("probably" with Humphrey's knowledge) to help Jackson as a way of stopping Carter.

Humphrey's shadow candidacy lent a certain credence to Carter's claims. In November, 1975, Hubert Humphrey told Congressman Paul Simon, "The Party knows where I stand. If they want me, I'm available, but I'm not going to lift a finger." And he told all the candidates who visited him that he might come in at the end. Throughout the spring he suggested that he would like the presidency, if not the competition of the primaries. He maintained an active speaking schedule, suggesting to groups like the National Conference of Mayors and the American Society of Newspaper Editors that he would be accessible after the primaries if there was no clear front runner. And as Carter quickly broke from the ranks, Humphrey began showing signs of nervousness. During the Illinois and North Carolina primaries he tried—along with Scoop Jackson and Bob Strauss—to encourage Wallace to stay in the race. Yet in late March he discouraged the efforts of several friends to put together a draft-Humphrey committee. And he insisted, on several occasions, that he was maintaining a neutral stance in all the state races.

Aside from Humphrey's ambivalent and sobering presence, however, there was no coalition against Carter during the early phase of the campaign. In New Hampshire the liberals had split their vote and the conservatives (Jackson and Wallace) had stayed out; in Florida there was, if anything, a pro-Carter cabal.

In Illinois, the truest of all political "bosses" had maintained a neutral stance toward Carter's candidacy. And in Illinois and North Carolina, Jackson and Udall had left Carter without any effective opposition from mainstream Democrats. In Wisconsin, despite some suggestions by R. W. Apple in *The New York Times*, Humphrey did nothing on Udall's behalf: "We wish he would," a Udall aide said.

Whatever Humphrey supporters and labor had planned for Jackson in Pennsylvania, it did not lead to any concerted action on his behalf. But it did give Carter more fuel for the fire. At a press conference on the afternoon of April 13, he showed reporters a copy of the Philadelphia *Bulletin*, which carried a lead story headed "Stop-Carter Alliance Is Formed." At this conference and later in his hotel room, Carter explained that this was the work of political bosses. He warned that if someone like himself, who had run all over the country, were to go to the convention and be denied the nomination by someone who had not, "it would be a very divisive thing . . ." Under these circumstances it would be hard to carry the South for the Democratic Party. "I'm not saying it as any kind of threat."

## Bandwagon

With Carter's impressive victory in Pennsylvania, it became clear that there would be no brokered convention in which Humphrey might play a role unless he would seek the presidency more actively. On Thursday, April 29, however, under the klieg lights in the Senate caucus room, Hubert Humphrey announced that he would not actively campaign. "The one thing I don't need at this stage of my life is to be ridiculous," he said, his eyes tearing.

After Humphrey's press conference, Scoop Jackson, out of money, flew back home to Seattle to announce that he was ending his active pursuit of the nomination. This left Udall as the only one of the original starters still in active competition with Carter. Bayh had "suspended" his campaigning on March 4 after he finished seventh in the Massachusetts primary. Shriver quit on March 22, and Harris followed suit on April 8. (Both needed the federal matching funds due them, so they technically remained in the race, leaving their names on the ballots in several states.) With Jackson now out of the race, Udall tried to rally the Washington Senator's support behind himself. In New Brunswick, New Jersey, he appealed for Jackson's supporters even before Jackson's exit from the campaign was official. Yet Udall did not get Jackson's endorsement—as he had been unable to get the earlier dropouts' support. To a certain degree this was caused by the bitterness of their early fights with each other to "clear the field."

With no one to back, the uncommitted slates began to fall apart. Humphrey's refusal to enter the New Jersey primary, for example, undermined the attempt by New Jersey's Democratic Party chairman James Dugan to field a slate of prominent delegates who were officially uncommitted but actually backing Humphrey. People also began to buy Carter's view that the opposition to him, at this point, was wrong. On Monday, May 3, George McGovern—who had been supporting Udall—publicly fired two of his top aides, Alan Baron and Jack Quinn, for their participation in stop-Carter meetings. Mentioning the Anyone But McGovern movement of 1972 and Carter's participation in it, McGovern said that the convention could not ignore the long string of victories Carter had won in the primaries.

While the opposition seemed to be folding, the polls were suggesting that Carter could be a winner in the fall. One *Time* poll (by Yankelovich, Skelly and White) showed Carter leading Ford by 48 percent to 38 percent—a startling change from the 46 percent to 38 percent lead Ford had held only seven weeks previously. Also, 50 percent to 27 percent of those polled wanted to see a Democrat as the next U.S. President, assuming Republican and Democratic candidates of equal ability. And 48 percent of the total voting population saw Carter as the strongest Democratic candidate, as opposed to Humphrey (34%) and Jackson (3%).

Looking ahead, a Carter romp to the finishing wire seemed imminent. The Southern primaries—Louisiana, Texas, Alabama, Georgia, Tennessee, Arkansas, and Kentucky—were clustered in May, and Carter had entered each one of them. With Wallace and Bentsen out of the race as serious contenders, Carter's bandwagon going, and his Southern charm winning over that region, Carter stood to win in all these states, except possibly Alabama, where Wallace was fighting a rear-guard action against him. There were at least 200 delegates that would go to him without any serious effort on his part.

Carter had had some problems in Georgia. Back in July, 1975, the Darden poll had shown Wallace beating Carter on his home turf by a slim margin of 49.1 to 42.2 percent. And Georgia influentials had been slow to endorse Carter. The state's congressional delegation was not present when he declared his candidacy at the National Press Club luncheon in Washington. As of mid-March, 1976, the list of Georgia Democrats who had *not* endorsed Carter included: Governor George Busbee, U.S. Senators Herman Talmadge and Sam Nunn, nine of the state's ten Congressmen, the state partly leadership, and four of the five living ex-governors (not counting Talmadge and Carter).

Carter had been able, however, to postpone the date of the Georgia primary—from the originally scheduled March 9 (the day of the Florida primary) to May 4, by which time, with the Carter bandwagon rolling, the Georgia problem evaporated. Governor Busbee, on April 22, announced that he was going to vote for Carter and assailed the party bosses for their apparent prejudice against a Southern candidate. He said: "I've never felt this discrimination before and for it to erupt in this campaign is wrong. It could destroy the Democratic party were it injected in this way." At an afternoon press conference the same day, Maynard Jackson, the black mayor of Atlanta, endorsed Carter, calling him "a president for all the people." Jackson then flew to Philadelphia to do some campaigning for him.

When Georgia finally went to the polls, Carter won 84 percent of the vote. The turnout was low, however, possibly because there was no real contest by that time. Wallace, who was Carter's only real competition in Georgia by them, had been effectively pushed out of the race. None of Carter's other competitors—and there were many slated in Georgia—really ran a campaign against him there. On May 1 Carter had taken Texas, despite Bentsen's favorite son candidacy. On May 4, in addition to Georgia, he took Indiana with 68 percent of the vote. He won Tennessee on May 6, but lost Alabama the same day. In short, two thirds of the way through the race Carter seemed to have the nomination sewed up.

Not all Democrats were happy with this rush to Carter. After Pennsylvania, as one *Time* poll showed, Carter remained the choice of a minority of the Democratic Party—39 percent—to 59 percent for other candidates. And more Democrats would prefer Humphrey if they were voting on the basis of economic, defense, and foreign policy issues only. On May 4, moreover, Carter suffered a surprise defeat (his first since New York) at the hands of an uncommitted slate in Washington, D.C.—the only political unit in which blacks, with whom he was purportedly strong, constituted a majority of the voters.

### Rocks in the Road

Two late-comers to the presidential lottery were to place some new hurdles in the path of the Carter bandwagon: Idaho's Senator Frank Church announced his candidacy just after the Illinois primary and laid claim to the mantle of Morris Udall; California Governor Edmund G. (Jerry) Brown, Jr., casually made his announcement to four reporters in his Sacramento office, without so much as informing his staff first.

Carter's reaction to this turn of events was mild. Neither Church nor Brown presented a major threat, he told reporters. Jackson's withdrawal and Humphrey's decision not to campaign actively improved his chances. And though he vowed he would not take anything for granted, Carter said he would cut back his campaign pace and concentrate on unifying the party, identifying the issues, and preparing for the November election.

Brown and Church, as it turned out, did manage to slow down the Carter bandwagon. On May 6 Brown asked fifty Congress members to postpone endorsements of Carter for a week, and several were willing to do so. House Speaker Carl Albert called Brown "astute" and "attractive," and predicted that he was the only one who could stop Carter now. Five days later, on May 11, Church beat Carter in Nebraska by one percentage point—but a "win." In Maryland, Brown was now drawing the kinds of enthusiastic crowds Carter had never seen. And he was contesting Carter's outsider image in a way Washington insiders could not. On Carter's promise of governmental reorganization, Brown said, "It kind of reminds me of the secret plan that Nixon had about Vietnam." On Carter's reorganization of the Georgia government, he pointed out that the number of state employees had risen during Carter's time in office. He called Carter's plans for federal zero-based budgeting "a form of consumer fraud in the political arena . . . a slogan that holds out the false promise that somehow there is an easy way to make the federal budget go down. There is no easy way."

Carter could have chosen to downplay Maryland. Brown had entered too late to field delegates, so all that was at stake was the popularity contest. But Carter tried to beat Brown by campaigning against him in Maryland. His pitch was not honed to meet the concerns of these particular voters—many of them government employees. Accusing the California governor of being against governmental reorganization, Carter pledged to cut the 1,900 federal agencies down to a "manageable" 200 (he gave no indications of which ones would go). On primary day, May 18, his blunder was translated into a solid Brown victory—48.3 percent to 36.9 percent.

The day was nearly a total disaster. Carter narrowly escaped defeat in Michigan—beating Udall 44 percent (306,301 votes) to 43 percent (304,297 votes). (Shriver with 6,163 votes, and Harris with 4,323 probably kept Udall from being the victor.) The narrowness of Carter's margin was even more a problem because he was the front runner. He had momentum, as well as the support of major segments of the Michigan establishment. (Henry Ford of Ford Motor Company, UAW President Leonard Woodcock, and Detroit Mayor Coleman Young all supported Carter and worked for him to varying degrees.)

Suddenly, as Ken Bode wrote in the *New Republic*, "Carter's setbacks rather than his successes were the subject of note." At just the time when attention might have shifted to his delegate totals, attention was diverted to the popularity contest. "With his front runnership well established, the preference contests have become a referendum on Jimmy Carter; they indicate how much support he does not have, how substantial a task he faces in unifying the Democrats if he does win the nomination."

Within the next two weeks the Carter bandwagon ran into a rockslide. On May 25 he lost Oregon and Idaho to Church, and Nevada to Brown. On June 1 he suffered a dismal defeat at the hands of Church in Montana, 59.9 percent to 24.8 percent. And Rhode Island went to a slate of ostensibly "uncommitted" delegates-really pledged to Brown or Humphrey—in an extremely close contest (only 798 votes separated this slate from Carter). Looking ahead, these losses portended future problems for Carter in the last primaries—the Big Three (California, New Jersey, and Ohio) scheduled for June 8. Brown would almost certainly be victorious in California. The slate of uncommitted delegates in New Jersey had held together and now emerged as a fairly solid stumbling block for Carter. Only Ohio looked good: Udall and Church were both entered there and Carter could once again anticipate divided opposition.

Yet Carter was able to minimize the psychological impact these losses might have on his bandwagon. His strategy of running everywhere was now paying off: for each primary day on which he suffered a loss, he also managed to pull out a victory. On the evening he lost in Nebraska, he achieved a narrow win over Udall in Connecticut (where Church split the liberal labor vote). The night of his defeats in Idaho, Nevada, and Oregon he had compensatory wins in Arkansas and Kentucky. Most important, the night he lost Rhode Island and Montana, Carter managed to dominate the headlines with an unexpected conquest of George McGovern's home state of South Dakota. He had not disclosed the results of a favorable poll there showing his front runner status in order to maximize the surprise effect and the good press he would receive as a consequence.

At this phase of the campaign, moreover, the delegate count was what mattered. The Democratic Party had recently abolished winner-take-all primaries. Now delegates would go even to those candidates who did not "win" the state. Carter was still accumulating delegates faster than his opponents—picking up most in the Southern states where he had no real opposition, and winning almost as many in the Northern states where he "lost."

Carter played up these strategic considerations. Even while it became apparent that he was losing Oregon, Nevada, and Idaho, Carter told reporters in New York City that his wins in the three Southern primaries and some caucus states had put him over the 1,000 mark in his totals. While campaigning in Los Angeles in early June, Carter advised Jerry Brown to count delegates. ". . . I would say that someone who has 1,000 delegates is ahead of someone who has 25. That is just my twisted logic. Maybe it would not stand up in front of a Zen Buddhist analysis."

The press was counting, too. In looking ahead to June 1 and June 8, Hal Gulliver said, "If Carter suffers only one or two more "defeats' comparable to these past two Tuesdays, on which he picked up 100 delegates plus each time, he will comfortably have locks on the nomination well before the Democratic convention begins."

These reversals in May, however, put hope back into the draft-Humphrey crowd. Before the returns of the May 18 primaries had even come in, Joseph Crangle, the Buffalo, New York, Democratic leader, checked into the Hay-Adams Hotel, across Lafayette Square from the White House, and started formulating a strategy to draft Humphrey into the ongoing presidential race. Making up for lost time, he assembled in his room four of the best party operatives: Alan Baron, staffperson for George McGovern; Robert Keefe, Scoop Jackson's campaign director; Jack Quinn, a former manager for Udall; and Mark Shields, another Udall man. Their job, as one participant saw it, was to come up with "an insurance policy against the extremely small odds that Carter doesn't make it." A week later the group held a second session.

For a moment it looked as though Ted Kennedy might help out. In New York on May 25 to receive the National Father of the Year award, Kennedy roundly criticized Carter: "Mr. Carter has in his appearance before the Democratic Platform Committee intentionally made his position on some issues indefinite and imprecise, as far as I was concerned." He said Carter's vagueness was a "tactic . . . which has shown to be successful and which he has justified" by winning 11 primaries so far and gathering 745 delegates." But Kennedy's motive was not to stop Carter. Sources close to him were quoted as saying he was annoyed over Carter's lack of commitment to various issues, and that his hints that he might run either for President or as a vice-presidential candidate with Hubert Humphrey were meant to spur Carter into being more specific. The following day ABC reported that Kennedy would not run—that he wouldn't even attend the Democratic convention. Kennedy absolutely refused to join in the effort to push Humphrey.

On June 1, with only six weeks to go before the convention, a Humphrey-for-President headquarters opened on Capitol Hill. Supporters spoke with uncommitted delegates all across the country. (Organizer Joe Crangle insisted that Humphrey supporters were not trying to stop Carter—although he did admit that he talked with former McGovern aides, Alan Baron and Jack Quinn, who had been fired for the doing just that.) On June 4 Humphrey was still insisting that he would not enter the race—"unless Carter suffers a serious setback." He went off to campaign in New Jersey, though he stressed he was not working for himself.

By this time the only hope left for Carter's opponents was the outcome of the June 8 primaries—in California, Ohio, and New Jersey—where 540 delegates were up for grabs.

## Home Stretch

Carter had some problems. California, which normally attracts the most attention of the day, had become virtually a noncontest. (A Field poll published shortly before the primary showed Brown running ahead of Carter with 51 percent of the vote, compared to Carter's 20 percent.) Deciding to take their loss, the campaign minimized Carter's efforts in the state and canceled all but one short trip designed primarily to help raise money and the morale of his campaign workers. The situation in New Jersey was almost as bad; State Chairman Dugan had managed to hold together his "uncommitted" slate. Moreover, both Humphrey and Brown—joined by Brown's father, former California Governor Edmund "Pat" Brown, Sr.,—were campaigning in the state and infusing some old-style Democratic enthusiasm into the race.

Ohio, however, looked good for Carter. With momentum in his favor, he was better able to secure the endorsements of some of the state's influentials, including the liberal former governor, John Gilligan. Most important, Carter was running against a divided opposition; for all the talk of Anyone But Carter, it wasn't working in Ohio, where Udall and Church were ensuring a divided liberal vote.

As the "Big Three" showdown approached, political commentators outlined Carter's problems. Albert Hunt noted in *The Wall Street Journal* that "Mr. Carter's prospects depend heavily on winning the Ohio and New Jersey primaries . . . The loss of either Ohio or New Jersey along with California could send the Carter campaign into a tailspin from which it mightn't recover . . ."

Such statements were troubling to the Carter campaign. Its members knew from their polls that they were going to lose New Jersey as well as California. To avoid a possible last-minute "tailspin," they had to make Ohio the proof that they were going to obtain the nomination.

Carter had been wooing Mayor Richard Daley of Chicago for quite some time—placing weekly calls to him throughout the campaign. According to Greg Schneiders: "We would place a call to Daley every week or ten days . . . Carter himself always talked to Daley." One incident best illustrates Carter's deference to Daley. Carter had accepted an invitation to a fundraising affair that was to be dominated by Daley's arch-rival, Governor Dan Walker, and his allies. After receiving word from Alex Seith (chairman of the Cook County Zoning Board and a prominent Chicago attorney) that Daley was "damned mad" about this turn of events, Carter told Seith: "I'm going to cancel the thing. My friendship with Mayor Daley is too important." On Monday, June 7, Seith told Daley that Carter had not been aware of the situation and would call him to set the record straight.

On Tuesday, June 8, the day of the Big Three primaries, Carter called Daley to make his peace. Carter also told the mayor that he was going to lose California and New Jersey, but that he would win in Ohio. Shortly thereafter, Daley strode out and held a press conference. Speaking of Humphrey, he said that no one should have the nomination handed to him after refusing to take part in the primaries: "who said that's the man who should be knighted on a white horse. . . . Our party isn't in bad enough shape to have to go to someone and demand him and draft him." He had some kind words for Carter.

This man, Carter, has fought in every primary, and if he wins in Ohio, he'll walk in [to the convention] under his own power. . . . I've known him for years. He's got courage. I admire a man who's got courage. He started out months ago and entered into every contest in every state and he won 'em and he lost 'em and, by God, you have to admire a guy like that. . . . He's got a religious tone in what he says and maybe we should have a little more religion in our community. . . . The man talks about true values. Why shouldn't we be sold on him?

That evening Carter lost disastrously in California—Brown took 59 percent of the vote and 204 delegates to Carter's 21 percent and 67 delegates. In New Jersey the uncommitted Brown/Humphrey slate received 42 percent of the vote and 83 delegates to Carter's 28 percent and 25 delegates. But with Daley saying Ohio was the state to watch, that's what everyone did. There Carter captured 52 percent of the vote compared to Udall's 21 percent and Church's 14 percent. He also won 126 delegates, bringing his total count for the day to 218 of the 540 selected.

Election night Carter telephoned his remaining opponents—Church, Udall, and Wallace—each of whom indicated that he thought Carter had pretty much secured the nomination with his Ohio victory. After that the opposition crumbled.

At a press conference in Montgomery, Alabama, the next day, Wallace withdrew from the race, requesting that his 170 delegates cast their first ballot votes for Carter. In Chicago that same day Major Richard Daley told reporters that he would vote for Carter at the Democratic convention, but what the rest of the delegates did was up to them. Humphrey followed suit, and Udall released his delegates. On Thursday, Jackson announced that he would ask his 220 delegates to vote for Carter on the first ballot. Governor Milton Shapp of Pennsylvania and Philadelphia Mayor Frank Rizzo also fell in line. The next Monday (June 14) Church and Harris released their delegates and offered their full support to Carter. Udall freed his delegates to vote as they pleased, but said he would remain in the race.

Jerry Brown continued the contest, however. The day after the Big Three he said that it was possible that Carter was not so popular with the people as he was with the delegates. Two days later he traveled to Louisiana, where he picked up nineteen uncommitted delegates from Governor Edwin Edwards. He said that New Jersey, New York, Missouri, and Illinois would be his next stops. Almost three weeks later Brown had to recognize that his opposition was chimerical. On Friday, June 25, in a nationally televised speech, he conceded, saying: "Governor Carter appears certain to be nominated, and, if he is, I will enthusiastically support his candidacy in the fall."

## How He Did It

Carter had been preparing for this bandwagon from the very beginning of his campaign. During the early primaries he had used the polls to illustrate his broadly based support, showing him sweeping the black vote and the Wallace vote, the labor vote and the business vote, the liberal and conservative vote. As he became well known, he built on the Democratic desire to win. A Carter television commercial, "Bandwagon," aired in New York shortly after the Illinois primary, carried this message: "A recent Gallup Poll," the narrator (dressed in a gray suit) seriously and confidentially tells the audience, "shows that only one Democrat can beat Gerald Ford for the Presidency. It isn't one of the Washington insiders and it isn't the Democrat who tied on with the political bosses and king-makers. The only Democrat who can beat Gerald Ford is Jimmy Carter."

As he moved out front, Carter and his supporters envisioned ships and trains departing from points all around the country. In his March 16 meeting with Jerry Wurf, president of the liberal public employees union (AFSCME), Carter noted that the submarine was leaving the dock and they (the union members) had better climb aboard. At a breakfast fundraiser (on Wednesday, May 13) at the Plaza Hotel in New York, New York City Councilman Matthew Troy remarked, "The boat is leaving and the gangplank is going in." William

Vanden Heuvel supposedly offended New York Governor Hugh Carey with the statement, "The train is leaving the station," suggesting Carey had better climb on.

To soften possible resistance at the end, Carter wooed his former opponents as they dropped out of the race. Shortly before the Indiana primary Carter called Birch Bayh, and the day before the election there Bayh endorsed him. In the late spring, when Wallace was no longer a threat, Carter softened his statements about him: "People wrote him [Wallace] off because they considered him a racist. But he made some valid points about Washington's inability to respond to the average person's needs, black or white." And after his Ohio victory Carter made a drive to mend fences with Morris Udall.

Aside from his own efforts, Carter was aided by luck. Hubert Humphrey's decision not to enter any of the early primaries helped Carter. The polls at the beginning of the season suggested that Humphrey could have won the nomination had he really gone after it from the beginning. His shadow candidacy, however, cast a pall over the campaigns of the other candidates opposing Carter. Labor and old-line politicians, assuming that Humphrey would come in later, did not face the necessity early in the campaign of getting behind some candidate other than Carter. Jackson especially was weakened because he was perceived as a stalking horse for Humphrey. His win in New York was depreciated; and in the crucial Pennsylvania election, labor and its political allies never really consolidated their efforts because they thought they would still have some room for maneuvering afterward. Right after the Pennsylvania primaries, while Humphrey might have entered the race and made a difference, he simply backed off. It was the last moment when he still might have had a chance to run what would be perceived as a legitimate campaign.

In May, when Carter began to falter, there was no one left to pick up the pieces. Udall had never "won" a primary—partly because Shriver and Harris stayed in the race past their active campaigns in order to qualify for federal matching funds. And he was never able to secure the endorsements of the others as they dropped out of the race. Brown and Church, despite their impressive shows, were simply too late to catch up or do any damage. Further, they were unable or unwilling to get together and divide up their territories so Carter would face them one-on-one in the final phases of the campaign. Udall was interested in making some accommodations in that regard. According to John Gabusi, Udall's campaign manager, members of the three campaigns met to discuss the possibilities for combined efforts after Pennsylvania: and whether it was planned or not, Udall stayed out of Nebraska, where Church had been campaigning hard, and left Maryland to Brown while focusing his own efforts on Michigan. Udall also called on Church to stay out of Ohio and Connecticut, to give him a chance finally to meet Carter head-on. But Brown and Church pursued their own rather contradictory courses. Brown competed with Church in Oregon and came close to throwing that primary to Carter. Church insisted that it was Udall who should drop out and, by competing with him in Connecticut and Ohio, generated Carter victories there.

Nor were the Wallace-Jackson supporters warm to the idea of rallying behind one of the "liberals." Charles Snider, Wallace's campaign manager, noted later, Wallace himself didn't want Humphrey to get the nomination. For him the choice was between Governor Carter and a Republican. After Wallace's endorsement of Carter, Snider said, ". . . I had the task of actually calling and talking to each one of our delegates, about one hundred and sixty of them. Of these, only about fifteen—from Florida—objected to giving their votes to Carter." Said Jackson manager, Robert Keefe: "There was a growing respect for Carter. Even had Humphrey gone in, many of the Jackson delegates would have gone for Carter, just on ideological grounds."

There was another reason why the Democratic insiders did not get together. Democrats were not ideologically polarized as they had been in 1972. As Ken Bode noted, there was no "critical mass" for a stop-Carter movement. Further, Democratic activists in all camps were eager to win—ready to give up the stubborn insistence on political purity that had characterized both McGovern's support and his opposition in the final phases of the 1972 campaign. As Peter Hart (pollster for Udall) noted of a survey he did of 2,000 delegates to the Democratic forum in Louisville in 1975: "The one thing that struck me in that poll was the indication of a tremendous desire to win on the part of all the various Democratic factions. This was important in the general election and the way in which the Democratic party came together, and it was something we saw very early." This, in essence, was the key to Carter's victory. He had established himself as the candidate who could win.

## Campaign Finance

The fuel for the Carter bandwagon was money. It took dollars to keep him and his aides on the road, to hire the phone banks, to produce the radio and television advertisements, to pay the staff in Atlanta that handled the publicity releases and did the advance work.

In their early fundraising activities Carter and his staff had shown considerable ingenuity. To qualify for federal funds, which required that a candidate raise at least $5,000 in each of twenty states, Carter had to work fundraising parties around the country. In June, 1975, for example, he breakfasted with 20 prominent Tennesseeans who paid $100 a plate, and lunched with 200 others, who paid only $10—a day's work that brought him close to the minimum amount to qualify in that state. At a Washington, D.C., fundraiser in October, Carter distributed peanuts, while "Jimmy Carter for President" T-shirts were being sold for $5 each. So that the $3.50 netted on the sale of each shirt could be used to secure federal matching funds, the purchasers of the T-shirts were asked to fill out cards with their names and addresses. Later that same year, Carter's old Navy friend, Warren Colegrove hosted a fundraiser in the Annapolis area. (Though the charge was only $10 a head, and all of the state's political organization was invited, only the state comptroller showed up.) In Georgia, where Carter raised most of his money, the campaign also relied on fundraising parties—from a pool party in the summer of 1976 to a $100-a-plate dinner for 1,000 at the Atlanta Hyatt Regency in March, 1976. Each member of the Peanut Brigades, moreover, paid for his own share of a charter flight—and this travel contribution could then be matched with federal funds.

Equally important were the rock concerts. Taking a page from the McGovern campaign of 1972 (which the Carter campaign did with some frequency), Phil Walden of Capricorn Records (the largest independent recording label in the United States) persuaded performers under contract with him to do benefit concerts for Carter. At crucial times in the campaign, in the fall of 1975 and the spring of 1976, groups such as the Marshall Tucker Band, the Allman Brothers, the Charlie Daniels Band, and Elvin Bishop, all gave benefit concerts for Carter. Rather than charging benefit prices, with tickets ranging from $10 to $500, as McGovern's performers had done, they charged standard concert prices—asking each patron to fill out a ticket stub so that he/she could be listed as an individual campaign contributor. This enabled the Carter campaign to secure federal matching funds for each ticket sold, thus doubling his take from each concert. Overall approximately $400,000 was raised this way. One former staffer, quoted in *New Times*, said: "If it hadn't been for Phil, Jimmy would have been dead. Jimmy owes Phil an enormous debt."

Carter himself worked some of these concerts. On May 17, 1976, Carter raised $25,000 from the stage of a rock concert in Nashville. Surrounded by jeans-clad musicians wearing cowboy hats, Carter spread his arms to the audience saying, "I would like to introduce you to one of my closest friends in the world—Charlie Daniels." He obtained the names and addresses of the 7,000 people who attended—because the tickets noted that an address and a signature would qualify the ticket holder for a drawing to win a stereo and a collection of record albums.

Carter also raised a good deal of money through direct mail solicitations—a technique that would remain a central fundraising strategy throughout 1976. The $40,000 purse with which Carter started his active campaign had been secured mainly through a confidential letter he had sent to potential Carter "insiders," giving them advance word on his plans. This was followed in early 1975 with letters to opinion leaders around the country, which attempted to tap the anti-Wallace sentiment while requiring only a provisional commitment to Carter. By December of 1975 Carter had secured the services of Morris Dees, one of the top direct mail advertisers in the business, as his national finance chairman. Shortly after his appointment, Dees introduced a two-phase direct-mailing plan: everyone who had donated $100 or more was asked to double what he or she had already given. Then there were monthly follow-up letters asking the contributors to give again. Eventually Dees raised more than $1 million this way.

As the Carter bandwagon began to roll in February, it acquired another source of revenue. The large press entourage Carter had begun to accumulate after his Iowa "victory" required the chartering of airplanes. This was expensive, but it cost him nothing. The media people and the Secret Service men paid their own share of the traveling expenses. In fact, the Carter campaign charged the journalists one and one-half times the commercial first-class fare, which led to some grumbling that the campaign was making money from the press. (The Udall and Ford campaigns also charged more than full fare.) Actually, the extra money was used to provide good transportation for the press. At times, when ground transportation was supplied by local volunteers, the campaign did make money on the trip. Carter aides claimed this made up for their losses on others.

Most important to Carter's money-raising efforts were his early primary and caucus wins. The smart money would follow the winner, and Carter seemed to be that. In January, Carter had been running behind Jackson in total contributions received, tying with Udall for second place. In February he was outpulling everyone except Wallace (who peaked, raising over $2 million that month.) After the Florida, Illinois, and North Carolina primaries, Carter outpulled all his competitors in the amount of money he received (including late entries Frank Church and Jerry Brown), and the trend line was strictly uphill. Immediately after the Pennsylvania primary in late April, Carter soared way above all the others, reaching a peak of $2.25 million by May 31 (fully $1.5 million more than Brown, his closest competitor). It leveled off to a little more than $2 million during June.

Not only does private money follow the potential winner, so does the federal dollar. In the beginning of January, Carter received $100,000 in federal matching funds. His matching funds at the end of the month rose to approximately $550,000 and continued at that level or above for the subsequent pay periods. His total federal donation would come to $3.4 million for the primaries.

The freeze on federal funding from March 22 to May 21 (because of problems in how FEC members were chosen and some heel dragging by both Congress and Ford in correcting them) inadvertently redounded to Carter's advantage. Udall and Jackson, who had been depending on federal matching funds for their Pennsylvania campaign, had to curtail their advertising. And Udall was forced to squander precious time by having to fly on commercial airlines. Neither man, given his uncertain future, was willing or able to take out loans to finance a greater effort.

Though Carter had his problems, he was able to come up with the money he needed to conduct aggressive campaigns in Pennsylvania and the other states with April primaries. Pat Caddell later described their advantage in Pennsylvania: "We had a big jump on the media. We were the only ones with the money for it. We were on for about ten days unchallenged." And the surge in contributions that followed Carter's Pennsylvania victory would carry him over the later primaries.

Most important, Carter took advantage of a loophole in the federal campaign finance law. The Supreme Court had ruled that a candidate could spend as much of his own money as he wanted. (However, it upheld the $1,000 individual donation limit to one candidate, the $5,000 donation limit to one candidate by any Political Action Committee [PAC], and the $25,000 ceiling on contributions by one individual to all candidates.) This opened up new possibilities for Carter. With his personal wealth, his friends in the banks of Georgia, and with his bright prospects in the presidential lottery, Carter was able to guarantee large loans to fund the Pennsylvania and later campaigns. From March through May, Carter and the Committee for Jimmy Carter borrowed a total of $775,000 from various Georgia banks. On March 15, he was guarantor for $70,000 from the Citizens and Southern Bank of Atlanta. In April he guaranteed additional personal loans: $105,000 from Citizens and Southern and $100,000 from the Fulton National Bank of Atlanta. In May he secured five more loans—$500,000 in all—from the Fulton National Bank. He also ran up a bill of $500,000 with Gerald Rafshoon, who was doing his radio and television advertising. Thus, Carter went into debt to the tune of approximately $1,275,000 during his primary campaigns.

He did it with virtually no collateral or guarantees other than his political prospects and his ability to raise money and receive future payouts from the FEC. His peanut business could not have been used as an asset, had he wanted to, for the family corporation had recently borrowed approximately $4.9 million against it. (One million dollars of this was secured from the National Bank of Georgia, of which Bert Lance was president, to purchase a peanut shelter and construct a new warehouse. Later, it was learned that this loan was above the amount actually spent or the value of the property as reported for local tax purposes, raising questions about the possible use of these funds in the Carter campaign, which would have been illegal. When this information became public, Carter "voluntarily" paid more taxes. Special Prosecutor Paul Curran, appointed by Attorney General Griffin Bell, eventually exonerated him of any wrongdoing.)

As was the case with so many things in his campaign, Carter made his fundraising efforts do double duty. The statements and press releases that were dispensed to the media, as well as the FEC reports themselves, had a good public-relations effect. After a meeting with Rafshoon in November, 1974, Kirbo wrote Carter that he might make an "oblique stab" at Jackson, Bentsen, and Congress over the new campaign finance laws. He should suggest that the President and the Congress had allowed the new legislation to go into effect at a date later than necessary—to give the Washington candidates the opportunity to accept large contributions before the law became relevant. On December 14, 1975, Carter did just that, accusing Jackson and Bentsen of seeking large contributions before the new law became effective. The next day on NBC's "Meet the Press," with the other candidates, Carter insisted that "the spirit of the law is being violated." Both Jackson and Bentsen retorted that they had voluntarily placed limits of $3,000 on donations from others before the new law had been passed.

Throughout the famine days of 1975, Carter aides confided to the press how careful and efficient they were. They seldom spent beyond what they had. Further, their financial operation was a "grass roots" effort. In his final reports to the FEC Lipshutz pointed out that the campaign had eighty-three bank accounts in thirty-nine states, Washington, D.C., and Puerto Rico; that campaign contributions came from 95,000 individuals and political action committees, representing a total of 130,000 contributions. Lipshutz concluded, "We believe that these reports represent the most comprehensive and accurate representation of political campaign financial activity in the history of American politics."

It was a good picture, suggesting that Carter would be indebted only to the people and that he would be as careful and prudent with the public's money as he was with his own. Carter was not, however, the candidate of the small contributor, as the FEC records show. Moreover, his campaign workers did not carefully plan their efforts to keep them in the black. They spent more money than they had brought in in the fall of 1975—simply to survive. According to the FEC report for 1975, the campaign had taken in $504,587 and spent $506,518. And when federal funds were temporarily interrupted—just before the crucial Pennsylvania primary—they borrowed heavily to assure that Jimmy would win the state that was critical to his whole endeavor. Particularly interesting is the contrast between the FEC reports filed by the Carter organization during the campaign and the amended reports filed after the fall election. Consistently, the figures in the two reports present two different stories. The original reports ordinarily show the Carter campaign in the black. The amended reports for the same months indicate that the organization was in the red much of the time. (The other candidates also showed some discrepancies between the monthly and amended reports, but the gaps were not as great and the amended reports did not always show a greater indebtedness than the monthly ones.) Though no one suspected it at the time, the Carter folks were really high rollers, putting out money when they needed it early in the campaign and gambling on later "wins" to bring in the funds to finance their operations.

Nor was the financial structure as decentralized or efficient as Lipshutz suggested. There were serious conflicts between the people in Atlanta and the campaign efforts in at least two states—Ohio and California. The biggest problem for James Kittelman, Carter's in-state coordinator for Ohio from September, 1975 to February, 1976, was the centralization of the campaign in Atlanta. On one occasion Kittleman's committee sent out approximately 1,000 post cards to Ohio Democrats, telling them of Carter's forthcoming appearance on "Face the Nation." Though the mailing was approved in Atlanta, it wasn't paid for for eight months. They never had certain things Jordan had promised them: a bank account for the state effort or a state headquarters. Herbert Hafif, a well-known trial lawyer, Carter's chief fundraiser in California, was to experience similar problems.

Working in a situation where "the historical financial bread-basket in California had already gone to Brown . . .", Hafif had to develop "a completely new and different group of donors, schedule dinners, break down the state into fundraising areas and deal with the existing ineffectual structure, etc.—all in about sixty days." He brought in some new support in the Hispanic community: a leading Chicano television producer, Moctezuma Esparza, made Spanish-language television advertisements at no expense to the Carter campaign; a Viva Carter organization was organized, along with other outreach programs to Chicano communities. Hafif also got Wesley "Tiny" Harris, a disabled former union official to raise money: within thirty days he had secured over $15,000—with $40,000 more in pledges. "Tiny" helped Carter win 37 percent of the primary vote in the Sacramento area (as compared to the statewide 21 percent). The president of the California Trial Lawyers Association, Wylie Aitken, who had impeccable connections with the environmentalist and consumer movements, was also brought on board; he proved to be the largest single fundraiser in California.

Overall, during the three months or so that Hafif directed the fundraising activities in California (during the Supreme Court's freeze on federal monies) about $1.5 million was brought in. According to Hafif, for one two-month period, one out of every four dollars raised nationwide for Carter came from there. He observed that about 25 percent of the Pennsylvania media budget was raised in California at a time when Carter was in "absolutely desperate straits." However, Hafif soon found himself at odds with the Atlanta staff, which he felt was exercising too much control over their operations and keeping him from getting through to Carter personally. Eventually, Hafif was "fired" by Jordan. Many other people left the California organization when he did.

For all the purported efficiency, the Carter campaign people would argue differently when the news was leaked in late August, 1976, that unreported campaign funds had gone to black minister in California (some of it possibly for rental space and cleanup). Carter explained this episode: "I don't have any doubt that in our massive campaign, that is nationwide in scope, there are those who keep the money, both black and white. That is something that is impossible to prevent." Later the press reported that another $4,000 had gone as "travel advances" to the head of Carter's primary organization in Cleveland, Ohio, and was used to pay young black workers to canvass minority neighborhoods. To Emanual Eaves, the supervisor of Carter's minority vote-getting effort, this was an accounting error caused by "ineptness on the part of the people keeping the records." Campaign treasurer Lipshutz called it a "mistake" and admitted that there might possibly be similar discrepancies in other states. (The FEC, in its final report, absolved the Carter campaign of any legal wrongdoing in this kind of situation.)

There were some violations of the new campaign finance law, for which the FEC would later penalize the Carter for President Committee. Bert Lance had made the National Bank of Georgia's plane available to the campaign without noting this as a contribution. For this, the FEC, in 1977, fined the committee $1,200 and the bank $5,000. It also ordered the committee to pay more than

$3,200 to the federal government for acceptance of illegal campaign contributions from Edgar Bronfman (the Seagram liquor heir), a Coca-Cola political action committee, and auto magnate Henry Ford, who had put up funds for a lavish luncheon at New York's elegant 21 Club." And it levied another $1,000 fine against the Carter for President Committee and ordered it to repay the government more than $15,000 for paying workers during the transition period out of federal campaign funds.

In his financial operations, in short, Carter showed the blend of skill, luck, and willingness to take chances that generally characterized his campaign. During the lean days he showed considerable ingenuity in just remaining afloat, but once he was ahead, he used all his assets to put further distance between himself and the other contenders. His campaign finances were given a public-relations gloss that put a flattering light on his organization's operations. Carter and his aides were not, in fact, the neat, careful, always-in-control bookkeepers they described themselves as being. They were high rollers. And given the stakes they were playing for, and their starting point, gambling would pay off.

## Outsider, Insider

Paralleling Carter's electoral and fundraising successes was his wooing and winning of influentials across the country. He had met with people from top Wall Street firms early in his term as governor. His spadework had won him membership on the Trilateral Commission and gained him access to other distinguished people in the nation. As noted earlier, he had traveled to New York City in 1974 for luncheons with *New York Times* publisher Arthur Ochs Sulzberger and *Wall Street Journal* president Warren Phillips. He had met editors and publishers of other papers by February, 1975, saying, "The only ones we've missed so far are the *Boston Globe* and the *Christian Science Monitor*."

In November, 1975, when he was still practically unknown in the country as a whole, Carter met several important bankers, lawyers, and major campaign contributors at a cocktail party in New York City in an attempt to win their support for his campaign. In the spring of 1976, a Wall Street Committee for Carter was organized by Roger C. Altman (a partner in Lehman Brothers), Michael Taylor (a vice-president of Paine, Webber, Jackson and Curtis), and Thomas Murtagh (of Dean Witter and Company). They saw Carter as a good manager and fiscal conservative. As Taylor noted, "Carter's positions on some economic issues are closer to traditional Republican positions than are those of other Democrats." His well-organized campaign effort, with its sound management techniques, had impressed Altman: "It's less difficult to talk to people about Carter and to raise contributions for him, than for any candidate I've ever known."

Carter had also been wooing traditional liberal Democratic "fat cats" for some time. In May, 1975, he met former McGovern supporters over lunch at Maxim's in Chicago, and carried off one important recruit—fundraiser Louis

Manilow, a past contributor to McGovern and other liberals. He won over liberal fundraiser Max Palevsky (former chairman of the board of Xerox and a large contributor to McGovern, who pledged to support him—at least through the Florida primary campaign.

Despite his outsider stance, Washington influentials and political activists were objects of his courtship. Peter Bourne and Mary King had been making contacts for Carter in Washington since 1973, working out of Mary King's public-relations office in Washington, D.C. Carter, in a visit to the Brookings Institution in the summer of 1975, interested some of its foreign policy people in preparing issues papers for him.

Once the 1976 campaign began, Carter made other overtures to the Democratic Party elites. Shortly after the Iowa caucuses he met with several former McGovernites at a dinner party at the Georgetown home of Liz Stevens. Among those attending were Frank Mankiewicz (Robert Kennedy's press secretary in 1968 and McGovern's right-hand man in 1972); Ted Van Dyke (a top policy adviser for McGovern in 1972); Joe Duffey and Anne Wexler (largely responsible for the final effort for McGovern's 1972 nomination); Richard Holbrooke (managing editor of *Foreign Policy* magazine, a foreign policy official who had resigned after the Cambodia invasion in 1970); and James Flug (formerly aide to Teddy Kennedy and on the staff of the Energy Action Committee). Carter, who initiated the meeting, bluntly urged the guests to join his presidential bandwagon before it was too late. Though only Holbrooke signed on at the time, Carter made "a most favorable impression and stored up potential support."

After his triumph in Florida, Carter was able to draw some of the most influential people in Washington to his campaign. On Monday, March 15, he met with and charmed what *Time* called the Democratic power structure over a dinner of pink champagne and lamb at the Georgetown home of columnist Clayton Fritchey. Among the forty people present were Clark Clifford, Katharine Graham, Eric Sevareid, Senator Gaylord Nelson, Sol Linowitz, John Gardner, and Joseph Alsop. The next morning, Carter had appointments with Congressman Andrew Young, labor leader Jerry Wurf, and *New Yorker* journalist Elizabeth Drew; he lunched with the editorial board of the Washington *Post* and conferred with the Congressional Black Caucus. That evening he played to a full house at the Georgetown home of the Smith Bagleys (he was an heir to the Reynolds tobacco company fortune, and they had both supported Terry Sanford first). Carter earnestly told this group of Washingtonians that the motivation behind his campaigning was simply to bridge the chasm that had developed between the American people and their government. He offered his customary "down home" invitation to visit or telephone him in Plains. "If you can't remember my last name, just make it 'Jimmy, Plains, Ga.'" (Interestingly, the reports of this fundraiser appeared on page 1 of the "Style" section of the Washington *Post*; a similar event for Washington insider Frank Church that evening was relegated to page 8.)

Carter also whetted political appetites by throwing out hooks to policy influentials in the form of invitations to join his advising groups. As a relative newcomer to the national scene, he was not already surrounded by a phalanx of advisers, speechwriters and future assistant secretaries of State or Treasury. By late April many people in Washington were fancying themselves in offices in the White House, the Executive Office Building, executive offices in the State Department. His Foreign Policy and Defense Task Force, announced on April 22 immediately before the crucial Pennsylvania primary, was described by the Washington *Post* as "a biographical register of the New York–Washington foreign policy axis." The roster included: Zbigniew Brzezinski, Cyrus Vance, Theodore Sorensen, Paul Warnke, Charles Yost, Anthony Lake, Richard Holbrooke, Richard Gardner, Paul Nitze, and later, Averell Harriman. While the list showed that Carter could collect some of the best people, it was less revealing of the candidate's own policy preferences. It included both defenders and critics of the Vietnam war, both hard and soft liners on weapons developments, both hawks and doves on the United States's relationship with Russia. This intermingling of ideological types made it possible for Carter to eschew identification with any single policy constellation. He could emerge as a person concerned with research and the facts, without paying the price of being closely identified with one specific policy orientation.

The last persons Carter would win over were the other national politicians in his party. He had not had much success with them in the early stages of his campaign. During one trip to Washington in 1975, for example, he dropped in to see then House Majority Leader Thomas "Tip" O'Neill of Massachusetts. When Carter told him, "I'm going to be the next President," O'Neill just smiled and shrugged. Carter told a newsman several months later that "It had been very difficult for me to get a telephone call returned or an appointment" in the early months of his campaign. Even his fellow governors failed to back him. Reubin Askew was neutral in Florida, Marvin Mandel had helped Brown in Maryland. Others, like Calvin Rampton of Utah, were explicit in their distrust of Carter (in the gubernatorial fraternity he would rank Carter about forty-ninth, he said). As Jules Witcover noted: "In the gubernatorial fraternity, in which the ability to relax is a powerful requisite for acceptance, Jimmy Carter was just a bit too conscientious—some said devious—for his brethren."

As he neared the end of the primary trail, Carter realized he would have to improve his relationships with other leaders in the party. Thus, he reassured several freshman Congressmen in May: "I'm not anti-Washington. I've never made an anti-Washington statement. I've pointed out some things that ought to be done. . . . The programs we put together for congressional approval will be put together by me and the leaders of Congress." Just before the Big Three primaries, he announced that Frank Moore, who had been gathering delegates for him in the Southern states, would act as a full-time congressional liaison officer, dealing with Senators and Representatives. The Carter organization also went after the congressional staff. On June 8 more than forty Capitol Hill staffers were invited to a meeting with his aides, and many of them would later draft position papers and foreign policy statements for him.

After his nomination was certain, Carter did some more political fence mending. In Washington, D.C., on June 25, he attended a luncheon with sixty members of the Senate Caucus (where, upon the motion of Senator Hubert Humphrey, he received the unanimous endorsement of that group). He met behind closed doors with several leaders of Congress, made a courtesy call to the Democratic National Committee, and attended a reception for Democratic members of the House. Once again Carter was telling the Congressmen that he had never been anti-Washington. (And Andrew Young, who accompanied him on most of his rounds, explained that the anti-Washington theme was simply a press explanation of the Carter phenomenon.) Carter even implied that his choice for a running mate would most likely be a Washington insider. And at the reception for House members (where 250 Congressmen lined up to be photographed with him) he noted humbly: "If there is one aspect of my experience which has sadly been neglected, it is my lack of knowledge of the inner workings of Congress."

Next, Carter solicited support from the nation's mayors. In Milwaukee, he told the U.S. Conference of Mayors that "if I become President, you, the Mayors of America will have a friend, an ally and a partner in the White House." From the mayors he moved on to governors and their national conference in Hershey, Pennsylvania, on July 6. His visit was rewarded when, at a meeting of the Democratic governors, Maryland Governor Marvin Mandel, who had opposed Carter during the primaries, sponsored an endorsement resolution. Carter promised that he would consult with the governors throughout the rest of his campaign.

Carter had conducted his campaign at two levels from the very beginning. While running as an outsider, he was trying to win the insiders over to his side. And the antiestablishment rhetoric, which served to attract voters to him in the initial stage of his campaign, gave way to public assurances that he really was no threat to the influentials and their power. Carter, in other words, seemed to be simply an outsider who was trying to get in. There was considerable truth in the statement he had made at the Smith Bagleys' fundraiser back in March: "I am not running an anti-Washington campaign. If I had anything against Washington, I would not be running so hard to get there."

# FOURTEEN

# Securing the Nomination

## *Heir Apparent*

C ARTER BEGAN TO ACT LIKE his party's nominee even before the primaries were over. His vice-presidential search began in mid-April, when he asked Greg Schneiders and Ted Sorensen and others to think about the process of vice-presidential selection. By early June they had compiled a list of prominent Democratic mayors, governors, and Congresspersons, from which his aides compiled a shorter list of about two dozen prospects. Pat Caddell, shortly after the Big Three primaries, dispatched poll takers to question 200 representative Americans about approximately fourteen potential vice-presential candidates. The results—intercepted and published by the Boston *Globe*—were fairly predictable: Democrats with name identification—like Ted Kennedy and Edmund Muskie—scored highest. Others included in the poll results were: Adlai Stevenson, Walter Mondale, Alan Cranston, John Glenn, Frank Church, Birch Bayh, Peter Rodino, Hugh Carey, Michael Dukakis, Wendell Anderson, Tom Bradley and one woman, Barbara Jordan of Texas. Of these, John Glenn was the only one who could bring in votes for Carter; the others would lose votes for him, Carter aides told the journalists around them.

The whole process had been a coalition-building exercise. The initial longer lists included blacks, women, Jews, and politicians from outside of Washington. (In Washington, on June 26, Carter told reporters that he might choose a black or a woman.) The mere fact that they were listed, even if never seriously considered, served to flatter and win over some individuals. Further, Carter and his aides, in calling "distinguished Americans" across the country and seeking their advice on various candidates, made these individuals feel like camapign insiders in the process. The search also gave Charles Kirbo the opportunity to go to Washington in late June and early July to touch base with the major politicos there.

On his visit to Washington in late June, Carter said that the person chosen would have to be someone "politically and personally" compatible with him—to assure that, in the event of succession, Carter's programs and campaign promises would be pursued. The last phases of the screening process helped guarantee that. Each person being considered had to fill out a questionnaire in which he was asked about past financial statements, possible arrest records, psychiatric treatments, and "anything in your personal life or in that of a near relative which you feel, if known, may be of embarrassment in the forthcoming campaign." (There had been some discussion of having the FBI do background checks on prospective candidates, but when it became clear that federal law does not empower the government to undertake background checks on behalf of a political party, Powell and Jordan shifted to the questionnaire and interview techniques.) They also had Atlanta newspaper people call local associates around the country to gain further information about the candidates. Three of the candidates (the "finalists" for the job as it turned out later) made trips to Plains—the "Court of St. James's" as one reporter called it—for a personal interview with Carter. (Earlier, *Newsweek* had reported that Carter's aides had told him that summoning Senators and the like to Plains to "walk in the fields" with him was "demeaning." They evidently had not convinced him.)

Early on the Fourth of July, Ed and Jane Muskie left their remote fishing camp in Maine to begin a series of commercial flights that got them to Atlanta at midnight. There they were met by Chip Carter and flown by small private plane to Plains. After arriving around 2:00 A.M. and talking with Carter until 3:30 in the morning, Muskie was finally allowed to get some sleep. At 9:00 the next morning he was awakened by a cheerful Carter—for a three-hour meeting. Afterward, the two men held a press conference on the front lawn of the Carter home, followed by a walk down Main Street to the train depot.

At the time of his meeting with Muskie, Carter had noted that the Maine Senator "has been willing to present himself to the American people"—a crack at Mondale, who had closed his own presidential campaign in December, 1974, because he said, he did not like traveling. On the morning of July 8, Mondale arrived at the Americus airport for his interview; he was left to cool his heels awhile before he was met by someone from the usually punctual Carter crowd.

When they did meet, things went well. Mondale, who had earlier been noted as an advocate of busing to achieve racial integration, explained that he had simply advocated support of federal court orders. They also discussed the ways they might work together (Mondale later recalling that Carter kept emphasizing the importance of "compatibility"). And Mondale assured Carter that he would get out and campaign hard—joking that he now liked Holiday Inns and promising to resign from the Senate should he receive the nomination. After their meeting the two men emerged for a leisurely stroll down Main Street, providing the press with many "photo opportunities."

Later that same day John Glenn was in Plains for his interview with Carter. The press, attentive to small signs of favor and disfavor, noted that his visit with

Carter lasted only two hours and concluded with a short press conference—without the walk down Main Street. (Carter's interviews with the other four candidates—Senators Frank Church of Idaho, Henry Jackson of Washington, and Adlai Stevenson of Illinois, and Representative Peter Rodino of New Jersey—were scheduled for New York City during the Democratic convention.)

Hoping to avoid any divisive displays at the convention, the Carter people went to work in June to paper over differences in the party and secure a unity platform. (Carter had asked the party not to enact a "wish box or Christmas tree" for a platform.) Before the convention began, the major issues that could have opened up old cleavages had been compromised in some way. A strong plank on breaking up the vertically integrated oil interests was hedged in favor of a vague commitment to free competition in the crude oil industry. Red flag issues, such as decriminalization of marijuana and protection of homosexual rights, were avoided altogether. Southerners agreed to sidestep the busing issue. Blacks agreed to a restricted welfare reform plank. Former antiwar protesters agreed to a provision to permit the President to grant pardons to deserters on a case-by-case basis, dropping a previous plank pledging blanket pardons for Vietnam veterans in legal or financial jeopardy because of their opposition to the war. Even labor (which would be strong at this convention—up from 16 percent to 20 percent of the delegates) agreed with general statements on full employment and national health insurance, forgoing specific references to the Humphrey-Hawkins full employment bill or the Kennedy-Corman national health insurance bill.

## The Big Apple

As the delegates arrived in New York City, there was still potential for conflict. Women delegates, welded into a cohesive body by the National Organization for Women (NOW) and the National Women's Political Caucus (NWPC), and the women's caucus of the Democratic National Committee (DNC) were pushing for a minority report calling for quotas requiring 50 percent female representation at the 1980 convention. On Sunday afternoon, just before the convention, Carter met with a group of about fifty women. He asked Jane Patterson—a North Carolina delegate and the force behind the 50-50 proposal—to gather a smaller group to meet with him the next day. Admitted to Carter's inner sanctum on the twenty-first floor of the Americana Hotel on Monday, Patterson, Bella Abzug, Pat Derian, and others were persuaded by attentive Carter charm to settle for a platform compromise. Instead of specific quotas, he pledged himself personally to promote equality at the 1980 convention, a work for the Equal Rights Amendment, and to appoint women to high-level posts in his administration.

On Tuesday morning more than 1,000 delegates, alternates, and onlookers attended a meeting of the women's caucus. After an hour-long heated debate, the women went along with Abzug and the other "negotiators," with an over-whelming vote in favor of Carter's compromise proposal. (Partly it was because they knew—as a poll of the delegates had indicated—that the 50 percent requirement would be defeated on the floor anyway.) But it was also because Carter made them feel like insiders. As Jo Freeman said: "This was the first time a presidential candidate had seriously talked with them (women) on their own terms. The outsider to the Washington establishment had made them feel like insiders. They began to feel that he could be trusted." The mother of con-temporary feminism, Betty Friedan, told Kandy Stroud over lunch at *The New York Times* that she had been "moved to tears by Carter. He made a commit-ment to us in such a substantive way that unless he's an absolute liar, he'll be doing something for women." She had the feeling that "it was the way he spoke about his mother and his wife working."

Carter was similarly persuasive in his dealings with leaders of the black caucus. On Monday morning, members of the caucus questioned Carter on several key issues of concern to them. Though Carter ruled out Los Angeles Mayor Tom Bradley, a black, as a vice-presidential possibility, (he wanted someone with "Washington-based" experience), he did agree to support the reelection of Basil Patterson as vice-president of the DNC and, to push for stronger affirmative action programs. He even pledged to "exceed the demands of the Black Caucus" in his administrative appointments, and he asked them, on the spot, for the names of people they would like to see on his task force and in his Administration. As the session came to a close, most of the caucus members were satisfied with Carter's promises and proposals, and pledged their support to him "without reservation." In short, as Nora Sayre later noted, "Carter gave the impression that he would do more to equalize the sexes and races than any previous President, and consequently received their robust backing. His tactic has been summed up as 'Sleep with me now and I'll marry you someday.' "*

Having headed off potential conflict on the floor, the Carter people took steps to make sure that they would hear what they wanted from the podium. Back in October 1975, Robert Strauss had selected keynote speakers and other major presentors so as to show the party as a varied but united lot. The remain-ing access to the podium (and thus potential exposure on national televi-sion)—to read speeches, to deliver reports of the credentials or platform com-mittees—would be equally controlled. Sometimes access was traded for support. Michael Harrington, the Democratic Socialist, for example, was of-

---

* The Carter people also had to clear up some problems with the AFL-CIO. On July 14 Hamilton Jordan and Landon Butler, in a private meeting with AFL-CIO officials at the Americana, backed off from an earlier agreement to bring a member of the Machinists Union onto the convention floor as "the representative of labor." (The Machinists Union was a member of a liberal coalition at odds with the AFL-CIO hierarchy.) As the labor officials explained to Jordan, the AFL-CIO opposed the idea of a labor representative of any kind, not just one from the liberal coalition. In the end, Jordan promised to deal with a variety of demands by the AFL-CIO, and the AFL-CIO leaders promised their full support at the convention and in the fall.

fered ten minutes of TV time in exchange for supporting a rules change the Carter people were backing. (He refused.) Ted Kennedy was offered one minute to read the section of the platform on national health. (He also refused.) And though Kennedy never made this offer public, at a New York party on Tuesday of convention week he quipped: "I'm having trouble getting a perimeter pass to the Convention." (In lieu of the one-minute spot, he had an interview with Walter Cronkite on Wednesday, his only appearance on television, where he said little about Carter and promised to work hard on the Senate Judiciary Committee. As he told Cronkite: "You don't have to be a president of the United States to make a difference in this country.")

Carter's other worry was Jerry Brown, who was still meeting with delegations, talking like a candidate. Brown, they feared, might try to address the convention in an attempt to instigate support for himself for the vice-presidential slot. The first strategy was to ignore him. As Strauss told Charles Kirbo, they could play it cool. "Let's just wait. We'll keep our hands off. . . . He's like a pimple on your face. If you touch 'em too soon, you get a red blotch. If you wait till the right moment, they just pop."

When the convention opened, Carter and his aides were in position. They would be making decisions from three major control centers. The candidate and his family would be sealed off in a suite on the twenty-first floor of the Americana Hotel (the suite used for filming *The Godfather*). The flow of visitors and phone calls to the candidate was strictly controlled by Carter's top aides, located in offices on the twentieth floor.

Down in Albert Hall, in the lobby of the Americana, there was a sham campaign office (called the "zoo") which was designed to keep the pressure off the real operations center on the twentieth floor, all the while making the naive convention outsider feeling like an insider. There was a door marked "Hamilton Jordan—Campaign Manager" and a polling desk with Pat Caddell's name (misspelled) on it. Staffed by volunteers, the office was mainly a recruitment center—where 400 people each day were signed up for the fall campaign.

Several blocks away at Madison Square Garden, just off the convention floor, there were three Carter command trailers arranged in the shape of a Y—with the trailer on the tail reserved for VIPs. There were telephones to floor captains and delegation leaders on the convention floor as well as to Carter and Jordan at the Americana.

With the compromises worked out and Carter's people in position to control the convention, there would be few discordant notes in anything that followed. The formal opened on Monday, June 12, at 8:15 P.M. Several New York State and national party leaders came to the rostrum to celebrate the unity of the party and the Democrats' return to the city of New York. John Glenn gave an unexciting keynote address, as television cameras panned the audience— revealing scores of sleeping and chatting delegates. Barbara Jordan, the other keynote speaker, followed him with another kind of speech—her rolling rhetoric tapping a hunger for enthusiasm and passion in the crowd and causing a temporary flurry over whether or not she might be a vice-presidential candidate.

On Tuesday evening party officials presented the reports of the Compliance Review Commission and the Credentials Committee, highlighting the contrast between the harmony and order of the 1976 processes and the problems and disorders of 1972. The Rules Committee, which recommended the adoption of most of the 1972 rules, presented a proposal that would increase the percentage of committee members' signatures needed to support a minority report—from 10 percent of the members present to 25 percent of a committee's total membership. The committee also proposed a delay in the discussion of changes in the basic bylaws and resolutions to the final day of the convention. The proposal on minority reports would make it more difficult for outsiders to raise new issues at future conventions; the delay of discussion would put off any battle over the changes until after the nominations had been made—thus downplaying their importance as an early test of strength between contending factions at a convention.

A minority report from the Rules Committee sparked the only real conflict at the convention. Three delegates (including Jean Westwood, McGovern's choice to head the Democratic National Committee during the 1972 convention) argued for a proposal that would permit debate on the platform or any section thereof, provided at least 300 delegates from ten states had so petitioned. If there were more than three such petitions, the chairman would choose the three with the greatest number of signatures.) The Carter organization, concerned that the right to life people and those favoring a plank on pardons for Vietnam deserters would get some television time, flooded the convention aisles with their floor leaders to work to guarantee the defeat of the resolution. Georgia, which led the balloting, gave the cue—casting its fifty votes against the resolution. And the delegates responded with a whopping 1,957 votes against the resolution (735 in favor). The convention then adopted, by a voice vote, the report of the Rules Committee.

These matters disposed of, the presentation of the party platform would become less an occasion for discussion than a parade of celebrants signifying by their presence that the Democratic Party was now a family. (The journalist Richard Reeves called it "losers' night.") Running against the All-Star Baseball Game on ABC, the parade included: Senators George McGovern, Frank Church, Hubert Humphrey; Governors Michael Dukakis, Wendell Anderson, George Wallace; Chicago Mayor Richard J. Daley, Detroit Mayor Coleman Young; Miami Mayor Maurice Ferre; civil rights leader Coretta King; labor leader Jerry Wurf; and Admiral Elmo Zumwalt.

On Wednesday night four names were placed in nomination for President: Carter, Udall, Brown, and Ellen McCormack, the antiabortion candidate. A random drawing held that afternoon determined that Carter would be the first candidate to be nominated. New Jersey Congressman Peter Rodino of Watergate fame made the first nominating speech, saying: "He [Carter] has brought a united South back into the leadership of America and a united America back to a position of respect and esteem in the eyes of the world." Margaret "Midge" Costanza talked of how she had been attracted to Carter's "sensitive character" when they first met. "He is a decent human being." Andrew Young spoke of Carter's roots and how they had prepared him for the presidency: he hailed from a part of the country that had already laid down "the burden of race"; his rise "from the grass roots" would make him sensitive to the problem of poverty; his military background had given an understanding that "we can be a strong nation without pouring all our wealth and all our money and resources into those things which destroy."

By 10:45 P.M., the roll call of the states began. And at 11:16 P.M., Christine Gitlin, one of Carter's first supporters in Ohio and the chairperson of the Ohio delegation, intoned the magic words that put Carter over the top: "Madame Chairman. . . . I am proud and honored . . . to cast in the spirit of unity, love, and victory in November, 132 votes for Jimmy Carter!" Peter Duchin's orchestra struck up the old FDR song, "Happy Days Are Here Again." Back in the trailers, the Carter staffers burst into a "swaying, stomping, hollering, back-slapping, hair-mussing, kissing, hugging, weeping mass." At one point Hamilton Jordan bounded up the stairs to the top of one of the trailers to make a boisterous, joking announcement: "Now that we're through the primaries . . . I'd like to announce that we're firing all the women and blacks!" Then, for one brief moment, Jordan became serious: "It's hard to grasp what's happening . . . Not bad for a bunch of dumb southerners!"

Back on the convention floor, the roll call of the states was finished. The final vote was: Carter, 2,238 1/2; Udall, 329 1/2; Brown, 300 1/2; Wallace, 57; McCormack, 22; and a scattering of votes for others.

Jerry Brown, from the California microphone, began the switch to Carter. "It's a long and difficult struggle within our environment to work together and bring about justice," he told the convention. "I think Jimmy Carter can do that." Then: "I just want to be able to announce that the California delegation votes 278 votes for Mr. Carter, and we're on our way to bring this country back to the Democratic column." After Brown began the switch, Rhode Island's Governor Philip Noel proclaimed all of their votes for "Jimmy Brown," but quickly corrected himself. Then Georgia Governor George Busbee moved to suspend the rules and nominate the state's native son by acclamation.

To keep some measure of exitement in an otherwise dull convention, Carter had decided to withhold the announcement of his vice-presidential choice until shortly before the actual balloting would take place. Carter aides, in the meantime, had kept the corridors buzzing with their small confidences to various and sundry reporters. (Columnist Jane O'Reilly later recalled one of her huddles with Pat Caddell: "He told me a lot of inside stuff, which I later saw everywhere in the press.") Frank Church, touted by aides as almost a shoo-in back in early June, was now being dismissed as too "pompous" on television; and Carter had been turned off by all the wheeling and dealing on his behalf. The consideration of Henry Jackson was mainly a courtesy to the veteran Senator. As a foreign policy hawk and a conservative on social issues, he would appeal mainly to those independent and conservative Democratic voters with whom Carter was already strong. Ed Muskie, the aides whispered, drank too much and was a mite lazy. Adlai Stevenson was not even treated courteously. Jerry Rafshoon told Chicago columnist Mike Royko and others at the convention that Adlai wasn't bright enough to find the men's room. As Royko later wrote: "[There were] sneering, arrogant, patronizing remarks about Stevenson's mental deficiencies. Naturally, the sources were never identified by name." John Glenn, whose star had risen earlier as Church's declined, had emerged as the top contender in a Caddell poll. But Carter aides were now saying he was too much like Carter in background, philosophy, and style; and there was concern about his weak record on labor matters and his use of tax shelters.

In the vice-presidential guessing game, *The Children's Express* a newspaper put out by youngsters, outscooped the other media. On Wednesday they named Mondale as the vice-presidential nominee. As Gilbert Giles, twelve, pointed out, they had some sources the other ignored. "My main advantage is that adults don't think children listen or understand."

On Thursday morning, at 8:30 A.M., Carter asked Mondale to run as his Vice-President. Shortly after 10:00 Carter arrived with Rosalynn at the Georgian Ballroom of the Americana Hotel to announce his decision. Mondale, he said, had a "comprehension and compassion for people who need services of government most," and he had "the trust of a wide range of Democrats . . . and the clear concept of what the Presidency should be." Moments later Joan and Walter Mondale arrived and the two couples joined hands and smiled.

Mondale showed that he had met Carter's compatibility test. In response to a question about how he prepared for his job interview in Plains, Mondale joked: "The first thing I did was to read the most remarkable book ever written, called *Why Not the Best?*. I found every word absolutely brilliant."

Shortly afterward, when the wives of the two candidates had their own session with the press, Rosalynn made it clear that she would be the boss on the distaff side. Joan Mondale, asked what sort of activities she would want to pursue if her husband was Vice-President, responded that she was interested in day care centers. Before she could finish, Rosalynn (perhaps recalling the military tradition, where the general's wife sets the tone for the other wives) stepped to the microphone, saying, "I've become very concerned about day care centers . . . and I'm sure Mrs. Mondale would be very capable of helping me with anything I try to do."

Throughout the convention Carter had remained pretty much ensconced in his suite at the Americana—interviewing vice-presidential candidates, negotiating with various groups, watching the convention on television, calling a few VIPs on the phone (Kennedy, for one, after he appeared with Cronkite), revising and practicing the delivery of his acceptance speech. Only occasionally did he venture out. On Sunday he went to the NBC studios for a session on "Meet the Press," and to church services at the Fifth Avenue Presbyterian Church. Afterwards he walked down Fifth Avenue and attended a brunch in Strauss's honor at the 21 Club. On Monday night his family went to Mamma Leone's for some good northern Italian food. On Tuesday, he met with the New Jersey delegation (where he ignored Governor Byrne, who had unsuccessfully headed the Carter delegate slate, while courting Dugan, who had not) and on Wednesday he met with the California delegation where he joked about Governor Brown's suite, "excuse me, his 'room.'"

Carter's first formal appearance before the convention came on Thursday evening, when he made the traditional acceptance speech. Strauss, determined not to repeat McGovern's 1972 experience, when the South Dakota Senator had poured out his acceptance prose at 3:00 A.M. (EST) to a sleeping nation, asked for and received at the very first session of the convention the unanimous consent of the delegates for a special order stipulating a certain time—9:30 P.M. on Thursday—for the candidates' acceptance speeches.

At 9:50 on Thursday evening, Frisbees were sent floating across the Garden and placards (one spelled out "Texas Loves New York City") bobbed up and down, spreading the good news that the Democratic Party had reunited. When Mondale approached the platform to deliver his acceptance speech the good-natured crowd cheered and applauded. His speech (which he had sent to Patrick Anderson beforehand) was a tribute to the Democratic presidential nominee and the new unity of the party. "Jimmy Carter is the embodiment of the hopes and dreams not only of we Democrats, but of all Americans . . . What this convention represents above all is the end to the divisions of the past . . ."

Carter was introduced to the convention by a film prepared by Rick Goodwin—a fourteen-minute testimony to his humble origins, unparalleled perseverance, and outstanding career in public service. There were even some cartoons included for humorous relief. When the film ended, it was Carter's time to appear. The original plan for his entry, pressed by his aides and opposed by the televison networks, was pure Hollywood. It called for a darkened hall and a sudden beam of light on the podium, where Carter would dramatically appear. But this plan was junked when Carter noted approvingly, how the television cameras picked up the enthusiastic crowd's response to Mondale. Carter made his entry, not from behind the podium as one might expect, but from the back of the hall, so he could walk though the crowd on the floor and up to the dais. (The imagery was much like a campaign TV ad in which Carter moves from being outside with the people to the interior of an open White House.) For a short while there had been a rumor circulating on the floor that Carter might walk up to Mayor Daley, shake his hand, and welcome him back into the Democratic fold. But that was not Carter's kind of symbolism—it might suggest indebtedness to someone else.

With his opening line Carter won a round of laughter: "My name is Jimmy Carter and I'm running for President." Carter then gave the speech that he and Patrick Anderson (in consultation with dozens of other Democrats) had prepared. Carter evoked the names of Roosevelt, Truman, Johnson, and Kennedy, and identified himself with the party: "I have always been a Democrat." But he was still the "outsider" and the "populist." "I have never met a Democratic President," he said. And he inveighed against "special influence and privilege." He saw "no reason why big shot crooks should go free and the poor ones go to jail." He called for a fairer tax system, denounced exclusive private schools, and the self-perpetuating alliance between money and politics. And he took aim at the "establishment": "Too many have had to suffer at the hands of a political and economic elite. . ."

It was unusual material coming from a man whose forces had successfully knocked out of the party's platform proposals calling for breaking up vertical integrations in the oil industry, and had softened other proposals calling for government support of full employment and medical programs for the public. But at this point the euphoria kept most people from considering contradictions like this.

After the speech Bob Strauss called up Democrat after Democrat to join Carter on the podium in a final cheer for unity: Jackson, Udall, Church, Brown, Wallace, Muskie, Glenn, Daley, Humphrey, Barbara Jordan, Mayor Beame, Governor Askew. . . . And they all linked arms—as if to signify their unity in the forthcoming campaign and the return of the Democrats to power in Washington. Then Martin Luther King, Sr., gave the benediction. He called for silence, got it, and with his prayers, turned the audience into a large, emotional organism. Everyone joined hands and sang "We Shall Overcome." And King said: "Surely the Lord sent Jimmy Carter to come on out and bring America back where she belongs."

There was something wrong with this picture, however. For the first time since 1952, there were no Kennedys on the podium. And for all the harmony and talk of Carter's having united the old Democratic coalition, he had not really done that. All those Democrats standing on the convention platform with arms linked had one thing in common—their desire to win. But they had not really agreed on what their common goals might be.

# IV

# Rhetoric: Love Sweeps the Nation

# FIFTEEN

---

# Media

CARTER'S MEDIA STAFF had grown from three in the summer of 1975 to eight paid aides and numerous volunteers by March 1976. They provided the necessary amenities for the traveling press corps. In Plains, in what had been Earl Carter's Main Street office, they set up a press headquarters complete with telephone banks, typewriters, desks, teletype machines, and a coffee urn. The staff kept the press informed through notices on an announcement board, mimeographed handouts of the daily schedule and names of visitors, advance copies of speeches, issue papers, schedules for press conferences, photo opportunities, and interviews.

## Strategy

In addition to taking care of the press, Carter's aides tried to get reporters to focus on certain events and to interpret them in ways most congenial to campaign objectives.

Throughout the primaries, they worked at influencing journalists' views of the political field and Carter's advance within it. Their first important technique was the strategy leak. Jordan, Powell, and other "insiders" such as Peter Bourne or Pat Caddell would take reporters into their confidence about long-term strategies, sometimes giving a reporter a peek at a strategy memo, heightening the suspense and the value of the information by keeping it "secret.' By the time Kandy Stroud was allowed to see Jordan's original strategy memo, the procedure had become carefully ritualized:

The Jordan memo was treated like the Magna Carta. The original was kept under lock and key and copies were not available to the press. Anyone wishing to read the memo was required to make a special appointment in Jordan's office and any excerpts were to be approved by Jordan himself. The day I went, although I had an appointment, I was asked to wait until Jordan returned before I was allowed to begin reading. Jordan wheeled in a typewriter next to his secretary and insisted that I sit there to excerpt it while she watched. My eight pages of typed notes had to be O.K.'d by Jordan. Only three pages were returned to me, and those had been retyped and edited by his secretary. No exact quotes were to be used.

During the fall campaign, a similar technique was used in disclosing state by state priority ratings. Though Jordan allowed Jules Witcover in to see the map that traced the programmed travels of Jimmy, Rosalynn, Fritz Mondale, and the others, he ordered aide Rick Hutcheson to cover the priority ranking on the giant map with large sheets of wrapping paper.

Such leaks during the early phases of the campaign served to make Carter's long-shot candidacy credible. Later, when the campaign began to unfold as the Carter people had said it would, their plan took on a prophetic quality. Jack Germond of the Washington *Star*, for example, had received a complete outline of the upcoming campaign from Carter and his associates in early 1975. By March, 1976, though he still had doubts, he couldn't help noticing that the campaign was exactly where Carter had said it would be.

The Carter organization also knew how to position the candidate to secure the most beneficial coverage. On election nights and/or the mornings after, Carter was readily available for interviews. The morning after the Iowa caucus, Carter was in New York City in time for television interviews on the network morning programs. On the night of the New Hampshire primary, Carter was on hand for interviews in Manchester, where all the networks had set up camp. He was able to minimize the Massachusetts fiasco by staying in Florida. On April 6 Carter was in Wisconsin for that primary, where he had a chance, avoiding New York, where he did not. In the post-Pennsylvania primaries, which he lost to Brown and Church, he located himself so that the emphasis would be on the states he won, not those he lost. On May 25, when Kentucky, Tennessee, Arkansas, Idaho, Nevada, and Oregon were all voting, the only real contest appeared to be in Oregon. By staying in New York City, Carter was able to reap the benefits of the Southern victories and go to bed just when the Pacific time zone states were beginning to count the votes. The press, with their own deadlines, emphasized his three Southern wins; the victories of Brown in Nevada and Church in Oregon and Idaho were not discussed until late the next day. Even the Los Angeles *Times*'s morning headline was on the Carter victories. For the Big Three primaries on June 8, Carter put all the emphasis on Ohio by personally campaigning there, skipping California, where he knew he would lose, and cutting short his effort in New Jersey, where there was a close race.

The decision to base the candidate in Plains also had a subtle influence over the media. In Washington he would have been in competition with not only all the other candidates, but the entire government. Also, if he had been based in Atlanta, where the real campaign operations were, stories about Carter's governorship and staff operations could be more easily checked out by reporters wandering over to the state capitol, the Georgia Archives, or campaign headquarters. In Plains the press corps had nothing to do but write human interest stories and talk to Carter's friends.

The staff also used access to Carter as a subtle means of winning friends and shutting out enemies. Early in the campaign Carter had to take media attention when and where he could get it. After Iowa the balance began to shift as Carter attracted a large press retinue. And after New Hampshire access to Carter had become a valuable commodity. With demand high the Carter staff controlled the supply. Indeed, as Jody Powell later explained, their decision to hire a small hotel ballroom for Carter's New Hampshire victory statement did just that. When Carter was declared the winner, there was insufficient room in the hall for Carter supporters, volunteers, and the press. This gave Powell a legitimate excuse for admitting the press on a priority basis, putting them in his debt, while supporters and volunteers waited outside. As Jerry Rafshoon said, commenting on the difference this victory made:

I got kind of a kick in New Hampshire listening to a guy from ABC arguing with Jody that he had been double-crossed. I can remember a year earlier if we could have a two minute shot on ABC, we'd have flown out of Georgia, gone up there, waited in the reception area, gotten his two minute thing, and flown back. . . . [They said] "it's just going to kill us to see him with Cronkite before Reasoner, we're going to lose face" . . . and, it was really, I guess a feeling of satisfaction that now it's a case of "rationing" his time to national media.

By the Florida primary Carter was in such demand that he could obtain media attention almost any time he wanted it. The evening of the Florida primary, Walter Cronkite did a Carter interview, interrupting CBS's prime-time schedule to watch Carter watching the returns in his hotel room.*

Whereas in the fall of 1975, a casual request to Powell was enough to gain a half-hour interview, after New Hampshire, as Kandy Stroud recalls, "Attempting to set up an interview with Carter was tantamount to all-out war." Over a ten-month period she called Powell dozens of times and never received a return call. Having had an interview with Carter scheduled and then postponed several times, Stroud finally just went to Plains with a filming crew from NBC. She talked to Peter Bourne, who suggested she just show up at the house with the film crew as planned: "Jimmy will never turn you down." Unwilling to do that, Stroud called the house. " 'I don't know anything about any television interviews,' Carter said coldly. 'No. Jody never talked to me. And if he has set up an interview on my one day off, I'll fire his ass.' " After she told him of Peter Bourne's suggestion, Carter said, " 'If Peter Bourne suggested that, I'll fire his ass too.' " She continued cajoling Carter until she felt her voice crack: "In all my life I had never shed a tear over an interview, but somehow I felt I was dealing with the military. I began to say thank you and hang up before I sounded like a complete idiot, when Carter sensed he had brought me to tears.

---

* The campaign could also deny access to infiltrators from the other side. In late April, for example, Jay J. Pike, a young correspondent openly working for *First Monday*, the monthly magazine for the Republican National Committee, had received credentials and been booked on the Carter press plane. After the plane took off, the Carter staff recognized their mistake. When they landed at Austin, Texas, Pike and his luggage involuntarily disembarked.

'Don't cry,' he said softly. 'You know I love you. Can you be here by two o'clock?' "

Robert Scheer of *Playboy* had better luck. With the help of Powell and Jordan, he managed to log more interview hours with Carter than any other newsperson. The day after the Democratic convention Powell told him: "Listen, Scheer, I'm not going to kid you. Now that he's the nominee, I've got over 700 requests from all over the world for interviews. He's told me to cut back, but I've got a prior commitment to you guys and I'm going to honor it. So hop a plane down to his place in Plains. We'll just cut out an appointment with some future Secretary of State." Scheer and *Playboy* had paid their dues. As Scheer remembered, "*Playboy* and I both hung in there through the months, taking (and paying for) flights halfway across the country on the tentative promise of yet one more hurried chat."

## Providing Good Copy

The genius of the Carter media effort was also evident in the molding of an attractive and newsworthy candidate. In this, Carter's early anonymity was an advantage. Having no national track record, he could come into the presidential race without a fixed image or label. He would be the one to introduce background information on himself. Before an interview, for example, reporters were expected to read *Why Not the Best?*, with its idyllic portraits and summary of Carter's religious and political life. Atlanta journalist Jim Merriner noted, Carter would ask: "Have you read my book?" Elizabeth Drew experienced this. Riding with Carter between some Chicago campaign stops in March, 1976, she asked him about his master plan. "It's in the book . . . how I decided to run for the Presidency, and the plans are in the book. There's no point in our talking about these things when they're in the book." When Drew explained that his staff was attempting to locate a copy for her, he replied icily, "It's in the stores."

When they made the decision to run, Carter and his aides had also discussed potential themes and images for the campaign. Carter himself raised the question of how he should run, "As a farmer, a non-office holder? A Georgian? Do you see any negatives there?" Peter Bourne, as noted above, had impressed upon Carter the need for appearing self-confident. And Rafshoon laid out a four-phase program for the evolution of his image. The first phase would focus on Carter as a "heavyweight governor," promoting a "good guy" brand of populism. The second phase would show him as a leader of the Democratic Party. The third would establish Carter as a "heavyweight thinker," while the final one would simply portray him as a presidential candidate.

At a more personal level, Carter had been advised to accentuate the John Kennedy likeness, and a photo of him sitting in a rocking chair on the patio at the Georgia governor's mansion had been widely circulated. By 1976 he had switched from a "wet-head" hairstyle to a fashionable shaggy, over-the-ears style, created by former Playboy bunny Betty Swims, and kept in place with Pantene Hair Groom Spray. Although his jeans, workshirt, and boots were the vogue for Plains, when traveling, Carter was impeccably tailored, so much so that in February the Fashion Foundation of American named him the best-dressed man in public affairs.

Carter's staff also worked with him on his formal speeches. As early as 1973 Powell was suggesting that he keep his speeches to a maximum of twenty minutes, preferably fifteen, and stick to the prepared text. Most of the applause, Powell noted, came during the prepared, not the extemporized, parts of a speech.

His announcement speech went through at least four drafts and many marginal notes suggesting changes. Eizenstat felt Carter's Rickover story was "hokey," that his statements about his Christianity smacked too much of the "old South," that at several points Carter got into the "McGovern trap of the too specific." On foreign policy matters Eizenstat suggested Carter take care not to promise "an overly hard line and paint ourselves into a 'Jackson corner,' " and said his suggestions for arms limitation were "too simplistic." (It was Carter who made the final decisions, however. The "hokey" Rickover story remained in his announcement speech. He dropped some rhetoric that alluded to the Soviet Union as a "warlike power" in favor of a softer comment on "other world powers." But he labeled himself as a "Christian," even though Jody Powell and others preferred "churchgoer." Carter also continued to ad-lib speeches when the mood struck him.)

Carter's informal style on the stump was also a product of practice. Early in the campaign his staff would evaluate his appearances on a scale from "A" to "C." Key passages of his talks were filmed again and again until at least one "A" performance was on tape. On some occasions, several takes were required before Rafshoon was satisfied. Reportedly, four separate takes were required to get an "A" piece of videotape of Carter's famous promise: "I'll never tell a lie. I'll never make a misleading statement. I'll never avoid a controversial issue. Watch television and listen to the radio. If I ever do any of those things, don't support me."

Carter was an apt student. As journalist David Halberstam noted, Carter used the television camera effectively to reach people and to minimize his potential weaknesses. On TV he didn't look short. Though said to be cold and aloof, on TV he didn't look it. Halberstam was particularly impressed by his pacing, his sense of control, his soft low-key manner. "Carter used 'pauses'— they were reassuring and echoed his own self-confidence."

He also had a keen sense of what would provide a good photo opportunity. The night of his Wisconsin victory he had immediately struck the Trumanesque pose with a copy of the Milwaukee paper declaring Udall the winner. When he met Morris and Ella Udall in Pennsylvania Carter managed to upstage Udall and obtain a front-page picture of himself kissing Mrs. Udall "hello" while her husband stood in the background. During his postconvention stay in Plains every incident provided a "photo opportunity"—his emerging from church on Sunday, or his walks down colorful, nostalgic Main Street with Jerry Brown or some other visitor, his wading in the mud to help clean a pond, his almost sensual caress of a peanut plant.

The good copy Carter obtained was based, in part, on his ability to establish a different, but not too different, continuing story line with a full complement of conflicts and supporting characters, an attractive drama, particularly in the wake of the Watergate and Vietnam experiences. Aside from the trials and tribulations of Jimmy seeking his conquests on the campaign trail (where the insiders were ganging up against him), there was the full panoply of interesting characters in Plains. Billy and Lillian Carter, interesting in their own right, provided relief from Jimmy's pieties, all the while reinforcing his basic claims of intelligence, morality, and dedication. Ruth, the vivacious evangelist sister, who traveled around the world on her healing mission, was also good copy with her emphasis on Jimmy's born again experiences and healthy personality. Gloria, the "motorcycle fiend" and farm wife, was in many ways the touchstone with "normalcy." Then there were the relatives and townspeople: Uncle Alton, the old-style elder, and his antique store; Cousin Hugh, the world's largest worm farmer; the Williamses and their "competing" feed seed business. The town itself was an important backdrop. Big-city reporters could see for themselves the redeeming virtues of a beautiful and friendly small town, unspoiled by urban blight and smog and anonymity. Even the peanut became a symbol. According to Elizabeth Drew, Carter and his staff had discussed the role of the peanut in the campaign. Some argued that it was too corny; but when it was discovered that the peanut had a kind of humble quality, it became important to a campaign in which, as one aide noted, "Humility was not our long suit."

## Coverage

Carter had been marked as a man to watch, as we have seen, even before the primary season opened in 1976. His "win" in Iowa made him a national figure and guaranteed him a long following of newspersons in his New Hampshire campaign. When Carter received the extra few hundred New Hampshire votes, which qualified him for "winner" status, he received a veritable "orgy of publicity." His face was on the covers of *Time* and *Newsweek,* the stories totaling 2,630 lines, compared to 96 for Udall, the second place finisher. In the week following New Hampshire, Carter received three times the television news coverage and four times the newspaper coverage of his competitors. As Morris Udall observed: "We all said we weren't going to let New Hampshire do it to us again, and New Hampshire did do it. We all said the Iowa caucus wasn't that important, and the press made it that important. . . . Once that avalanche starts down the ski slope, get out of the way."

Even before the New Hampshire primary there were stories in UPI and in *Time* which marked him as the potential front runner. After New Hampshire,

Roger Mudd saw Carter as "the one with momentum, the one now who must be stopped." NBC's Tom Petit called him "the man to beat." This discovery of Carter as a front runner—the protagonist of the campaign drama—subtly influenced press treatment of the other candidates. They were now the challengers, the people who might gain or lose on the front runner, or slow his momentum. Thus, Jackson's Massachusetts win did not dislodge Carter as the front runner. As *Time,* magazine saw it, Massachusetts had "slowed the momentum" for Carter and to "recapture that forward thrust" he had to "run strongly [not win] against Wallace" in Florida, Illinois, and North Carolina. Walter Cronkite said only that, "Massachusetts . . . put Senator Henry Jackson alongside Jimmy Carter in front of the Democratic pack." And Roger Mudd noted that "Henry Jackson's strong finish surprised everyone." Even Jackson's win in New York did not change expectations. Roger Mudd pointed out that Jackson's victory came from a coalition of the right, the center, and Jews, which appeared "peculiar to New York and may not be duplicated anywhere else." *Time* gave New York short shrift, covering instead Carter's Wisconsin victory and his troubles and apology for his statement on "ethnic purity." In *Newsweek,* Carter's New York loss and his narrow Wisconsin victory were portrayed as less troublesome than the possible candidacy of Hubert Humphrey and the row over "ethnic purity."

This early designation of Carter as front runner was premature in several ways. It could not have been based on the popular vote totals in the early primaries. In New Hampshire, Carter, with 30 percent of the vote, won approximately 23,000 actual votes; in Massachusetts, Jackson's 23 percent of the vote translated into 163,000 votes. After the New Hampshire, Massachusetts, Vermont, and Florida presidential preference primaries, Carter had received only 590,500 of the 2,170,043 votes cast—27 percent. During the remainder of the campaign Carter's vote fluctuated, depending on each state's primary structure. By the end of the primaries Carter had received approximately six million of the reported sixteen million popular votes—39 percent.

Nor had Carter locked up the committed delegates. By March 31, after the Illinois and North Carolina primaries, only about 23 percent of the convention delegates had been chosen, and of those, Carter had won about one third of those committed to a specific candidate. After the Wisconsin and New York contests, with about 33 percent of the delegates chosen, Carter had 27 percent of the total (compared to Jackson's 21 percent). After the Pennsylvania primary Carter had 28 percent of the total number of delegates chosen, while 18 percent were still uncommitted (Humphrey's potential strength).

Carter was not even the favorite of Democratic voters in the national polls. A Darden poll published in mid-January, 1976, showed Wallace leading Carter in the South 41.6 percent to 34.6 in a one-on-one contest. That same month a national Lou Harris poll of independents and Democrats had Carter in a tie for fifth place (with Muskie, Brown, and Bayh) at 4 percent—trailing Kennedy (24 percent), Humphrey (18 percent), Wallace (12 percent), and Jackson (6 percent). With Kennedy and Humphrey out of the listing, he still secured only 12 percent of those with a preference, running behind Wallace and Jackson. Further, exit interviews done at the Florida, Illinois, New York, and Wisconsin polls suggest that Humphrey could have won each of those states.

But such things are subject to interpretation. In 1976 the media were reacting against the mistake of 1972, when George McGovern's candidacy had been ignored because of his low showing in the early opinion polls. They were not about to write off any challenger who seemed to be expressing an opinion tide. Also, there were other special considerations in 1976. The top three front runners were disqualified for one reason or another: Kennedy was not in the race; Humphrey had not entered any primaries; and Wallace was not a credible candidate, given the strong negative reactions to him among elites and other segments in the party. Equally important, as Carter won primaries and gained media exposure, he climbed in the polls, which suggested an upward trend in the future.

The network exit polls also showed that Carter had the ability to draw support from a broad spectrum of voters. And early in the season he surfaced as the strongest candidate the Democrats could run against Ford. A February Gallup Poll had shown Carter as the only Democrat who could beat Ford one-on-one. A survey of Illinois voters in late March showed Carter and Ford running neck and neck in that state. By early May, Lou Harris's national polls showed Carter defeating Ford 47 to 43 percent.

The polls, when joined with his primary victories, subtly undermined the legitimacy of his opposition in the later primaries, as well as any attempt to form a coalition against him or allocate the remaining primaries so that Carter would have to face only one opponent in each. As early as March 15, for example, NBC's David Brinkley publicly worried about the value of the primaries if the politicians at the national convention ended up choosing the candidate in spite of them. And the Washington *Post*, in an April 29 editorial discussing the Pennsylvania primary (the primary that helped convince Humphrey to stay out of the race), noted: "A whole lot worse things could happen to the country than for Hubert Humphrey to be his party's nominee. But it matters how he gets there. For few worse things could happen to either Humphrey or his party than for there to be a recurrence of the fissuring of the Democrats and all the attendant bitterness that gave a grateful nation Richard Nixon two times running. . . ."

In short, the early electoral process produced a circular effect. The media's attention to Carter helped him secure his first victories, which brought further press attention, which brought further popular recognition and helped Carter soar in the polls, which brought more favorable press attention, and so on.

### Banana Peels

The real danger to the Carter candidacy in the spring of 1976 was that he might do or say something so out of character, so unpresidential, that the press as a whole would turn on him and give the story major press play. Such an event would have seriously undermined his campaign.

In the past other candidates had fallen victim to this "banana peel" effect. In August, 1967, former Michigan Governor George Romney, campaigning for the Republican nomination, had told the host of a Detroit talk show that he had had "the greatest brainwashing that anybody can get when you go over to Vietnam." The subsequent press coverage suggested that Romney was too "impressionable," and he was finally forced to withdraw from the race. In 1972 Edmund Muskie, in an emotional scene outside William Loeb's Manchester *Union Leader* office, derided that publisher for a nasty, unwarranted attack on Mrs. Muskie. Reports that Muskie had broken into sobs at one point were widely interpreted as signs of weakness. The story probably contributed to his unexpectedly low showing in the later New Hampshire voting.

There were three potential banana peels upon which Carter's primary campaign could have slipped—an article by Steven Brill in *Harper's*, the "ethnic purity" statement, and the resignation of Robert Shrum from his campaign staff. Carter managed to survive all three.

Rumors that a critical article on Carter would be appearing in *Harper's* in the spring had been circulating through the campaign world since the end of 1975, when Steven Brill had received the go-ahead for the piece. By the end of January the article, entitled "Jimmy Carter's Pathetic Lies," was set for publication in March. Jody Powell requested and obtained an advance copy, giving his word to *Harper's* editor Lewis Lapham that he would not circulate the article prior to its appearance in the magazine. What Powell read had real potential for halting the Carter bandwagon. There had been other critical articles in the press, but for the first time, in a widely circulated and reputable magazine, an author had documented his critique with materials from the governor's papers in the Georgia Archives, as well as interviews and old newspaper stories. The portrait that emerged showed Jimmy Carter as a wily politician who wheeled and dealed with the best of them—a portrait incongruent with his self-presentation as a man above politics, a born again Christian who would restore morality and harmony in America.

Powell immediately set the staff to work on a rebuttal that ultimately ran as long as Brill's 6,000-word article.

Members of the press, catching the scent of the brewing storm, asked Carter about the article on Sunday, February 1. The smile on his face faded; his eyes iced over. Characterizing the story as "a collection of lies, distortions, and half-truths," he said, "I've read it. He [Brill] said he was coming down to gut us and has had a close association with our opponents. What else could you expect?"

The next day, Powell circulated both the still unpublished article and his refutation. Brill, as it turned out, was vulnerable on a few points. Though he had put his finger on several sensitive aspects in Carter's earlier career, he had not read the fine print. Thus Powell could correctly deny that Carter had ever urged people to "protest William Calley's conviction," as Brill had phrased it.

As Powell pointed out, Carter had said "he believed Calley had been used as a scapegoat for higher ranking officers and that this would damage the morale of American soldiers" and had responded with a day "honoring American fighting men which clearly omitted the slightest indication of support for Calley." Nor had Carter called Maddox "the essence of the Democratic Party"; he had said that "THE WAY MADDOX CAMPAIGNED [going directly to the people, not depending on 'big shots,' etc.]" was the essence of the Democratic Party. Powell was off base on another response, however. The letter in which Brill had quoted Carter to the effect that he and George Wallace shared the same political philosophy, Powell said, "was written by a staffer, never seen by Governor Carter, and did not accurately express his views. . . . Had the writer of the article asked, he would have been told of the three-letter-initial code used to identify staff letters." (Certainly the letter went out under Carter's name, and the initials on the letter were Jody Powell's.)

Having raised questions about Brill's work, Powell also attacked the author himself. Powell seems to have informally spread the word that Brill had flunked out of Yale Law School (Brill graduated), that the article had been commissioned by Birch Bayh (completely false, according to Lewis Lapham of *Harper's*), and that Brill was known for incompetent work. Powell referred to an article Brill had done on Henry Jackson as a "hatchet job." (The Carter campaign itself later circulated the article.)

The heat was now off Carter—he could remain above the fray while aides pointed to Powell's refutation of Brill any time a question was raised. Having their answers ready for simultaneous appearance with the charges, the Carter people guaranteed that (given the press's concept of objectivity) the two would run side by side in newspapers. Any questions that might give reporters the incentive to investigate the charges appeared to have been answered. And by getting the refutation into circulation before the actual appearance of the article in the March issue of *Harper's* and raising questions about Brill's accuracy and motivations, Carter's staff put Brill, Lapham, and *Harper's* on the defensive. Instead of Carter's, Brill's credibility and motives would be the center of focus.

Jack Germond of the Washington *Star* noted on February 4, "the latest round in what has become a liberal assault on Carter" saying it was possibly the most severe "in harshness and intensity in any presidential campaign of the postwar period." *Time* magazine's report, "Doing a Job on Jimmy," portrayed Brill as kind of a liberal hired gun, saying that he had been hired by the Americans for Democratic Action to prove that Henry Jackson was not a real liberal on domestic issues, that he had done an article based on an interview with George Wallace that Wallace denied took place, that rumors of Brill's "hatchet job" (the same phrase used by the Carter campaign) on Jimmy had been circulating since November, 1975. They also quoted a "Washington-based political correspondent" saying, "Brill is a hit man. He's the liberal enforcer." In discussing some of the actual criticisms of Carter made by Brill, *Time* discounted them, not with facts, but with statements such as: "Carter has already refuted";

"some are absurdly trivial"; "many others are open to serious questions"; and "a dozen other points in the piece are challenged by sources in Georgia and elsewhere." The only charge *Time* acknowledged as true was the relatively harmless statement that Carter had "led anti-McGovern forces in 1972." (Actually Carter did not "lead" the anti-McGovern forces as noted above.) Atlanta *Constitution* columnist Hal Gulliver was even less subtle, calling the Brill article "the shabbiest piece of political journalism of the season." He not only attacked the "hatchet job," but also the author: "Calling Brill a journalist is a bit like accusing the Happy Hooker of being a suburban housewife."

A few journalists investigated the Brill charges. (An AP story in the February 18 *New York Times*, for example, supported Brill's findings that the reorganization of the Georgia government had been more cosmetic than functional.) But generally the discussion degenerated into accusations, denials, and cross-accusations—not between the Carter staff and the press over substantive questions raised, as one might expect, but rather over isolated comments and claims made against and for Brill.

Not long after this episode Carter almost slipped on a peel he dropped himself. On April 2, in flight across northern New York State, Carter gave an interview to Sam Roberts, the chief political correspondent of the New York *Daily News*. Two days later, a summary of the interview was printed. Tucked away in the sixteenth paragraph, Carter was quoted as saying (in response to a question about scattered-site public housing): "I see nothing wrong with ethnic purity being maintained. I would not force a racial integration of a neighborhood by government action. But I would not permit discrimination against a family moving into the neighborhood."

At first very little attention was given to the use of the phrase "ethnic purity" (least of all by Roberts, who made no comment about it). Then Marty Plissner, the political editor of CBS News, asked Ed Rabel, the CBS correspondent traveling with Carter, to get an elaboration on the statement. Rabel did so at a press conference in Indianapolis on Tuesday, April 6 (the day of the Wisconsin and New York primaries). His question: "What did you mean by 'ethnic purity'?" Carter replied that he supported open-housing laws, but only for those who wished voluntarily to live in such neighborhoods. He surprised Rabel by using the phrase again and adding some new ones. He opposed government programs, he said, "to *inject black families* into a white neighborhood just to create some sort of integration." But he was not opposed to a community "made up of people who are Polish, or who are Czechoslovakians, or who are French Canadians or who are blacks trying to maintain the ethnic purity of their neighborhoods. This is a natural inclination." (Emphasis added.)

The words Carter used astounded the reporters—and they gathered in the back of the press bus and played their tapes again. Then the pack instinct took over. In South Bend that same day, the press peppered him with questions. Asked if he would favor federal or state programs to provide public housing in the suburbs or middle-class areas, Carter dug in further. "To *artificially create* within a community that's homogeneous in racial or economic status a *diametrically opposite kind of family*, I think is bad for the community on both sides . . ." (Emphasis added.) Carter began perspiring heavily; he looked tense and angry. "If you're trying to make something out of nothing," Carter told Chris Lydon of *The New York Times*, "I resent that effort."

After this exchange Carter evidently felt off balance and he wanted to restore it. Back in the press plane after a successful visit at the University of Notre Dame, Carter sought out Lydon. They small-talked for a while, but the conversation soon turned to the topic of the day. Lydon told Carter, "For a person who chooses language with a surgeon's precision, you have chosen some very strange words to use today. I never heard you talk that way—black intrusions, alien groups, a different kind of person—what were you trying to say?" Carter gave Lydon his cold blue stare and responded, softly, slowly: "I don't know how to use the English language if you don't know what I'm saying."

For a moment this looked as though it might be *the* banana peel on which Carter's candidacy would eventually slip. Black leaders began to wonder about him in public. Atlanta Mayor Jackson pondered, "Is there no white politician I can trust?" Jesse Jackson called Carter's views "a throwback to Hitlerian racism." Julian Bond said that the statement smacked of "Nazi Germany." Hosea Williams said, "You can't be for ethnic purity and open housing too. You can't have your cake and eat it too. The man is trying to say what he can to please everybody. . . . I'd rather support a southern white man who says he's for segregation and keeping blacks totally out of neighborhoods than a sophisticated racist like Jimmy Carter. At least with the segregationists I know where I stand." Even Andrew Young was distressed. He joined the Congressional Black Caucus in a telegram attacking Carter and his statements. And he indicated that much of the work he had done for Carter might now be destroyed: "A lot of people who said 'You can't trust a Southerner' are going to say, 'See, I told you so.'"

When Greg Schneiders and Betty Rainwater first heard Carter use these phrases and saw the press reaction, they urged him to lay off. After two days of headlines and negative reactions from blacks and members of the press, Carter tried a reluctant backdown at a press conference in Philadelphia. But it was accompanied by a defense of what he had said, which required a further backdown. He said: "It was an unfortunate use of a phrase. I know how I feel. I know my record in Georgia. I would make sure that anyone who wanted to move into a neighborhood would have the right to do it." When asked if what he was saying was "there is nothing wrong with the thought, just that it was a poor use of words," he replied: "Yes." When pressed further, he admitted the other phrases—"black intrusion," "diametrically opposite kind of family," and "alien groups"—were "unfortunate too." Asked to give an example of what he now said he really opposed—the arbitrary power of the federal government to change the ethnic character of a neighborhood—he could not. Was he "talking about a straw man, something that does not exist?" one reporter asked. Carter was forced to reply, "Yes, that's correct."

. This apology did not end the political storm. Carter was still queried about it by reporters. And other politicians spoke out on the subject. Udall said he respected Carter for his apology, but added: "Choice of words are revealing of basic attitudes. It's remarkable to me that this happens when it does, when Wallace is leaving the race and Pennsylvania and Michigan are coming up."

The "ethnic purity" flap was finally put to rest after Carter succeeded in putting together a rally of black supporters in Atlanta (details are in Chapter 17). But in addition to whatever insight it provided into Carter's racial attitudes, it revealed an interesting attitude toward journalists on the part of his campaign. Members of his staff viewed the entire episode was a ritualistic test of strength between Carter and the press rather than a search for Carter's real position on racial issues. According to Jody Powell: "I really think in some ways the best thing we did to get it over with . . . let them ask their questions, hostile or otherwise, [and] demonstrate that he could handle it. . . . I think that's what the press is looking for . . . they're a lot more interested in how, whether he could handle the problem, than they were in whether he was a racist or not." Charlotte Scott, Carter's Pennsylvania press secretary, saw the press looking for a fight: "Everything had been going so smoothly; he'd been winning; there had been no mistakes; he was the ideal candidate; he was picking up support; and, all of a sudden, there was a chance, something to level in on. There hadn't been an opportunity beforehand . . . Everyone made a living off it for two weeks."

This view is supported by the relative lack of curiosity about Carter's actual record on open housing while governor of Georgia. Julian Bond, at the time of the flap, contacted at least three reporters—from the Washington *Post*, the Los Angeles *Times*, and *The New York Times*—telling them that there had been no fair housing laws passed in Georgia during Carter's term, though Carter said there were. Only one reporter seemed to pursue the lead; and none of the papers dealt with Bond's charge.

Less than two weeks after the ethnic purity flap, Robert Shrum joined the Carter campaign, leaving his job as staff director for the Senate Select Committee on Nutrition and Human Needs. He was one of the best speechwriters around (he had written for John Lindsay, Edmund Muskie, and George McGovern). And his decision to join the Carter staff was a sign to insiders in Democratic politics (as Robert Sam Anson later noted), that "you have arrived, that, on important issues, you are okay." He had joined Carter for two reasons: to promote "both purpose and power for the Democratic party" and to fulfill his desire to be a presidential speechwriter—a role he saw as a "means of advising and verbalizing for a president."

Shrum stayed with the Carter staff for only nine days. His last duty was to draft the Pennsylvania victory statement, which he read, pronounced "good," and decided, "I didn't believe it." On the day of the Pennsylvania primary he drafted a letter of resignation, left a copy in Jody Powell's box, and went to stay with friends. A few days later he made his resignation letter public. In it he said: "I share the perception that simple measures will not answer our problems; but it seems to me that your issue strategy is not a response to that complexity, but an attempt to conceal your true positions. I am not sure what you truly believe in other than yourself."

Shrum, later summarized his experiences and reasons for leaving:

I resigned after days of increasing doubt, which I couldn't suppress, though I tried to. It was as though I passed through a door and once inside the campaign they showed me the trick. The assumption was that everyone wanted to play it for power. Every promise to me was kept except one—the promise of Carter's character and belief. My problem wasn't that I lacked access, but that I had it.

The "dichotomy [between the] private man and public figure" he said was pervasive: "public compassion, private callousness; public indignation over tax loop holes, private concern to molify special interests; public allegiance to new priorities, private sympathy for the military-industrial complex; public smiles, but no private smiles." While in public Carter spoke "fervently" of mine safety with "the timbre of his voice plucking chords of credibility for his words," in private, he dismissed as too radical proposals to increase benefits for miners possibly afflicted with black lung. While in public he had said he favored diversion of the highway trust fund to mass transit, in private he wanted to mollify the trucking industry and tell them that his first objective would be completion and maintenance of the interstate highway system.

Shrum's disappearance had made the Carter press entourage curious. When first asked about him (one Friday in Alabama), Carter had evidently not heard the news and he praised Shrum as a person and a speechwriter. After Powell and Caddell had told him of Shrum's defection, Carter at first declined comment, saying he had not yet seen the letter of resignation (public by then). But when Charles Mohr of *The New York Times* persisted, inquiring specifically about the charge that Carter had dissembled by advocating defense cuts publicly, while privately admitting that the defense budget might actually have to be increased, Carter retorted: "Shrum has never been on my payroll. I don't feel inclined to comment on this young man's statement. . . . [Shrum] obviously wrote the letter for the news media. . . . I'm not a liar. I don't make any statements in private contrary to what I make in public." The next day, after Carter had seen the letter and had a briefing, Carter said that Shrum had been "quite mistaken about two or three statements he made about me in the letter." Carter said: "[I] think he felt when he came to work for us that because of his superlative writing ability I would just accept his speeches and parrot them to the public." (Later, in the *Playboy* interview, Carter went even further: "Shrum dreamed up eight or ten conversations that never took place and nobody in the press ever asked me if they had occurred.")

Powell told members of the press that Shrum had never been on the payroll and had been working on a trial period. (Technically, this was true, since Shrum had not filled out the required tax forms—nor was he ever paid for his nine days of service.) "What he's doing is childish and hurtful. He's made a very hasty judgment about people he doesn't know and understand." Shrum, Powell suggested, had been under pressure from liberals and had in fact entered the campaign with the intention of sabotaging Carter: "I understand that he kept a secret diary from the very beginning, which makes me suspicious. . . . It is highly improper on the face of it." (Robert Sam Anson also noted that rumors "of uncertain origin" began circulating around the press that Shrum had a history of mental illness and that he was a drunk—he is in fact a teetotaler.)

Though *Newsweek* gave the resignation a column and a half, the story did not create much of a stir. The Washington *Post*, for example, ran it on page six between ads for a men's clothier and a liquor store. *Time* buried the story in two paragraphs at the end of a large Carter piece and called Shrum a "disgruntled liberal."

This lack of attention is partially understandable in situational terms. The story came shortly after the "ethnic purity" flap; the press and public had already been drained by press crises. It was also drowned out by the other big stories—Carter's victory in Pennsylvania, Jackson's suspension of active campaigning, and Humphrey's decision against actively entering the campaign—all of which suggested Carter had the nomination locked up.

After the Shrum resignation there would be no more press crises for Carter until the fall campaign. Occasionally some incongruent story would surface—of how campaign funds had been converted into "walk around money" in some black districts, of staff conflicts (e.g., the firing of Herbert Hafif from his position in the campaign) and goof-ups (e.g., a press release listing George Bush as an example of the "failures" and "political hacks" appointed by Ford, circulated the same day Bush was in Plains advising Carter on national security). But these were all isolated incidents that did not touch Carter personally, and most of them were passed on by the reporters to die benignly in the bottom paragraphs or back pages of their newspapers or magazines.

### The Boys (and Girls) on the Bus

This is not to say that there was no criticism of Carter in the American press. Though he had basically received favorable coverage in the national media, there was some critical counterpoint. Syndicated columnists like Rowland Evans and Robert Novak, William Safire, Patrick Buchanan, Joseph Kraft, and David Broder did raise questions about Carter and his campaign. Newspapers both liberal and conservative, such as the *Village Voice*, St. Louis *Post-Dispatch*, Boston *Globe*, Detroit *Free Press*, *Arizona Republic*, carried stories that critically probed Carter's claims of past accomplishments and pointed out some of the contradictory aspects of his campaign rhetoric. Even the television networks, in a few of their early biographical pieces on the candidate, noted some of the negative aspects of Carter's past.

Moreover, individual reporters on the campaign trail or during the summer in Plains did probe and push Carter on varying subjects. Jules Witcover of the

Washington *Post*, for example, dogged him through the snowy hill roads of New Hampshire for over an hour trying to get details on his reorganization of Georgia government. David Broder, also of the *Post*, discovered during the New Hampshire campaign that Carter had written a letter supporting the "right to work" clause of the Taft-Hartley Act, an issue he was hedging on. Robert Turner of the Boston *Globe* generated considerable criticism from Carter for soliciting reaction to Carter's comments before the League of Women Voters concerning the home mortgage income tax credit. Wes Pippert of UPI was one of the few reporters who went to the Sumter County Courthouse and other places to dig into Carter's land holdings and other background. Tom Ottenad of the St. Louis *Post-Dispatch*, who had covered Carter since the governors' conferences, later wrote a piece for *The Progressive* magazine that put all of the criticism together concluding in a portrayal of Carter as a snake-oil salesman—the free-wheeling opportunist.

Other reporters were also tough questioners on specific issues. During press conferences Charles Mohr of *The New York Times* was persistent in questioning Carter on Robert Shrum's resignation. Curtis Wilkie of the Boston *Globe* probed Carter on his aides' supposed meetings with William Loeb. Even friendly journalists would report Carter comments that didn't quite fit with his campaign persona. David Nordan of the Atlanta *Journal*, for example, reported that when questioned privately about Senator Kennedy's possibly joining the stop-Carter movement, Carter had responded, "I don't have to kiss his ass." None of this, however, was more than the routine probing any national candidate can expect.

There were other little glimpses of Carter's personal faults that some of the less beguiled reporters caught. One young journalist, Eleanor Randolph of the Chicago *Tribune* (a Southerner by birth) later wrote that the day-in, day-out exposure did give the astute observer unintended glimpses of the candidate's personality that didn't quite fit his public image. His humor came from poking fun, criticizing and even demeaning those around him—"Carter likes to carve up an opponent, make his friends laugh at him and then call it a joke." She said that he had "stretched the truth to the point where it becomes dishonest to call it exaggeration." Yet, she recalled, "most of us called it exaggeration or a wilful bending of the truth." Further, "the other characters in the Plains tableau kept wandering out of their roles, showing new dimensions of themselves, of course, but also giving special insight into the character of their husband, brother, cousin, nephew or son, Jimmy Carter."

Somewhat paradoxically, given all the attention to Carter's personal life, few of these "insights" were publicly discussed at the time. As Randolph concluded:

The Nixon Presidency helped create a whole breed of political journalists, who appeared in great numbers in 1976 to explain the character of Presidential candidates. It was a kind of Teddy White-ism gone wild, and yet for all of us out there trying to explain what kind of person Jimmy Carter was, most of us didn't or couldn't and opted to call him an enigma. Perhaps that was the easy way out. Maybe it was better to say that Carter was an enigma than to say directly, in the middle of the campaign, that he wasn't a particularly nice guy.

Aside from this tendency to gloss over his faults, the press in the spring and summer of 1976 reflected to a great extent the candidate as he projected himself, his campaign, and even his opponents. The extent of this mirroring effort, evident to some degree in much of the media coverage of Carter, will become more obvious in subsequent chapters. For now, it is important to look at some of the factors in the press corps which may have created this predisposition to take Carter at face value.

### The Reasons Why

By January, 1976, the networks and wire services began assigning film crews and reporters to individual candidates. In March, after the field of candidates had been winnowed down by New Hampshire and Massachusetts primaries, the major print media also moved from their earlier zone coverage (i.e., assigning reporters to the contests rather than the candidates) to covering individual candidates. As the field of contestants narrowed even further, reporters covering the dropouts were assigned to the survivors—thereby increasing the press retinues of the leaders.

Whatever the advantages of this system of coverage, the procedure tends subtly to color the journalists' perspectives on the campaign. Working and traveling and joking together, both sides have a shared interest in getting publicity—the candidates for the obvious reasons, and the reporters so they can advance their own exposure in their medium and thus further their careers. So the candidate and his managers "help" the reporters, providing the routine necessities, telephones, space to write, transportation (which is organized by the campaign and then billed to the reporters's paper or network). They also give them stories—arranging for interesting events, providing background on campaign strategy and the private life of the candidate, scheduling interviews. The result, as Timothy Crouse shows in *The Boys on the Bus*, (his study of the 1972 campaign) is an almost symbiotic union between the journalists and the candidate. In 1976 as David Jones, national news editor of *The New York Times*, explained: "the experience of our political reporters is that when they get on that campaign plane, they get trapped; they're in a cocoon and it distorts their perception of everything that's happening in the campaign because they don't see the broader dimensions."

In Carter's case another factor heightened the symbiotic relationship with the reporters. Because he had been unknown (and because the media were also covering the hot Ford-Reagan contest), he had initially been assigned many young journalists. Several of them were also Southerners—for example, Curtis Wilkie of the Boston *Globe*, James Wooten of the New York *Times*, Eleanor Clift of *Time*, a fact which Jordan had suggested in his 1972 memo might be significant. (The older, more experienced, and better established Washington-based journalists, who were or would be Carter's chief journalistic critics, would not come on board until late in the primary season or the general election in the fall.) Some of these less established reporters saw themselves as challenging, along with Carter, their own establishment. As Richard Reeves later wrote:

> Jimmy Carter, it turned out, was my candidate. I should have figured that out before. He was, as I thought about it, the candidate of a frustrated generation of American political reporters. My generation—people like Johnny Apple and Jim Wooten of *The New York Times*, Jack Nelson of *The Los Angeles Times*, Marty Schram of *Newsday*, Patrick Anderson, and a lot of others. For years, we had seen our business defined by a generation that came along with John F. Kennedy—the Hugh Sideys and Joe Krafts—who had been able to report politics as the institutionalized ambition of their candidates, the Kennedys, Nixon, Humphrey, and Rockefeller.
>
> Then *we* found someone *they* didn't know—an outsider. We began touting Jimmy Carter in early 1976; they began mocking him. To me, he was a transitional figure who understood symbolic communication in mediaworld; to James Reston, he was the slightly laughable "Wee Jimmy." The lines were drawn—in shorthand: Carter vs. Humphrey.

In fact, the young reporters were on the climb and many of them tethered their career aspirations to Carter's own climb. As Reeves said, "We knew him, we had forecast his triumph, we had checked out our new desks at the White House, and we had begun our Carter books—the books we expected to take us into the first rank of our little business." Ken Auletta of *More* magazine elicited similar comments when interviewing other reporters covering the Carter campaign. Curtis Wilkie said: "I'm going to be in a position to actually know a President and Vice President of the United States and be able to say to my kids—if Carter wins—that I covered probably the most remarkable political story of the century. The political thing to do is to say it doesn't matter to me . . . it does . . . if Carter ever sees me, he'll know who I am. No President ever knew who Curtis Wilkie was."

## Ambivalence

Despite the good press Carter had secured and the skill he and his aides showed in bringing it about, he had an ambivalent attitude toward the media.

From the beginning of his political career he had been wooing and charming publishers, editors, and individual journalists. When he was governor, national journalists traveling to Atlanta could be almost assured of an invitation to stay the night at the governor's mansion. And Carter, on his early travels for his presidential campaign; met with editors and publishers across the country. His manner was cool, and he showed that he was smart and had done his homework. As Witcover noted, he was very good at this: "Newspaper editors whom he visited as he traveled around the country were invariably impressed by him."

On occasion Carter noted the favorable coverage he had received. In the spring of 1976, for example, he described his local news coverage as "almost perfect." He continued: "The aftermath of my visit around the country has been favorable without exception. . . . The *New York Times* has really been favorable to me." In an October *TV Guide* interview, Carter said that "throughout the last 21 months since I've been campaigning, I've been treated fairly. And I think the coverage of the campaign in its totality has been adequate." (Carter also promised that good things would come if he were elected President: "I intend to hold news conferences every two weeks, with a minimum of 20 full-scale news conferences per year. I intend to restore the format of the fireside chat, using television or radio or both, depending on the importance of the subject. I would like to have them fairly frequently, maybe once a month on a subject of major interest to the American people.")

Yet Carter and his close associates displayed a certain defensiveness about the media. In late January, 1976—before the Brill article appeared in *Harper's*—Carter was expressing concern. He told Jules Witcover on a drive to a dinner party at Brattleboro, Vermont, "To have this concentrated attention on myself and the other candidates by the press at this early stage is really extraordinary. I think that [it] possibly will make the press more demanding than they should be on final answers on complicated questions at the early stage of a campaign . . ."

When members of the press corps wrote stories he did not like or pushed him too hard in press conferences, Carter and his staff would openly confront them. Powell, on occasion, would belittle reporters in front of their colleagues. Carter himself would sometimes show his irritation, or deeper anger. After the Boston *Globe* had published several articles Carter disliked, Curtis Wilkie asked Carter if he had any of the self-deprecating humor displayed by Morris Udall. Carter responded: "I don't know. I would have to check my character analysis in the *Boston Globe* to find out." When Christopher Lydon of *The New York Times* and Joel Weisman of the Washington *Post* pressed Carter with several questions about the meaning of his statement that all income would be treated equally under his tax reform program, Carter said: "All right. I'll give you the same answer three times. . . ." His fury evident—a vein in his temple began to throb—he continued, "I'm not qualified to give you specifics now, . . . but when I'm President this is going to be done . . . I'm not trying to be evasive." On a later occasion when Jim Wooten of the *Times* tried to articulate Carter's distinction between a pardon and an amnesty for Vietnam draft resisters, he was abruptly cut off by Carter, who said, "Do you have a question?"

When feeling particularly threatened, Carter and his staff might even question the motives of a reporter. As we have seen, both Stephen Brill and Robert Shrum were portrayed by Carter and his aides as disgruntled liberals out to get him. On another occasion Carter confronted Charles Mohr of the *Times* on a piece he had done that contrasted Carter's campaign statements on Vietnam and the fact that while governor he had declared an "American Fighting Man's

Day" at the height of the Calley controversy. When Mohr told Carter that he had a Vietnamese daughter, Carter said: "But you still think you can be objective?"

Sometimes Carter would show his displeasure by complaining to those with power over the media or reporters. When James Gray, who runs a television station in Albany, Georgia, did not run the whole five hours of an early fundraising telethon, the Carter organization filed a complaint with the FCC. (Though Gray won, 7-0, before the complaint board, he was worried that Carter might be vindictive toward the press in general: "He's a tough nut. He went after me to the fullest.") After Washington *Post* reporter Jules Witcover prodded Carter in New Hampshire about the Georgia reorganization, Carter let it be known to some members of the press that he had complained to publisher Katharine Graham that he didn't like the tone of the paper's coverage of him. "I told her that the *Post* was the only major newspaper so far that had not recognized the substance of the campaign," Carter said. At another point, Carter was so upset with the coverage from the Boston *Globe* that he went to Editor Thomas Winship to complain about Curtis Wilkie's reporting and the newspaper's editorial cartoons. Later Carter wrote a letter to *The New York Times* deploring William Safire's criticism of Pat Caddell's retention of an $80,000 contract with the Saudi Arabian government. When CBS and ABC ran stories about the eviction of a black family from a dilapidated house across the street from Carter's home in Plains, Jody Powell called the offices of the two offending networks to complain—and then called NBC to congratulate them for not running the story. (As a result, all three networks were perturbed.)

Carter displayed an underlying distaste for the press in a relatively private moment at one of the fish fries during the summer camp in Plains. Escaping from the mass of reporters invited to the event by Powell, Carter walked onto the porch where he joined his sister Gloria and her husband Walter Spann, and Robert Scheer. Ignoring Scheer's presence, Carter greeted Gloria and Walter. Walter said: "Guess it's hard for you to get away from all those reporters. They're like gnats swarming around." Carter, who was eating a piece of catfish, replied, "The press people are afraid I'm going to eat a fishbone and choke on it. They're afraid they won't have a picture when it happens." As Scheer later reported, the tone was "on the bitter side."

Basically Carter saw most press criticism of him as unfair. The "fuzziness" charge, he said in April, is the result of "the Washington political figures, including the news-media persons" being upset "that someone unknown to them could be a success without their knowing it." In the summer he told Scheer rather vehemently: "The traveling press have zero interest in any issue unless it's a matter of making a mistake. What they're looking for is a 47-second argument between me and another candidate or something like that. There's nobody in the back of this plane who would ask an issue question unless they thought he could trick me into some crazy statement."

To some extent Carter was zeroing in on the general vulnerability of the press. Yet there was a special irony in Carter's criticism. As Charles Mohr noted later in the year, Carter's candidacy from the very beginning had not been an issue-oriented one and Carter's favorite reporter had been Jack Germond of the Washington *Star,* who stressed the horse-race aspects of the campaign rather than the issues. Actually, Carter's defensiveness toward media criticism suggests that he would have been happy with nothing less than a mirroring of his self-presentation, of his finely honed issue papers and his campaign images.

# SIXTEEN

# Promises, Promises

O CARTER AND HIS AIDES, issues played a minor role in winning a campaign, and a possibly major role in losing it. As early as 1973 Jody Powell had written Carter that McGovern's mistake in 1972 had been making Vietnam an issue: he had not realized that the goal of a political party is to "put together a winning coalition." Peter Bourne's early strategy memo expressed a similar sentiment: opposition to the Vietnam war had not been the critical factor in building support for McGovern.

Carter shared these views. In a 1975 interview he had argued that McGovern's biggest mistake was in making Vietnam the major issue of his campaign—"That's not how it works." Or, as he told a group of top network executives and correspondents on another occasion, "the only Presidents he knew of who [had] emphasized the issues were Dewey, Goldwater, and McGovern."

This philosophy did not prevent Carter from making issue statements—many of them—during his campaign. Over the course of his run, the Carter organization produced papers on everything from abortion and agriculture through gun control and housing to zero-based budgeting.

In evolving his issue stands, Carter was aided by Stuart Eizenstat, who had performed the same function for him in 1970. Early in the presidential campaign Eizenstat sat down with Carter, throwing out issues to him by going down the alphabet from "A" to "Z." Most of their stances had been worked out this way by the end of 1975. Later, with a staff of about twelve young people, Eizenstat coordinated the efforts of several loosely organized task forces. Aside from winning over those on the task forces, the process resulted in numerous issue papers, which were distributed to interest groups throughout the country. Eventually there were enough papers to fill two thick loose-leaf books, on file by 1978 with the DNC.

The final choices were rooted, Carter himself freely admitted, in the public mood. As he wrote in *Why Not the Best?*, "dozens of issues are considered during a political campaign, but candidates do not create the issues. They exist in the minds and hearts of our citizens." To be successful, he later explained, he would have to develop a presentation that "reflected" what the people wanted rather than what the candidates "want for them." Then, "what we learned, we gave back to them in a political program that reflected what they wanted."

In certain politically neutral areas, Carter spelled out some specific reforms. Complaining that "we have the worst bureaucracy in Washington," he promised to reduce the federal government's 200 advisory commissions and 1,700 agencies to a more manageable 200 (though he would not specify which agencies would be eliminated and how the recombination would work). He pledged to break up the gigantic Department of Health, Education and Welfare into independent agencies and create a separate Department of Education. Zero-based budgeting, which he would introduce to the federal government, would bring new economies.

Many of Carter's issue stands were not stands at all, but abstract statements of principles to which few could object. In his announcement speech Carter noted that government should be honest and open, with substance and logical direction. It should reflect the principles of rationality and businesslike administration, but also have simplified, fair, and compassionate welfare programs. The veils of secrecy surrounding governmental operations and the presidency should be lifted. The system of justice should be revised so laws would be administered in an evenhanded manner, and government officials should be chosen on the basis of merit, not political payoffs. In his stump speeches and in his television and radio commercials, Carter backed the work ethic, efficiency in government, a halt to inflation, and jobs for all who could work and welfare for those who could not. In one ad, for example, Carter noted that the problem was not the 6.5 percent inflation rate, but how people would pay their grocery bill, mortgage, taxes, and college costs for their children when "our hard work and our savings [are] thrown away by a far away unconcerned bureaucracy." In the nation's foreign policy and national defense, Carter said, the No. 1 responsibility of a president, above everything else, is to guarantee the security of this country—freedom from fear of attack or blackmail, the ability to carry out a legitimate foreign policy.

Further, most of these values could be obtained without any need for trade-offs at the margin. His reorganization of the federal government would cost no federal civil servant his job. (At one point Carter said the number of bureaucrats would probably increase somewhat.) The national budget could be balanced without the sacrifice of social programs or a strong national defense. ("If we had some tough competent management and eliminated the tremendous waste in Washington, we could start reducing this nation's sixty billion dollar annual deficiency.") Though the nation needs weapons sufficient to meet "the strategic needs of our country and to meet our legitimate obligations to our allies," he could trim $5 to $7 billion from the military budget and still end up with a more "muscular" Pentagon.

In his tax reforms Carter would plug loopholes and aim for "truly progressive tax rates." Yet businessmen and wage earners would be treated "equally" on tax deductions, private investment would be encouraged, and income would only be taxed once. His plan, he promised, would result in about a 40 percent reduction in income tax for the average taxpayer. But this would not cause any decline in revenues because the additional money in circulation would improve the economy. Welfare rolls could be cut without hurting those in genuine need. The few people ("ten percent") who were on the rolls but could work "should be separated from the other ninety percent and treated as part of our unemployed work force, with respect and dignity." Thus, the number of welfare recipients would be decreased, the labor force increased, and everyone would be taken care of, without an increase in government expenditures. On the economy in general, Carter thought inflation could be down to 3 or 4 percent by 1979 or 1980, while at the same time unemployment could go below 5 percent "without inflationary pressures."

Occasionally Carter edged toward a controversial stand, a hard statement of priorities. In a New Hampshire advertisement he promised to give highest priority to a nationwide comprehensive mandatory health insurance program, and shortly before the Pennsylvania primary he gave his highest priority to the achievement of full employment—"a job for everyone who wishes one." After the party convention he told the Committee of 51.3% (so named because women make up 51.3 percent of the national population) that he would push for passage of the ERA.

## Obscuring Technique

Mostly Carter skillfully fudged on the controversial issues. He did this by sending out complex messages that various listeners could interpret according to their own predispositions. From the multitude of signals—a word, a condition, a posture—Carter was able to send different people different signals about his positions.

One prime technique was the hedge. Carter would make general value statements reflecting the sentiments of one sector of his audience and then tack on conditions or operational statements that would satisfy another segment. Though such statements might be inconsistent or contradictory, many of the people listening would only hear the part that conformed with their own views and ignore or discount the other material. David Nordan pointed out how this worked: "It [the Carter statement] pointed up the essence of Carter on the issues. The bottom line is usually clear, although the rhetoric leading up to it often is carefully programmed to strike harmonious chords on both sides of the argument."

There are many examples of this technique. For instance, Carter supported in principle the "right to work" provision of the Taft-Hartley Act (really a constraint of the union shop); a provision strongly opposed by labor and strongly supported by business; but he would *not* oppose legislative measures to do away with it. Also, he was not in favor of mandatory busing to achieve integration ("the only kids I have ever seen bused are poor children"); but he did support a "voluntary busing program" similar to the Atlanta plan, which he saw as a model for the rest of the country; and as a presidential candidate he was opposed to a constitutional amendment to ban busing. He told an audience at the Iowa State Fair that he would "stop embargoes [on grain exports] once and for all," but he later admitted that such embargoes could be "mandatory" if the country did not have "adequate grain stocks." On the Panama Canal, he opposed "relinquishing actual control" but was willing to remove the word "perpetuity" from the treaty. He implied that the United States should withdraw troops from Korea: "We are spending too much on troops overseas. The Korean War has been over 20 years. We have 40,000 American troops in Korea." On some occasions he committed himself to withdrawal over a five-year period. But, as he told an audience in Florida, "I do not believe we should withdraw Americans from Korea, *except on a phased basis*" (emphasis added). In a subsequent interview with Bill Moyers, Carter presented yet another possibility: "I would never again . . . get militarily involved in the internal affairs of another country." But as for South Korea, "Well, we're already involved there. And we have a commitment made by Congress, the President, the people and the U.N. in South Korea."

This technique is exemplified in Carter's handling of the abortion question. In Iowa, Carter made statements about his personal moral opposition to abortion, suggesting that under certain undescribed circumstances he might accept some kind of restrictive national legislation on the matter. But he did not favor attempts to pass a constitutional amendment prohibiting abortion. Some leaders of the Iowa antiabortion movement missed Carter's conditional clause, and one Catholic newspaper urged their readers to support Carter because he was the only candidate who backed a "right to life" amendment. Only after talking to Sargeant Shriver's Iowa campaign manager and calling Carter's Atlanta headquarters did Monsignor Frank Brady of Sioux City discover that Carter really opposed an antiabortion amendment. Monsignor Brady then went on local television to denounce Carter and his abortion stand. But it was the night before the primary, and many antiabortionists did not get the message. (According to Evans and Novak, Carter's ambiguity on abortion "made the difference between first and second place" in Iowa. True or not, Carter was certainly able to undercut Shriver, the only Catholic in the race, whose position on abortion was indistinguishable from Carter's—except he said his more clearly.)

Though Carter maintained this position on abortion throughout the campaign (similar confusion arose over it during the Rhode Island contest), at the Democratic Platform Committee, Stu Eizenstat, trying to win over the women activists, agreed to a provision that specifically opposed a constitutional amendment.

Whatever their own contributions to the confusion, the antiabortionists, believing they had been misled, remained angry at Carter, evident in the nominating speeches for antiabortion candidate Ellen McCormack at the Democratic convention. After the Republican convention, which endorsed a plank supporting the antiabortion constitutional amendment, the "antichoice" people could more clearly target Carter as the enemy. One of their newsletters, for example, pointed to his warm remarks about family planning in the forward to a book published in 1973, which endorsed the right to abortions when birth control fails.*

By the late summer Carter's advisers were suggesting it would be best for him to ignore the abortion issue altogether. But Carter, showing an almost reckless faith in his own ability to charm and persuade, arranged a meeting with a group of Catholic bishops on August 31 in Washington, D.C. He told the bishops that, though he was personally opposed to abortions and thought the government should do nothing to encourage them, he opposed a constitutional amendment prohibiting them. Then he tried to move to other issues on which he and the group could agree. The prelates refused to budge. Archbishop Joseph L. Bernardin of Cincinnati read a prepared statement saying that until the bishops and Carter got the abortion question resolved, nothing else should be discussed. Finally Carter conceded that he would not flatly oppose all possible constitutional prohibitions regarding abortion. Though he had not yet seen a version he cared to support, someone might compose one that he could. Shaking hands all around at the conclusion of the meeting, Carter, in a slip of the tongue, told the bishops he hoped their relationship "will grow after this embryonic start." But Carter did not even get the standard postmeeting photographs with the group. And in a statement to the press Archbishop Bernardin noted that he could not get Carter to accept his position, and that he was outraged with the abortion plank of the Democratic platform. (Carter explained to the press that he had not changed his position when he told the bishops he might favor some new version of an antiabortion amendment; he simply didn't want to rule out anything that he had not yet heard of.)

Carter's hedge before the American Legion's convention also did not work. Wearing his Legion hat from Post 2 in Americus, he started by striking responsive chords with the audience. He traced the military history of his family from the first Carter in Georgia, who served in the Revolutionary War, through his father, who, he inaccurately said, had "served as a first lieutenant in the Army during the First World War," to his own service in World War II (actually he was a midshipman until 1946) and Korea, and his son Jack's in Vietnam. Carter continued with several themes close to the hearts of his fellow Legionnaires: maintenance of adequate military strength, firmness in honoring commitments, revitalization of patriotism and promotion of national security, develop-

*The antiabortion forces overlooked some potentially even more damaging ammunition. In a statement at the fall, 1971, Goals for Georgia health conference, Carter came close to endorsing the "choice" alternative. He pointed out that 84.5 percent of those answering a questionnaire circulated by his goals for Georgia program favored allowing early abortions. As public attitudes changed, he said, "health officials' attitudes and more liberal policies will come." The conferees, he suggested, should seriously consider proposals supporting voluntary abortions and sterlizations.

ment of a strong and responsive Veterans Administration and veterans' benefits.

Then he took his stand on amnesty, calling it "the single hardest decision I
have had to make during the campaign":

Where I come from, most of the men who were sent off to fight in Vietnam were poor.
They didn't know where Canada was, they didn't know where Sweden was, they didn't
have the money to hide from the draft in college. Many of them thought it was a bad
war, but they went anyway. A lot of them came back with scarred minds or bodies, or
with missing limbs. Some didn't come back at all. They suffered under the threat of
death, and they still suffer from the indifference of many of their fellow Americans. The
Vietnam veterans are our nation's greatest unsung heroes. I could never equate what
they have done with those who left this country to avoid the draft.

But then came the shift.

I think it is time for the damage, hatred and divisiveness of the Vietnam war to be over. I
do not favor a blanket amnesty, but for those who violated Selective Service laws, I intend to grant a blanket pardon. To me there is a difference. Amnesty means that what
you did is right. A pardon means that what you did—right or wrong—is forgiven. So,
pardon yes; amnesty—no. For deserters, each case should be handled on an individual
basis in accordance with our nation's system of military justice.

In this instance the hedge did not work—at least with the audience on the
spot. The amnesty passage was interrupted by "boos" and thumbs-down gestures. Carter was visibly upset—his eyes down at first, then darting about while
the national commander quieted the convention hall. Carter finished his
speech with a brief discussion of the horrors of nuclear war and left the hall to a
short, but polite ovation.

In addition to the hedge, Carter's other major technique was to use code
words or phrases—symbols that denoted a wide range of attitudes and views
that he did not have to spell out to the knowing and which evoked little meaning to the unknowing.

His most obvious use of code words was revealed in Carter's effort to find
some common ground between himself and his audience that would enable
them to attribute to him desirable attitudes and values. In his 1974 announcement speech, for example, he identified himself as "a farmer, an engineer, a
businessman, a planner, a scientist, a governor, and a Christian." In Why Not
the Best? he added other identities: "I am a Southerner and an American . . . a
father and a husband . . . a naval officer, a canoeist, and, among other things, a
lover of Bob Dylan's songs and Dylan Thomas' poetry."

When talking about his Christianity, Carter used language that would ring
bells of recognition in diverse religious groups. As a boy raised on a farm that
"resembled farm life of fully 2,000 years ago," and a "born again Christian"
inclined toward literal interpretation of the Bible and enriched by missionary
work with people speaking a language other than English, Carter could evoke
all kinds of associations with evangelicals and conservative Christians. But his

quotes from Niebuhr, Kierkegaard and Barth made it clear, to the intelligentsia at least, that he was not really a fundamentalist or a radical conservative.

By using symbols out of his own past—his small town, farm, church, and family—Carter could also convince social conservatives that he was like them. But his comments on his close relationship with the Allman Brothers Band and others of the country-rock set sent a message to their fans that he was not a strait-laced Bible-beater and didn't mind the partying, drinking, and even the drug use of that particular group. (The Allman Brothers Band members were his friends, he used to say, and if people didn't like what they stood for, they could simply not vote for him.) Even his musical tastes signaled as much. Saying that Bob Dylan's song "Maggie's Farm" (which describes the burning resentment of poor whites toward the middle class) was his favorite sent a message that Carter might really be a closet radical interested in redistribution of wealth.*

When dealing with smaller, more specialized audiences, Carter could pull out the most relevant signal without contradicting himself. Through the hedge, he could subtly accentuate his main thesis—or his conditions to it; or he could reach in his bag and pull out one or another of his code words, depending on the audience. As T. D. Archer, president of the North Georgia Building and Trades Council, noted, "At a labor gathering, he was a labor man. But if you heard him at a chamber of commerce meeting, he was a chamber man."

Carter told most of his audiences that the United States needed nuclear power to ease the energy crunch, but in New Hampshire, where environmentalists and others were bitterly fighting the Seabrook nuclear plant, would say only "as a last resort would I continue to use nuclear power." In Minnesota, Carter promised to cut the defense budget by billions. In Pensacola and Jacksonville, Florida, with their large military bases, Carter spoke of the need for a strong defense. (When questioned, Carter said his cuts would be made without having to close the Florida bases.) Most places Carter said, "We don't have to build a B-1 bomber. The Russians don't even have a comparable plane to our B-52." But in Omaha, Nebraska, headquarters of the Strategic Air Command, Carter emphasized that he would continue research and development funding for the B-1.

There is evidence that Carter was fully aware of what he was doing. If he had read all the presidential biographies, as he said he had in *Why Not the*

---

* This technique also appeared in his advertisements. In 1976, when Carter wanted the black vote, one radio advertisement aimed at black voters had the narrator saying, "Last year Jimmy Carter went to Iowa as a political *black* horse" (emphasis added). The usual phrase is "dark horse," but for this commercial, Carter seemed to be reaching out for a clear identification with his audience. Another commercial, playing up the similarity in name of Senator Henry Jackson's home state and the nation's capital quickly brought to mind his campaign against Washington. Carter said: "Well the *Senator from Washington* is advocating massive spending programs when he doesn't even know where the money is coming from. It's just another example of how the Washington insiders have put this country in the economic mess it's in now" (emphasis added). Though superficially slips of the tongue, given their usage in commercials, they seem purposeful.

*Best?*, Carter would have discovered that Lyndon Johnson used to identify himself by a string of labels (which in many ways could have been a prototype for Carter's own richer, fuller string of embellished self-identifications). In the drafting of his announcement speech there was quite a discussion on the phrasing of his religious identification. Originally Carter had proposed saying, "As you know, I am a Christian, and will try at all times to represent the finest aspects of my own faith." Jody Powell suggested this be changed to "a church member." But Carter preferred and used ". . . I am a farmer, an engineer, a planner, a scientist, a governor and a Christian." On the campaign trail Carter generally included Martin Luther King, Jr.'s name when listing great Americans before black audiences, but dropped it when speaking to conservative white audiences. When a reporter questioned Carter about this, Carter abruptly said that he knew what he was doing and would not do it again. On the rest of that tour, he dropped King's name from the list before all audiences.

In February, 1976, Carter said he was "always very cautious" about what he said. Later, in an off-the-cuff comment to reporters, he noted, "I never do anything unintentionally, even if it looks unintentional." And though he fervently denied that he had ever intentionally misled, Carter admitted that he tried to please different publics: "I don't see anything inherently wrong in trying to say things in such a way that I don't irritate people, as long as I remain consistent with my basic position."

Carter's aides and supporters were aware of his techniques. As Charles Kirbo explained: "Whatever people say, Jimmy's got the capability of leading them—each a little differently—in the same direction." In this way, Kirbo added, Carter might be in a position where he could disagree with people on particular matters and "still get their vote." Deputy campaign manager Ben Brown noted, "You don't ever really know precisely where he's going . . . people just believe in him as a person." And Jody Powell commented, "Sure, Jimmy has worked out answers on controversial issues so as not to anger people. Why not try to find a solution—a way of getting it done—so as not to piss off a lot of people and create more problems than we started with?" Some of them even helped in conveying these mixed messages. While Peter Bourne and Mary King told the liberal Georgetown set Carter was really a closet progressive, Charlie Kirbo confided to his business friends that Carter was really a closet conservative.

## The Reasons Why

Actually, as Carter admirers and supporters were to point out during the campaign, obscuring or ducking on controversial issues is part of the art of winning elections. This tendency is not necessarily a reflection of the poor character of politicians, as Americans have increasingly come to assume, but rather a reflection of the make-up of the electorate and the fact that an individual needs to appeal to a sufficiently large group to win an election.

American voters have recently moved away from programmatic politics and strong party identifications. As Ira Carmen has pointed out, the "alienation phenomenon" caused by the events of the 1960s and early 1970s has lessened popular interest in voting. Fewer people experience a sense of civic duty or feel that voting affects political events. (In the nineteenth century voter turnout frequently exceeded 75 percent of those eligible, while the Nixon-McGovern and Carter-Ford contests barely reached a 55 percent turnout.) While "dramatic political events" may still activate some citizens to vote, or not to vote, effective political action is increasingly being identified with working through special-interest groups. The result: "candidate perception" and stands on single issues are becoming increasingly important factors in electoral contests. (To Carmen's conclusions I would add that these factors may be especially important in primary elections, where individuals vote within a party rather than choosing between parties.)

As a consequence, elections are increasingly determined by a large, fluid group in the political middle who vote for the "best man" (and occasionally, in Congressional and local elections, the "best woman"). And because there are only two major parties in America, "ideologists" to the left or the right of center have no alternatives except to go to an ineffective and unsuccessful splinter party or stay home on election day.

This creates a great deal of pressure on the candidate to go to the floating middle. Yet here there is a problem. Beneath the apparent consensus on mainstream values is a great diversity of interests and values. In recent years there has been a proliferation of pressure groups in the center, demanding that their specific benefits or interests be maintained or increased, while the parties— which traditionally have paid attention to the systematic consequences of various particular issues and tried to reconcile them—have become increasingly weak. Add to this the demands by some groups for the universalization of their specific ethnic or social values (values not necessarily held by a majority of the total electorate) and the problem of forming a winning coalition increases substantially. It has reached a point where to win a national election, a candidate almost has to take conventional stances on mainstream values, all the while appealing to some conglomeration of specific but diverse interests of a majority of the voters in such a way as to avoid antagonizing any important segments. In these circumstances a premium is apt to be placed on obscurantism. In some respects Carter's victory in 1976 was due to his ability to "out-fuzzify" all his opponents.

## Spanning the Political Spectrum

Where Carter differed in essence from his opponents was in his eagerness to appeal to everyone and in his refusal to connect his various individual stands in terms of some philosophic framework that would place him somewhere on the traditional spectrum of social and political values. This unconnected quality was noted by one writer in *The Wall Street Journal:* "Mr. Carter has taken a reasonably large number of specific stands on specific issues, but upon reviewing his positions, one comes away with the impression of a shopping list ordered up from the local delicatessen. There is no feel for the instincts of the man, and certainly no feel for the depth of his conviction on any issue."

Generally, political leaders as well as their parties have accentuated one value cluster or another, with the Republicans leaning toward the puritanical values and the Democrats toward the compassionate ones. Carter, however, gave almost equal play to both. In several commercials Carter stressed his commitment to the value of hard work and how he had lifted himself by the bootstraps through it. In one commercial (run in English and Spanish) Carter said: "I'm just like you are, I worked almost all my life, manual labor. My folks have been in Georgia 200 years. Nobody in my daddy's family ever finished high school before me. I grew up on a farm during the depression years. We didn't have electricity or running water but I had a good life." And in other advertisements Carter said, "And I think our country needs just an understanding of working people and not an understanding of big shots who have enough money to hire high powered lobbyists." Or, "I believe in the work ethic." Or, "Sometimes I think that a lot of our Washington officials don't know what it means to work for a living." These ads usually showed Carter working—pulling weeds in a field, moving among corn rows, handling peanuts at his warehouse.

Carter also pulled on his background to show he valued balancing the budget: "When I ran my farm I balanced the budget. I ran my business and balanced the budget. I was Governor of Georgia for three years. We had a balanced budget every year and a surplus and if you elect me president, before this next term is over, we are going to have a balanced budget in Washington and you can depend on that."

When the opportunity arose, Carter could emphasize with equal ease his compassionate values. In one New Hampshire commercial he combined his belief in the work ethic with an expression of the need "to reverse our spending priorities to spur employment. When we spend for instance a million dollars to improve the quality of people's lives on transportation, pollution control, health, recreation, education we create almost a million dollars worth of new jobs." A fall advertisement showed an elderly man being examined by a doctor, the stethoscope pressing into his frail rib cage while his wife stood obviously worried. This was followed by a photo of an elderly woman sitting on a broken park bench and another photo of a woman looking out through a dirty, barred window. All the while Carter's voice is saying: "Gerald Ford voted against medicare, against food stamps for the elderly, against adequate housing. Isn't it bad enough that elderly people are the worst victims, the easiest victims, of hoodlums and criminals? Must they also be victimized by their own government in Washington? I'm Jimmy Carter; I couldn't live in the White House without helping them." In another advertisement he portrayed the country as falling apart: "The Republicans in their TV commercials are saying that the economy's healthy, employment is high, our place in the world is honored, our leadership is great." But he looked around and saw "eight million people—everyone of them out of work; every trip to the supermarket, a shock; cities collapsing; suburbs scared; hospitals closing; teachers fired; crime growing; police departments cut; fire departments cut; day care centers shut; welfare sky rocketing; energy in foreign hands."

Not only did Carter refuse to choose between the puritanical and the compassionate values, he also refused to apply any of the conventional political labels to himself. In January, 1976, Carter noted, "I never characterize myself as a conservative, liberal or moderate and this is what distinguishes me. . . ." In one discussion Carter sounded like the Red Queen in *Alice in Wonderland*: "I don't see myself as a liberal or conservative or the like. I'm a farmer, you know. Now you ask most farmers whether they are liberal or conservative, and they often say conservative. The same with businessmen. And I'm a businessman, too. But that isn't to say that all businessmen and all farmers are conservative." And he told the "Face the Nation" audience in March, 1976, "I don't think the voters are in doubt about what I say; they just feel that I'm the sort of person they can trust, and if they are liberal, I think I'm compatible with their views. If they are moderate, the same; and if the voter is conservative, I think they still feel that I'm a good President."

## Populism: New Style

There was one label Carter was willing to apply to himself—populist. In an interview in Plains after his speech accepting the Democratic nomination Carter said it "was uniformly populist in tone. That is what I intended it to be." When later asked if he regarded himself as a "populist," he replied, "I think so."

But Carter never spelled out what this populism would mean—whether it would accentuate some values over others or accept some governmental precepts while downplaying others. Indeed, when pressed to explain what he meant by the term "populist," Carter responded somewhat defensively: "I will let you define it." (A problem when one considers that even those who knew Carter best could not define it. Charles Kirbo, for example, remarked in July, 1976, that while Carter had "a wide area of populism" in him, "I'm not sure what, politically, he cares about. Right now, I imagine he's caring about being President more than anything else.")

Carter actually did make a few old-style populistic promises to open up the government. In *Why Not the Best?* he said: "We must strip away secrecy from government in every possible way; open up to the people the deliberations of the executive and legislative branches of government." He said he would require his Cabinet officers to meet periodically with the houses of Congress in "public interrogation sessions." In July, 1975, when he released his personal (as distinct from his business) financial records (which he said was in accordance with a promise made during the gubernatorial campaign), Carter called for a disclosure law requiring "an annual statement of all financial involvements which might constitute a conflict of interest." And in his announcement speech Carter proclaimed the need for sunshine laws that would open up government agency meetings to public scrutiny.

As noted earlier, however, Carter's populism was mostly stylistic—a reliance on the rhetoric of the "outsider" and the outsiders' resentment of those in power. On foreign policy matters he traced recent problems in the United States to the government's loss of contact with the people and secrecy in decision making. As he told the American Chamber of Commerce in Tokyo in May, 1975, one of the lessons of Vietnam was that "we must never again keep secret the evolution of our foreign policy from the Congress and the American people." At the National Issues Conference in November, 1975, he said, "almost everytime we've made a serious mistake as we relate to other nations—and we've made a lot of them—it's been because the American people have basically been excluded from participation in the evolution or consummation of attitudes toward other countries around the world." The involvement in Vietnam was the result of this secrecy. Carter told Robert Scheer: "there was a governmental consciousness to deal in secrecy, to exclude the American people, to mislead them with false statements and sometimes outright lies. Had the American people been told the facts from the beginning by Eisenhower, Kennedy, McNamara, Johnson, Kissinger and Nixon, I think there would have been different decisions made in our government." Further, early in his campaign he railed against American covert interventions abroad: "We must not use the CIA or other covert means to effect violent change in any government or government policy."

Carter targeted specific leaders. Secretary of State Henry Kissinger, he told the Chicago Council on Foreign Relations, was the embodiment of this degrading secrecy. His success was tied "too closely to his personal reputation. . . . He is trumpeting achievements on paper while failing to insist on them in practice . . ." In another interview he characterized Kissinger as a kind of "Lone Ranger" with a secret foreign policy attitude, "which almost ensures that there cannot be . . . a coherent evolution on foreign policy. . . ." Political contributors who had won ambassadorships under the Republicans were another subject of his scorn: When he had gone into other nations and called on the American Embassy and seen an "ignorant, rich, major contributor to a Presidential campaign who can't even speak the language of the country in which he serves . . ." he found it insulting to himself, to Americans generally, and to the people of the country in which such an appointee serves. "And it ought to be changed."

Carter may have been correct in his diagnoses of some of the reasons for recent American foreign policy failures, but his recommendations involved no institutional changes, or even any reconsideration of the premises of America's role in the world. Rather, they were a restatement of traditional stances.

Foreign policy, he said, should not be made part of partisan politics. "Appointments to our U.N. delegation, to other diplomatic posts, and to international conferences should be made exclusively on a merit basis, in contrast to the political patronage that has characterized appointments under this administration."

For all his inveighing against secrecy, Carter also had the traditional concern for protecting national security secrets. As governor, he had expressed support for a national secrets act that would make it possible for the government to prosecute those who published material adversely affecting national security. And in 1976, when forced to get down to specifics, Carter opposed dissolution of the CIA as well as "any cessation of its covert operations—I never joined those who wanted to prohibit covert activities. I never attacked the need for the best intelligence apparatus in the world." He would take responsibility to see that the CIA acted within the law. If the agency ever made a mistake, Carter promised a University of Illinois audience "I'll be the one, as President, to call a press conference and I'll tell you and the American people this is what happened, these are the people who violated the law, this is the punishment that I recommended, this is the corrective action that needs to be taken and I promise you that it won't happen again."

In general, Carter simply exhorted Americans to return to an ideal standard. "A nation's domestic and foreign policy actions should be derived from the same standards of ethics, honesty and morality which are characteristic of the individual citizens of the nation. The people of this country are inherently unselfish, open, honest, decent, competent, and compassionate. Our government should be the same, in all its actions and attitudes." Carter himself would exemplify those principles. He told Robert Scheer: "I don't ever want to do anything as President that would be a contravention of the moral and ethical standard that I would exemplify in my own life as an individual or that would violate the principles or character of the American people."

From Carter's perspective there was no need to assess the impact of changing power relations on America's role in the world. In his travels Carter had found a "growing distrust of our government," but "a natural friendship toward the American people." Therefore, if the government would simply "treat the people of other nations as individuals, with the same dignity and respect as we demand for ourselves," the distrust would change to friendship. Through these moral fundamentals he would once again restore America's tradition and mission in the world: "There is only one nation in the world which is capable of true leadership among the community of nations, and that is the United States of America."

On domestic matters the pattern was similar. Carter used words that express a kind of resentment towards the "big shots." In his acceptance of the Democratic nomination, Carter articulated the resentment the poor often feel:

Too many have had to suffer at the hands of a political and economic elite who have shaped decisions and never had to account for mistakes or to suffer from injustice. When unemployment prevails, they never stand in line looking for a job. When deprivation results from a confused and bewildering welfare system, they never do without food or clothing or a place to sleep. When the public schools are inferior or torn by strife, their children go to exclusive private schools. And when the bureaucracy is bloated and confused, the powerful always manage to discover and occupy niches of special influence and privilege. And unfair tax structure serves their needs. And tight secrecy always seems to prevent reform.

In specific areas of concern, the same rhetoric prevailed. Back in 1975 Carter had called Ford's tax plan (which would slash taxes and the budget by $28 billion) an "abdication of leadership." He said "I am always suspicious when I hear voices from Washington talking about a tax reform to help the working family. No matter how rosy it sounds at first, by the time the special interests get through, the big shots always end up with the break and the working people get the crumbs."

Carter had no greater regard for Ford's energy policies. In February, 1975, Carter told the Nebraska General Assembly that Ford's planned gas rationing and tax increase on oil imports was "too much to ask the American . . . consumer to bear at this time." Later, Carter branded Ford's imposition of a dollar-per-barrel tariff on imported oil as likely to have a harmful effect on already painful levels of inflation and unemployment and discriminatory toward certain regions of the country, such as New England, and on certain groups in our society, particularly farmers and those who must travel long distances to work. In essence, the "Gerald Ford/Oil Industry Policy" resulted from the lack of leadership in the presidency that allowed the oil companies—the big shots—to take over energy policy.

When it came right down to it, though, the only major domestic reform Carter recommended was a change of the guard. Carter pointedly said in some of his commercials, "The fundamental question for 1976 is whether we are going to have major changes in the way this country is run." Or, "we know from bitter experience that we're not going to get the changes we need simply by shifting around the same group of Washington insiders. They sit up in Congress every year making the same political speeches and the same unkept promises." Carter, the outsider, was the man to make these changes. "There is one major and fundamental issue. And that is the issue between the insiders and the outsiders. I have been accused of being an outsider and I plead guilty." One advertisment showed this whole change quite graphically. After showing pictures of people and events across the country interspersed with shots of Carter, the commercial concluded with the camera panning into a close-up of the White House, which dissolved into a close-up of Carter.

Certainly Carter's populism did not mean, as it had for the populist of the 1890s, that he embraced any programs for the redistribution of the tax burden or the institution of new programs for the poor. As we have seen, Carter has always been friendly to big business. As governor, he had held up the corporate model of "efficiency" as the basis for his reorganization plan and secure business support and contributions for it; he had also promoted Georgia business abroad, pushing Lockheed in Brazil and Coca-Cola and Lockheed in Europe. At times he made his probusiness views quite explicit. In Alabama in May, 1976, he expressed his opinion that "it is not business that has corrupted government so much as the other way around."

When it came to spelling out the details of his own energy program, Carter was never on radical ground. It is true that he had recommended, in a speech before the Washington Press Club in July, 1975, a mandatory limit on foreign oil imports, a resumption of fuel allocation by the federal government "if it becomes necessary," presidential stand-by authority to levy excise taxes on petroleum products, and the continued regulation of the price of "old" oil and natural gas. Carter also said that he favored government programs to develop alternative energy sources, including "properly planned" atomic power, as well as government controls to alter the electrical rate structure in order to discourage consumption, strong enforcement of antitrust laws, mandatory motor vehicle efficiency standards, and strict enforcement of low speed limits on the highways. In December, 1975, he did a little saber rattling, saying that the United States should consider an "economic declaration of war" against the oil-producing nations should they try to impose another oil embargo.

As the campaign progressed, Carter found it necessary to soften these stands. By February he shifted his position on continued regulation of natural gas prices, saying that he would support temporary deregulation. Later "temporary" became a five-year trial period for deregulation of gas not already committed to users. And though Carter had expressed concern about the oil lobby, he showed no great alarm about either horizontal or vertical integration in the energy industry. After his August energy briefing he found value in Oklahoma Governor David Boren's suggestion for vertical "accountability," while expressing his own opposition to vertical divestiture "as long as I'm convinced there's an adequate degree of competition." His own concern he said in answer to a question, was "more in horizontal investment—the oil companies investing in coal and uranium and geothermal—than it has been in the vertical integration." Yet his concern could not have been too great for he admitted that the issue had not been "discussed . . . at all this afternoon." Actually, his position on horizontal divestiture differed only in the emphasis: "Unless I'm convinced that there is an adequate amount of competiton there, I would look with favor on horizontal divestiture."

In his address before a blue chip establishment group at New York City's 21 Club in August, Carter offered assurances that he would propose no changes in the tax laws for at least a year, and then only after a careful study of the matter. And he reiterated his commitment to a simplified tax system which—with a few exceptions—"treats all income the same" (i.e., no higher tax on income from dividends). Responding to questions, he pledged not to make the multinational corporations the consumers' "scapegoat" because it was politically expedient. Nor would his Administration subvert or impede foreign investment by American business. He favored retention of the foreign tax credits whereby American-based businesses deduct the taxes paid to foreign governments from their American taxes. His commitment was to a "minimum interference of government in free enterprise." And though he "would not give anyone a special favor," he told reporters after the meeting, "I will be a friend to business."

After Carter had secured the nomination, his friends also assured business leaders that Carter was no dangerous radical. Philip Alston wrote and talked on the telephone to business associates throughout the country. Bert Lance traveled to Texas in October to meet with economic leaders, and other friends from the Atlanta business community reassured their friends that Carter was "safe." And they got the message across. *Fortune* magazine noted in a September, 1976, editorial, "though he calls himself a populist, he doesn't look like a threat to the established social order."

## The Fuzziness Charge

In casting such varied appeals there were bound to be many puzzles in Carter's presentations. And some of his opponents did attack him on this. In New Hampshire, Bayh and Udall accused Carter of speaking out of both sides of his mouth on abortion and the 14B "right-to-work" clause of the Taft-Hartley Act. Udall said: "Carter's tried to fudge. He was asked about abortion and he fudged. He was asked about 14B and he fudged." Birch Bayh, who prided himself on being a politician, asked about Carter's "business of running against the government": "Who are we kidding? . . . I want to make the government run." In Florida, as noted above, Jackson accused Carter of saying one thing in the sun and another thing in the snow. Udall charged at one point that he could not get Carter to specify a few of the 1,700 agencies that would be cut in Carter's government reorganization—"I've been asking him to name just 17." During the Michigan campaign, Udall used a commercial featuring cartoon faces of Jimmy Carter—alternately smiling and frowning-while actor Cliff Robertson (who had played Jack Kennedy in the movie *PT-109*) enumerated Carter's flip-flops on various issues. Udall also produced a "Quick Carter Quiz" asking questions on Carter positions concerning specific issues: "welfare reform, right-to-work, and the reduction of specific federal agencies."

The "issues" issue was a topic of discussion in the press as well. Alan Eberhard, for example, noted in the April 25 Washington *Post* that Carter seemed to have learned a great deal from Senator Joe Biden, of Delaware, who after his own 1972 campaign had said: "I don't think issues mean a great deal about whether you win or lose." Eberhard quoted George McGovern: "Do you get the impression that these candidates (who do not discuss issues) are running because they want to be President, rather than because they have anything in mind to deal with the problems of the country . . . ? I would have never even thought of running for President if I hadn't been fed up to the eyeballs with what was going on. I didn't run because I wanted to sit in the White House."

*The Nation* editorialized on May 15 that they had "a certain difficulty in getting a handle on the policy views of James Earl Carter Jr." Most disturbing was that "every time we think we have a firm hold on them they seem to slip from our grasp." Even *Time* magazine, in late May, noted Carter's tendency to use code words and discussed Carter's fuzziness, recounting popular jokes on the subject. ("In a bridge game, after an opponent has raised the contract to three spades, Jimmy says, 'Well, then I'll bid four.' 'Four what?' 'I'll tell you after the convention.'" And: "When his father asked young Jimmy if he chopped down the family's beloved peach tree, the lad responded, 'Well, perhaps.'")

By late March there were indications that the voters, too, had become concerned about Carter's fuziness. The network exit polls in Wisconsin showed the "fuzziness" issue as Carter's greatest weakness among voters. A CBS–*New York Times* survey in late April showed that while Carter had gained strength between March and April among Democrats, he dropped twelve points with college graduates and self-identified "liberals" and twenty-seven percent with Jews. Carter staff members admitted in late April the impression that Carter is intentionally vague "has been growing geometrically" in Caddell's polls.

Carter and his aides had tried to deal with the fuzziness issue even before it became a hot item in the news. At the time of the Florida primary some of the commercials were revised—the old advertisements featuring Carter making general statements about work, welfare, unemployment, and so on were now introduced with a new voice-over: "Jimmy Carter on the issues." By the Pennsylvania primary, as Rafshoon noted, they were getting on the air earlier with these revised commercials, successfully diffusing the anti-Carter advertisements being used by Udall and Jackson.

On the campaign trail Carter began to emphasize specificity on the issues. Just before the Pennsylvania primary he gave his national health policy speech before the Student National Medical Association (April 16) and distributed a paper outlining his general economic philosophy to the press (April 22). In the late phases of his campaign Carter came to rely increasingly on prepared addresses on the issues. In Elizabeth, New Jersey, (June 6), he outlined his Middle East policies and stressed his commitment to Israel. His urban policies were outlined before the U.S. Conference of Mayors in late May and his views on Federal-state relations were detailed to the National Governors' Conference in late June.

Sometimes he would overwhelm his audience with specific policy stands. In one speech before the Oregon primary, Carter touched on governmental reorganization, zero-based budgeting, long-range planning, health care, welfare reform, tax reform, environmental quality. And if people wanted to know about his position, all they had to do was write to Box 1976 in Atlanta and the campaign would mail them his paper on the subject.

Carter insisted that he was not really "fuzzy" on the issue. His critics simply could not understand what he was doing. During the Wisconsin campaign he suggested he was simply more thoughtful than others. When asked about Udall's statement that he was more inclined to support public-sector jobs than Carter, Carter responded: "I hate to be critical but Udall almost with a knee-jerk reaction supports any kind of bill that's introduced of that nature. When Humphrey introduced the Humphrey-Hawkins bill, he [Humphrey] announced publicly that it had no chance of getting out of committee in its original form but it was a good subject around which debate could be raised. So immediately Udall endorsed the bill as it was. I don't know if he'd read it or not. This has been a difference between myself and him." Later he said that those who complained of his handling of issues were simply looking for "shallow, easy answers." "I think it's just as misleading to give a simplistic answer to a complicated question as it is to avoid an issue. I've never avoided an issue. Although my answers might be complicated, and might present both sides of a question . . . They are complete." In his interview with Robert Scheer, Carter suggested that the fuzziness issue had arisen because he was more of an independent thinker than others. "I'm not an ideologue and my positions are not predictable. Without any criticism of McGovern, if the question had ever come up on abortion, you could pretty well anticipate what he was going to say. . . . But I've tried to analyze each question individually; I've taken positions that to me are fair and rational, and sometimes my answers are complicated."

Actually, Carter accomplished what he set out to do in the issue area of the 1976 campaign. He had avoided the controversial political commitments and the traditional political labels, which could have lost him important segments of the voting public. To counter the cost of this strategy—the fuzziness charge—he dazzled his audiences with general and specific statements that effectively skirted or confused the real questions—effective rebuttal for those believing one can hedge only through avoidance or blatantly abstract generalizations. Moreover, he provided plausible explanations for the alleged fuzziness that put him in a good light and satisfied those without the time or inclination to look beyond his own explanations.

It is not possible, however, to understand Carter's positive impact on many Americans simply in terms of his skills in escaping controversy. Rhetorically, Carter operated on two levels. As he explained it, "At one level . . .there is the traditional debate over such issues as defense, health care, tax policy, and the economy. But . . . the other level of this year's campaign, the less tangible issue, is simply the desire of the American people to have faith again in government, to want a fresh start." As Jody Powell said after the election in 1976:

I think people draw an artificial distinction between what's an issue and what's a non-issue. There was a tremendous yearning in the country this year for something of substance that you could put some faith in. This all followed the disillusionment with causes that start out in a blaze of glory and end up in disappointment. People all over the land were looking for something they thought they had known once and somehow had lost touch with. I think that pine trees and home towns said something even to people who had never seen a small town, because they suggested something that they wanted. If we say that this is not an issue in this country, then we miss what's going on with people out there.

Carter's magnetism was based on the appeals he made at this other level. Where he differed from most other candidates was in his recognition of these deeper longings of the voters, and his ability and willingness to make bold, breath-taking, and original claims that he was the one who could satisfy those longings.

# SEVENTEEN

# Race, Religion, Region

UAW LEADER LEONARD WOODCOCK in explaining his endorsement of Carter, caught the essence of the Georgian's gaining appeal to the traditional party elites. "If a political genius had offered to produce a candidate who could carry the working class as well as the crucial black, moderate, and liberal votes in the North, and at the same time defeat the strident segregationist of the South, he would have been called a dreamer. And yet, that is what Jimmy Carter has done."

Carter captured this broad group through his skillful use of what reporter Tom Ottenad has called the "three R's"—race, religion, and region. They could have been disadvantages for a less skillful politician, but for Carter, they became his most important assets.

### Race

Carter's appeal to blacks was less a matter of his past record and/or concrete policy proposals than certain mythic accounts (a rich elaboration on the facts, mostly) of what he and his family had done—topped off with his ability to relate to black people on the campaign trail and to win the endorsements of black political leaders.

In *Why Not the Best?* Carter offered a narrative of his own past which established his civil rights credentials. As a young child in the rural democracy of Plains, he had swum and played and worked with blacks on an equal basis, not recognizing the strict caste lines that separated the races. As a young businessman in Plains in the fifties and in the early phases of the civil rights movement, he had innocently gone along with the mores of the time. But he had finally taken some stands—refusing to join the Plains White Citizens Council and standing up in his church to keep it open to blacks. As governor, he recalled, he appointed blacks to posts at every level of state government, hung Martin Luther King's portrait in the state capitol, set up a biracial "disorder unit" to mediate clashes between whites and blacks. He overhauled the mental hospitals and state hospitals (which contained a large black population; and deputized high-school principals as registrars so they could sign up voters in their schools.

His campaign radio ads for blacks repeated these themes, suggesting without actually saying it, that Carter had been in the forefront of the civil rights movement. In Mississippi, for example, one advertisement quoted Carter as saying: "The best thing that happened in the South in my life time was the passage of the civil rights acts and the granting to blacks and other minorities [the right] to live a decent life and have equal opportunities." In a radio advertisement used in the New York primary, Carter recalled his inaugural statement that the "time for racial discrimination was over," noted his daughter's attendance at a "typical south Georgia school," where about "60 percent of her classmates are black . . ." And an announcer said: "The black people of this entire nation are come to know the difference between a civil rights record that consists of raising your hand in Congress and the lifetime commitment of Jimmy Carter." Then the announcer pushed the black bandwagon: "In all the primaries so far more black people have voted for Jimmy Carter than any other candidate. Let's keep it going."

In his personal appearances before black audiences, Carter not only played on emotionally powerful themes, he did it in a way that suggested he really felt what he was saying, that he really had a loving connection with those he was addressing. A stiff and formal speaker in front of most groups, in front of black audiences Carter would relax and fall into the loose, rolling style of the old circuit-riding preacher. "There was rapport between them," Kandy Stroud observed. "A soul thing. An unspoken magnetism." Whether or not he was speaking in a church, his style was very much like a preacher's, and blacks reacted, not with applause, but with "Yes, suh," and "Amen, Brother."

This ability to relate to blacks was especially evident in his speech at the Monument of Faith Evangelistic Church on the South Side of Chicago, shortly before the Illinois primary. Elizabeth Drew described it:

Carter speaks softly now. He talks of growing up with blacks. . . . He speaks slowly, rhythmically, with frequent pauses, like a preacher. The vast church is dead silent except for the sound of his soft voice. He tells of unveiling the portrait of Martin Luther King, Jr., at the State Capitol when he was governor, of how Coretta King and Daddy King and Andrew Young were there, "and we sang together 'We Shall Overcome.' " He quotes Reinhold Niebuhr (as he does in his book), saying that the purpose of politics "is to establish justice in a sinful world." It appears to be the one line from Reinhold Niebuhr he quotes. "You don't see any rich people in prison," he tells them. He talks about John Kennedy, about government. Again he has perfect pitch for his audience. "We all feel like we're outsiders," he says. He talks of his defeat of George Wallace and says, "In Massachusetts, I didn't come in first. But in Roxbury [pause], where the black people live [pause], I came in first."

Later in the campaign, in a sermonlike speech before the quadrennial conference of the African Methodist Episcopal church, Carter offered another black audience his very best. He told jokes: "I can't deny the fact that one of the reasons I wanted to come tonight was to be on the stage with these bishops to learn a little about politics." He talked of his boyhood in Archery, lauding Bishop William D. Johnson, who had been minister of the Archery church during Carter's childhood. He recounted how he had visited the Archery AME church "many times," despite the earlier segregationist traditions. He identified with them: "This church of yours, the church of Christ, has provided a basis on which we could eliminate disharmony." He talked of how religion should be put into practice: "Jesus Christ never hid himself seven days a week in the synagogue . . . He walked the streets [shouts], He touched blind eyes [shouts], He healed those who were crippled [shouts], He pointed out injustice [shouts]. He brought about compassion and brotherhood and love. . . ." Then he showed his caring: "When I was governor I visited all the prisons in the state to learn about those who were in the prisons and what could be done for them. . . . There are a lot of old people, retarded people, poor people, uneducated people in prison, but not any rich people." He concluded: "We've got that something that never changes [Shouts and applause]—faith in God [That's it!].*

Carter himself would frequently suggest that the South's two races were at that time more congenial, less angry, with each other than blacks and whites in cities such as Boston. "It is a great tribute to the South that we have been able to overcome this problem [segregation] and we are recognized throughout the world for the progress we have made." As Carter said at the groundbreaking ceremonies for the Martin Luther King, Jr., Hospital in Watts, "I sometimes think that a Southerner of my generation can most fully understand the meaning and impact of Martin Luther King's life. He and I grew up in the same South." On other occasions Carter was fond of saying: "I stand with my daughter. She's not in some all-white suburban school, or some private school with a black or two in it for show; she's in a class that's more than half black, and she doesn't keep count, I'll tell you." (Andrew Young also noted this special relationship with blacks: "He grew up with black people, he empathizes very well with poor people generally. He's known the effects of racism and poverty first hand. He didn't learn about it in sociological textbooks.")

Carter was well aware of the importance of black endorsements to his candidacy and took care to secure them. As he told Kandy Stroud:

There's a complicated infrastructure among black people. They have leaders whom they trust. . . . Blacks were persecuted for so long that there were only a certain few spokesmen . . . that communicated with the white world and were emissaries to the white political structure. The spokesmen, often preachers, would come back and tell their congregation what was best. The bonds between the congregation and the pastor far transcend the religious world, as well as the political, economic and social worlds. . . .

* Rosalynn Carter, who did most of the campaigning for the family in the black districts, also showed a special way of relating to blacks. Going into black neighborhoods and most of the time accompanied only by another white woman and a driver, she stayed in black-run hotels, ate at black restaurants, and spoke at black churches. One observer noted that she was a "living refutation of the myth that Southern white ladies don't dare venture into black neighborhoods."

In obtaining his endorsements, Carter had a distinct advantage over the other Democratic presidential candidates. As Andrew Young points out, Carter "was governor of the state with more elected black state representatives than any other, where a third of the electorate is black, and he lived for four years in a city (Atlanta) where he had to deal with the most sophisticated black leadership in the country."

Most crucial to Carter's future campaign were the friendly relations he had established with the father, widow, and aides of Martin Luther King, Jr. Like many black political leaders, Martin Luther King, Sr., "Daddy King," was a political pragmatist. He had supported Gene Talmadge in previous elections, and when Carter first came to him for support in the presidential race, King told him that Nelson Rockefeller would be his first choice—should he run. But then, in February, 1975, King publicly endorsed Carter before a group of students at Georgia Southwestern College—an endorsement later used in handbills and full-page ads run in black newspapers. A 45-rpm record was also made of King's statement and played on black radio stations and in black churches the Sunday before primaries. He said: "I have never met a finer person than Governor Carter. He's a good man. A man who loves all the people. I don't remember ever meeting a man who is more sincere than Jimmy Carter. . . . I am with him all the way. . . ." This endorsement was followed by a voice saying: "Let's follow the lead of Reverend Martin Luther King, Sr., and vote for Jimmy Carter. . . ."

Congressman Andrew Young, from Atlanta, played an even more crucial role. He was one of the first Georgia politicians, black or white, to endorse Carter. At the Democratic miniconvention in December, 1974, he stated that he intended to work for Carter to "make sure that Jimmy Carter is given real consideration as a candidate by the American people." At first, his support was guarded—"I don't want to be locked into his candidacy." (As Young later explained, he started working for Carter "mainly because of the South and Florida" where he thought a win for Carter would eliminate the threat of George Wallace and probably gain Carter a shot at the vice-presidency.) The reserve had dissipated, however, by January 1976 when the *Village Voice* published an anti-Carter piece that Young regarded as unfair, anti-Southern. He wrote a long answer to the paper, saying: "Carter is one of the finest products of the most misunderstood region of our nation. You are probably right in questioning Jimmy's doctrinaire liberalism, but progressive politics in 1976 must be based on a tough mind and a tender heart and a loving sensitive spirit." According to Young, "I really got kind of carried away . . . The next thing I knew there were 50,000 copies of that letter being printed and distributed around New York. I just got involved and couldn't get uninvolved. I kept getting in deeper and deeper and deeper."

Young's most important contribution, however, was the yeoman's work he did for Carter among the black and liberal groups early in the campaign. Throughout the primaries, he visited churches, and old civil rights and antiwar groups. He got there before any of the others, so there was no competition for early connections. (In fact, no other candidate except Brown even tried to lay down a structure in the black communities.) He contacted labor leaders as well, "trying to get them not to do to Jimmy Carter what they did to McGovern." By October, 1976, Young had visited approximately twenty-seven states and fifty-one cities on behalf of Carter. As Julian Bond, a Carter critic, observed: "Reverend King's and Young's endorsements have been the key. They made Carter legitimate in the eyes of blacks all over the country."

Some other blacks were more reserved about Carter. According to Bond, Carter had called him to the governor's mansion in 1974 and told him he was planning on running for the presidency. He wanted to know if Bond would support him on some lecture tours. Bond jokingly said that he, too, was a candidate. Would Carter help him? Bond did support Carter through the Florida primary—to help beat Wallace. But then he shifted his support to Udall. As he later explained it, he saw no basis for supporting Carter on either his past record or his concrete promises for the future. Hosea Williams, a state representative and president of Metro Atlanta Southern Christian Leadership Conference (SCLC), never endorsed Carter either. At a news conference at the Georgia state capitol in March 1975, he blasted Carter's civil rights record while governor and pointed out that Carter had no blacks on his national campaign at that time. Williams also charged that "black leaders jumping on Jimmy Carter's bandwagon at this time are political prostitutes, because if the support Jimmy based on his civil rights records as governor, they can support ex-Governor Lester Maddox for president." (Carter handled this attack as he would many others during the campaign. His spokesman said, "He [Carter] was not in the habit of responding to anything Lester Maddox said, and would not find it useful to respond to Hosea Williams.")

Excluding Bond and Williams, most Georgia black leaders jumped on the Carter bandwagon as it rolled along. These included State Senator Ben Brown, who worked as a Carter volunteer beginning in 1974 and joined the paid campaign staff in 1976 as deputy campaign director. (It was his work in Florida and Pennsylvania that helped demonstrate Carter's support in the black community.) Others who endorsed him were Coretta King, widow of Dr. Martin Luther King, Jr.; Jesse Hill, a wealthy Atlanta insurance executive, who provided seed money for Carter even before he publicly announced his candidacy; Herman Russell, wealthy plastering contractor and part of the group of businessmen supporting Carter as early as 1974; John Cox, a former YMCA director and later community relations consultant; Vernon Jordan, Jr., executive director of the National Urban League; Carl Holman, president of the National Urban Coalition and later a member of the transition team. The mayor of Atlanta, Maynard Jackson, was not quite so enthusiastic, though he finally endorsed Carter in April 1976.

Not only did Atlanta blacks promote Carter to their "brothers" and "sisters" elsewhere in the nation, they also bailed him out of serious trouble in early April during the "ethnic purity" flap.

After days of heated controversy over Carter's use of that phrase and others ("inject black families," "diametrically opposite kind of family") he and his aides decided to contact Jesse Hill, who agreed to put together a rally to show black support for Carter. On Tuesday, April 13, in a downtown Atlanta park, Carter was absolved of any misdeeds. Flanked by Jesse Hill and R. Benjamin Mayes, Carter listened intently as Daddy King called Carter's remark a "slip of the tongue that does not represent his thinking." King assured all that he "forgave" Carter: "I'm with you all the way. I want to find that man who has never made a mistake. I know I have. But if a man apologizes, this nation has no choice but to accept it." His statements, he said, carried the endorsement of other black leaders, including Andrew Young, Detroit Mayor Coleman Young, and Southern Christian Leadership head Ralph Abernathy. Though Hosea Williams was marching in protest at the other end of the park, the crowd paid no attention to that. They cheered King. Carter beamed. And the ethnic purity affair, for all practical purposes, ended permanently.

Carter, however, would take further steps to obliterate any lingering doubts on the part of blacks in his preparation for the next primary in which their vote would be a major factor. A radio advertisement was aired in Washington, D.C., before that city's primary, suggesting that Carter was really committed to open housing: "To rent or purchase housing is one of our basic rights," he said. "As president I will fight for equal and open housing just as strongly as I did as governor in Georgia." A voice then said: "It was Jimmy Carter who was responsible for having the Georgia General Assembly pass the first open housing law in that state's history."

Throughout the primary season, the black vote helped Carter to victory. It helped him in the South, where the threat of George Wallace loomed large through the early months. (Carter won 70 percent of the black vote in Florida and 90 percent of the black vote in North Carolina.) And in the North, black support was also important to at least three big Carter victories. (In Illinois Carter won the primary with the help of a two-to-one black vote. In Pennsylvania, where "ethnic purity" could have thrown the black vote to Udall or Jackson, Carter won more than 50 percent of the black vote. And in the extremely close win in Michigan, the black vote provided him with his victory margin.)

Not every black leader was pleased with this rush to Carter. In early April, Julian Bond, John Lewis of SNCC, and Congressman John Conyers of Detroit saw Carter's strength with blacks as a failure in black leadership. As Bond observed: "Carter is getting the black vote by default, and it's wholly undeserved. There is no ideological reason to be for him; on international issues, he is a subdued Scoop Jackson; on domestic issues that are important to blacks— things like food stamps—I'm convinced he would be punitive and preachy. The black voters have evidently stopped making decisions in terms of racial self-interest." (Later, in July, Bond elaborated: "I am disturbed by the malaise afflicting blacks . . . They are supporting Carter because they think he has a good chance of winning and they want to be on the side of a winner." Carter responded to Bond's remarks as he had to criticism from Hosea Williams. "I have never tried to respond to Julian Bond or [former governor] Lester Maddox," Carter said. "What their motives are, I don't know. I think they both thought they ought to be president.")

There was some resistance to Carter's bandwagon at the May meeting in Charlotte, North Carolina, of the Caucus of Black Democrats. Along with the other candidates Carter made an appearance at the conference to answer questions and give his own viewpoints. Behind closed doors with caucus leaders Jackson, Mayor Richard Hatcher of Gary, Indiana, and the caucus chairman, Basil Patterson of New York, Carter said that he could not "win the election without the support of blacks inside of Georgia." He agreed to appoint blacks to a fourteen-member policy task force to help him draw up his stands on issues, and to name more blacks to key administrative posts once elected. But when Hatcher told Carter "we want 25 percent of the action in the Cabinet, the convention, and everywhere else," Carter replied: "I think that figure may be a little high, or it may be a little low."

The caucus did not endorse him, or anyone else, at this time. Said Hatcher, "Any candidate running for President who feels that black people have no other option, no place to go, is in for a rude awakening. If we choose not to support any of the candidates, we could just stay home."

In June, Carter tried to send out other signals to the blacks. He indicated that blacks were included in the list of candidates from whom he would choose a vice-presidential running mate. He made an appeal to the state parties with at-large positions yet to be filled to increase the number of black and women convention delegates. (Nevertheless, the number of black delegates dropped from their 15 percent level of 1972 to about 11 percent at the 1976 convention.)

Aside from winning some early primaries and proving his broader national appeal, there were more concrete reasons for Carter's need to prove himself with blacks. Since the New Deal most black voters have voted Democratic. They are clustered in a few key Northern states and can make the difference in the general election—determining whether or not a Democratic presidential candidate wins or loses several of those with large electoral votes. In Illinois, for example, blacks are 12.4 percent of the total voting age population; in New York, 12.6 percent. With the rise in black voter registration in the South, blacks were potentially important in several Southern states, as well—in Georgia, 23.7 percent of the voting age population was black. If a Southerner could win the black vote nationwide and hold his own in the South, he clearly had an advantage in the race for the nomination, and a good chance of winning the election.

One might speculate that in their support for Carter, voting blacks, led by black pastors and politicians, were voting on the symbolic issue of the South more than on issues of substantive programs of social change. They were voting out of nostalgia, trust, and hope—nostalgia for the rhythms and religion of rural Christianity, trust in the leaders who told them Carter was all right on race issues, and hope that a man who grew up with and cared for blacks could make the transition into the new South of equality and justice more readily than a Northern stranger.

## Religion

Flying through a blinding snowstorm over the White Mountains Jimmy Carter talked about a great religious leader with some of his fellow travelers. He had noticed in his reading of the Book of Acts in the Bible the previous evening that Saint Paul had visited a town named Cos during his missionary travels. Now Carter was traveling to Coos—Coos County, New Hampshire— where he was scheduled to speak at a school in the town of Berlin.

At St. Patrick's Catholic West School later in the day, children crowded into the gymnasium and gathered in a circle around him, sitting on the floor. He invited the children to visit his daughter, Amy, at the White House, and he told them: "Amy came to Berlin three weeks ago . . . she's never seen snow before." He continued, as Witcover recounts it:

"How many of you have mothers who vote? Raise your hands." And they did. "How many of you have father who vote? Raise your hands." And they did. "Grandmothers? . . . Brothers? . . . Sisters?" And, finally, "Do you know what my name is?" A chorus of small voices shouted in unison: "Jimmy Carter!!" Grinning broadly, he then launched into his government-of-love sermon again. The children sat absolutely rapt as he spoke in a low, almost reverent voice. And when he said, simply, "Thank you very much. I love all of you," as he raised his arms high, out over their heads, an interesting thing happened. As if on cue, the children sprang to their feet and swarmed up to him. He reached down, picked up one and hugged her, set her down and picked up another, and on and on. Others clung to his legs and tried to scamper up into his reach. My colleague from *The Washington Star*, Jim Dickenson, shook his head with wonder. "Suffer the little children to come unto me," Dickenson said, and that's about how it was.

Carter's special ability for emotionally charging his relationships was also evident with individuals. On that trip to Coos County, one volunteer had noted: "Well, the last time he was here he said: 'You may hold this against me, but I'm a very religious man.' . . . that made a deep impression on people. A lot of nuns up here like that. They feel that unless we return to moral values, the country is in deep trouble . . . They also know he risked his life over the mountains in a little plane to see us and they like that, too."

As Tom Whitney, the Iowa State Democratic chairman, remembers his first meeting with Carter, they spent about two hours talking about Christian love. "We explored the 'I Am Third' process in which God is first, family and friends second, and I am third. This nation needs a totally loving president." Whitney also recounted how Carter had reached out to a person in distress. Upon learning that a woman, important in the Iowa Democratic Party, had a son hospitalized for alcoholism, Carter took it upon himself to call on the son and tell him, in a very personal way, the difficulties he had in his own life. Whitney noted: "That quality within him ought not to be viewed cynically . . . He's got a lot of quality and style—a lot of style. Most people feel perhaps on occasion he tells them less than the whole truth. But they want to believe.")

Carter had seen others in his environment relating in these ways. As a boy he had visited Bishop Johnson's church to witness that loose, interacting style of the Southern evangelical preacher. In his own church in Plains in 1976, the young minister routinely brought the children around him during the regular service, telling them stories and making them happy, much as Carter had done in Berlin. Billy Graham, in whose crusades Carter had participated, had similar ways of making contact with individuals in a crowd.*

Carter himself would trace the extraordinary quality of his ability to relate to strangers to his salvation experiences. As he said in one interview:

. . . one of the things that I derived from it [his salvation experiences] in a—again in a kind of embarrassing way—is that when I stand on a factory shift line, like I did this morning in Erie, Pennsylvania, the General Electric Plant, everybody that comes through there—when I shake hands with them, for that instant, I really care about them. In a genuine way. And I believe they know it. A lot of times. Quite often I will shake hands with a woman who works in a plant, say an older woman, and I just touch her hand, and quite frequently they'll put their arms around my neck and say—"God Bless you, son" or "Good luck."

Aside from noting his charisma and his ability to weave a spell with different types of audiences, the press at first paid little attention to the religious theme Carter had introduced early in his campaign. (In *Why Not the Best?*, which was published in the fall of 1975, Carter outlined his religious history and mentioned his salvation experiences, though he had not been very specific about them.)

Then, March 12, 1976, shortly before the North Carolina primary, Ruth Carter Stapleton's interview in the Washington *Post* catalyzed the national media to press Carter for more information about the role of religion in his life. (She told of a long private conversation with Jimmy in late 1966, and at the time it seemed to be the first detailed description of Carter's "born again" religious experience.) To check the story with Carter, the *Post* dispatched Jules Witcover to North Carolina, and on a ride to a Winston-Salem fundraiser, Carter told Witcover that Ruth's story was basically correct—though he did not share her recollection of his crying or saying that he would be willing to give up his politics for Christ.

At the fundraiser, Carter shared his religious experiences with approximately seventy wealthy contributors, the national press, and the American public as a whole. The house was crowded; it was a balmy spring evening, so the group made their way onto the veranda of the luxurious home. Carter explained that in 1967 (Ruth said her exchange with him was in 1966) he had

*As Billy Graham describes his interaction with those who come forward to be saved: "Many times I look right down into their eyes. In fact, I try to look at each one for just half a split second if I possibly can so as to give them a little sense of personal relationship and the fact that I'm happy that they're making this commitment . . ."

undergone a deeply "profound religious experience that changed my life dramatically." For the first time, he said, he recognized that he "lacked something very precious—a complete commitment to Christ, a presence of the Holy Spirit in my life in a more profound and personal way, and since then I've had an inner peace and inner conviction and assurance that transformed my life for the better . . ." He said that he "spent more time on my knees the four years I was governor in the seclusion of a little private room in the governor's office than I did in all the rest of my life put together because I felt so heavily on my shoulders that the decisions I made might very well affect many, many people."

Such an intimate revelation was bound to raise further questions. The next day, at a press conference in Wake Forest, Carter again discussed his "born again" experience. He declined to be more specific about when the experience took place, yet he reassured his listeners that he was not a religious eccentric. "It wasn't mysterious. It might have been the same kind of experience as millions of people have who do become Christians in a deeply personal way." In Kenosha, Wisconsin, at 7:00 A.M. at an Italian restaurant, he told another group: "The most important thing in my life is Jesus Christ." The crowd responded with warm applause. But he quickly reassured the group of his belief in the separation between church and state, and that he didn't want anybody to vote for him because he was a Christian. When asked about his relationship to God at Marquette University (a Jesuit school in Milwaukee), "an embarrassed tenseness seemed to settle over the room." Carter cut through the tension, however, with a relaxed statement: "The presence of my belief in Christ is the most important thing in my life . . . It is a matter of privacy, but also a matter of which I'm not ashamed . . ."

The next Sunday, back in Plains, some journalists followed Carter into the men's Bible class at the Plains Baptist Church. The teacher, Clarence Dodson, turned the class over to Carter to talk on the topic of the day, the second coming of Christ. "Suppose you were informed this afternoon that Jesus was going to come tonight and you just had five more hours to live . . . What would we do to get ready for Christ's presence? You might think of all the people you had hurt, or of those for whom you had hatred in your heart, and you might get on the phone and call them and say, 'Look, I'm sorry.' You might talk to your wife about something you had said to her, or you might think of something you had never admitted you had done . . ." Carter concluded: "We should live our lives as though Christ were going to come this afternoon, so we would be prepared when Christ put out His hand and said, 'Frank, or Clarence, or Hugh, . . . here we are together now.' " Later that same day on NBC news, Carter told John Hart that he never prayed for his election to the presidency, nor did he see himself as anointed for that position. "But I do ask God to let me do the right thing, whether I win or lose."

In an interview with Bill Moyers on public television in early May, Carter elaborated on several of these themes. Despite an earlier story in *Why Not the Best?* (of how he had once told a visiting pastor who called politics a "disgraceful profession" that the vocation of politics was the equivalent of a pastorate), he told Moyers he didn't look on the Presidency as a pastorate. It simply gave him "a chance to serve," to magnify his influence. Nor was his prayer life especially unusual—he never petitioned God for his own victory. In fact, "I never asked God to let me win a single nomination. Never." When asked how he knew God's will, he said: "Well, I pray frequently. Not continually, but many times a day. When I have sensed a peace and just self-assurance—I don't know where it comes from—that what I'm doing is the right thing, I assume, maybe in an unwarranted way, that that's doing God's will." And though he clearly had been seeking power, he was not motivated by any "unfulfilled, all-obsessive hunger—no. I feel powerful enough now. And secure enough now."

Carter, in short, was no religious fanatic. As he explained it, he had no sense that God had chosen him for a special mission, he saw himself as no better than anyone else.

Moreover, despite the prayer, Bible reading, and Sunday school lessons, he was no narrow-minded Baptist—as *Time*, *Newsweek*, and others soon pointed out. He could enjoy the little pleasures of life. He and Rosalynn enjoyed dancing and had belonged to several dance clubs. Amy was a "clogger." Nor was Carter a teetotaler—he had an occasional scotch (which he had sworn off for the duration of the campaign) and both he and Rosalynn drank wine. Later in the campaign, to the distress of a few of his stricter brethren in Plains, he even took to playing softball after church on Sunday.

Further, he did not impose his own lifestyle on others. One of his first acts as governor, as *Time* noted in early May, had been to put an end to the religious service that Lester Maddox had held in the state house every morning. Carter thought that the service was pointless. And he had "outraged some Southern Baptist clergymen" as governor by opposing Georgia's "blue laws" (a statute banning the sale of liquor on Sunday). Reporters who traveled the campaign trails with him were reassured when they realized that Carter tolerated those hard-drinking, tough-talking, and sometimes womanizing members of his personal circle. He would not impose puritanical values on those closest to him.

*Time* and *Newsweek*, taking their cues from the quotes of Niebuhr, Tillich, Kierkegaard, Dietrich Bonhoeffer, and Karl Barth that laced his book, speeches, and interviews, began to portray him as a highly educated student of theology—a kind of existentialist Christian. One commentator noted that "one would also like to think that his Niebuhrian sense of limits might check the pretension that often lurks within Protestant fervor . . . Such an internal system of checks and balances could turn out to be a presidential virtue."

Throughout April and May, Carter's religion was the object of considerable press attention. (Carter himself said one reporter had told him that about 100 articles had been written about his religious life by late May.) The fact that his first two major addresses after the June 8 primaries were before religious groups—and that he showed his two distinctly different styles and somewhat different themes in them—guaranteed that his religion would continue to receive a lot of press attention.

On June 19, before a national conference of laymen of the Disciples of

Christ at Purdue University in Indiana (a predominantly male, white, middle-class group), he outlined his own religious history, elaborating on themes and giving detail beyond his earlier presentation in *Why Not the Best?* and the Moyers interview. His own pride, he said, had been challenged and deepened through his missionary works. And he detailed for the first time two places he had visited as a missionary and what he had learned. He talked of how the nation had fallen short—giving his own disillusionment with it as an example of the learning process. And he called for a new type of leadership. Men should strip away the kind of pride they have in becoming strong, independent, and unemotional, he said, to find a truer strength in which there is "concern, compassion, love, devotion, sensitivity, and humility . . ."

Later that same day, in an address before the black ministers attending the quadrennial convention of the AME, Carter showed a different style and gave a somewhat different message. This time he exploded into a hymn of praise to the nation. "We've got a good country, *the greatest on earth*. Richard Nixon hasn't hurt our system of government; even Vietnam and Cambodia haven't hurt our system of government; or the CIA hasn't hurt our system of government. It's still clean and decent, the basis on which we can ask the difficult questions, correct our nation's shortcomings, but we've got to keep searching." In Plains the next day, he was back to warning against national pride. In his Bible class he cautioned: "America is learning God is not automatically on its side and in the eyes of God, we're no better than anyone else."

The following Sunday, Carter did not take over the Sunday school class. But after the session he passed out copies of the text of that day's lesson. As noted in the pool report, Carter had underlined several words in a lesson, including a passage which said, *"the church and the state are—and must ever be—separate!"* And: *"We can and we must make our Christian use of our ballot, and God intends for government to be dedicated to the welfare* of his subjects. This *does not mean a blanket approval of every kind* of welfare state!"

By this time Carter's "Sunday-go-to-meeting" appearances at the Plains Baptist Church when he was in town had become a major happening. Each Sunday morning throughout the remainder of the campaign, tourists and reporters would crowd around the church, hoping to meet or see the candidate in his natural habitat. Many of them followed Carter, his retinue of Secret Service men and reporters into a small room for the men's Bible class, where Carter might even conduct the lesson for the day. After the class everyone would move to the chapel for the regular church service. While the dynamic young preacher, Bruce Edwards, conducted the service, the tourists strained to catch a glimpse of Jimmy and Rosalynn in their pew (the third on the right) and to see if Lillian was there that Sunday (not often!). They saw a man in his own element—comfortable, relaxed, accommodating. Some noticed how he so naturally put his arm around Rosalynn, even in church. Carter himself welcomed tourists into the church for the service. "Y'all come on in, you don't have to be Baptist," he told one couple who stopped him for a photograph with their two children.

Eventually the crush of tourists and the assault of flash cubes became too much. One Sunday the tourists even took the Carters' pew. The men's Bible class became so crowded (the room had already been changed once) that Carter suggested the deacons issue passes to ensure that only local men forty to sixty years of age could attend. "I hate to do it," Carter said. "The only purpose of the Sunday school lesson is to study about Christ!" Aides pointed out that this reflected "his concern about too much public attention to his religious beliefs." The press, however, was admitted, having worked out an arrangement with Jody Powell for a rotating pool of four reporters to cover the class.*

Although Carter himself never explicitly stated that people should vote for him because of his religion, others around him were not so shy. His sister Ruth made available to his campaign organization a list of her followers in Iowa and Illinois. Shortly before the Illinois primary she sent letters to people on her Illinois list, soliciting their support:

My reason for writing you is to acquaint you with a most important facet of Jimmy, one that couldn't possibly be pursued with any depth by the press or television, and that is his quality of deep personal commitment to Jesus Christ and his will to serve Him in whatever capacity he find himself. . . . What usually is ignored in . . . analyses [by national commentators] is that our nation's greatest need is for a President who will render spiritual leadership. This, in my opinion, is one of Jimmy's greatest qualifications. . . . On Tuesday, March 16, the Illinois Primary will be held. Please call your friends and neighbors to go with you and cast your vote for Jimmy in the Preferential Primary and for his delegates in your particular Congressional District.

In an interview she gave in April, Ruth predicted that Carter would win—it would be the first time in recent years when there would be a President "who has made a total commitment to Christ and who practices the principles of Christ and puts them into politics." And at the end of the primary season, while decrying the use of religion as a "tool" to curry public favor, she thought it "very important that the candidate be a man of faith."

Rosalynn, in her appearances in black churches, also spoke of Jimmy's religion. At the Gillies Memorial Church in Baltimore, for example, she said, "Another thing I want you to know about my husband is that he's a Christian man. He has told me many times that he spent more time on his knees as governor of Georgia, than in all the rest of his life put together. . . . We need your help, so that with your help and the help of our Lord Jesus Christ, Jimmy Carter can be a great president of these United States." In Maryland, Carter's Aunt Sissy appealed to Baptists on her nephew's behalf. "If all you Baptists vote for him, he'll get in because there are more Baptists than anyone." In Florida

---

* There was a small hitch at the beginning, however, as Plains had its first "segregation" crisis. Women reporters were initially to be barred from the pool arrangement. Protests came from the National Press Association—that this kind of barrier would keep the women from performing their professional duties. And the journalists in Plains decided to confront Carter and the church by assigning two of their women members to cover Jimmy the next Sunday. Carter, who had at first appeared to go along with the ban, concluded that he could not go to church that Sunday unless it was lifted. The next morning the women reporters showed up and were admitted. As the Reverend Edwards explained afterward, Jody Powell had called him the previous night to work the thing out.

his son Chip told voters that his father's Christianity was a source of his ability to lead. When a French journalist asked why Lillian Carter thought her son would be a good president, she replied that his Christianity guaranteed it. The journalist, who was Jewish, asked how. If she had to ask that question, Lillian Carter said, she simply could not understand.

Another Carter supporter, Detroit Mayor Coleman Young, specifically asked blacks to vote against Udall because of his religion and for Carter because of his: "I'm asking you to make a choice between a man from Georgia who fights to let you in his church, and a man from Arizona whose church [Mormon] won't even let you in the back door."* (Young's statement was erroneous. Blacks could visit and have membership in a Mormon church, though they could not be in the priesthood. Further, Udall had specifically left the church years earlier precisely because of the limitations the church placed on blacks.)

Later, in July, a full-page ad entitled "Does a Dedicated Evangelical Belong in the White House?" (the answer was "yes") appeared in an issue of *Christianity Today*. It was paid for by Citizens for Carter, described in the ad as an independent political action committee of Christians for American Renewal. The Carter people said they hadn't placed the ad and were unable to reach the group's named chairman.

With all this activity, Carter seemed to be getting God in his corner—and it frustrated his political opponents. George Wallace, in an interview with Elizabeth Drew just before the North Carolina primary, said: "That little room where he said he spent all that time on his knees—that's where he made that little agreement with me [that in 1972] . . . ." "Scoop" Jackson intimated in one press conference in May that it was in bad taste for Carter to discuss his religious views. Jackson said: "When people go around telling how religious they are I generally get suspicious."

Arthur Schlesinger, Jr., raised other questions in *The Wall Street Journal*. "Mr. Carter's dominating theme appears to be 'Trust me, trust me.' But what is really troubling is the implication that evangelical principles can solve the social, economic and international perplexities." Charles P. Henderson, a Presbyterian minister and author of *The Nixon Theology*, observed in *The Nation*: "One hesitates to object when Carter asserts that government can be 'filled with compassion and love'—especially when one considers the alternatives, . . . Yet Carter's sweeping affirmations mask some critical distinctions between politics and the life of the spirit." Roger Rosenblatt wrote in *The New Republic* shortly after Carter secured the nomination:

Yet the candidacy of Jimmy Carter seems only to prove that we prefer grand illusions to petty ones, and that we may be willing to lie to ourselves more readily than we will ac-

* Udall promptly asked Carter to disavow Young's comments. Instead, Carter called upon Udall to "apologize for all the misleading statements he has made against me." (Carter said that Udall had run "an almost entirely negative campaign" with an attack on "religious grounds" in New Hampshire. Reporters who had covered that campaign were unable to recall any such attack. And when Powell was asked about it, he dodged: "I'm not sure he [Udall] personally said anything about his [Carter's] religious beliefs, but it's been a fairly consistent theme" among Udall campaign workers.)

cept the lies of others in order to preserve these illusions. I'm thinking of that old-time religion that Carter uses—not his personal faith in God, but religion as popular culture. No one since Oral Roberts has practiced it so vehemently. . . .

Carter himself disclaimed any responsibility for the way religion came to be played. He was quick to remind various reporters that the subject of his faith existed only because "you news people constantly ask questions about it." He told Sally Quinn: "I wish the subject had never come up. When one reporter wrote that I was spiritual I knew then that it was going to happen. And this time I haven't had a chance to talk to Rosalynn about it. I just hoped the news media would not pick it up. There is no way I cannot make a misleading statement, or give a false impression." (As Quinn noted, Carter was nervous in this part of the discussion, saying, "I don't like to explain something I haven't thought out.")

On the campaign trail Carter told voters he did not want them to vote for him because of his religion, that he would never try to "mix religion with politics to get votes." And he assured potential critics there wasn't "anything political" about his missionary work. "I was in a town in Pennsylvania where I never dreamed of going back to, and I've never been back there. And very few people knew who I was, and nobody knew I was a candidate for governor, even the folks that were working with me. I had been defeated in '66 and I went up there as a farmer, as just a Christian layman."

Whether or not he consciously planned it that way, the very manner in which Carter showed his religion in the primary campaign almost guaranteed substantial press coverage. In displaying his piety and discussing his relationship to God with journalists and would-be voters, he guaranteed that it would become a matter of considerable interest, as did the decisions of his minister and friends in the Plains Baptist Church to permit the reporters in his Sunday school class, as well as his own willingness to take over the lessons when they were present.

Further, by revealing his religion in bits and pieces, he whetted the appetite of a press only recently acquainted with him and wanting to know him better. His first presentations—that he was "born again," that he had experienced some deeply moving religious experience, that he had done missionary work, and that he prayed many times daily—naturally raised the question of whether he was a religious fanatic. And his reassurances that he was not were part of the dialogue.

Carter aides, at first worried about the religion issue, came to see it as an asset. One told Elizabeth Drew: "It may not go over well in the suburbs of Washington or in Manhattan or in Beverly Hills, but it goes over well with the rest of the country." This was particularly true with Southerners and evangelical groups as Michael Novak explained: "There is a hidden religious power base in American culture, which our secular biases prevent many of us from noticing. Jimmy Carter had found it."*

* This power base included Carter's coreligionists—the 13 million members of the Southern Baptist Convention, clustered in the South but found in all fifty states. The broader "evangelical group"

With his commitment to old-fashioned values Carter tended to be reassuring not only to evangelical Protestants, but also to traditional Democrats, Protestant and Catholic, alarmed about the pace of change, about such issues as abortion and busing, about the liberal tenor of Democratic leadership. He could win back many such defecting Democrats to the party.* As the CBS–*The New York Times* polls showed, Carter even won over many Protestant Republican types. Aside from blacks, the major Carter supporters were affluent suburban and rural people, whom the pollsters called "Republicans in disguise."

But Carter's religion did arouse anxieties among other groups that had been part of the old Democratic coalition. In the Florida primary he lost urban Jews to Jackson. In Maryland and California, Jewish voters turned against him by margins as high as eight to one. He ran weakest in states with large Catholic populations: Massachusetts, New York, New Jersey, Rhode Island, and Maryland.

Carter had anticipated problems with these groups in interviews and early television ads. Some Carter aides went beyond this, suggesting that questions about the way religion was played in the campaign represented some irrational response to the candidate. One book on Carter reports the following scene:

"Why do they hate him?" asked a Carter campaign aide, while draped comfortably across a seat on the campaign plane, a pile of discarded newspapers spilled across the floor below him. "Just listen to this," said the Carter aide, reading a statement, purportedly from an aide to Morris Udall, which questioned Carter's monopoly on goodness and suggested he was dangerous: " 'I'll never support Carter. I'd rather vote for Ford. Carter's so damn slick.' "

"Now does that make sense to you?" the Carter aide questioned. "He hates the governor because he uses the word 'God' so often, and because he admits that he prays for guidance before he makes a major decision. . . ."

Even on the press bus, some voiced concern that the centrality of religion in the campaign was provoking some animus or prejudice against Carter. James Gannon in *The Wall Street Journal* said, "Such reactions to Mr. Carter's religion may reflect prejudice, partisanship or jealousy as much as anything else." And E. G. Puckett of the *Maryland Baptist* charged that there was an "appar-

---

(i.e., persons, mainly Protestant, who believe in an active, loving God and want to share that experience with others) consists of an estimated 40 million people. Concentrated in eleven Southern states and six border states (Maryland, West Virginia, Delaware, Kentucky, Missouri, and Oklahoma), this group also is strong in several Midwestern and North Central states (Illinois, Indiana, Iowa, Kansas, Nebraska, Ohio, and Pennsylvania). When one adds, in addition to this, the charismatic movement, which cuts into the Catholic religion's bloc as well as the Protestant evangelical group, one finds 50 million Americans (or 31 percent of the total population) reporting having had "a religious experience of a sudden or dramatic nature. One person in four, in short, like Mr. Carter, is a 'born again' Christian." Both groups—evangelicals and charismatics—tend to be socially conservative, and like Protestants as a whole, tend to vote Republican more than Catholics or Jews.
* Nixon had won over many "silent Americans" with the old-time values and his frequent invitations to Billy Graham to preside over White House church services. In 1968 and 1972, while a majority of the Democratically identified upper-middle-class voters stayed with the Democrats, their working-class counterparts voted for Nixon.

ent smear campaign against Jimmy Carter . . . because he is a Southern Baptist
. . ." Another Baptist editor blasted the liberal press for their "bias," claiming
they had urged voters in 1960 to refrain from making John Kennedy's religion a
campaign issue while they were, in fact, encouraging voters now to make an
issue of Carter's religion. Even R. W. Apple would write that "Carter has a
Catholic problem because of a pervasive Catholic suspicion of southerners and
especially Baptists."

To explain Catholic or Jewish concerns about Carter's religion as a case of
prejudice is too simple. Both groups have voted generously in the past for Protestants of many varieties, delivering 78 percent of their vote to Lyndon Johnson, a Seventh-Day Adventist and a Southerner, in 1964. They voted heavily
for Harry Truman, a Baptist. A northern Baptist, Nelson Rockefeller, regularly
received a handsome plurality from Catholics in New York.

The problems with these groups were caused partly by the salience of Jimmy's religion, the political function it served, and the blurring of some of the
traditional cultural boundaries between the sacred and the secular. Also, the
symbols and references that stirred believers in salvation through grace and the
fellowship of the true believer did not resonate in the same way with those who
were not in that culture. ("Carter makes people nervous, especially those who
are Catholics," a writer in the moderate Catholic publication, *The Tablet*,
noted in the middle of June. "It is not just because he is a Baptist. . . . Rather,
it is a whole cultural style and delivery that is foreign to people who are not
rural, Southern fundamentalists.") Carter's nostalgia for the past had a double
edge to it. For Catholics and Jews, as several Jewish and Catholic publications
suggested, the "old South" held bad memories—of the Ku Klux Klan, and the
anti-Semitic populism of Tom Watson (whose magazine in 1915 had influenced
crowds enough to lynch Leo Frank, the only Jew in American history to be
lynched). A writer in *New York* magazine even recalled an Anti-Defamation
League study (published in 1966), which showed 80 percent of those polled in
the South held a literal interpretation of Christ's death—believing that the
"Jews" were responsible for the Crucifixion. As *The Tablet* editorialized:
"There is nothing tougher for a Catholic than listening to a devout Baptist talking about the good old days."

Some had reservations about the optimistic content of Carter's Christian
message and its relevance to politics. "It's hard to walk Cleveland streets believing in the goodness of man," one observer wrote. "One can respect ruthlessness. But hide one behind the other and you remind too many folks of that
early period when the Nixon staff had a righteous, religious preachy air. Morality scares people."

Carter had tried to correct for these problems along the way. His attention
to the Catholic groups would have to wait until after the convention, but during
the New York primary campaign Carter workers distributed a letter from several prominent Atlanta Jews, explaining how he was committed to the independence of the state of Israel and how his religion should be of no concern to

them. Later his Jewish backers (and there were many of them) arranged meetings with other Jewish leaders, to reassure them that he was sensitive to their concerns. Howard Samuels, for example, invited 150 Eastern Jews to a meeting with Carter. When only 40 showed up, Samuels complained: "They don't want to listen. They totally misunderstand the man and they're scared to death of him."

Shortly before the California primary, Carter met with Jewish leaders in his Los Angeles hotel suite to deal with their apprehensions about him. "I'm going to tell you something you don't like. I'm a devoted Southern Baptist," he said, which was certainly not news by then. But then he reassured them: "I worship the same God you worship." A leader of the Jewish community had told him, he said, that Jews were concerned about his commitment to the Great Society and New Deal programs. But Carter explained how he was comfortable with these programs, and he spoke of his trips to Israel and his close friendship with Golda Meir.*

Carter's religion, whether he intended it or not, was an important influence in his winning the Democratic nomination. He did lose some Catholic and Jewish votes, but except for Massachusetts this registered late in the campaign after he had shown "momentum." Further, what he lost there was compensated for by the appeal he was able to make to middle-class white Protestants—Northern and Southern—and to blacks everywhere. This (along with the shifting candidate structure which did not give liberals one clear alternative) were important in his successes in Iowa, New Hampshire, Florida, and Illinois. And with Wallace eliminated from the race, he had no competitors in the Southern primaries, which enabled him to dominate in the delegate count during the middle phase of the primary season, when he was losing some races outside the South.

At another, deeper level, the emphasis Carter placed on his religion served to quiet whatever apprehensions Carter watchers may have felt when they saw his darker, enigmatic side. Whatever uneasiness one might have at those times when he seemed rough or tough or manipulative, it could be put to rest by the conviction that here was a deeply moral man—those other traits could not be significant. At least that was the thinking at the time.

## Region

In some of his early fundraising letters Carter explicitly argued that Northern liberals should support him as the "good" Southern alternative to the "bad"

---

* Actually, Carter had met Mrs. Meir only twice—during his Israel trip in 1972 and during the spring campaign. The latter tête-à-tête was at Carter's request. Mrs. Meir, who had come to New York City for some hospital treatments, agreed to meet with him with the provision that he bring none of the press with him. She did not want to be used by anyone in the presidential campaign. Carter complied with her conditions. But as he stepped out of the door of her hotel, the Waldorf Towers, the press was there, having received a leak about the meeting from someone. So the next day the newspapers showed pictures of Carter leaving the meeting and quoted Carter as saying that it was a personal visit with "an old friend."

Southerners they feared. He had never "stood in a school house door to bar the entrance to a school child [a reference to Wallace] and never passed axe handles with his name on them [an allusion to Maddox]." A governor of a Deep South state, he said, "doesn't have to be a redneck or a bigot."

With the passing of the Florida primary and Wallace's hopes for the nomination, Carter deemphasized the "good"/"bad" Southerner dichotomy, accentuating instead a motif that would solidify the entire South behind his candidacy—the new South as a political force and as the source of a new morality for the nation.

Carter had been talking about the rise of the South for some time. In 1974 he spoke to the Georgia Press Association of a "new and exciting trend of national influence" coming from the South. Our people, he said, "are recognized for the greatness of their character. . . . We've always been intensely patriotic, church-going . . . We don't want government to push us around, but want to control government." And in one of his 1976 television advertisements he said: "I'm proud of our heritage and values—a love of the land, respect for hard work and the value of a dollar, pride in our families and communities, a sense of belonging, a feeling of deep patriotism and concern for our country . . . the time has come for the South to assume once again its rightful place in the affairs of a great nation."

Carter also solidified his Southern base by playing on widespread feeling that the South had been the victim of cultural and political discrimination in the past. As governor, he had expressed this theme on several occasions. In a tribute to Senator Richard Russell shortly after his death in 1971, Carter said: "Simply because he was a Southerner, the Democratic Party lost a powerful presidential candidate and the nation was denied a great president." In 1976 Carter would equate his own rise with the vindication of the South. And once this identification was made, he would be able to treat opposition to his candidacy as just another manifestation of the old Northern bias against the South.

At first, such suggestions were tentatively made. In his original fundraising letter, which asked for help in stopping Wallace, he said: "The enclosed envelope, addressed to Atlanta, Georgia, might cause you some hesitation if you're not from the South. You may have reservations about helping a Southerner become President. Please look at it as an opportunity to give a progressive new area of national leadership a chance." During the New Hampshire and Massachusetts campaigns a television commercial was featured in which he stated: "Some people say the nation will never vote for a Southerner for President but they said in 1960 that the South would never vote for a liberal Irish Catholic senator from Boston. When the returns came in, John Kennedy got the biggest margin of victory not in Massachusetts but in Georgia. And I believe that the people in New England will be just as open-minded in 1976."

Later, Carter wondered if anyone from his part of the country could please some people from the North—"the ones who cheered me when I took on George Wallace, but then walked away shaking their heads and upset with this or that after I beat Wallace." And in his interview with Robert Scheer Carter protested: "I'm not a packaged article that you can put in a little box and say, 'Here's a Southern Baptist, an ignorant Georgia peanut farmer who doesn't have the right to enjoy music, who has no flexibility in his mind, who can't understand the sensitivities of an interpersonal relationship. He's gotta be predictable. He's gotta be for Calley and for the war. He's gotta be a liar. He's gotta be a racist.' You know, that's the sort of stereotype people tend to assume and I hope it doesn't apply to me." The idea that Carter's election would vindicate the South was played up in the fall. On one radio ad used in the fall an announcer said: "On November second, the South is being readmitted to the Union. If that sounds strange maybe only a Southerner can understand. Only a Southerner can understand years of coarse anti-Southern jokes and unfair comparisons. Only a Southerner can understand what it means to be a political whipping boy. But then, only a Southerner can understand what Jimmy Carter as President can mean." Another ad carried a similar message: "Some people in this country say that a Southerner isn't good enough to be President. They still use words like backward and ignorant. But the thing that really bothers me is that come November 2, a Southerner might just be elected President."

Such seeds were planted in fertile ground and some Southern journalists and academics cultivated them. Larry King, a native of Texas and a nephew of Sam Rayburn, Jr., wrote in an *Esquire* article entitled "We Ain't Trash No More!":

Me and Jimmy Cah-tuh, we lost a war together in 1865. . . . We know that Tennessee Williams ain't exaggerating when he writes of delicate ladies who stare into space and hum a whole lot and always depend on the kindness of strangers. We know it's silly to go to a shrink at a cost of fifty dollars an hour when you can confess to a whole congregation for free and get your hand shook for it. We've been down with the pip and understand the importance of football. We're not ashamed to love our daddies or to cry when we've gazed on the wine a bit much, and our history temporarily overwhelms us. One of y'all Yankees break down and cry and everybody looks away or commences analyzing him. We just hug each other, knowing that shared misery creates a bond. It don't have all that much to do with class or economics, either. More to do with time and place and blood.

Jody Powell phrased it succinctly in the summer of 1976, "Everybody, black and white, now recognizes you don't have to be ashamed of turnip greens." Many, like Lew Grizzard, native Georgian and executive sports editor for the Chicago *Sun-Times*, "voted for him simply because he talks like we do."

Along with the Southern pride there was an underlying defensiveness prompted by the perception of a subtle anti-Southern bias in the North. Northerners were against Jimmy Carter because of their prejudices. Pat Derian, Mississippi's liberal Democratic National Committeewoman and a Carter worker (later Assistant Secretary of State), was quoted as saying: "It [the Anyone But Carter movement] has to do with the bias against the South. He's not a member of an Eastern liberal club. They don't have any lines to him." Charles Morgan, Jr., Alabama attorney and then director of the Washington office of the American Civil Liberties Union, said, "the real reason the Northern liberals don't like

Carter is that they don't have their hooks in him." Robert Coles suggested that Carter critics were guilty of class, as well as regional, prejudice. "There has been and no doubt will continue to be an element of sectional mistrust of Carter. Substantial opposition to him is based on class preference if not prejudices." Back home in Georgia, Jim Merriner of the Atlanta *Constitution*, articulated the feeling. "During the '76 run for the White House thousands of words in countless analyses have tried to illuminate what I call the peculiar prosecution (PP), that strange disdain the North has for the South. After all these years, since the Civil War, it is still there, that condescending, patronizing air from the North."

Actually, the national opinion polls indicate that there was little conscious discrimination against Carter because of his Southern roots or religion. But the extent to which Carter, his aides, and reporters talked about it made it a functional truth for many. As one writer in the Atlanta *Constitution* noted: "There's no one quite so bitter as a Southerner who thinks he is being dumped on because he's a Southerner." This reaction is evident in a statement by Georgia-born Dr. William W. Abbot, a University of Virginia historian and former editor of the *Journal of Southern History:* "I don't like Carter until people begin to attack him, and then I just get fighting mad . . . I don't like it when I hear them mocking his accent, making fun of his religion . . . And a lot of people do."

Carter was even able to convince some Northerners that concerns about Carter were based on such prejudice. TRB of the *New Republic* wrote: "I have a political activist friend in Washington who burst out against Carter with a vehemence that startled me: 'He's a two-faced louse!' he ejaculated or words to that effect. My friend thinks Carter's a hypocrite; maybe he is prejudiced; deep down perhaps, he is asking a variant of that old question, 'Can anything good come out of Georgia?' " (Even David Broder attributed the unease about Carter to a reaction against his Southern roots: "There are still a great many people out there—in labor, religious, and ethnic groups and in academia—who have not totally reconciled themselves to the idea of a dixieland governor for President.")

The Southern themes in Carter's campaign could have backfired if they had been played clumsily, turning off non-Southerners. But Carter avoided this problem by identifying his own rise with a broader movement in the South and in the nation whereby the people—the "outsiders"—would increasingly participate in the government.

In Carter's campaign for the governorship of Georgia in 1970, he had emphasized "down home" roots in the country and attacked city "big shots" for their fancy ways and their distance from the people. As governor, Carter had equated the people's movement in the South to a national trend. "Our problems are not peculiar to the South alone," he said in 1971. He saw the movement in the South as a "new expression of freedom. . . . I don't think we are going to go back to old days when the powerful made the decisions, when decisions were made in closed rooms." In 1976 the theme of the "average folks" versus the "city slickers" was neatly adapted to the national scene—with Washington rather than Atlanta as the foil. As the representative of all "outsiders," Carter could unify not only the South—city and country, progressive and populist—but the blacks and Hispanics and the poor across the nation. Nor were the outsiders he represented simply the ethnic and social minorities. His proud display of his humble origins, his old-style values of piety and patriotism, and his simple tastes and habits (making his own bed, washing his own socks, doing his own mending, and wearing jeans) helped solid, responsible middle-class people feel kinship with him. And his attacks on the bosses and the Washington establishment caught the same social resentment toward the privileged that Wallace had expressed in less respectable forms.

This appeal had some power even for sophisticated observers. As Robert Coles wrote in the summer of 1976: "He won, an underdog fighting the capital city boys, the big interests, the self-confident and well-to-do and proudly urbane Atlanta businessmen and bureaucrats, with their Brooks Brothers suits and revolving restaurants and exposed elevators, and plastic credit cards and guardedly liberal pieties . . ." Larry King openly delighted in how the "hicks" had outmaneuvered the sophisticates: "They started out so anonymous they might have robbed liquor stores without masks, and about all they seemed to have going for them was boatloads of ambition and oceans of gall. Yet they soon wasted the Democratic establishment as effectively as William Tecumseh Sherman once reduced Atlanta." David Nordan, political editor of the Atlanta *Journal,* took some perverse pleasure in watching the Eastern elites (who a "few months ago would have sneered at giving Carter an audience in their New York or Washington office") "bite the dust" at a briefing session in Plains in the late summer. "It brings a certain glow to a country boy's heart, to watch a dozen or so experts from Harvard and Columbia and Brandeis step off a rickety old bus into the choking red dust of a rural Sumter County road—not particularly because they wanted to, but because The Man sent for them." He delighted in Zbigniew Brzezinski's rumpled green jacket and his comment that riding on that bus gave one a sense for populist politics. He found humor in Ruth Morgenthau, head of the political science department at Brandeis, trying to keep her pink beret on her head while taking "intellectual swats" at gnats swarming around her. And he concluded that the experts were not even that smart—bringing nothing to their briefing session with reporters that hadn't "already been thoroughly covered in Carter's speeches and his platform." Looking at Jimmy Carter in his old jeans and chambray shirt, Nordan also had the feeling that, behind his expressionless blue eyes, Carter was taking the same pleasure in "giving the Harvardites a real lesson in 'populist' politics. . . . George Wallace would have loved it."

Carter's Southern roots not only provided a basis for identifying with him in the "populist" cause; the details he offered of his own personal family history gave "proof" that he would not forget the dispossessed once he obtained power. Carter's accounts of his early life in Archery and Plains (the mother who had to work twelve to twenty-hour days, the house without central plumbing or electricity, the 4:00 A.M. awakenings to do chores, the lack of doctors in his home county) suggest that he was touched too personally by poverty to forget it. One of the most important experiences he would bring to the White House, he said, was his own past relationships with poor people. "That's where I came from. That's where I lived. Those are my people—not only whites, but particularly blacks—and it's no accident that Andy Young and Daddy King support me. They know I understand their problems."

The rich and idealized description of Carter roots during the campaign also tapped some broader national impulse to escape from the anomie of contemporary society and its social and political fragmentation by a return to the past. As Carter told James Reston in early August, "There's a lack of personal security in the country now, I think, and maybe a feeling that the few precious things that were never supposed to change have gone." By looking to Plains and the values there, one could find the spiritual and social solace that seemed lacking throughout most of the nation.

In *Why Not the Best?* Carter portrayed an idyllic youth in which the older virtues were honored, the people were happy, and the pleasures were simple. "We felt close to nature, close to the members of our family, and close to God." On the campaign trail he recalled his childhood as a time when there was always someone to turn to in time of need: "When I grew up on the farm and when I got hurt, my mamma and daddy were always there—on the edge of the field or not too far from the creek. If I got thrown off a mule, my daddy was close by to pick me up."

Not only had this early life been good, one could always draw nourishment by going back: there was something about rural life, about Plains, that was healing and made a man feel whole and moral. Carter told Bill Moyers in his May 6, 1976, interview: "I had stability there. You know, when things started going wrong in my own life, my mother and father were there, and my community was there—which never did change; never has changed yet—but there was something there around which I built my life. In the modern-day world, you don't have that." On his return to Plains after the Democratic national convention, Carter talked of how touching base in Plains gave him the stability he needed. Just before the formal kickoff of the fall campaign, he reiterated this theme before his Sunday school class in Plains: "If there is one thing that gives me stability, and continuity to my life in the hurly-burly and pressures of political campaigning, it's coming back home to Plains and to church."

He proposed to recreate that stability, that simplicity in the nation as a whole. As he suggested in *Why Not the Best?*, the sense of community one had in Plains could become the national experience as well: the people there represent "very well" the people of the nation, he said. "We live and work together in a spirit of friendship and harmony. Our 250 white citizens and our 350 black citizens learn from one another. . . . rural people sometimes have the reputation (perhaps undeserved) of living close to the earth, close to God, close to poverty, and closer to their government."

On the campaign trail he implied that he could make the whole nation a caring people—he would make America like his family. "I've got a good family," he said. "I hope that you'll be part of my family." Through a return of its roots America would find a nourishment and a connection that would heal and bind the nation together. Carter thus presented himself as a metaphorical good father who could lead the nation forward to a new wholeness.

# EIGHTEEN

# The Extraordinary, Ordinary Man

CARTER ESPOUSED A concept of the presidency that was in the "great man" tradition. As he told Bill Moyers in the spring of 1976, "There is only one person in this nation who can speak with a clear voice to the American people. There's only one person who can set a standard of ethics and morality and excellence and greatness or call on the American people to make a sacrifice and explain the purpose of the sacrifice, or answer difficult questions or propose and carry out bold programs, or to provide for defense posture that would make us feel secure, a foreign policy that would make us proud once again, and that's the President." He continued, "In the absence of that leadership, there is no leadership, and the country drifts."

While adhering to these views of the American presidency, Carter projected himself in ways that indicated he had the personal qualities requisite to providing such aggressive and innovative political and moral leadership. (The extent to which Carter actually had these traits and the degree to which he internalized this persona will be discussed later.)

From the beginning of his campaign, as has been shown, Carter exuded self-confidence, noting that he "did not intend to lose" and presuming victory with talk of his inauguration, his Cabinet, and his presidency. Typical was his reflection in early March, 1976. His success so far, he said, hadn't really been a surprise to him. "We were confident two, three years ago I would be elected. I feel as good now as I did when I began to campaign." And when reporter Vermont Royster asked Carter to explain his "audacity," Carter responded that he "always had self-assurance" and that he always knew he "could meet any challenge as well as the next man." He also had a near complete inner assurance. "Without being arrogant about it," he said, "I am sure of myself. I'm almost at complete peace with myself and the world around me. There's a certain equanimity in my character as I approach a difficult question or a challenge. I'm sure of my relationship with most intimate friends, family members, staff members."

Not only did Carter project self-confidence, he also showed that he had the qualities of toughness seen by many as necessary to good political leadership. His accounts of his role models—Earl Carter and Hyman Rickover—and of his early political life showed that he was competitive, tenacious, and unimpeded by false sentimentality or compassion for those on the other side. His campaign for the presidency, he promised, would be "tough, hard-hitting, combative." And he predicted that his presidency, "might be very contentious; it might be very competitive and it might even be combative—but I think the Congress is eager for some strong leadership, too, and I intend to be a strong leader." Despite the soft-spoken manner, Carter indicated, he would not be pushed around.

His associates also gave testimony to this toughness. According to Hamilton Jordan, Carter was a demanding boss, "He'll say mildly, 'Ham, I asked you last night to draft a one-hundred-fifty-page memorandum and I'm disappointed not to have it today. I'm sure there must be a good reason.' You'd rather he hit and cussed you." Charles Kirbo contrasted his own reluctance to "let the heads roll" to Carter's sang-froid when they began to organize Carter's administration in Atlanta: "I said, Jimmy, I wish we could hurry up and get done with all the firing of folks, I even hate to go into that office." Carter's reply, according to Kirbo, was: "Hell, I can't wait to get there." Further, Jordan, while denying reports that Carter was "vindictive," let it be known that Carter could remember friends and punish enemies as well as anyone:

For example, somebody said, well, weren't we vindictive by kicking Carl Sanders off the platform committee this year [1976]. First of all we had our own person, Stu Eizenstat, that we wanted there and he performed beautifully. Secondly, Carl Sanders has never done a damn thing for us. He was one of those encouraging Senator Humphrey to run until the very last minute. That's politics, not vindictiveness. Jimmy can be tough—he can be tough on his opponents and he can be tough on people who have fought him over the years. He never appointed people to boards and commissions that have fought us just continually . . .

Even one of Carter's admitted faults—stubbornness—was translated into a virtue—moral tenacity. As he explained: "I don't know how to compromise on any principle I believe is right. Georgia Secretary of State Ben Fortson once called me as 'stubborn as a South Georgia turtle.' Unthinking non-compromise is, of course, foolish; but maybe this is a time, on matters of principle, for an absence of compromise." In another interview Carter said: "I believe that I am stubborn, which may be a weakness or a defect. Tenacious is another word. Once I set my mind to do something, I find it very difficult to deter from it." Charles Kirbo found value in the Carter stubbornness: "I was one of those early critics of him being stubborn. But I found out that, like most other attributes he has, he uses them to an advantage. There's a time to be stubborn. . . . He's a tough horse-trader, real tough. . . ."

Carter demonstrated, in many little ways, that he had the qualities he claimed for himself. His toughness was manifest in the demanding schedule he ran during the campaign. Elizabeth Drew noted the "brutal" pace he had set for himself when she traveled with him through Illinois just after the Florida primary. Kandy Stroud thought "he punished his body beyond endurance, working longer and harder than anyone else. While other candidates started often as late as nine o'clock, Carter started at 4:30 or 5:00 am. . . ." Further, he acted as if his grueling pace was the most ordinary thing in the world. "I've always worked this hard," he told Stroud as she collapsed into a swivel chair on his campaign plane. "I didn't work any harder than I did ten or fifteen years ago." And he went on to explain how he would have done about the same thing had he remained a student or an engineer, a naval officer, or gone to work in a major corporation (which he recalled he had almost done). All this activity and planning is "very pleasant for me, almost like a solitary chess game."

There were other signs of his sang-froid. Reporters who lagged behind were left behind. His plane moved when he was there—on time. (Stroud seemed to prefer this to Jackson's campaign leadership: " 'Super Scoop,' . . . ran his campaign like a sophomore's tour of Europe. While Carter would desert reporters on the runway in order to be on time for an appointment, Jackson would lollygag around waiting for journalists to make phone calls, even when he was way behind schedule.") Not even the weather could stop him. During an early December swing through Iowa, the wind became so bad the Secret Service men told Carter's staff it was too dangerous to fly. But Jody Powell insisted, so the plane left on schedule, bouncing "like a cork in a fast moving Georgia stream," and Carter arrived on time. To get to Berlin, New Hampshire, as we have seen, Carter braved a blizzard. He even helped scrape ice off the plane's wings. "People are waiting for me . . ." he said as he took off.

Carter's intensity in sports and games reinforced this tough image. In the summer of 1976, after hunkering down in Plains, Carter showed his competitive streak in the softball games between his team of Secret Service men and the newsmen. He played hard and was a leader. As Helen Dewar noted, Carter at one point barked: " 'All right, let's calm down,' to several Secret Service agents who weren't playing up to Carter's standards. They immediately snapped to attention." And when one of his staffers, serving as umpire, began helping the newsmen with his calls, Carter threw him out of the game even though the Carter team led by about thirty runs. As Billy Carter pointed out, drawing the moral from these dramas, "Jimmy enjoys both the sport and the competition, but I would figure it's the competition more than the sport . . . He's always been that way, liking to win." Helen Dewar wrote: "As in his campaign, he set tough standards for himself and expects others to do the same."

Another important Carter virtue was intelligence. In *Why Not the Best?* he relates a charmingly disarming story of how he, as a boy, had read Tolstoy's *War and Peace* at least three times after Julia Coleman had recommended it to him, even after discovering it was not the cowboys-and-Indians tale he had anticipated. (However, a gift from his godmother when he was four—the complete works of Guy de Maupassant—was not read until much later in his life.) Even his account of that first meeting with Admiral Rickover, though it shows him falling short and quivering in front of a "great man," carries a secondary message—that Carter could have been at the top of his Annapolis class had he really concentrated his efforts. When asked by Rickover if he had done his best at Annapolis, Carter recalls that he started to say yes but then remembered the "many times . . . when I could have learned more." And his brief mention of his depression at not having received a Rhodes scholarship shortly after his graduation suggests that he had been a real contender for that honor—having exhibited at the Naval Academy the high scholarship, leadership, and athletic skills required to win it.

Writing of his voracious reading appetite ("three or four books each week"), Carter said it was "easy and natural to revise my reading lists to encompass subjects relating more toward foreign affairs, defense, and economics" in preparation for his presidential bid. He further "accumulated and read histories and biographies concerning our nation and the presidency, and, in order to avoid mistakes, even studied the campaign platforms of all the unsuccessful candidates for president since our electoral process began."

Carter suggested that he had a scientific cast of mind. Throughout the campaign, he identified himself as a scientist or nuclear physicist or nuclear engineer. Moreover, the scientific cast of thought was evident in the campaign operation. Carter and his aides showed how thorough and confident they were, telling various newspersons how they utilized computers and quantitative techniques (giving exact numeric value to primaries and states for example) to determine their campaign schedule. They confided that they employed marketing techniques to target their television advertisements, polls to sound out the political waters to determine what to say and where, and nationwide searches for vice-presidential candidates and other members of a potential Carter Administration to secure the most "qualified" individuals.

Yet Carter projected himself as no mere technocrat. He appreciated classical music: "I used to be obsessed with classical music when I was a midshipman and when I was in the navy." But neither was he a snob. "I started to listen to Bob Dylan's music primarily because of my sons, but I got to like it and I used to spend three or four hours a day listening to Paul Simon, Bob Dylan and the Allman Brothers. At home I'd study government reorganization or budgeting techniques while I listened to rock." And he had a taste for good literature. His favorite poet was Dylan Thomas. Indeed, as he told one interviewer, he, Rosalynn, and the boys used to listen to recordings of Thomas reciting his own poetry and then analyze one poem each week to "see what every word of his poems meant." Aside from *War and Peace*, Carter said his favorite book was James Agee's *Let Us Now Praise Famous Men* (his favorite study of Presidents, as noted, was *The Presidential Character* by James David Barber). His sensitivity was evident in his love of nature. He spoke eloquently of his favorite places in Georgia: "We studied the wildlife programs on our isolated game preserves, and inspected the virgin cypress groves on Lewis Island in the mouth of the Altamaha River. Our favorite place was Cumberland Island, off the Southeast Georgia coast, where one can see dozens of sea turtles coming ashore to lay their eggs in the early summer. We would watch the sun rise over the Atlantic, and drive down twenty miles of the broad white beach without seeing another living soul." Further, as he told Sally Quinn, he was a sportsman of sorts—a hunter, fisherman, canoeist, as well as a tennis player and softball star.

Throughout the presidential campaign Carter's family also testified to his widespread intellectual and aesthetic interests and abilities. Rosalynn recalled their early married life: "We used to study books of the great artists. We would memorize Shakespeare and read the great philosophers; I remember reading *War and Peace* then, because Jimmy had talked about it so much. We'd listen to records—Tristan and Isolde and Rachmanioff concertos played by the great pianists." Billy testified to his brother's intelligence. "I'm not just saying this because he's my brother, but Jimmy's the smartest human being I've ever known. I say, from both learning and the ability to learn, and to change. He can take a subject he knows absolutely nothing about and by talking to people and by reading and breaking down what he's heard, in a very short time he knows as much about it as anybody. I know more about peanuts than Jimmy does, but I won't let him know that because in a couple of days he'll know more than I do."

This self-confidence, this toughness, this intelligence—in short, this unusual capacity—could have been frightening had it not been linked with a complementary quality—Carter's ability to care for others, his compassion for the less fortunate, which was always in the foreground.

The need for a compassionate government was made explicit in many of his campaign advertisements and speeches. Exemplary was Carter's expression of concern for the victims of our criminal justice system in the 1974 Law Day Speech: "My heart feels and cries out . . . that now we assign punishment to fit the criminal and not the crime. . . . You can go to the prisons of Georgia, and I don't know, it may be that poor people are the only ones who commit crimes, but I do know they are the only ones who serve prison sentences." A point made in his announcement address, that "a simplified, fair and compassionate welfare program" was not beyond the capacity of government, was reiterated frequently throughout the campaign. Anecdotes in *Why Not the Best?*—of how moved he was by Eloy Cruz's dealing with the distraught young father who had tried to kill his own child, and his own moving description of how a forty-five-year-old Mongoloid woman lit a candle in a ceremony he had observed—show that he had feeling for those who are vulnerable.

His concern for the poor was symbolized by his favorite Bob Dylan song, "Maggie's Farm." And his favorite poem (often quoted on the stump), Dylan Thomas's "A Refusal to Mourn the Death, by Fire, of a Child in London," suggested that he shared the poet's distaste for war. His sensitivity was underscored with repeated references to his kinship with Bob Dylan, a voice of the 1960s. "I really like rock music and Bob Dylan and I get along really well. He's very, very shy. Painfully so." When challenged about his friendship with various rock stars, Carter responded about them, and indeed about any others different from himself, "I care for these people." In his interview with Bill Moyers, Carter talked of his mother's compassion for others in the same context, saying he thought he was more like her than like his father.

Taken together, the projections from Carter amounted to a kind of Renaissance man, possessed of a cultivated aesthetic sense, finely educated in contemporary science and technology, yet at the same time tough and combative—capable of meaningful action in the real world. Occasionally a person with these skills and virtues may appear on the political scene, and Carter, no doubt, possessed some of the qualities he projected. What was truly extraordinary was that he apparently combined so many virtues—each one developed to a fine perfection.

He was imbued with great certainty about his ultimate goals. When Bill Moyers asked if he had any doubts, Carter responded:

I can't think of any . . . Obviously, I don't know all the answers to the philosophical questions and theological questions—the kind of questions that are contrived. But the things that I haven't been able to answer in theory or supposition, I just accept them, and go on [to things that I can influence or change]. . . . I do have, obviously, many doubts about the best way to answer a question, or how to alleviate a concern, or how to meet a need. Or how to create in my own life a more meaningful purpose, and to let my life be expanded, in my heart and mind. So doubts about the best avenue to take among many options is a kind of doubt. That is a constant presence with me. But doubt about my faith? No. Doubt about my purpose in life? I don't have any doubts about that.

He has never experienced fear. In an interview with Mike Barnicle he shows that side of his personality:

Q. (Does the idea of being president scare you at all?)
A. "No. I know that I can be a good president."
Q. (Have you ever been afraid?)
A. "No."
Q. (Never?)
A. "Not in the sense of the word fear. There have been four or five times when I faced the possibility of death. I know enough about myself that I wasn't afraid. Once, on a submarine in the spring of 1949, I was officer of the deck . . . and we were caught in a storm. I was swept off by a huge wave. I could have disappeared in the ocean and no one would have noticed. But I didn't. I survived. I'm a fatalist, I guess."

He had the capacity to love anonymous people he met while campaigning, as we have seen. And he would be an effective President because of his "genuine affinity or intimacy with a wide range of voters. I feel completely at home with black groups, environmental groups, farmers, young people, very conservative business executives and so forth. And I think they know it, they feel it. And I derive from them very strong, very fervent, very dedicated support." He compared himself to a previous President in this regard. "Lyndon Johnson was never accepted by the liberal Eastern establishment. He did things that had been talked about for generations, in the field of social progress and alleviating discrimination—Voting Rights Act, Civil Rights Acts. For some reason, he was never quite accepted. I don't know why . . ." But Carter thought he himself would be accepted by the "Eastern liberal establishment." "I'm sure of myself. I'm not sure that Johnson was ever sure of himself when he was President. I don't feel ill-at-ease when I'm in a Harvard professor's house and there's two or three hundred people around asking questions."

Carter projected himself as an extraordinary man, capable, perhaps, of greatness. This theme was particularly explicit in one of Carter's late spring commercials. The ad began with actor E. G. Marshall saying:

> I've always felt that when Franklin Roosevelt died that was the end of the good and great presidents. And then after Harry Truman I thought, well that's the last of them. And then we had Jack Kennedy. For such a short time, too. I learned something from them. I learned that in the proper time the man and the moment can meet, so to speak. A good man can become a great man. A person with a vision can become a president with a vision. Take up a country and lead it into a more secure future. Where the goal truly is justice for all. I look forward to voting for Jimmy Carter. That's the truth of it. I feel it's in the air that we are going to have a new Democratic president. In the tradition of the best Democratic presidents.

He was followed by a narrator saying, "We need a president who speaks for us for a change." And the commercial concluded with Jimmy Carter's compassionate but tough voice: "We love our country. We love our government. We don't want anything selfish out of government for ourselves. We want to be treated fairly. We want to have a right to make our own decisions."

Shortly after his nomination Carter himself suggested that he might combine all the virtues of the previous Presidents: "I've studied the finer aspects of previous Administrations, the humility and courage and tenacity of Mr. Truman's Administration, the inspiration of Kennedy, the elimination of discrimination and inequity by the Johnson Administration. I would like to exemplify the finest aspects of each one of those great Presidents of the past. Whether that would be possible it is too early to say, but that's my goal."

These claims could have created envy or resentment or touched off growing apprehensions about the "imperial presiency" if he had chosen to set himself above others. But Carter avoided that pitfall; his perfection was tempered with assurances that he was one of the people. "I have never claimed to be better or wiser than any other person," he said on one occasion. "I think my greatest strength is that I am an ordinary man, just like all of you, one who has worked and learned and loved his family and made mistakes and tried to correct them without always succeeding."

Carter did not just tell Americans that he was humble, he showed them. He was the presidential candidate who carried his own luggage and washed his own socks and made his own bed. "He could roll up his sleeves, stalk through farmers' markets, slog through mines, or fox-trot with senior citizens with as much ease as he could mingle with the stars of Hollywood or the millionaires of Manhattan." At home, he relaxed in workshirts and blue jeans. Further, Carter did what most Americans, let alone presidential candidates, never do: he would give his phone number and address to campaign crowds and urge them to keep in touch with him and let him hear how they felt the campaign was progressing. In a different way, he seemed to be trying to make this same point in his interviews with Robert Scheer (for *Playboy*) and Norman Mailer (for *The New York Times Magazine*), to be discussed below.

Moreover, Carter professed to having no selfish interest in seeking power. "I don't want anything selfish out of government," he often said. "I think I want the same thing you do. And that is to have our nation once again with a government as good and honest and decent and truthful and fair and competent and idealistic and compassionate, and as filled with love as are the American people."*

The administrative structure Carter intended to have reinforced these attitudes: "There will be no all-powerful 'palace' guard or 'shadow' cabinet in my White House. There will be no anonymous aids, unelected, unknown to the public, and unconfirmed by the Senate, wielding vast power from the White House basement." Commenting on the tendency of Presidents to select Cabinet members on the basis of political considerations, he said, "I will pick my Cabinet on the basis of merit, not politics, and I will restore my Cabinet to its proper role as the President's first circle of advisors." And he would avoid the "wagons-in-a-circle" psychology of the Nixon Administration. His staff, having "free access" to him, would be encouraged to tell him when he was wrong. He would keep himself open to criticism and discussion; "an almost unrestricted debate within White House circles" would exist.

Carter's virtue was the ultimate assurance that one need not fear power in his hands. He promised to apply the same high standards he had in his private life to the public realm. And where shyer men might have held back, Carter looked America in the eye and said, "The President ought to tell the truth

---

* Carter's staff expressed a similar lack of interest in personal gain out of service to him. Pollster Pat Caddell insisted that he was not interested in a White House post: "Oh, I enjoy the power. I'm fascinated with it. It enables you to do things . . . But I'm not interested in going to D.C. and heading up the Census Bureau . . . I don't want to work that hard, I'm spoiled by my own independence . . . I'd rather be in a position that I didn't need the White House job." Stu Eizenstat, when asked of his own motives, responded, "I don't know. Certainly not greed or ambition. I guess it's the desire for excellence. I'm Jewish for one thing. And I care deeply about people, especially people who are not able to help themselves like other people can . . . And I think the government has the responsibility to play a role and be an active instrument for change." Charles Kirbo dismissed the possibility of going to Washington with Carter: "I'm just interested in the moral factor in decision-making, having a voice in what is the right thing to do, the proper thing to do." And Andrew Young insisted he wanted to remain in Congress. "I really kind of sold him to the liberal community and the black community generally and they're holding me accountable," he said. "In Congress, I'm free to be a critic and still be a friend. Even though I like him, once I get in the Cabinet I'm an employee and I have to defend his administration." In another interview Young was more direct: "I have no personal ambition and Carter owes me nothing personally."

always." "I'll never lie to you . . . never make a misleading statement . . . never betray your trust." He added, "If I ever tell a lie . . . I want you to come and take me out of the White House." (In his interview with Moyers, when asked if he would ever resign because of evidence that showed he had, indeed, lied while in office, Carter equivocated. "Well, I can't say that. But there will be times when I'm asked a question that I might refuse to answer. But if I give an answer, it will be the truth.")

Indeed, the very suggestion that in promising never to lie or mislead, he had promised too much, perplexed Carter. "One of the great surprises to me in the campaign was that when I made that simple statement 18 months ago—not in a fervent way, not even in a way to surprise anybody . . . that it became so controversial." He suggested that given the nature of the national media, it would not be possible for him to lie to them. "If he [any candidate] fed different lines to different audiences," Carter said, "the reporters would simply broadcast the tapes back-to-back and that would be the end of him."

Jimmy Carter's campaign persona was that of a "great man" destined to be a great president. This man in jeans with red Georgia dust on his work boots offered a set of virtues that were complementary and reassuring. He was self-confident but humble, tough but compassionate, intelligent but still one of the boys, religious but accepting of differences, always working toward what he wanted by not wanting anything for himself. He was, in essence, extraordinary but ordinary.

# NINETEEN

# Fantasies

O N AUGUST 7, 1976, a hot, humid evening in Plains, Carter
met with Ralph Nader in the office of his Woodlawn
Drive home. From 9:00 P.M. until sometime after midnight, Nader lectured him on the way government
works, talking of Washington and warning him of the
potential booby traps in the presidency. Carter listened intently, contemplating examples and nodding his head—showing Nader he understood.

A young man sitting in the corner of the study was exhilarated by what he
saw in Carter. "That is the difference with state governors," James Fallows told
himself. "While senators are prancing about with new ideas and noble intentions, governors see what happens when the payroll is met, the program administered, the intention converted to result. The last governor to become
President was Franklin Roosevelt, and I told my friends that summer that
Carter had at least the potential to leave the government forever changed by
his presence."

From other fragments of Carter's past and his rhetoric, Fallows—formerly
editor of the *Harvard Crimson* and an associate of Nader's, a Carter campaign
worker at the time of this meeting, and in the future a speechwriter for the new
President—had built a whole set of great expectations for this new political figure. Carter's Law Day speech in 1974 and Hamilton Jordan's assertion that the
government would be run by the people had led him to the conclusion that
Carter had a deep commitment to the common citizen. From Carter's discussion of his mentor, Hyman Rickover, Fallows concluded that Carter would be a
tough professional. Carter's proposal for eliminating the mortgage tax deduction, he assumed, was part of a well-thought-out general approach to tax reform; his approach to defense would provide a careful and tough balance between the need for a major new defense system and the widespread desire for
defense cuts.

Carter had been evoking similar responses long before he was a front run-

ner in the presidential race. This is most evident in the reaction of several reporters who covered Carter during the early phases of the campaign. Several
saw him as a serious populist. Hunter Thompson's response to the 1974 Law
Day speech at the University of Georgia, already noted, exemplifies this tendency. From Carter's identification with the victims of injustice in some phases
of the address, Thompson concluded that he was an "angry agrarian populist."
In the heat of the '76 campaign, others began reading Carter as the spokesman
for the dispossessed. As Anthony Lewis said, "He cares about the powerless in
society—genuinely I am convinced. He instinctively identifies with the victims
of official abuse." Simon Lazarus and Harry Huge, writing in the *New Republic,* saw the possibility of a Carter presidency as "a unique, totally unexpected
chance to generate nationwide consent for the equalitarian principle. In hard
political terms, . . . Carter's candidacy has significantly expanded the potential
constituency for progressive policies." Neal Peirce (a Southern-born columnist
and contributing editor of the *National Journal*) was impressed by what he saw
as Carter's reason for wanting power: "to correct the inequities as I discern
them," and to be a "strong spokesman" for those who are weak. Tom Wicker of
*The New York Times* reasoned that because he and Carter shared a common
background (they were only one year apart in age and Wicker hailed from a
North Carolina railroad town only slightly larger than Plains), Carter must
share his own enormous empathy for the underprivileged: "I feel reasonably
sure that I can detect in Jimmy Carter what I long ago recognized in myself—an
indelible class sense, ingrained in us while growing up in the South during the
Depression, and fundamentally unaltered by later affluence."

Others, as we have seen, saw Carter as having a deeper religious conviction
than his competitors. Wes Pippert, who covered Carter in Plains for UPI in
August of 1976, was convinced that Carter's emphasis on his religious faith
showed that he was a deeply moral and compassionate man. Himself a small-
town boy and a deeply religious born again Christian, Pippert also deduced,
later on, that Carter's Christian faith guaranteed his humility as well. Criticizing his colleagues for missing the true moral dimensions of the man, Pippert
wrote in his book, *The Spiritual Journey of Jimmy Carter,* that "some reporters
interpreted Carter's claim to a relationship with Christ as arrogance. . . . this il-
lustrated a basic lack of understanding of the Christian faith. For the person
with a personal relationship with God *by definition* has experienced the humiliation of acknowledging his or her sins (emphasis added)."

Garry Wills, who was never completely caught up in the emotional sweep of
1976, nevertheless wrote:

When Birch Bayh goes to his native hamlet and says he never feels closer to God than
when he is there, we do not care because we know he does not mean it. When Nixon
used Billy Graham to bless the billy clubs of the sixties, the insincerity gave us at least
the relief of mockery. Kennedy's Catholicism was made up of gestures. But when a man
*means* what he says in this awesome area, he drifts outside the ties and shared weak-

nesses that keep us in touch with each other. Carter says he will not be compromised. The claim has been dismissed as unkeepable. But I wonder. The scary thing is that he might have some way of keeping it.

For Wills, even Carter's Southernness was somehow more genuine than that of other politicians. To be a "real Southerner," Carter could "not just be a front man for Northern liberals (like Terry Sanford or Reubin Askew)." But he would not be a military hawk. Like Eisenhower, Wills implied, Carter has seen the military from the inside. "That experience can be more disillusioning than inspiring; and Carter has shown a healthy skepticism about the top-heavy military staffs. He gets the best of two worlds—a Southern respect for the military without the awe that naval amateurs like the two Roosevelts displayed."

Many observers concluded that Carter was some kind of genius. Pippert, in the summer of 1976, told the author in a casual conversation that he saw Carter as the most impressive presidential candidate since Roosevelt. Neal Peirce concluded that Carter "does have a first-class mind—probably one of the more impressive intellects in the history of presidential politics." (Later, after Carter had been in the White House for a few months, Robert Pierpoint, CBS White House correspondent, had this to say: "Intellectually, Carter is the smartest President I've covered. He's quick, perceptive, industrious, and an incredibly fast study." Even Fallows, writing in 1979 said: "He is probably smarter, in the College Board sense, than any other President in this century.")

As the campaign rolled on, some reporters discounted the contradictory images Carter was projecting, denying what was before their eyes. Lazarus and Huge, for example, concluded that Carter hadn't really been fuzzy on the issues. And late in the primary campaign James Reston stated that Carter had "answered more questions, and been more specific than Ford, Reagan or most of his Democratic opponents"; he also noted the "fallacy of the 'anti-Washington' tag pinned on him by the press."

Other reporters, noticing some of Carter's flaws, decided they were unimportant. Norman Mailer, after his late summer visit to Plains, saw that Carter was an intellectual name dropper. He concluded that "Carter was not necessarily one of America's leading authorities on Kierkegaard." But he excused Carter on the grounds that Mailer himself had not been above quoting "an author he had not lived with thoroughly. . . ." Indeed, Mailer gave Carter magical powers: "Yes, he was quiet in his charisma; and no massings of energy rose like thunderheads from his brow. . . . Nonetheless, his aura was hardly the same as other people's. Happiness came off him. It was as if he knew that God had given him intelligence and good work that would make sense, and so he could give his strength to the world and get new strength back." Mailer concluded that Carter lay "within range of the very good and very decent man he presented himself to be." His evidence: "After all, it was not every day that you could pull the lever for a man whose favorite song was 'Amazing Grace, how sweet the sound that saved a wretch like me—I once was lost, but now I'm found, was blind but now I see.' " Scheer noted Carter's defensiveness, but concluded it was not important. "He *is* thin-skinned, as others have reported, and he'll glare at you if he doesn't like something you've asked." But Carter could "take it as well as dish it out and, unlike many other politicians . . . , he'll eventually respond directly to a question if you press him hard enough." And while Neal Peirce saw a "cruel side" ("Carter's occasionally mechanical smile, his icy blue eyes in anger, his lashing out at opponents, his exaggerating his own public record while promising never to tell a lie"), he concluded that these things were outweighed by the compassion which "appears again and again."

This author's own experiences in the Plains of August, 1976, suggest that some of the younger reporters had internalized Carter's own self-defenses. Seated with four reporters at a table in the Back Porch Cafe, I was asked what I thought about Carter. I told the group that I really didn't understand him. One of them told me that was because I was not a Southerner.

"But I understood Estes Kefauver," I said.

"Kefauver was not from the DEEP South."

"What about Lyndon Johnson," I countered.

"That is really the Southwest."

"Well, I did a study of Walter George and I think I understand him. He was raised in Preston, Georgia, ten miles from here, and had his permanent home in Vienna, Jody Powell's hometown. He was a clear, responsible conservative."

"For what period did you study him?"

"When he was chairman of the Senate Foreign Relations Committee and the Senate Finance Committee."

"Aha! The Washington influence!"

I pressed on. "What do you think of the way Carter's religion was used in this campaign?"

"Carter didn't introduce his religion into the campaign. He only answered our questions about it."

"But he had a chapter of his born again experiences, his religion, in *Why Not the Best?* It was written in early 1975 and published later that year.

With that the gathering broke up—in thirty seconds flat. One reporter remembered he had another engagement. One saw a friend across the room. So did another. The fourth muttered something I did not catch and left.

Politicians and ordinary people picked up similar themes. As Carter wrapped up the nomination in June, Democratic leaders in Congress saw him as having the earmarks of greatness. House Speaker Carl Albert predicted that Carter would win the presidency with a landslide greater than Lyndon Johnson's in 1964. Senate Majority Leader Mike Mansfield saw Carter unifying the Democratic Party in much the same way Franklyn Roosevelt had. Martin Luther King, Sr., in his closing prayer at the convention suggested that God had sent Carter to America in its time of need. In the late summer, on the day before the opening of the fall campaign, Clarence Dodson, the president of Carter's Bible class in the Plains Baptist Church, compared Jimmy Carter to

Saint Paul. Using a lesson from the Book of Galatians (in which the critics of Paul question whether or not he was one of the twelve original Apostles), Dodson turned to Carter, who was in the class, saying, "Here the people are accusing Paul, like the people . . . trying to cut you down, saying all manner of things against you that are false."

Those around Carter shared a reflected glory. Scheer, in his *Playboy* article, for example, described Carter's aides as tough and effective packagers—like Nixon's palace guards in these respects. But they were not the same in crucial respects. "I found it increasingly difficult to think of them as possessing that cold-blooded uniformity of the Nixon gendarmes." Jody Powell was not "tight-assed." At least some of them were as "hard-drinking, fornicating, pot-smoking, free-thinking a group as has been seen in higher politics." Worries about their throwing up the "palace guard" faded as one stayed up drinking with them in "some redneck bar." Even the devotion to Carter was seen positively. As Margaret Shannon noted in April, 1976, Carter's top aides "are one-candidate men, and Carter is the candidate. They don't have the sort of track record so common among political professionals for hire—one candidate this time around, his opponent or opposite the next time around."

This idealizing tendency covered Carter's family as well. Gail Sheehy portrayed Rosalynn as an equal partner to Jimmy in her article "Ladies and Gentlemen, the Second President—Sister Rosalynn." She was like the pioneer women of old: "Sister Rosalynn is the very essence of the pioneer wife, the kind you've seen in the 'big sky' movies, the one who draws a weary hand across her brow at the end, straightens her apron, picks up the drowned child, determined to get the seed in the ground for next season." Lillian Hellman, in a fall article, saw a very different Rosalynn: to her Rosalynn was surely going to be another Eleanor Roosevelt as First Lady. To Norman Mailer, Rosalynn was the wonderful, unpretentious archetypal American woman:

With her heart-shaped face, her large eyes, her direct features, her absence of patrician hesitation to approve or to judge, she could even have been a hostess or a waitress, but a most marvelous, intelligent and attractive waitress—a movie star of a waitress in a good 30's film—the sort who gives you cheer about the future of the human condition. . . . Something of that pent-up vigor, and practicality, and tough confidence that lives in 10 million American housewives was in her, but with the difference that the vigor was hardly pent-up, and the intelligence was active.

Lillian Carter epitomized the rooted, moral, and compassionate mother— the source of Jimmy's ambition and caring. Orde Coombs, in a profile on the candidate's mother for *New York*, described Lillian as a woman who has "traveled to many countries around the world, but she has remained a small-town woman, anchored in Christian beliefs and in an unflinching devotion to what is right." But she was no shallow Christian, she possessed a deep insight and a passion for the good. She was proof of Faulkner's suggestion in *Intruder in the Dust* that great things come through the women and children. As Coombs said,

"Faulkner knew that women like Lillian Carter existed, and they always worked on the circumstances and always broke the rules when the heart had its reasons." Indeed, in understanding Lillian one can unlock the mystery of Jimmy Carter: ". . . as I look at those watering gray-blue eyes, I understand the passion and pain of Jimmy Carter, and I sense where the chinks in his armor lie, why he plays it both ways . . . All of Lillian Carter's morality works for her son in 1976. It is a morality based simply on doing for your neighbor what you would like him to do for you . . . it is essentially a morality of the past." For Henry Allen, Lillian Carter was the representative of the doers in the South— the rural, middle-class families wedged between the celebrated plantation owners of *Gone with the Wind* and the desperate, impoverished folk of *Tobacco Road.* "It's a class which has built the churches, 'carried' the farmers on loans from planting to harvest, ginned the cotton, sold the dry goods, and controlled the politics. . . . Rich enough to be proud of 'taking care' of their blacks, but rich enough, too, to buy the farm machinery that drove them off the land."

For some observers the entire Carter family transcended the petty rivalries, jealousies, and competing interests that plague many families. As James Neyland wrote: "Gloria and Ruth didn't take anything away from themselves or their families by going out and campaigning for their brother; Miss Lillian didn't take anything away from herself by looking after Amy while Jimmy and Rosalynn were traveling around the country. And Amy hasn't missed out on any love by spending time with her grandmother at the Pond House; if anything she has gained." Indeed, healing was what the Carters were all about. Miss Lillian, a nurse by profession and a Peace Corps worker by choice, committed herself to the task of serving the sick in Sumter County and, for a brief time, in India. Ruth, in her lectures and writings, appeals to those seeking inner, spiritual healing. And Jimmy, some felt, was destined to heal the wounds of the entire nation. Many agreed with Norman Mailer's vision of Carter as a "man who saw it as his purpose to save America, and the wonder of it was that he was believable."

And for some the tiny town of Plains became a kind of rural Camelot, a haven from commerciality and unrest in contemporary society. Norman Mailer wrote:

A place like Plains could be modest by the measure of its income and yet offer an unmistakable well-ordered patina, a promise that the mysterious gentility of American life was present, that there were still people interested in running things without showing the traces, that the small-town establishment remained a factor to be taken account of among all the other factors like exhaust roar and sewage slick and those plastic toylands stretching to the American horizon.

Reynolds Price was utterly enchanted with the healing powers of Plains after an evening with Carter in a café in the summer of '76. As he later wrote:

With all the cold fears our past four Presidents have drenched us in, all the seedy disbeliefs they've sowed, I left . . . that night feeling better for my own kin's chances now and lighter on my feet, which slid in Georgia mud—purple [royal orange perhaps] Sumter County clay, the ground of many Carters over 125 years; apparently a national family at last to feed us with stories and the actions they cause: varied fare and nutritious, the stories of care and honest consolation that we've needed for very much longer than was good.

Some of these surmises about Jimmy Carter, his people, and his place undoubtedly reflected some real and positive qualities. But the conclusions themselves were based less on solid analysis of his political past and surroundings than on a tendency to catch fragments from his campaign behavior, from a parable in his autobiography, and from stories told by the family or neighbors, weaving out of them a flimsy but rich tapestry portraying Carter's overall virtues and mission. Sometimes the conclusions drawn were so glowing, so perfect, that they could not actually apply to any mere human being. In short, many Carter watchers (including several modern-day bards—the campaign's traveling press) were caught in a process of fantasy—"the power, process or result of creating mental images modified by need, wish or desire."

What was there about Carter that encouraged such mental processes? How was he able to evoke such fantasies?

As Patrick Caddell has suggested, Carter's anonymity was an asset, making it possible for "large parts of the electorate [to] project their own desires on to Governor Carter."

This anonymity, as we have seen, gave Carter an extraordinary freedom to present himself and his themes, sometimes in an emotionally rich, fablelike form. Moreover, his technique of sending out so many different signals about where he stood politically as well as what he was like perpetuated the ambiguity. In a situation where so many individuals were called upon to respond to him without any independently derived prior knowledge of him, there was more than the usual tendency to respond to these complex signals by picking out the ones that fit ones predisposition, ignoring those other signals as some kind of irrelevant noise.

James Fallows's response to Carter, given above, is a fairly explicit description of this psychological process. In another passage he describes Carter's role in the whole process. In winning people over to his side, Carter

was a genius at using a phrase, a gesture, a code word that his listeners assumed to be of greater significance than it was. He led call-and-response like a preacher in a black church; he talked with environmentalists about the sins of the Corps of Engineers; he told the American Legion about his family's three centuries of military service; and he told everyone in back-room meetings that, while he could not promise a single appointment to a single person, 'I think you'll be pleasantly surprised by the choices I make,' and 'I think you'll agree with what I do 95 percent of the time." Espying these chunks in the water, each onlooker viewed them as tips of icebergs, indicating vast, hidden extensions below.

This tendency was evident in the assumption of many liberals that Carter would really be more liberal than some of his conservative statements suggested. TRB, for example, suggested in the *New Republic* that "Carter will be more liberal than is commonly supposed. There is a ring to that speech he gave as governor on Law Day. . . . It was a speech, quietly delivered, challenging 'the powerful and the influential' to unfreeze the status quo. . . . Quite a speech." Stanley Cloud of *Time* magazine predicted that "conservatives may feel deceived when they discover Carter's basic liberalism borders on populism." When Carter talked conservatively, well, he was simply doing what they viewed Roosevelt as having done in 1932—hiding his populist light under a conservative cover so he could win an election. Scheer in the *Playboy* interview even confronted Carter with the idea that he might be more liberal than he appeared: "Still, not everybody's sure whether you're a conservative in liberal clothing or vice versa. F.D.R., for instance, turned out to be something of a surprise to people who'd voted for him, because he hadn't seemed as progressive before he was elected as he turned out to be. Could you be a surprise that way?" Carter, to his credit, denied both the Rooseveltian parallel and the clothing problem, maintaining that the Democratic platform on which he was running was "very progressive, very liberal, very socially motivated." He had made many promises toward progressive action during the campaign, and did not think there would be many people "disappointed—or surprised" when he carried out those commitments as President.

It was not just the reporters who built fantasies about Carter; the voters, too, seem generally to have interpreted Carter to fit their predisposition. Surveys taken by *The New York Times* and CBS throughout the primaries indicated that conservative voters saw a conservative Carter, moderates a moderate Carter, and liberals a liberal Carter. This is supported by a poll done by President Ford's campaign after the Pennsylvania primary. Comparing the normal Democratic voting pattern in terms of demographic and geographic factors in Pennsylvania with Carter's vote, Robert M. Teeter, Ford's director of research, found that Carter had won more votes in every category than he should have statistically, with one exception—the Catholic voter. In a poll Teeter did right after the conventions, respondents consistently placed Carter near themselves on two attitude scales (the partisan dimension: economic liberal to conservative; and traditional values: attitudes toward marijuana, abortion, and pornography). Most interesting, on the traditional values scale Carter was perceived as substantially more conservative than Ford (though on the partisan dimension scale the expected Democratic/Republican split prevailed).

The tendency to read ambiguities to fit one's own predisposition is a general human one. In Carter's case several specific factors helped predispose people toward him.

Personally, he was a spellbinder, with some groups. His ability to weave his magic over a wide variety of people—blacks, county sheriffs, children, college students, residents of "old folks" homes—impressed reporters and political activists alike. As Tom Wicker noted, anyone who doesn't understand "the mystical appeal of Jimmy Carter to the American people in 1976" should have attended a senior citizens' center gathering near Harrisburg, Pennsylvania. Carter attacked America's problems with Vietnam and Watergate while his audience was "rapt throughout these formulations except for a few heads nodding sagely." David Broder of the Washington *Post* described Carter's magic with a black YMCA crowd in Milwaukee. Carter spoke "with an eloquence, a simplicity, a directness that moved listeners of both races. . . . One would have to be made of stone to be unmoved by the surge of emotion—the communion—between those black listeners and that white speaker who hopes to be their president."

This charm was most directly related to Carter's ability to connect, seemingly on a personal and intimate basis, with many different types of people, whether individually or in groups. When he sees a pretty woman, Helen Dewar observed, he will stop "for a tender second over a hand clasp . . . [that] exudes appreciation and susceptibility. He is, incongruously, a toucher—a hand passes lightly over a fine blond head or flicks a flawless young cheek." She continues: "He has one truly remarkable platform gift—the ability to establish a sense of intimacy with each member of an audience." College students, for example, "with their distrust of bombast, dig him, in part because he appears to be innocent of demagoguery even when delivering the demagogic string of emotion-stirring words that usually bring his talks to a close." According to Fallows, "His intelligence and magnetism soon banished all thought of the limits of his background. . . . He was fully aware of this power and used it whenever he could. Early in the campaign, when trying to convince people that his candidacy was not a joke, he placed high hopes on his meetings with newspaper editorial boards."

His charm, for some, was also the result of his personal "power"—his impudence, his daring, his skill in doing the unusual and carrying it off. Not only did he seem to be free of the constraints of shame and fear that humble so many human beings, he was successful. Garry Wills had been initially intrigued by Carter's ability to get a group of potentially hostile south Georgia sheriffs to eat out of his hands through his soft, schoolmarmish ways. Hunter Thompson was hooked by Carter's ability to discomfort Ted Kennedy, his verbal pyrotechnics in assaulting the establishment (the lawyers and judges present for the Law Day speech), and the show of extemporaneous skill. And TRB was impressed and astonished by

the calculated impudence with which he told what he planned to say in his inaugural. . . . I never met a candidate like him before and *it was swell copy* (emphasis added). The confrontation of Southern and New England cultures was wonderful, too; when the clean-cut YMCA-type young man at Durham made the reticent Yankee ladies cringe by asking Carter straight out, had he been saved?—and Carter answered quietly, yes, that he was a 'born-again Christian' and what was the next question?

ABC's Sam Donaldson took note of the aplomb with which Carter would try things (such as helping clean the mud pond in Plains) no other candidate would ever think of.

Some were even attracted by the little dark corners they thought they saw in Carter's soul. David Nordan and Curtis Wilkie were fascinated with the treatment received by the "Eastern establishment" when its representatives trekked to Plains. Wilkie, a Southern native working for the Boston *Globe* also showed some veiled delight at Carter's behavior under pressure. On a flight over New Hampshire, Wilkie had asked Carter if he had talked to William Loeb (right-wing editor/publisher of the Manchester *Union Leader*). Carter assured him, "I have not."

"Has any of your staff met with him?" Wilkie continued.

"I said I didn't see him."

"But did any of your aides see him?" Wilkie persisted.

"I said I did not see him." "And he looked at me with those icy, bright-blue eyes," Wilkie recalled with a shudder of apparent relish at the memory of Carter's barely suppressed fury.

Larry King, a native Texan, explicitly expressed his "left-handed" admiration for Carter: "Jimmy Carter has proved he's smart and tough. I also suspect he's half mean . . . There's this history of the South having been shut out so long that even us longtime expatriates defensively feel that should Jimmy Cah-tah prove to be a sumbitch, then he's at least *our* sumbitch."

As one Carter observer noted, the little signs of Carter's manipulativeness were appealing to some.

Distrust is precisely Carter's appeal. Cleverly, he manages to appear slightly dishonest. Allegations that he had been less than honest in the past do not hurt him; they play into the scheme. . . . Like most victims of con men who are lured by the prospect of easy gain, many of Carter's supporters think he is really one of their own and that he is just stringing along their opponents for the votes. . . . Southern whites see him as a redneck after the black votes, and blacks seem him as the liberal's liberal conning the rednecks.

In short, Carter's anonymity at the beginning of the race, his ability to forge out of that situation an idealized self-presentation that most people bought, a complex set of values and issue stances that could be variously interpreted, his personal power manifest in his ability to weave a spell over the people as well as the elites, and the final proof of his extraordinary ability in the miracle he pulled off—those were all elements in making him the subject of so many fantasies.

Yet one cannot understand Carter's appeal to the public, especially to the millions who voted for him and never met him, without looking at the content of his themes and its relation to some deeper need in the American people as a whole. TRB of the *New Republic* said in early 1976: "My impression is that audiences yearn to believe Jimmy Carter. They are looking for something. It is in his manner and tone."

What were so many Americans looking for in 1976? More important, how did the Carter themes meet their needs? Americans in the past had always looked to the President for psychological assurances as well as political leadership. He has symbolized the nation, embodying its hopes and fears and making crucial decisions for it. His fate has been viewed as the fate of the nation as a whole.

This feeling has generally been accompanied by a tendency to idealize the man in the office. In the past, standard public opinion polls show the President rated consistently as one of the "most admired men" in America. In a 1945 poll, for example, when people were asked, "In your opinion, who is the greatest person living or dead?" Roosevelt ranked first—with Lincoln and Jesus Christ appearing second and third respectively.

The existence of an emotional attachment to the President, moreover, is evident in the response of the public to his unexpected death while in office. After John Kennedy was assassinated many people felt a deep personal grief, as if they had been personally bereaved. In one poll 50 percent of those sampled said they had wept, 43 percent could not eat, 48 percent experienced insomnia, 68 percent acknowledged "a sense of nervousness and tension."

These attachments were particularly clear in children. For them the President has traditionally been viewed as a friend, someone to trust. Indeed, in the minds of one sampling of schoolchildren the President took on heroic proportions. As David Easton and Jack Dennis pointed out: "From the earliest grade the child sees the President as on a commanding height, far above adults as well as children. The President flies on angel wings, smiling, beneficent, powerful, almost beyond the realm of mere mortals. Young children view the President as a storehouse of inexhaustible virtues—wisdom, benevolence, power, trustworthiness, and exemplary leadership. . . . He has power to do what is best and does."

This idealizing does not stop with children. The authors of college textbooks covering the presidency give the incumbent similar virtues of omnipotence and benevolence. The President, as Tom Cronin notes, is usually portrayed as the "strategic catalyst" and "genuine architect" of American political and public policy. He is a central figure on the world scene and the nation's personal and moral leader., " a symbol of all good past and to come." If, only if, the right man is placed in the White House all will be well, and, somehow, whoever is in the White House is the right man."

But this tendency to trust and idealize the President began to decline as America went through the traumas of Vietnam and Watergate. The policies that didn't work, the widely publicized statements by the President that turned out to be lies, the questionable use of presidential authority—all undermined the faith in the wisdom and morality of the President ingrained in so many. The polls show the diminishing popular satisfaction with Presidents. While Eisenhower received an overall 57 percent satisfaction rating, Kennedy, 52, Johnson was down to 32, and Nixon reached the then all-time low of 28 percent. Further, in 1972 only 27 percent of the American people had a "great deal" of confidence in the executive branch (down 14 points since 1966). In 1973, 75 percent of the American people believed that the government had lied to them to some degree.

This dissatisfaction has since extended down to the grammar-school level. By 1973 children were seeing the President as a negative figure. In a study done in Texas, Professor Harold Barger found "so strongly a massive disenchantment with the President that even if it were possible to theoretically separate the man from the office for children and adolescents, the residue of cynicism and confusion might well effect their perceptions of subsequent men in the office for some time to come." He found this disenchantment in all ages and ethnic backgrounds, and so negative it exceeded "even the unprecedented low ratings and cynical responses of adults." Indeed, by 1973 political alienation and cynicism had reached such a point with all members of society that Stanley Hoffman noted that "now, no administration can ask for basic trust."

Ironically, trust was precisely what Carter was asking for—and apparently receiving. As Carter himself pointed out, while Americans retained deep concerns about specific issues, "that's not why they're voting." What they were looking for, he explained, was "somebody they can trust." And the trust he asked for was an unusual kind; it necessitated a leap of faith, a giving of the heart to an unknown stranger. There was a long period of testing, proving, and getting acquainted to justify the trust.

Carter's ability to reverse the prevailing trend in public opinion can be explained in part by his attempt to articulate this demoralization. Further, he had some answers as to what had gone wrong in our national life—we could look to him for some type of correction. His answers were soothing, easy, and did not demand much of us, while promising a restoration of national self-esteem.

Carter attributed America's troubles, as we have seen, to a clique in Washington: the people were really good, their values the correct ones. To transcend and reform the government, all that was needed was a leader from the outside who was his own person and represented an idealized version of the American people—good, compassionate, moral. He would be the vehicle whereby America would once again have a government as good as its people. To deal with the longer term problems—the fragmentation and anomie of modern industrial society as well as the breakdown of traditional moral structures—he summoned a national nostalgia for a romanticized past. We simply needed to reaffirm the older values by electing a man to office who embodied them in his own life, while extending the morality and love shown in our own idealized private lives of the community as whole.

His populism, as we have seen, went down easily. There was no dealing with the problem of updating an individualistic morality so it would provide real guidance for the mass industrialized society. In identifying himself with the people and presenting himself as an outsider, he was able to attract strong emotional identification from a large spectrum of the populace who felt depressed and resentful. And while demonstrating his ability to win the people's trust and his capacity for "rule," he was also assuring members of the elite that his election would legitimate and restore political authority in America.

Carter's real genius was in seeing that beneath the demoralization, Americans were still yearning for the good authority they thought they had had in the past. As we have seen, Carter held a traditional conception of the presidency (in essence, the "imperial presidency") and projected himself as possessing the extraordinary combination of traits that made him equal to that exalted office. At the same time Carter showed himself as different from those who had betrayed us in the past. His own career and past seemed to be anchored in religious and moral values that suggested that he had the kinds of inner constraints lacking in some of our past Presidents. For some, it was simply that Carter said he would never lie. Liberals should support Carter, ACLU leader Charles Morgan said, because "He's the only candidate who's comfortable saying he won't lie." The whole Washington community, he continued, is "permeated with lies." And acceptance of that situation "cuts across the heart of democracy."

Actually, this desire and need for powerful authority is not unique to Americans. It runs deep in most political communities and cannot be treated simply as some infantile aberration. When we are in dependent situations, as all human beings are (first as children in a family, then as citizens in a complex polity where decisions affecting the existence of the entire group are centralized in the hands of its leaders), we want that authority to be both strong and good—so that the power will be used on our behalf rather than against us. If our leaders are portrayed to us in their individuality, we may even come to see them as friends, as people we know and care about and love. The affective connections, one-sided though they may be, are nonetheless powerful, as reactions to the death of a President show.

But Carter's spellbinding, hypnotic, fantasy-evoking effect cannot be accounted for simply in terms of a rational, more or less conscious, desire for a good and strong leader. Any political leader can be expected to attempt to fill this need by presenting himself as a potentially competent and "good" President. In his presentation however, Carter went beyond simply showing these traits as part of a campaign. Hearkening back to the images of the President found in the minds of children and the oversimplified college textbooks of the past, Carter projected himself as a man destined for the office, with a perfection of the requisite virtues (including a becoming modesty) that we associate with the presidency.

To understand the psychological dynamics of this kind of appeal, the description by psychoanalysts of the nature of the charismatic leader and the charismatic tie is helpful. Heinz Kohut has argued that the spellbinder often makes grandiose claims for himself that are all the more persuasive because they are deeply based in his personality. As a result of his own feelings of infallibility, this kind of personality tends to "formulate certain simple and clearly depicted goals—whether in the realm of religion or of politics." Further, "although these goals may be rational in appearance, they are, nevertheless, the manifestations of an archaic self which, in accordance with the solipsistic conceptions of early life, is still experienced as possessing absolute power and un-limited knowledge. It is this connection with the archaic self which lends dog-matic certainty to the opinion held by such individuals, and it explains the ruthlessness with which they are able to pursue their goals."

Moreover, Kohut suggests that these qualities are apt to be deeply attrac-tive to others, exerting a "quasi-hypnotic effect" on many people. This is be-cause "deeply rooted in our earliest childhood there remains in us a longing to merge with an all-powerful and all-knowing figure. This yearning finds an ap-parently irresistible fulfillment for many in their total submission to a Mes-sianic leader and to his dogmatic beliefs."

Irvine Schiffer, in his work on the charismatic leader, sees a similar pattern. The charismatic leader, he argues, adopts themes that permit others to identify with him and to project their own solipsistic (i.e., self-centered) tendencies on him, perhaps working "their own creative ambitions for themselves" through his career. Certain themes typify this kind of leadership. The charismatic leader is apt to have an aspect of foreignness about him (because in our growth toward independence, we displace our identifications onto nonfamiliar figures) but also some familiarity (so we can engage in the delights of self-recognition). He is "blessed" with minor blemishes or weaknesses that enable us to identify with him (he "needs us, as we need him"). He has a calling to be a public ser-vant—which is confirmed by his ability to attract an organized following. He is combative, active, willing to fight—ready to become the victor or the victim, the winner or the loser. He may have money, but it is best if he is a self-made man and if the money is not used for personal gain but to obtain love. (In con-trast to his bold quest for power, "the ego of the charismatic figure shapes a libidinous plea for confirmation from an outside world.") He can even engage in play-acting with the "blessing" of his public. If he believes his people want a strong person, he is capable of acting strong; when they want humility, he acts humble.

Whatever Carter's underlying character structure, he projected himself in ways that tapped some of these charismatic themes. In his persona he showed that supreme self-confidence Kohut has described. In his rise to power he evoked the themes outlined by Schiffer. He was different—an "outsider," a born again Christian, a Southerner. And he did things other candidates did not—bearing testimony of the gospel on the campaign trail, for example. But he was not all that different when one got to "know" him. He believed in sepa-ration of church and state, had traditional values, and would not force his values on others. Despite his strength, he had some weaknesses—he had been a phar-isee in his younger days and was stubborn in the present. He was aggressive, combative, active—but he also needed the people who worked for him and believed in him. And if there was a touch of posturing, a little innocent political fooling of some people, that was all right. He had to win the office and such act-ing was a necessity to gain the power.

A man projecting himself in this way, however, has certain vulnerabilities.

He is apt to be found out—no human being is so all-powerful and all-good. Further, his relationship with his public is apt to be shaky, particularly if he does not deliver on his promises. Though others project onto him (as an ideal figure) a wide variety of their own desires and qualities, no real relationship is formed. Further, fantasy provides insubstantial fare for the human psyche, and the tie based on it is apt to be ephemeral. Any political leader who depends on fantasies in a major way is building a fragile base—especially if he holds the kind of office where his actual virtues and vices stand to be revealed.

There was evidence in some of the polls that Carter's tie to many voters was fragile. Though he was about fifteen points ahead of either Republican alternative in some of the opinion surveys conducted in June, almost half his supporters could not answer correctly most questions concerning him and approximately one third had difficulty answering any of them correctly. As Patrick Caddell noted, "he was perceived as a strong person, stronger than Ford, but people were uneasy with him as a person." (Some wondered, however, if he was qualified to lead in the foreign policy area). In his own postconvention polling, Caddell still found this uneasiness; though Carter was viewed as being in harmony with most people's thinking, many had doubts about him.

Robert Teeter, in his polling for Ford, found a similar pattern. Carter was widely viewed as a competent, strong, moral, and Christian man. But people seemed to have two major questions about him: Was he qualified to be President? Wasn't his religion a little bizarre? Caddell, in the later polls, saw essentially the same pattern. Carter was widely perceived as having the qualities he claimed for himself. But as Jordan noted, "we suffered from the weirdo factor. Here was a guy from a different part of the country who talked quite openly about his religion, who had never served in national office before."

Individual reporters, commenting on their own reactions to Carter, give an even clearer picture of the nature of the tie. Exalted perceptions of Carter were accompanied by glimpses of the contradictory cues he emitted and the fragmentary nature of the data they did have about him. And feeling that what they did see somehow did not add up would surface now and then.

Kandy Stroud expressed a definite ambivalence:

My perceptions of him over a two year period were as complex and contradictory as he was himself. At one moment, he seemed unimpressive, small, average, pleasant enough, but hardly presidential. At another moment, he could be the statesman, grappling with the most complex issues of our day. He could put an audience of labor leaders to sleep, stir an audience of blacks to tears . . . Personally I find when I am in Carter's presence I am mesmerized, overcome by his charm. He can be as hypnotic as a snake, tantalizing as a spider, and he is as disciplined, spiritual and brilliant a man as I have ever met. And yet, five minutes after I've left him I find myself questioning the favorable impression.

Sam Donaldson of ABC television experienced similar competing emotions.

One part of me says I know him, that I grew up with him, or at least in the same kind of environment. He does things no recent President has done (e.g. wallow in a mud hole). But the other side of me says I need to know a lot more about him. He is the best politician in the technical sense that I have seen—best understood how to please the people and get the votes—he's like an electronically-guided self-correcting missile—automatically corrects himself. He is skillful, brilliant and has an amazing political ability. . . . Carter always manages to remove possibilities of controversy when the press is grasping for it.

Robert Scheer spelled it out another way. He felt Carter was some new face needed in the United States. But sensing a disturbing, "performancelike" quality about the Carter operation, he wrote: "It's not that Carter is shallow and exploitative but that he and his staff have decided to submit to . . . campaigning that is inherently shallow and exploitative." One senses that Carter is a good man who cares for his family and his real roots. "My editor tells me, 'Hey, I really like this guy.' Then, not thirty seconds later, he wonders aloud if we've been had. Which is how it always is with a James Earl Carter performance."

Mike Royko expressed this ambivalence in its most black and white form. He saw Carter's rise as possibly something special:

The American dream of anybody making it to the highest positions in our country is a beautiful concept that most of us don't believe in anymore. We feel anybody who makes it big in politics has strings attached to him, and we figure he's in it for what he can grab for himself and his backer. So, in our Bicentennial year, of all times, along comes this grass roots character from a small town in Georgia, and nobody can figure out where the strings are attached, much less who's on the other end pulling them.

Indeed, Royko dared to hope that his "cornball American dream come true" would "be for real." It would be "so nice if it turned out that Jimmy Carter was everything he said he was in order to achieve his triumph—a man of decency, honor, compassion, love and truth." But there was another alternative he hoped he would not have to face: "if he isn't all the things he says he is, then, he is just the opposite—he is the single most cynical, deceitful, dishonest man in America. There can't be any in-between—not with the kinds of virtues that he is claiming as his own."

# TWENTY

---

# Victory

*Summer Solstice*

WHATEVER DOUBTS some people may have had about Jimmy Carter, they were not apparent in Plains, Georgia, in the summer of 1976. There was a magic in that town. Like some modern-day Brigadoon, Carter staffers joked, it seemed to materialize each morning just as the stream of journalists and tourists turned the corner on the road from Americus. Main Street with its quaint, newly painted stores and the refurbished Seaboard Coastline Railroad depot on Logan Square (which had not seen a train for some time and now served as Carter headquarters) seemed to have been lifted out of the 1890s. Moreover, the friendly townspeople, fresh air, clean sky, green fields, and red clay of southwest Georgia evoked a nostalgic memory of a preindustrial, preurban, pre-Vietnam pre-Watergate America.

Carter himself seemed loved by everyone in town. Beginning with his win in Pennsylvania, his friends had gathered at the train depot headquarters on Tuesday primary nights; there they would munch on "presidential peanuts" and sip fruit punch prepared by local volunteers while watching the election returns. Yells would rock the old depot when his victories were proclaimed, while volunteers would take telephone inquiries from reporters. The night he was nominated, some 4,000 people celebrated by dancing in the streets. On his return from the convention thousands of locals and tourists who had waited in the sweltering mid-July heat greeted him, waving flags and cheering. Members of the Plains Women's Club or the Peanut Brigade prepared food for all his victory celebrations. Others did their share by telling reporters, historians, and political scientists what a good boy, student, friend, man, and neighbor Jimmy was and had been. Some even elaborated a bit to make him more interesting—telling how Carter might have been valedictorian of their class had he not played hooky at the end of his senior year; or some would mention a girlfriend that he never really had.

This magical mood was fed by the men and women pouring into Plains. The tourists drove in on two-lane state roads from Albany or Columbus or Vienna or Interstate 85. (Shortly after the nomination Hugh Carter put the tourist count at 300 to 500 a day.) Generally they walked down Main Street hoping for a glance of Jimmy or, if not him, maybe Billy or Gloria or Amy. And if Miss Lillian was in town, they would file through the campaign headquarters in the train depot for a few lively words and pictures (but without flash bulbs, "Doctor's Orders," the sign on the wall said) with the matriarch of the Carter clan. They crowded around the train platform when press conferences were held and beamed when Jimmy mingled with them to kiss a baby or touch a hand. Some took the two-dollar tour (the only one at that time), in which an enterprising physics professor from Georgia Southwestern, David Ewing, pointed out forty points of interest, including where Jimmy had been born, his first home, his second, his tree house, the Lions' swimming pool he helped to build. But most of the time the tourists had to settle for Hugh Carter's store, where they could buy a copy of *The Miracle of Jimmy Carter*, prominently advertised by posters in the front windows, a stenciled twenty-five-cent map of Plains, or a more expensive Jimmy Carter bumper sticker. Or they could drift into Turner's general store or the Walters' grocery, which remained much as they had always been. They might even find a beer at Billy's gas station or at the recently opened Skylight Club, owned and operated by a black couple.

The politically powerful also came—by small private plane or chartered bus from Atlanta—for appointments with the Democratic nominee. In early August, Ralph Nader visited Plains; he umpired a softball game, talked for hours with Carter, and pronounced his stand on consumer affairs admirable, a "breath of fresh air." On the Wednesday before the Republican convention, Senator Walter Mondale flew into Americus for a visit. Later that same morning CIA Director George Bush arrived at the Plains airstrip aboard an Army helicopter, briefed Carter and Mondale for five hours, and departed. Later that afternoon California Governor Jerry Brown flew in for an overnight visit.* Throughout the summer experts were bused in from the airport in Atlanta to brief Carter in the Pond House in Plains—on matters of defense policy, economy, foreign policy, energy, international economics, and domestic policy. When it was over, they came into the yard or onto the platform at the train depot for a press conference, lining up behind Jimmy Carter and saying nice things about him. Carter, in his soft, monotone voice, summarized their discussions but avoided taking any stances himself except to say he was not concerned about the problems of vertical integration in the energy industries. Although

---

* Brown's attitude, as a challenger in the late primaries, was an important indication that the party leaders would pull together, though perhaps ambivalently, for the fall campaign. After a night in the Carter home, Brown and Carter strolled down Main Street. Wearing a suit and tie while the other men wore sports shirts, Brown also made a few sub rosa comments on the number of Carters in town and the idling motors of the Carter "gas guzzlers," which ran throughout the stroll. But in their press conference Brown pledged his support to the Carter campaign, noted his "intelligence and integrity" and how he had "confounded the experts." He has brought the people together, he said. "This is just the beginning of a process of reconciliation that has been a long time in coming."

the gnats were out and the reporters wiggled and slapped at them, Carter stood calm even when an insect would light on his forehead or crawl toward his mouth.

The high point of each day was the press conference or the photo opportunity. The pool reporters even followed the candidate to Rosalynn's family reunion (the Murrays) where they learned the hot news that the Carters had contributed a jar of butter beans to the "Groaning Board." When Carter visited the nearby agricultural experimental station, the press corps was with him to hear how Carter had turned to the researchers for information on the various uses of the peanut. They piled into a press bus for a trip to Macon for the fifth annual Capricorn Records Barbeque and Summer Games at Lakeside Park. They followed Carter to church on Sunday and noted his comments on the Bible. The bulletin boards at the press building and the Best Western Motel in nearby Americus were checked regularly to see if a softball game was scheduled for that evening. Indeed, those games had become a kind of mania in which Billy and a team of reporters ("The Newstwisters") put their all into a victory over Jimmy ("Big News") and his Secret Service team.

Amy and Rosalynn and Lillian and Billy and Gloria and Cousin Hugh and Uncle Alton were all watched and interviewed. Even the merchants on Main Street—the Williamses, Turners, Dodsons, and Godwins—appeared in the press. A few members of the press corps fanned out into the community and surrounding countryside—often with the aid of a volunteer from the depot headquarters—to locate former Carter school teachers, classmates, or employees. But even the most energetic were hard pressed to find any of the few local anti-Jimmy types who later turned up in the Ford camp. Occasionally a reporter might go to the Sumter County Courthouse in Americus to study old land records, or find the editor of the Americus *Time-Recorder* for an explanation of some old political story or another, running the considerable risk of missing a softball game.

Overall, there was a feeling that Carter was destined to become President. From time to time during the spring and summer Carter talked as if he were already President. (On "Face the Nation" he had said, ". . . I think they still feel that I'm a good President," and at the convention, speaking to the New Jersey delegation, he said, "it is my responsibility as President . . .") The operation of the Committee on the Transition, his issues task forces, and his Talent Bank 77 suggested that his major concern was not the election, but planning for the government he would soon lead. Carter's friends in town, assuming he would be President, sponsored a citizens' committee trip from Plains to Johnson City, Texas, to see how former President Johnson's hometown had survived the hordes of tourists. Cousin Hugh Carter was predicting the tourist flow would rise to 2,000 a day around the November election. And at the Plains High School reunion in June, the class of '41 made their plans to hold their next reunion five years hence—in the White House (just as five years earlier they had held their first reunion at the Georgia governor's mansion). Even Theodore H.

White, who has spent his life covering political leaders around the world, caught this extraordinary mood. Over coffee in the newly opened Back Porch Cafe, next to the press headquarters, White told a reporter from the *Americus Time-Recorder,* "I think Jimmy Carter has a chance to become the first candidate ever to win all 50 states in an election."

## Small Flags

For all the magic, a few stories suggested a more complex, more mundane reality. Early in the season Gloria's husband, Walter Spann, who had been involved in a project with three other south Georgia entrepreneurs to sell souvenir titles to plots of land next to the Carter farms, had the ground cut out from under him when Carter condemned the whole project in a statement to the press (the plots kept selling all the same). In early July, A. Z. Pittman, an elderly black man, his wife, and their seven children were forced out of their ramshackle home across the street from Jimmy Carter's house, when the owner, Marlin Poole, decided to tear it down. He had told Pittman that he would have to move because Mr. Jimmy was becoming President. (Pittman didn't blame Carter, he was a "fine Christian gentleman"; and Jody Powell and Pittman both explained to the press that Carter had known nothing of the eviction until after the house was demolished while he was at the convention.)

There were also some incongruities in the overall Carter image. Though he had pledged not to make Ford's pardon of Nixon an issue in the campaign, Carter proceeded to link the two men together, referring on occasion to their close relationship and calling Ford the "appointed president." On one of his few forays out of town, at a noontime rally on August 4 in Manchester, New Hampshire, he attacked Ford for "neglecting his basic responsibilities" so that he could "chase an ex-movie actor around the country in search of convention delegates." Later, when asked if connecting Ford to Nixon was unfair, Carter said: "It's not my fault Nixon is unsavory." Carter's "populism" was also hard to reconcile with the lobster claws and caviar at a late August party in Los Angeles (given for him by Lew Wasserman, board chairman of the Music Corporation of America) and the sleek limousine arranged for transporation to another party with Hollywood stars at the Beverly Wilshire Hotel. Yet he told the celebrities at the second party:

We can go out and get in our Chevrolet or our Buick or our Cadillac and Rolls Royce and go anywhere we want to. A lot of people don't have automobiles. . . . So I say, public servants, like me and Jerry Brown and others, have a special responsibility to bypass the big shots, including you and people like you and like I was, and to make a concerted effort to understand people who are poor, black, speak a foreign language, who are not well educated, who are inarticulate, who are timid, who have some monumental problems.

Later he told reporters that he would travel in regular cars, and when he got to Washington, he would cut down the number of limousines.

Carter's reign in Plains was to a great extent a conscious decision. As Tom Ottenad had written early in the summer after an interview with Charles Kirbo: "The Carter camp's aim is to create an aura of invincibility and inevitability about Carter's victory next fall. . . . The surprise plan for Carter to lie low from the end of the convention until the start of the fall campaign . . . is intended principally to develop a new public image of the still little-known Southerner as a man able to meet the demands of the presidency." The results were to their liking. As Jody Powell later said: "The type of publicity we were getting [during the summer in Plains] was the best we had gotten during the whole campaign period, certainly better than we would have gotten out on the road. If we could have stayed in Plains until October, as Ford stayed in the White House until October, we would have won by five or ten points."

## Planning

The break in active campaigning also gave Carter and his aides time to prepare for the fall campaign. To avoid any divisive fights, he asked the officers of the Democratic National Committee, including Chairman Robert Strauss ("the greatest party chairman I have ever known"), to remain in their positions. From within the party Carter formed a national steering committee (50 percent female) to meet about every two weeks and advise him on the campaign's progress. The party's role, however, would be limited to increasing voter registration and turnout, helping local and state candidates, and organizing a Truman-esque whistle stop tour for Carter. (Under the new campaign finance laws, which gave each party's nominee $21.8 million, the party was no longer needed for fundraising.)

The campaign would be run from Atlanta, where the Carter organization had taken over new offices on the top three floors of the Peachtree Center. The strategic decisions would be made by Carter's Georgia associates: Richard Harden, who had been forced out of his job as head of the Georgia Department of Human Resources, came on as the campaign's budget director. Tim Kraft became the national field director and with Phil Wise put together a field staff composed of regional directors and state field directors. To avoid local political rivalries and concentrate work on the Carter effort, the campaign took a page from Kennedy's 1960 campaign. Thus, the majority of the state organizers were not political influentials drawn from within the states but experienced middle-level political activists, most of whom had served Carter during the spring.

A few people from outside the Carter ranks found their way into upper-level jobs with the Atlanta staff. Ted Kennedy's former advance man, Jim King, joined the campaign as chief of scheduling and advance work. Walt Wurfel, press secretary for Humphrey's 1972 campaign, was brought in to strengthen the press staff. Milton Gwirtzman, who had been with Kennedy and served as a Carter speechwriter later in the campaign, helped coordinate the issues teams, aided by a Washington-based organization under old Democratic pro Joseph

Duffey, former head of the ADA and a McGovernite in 1972. Some of the field organizers came from other camps: Gerard Doherty, a Kennedy associate in Massachusetts, went to New York; Tim Smith from Mondale's earlier campaign staff went to Virginia; Margaret McKenna, a Department of Treasury consultant, to Rhode Island; and Arnie Miller of New York and McGovern's Michigan campaign to Maryland—to name a few.

In choosing members for the sixteen issues teams, the Carter organization also touched base with leaders from across the political and social spectrum. Professionals from Wall Street, major law firms, congressional committees, universities, think tanks, and other places were brought in. Presidents of corporations and universities, professors, the head of the Navaho coal development project in New Mexico, and other such leaders offered advice and counsel. Perhaps more important than their specific campaign functions, these committees and consultants brought Carter support based on new political grease—the spoils of anticipation. Because Carter had taken the stand throughout the campaign that he was not promising any jobs, that his appointments would be on the basis of merit, he was able to motivate people whose ambition could be appeased with visions of potential political plums. With contacts in the organization (and knowledge that by putting a "Z" on the envelope their letters would get to the people who counted), all kinds of people would fancy themselves in good position to have their talents recognized when it came time for specific appointments.

The most obvious ploy along these lines was TalentBank 77. Thousands of mimeographed letters were sent to blacks, other minorities, women, and middle-level professionals in business, government, and academia saying that the recipient was "qualified for executive-level government jobs." Recipients were asked to fill out the two enclosed information forms and a résumé for the TalentBank 77 files. (The sole black and the senior woman in the department of political science at the University of Illinois, for example, both received forms; mine arrived on Monday, November 1—the day before the balloting.)

For all these attempts to broaden their political base, the Carter people were halfhearted in their efforts to make party regulars part of the team. Caddell was to take separate pollings—one for the Carter organization and one for the Democratic National Committee. The list of party luminaries asked to campaign for Carter was short, and the time spent on his behalf would be brief. California Governor Jerry Brown and Senator Joseph Biden of Delaware, for example, were slated for the most days—six; Senator Henry Jackson and Representative Barbara Jordan, five days; Senator Ted Kennedy, four; Governor George Wallace, two.

The Carter organization mapped out their fall strategy. As Jordan pointed out in a memo on June 2, updated on August 9, the ten border and Southern states were almost sure bets. By adding all states that usually vote Democratic, Jordan figured that Carter could win by taking a few major states in the North. But they did not want to appear "overly dependent" on the South: "The strength of the South in the electoral college is quite obvious to the media. But to the extent that regional bias exists in this country—and it does—there would be a negative reaction to a candidacy that was perceived as being a captive of the Southern states and/or people. . . . Southern regional pride can be used to great advantage without unnecessarily alienating potential anti-Southern voters." At the same time they did not want to seem to be taking the South for granted. They struck a balance by arranging for Carter to make stops in the South on the way to wherever he was going in the rest of the nation. And Carter did pay considerable attention to Mississippi and Louisiana—the only Southern states where Jordan thought Ford had a chance. The goal was to "put Ford on the defensive, making him spend time and money in states he should carry." Mondale, as an integral part of Carter's strategy, was to be in charge of holding the traditional Democratic constituencies, campaigning mainly in the North among labor, minorities, ethnics, and party regulars. (As Robert Moe, Mondale's campaign aide, explained, "Historically, the presidential candidate has been nominated because he's had support of those constituencies, and then he has picked a vice presidential candidate to reach beyond; but this was the reverse.")

Carter would be aided on the campaign trail by members of the Mondale family as well as his own—to make the Carter presence felt where the candidate himself could not appear. A point value was assigned to each participant for each day's campaigning (e.g., Jimmy, seven points for a full day's campaigning; Fritz, five; Rosalynn, four; and so on). Trips were scheduled so that the total "visit points" accured by the various participants equaled the calculated point value of each state. All of this was mapped out, like troop movements, in the situation room of the campaign headquarters in Atlanta. From there Hamilton Jordan directed a staff that soon numbered more than 1,400 (600 in Atlanta and 800 in the field). On one map colored lines showed the routes of various campaigners; another map, with pins, showed where they had been; a third recorded the most recent polling information for each state.

## The Fall

One bright August morning just before the Republican convention, a plump, dark-haired man outlined Carter's future to reporters gathered on the grass across the street from the press headquarters in Plains. In a barely audible voice Patrick Caddell seemed to be predicting a landslide victory for Carter. Carter is ahead, or close to it, he said, in every state and in every major population grouping, except among Republicans and strong conservatives. A decline in support of the Democratic candidate was expected after the Republican convention—that is always the case. And Caddell admitted a certain softness in Carter's support in the Northeastern states—ostensibly because Carter had not conducted an extensive campaign there. ("It's not so much a problem, as a case where the perception and support are not as firm or as hard as they might be.")

Actually Caddell was trying to prevent any rush to negative judgment when

Carter's almost inevitable decline would appear in the polls. And none too soon. From a 33 percent lead over Ford in late July, Carter had already dropped to a 23 percent lead. After the Republican convention Carter's margin slipped rather dramatically to a 10 percent lead (49 percent for Carter to 39 percent for Ford). Outside the South he was running neck and neck with Ford (44 percent to 43 percent). No other candidate for the American presidency since the beginning of modern opinion polling in 1935 had experienced such a rapid decline in the period immediately following the two parties' conventions.

After the first flush of the Republican convention was over, Carter recovered some of his strength, rising to a 15-point lead. But his lead would decline, with some fluctuations, throughout the fall campaign. By election day it was not at all clear who would win. The final Gallup Poll showed Carter trailing Ford, for the first time, by 1 percentage point (46 percent to 47 percent, with 4 percent undecided). The Friday before the election Louis Harris, whose polls were showing the same trends, explained that the soft and undecided vote was then going to Ford. Carter's basic support had remained constant from the beginning of September up to the election.

In some ways the slippage could have been predicted. Carter had ridden to the crest by appealing to such a broad range of people that he had created an inherently fragile coalition (Julian Bond had characterized Carter's support as "a mile wide and an inch deep"). In a memo dated July 22, Caddell had noted that his own polls showed ". . . a third of all Carter voters in the South, the Deep South, and the Farm Belt were describing themselves as not very enthusiastic at all about their choice of Jimmy Carter." He found no state or area in which a majority of registered voters was very enthusiastic or even somewhat enthusiastic about Jimmy Carter. The lack of enthusiasm in the North was among liberals, and in the South among conservatives. In both regions the unenthusiastic voter was two to three times more likely than the enthusiastic voter to find Jimmy Carter "ambiguous (vague, two-faced, too political, etc.) on the open-ended question 'What do you dislike about Jimmy Carter?' "

Another Caddell poll showed Carter weak even within the traditionally Democratic constituencies—women, youths, Catholics, Jews, and self-identified liberals. In population groupings where a Democrat could usually be guaranteed at least a 25 percent margin, Carter was only slightly in front of Ford. "If I didn't know you were a Democrat," Caddell told Carter, "I'd never be able to tell it from these results." The severity of this problem was driven home to Carter in August, when the results of a series of in-depth, open-ended interviews by Caddell became available. A number of people who identified themselves as probable Carter supporters at the beginning of the interview concluded the session with confusion about who they were going to vote for. Caddell was aghast: ". . . they were defecting right in the middle of the interviewing. That's frightening. That is the classic example of a soft vote."

As if this were not enough, the Republicans had devised a strategy to exploit these vulnerabilities. Ford pollster Robert Teeter had discovered in polls done between the two conventions that issues were not statistically significant in predicting the vote of any large voting group—"it was almost entirely a candidate perception election." As noted in the preceding chapter, Carter was perceived as considerably more conservative than Ford in terms of "traditional American values." However—and this was important for the Republicans—the perceptions of Carter were not strong. Teeter said, "All our polling tells us that the feelings about Carter are thinly held, the perceptions are weak perceptions. People like Carter. They think he thinks the way they do. But they don't know him." Thus, the Ford people decided to base their campaign on changing voters' perceptions. They would zero in on Carter in two ways: emphasize his "liberalism" on economic matters and articulate people's apprehensions about him. "He'll continue to be all things to all people," Teeter said at one campaign staff meeting. "He'll try to seem liberal to liberals and conservative to conservatives. He will be a nonissue candidate. He has to be. But he'll be playing a dangerous game." The big question was simple: "Can that approach stand up to the test of a national election campaign?"

Carter was vulnerable because of the way he had run his primary campaign. He projected unusual virtue. He could appeal to all segments of the population. But this kind of imagery is difficult to sustain. Eventually he would have to make hard choices that could lose him the support of those who did not realize where he actually stood on issues of importance to them. Any discrepancies between his image and his behavior would become a matter of public scrutiny. No longer the outsider, Carter would now have to run as the insider chosen by his party. The antipolitician populist would occasionally look like a penny-ante politician. The pious Baptist would use salty language in public. The secure and confident leader would get nervous and tongue-tied in public debates. And the crackerjack organization, like all other groups of human beings, would make mistakes. Even his "roots" would lose magic as his people, staff, and church were revealed to suffer internal divisions. In short, Carter would not just appear fuzzy on the issues: his self-portrait would blur in a kaleidoscopic show of diverse images and styles. In advertising terms, he would fail to "position" his product.

In the formal Labor Day opening of his campaign at Warm Springs, Georgia, with Roosevelt's "Little White House" as a backdrop and two of Roosevelt's sons by his side, Carter noted a similarity between his forthcoming campaign and Roosevelt's in 1932. "This year, as in 1932, our country is divided, our people are out of work, and our national leaders do not lead. Roosevelt's opponent in that year was also an incumbent president, a decent and well-intentioned man who sincerely believed that our government could and should not with bold action try to correct the economic ills of our nation." He evoked Harry Truman, citing his slogan, "The Buck Stops Here," to emphasize the lack of leadership displayed by President Ford. And he identified with John Kennedy as another outsider, "because he was young and inexperienced and because of his religious beliefs. . . . This year, as in 1960, our country was drifting without inspiration and purpose . . ." He came to Lyndon Johnson, putting himself in the last phase of the great Democratic tradition: "When President Johnson went out of office, the unemployment rate was less than four percent. . . . Under this Republican administration, the unemployment rate has been the highest since the Hoover depression."

In Darlington, South Carolina, his next stop, Carter upstaged the opposition. Republican vice-presidential hopeful, Senator Bob Dole of Kansas, was also scheduled to appear at the Darlington 500 stock car race, and a deal had been struck that Carter would ride in the pace car, with Dole riding several cars back, as both men circled the track. Afterward Carter and Dole would retire to the VIP section to watch the race. But Carter went to the pit area instead and shook hands with the crews. Then, to the dismay of the Secret Service, he headed for the grandstand and found a seat with a group of average American citizens. The Republican vice-presidential nominee, meanwhile, sat dolefully in the designated VIP area. (Carter told the crowd he would invite the stock car drivers to the White House. "I have a lot of friends in the pit crews and driving the cars.")

However, the Carter campaign's "crackerjack" organization publicly fouled up at Carter's next stop, Manhattan's Columbus Circle subway station. It was 7:40 in the morning and aside from the press, there was no crowd. Someone had failed to note one detail: people would not emerge from that exit until later in the morning on their way to work. At a Brooklyn College stop Carter had to abandon his prepared text because the room was without a podium and the microphone wouldn't work. Later he missed an entire shift of factory workers at the Haddon Bookbinding factory in Scranton. And in Milwaukee on Thursday evening, he was forced to referee a shoving match between the local police and the national press corps because his campaign staff had failed to tell the police that the media was permitted to interview the candidate.

Meanwhile, Carter began to act like the public's image of a local politician. Responding to reports that FBI Director Clarence Kelley had had FBI staff carpenters install window valances in his private apartment, Carter pulled out his Watergate theme. "There's been a great contribution to the crime rate because of Watergate, because of the CIA revelation, and because of the disgraceful actions in the FBI," he said at Brooklyn College. At a later meeting with local black political leaders, Carter said yes—he would have fired Kelley. In North Philadelphia he noted that Kelley had been

caught with government employees using my and your tax money decorating his apartment. When people throughout the country, particularly young people, see Richard Nixon cheating, lying, and leaving the highest office in disgrace, when they see the previous Attorney General violating the law and admitting it, when you see the head of the FBI break a little law and stay there, it gives everybody the sense that crime must be okay. If the big shots in Washington can get away with it, well, so can I.

Carter himself became the object of hostilities. In Philadelphia, where he was trying out his neighborhood strategies (i.e., visiting white, ethnic urban areas), he was confronted by anti-abortion picketers, including two Catholic nuns carrying a small white coffin. That night in Scranton, he was met by a large, seemingly friendly crowd. Pleased by their enthusiasm, especially after that day's series of mishaps, he strode hopefully into their midst. But half of the assembled crowd were antiabortion protesters, and they encircled him with chants of "Life! Life! Life!" The next day, however, Carter advance man Jim King came through with just the media event needed. At Pittsburgh's Polish Hill, a priest turned out his elementary school en masse and kissed Carter on both cheeks. Carter proudly wore a T-shirt reading "Polish Hill."

Then, on Thursday, September 9, Carter ended his first week of formal campaigning on another incongruent, though upbeat, note. This time the outsider, the antiboss candidate was deep in the embrace of the biggest and best boss of all—Mayor Richard J. Daley of Chicago. After a daylong tour of Illinois, Carter arrived in Chicago for Daley's traditional election year fireworks extravaganza and torchlight parade (scheduled much earlier than usual). The parade concluded at the state Democratic convention at the Medinah Temple. There, Carter seems to have been carried away by the occasion. Coming to the podium jubilant, he was greeted with a standing ovation and pounding, rhythmical applause. He prefaced his speech with a tribute to Mayor Daley, his "very good friend." Then he began his speech about preventive health care. At one point he broke out with an unusual litany of his own childhood diseases. To the audience's astonishment, he hollered out: "Whooping cough, Cholera . . . Typhus, Typhoid, Diphtheria, Polio. They [Carter's childhood doctors] tried to immunize me against these diseases, and quite often they succeeded." One reporter later wrote, "It was an inexplicable close to an incredible evening."

Back in Plains, Carter rounded off a rather undistinguished week with one more exchange over Clarence Kelley. Ford, in the Rose Garden of the White House where he was to do most of his campaigning throughout September, had attacked Carter for his handling of the Kelley matter: "I hope that Governor Carter understood that Mrs. Kelley at that time [when the carpentry was done] was suffering from terminal cancer and that was a very sad and difficult time for the director of the FBI." Carter had the last word, bringing the whole discussion to a new low: "Obviously, I sympathize with anybody whose wife is dying of cancer," he told reporters, "but that doesn't have anything to do with it." And besides, Carter said, Ford had brought up the matter "after Director Kelley had announced that he was remarrying."

On September 20 Carter, accompanied by his wife, Mondale, and thirteen cars of reporters caught "The Democratic Special" at New York City's Pennsylvania Station for a whistle stop train tour through New Jersey, Pennsylvania, and Ohio. Inviting publicity that would make associations between his own and Harry Truman's whistle stop campaign, Carter mentioned the former President at several stops. "How many of you want another President like Harry Truman?" he asked the crowds.

The big item of interest on the train, however, was not Carter's whistle stop identifications, but his views on sin and sex. Shortly before the train's early morning departure, Barry Golson, an editor for *Playboy*, and Robert Scheer, a free-lance journalist and former editor of *Ramparts* appeared on the "Today" show to discuss their interview with Carter (the article was being rushed into print so it would circulate before the scheduled October 14 publication date). Though the interview covered many topics, what excited all the attention was Carter's statement that he had often looked at women with lust in his heart, and his use of sexual colloquialisms. Reporters on the campaign train, primed with questions from their editors, asked Carter about it. Carter tried to play it cool. Questioned about his use of the word "screw," Carter replied, "I don't remember." And sensing the need not to seem defensive or disturbed, the Carter staff nonchalantly passed out copies of the interview. As Carter left the train that night, it was the *Playboy* interview that was receiving big media play. The Washington *Star* final edition headlined "Carter on Sin and Lust": 'I'm Human . . . I'm Tempted.' " "Trust is Out," Georgia's Columbus *Enquirer* announced. "Sex, Sin, Temptation—Carter's Candid View" ran the Chicago *Sun-Times* story.

This interview had been one of the more revealing exchanges with Carter— outlining his world views (Vietnam, Chile) and giving clues about his theological predispositions. But the interview got attention because of the choice of forum and the language.* ABC waited until fifteen minutes before air time to decide whether to let Harry Reasoner quote Carter. At CBS, Walter Cronkite settled for saying that Carter used "words mild for Playboy but perhaps a little racy for Sunday school." The Atlanta *Constitution* and the Dallas *Times Herald* used "shacks up" but not "screw," while The *New York Times* noted that Carter had used "a common but mild vulgarism for sexual intercourse."

After the story broke, various people tried to point out that his theology was not that controversial. Joseph Duffey, associate campaign director for the Carter campaign and a nonpracticing minister, offered the explanation that Carter's remarks were "very classic, orthodox Christian doctrine. The street Greek in which the Bible was originally written probably includes words similar to those used by Governor Carter. I don't see that it is terribly damaging." Carter's Illinois director, the Reverend James Wall of *Christian Century* noted

---

* What Carter said in the controversial part is this:
I try not to commit a deliberate sin. I recognize that I'm going to do it anyhow, because I'm human and I'm tempted. And Christ set some almost impossible standards for us. Christ said, "I tell you that anyone who looks on a woman with lust has in his heart already committed adultery."

I've looked on a lot of women with lust. I've committed adultery in my heart many times. This is something that God recognized I will do—and I have done it—and God forgives me for it. But that doesn't mean that I condemn someone who not only looks on a woman with lust but who leaves his wife and shacks up with somebody out of wedlock.

Christ says, Don't consider yourself better than someone else because one guy screws a whole bunch of women while the other guy is loyal to his wife. The guy who's loyal to his wife ought not to be condescending or proud because of the relative degree of sinfulness.

that Carter's comments were not contradictory to "standard Protestant theology." Dr. Joe Barnhart, professor of philosophy at North Texas State University, agreed: "What he said is strictly in keeping with the evangelical faith."

Yet the whole *Playboy* discussion on vital moral and religious matters reinforced the concern that Carter was not what he seemed to be. The Reverend Harold Lindsell, editor of *Christianity Today,* commented, "Here's a man who professes to be a Christian. And then gets himself all tied up in speaking words which at best are questionable . . ." In metropolitan Atlanta a group of seventeen independent Baptist preachers denounced Carter as having "brought reproach on the Christian faith." The Reverend Bailey Smith, who had once been a strong Carter supporter, described his own conflict. In an earlier visit to Oklahoma, Carter had prayed with Smith before going out to speak to Smith's Baptist audience. "I, the preacher, just stood there, but Carter, the politician, got down on his knees and just prayed heaven down. He prayed for me. 'Dear God, bless this person as he preaches, fill this person with your presence.' He prayed that people be converted. He said, 'Help me to say what you want me to say. . . . I felt he would die for his faith." But now Smith couldn't reconcile Carter's use of "shack up" and "screw" in *Playboy* with this memory. "We're totally against pornography. And, well, 'screw' is just not a good Baptist word."

But even for those who were not so concerned about Carter's religious orthodoxy his language did strike a jarring note, raising questions of whether or not he was as politically astute as he seemed to be. At least this was the reaction of the press retinue on the train. As Kandy Stroud later recalled, when the interview came out, "disbelief descended on an already puzzled press and fanned whispers of impending doom." One CBS correspondent declared, "the campaign is dying right under our feet." Tom Wicker and James Reston were appalled at the political mudslide they were witnessing. As Hamilton Jordan would wryly note, it increased the "weirdo factor."*

In the midst of the fallout from the *Playboy* article, Carter's performance in the first of his three debates with Ford created another incongruity in his self-presentation. The calm, able Carter of the summer months was transformed, before a prime-time viewing audience of 100 million Americans, into a nervous, ordinary human being.

The encounter was being treated as a major sporting event. *Newsweek* gave a score sheet listing the strengths and weaknesses of the two candidates (e.g., Ford does not lose composure under fire, though he is a poor extemporaneous speaker. Carter can speak eloquently without notes, but can appear unduly aggressive on television.) *Time* noted how the two sides haggled over the details of the setting (Ford aides insisted that the candidates stand, thus empha-

---

* Any doubts that Carter had simply lowered his guard in an off moment were dispelled the next Sunday (September 26) when Norman Mailer's interview with Carter was published in the *New York Times Magazine*. The candidate actually used the renowned four-letter word, "that the *New York Times* has not printed in the 125 years of its publishing life."

sizing Ford's impressive height; Carter aides insisted that the podium be narrow, thus emphasizing Carter's more agile physique.) Stories came out of the two training camps—Plains and Washington—describing the preparations. Ford was portrayed as in very serious training. Aides were helping him hone his speaking style. He was using video tapes of Carter speeches in practice sessions. It was even reported that Ford used a Carter stand-in for his practice debates. (In fact, Ford drew the line at this.) On the other hand, Carter was portrayed as the cool candidate, confident of victory. Carter had earlier viewed the 1960 debates between Kennedy and Nixon, but Hamilton Jordan said they were "not going to go through an elaborate process," and Patrick Caddell observed: "Last minute cramming doesn't do anything but make you nervous." Carter, the stories said, was not being quizzed by his assistants (as Ford was and Kennedy had been). Nor was he going through a practice run-through. Jody Powell explained, "We are not going to turn Jimmy into some sort of TV star." One story even noted that Carter had been nonchalantly reading the comics to Amy one evening before the first debate.

The night of the bout, Thursday, September 23, 100 million Americans tuned in for the event, televised on all the major networks. When Carter entered the stage at Walnut Street Theater in Philadelphia, Kandy Stroud thought he "looked like Howdy Doody," with his robust red tie knotted slightly off center, and his cowlick. After the President had come on stage, she said, "Carter looked small and unimposing. . . . What had seemed boyish only months ago now looked badly worn." President Ford, in contrast, looked the epitome of "Presidential" as he entered the stage in his well-tailored, vested blue suit. Carter seemed to sense the difference. "When he shook hands with the President he extended his arm stiffly, holding Ford as far away as possible like a snake on a stick."

The first question, as decided earlier by a flip of the coin, went to Carter. As if to bury forever the charge that he was fuzzy, he poured out statistics and outlined detailed programs in a potpourri of information. Ford, in turn, hit out aggressively with a central theme of his fall campaign, that Carter was hypocritical on the issues and did not deserve the trust he asked for.

After fifty minutes of this, at 10:51 P.M., the sound system went dead. Neither man knew what to do. They froze—standing, not speaking to each other or the people on the stage, looking straight ahead. At one point, when assured the camera was off them, both wiped the perspiration from their faces almost in unison. After twenty-eight minutes, the sound returned. Carter picked up where he left off, as if nothing unusual had happened, in the middle of his rebuttal to a Ford answer.

Overall, as Caddell later said, the event was a "wash." "Both of them seemed overbriefed and overguarded," Elizabeth Drew noted, "almost afraid of spontaneity . . ." Gerald Rafshoon claimed, "no win, no loss." Actually, the first debate turned out to be a relative loss for Carter. A CBS–*New York Times* poll showed that 37 percent of those questioned thought Ford had won; 24 percent saw Carter as the victor. Part of the problem was that Carter had created very high expectations for himself.

The morning after the debate, on a campaign pass through Texas, Carter compounded his problems. His comments about Johnson in his *Playboy* interview had offended the Johnson family and many other Texans.* Party Chairman Robert Strauss saw a possibility that Carter would lose Texas. So right after the campaign plane, Peanut One, touched down at the Houston airport, Carter tried to explain his comments on Johnson to a group of Texas journalists gathered near the runway. *Playboy*, Carter suggested, had misinterpreted his remarks.

After the interview was over, there was a summary made that unfortunately equated what I had said about President Johnson and President Nixon. . . . I realize that, if you read it, it says that after the final session was over, there was an analysis that was made after the completion of the interview. My reference to Johnson was about the misleading of the American people; the lying and cheating part referred to President Nixon. And the unfortunate juxtaposition of these two names in the *Playboy* article grossly misinterprets the way I feel about him.

Sam Donaldson of ABC and Larry Knutson of the Associated Press edged over to the circle in time to hear Carter's answer. Donaldson whipped out a copy of the *Playboy* article, read the section Carter had been talking about, and asked him if those were his words. Robert Scheer, worrying now about his own recollection of the interview, ran back to the plane to get his tape-recording while Carter assured Donaldson he was not denying the accuracy of the quote.

On the plane to California that night, as Powell came out to talk to the reporters, one complained: "He's flip-flopping again, Jody. He's changed his goddamn mind in midstream. I got it right here on tape. He's saying he didn't call Johnson a liar. Just what the hell is going on?" Powell tried to defend his boss; certain reporters were just "grubbing in dirt." But nobody would buy that line. The conversation degenerated into a shouting match, with Powell accusing his antagonists of "nit-shitting." They in turn accused Carter of trying to "wing one past the provincials and themselves."

Later that evening Carter tried his hand at patching things up with the press in San Diego. About a dozen print journalists were invited to his hotel room for an off-the-record discussion. As the beer was passed around, Carter told the gathering how much he respected them and how he regretted the misunderstanding in Houston. They were all in the campaign together, and all anybody wanted was what was best for the country. Would they give him some "advice" on how his campaign might be improved? With his query Carter ex-

---

* In the interview Carter said: "But I don't think I would ever take on the same frame of mind that Nixon or Johnson did—lying, cheating and distorting the truth. Not taking into consideration my hope for my strength of character, I think that my religious beliefs alone would prevent that from happening to me. I have that confidence. I hope it's justified."

plicitly overstepped the boundaries of propriety. Several of the reporters present, already uneasy at having been singled out for this special meeting, saw this as an attempt to manipulate them into becoming part of his campaign. Martin Schram of *Newsday* told Carter that the press was not in the business of advising candidates. So Carter backed off. His complaint was not with the print media but with television. He insisted that he had not been playing word games in Houston. Charles Mohr of *The New York Times* and Carl Leubsdorf of the Baltimore *Sun* disagreed, quoting Carter back to Carter. Powell said that the campaign's openness had been abused by the press and this might force the Carter camp to close the campaign to them. To which they responded that if Carter decided to exclude the press from the campaign, they would have to write about that, too.

These rather explicit attempts at manipulation contributed to Carter's already deteriorating relations with his national press entourage. Mohr and a few other senior reporters who had not been with Carter throughout the campaign had been reporting some of the negative things they had seen in Carter for some time. But now even some of the younger people who had been enamored of him earlier were discouraged. One lamented, "You see we really care about the guy and it's getting to us to see Carter piss away his edge. Some of us have been with him since he was Jimmy Who? and hell, we have a lot at stake. We were around before the glamour boys got sent in, been aboard a long time, kind of got used to the big time." Even Scheer was distressed. He wrote in the November issue of *Playboy:* "I was surprised to find myself suddenly depressed by the prospect of Carter's defeat."

### Counterattack

As his relationship with the press deteriorated, Carter became snappish, curtailed his evening campaign activities by stopping at 8:00 P.M., and took to staying in his own forward compartment of the plane when en route to his various stops. He also became more aggressive in his attacks on Ford. Right after the *New York Times*-CBS poll showing the dimensions of his "loss" in the first debate was published, Carter escalated his rhetoric. The "bloated mess" in Washington, he said in Portland, Oregon, could only be cured by an outsider.

You can't expect any better from political leadership that's been bogged down in Washington for the last twenty-five or thirty years, deriving their advice, their counsel, their financial support from lobbyists, and special interest groups. They go to the same restaurants. They belong to the same clubs, they play golf on the same golf courses, they communicate with one another . . . in the absence of participation, understanding, control by the people. We can't run this government or this administration or this campaign from those private clubs or from the White House Rose Garden.

In another appearance that day Carter edged toward sarcasm: "I think you always should say something good about your opponent. President Ford has simply exemplified the leadership of the Republican party." Ford was in the "great tradition of Warren Harding, Herbert Hoover and Richard Nixon."

Back in Plains the next day the toll on Carter was beginning to show. At about 1:30 P.M. on Tuesday, September 28, he sauntered out of the warehouse in his unflared jeans, leather boots, and embroidered blue workshirt, to greet thirty or forty tourists. One observer noted: "His face wore no expression except a frozen smile. There were deep circles under his eyes. He looked to me as exhausted as anyone I had ever seen." Then he worked the crowd, seeming "to have been doing something he felt he had to, but for which he had little strength." But as soon as he stepped into the car, "his smile melted and he folded his hands in his lap. When the car drove away, he merely stared straight ahead, without even a glance at the tourists who observed him through the window."

His ability to recoup, however, was evident the next day, when he appeared at a press conference at the railroad depot. "He was in a very good mood; his smile seemed natural, the circles from his eyes were gone, and when a reporter was asking a question, Carter looked directly into his eyes, nodding to show that he understood, . . . the total impression (was) of control, self-confidence, and good humor."

There may have been reasons for the revitalization other than a good night's sleep. The previous evening the top two stories on all the three network shows had to do with Jerry Ford's golf outings with lobbyists and the investigation by the Special Prosecutor's Office into Ford's past campaign finances. And the same two stories were featured on the "Today" show that morning and in *The New York Times*.

For a week there had been ripples in the press to the effect that Special Prosecutor Charles Ruff was investigating charges that Gerald Ford had misused campaign contributions during his earlier career as a Congressman, that two maritime unions had secretly funneled contributions to him through committees in Kent County Michigan, and that he had gone on vacations paid for by the chief lobbyist for US Steel, William Whyte.

The stories won the attention they did because Ford's press secretary, Ron Nessen, announced on Tuesday night that as a Congressman Ford had been the guest of William Whyte, and that he had also played on Firestone, Alcoa, and Bethlehem Steel company golf courses, and stayed in US Steel guest rooms at Disney World.

But Ford's problems did not end with Nessen's announcement. Later in the week Judy Woodruff revealed on NBC that Secretary of Agriculture Earl Butz had just apologized for a racist (and vulgar) joke he had told right after the Republican convention, and after several calls for his resignation over the weekend, he reluctantly gave it on Monday. The air had hardly cleared of this affair when new stories appeared suggesting that the IRS was auditing Ford's taxes (for a period during his House career). Then John Dean, on the "Today" show, implied that Ford had perjured himself before the Senate during his vice-presidential confirmation hearings when he said he had not talked with members of the Nixon White House about pressuring Representative Wright Patman to discontinue the House Banking Committee investigations of the Watergate breakins. Finally, after almost three weeks of riding under clouds, Ford was relieved by Charles Ruff's announcement, on October 14, that he had been cleared of any wrongdoing.

While Ford was being deluged with all these difficulties, Carter could have sat back and watched. Indeed, Carter himself was politically vulnerable on such matters. The two unions that had contributed to Ford, the Marine Engineers Beneficial Association and the Seafarer International Union, had turned against him in 1974, when he vetoed a bill requiring that 20 percent of all U.S. imports be carried in American bottoms. In 1976 they were making contributions to Carter's campaign. (Jesse M. Calhoon, the president of the Marine Engineers, had sponsored a $1,000 per plate dinner on June 30, raising $150,000 for Carter's primary campaign.) Further, though the press did not know this at the time, Carter's friend Bert Lance had made the Bank of Georgia's plane available without charge to the Carter organization on a few occasions during the spring campaign. Moreover, Carter, as we have seen, had been the guest of various private companies in the past, during his governorship.

Carter, however, went on the attack himself. The day after Nessen's press conference Carter had found "a great difference" between his trips as governor and Ford's—all Carter's trips were to promote Georgia business abroad and involved no personal recreation on his part. On October 1, in Portland, Maine, Carter said: "I know the difference between one who gets his advice, his knowledge, his golf games, his obligations from special-interest groups in Washington—compared to one who derives all of my support, my advice, counsel, my strength, my criticism directly from the American people." That same day, however, the AP broke a story from Woodbine, Georgia, that raised questions about Carter's own weekend trips, hosted by private interests. The general manager of Brunswick Pulp and Paper Company was quoted to the effect that the company had been host for two weekends at its Cabin Bluff resort for Carter and his guests. They had picked up the tab for everything, including country-style cooking.

When asked about his own "vacation" trips, Carter admitted it was "wrong" to have accepted them, yet he proceeded to find other reasons to show there had been no impropriety on his part. His vacations could not be compared to Ford's golfing trips "because President Ford has never revealed the details of his vacation." Another difference, he noted, was in the frequency of hospitality—"I could have gone every weekend if I had wanted to." But he did admit that he would not accept such trips while President and wouldn't if he were governor again—because "standards have been raised on things like this since Watergate."

On the Butz affair, he said, that same day, "I don't think anybody could make any more . . . derogatory statement than Mr. Butz did make about black people. I thought it was disgraceful, and I don't believe I would permit that to be done by any of the people who worked under my administration while I was President." And just in case Italian-Americans and Catholics had forgotten Butz's earlier joke about the Pope, Carter reminded them: "I think it's [the black joke] similar to the kind of statements he has made in the past that were embarrassing to Catholics and Italians." After learning of Butz's resignation he told reporters that Ford's handling of the affair was the latest proof that "no one is leading the nation." One reporter noted how Carter savored his "rival's discomfiture."

Carter's aggressive mood was also evident in his handling of the second presidential debate on foreign policy and defense on October 6. He had gone into training, using a tape recorder to check his delivery. He was briefed on possible questions by Congressman Les Aspin of Wisconsin, Stu Eizenstat, Pat Caddell, *Foreign Policy* editor Richard Holbrooke, and Zbigniew Brzezinski the day before and the morning of the debate. (Aspin said later they had "picked out eleven of the thirteen questions that were asked.) And when the debate opened, the tentative, halting style displayed at the beginning of the first debate was gone; Carter moved confidently and aggressively in his answers to questions.

Ford, too, was holding his own—until Max Frankel of *The New York Times* suggested that the Soviet sphere of influence in Eastern Europe was being recognized in the Helsinki pact. Ford responded: ". . . we have an agreement where they notify us and we notify them of any military maneuvers that are to be undertaken. They have done it. In both cases where they've done so, there is no Soviet domination of Eastern Europe and there never will be under a Ford Administration." Frankel was startled. "I'm sorry, could I just follow? Did I understand you to say, sir, that the Russians are not using Eastern Europe as their own sphere of influence in occupying most of the countries there, and making sure with their own troops that it's a Communist Zone . . ." Ford dug himself in deeper:

I don't believe, Mr. Frankel, that the Yugoslavians consider themselves dominated by the Soviet Union. I don't believe that the Rumanians consider themselves dominated by the Soviet Union. I don't believe that the Poles consider themselves dominated by the Soviet Union. . . . Each of those countries is independent, autonomous, it has its own territorial integrity and the United States does not concede that those countries are under the domination of the Soviet Union.

When it came his turn, Carter piggybacked on Frankel's probe. "I would like to see Mr. Ford convince the Polish-Americans and the Czech-Americans and the Hungarian-Americans in this country that those countries don't live under the domination and supervision of the Soviet Union behind the Iron Curtain." Carter also attacked Ford for not meeting Aleksandr Solzhenitsyn in the White House, for the "terrible" grain deals with the Soviet Union, for suggesting that low unemployment during the Kennedy and Johnson administrations was a result of the Vietnam war. ("Karl Marx said that the free enterprise system in a democracy can only continue to exist when they are at war or preparing for war. Karl Marx was the grandfather of Communism. I don't agree with that statement, I hope Mr. Ford doesn't either.") But if Ford were too soft in his dealings with the Russians and Communism, he was also too hard. Carter attacked the Administration for its slow progress on the SALT talks and its "action in overthrowing an elected government in Chile and its helping to "establish military dictatorship." Carter even took a shot at Ford's intelligence after the President's reminder that SALT I would expire on October 3, 1977: "He has learned the date of the expiration of SALT I, apparently."

The next day the headlines concentrated on Ford's gaffe. As Ford pollster Robert Teeter later noted, "In the polling we did starting in the last minute of the second debate, between 11:00 and 1:00 that night, the question of who did a better job in the debate came out Ford 44 percent, Carter 43. . . . Between 5:00 and midnight the day after, it was Ford 17, Carter 62. Reports of the debate had reemphasized the president as a mistake-prone, inept bumbler, exactly what we had spent six or seven weeks trying to get away from."

Carter also called Ford on the matter. In Salt Lake City on October 7, he assailed Ford for this "serious blunder." In Albuquerque the next day Carter charged that Ford had been "brainwashed" while behind the Iron Curtain. In Cleveland he added, "It doesn't surprise me that Mr. Ford didn't know the condition of relatives of Americans in Eastern Europe. Mr. Ford doesn't know anything about Americans in America. . . . If we had wanted experience, we would have kept Richard Nixon. At least other Presidents knew whose tanks were in Poland."

Carter had been egging Ford on for weeks in an attempt to get him out of the Rose Garden. By the second week in October, Ford had taken to the road and was responding in kind. In Lawton, Oklahoma, he accused Carter of talking out of both sides of his mouth. At the Texas State Fair in Dallas he lashed out at the "14 distortions, inaccurate statements or untruths" made during the second debate. (For the record, White House press secretary Ron Nessen circulated a fact sheet that sought to back up the claims. It juxtaposed Carter's statement that he had never advocated $15 billion cuts in the defense budget with a quote in Savannah *Morning News* from Carter, saying that "approximately $15 billion could be cut from the defense budget and not weaken this nation's military capability.") In New York that night, Ford suggested that Carter had been playing "hide and seek." I have been "looking all over the country for the candidate who said, 'I'll never lie to you.' He seems to have disappeared."

Ford continued the assault on his own whistle stop, train, "The Honest Abe," as it rolled across Illinois in mid-October. Before a cheering crowd in Joliet, he described Carter as a man who "will say anything, anywhere to be President." In Pontiac, Bloomington, Lincoln, Springfield, and Carbondale, he persisted in his attack. "He wavers, the wanders, he wiggles, and he waffles."

Carter, he said, is misleading the public about defense cuts, taxes, and federal spending.

## High-Low Roads

In a memo of October 16, Patrick Caddell warned Carter about the damage that had been done to his campaign. His polls were showing a swing away from Carter by middle-income independents, liberals, and conservatives. Further, Carter's support was slipping in the West, the border states, and the South. In a memo of October 20, Caddell reported a serious problem with women voters, who were seeing Carter as less able than Ford in the area of foreign affairs; a majority of women even agreed with the statement: "Jimmy Carter would be a risk as President because we don't know what he would do." Caddell's conclusion: the Ford negative campaign is having an impact, particularly on women.

A change of tactics was in order: Caddell suggested a return to themes used before the second debate—"when we stressed our opposition in aggressive *issue* terms rather than aggressive *personal* terms."

Carter did attempt to tone down his attacks. In a meeting with journalists in Plains on October 18, he said he would try not to make any personal attack on Ford during the remaining two weeks of the campaign. And in the third and final debate with Ford on October 22, he displayed this new strategy. When asked to comment on the "low level" of the campaign, Carter offered an apology. "I have to admit that in the heat of the campaign . . . I've made some mistakes. And I think this is part of just being a human being." He pledged that during the ten days remaining before the election he would try to stick to issues and said his campaign would not run television advertisements and newspaper advertisements based on a personal attack on President Ford's character.

Yet an analysis of the text of the debate shows that Carter was not wholly living up to his promise. His pledge to take the high road in the remainder of the campaign, for example, was followed by: "I believe that the opposite is true with President Ford's campaign." He contrasted his standards in choosing a running mate to Ford's. "I don't want to say anything critical of Senator Dole. But I never heard Mr. Ford say that that [qualifications to be President] was his primary consideration." And when Ford defended the chairman of the Joint Chiefs of Staff, Air Force General George Brown [who had a few days earlier put his foot in his mouth with a statement about the British decline as a world power] Carter, reminding the audience of Brown's earlier statements about Jewish influence in the media and Israel's being a "burden" to the United States, suggested that Ford's own attitudes might be suspect unless he gave a public reaction to Brown's remarks.

Neither candidate came out a clear winner in the postdebate polls. In the Gallup Poll, for example, Carter was viewed as the winner by 32 percent of the audience, Ford by 27. Twenty-one percent called it a tie and 20 percent had no opinion—in contrast to the 8 percent who had had no opinion after the first two debates.

After the third debate there were but two weeks to go in the campaign. Carter would concentrate on the big industrial states in the North, plus Texas and a few other close states in the South. He would also tune down his sniping at Ford personally, accentuating domestic policies and more upbeat themes. The day after the last debate Carter told a New York crowd that Ford was a "decent man" and that his basic problem was his continuation of the conservative course set by Republican Presidents since 1922. At other stops he railed against "Republican economics" and reminded his audiences they were voting for a Carter-Mondale ticket. At an old-fashioned Democratic rally in Dallas on Sunday, October 31, Carter finally hit his stride. Though he had earlier shown signs of worry and fatigue, he once again displayed that charismatic touch as he went through a medley of campaign themes, his voice stronger and smoother than ever. Ford was a "decent man," but he could not provide the kind of bold leadership the country needed: "It takes a deep dedication to a cause, . . . to a way of life, that has been exemplified in the past by great Presidents who were Democrats." Then a litany of questions about Ford: "Can you think of a single program that he's put forth that's been accepted. . . . Can you think of a single thing?" The crowd responded with shouts of "no," "inflation" and "unemployment." Carter repeated the crowd's chants. The Ford Administration, he called out, was responsible for the highest inflation rate in 192 years, the highest interest rates since the Civil War, and a bureaucracy too big to address itself to the problems of the people.

The Carter organization also undertook a massive advertising campaign in the final days. There were some negative commercials, used mostly in the South, where Caddell's early October polls had shown Carter threatened with the loss of his most important base. One set emphasized Southern pride and resentment of past ridicule. Another series focused on Ford's "soft" dealings with the Soviet Union. Playing off the Ford Eastern European gaffe in the second debate, one commercial had an announcer saying that it "raised disturbing questions about the real intention of Mr. Ford's secret negotiations with Russia. Isn't it now clear why Jimmy Carter wants to put morality back in our government and isn't it clear that this Democrat has no illusions about Russia's intentions." In another commercial Carter piggybacked on Ronald Reagan's critique of the Ford-Kissinger détente policy. Reagan's comments were scrawled across the screen: "My view of detente is that it has been a one-way street. . . ." Then Carter said: "The Soviet Union knows what they want in detente and they have been getting it. And we have been outtraded in almost every instance." Another, entitled "Foreign Policy," featured a Reagan comment on Ford's lack of leadership, followed by Carter's suggestion that the President lacked authority. "As far as foreign policy goes, Mr. Kissinger has been the president of this country."

The one negative advertisement used nationally emphasized the relative popularity of the two vice-presidential candidates. (Mondale had clearly been the victor in his debate with Dole on October 15, and the polls showed him contributing at least three percentage points to the Democratic ticket.) The two men were shown side by side on a split screen, while the narrator reminded the audience, "four of the last six Vice Presidents have wound up being President; who would you like to see a heart beat away from the Presidency?" As Rafshoon later noted, this advertisement was used effectively almost every-where—except the South "because we were downplaying Mondale [there]."

Mostly, however, the national commercials reverted to the positive themes of the primary campaign. Carter's hour long election eve show was the high point of this approach. Comfortably seated in his book-lined library in Plains, Carter began by recalling how twenty-two months earlier he had been " a lonely candidate" with "a close personal individual direct relationship with the people of this country." Once again, he would let the people see "a direct personal relationship with the man who hopes to be the next President of our country" in an "untarnished and direct and unrehearsed" presentation. As if to lay the "fuzziness" issue aside forever, he answered a wide variety of questions from all kinds of voters, calling some by name (their comments and questions had been filmed on location the week before in a "man-on-the-street" format). For his conclusion Carter stood in front of his desk with a very serious, strong look on his face, no hint of a smile. He said: "We have got to pull ourselves together in a sense of unity . . . together we can restore the greatness that we lost. And prove once again that we still live in the most wonderful country on Earth." And with that the camera faded to a picture of the Carter home, peaceful in the dusk.

### Final Hurdles

The Ford organization was to zero in on Carter's vulnerabilities in the last two weeks of the campaign. Their most effective commercials were a version of the "man-on-the-street" interviews—spontaneous remarks, later edited for length. In one advertisement six different Atlantans observed, in soft Southern drawls, that Jimmy Carter had not been much of a governor. Another set of commercials focused on Carter's gubernatorial record. One opened on the last line of a Carter advertisement—"And what he did as governor, he will do as president,"—then cut to a map of Georgia, with an announcer proclaiming: "Government spending increased 58 percent . . . Government employees up 28 . . . bonded indebtedness up 20. . . ." Then flashing to a map of the United States, the voice concluded, "Don't let him do as president what he did as governor." For the print media an advertisement used the *Playboy* cover plugging the Carter interview (the cover pictured a nearly nude woman), run next to a *Newsweek* cover featuring Ford. ("One good way to decide this election. Read last week's *Newsweek*. Read this month's *Playboy*.")

Carter also had some problems that were indirectly the result of his campaign rhetoric. He had projected himself, his organization, and his roots in such ideal terms in the spring and summer that rather ordinary events could raise questions about what he was really like. On October 11, for example, the UPI had picked up a Knight News Service story about a 111-page campaign manual in use by advance persons working for Carter. Though the manual contained nothing especially shocking, it showed the behind-the-scenes operations that helped create the Carter "charisma." Included were suggestions on how to light Carter's head when he appeared on TV to highlight his hair and create a halo effect. Instructions were given on whom to put on the podium (a cross section of average Americans), what to put on the candidate's index cards (names of local politicians, local issues, etc.), on how to draw and keep an enthusiastic crowd ("Encourage pandemonium by scattering hard-core enthusiasts throughout the crowd." Organize "spontaneous cheering.") Advice was offered on how to "shrink the hall" by darkening sections of it or hanging banners. Fake identification could be used in telephone surveys to assess potential crowd turnout, and traffic could be stalled with broken-down cars to create crowds. The manual gave priority ranking for the media (first the wire services, then the networks, then individual stations or newspapers) and suggested that to maximize coverage, one should "dribble out" information. ("Never tell people more than they need to know to perform their function . . . by restricting knowledge you will be better able to control what occurs.") Once the story broke, Carter ordered the manual revised. Jody Powell said Carter had never seen it and quoted him as saying it was "not in line with the way I want to see this campaign run."

Stories about problems in the Carter political organization had also been filtering into the press since early October. Because his state coordinators were salaried officials, paid by the national Carter organization and not residents of the states for which they had responsibility, they had few alliances or local contacts within their assigned territories and often did not know which bases to touch or how. Some of them hurt their own cause by trying to exclude locals from the organizational machinery. Nor did the headquarters in Atlanta meet the massive demands placed upon it. Local politicos and field workers alike found it very difficult to reach either Ham Jordan or Jody Powell on the phone. A black member of the campaign's committee in Washington, D.C., complained, "As far as Carter is concerned, we don't exist. . . . He should get on the phone and talk to some of the old-time Democrats that he's going to need. But no one does. They still think they're running in the primaries." A similar lack of coordination was evident in conflicts between persons working with the Democratic National Committee and Carter operatives in the field. Mark Siegel, executive director of the DNC, later said the party structure and the Carter campaign had meshed very well "in terms of personal relationships and operating relationships." But there were problems between "our people in the field and the Carter field operatives." On October 27 Herbert Hafif, who had chaired the California State Finance Committee and co-chaired the Carter National Steering Committee during the early primaries, publicized his concerns about the Carter organization in a full-page advertisement in the Los Angeles Times: "Hidden behind the smiles and loose joking of the small Carter team is the fact that it is a team experienced only in campaigning with no higher goal, save getting their man the Presidency. . . . Twenty-nine-year-old 'old boys' from Georgia jealously guarding the palace gates of power are more than reminiscent of Nixon's style, they constitute its substance." Hafif concluded, "this country is not being asked to elect a Democratic president, but to elect another imperial president who will promise anything to get elected but whose words stand in stark contrast to his records and actions." It was a hard-hitting statement and it might have had some impact. Ron Nessen thought it would be "a bombshell."

But the story did not fly. On CBS, Walter Cronkite gave a very brief report that a rich California attorney had taken out an ad attacking Carter. The Atlanta *Constitution* ran a short story under the headline "Angry Ex-Carter Aide Takes It Out In Print." The advertisement only gained wide attention when the Ford committee ran the aid in newspapers across the country on October 31.

One late-breaking story of conflict in the Plains Baptist Church, however, had serious negative potential. On Sunday, October 31, the Reverend Clennon King, the black minister of a storefront church in Albany, Georgia, accompanied by two black women and a child, appeared at the Plains Baptist Church to attend the Sunday service. The church doors were locked. In the pesence of a large crowd of reporters, photographers, and tourists, the Reverend Bruce Edwards explained that the deacons had canceled the services. They had decided, he said, to enforce the 1965 ban barring "niggers and other civil rights agitators." Hugh Carter, standing beside Edwards, shouted, "No! No! It says negroes—N-E-G-R-O-E-S." The UPI at 1:34 P.M. circulated the story under an "urgent" heading.

Carter should have been prepared for this. His willingness to let the church become such a focal point in his campaign had been risky from the beginning. The publicity had unleashed a flood of journalists and tourists on the church. By late October many members were unable to find parking places and some were refused admittance until they could be identified by Edwards or a deacon. Tourists were occupying congregation members' usual pews and taking hymn books, offering envelopes, and rocks from the church yard as souvenirs. It is not surprising that local townspeople resented this invasion. Further, with the exception of an occasional black reporter or Secret Service agent attending when Carter was present, the faces in the Sunday school classes and worship services were uniformly white week after week. The old 1965 rule banning blacks and other agitators from membership still stood as church policy.

There had been clear indications for the whole week preceding the confrontation of what might happen. The previous Sunday veteran UPI reporter Helen Thomas had looked around at an all-white congregation and had asked Carter, "Why are there no blacks here?" Carter drew back, startled. "I can't answer that," he said, "guess it's because they don't come." The Reverend Edwards, who had not heard that exchange, said in his sermon that there should be no "color line drawn in worship." The next day Clennon King (no relation to Martin Luther King) dropped off a letter at the Plains parsonage stating that he intended to apply for membership. Edwards took the letter to his board of deacons, recommending repeal of the 1965 ban, and endorsed King for membership or, if not that, consideration of the application on its merits. He was unanimously overruled, and the ban was read and reaffirmed. When Edwards protested that he could not go along with such a decision, some of the deacons suggested, in effect, that he should start looking for another church. One deacon moved that the upcoming Sunday service be canceled and the whole issue put off until after the election. Shortly thereafter Edwards contacted Carter. Carter offered not strategy or advice, but prayers and assurance that Edwards would do the right thing.

On Sunday shortly after the story had gone out over the UPI wire, journalists traveling with Carter in Texas tried to ask him about it. He brushed them off. Even Powell was not on top of the story. One reporter who accosted him was greeted by an explosive "Fuck you." (Powell apologized later.)

Right after that, however, Carter made a statement. His church had always accepted all worshipers, he said, and it was his "own deep belief . . . that anyone who *lives in our community* and who wants to be a member of our church, regardless of race, ought to be admitted (emphasis added)." On his way to San Francisco he added, "I will seek church action to continue worship opportunities and also offer membership to those who *live in our community* and *who share our religious faith* (emphasis added)." These conditions, as Carter must have known, would enable his friends in the church to deny the locally notorious King membership in the church on grounds other than race.

Meanwhile, Jody Powell had studied the final Gallup Poll, which showed Ford edging ahead of Carter by one percentage point. He decided that further action was necessary and woke Carter, who had gone to bed early, for a telephone conference with Andrew Young and Ham Jordan. Both advised Carter to issue a further statement.

So the next day, at a press conference in Sacramento, Carter suggested that King's action was politically motivated. "Recently, I think because of my presence in the church, as a Democratic nominee of our party, there's been a deliberate effort made to force the issue by someone who doesn't live in the community; who's a Republican; who's not a Baptist . . . perhaps if I had been there—I'm not a deacon any more in our church—I could have had something to do with minimizing the problem." When reporters asked why he didn't resign from his church, Carter responded: "But I can't resign from the human race because there's discrimination . . . and I don't intend to resign from my own church because there's discrimination. I think my best approach is to stay within the church and try to change the attitudes which I abhor. . . . If it was a country club, I would have quit." One of Carter's top aides said that the incident was the "most emotionally complex moment for him during the campaign."

Carter was really saved by the black supporters who rallied around him as they had done during the "ethnic purity" flap. Mrs. Coretta Scott King, who had flown to Los Angeles to appear with Carter, issued a formal statement of support, and agreed to an interview on the subject. In Boston, Jesse Jackson reaffirmed his support for Carter. In Atlanta, Andrew Young and Martin Luther King, Sr., organized a show of support for him. Young charged that Clennon King was inspired by politics, not by God, as he had claimed. And three thousand people listened as Clennon King's highly respected brother, C. B. King, denounced his brother's activity, calling him "emotionally and mentally disturbed." The whole incident was "the antithesis of what Jimmy Carter stands for."

The suggestion that Clennon King's action was politically motivated was reinforced by the discovery that only minutes after the story went out on the wire services, the President Ford Committee had sent telegrams to some 375 to 400 black ministers stating that if Carter could not influence the decisions and opinions of his own church, could one expect him to influence the issues and opinions of the United States Congress? Betty Rainwater of Carter's staff immediately contacted the three television networks and other representatives of the press, charging collusion ("they [the PFC] knew exactly what was going to happen and they probably had someone down there"). As a result network news on election eve emphasized the Carter statement alleging political motivation and the reports of support for Carter from black leaders. There was little discussion of the actual policy of the Plains church.

Overall, the campaign of 1976 was a big disappointment to many close observers. R. W. "Johnny" Apple of *The New York Times*, who had helped kick off the Carter surge with his report of the early Iowa poll, complained on October 20 about the fall campaign. "Neither nominee," he suggested, "appears able to decide whether he wants to be a good guy or a rabbit puncher." Moreover, with the "confusion produced by thematic and stylistic contradictions, in the absence of substantive discussion of most issues, the campaign has focused on a strange series of mishaps." Martin Kondracke, in a Chicago *Sun-Times* commentary entitled "The Dirty Duo," saw an "increasingly petty, nasty, low-blow campaign, and if voters are turned off by it, it's hard to blame them." Overall, Jerald terHorst reported, there was a "turned-off electorate. . . . The inability of President Ford and Jimmy Carter to excite, arouse, and mobilize the country can be ascribed to many reasons. The principal one is that vast numbers of voters have looked at the two men and see no practical differences. . . ."

### The Prize

Ironically, the independent campaign of former Senator Eugene McCarthy, which had received little attention throughout the fall, now took on great importance. The Gallup organization was giving McCarthy only 2 percent of the vote in its final poll. But with the major candidates separated by only one percentage point and 4 percent still undecided in the last Gallup reckoning, Mc-

Carthy's pull could be a deciding factor. McCarthy was on the ballot in twenty-nine states, including Illinois, Ohio, Iowa, and Oregon. He could possibly swing enough votes away from Carter to give those states to Ford.

The most important factor in the election, however, was likely to be voter turnout. There are twice as many self-identified Democrats as Republicans in the United States, but they tend to vote at a lower rate. A relatively high turnout is thus ordinarily an advantage for Democratic contenders. The Democratic Party's major concern at the end was fighting the apathy that seemed to have overtaken the campaign.

One old Carter friend, Bob Smalley, predicted that the election would hinge on the weather, though he was not thinking of the turnout rate. If the sun shines, he explained, the voters will feel optimistic and willing to take a chance (Carter). If it is a gloomy, gray day, they will feel doubtful and prefer a known quantity (Ford).

The weather on Tuesday, November 2, was sunny, dry, and unseasonably warm throughout most of the nation. Yet after the first returns began showing, it became clear that the election would not be decided until late in the night. Though there had been a record turnout—more than 81.5 million Americans voted (up 4 million from 1972)—the turnout *percentage* was low. In the nation as a whole the turnout was only 54.4 percent, the lowest since 1948.

Not until 3:31 A.M. did a network—NBC—declare Carter the projected winner. Carter claimed his victory at 4:00 A.M., meeting the faithful who had gathered at the World Congress Center in Atlanta. He was happy, and the crowd was jubilant: "It's not going to be easy for any of us . . ." he said. But, "if I can tap the greatness that's in you and in the American people, we can make our nation's government great and a source of pride once again." Then he went into the familiar litany:

"Are you proud of our nation?"
(The crowd shouts back, "Yes")
"Do you think we can help to unify it and bring it back together?"
(The crowd shouts, "Yes")
"Do you think we can put our people back to work?"
(The crowd shouts, "Yes")

He concluded, "I want to thank all of you. I love everybody here. . . . Let's all get to work to make our country great once again. . . . I'll try not to disappoint you. Thank you very much."

In the early dawn, after a short nap, he went home, where it had all begun. With the sun climbing over the horizon, he stood on the platform at the train depot and greeted the crowd of friends, family, and followers who had come to share in the moment of triumph. Carter began: "I told you I didn't intend to lose." Obviously in the grasp of deep emotion, he tried to go on: "I came all the way through—through the 22 months, and I didn't get choked up until I . . ." Breaking off in midsentence, tears pouring down his face, he turned to embrace a weeping Rosalynn. Turning back to the microphones, he finished his sentence: ". . . until I turned the corner and saw you standing here and said, 'People who are that foolish—we can't get beat.' "

The climb had been long and hard, and he had come perilously close to failure. Whatever had motivated him in his pursuit, he had snared the ultimate prize. From relative obscurity as a peanut warehouser and one-term governor of Georgia, he had won the most powerful political office in the Western world.

## The Reasons Why

Carter's overall electoral strategy had worked. Its cornerstone had been the South, and he won eleven of the thirteen states in that region (Virginia and Oklahoma were the exceptions). He won the few Northern industrial states he needed to put him over the top—New York, Ohio, Pennsylvania—as well as Massachusetts, Delaware, Rhode Island, Wisconsin, Minnesota, Hawaii, and the District of Columbia. Ford had taken all of the Western states, most of the Midwest, as well as New Jersey, Virginia, Connecticut, Maine, and Vermont. McCarthy, as it turned out, could have made the difference had he been on the ballot in New York (which Carter won by 288,767 votes). As it was, he played a role in tipping Iowa and Oregon to Ford.

However, Carter had not won the big mandate he had hoped for in the summer. In the Electoral College his vote was 297 to 240 for Ford (one Washington state elector pledged to Ford cast his vote for Ronald Reagan)—the smallest winning total since Woodrow Wilson's victory over Charles Evans Hughes in 1916. Carter's victory in the popular votes was also slim. Taking 40.8 million votes to Ford's 39.1 million, Carter had a margin of 1.7 million votes. In percentage terms he received 50.1 percent of the vote to Ford's 48 percent, with 1.9 percent going to Eugene McCarthy and the other minor candidates. This was slightly larger than Kennedy's percentage relative to Nixon in 1960, but considerably smaller than Johnson's in 1964.

Despite the appearances suggested by the electoral vote, Carter's election did not introduce a new pattern of regionally based voting. Though his 53.7 percent of the vote in the South was larger than any other Democrat's since Harry Truman's in 1948, and larger than his plurality nationwide, his vote was not sufficiently high to indicate that a solid South was back in the Democratic fold. His lead was substantially lower than the 65.6 that Truman had obtained in 1948 (even with the Dixiecrat challenge) and substantially below what Franklin D. Roosevelt pulled (81.3 percent in 1932 and 74.1 percent in 1944). Moreover, the composition of Carter's majority was different—a consequence of the Voting Rights Acts of 1964. Only from blacks did he receive a majority in most of the South. Conversely, Democrats had not lost the West and the farm states permanently to the Republicans. Ford's victories were not consistently large— and were particularly small in California, Oregon, and Iowa. It was a close election everywhere. In only twenty states and the District of Columbia did one candidate pull over ten percent more than the other.

Ironically, the man who had run on his personality, as an "outsider," with appeals to individuals across the political spectrum, owed his victory to the traditional party vote. According to the Gallup Poll, Carter secured 82 percent of the voters who identified themselves as Democrats, 85 percent of the non-white*, 63 percent of union families, 58 percent of the manual labor vote, 57 percent of the Catholic vote, and, according to another poll, 68 percent of the Jewish vote. In economic and social terms his strength was where it normally is among Democratic candidates—the middle- and lower-income groups. Thus, Carter won 58 percent of the blue-collar vote, 58 percent of grade-school graduates', 54 percent of the high-school graduates' vote and of those in the less affluent areas of the South. (The fact that there was an 8 percent unemployment rate at this time may have contributed to this phenomenon.)

In some of these categories, however—Catholics, Jews, voters under twenty-one—Carter's margin was below expectations. The Catholic vote of 57 percent, for example, was approximately equal to Humphrey's 59 percent in 1968 (when Wallace was attracting the blue-collar vote) and considerably below the 78 percent secured by Kennedy in 1960 and the 76 percent secured by Johnson in 1964. †

Within the Democratic coalition, the two groups that did the most to secure Carter's overall victory were the blacks and the union members. Of all the socioeconomic groupings, they had given him the highest percentages. Blacks, whatever figures are used, roughly equaled the vote for Johnson (94 percent) in 1964. The union family vote for Carter was equal to or better than that given to any other candidate since 1952 except Johnson in 1964. (Kennedy received 65 percent of the vote in 1960; Johnson received 73 percent in 1964.) Most important, these groups turned out for Carter in the states where he needed them most. Without the largely disproportionate vote for Carter by union families, his success in New York, Pennsylvania, and Ohio would have been impossible. Blacks helped push Carter over the top in both the North (e.g., New York, where he received 282,000 black votes), and the South (e.g., Louisiana, Texas, and Mississippi, where there was a high black turnout and overwhelming preference for Carter).

This turnout was largely the result of efforts by the Democratic National Committee and other groups closely associated with it. The major task of the party during the campaign was voter registration—and approximately 3 million people were registered in fourteen targeted states. The concentration was on blacks, Latinos, the poor, and the young. The effort with blacks was aided by Jesse Jackson, Coretta Scott King, Barbara Jordan, Richard Hatcher, and others, working with the DNC-financed "Operation Big Vote" and "Wake Up,

* The exact percentage of the black vote varies from poll to poll—the Washington Joint Center for Political Studies gave Carter 94 percent of the 6.6 million black votes; CBS gave him 82 percent; Lou Harris gave him 87 percent.

† Religion, according to Gallup, was not the deciding factor in the Catholic voters' choices. Most of them saw Carter's religion as an asset, and few placed a heavy emphasis on the abortion issue. Catholics were inclined to support Carter because they saw him as closer to their political views than Ford.

Black America." The AFL-CIO, which had endorsed no one in 1972, had their computers at work as early as May, 1976, categorizing their 12 million members—spewing out lists for local unions, complete with name, address, telephone number, and the relevant state and national voting district information. In the final days of the campaign, as it became clear the election would be close and turnout important, major canvassing operations were undertaken. In Pennsylvania approximately 10,000 union members were working on Carter's behalf on Election Day. In Cleveland, Ohio, 900 labor volunteers did the same thing. The UAW was particularly important, utilizing many of their 250,000 retired members to canvass and staff the telephone banks throughout the nation. Perhaps their best organized effort was in Michigan, where union members handed out bags of peanuts and announced the UAW's support for Carter at virtually every plant gate in the state.

Overall, these various "get-out-the-vote" efforts were a crucial ingredient in Carter's victory. Of the 3 million new voters registered, approximately 2.4 million voted Democratic. Total black registration was 9.5 million—up 750,000 over 1972—and the black turnout rate was considerably above what it had been in 1972 (about 70 percent, as compared to 58 percent). The electoral significance of these efforts can be most clearly seen by a quick look at two states, North and South, that Carter carried in the end. The AFL-CIO helped register 500,000 voters in Pennsylvania. Carter's margin of victory there was 123,073 votes. In Mississippi blacks turned out at a rate 22 percent higher than in 1972 and gave Carter 134,000 votes. Carter's margin of victory in that state was only 14,483 votes.

There is another way of looking at Carter's election victory. Some other groups, though they did not give him a majority, voted for him at a higher rate than they normally have done for a Democratic candidate, and that difference may be viewed as putting him over the top. In winning 46 percent of the Protestant vote, he was 10 percentage points higher than the average Democratic candidate for President since 1952, and higher than any Democrat since Johnson in 1964. Among professional and business people, his 42 percent ran higher than any other Democrat's except Johnson's 54 percent. Carter's 52 percent from those over fifty years old was a full 10 percentage points higher than the recent Democratic average. Studies other than Gallup's show that Carter's support from suburbs, small towns, rural areas—which are becoming increasingly important with urban flight—was above the Democratic average. Rural residents gave Carter half their vote in many farm states, contributing significantly to his victories in such states as Wisconsin and Ohio. (However, he lost the highly volatile independent vote to Ford. With 38 percent of that vote; he did not do so well as John Kennedy in 1960—43 percent—or Johnson in 1964—56 percent.)

Carter's inroads in these groups were a reflection of the strategy he had followed from the beginning of the campaign (as well as his entire political career). He had pursued a minimalist strategy for his base support—relying as he did on party symbols, rhetoric, and organization in an attempt to keep it secure. But unlike his Democratic predecessors—McGovern, Humphrey, Johnson, and Kennedy—Carter had actively wooed other groups with simultaneous emphasis on conservative social and foreign policy symbols and domestic policy themes, normally the preserve of Republican leaders.

It is a risky strategy, however, and has its costs. Generally, it is likely to induce apathy in the home base—where individuals are apt to be puzzled and uncertain over the unfamiliar packaging of appeals. Some will drop out; others will be less enthusiastic than usual in their support. For the individuals being wooed who are not normally within the base coalition there is a volatility problem. As they become aware that the candidate is the standard bearer for the other group and will be indebted to it, they are apt to defect from him.

Carter suffered this kind of fallout in the campaign of 1976. Despite the early signs of Republican support, he received a very small portion of that vote. Before the Republican convention 27 percent of the Reagan supporters had said if Ford got the nomination they would vote for Carter. On election day, however, Ford carried 91 percent of the Republican vote, Carter less than 9 percent, about the same percentage normally received by Democratic candidates. There was an even greater slide among the independents. (At his peak in July, Carter had 60 percent of these voters, compared to Ford's 30 percent. By mid-October their positions had reversed, with Ford receiving 53 percent to Carter's 33 percent.) Though Carter picked up strength in the independent category after the third debate, his final support from them was the smallest received by any candidate to win the presidency since 1952 (38 percent).

Even in his own Democratic base (which in 1976 consisted of 48 percent of the voting populace as contrasted to the Republican's 23 percent) Carter had problems. He had not attracted very enthusiastic crowds toward the end of the campaign. Even the intelligentsia, the second most faithful group to the old Democratic coalition, was uneasy. In mid-October, Robert Kaiser had noted that this group was only "grudgingly" supporting Carter. There was a concern "that Carter is too flexible, too 'slippery', too willing to bend and remold his positions under political pressure," and this disaffection was evident in the final vote. Despite the efforts of the DNC, unions, and blacks, and Carter's own efforts to recover the centrist Democrats who had drifted away from the party in 1972, he won no extraordinary majority in the party. It is true that his 82 percent of the Democratic vote was above the average of all Democratic presidential candidates since 1952. But it was below the figures posted by the other two Democratic winners in that period—Kennedy received 84 percent of the Democratic vote in 1960 and Johnson received 87 percent in 1964. The more general apathy was evident in the relatively large number of undecided voters that persisted up to Election Day. In mid-October, Daniel Yankelovich (polling for *Time* magazine), reported that 52 percent of the electorate was "soft" or "undecided"—a figure almost four times that seen at the same time in the 1972 election.

This volatility in the vote, and the apathy with which it was associated, was related to widespread uncertainty in the electorate about what Jimmy Carter stood for and about what he would do as President. In late September, after the first debate, the CBS-*New York Times* poll showed that 66 percent of those polled agreed with the statement, "At least I know what kind of a President Gerald Ford will be. I'm not so sure about Jimmy Carter." Pollster Daniel Yankelovich observed the public's confusion about Carter. "The electorate feels that it has a fairly clear sense of what a Ford presidency would be like. A Carter presidency, on the other hand, is still somewhat of a mystery." Lou Harris in his mid-October polls, found a similar malaise regarding Carter. Only 42 percent of the respondents felt Carter more trustworthy than Ford (with 17 percent undecided).

Doubts about Carter did not end once the decision had been made. NBC News, in a postelection poll, discovered that only 40 percent of the voters felt that Carter could be trusted to do the right thing "most of the time"—just about the same figure as for Ford. Pat Caddell, in a memo written in December, concluded that Carter had emerged from the election campaign with four major initial problems: he was still viewed as inexperienced; as an individual who "flip-flops on issues and positions"; as a person who "overpromised"; and as a possible "risk" as President. "Because he is an 'unknown,' whose actions and behavior can only be discerned when he is finally in office, many voters worry."

This uneasiness about Carter, as his aides later sensed, was not just based on a concern over his issue stances. As Jody Powell said in December, 1976: "There was no way on God's earth we could shake the fuzziness question in the general election, no matter what Carter did or said. He could have spent the whole campaign doing nothing but reading substantive speeches from morning to night and still have had that image in the national press." Hamilton Jordan sensed the nature of their difficulty when he said, "I think that oftentimes voters described Carter as fuzzy when they were unable to verbalize what they really meant." Perhaps the voters called him fuzzy "because he was a Southerner," or because of the "weirdo factor."

Actually the problem stemmed partly from his attempt to appeal to such a broad political spectrum. In trying to win over so many, he raised questions with some about where he really stood on the traditional scale of political values. It was also caused by the actual zigs and zags of the fall campaign. Though some of the shifts made good sense tactically, the overall appearance was that he corrected his course too fast, too often—he never seemed on an even keel.

At the most basic level, Carter's image problem came from having cast himself in such a heroic mold. There had been a fantasylike quality to Carter's self-presentation in the spring and summer. No man has the extraordinary virtue that Carter seemed to claim for himself. No politician can survive as an "outsider," or not make trades of one sort or another with other politicians, or hold his own organization together without some of the usual spoils of office. No campaign organization can function as smoothly and efficiently as the Carter people had claimed during the spring. Nowhere do people live in the harmony portrayed in Plains. When the realities of who he was, where he came from, and what he would do as a politician became more apparent in the fall, questions about him began. In elections the bottom line is victory, and that Carter had achieved. But the election did not answer the questions raised by the campaign—or those that would be raised by his presidency.

# V

# Presidency

# TWENTY-ONE

---

# Symbols and Spoils

THE INAUGURATION would be the high mark of Carter's populism as President. Three hundred thousand invitations were sent out—many to people whom Carter had met on the campaign trail and to whom he had promised this invitation. Although the basic invitation was a souvenir piece that only invited the recipient to come to Washington, the inaugural committee did schedule many free events—concerts, fireworks, and a huge square dance the night of the swearing-in. Admission fees were charged for most of the other events, but as journalists covering the event noted, the fees were low compared to the tariffs Nixon had charged at his 1972 inaugural.

For the swearing-in ceremony in front of the Capitol, Carter wore an ordinary three-piece business suit (bought in Americus for $175) and used his campaign name, "Jimmy Carter," rather than the formal James Earl Carter, Jr. He took his oath of office on a Bible that had been in the family for four generations. His unusually brief address promised both a new beginning and a "fresh faith in the old dream." More is not necessarily better, he said. Even our great nation has its limits. Yet together, "in a spirit of individual sacrifice for the common good, we must simply do out best". When the parade began, to the amazement of all, Carter broke precedent by walking the mile and a half down Pennsylvania Avenue to the White House with Rosalynn and Amy at his side. Though the security staff and police were upset by Carter's decision to "walk it," one security policeman, questioned by the press, said: "For a populist president, it's a good move."

There were many other symbols. A practice of the past, a show of religious unity, was evident in the inclusion of religious leaders of many faiths in various worship services. The reviewing stand at the White House used solar energy— a sign of the future. Even the décor was chosen to reflect the populist theme. J. Perry Kelly, the designer of the color decorations, chose warm colors (red, pink) to reflect "the glowing, warm and exceedingly human Carter people." There were no flowers, except in rooms for the Carters. Flowers, Kelly said, were too expensive. Overall, the tone of the inauguration as relayed by the press was one of folksiness, harmony, and frugality.

Carter continued to use "populist" symbols after the inauguration. In one of his most widely publicized acts, nine-year-old Amy was enrolled in the fourth grade at a predominantly black school near the White House—the first President's child to attend a public school since Theodore Roosevelt's Administration. At the swearing-in of eight Cabinet officers and four other Cabinet-level officials on January 23, Carter called attention to his "first official and completely open ceremony" and announced that he would forego the traditional playing of "Ruffles and Florishes" and "Hail to the Chief" by the Marine Corps band. The next day, after the first Cabinet meeting, press aide Rex Granum gave a detailed briefing on what Carter had told its members. He had announced that he was eliminating chauffeur service for his White House aides (which would reduce the number of vehicles in the White House motor pool by at least twenty cars) and suggested that his Cabinet members follow his lead with their own staffs. Foreign dignitaries would be greeted without the usual amount of military and other ceremonial display, and travel abroad by department heads should be limited to the absolutely necessary. Lawyers, he charged, had created "oceans of paper" for lack of anything better to do. Granum quoted Carter as saying, "I am determined to stay in touch with the people," and he asked the Cabinet officers to give him, in writing, their plans for doing the same.

Carter elaborated on his themes in several media events following the inaugural. On February 2, in his first fireside chat, the President wore a sweater carefully chosen for its warmth (to emphasize the conservation-mindedness of the wearer) and casualness. He made several promises. Government regulations, he said, would be written in "plain English" and would carry the author's name (an impossible promise, given the number of parties and compromises behind each official act). Honesty in government would be guaranteed by his strict rules on financial disclosure by his appointees. And he promised to "close the revolving door between the government regulatory agencies on one hand, and the business they regulate on the other."

In his fireside chat Carter used some visual images that had worked well for Franklin D. Roosevelt. In early March he tried something new to the White House, but previously successful for him—the call-in show. On March 5, for two hours, he was available to any American who could get through the jammed switchboard (over nine million people tried). He received and answered the questions of forty-two respectful Americans. And as he told Walter Cronkite, who screened the questions, the American people, were telling him "what they were concerned about" and asking questions never "asked of me and reported through the media."

During his first months in office Carter had another way of showing his ties to the people. In late February he announced his plans to make sure that 5 to 10 percent of the guests at state dinners would be average Americans. (At first, the "average Americans" were those who had helped in the campaign.) And even though some White House aides were worried that Carter's meet-the-plain-folk program might be perceived as a political gimmick, the response was favorable.

Drawing from his own practice as governor, Carter also took "power" (i.e., himself in the full trappings of office) to the people. As President he used the format of the town meeting. In mid-March he went to Clinton, Massachusetts, where he mixed with the people and answered their questions, while an uncomfortable Ted Kennedy and other Massachusetts dignitaries looked on. Shortly thereafter he did a repeat performance at Yazoo, Mississippi—in a sweating hot auditorium. The President took off his jacket and, probably for the first time in public, admitted that he, like most of them, had not been on the cutting edge when others had advanced racial justice in the South.

On these trips Carter often visited in homes of "average people." At Clinton, for example, he stayed overnight with a blue-collar family. Later these visits would be held in the homes of Democratic Party workers or volunteers from his early campaign. Each trip would be reported, with relevant stories showing the human side of Carter. He would stop at an elementary school class which had written him a letter, or make an unexpected phone call to individuals who had written the White House about some problem. Often the trips would be accompanied by a political announcement of interest to the local constituents. In addition to these attempts to keep close to the people, Carter sent out 450,000 letters to the public, asking their suggestions about energy.

Carter would also be open to the press in his first months in office. During the campaign he had promised to hold press conferences twice a month, and that first month, on February 8 and February 23, he did so. At his first conference, Carter pledged to hold twenty such conferences per year. By the end of the year he had held twenty-two.

Not only did Carter suggest he would keep down the barriers between himself and the people, he signaled that he would run an open Administration. During the campaign and transition, Carter promised that he would create a strong Cabinet that would provide real policy input. And after his first meeting with the Cabinet, deputy press secretary Rex Granum announced that the President had even suggested that the meetings might be open to the press. Further, Carter indicated that he would avoid a bulky, hierarchically organized staff. During the campaigning Powell had put forth the "spokes of the wheel concept"—explaining Carter's preference for a balanced circle of advisers rather than a powerful chief of staff through whom everything would be funneled. Hamilton Jordan, appearing on CBS's "Face the Nation" in mid-November, said: "The concept of a chief of staff is alien to Governor Carter and those of us around him. He's always had a strong team effort." On the same subject Carter, himself, said: "There will never be an instance while I am President where the members of the White House staff dominate or act in a superior position to the members of our Cabinet."

Further, there were "deeds" which suggested Carter was serious about pursuing these values. In his fireside chat he had talked about reorganizing the federal government:

The place to start is at the top—in the White House. . . . I am reducing the size of the White House staff by nearly one-third, and have asked the members of the Cabinet to do the same at the top staff level. Soon I will put a ceiling on the number of people employed by federal government agencies, so we can bring the growth of government under control . . . We have eliminated expensive and unnecessary luxuries, such as door-to-door limousine service for many top officials, including all members of the White House staff. Government officials can't be sensitive to your problems if we are living like royalty here in Washington.

Right after that the White House took steps to implement these objectives. The plans were to organize the White House office along functional lines, as opposed to a line-of-command setup. Zero-based review techniques would be applied to each White House unit's operational budget and personnel requests, to reduce the cost and size of staffs. A management committee composed of nine senior presidential aides would assume some of the functions previously assigned to a chief of staff. The old Domestic Council was disassembled, to be replaced by a domestic policy staff under the direction of Stuart E. Eizenstat. Another group supervised by Jack H. Watson, Jr., would act as the secretariat for the Cabinet. Looking at these plans, one observer concluded: "the changes could form the framework in which he is presented as a truly public President." Carter, in short, gave signs that he was going to be a frugal, simple, open, people's president.

Carter also moved quickly to show he would be an aggressive President in policy terms. The day after the swearing-in, he issued his first executive order to pardon the Vietnam draft evaders, indicating that he would keep his campaign promises and act quickly and clearly on controversial issues. He announced in early February that plans for a new Energy Department would be sent to Congress on March 1. And he promised to have a comprehensive energy program ready to present to a joint session of Congress by April 20. At a press conference on March 9 he offered a large number of domestic programs and new foreign policy departures: a Youth Conservation Corps program, a Middle East compromise, gradual withdrawal of U.S. troops from South Korea, and arms negotiation with Russia. He also brought forth his tax rebate program, his authorization to reorganize the government, and his opposition to "wasteful" water projects for the West.

To many close observers, however, it appeared that his basic economic and social policies would not depart substantially from the status quo. As early as December 29, 1976, Carter had suggested that his welfare reform package might have to wait for economic recovery. He claimed that he never promised to reduce the defense budget by $5 to $7 billion annually. (What he had said was that, through his efficiency measures, the budget could be cut $5 to $7 billion below the *increases proposed* by the Ford Administration.) And he assured the business community that he was no radical by indicating he would move slowly on tax reforms. Moreover, the range of his appointments suggested that he would rely heavily on old establishment figures, with a few women and minorities added to satisfy Democratic voting groups. It was a reflection of his more general tactic of trying to appeal to many factions and thus avoid identification with a clear-cut ideology. Overall, he had established, even before coming to office, the pattern he would follow throughout his Administration—making ad hoc adaptations to the strongest forces that typically influence politicians, while also making gestures (in appointments and minor legislative rewards) to the more liberal traditional groupings in his party.

The basic strategy had been suggested to Carter by Patrick Caddell in a fifty-six-page memo in December, 1976. Carter, he suggested, should emphasize style rather than substance in the early days in the White House. He should continue "campaigning," using fireside chats, town hall meetings, and the cutting of limousine service, while emphasizing the Southern elements, to keep Southern support. The problem, Caddell suggested, was that Carter did not have a strong mandate to lead the country. He had narrowly won the election and, to gain a broader voter base, he should use the honeymoon period to reassure and win over broad segments of the American public.

In some respects the strategy worked. Shortly after the election 61 percent of the populace positively expected the President-elect to do a "good" to "excellent" job. (There was however, a 59 percent majority who thought Carter would try to be "all things to all people.") During the transition period Carter's approval rating climbed to 70 percent, with 19 percent disapproving. The March Gallup Poll showed him up further, winning a 72 percent approval of his overall performance, with only a 10 percent disapproval.

But Carter also showed his proclivity for overdoing a good thing. At the very beginning the press uncritically relayed all this symbolic action. When commentators discussed it, they saw Carter as a superior politician—good at using the media, especially where symbols were involved. As early as his first fireside chat, however, a few journalists were seeing them as contrived and overdone, and wondering if the presidency was to be one of gestures rather than decisive action. David Broder suggested that almost everything Carter had done from the time he had taken office was public-relations tactics rather than meaningful decision making. Tom Wicker in *The New York Times* suggested he was trying to govern by television and public appeal. Gary Trudeau, in his popular "Doonesbury" comic strip, satirized the emphasis on symbols, showing a White House with a Secretary of Symbols who went around looking for "average people" (including one young woman who was insulted by the designation) to invite to dinner parties. And occasionally inconsistencies were spotted. William Safire criticized Carter's hiring of his nephew, Hugh Carter, Jr., as a White House aide as a form of nepotism. Joseph Kraft wondered why the White House did not release the written argument by Attorney General

Griffin Bell on the constitutionality of Carter's one-house veto for government reorganization. How did Carter decide on Stansfield Turner as CIA head, and why did Turner fly a Concorde from Europe? To Kraft and other reporters' skepticism about the White House's continued use of symbols with "nothing to show," Jody Powell replied that the press was taking the whole thing too seriously.

## *Early Spoils*

During the campaign Carter had played to a widespread public desire to transcend politics, a dominant theme in reformist politics of the United States. He would eliminate the spoils system and choose government officials only on the basis of merit. But Carter was not so politically naive as to follow this campaign rhetoric once he was in office.

In his Cabinet appointments, Carter brought in his own personal supporters to the nerve centers of government. Carter's old friend, political ally, and personal banker, Bert Lance, was named director of the Office of Management and Budget, which controls the budget for all the agencies of government. The director of the Georgia Office of Planning and Budget, James McIntyre, Jr., was named deputy director. The new Attorney General, Griffin Bell, a former judge on the Fifth Circuit Court of Appeals (serving the Deep South states), was an old acquaintance from Americus and a member of the Atlanta law firm to which Carter adviser Charles Kirbo also belongs. (The top slots in Justice had been set before the fall election according to one of my informants. In addition to Bell as Attorney General, a Carter supporter and former head of the ABA was slated to become Solicitor General. This latter appointment was dropped, going to Wade H. McCree, Jr., when disappointed blacks and women rallied against the appointment of Bell.) Carter also brought Michael Egan, the Republican minority leader of the Georgia House, who had backed Carter's reorganization plan, into the Justice Department. Peter Flaherty, the Pittsburgh mayor, who had been an early Carter supporter, was named Deputy Attorney General. Andrew Young, who had said during the campaign that he expected no position in the new Administration, was given one as ambassador to the United Nations.

For the key positions in the White House staff, Carter again chose Georgian political intimates. Jody Powell was named press secretary and the only aide about whom Carter said, "he is empowered to speak for me." Hamilton Jordan as special assistant was clearly going to be Carter's major trouble-shooter within the White House. Robert J. Lipshutz, the financial campaign manager in 1976, received the position of legal counsel to the President. The main adviser on domestic issues would be Stuart E. Eizenstat, the issues director during his campaign. Frank Moore was made Carter's assistant for congressional liaison. Richard Harden, despite his problems with the DHR in Georgia, was back as the man in charge of office procedures. Hugh Carter, Jr., was given the job of cutting back on White House luxuries. Indeed, of the seven top White House aides, only one (Margaret Costanza, assistant to the President for liaison for special-interest groups) was not from Georgia.* (Other key non-Georgian campaign aides received important posts. Tim Kraft, campaign field coordinator, became Carter's appointments secretary. Dr. Peter Bourne, a member of Carter's inner circle since 1972, was named special assistant for drug abuse prevention and mental health.)

Carter also rewarded his political friends with ambassadorial posts. Philip Alston, Jr., was named ambassador to Australia, Anne Cox Chambers to Belgium. Louis Lerner (one of his early Illinois supporters and the publisher of a string of neighborhood newspapers) was appointed ambassador to Norway; and Patrick J. Lucey, the governor of Wisconsin, one of Carter's early supporters, was rewarded with the embassy in Mexico (although he did not speak Spanish). Within the State Department, Patricia Derian, Carter's campaign manager in Mississippi, was named Assistant Secretary for Human Rights and Humanitarian Affairs. Hodding Carter III, Joseph Duffey, Richard Holbrooke, John Gilligan, and other such supporters also gained top positions.

Aside from placing his own people in important positions, Carter drew from the traditional elites for some of his top-level policy appointments. Cyrus Vance at State, Harold Brown at Defense, and Joseph Califano at HEW had been directly involved in decision making in the Johnson Administration. Zbigniew Brzezinski, Theodore C. Sorensen (whose nomination for Director of CIA was withdrawn), Patricia Harris, and W. Michael Blumenthal had also served previous Democratic administrations. None of them were "outsiders." Indeed as journalist Hugh Sidey said: "On occasion these days the Washington observer gets the feeling that the past eight years were just a dream. . . . Surveying this scene, one might be led to believe that the government of eight years ago will resume at noon on January 20."

How would Carter control it? "Grafting the head of this Administration to its body is going to be one of the most fascinating bits of political surgery of this century," Sidey mused. "Can the brain of Carter change the condition and function of the middle-aged limbs and trunk of this government, so conventional and familiar?"

For his appointments Carter also drew from the young political activists who had earlier been attached to the campaigns of George McGovern, Eugene McCarthy, and other Democrats. Sam Brown (named head of ACTION) had been on McGovern's campaign staff, and Larry Brown (named head of Peace Corps operations, replacing Howard University psychologist Carolyn Payton) had worked for Eugene McCarthy. John Gabusi in the Community Services Administration had been Udall's campaign manager. Mark Siegel, who had been executive assistant for the DNC in the fall of 1976, was brought into the White House as special liaion to the Jewish groups in the United States.

There was no consistent policy for the political appointees in the depart-

---

* The Georgia appointments were by no means limited to the President's assistants. Of the top federal appointments by Carter in 1977, twenty-one went to people who were Georgians by birth or work. In 1978 thirty-seven appointments to major federal jobs went to Georgians.

ments. Genuine open competition based on merit standards was not the policy, as the Talent Bank had suggested. Indeed, the questionnaires, returned by thousands of political hopefuls, were packed away in crates and stored in the Executive Office Building. No one ever read through them. But in several of the departments Carter did not follow an absolute policy of placing his own people in top positions. The Cabinet officers chose most of their own aides because Carter delegated political appointments in the departments to them. These men and women usually had no connection with Carter's grass-roots campaign workers. So the lower-level campaign workers who had been with Carter from the beginning were finding themselves out in the cold. From one account it appears that of 575 campaign workers seeking jobs, only 263 were given temporary appointments, which were to expire in May 1977. "Suddenly the campaign did not count for much," one reporter noted.

In relinquishing control of many department jobs to the relevant Cabinet officer, Carter also created future problems for himself. Each department head was in a position to create his or her own power base, choosing aides with no special allegiance to Carter. Eventually Carter and his loyalists would find themselves at odds with officials at the assistant secretary level in the departments. Without a common economic and social philosophy to bind together his Administration, Carter would have to call on personal loyalties, and at first he lacked that in several departments.

Later on, Carter's organizational reforms gave him new jobs to fill. In 1978 Congress passed the Omnibus Judgeship Act, creating 117 new district judgeships and thirty-five more court of appeals posts. Carter tried to increase the President's role in filling these slots. He issued an executive order suggesting (not requiring) that merit selection commissions be established in each state to recommend judicial candidates, thus bypassing the senatorial patronage system. The final selections, of course, would be his, and he could choose from a panel presented to him.* The Civil Service Reform Act, passed in 1978, would also give the President a new source of spoils—the census takers at the local level. At the time these arrangements looked only like reforms; Carter's deployment of these opportunities for his own reelection campaign would not become obvious for some time. Overall, Carter's populist rhetoric would obscure the extent to which he was acting as a traditional politician all along.

* The idea, however, did not receive enthusiastic support of Congressmen, and merit commissions were established in only twenty-four states. (Moreover, there is an indication that the merit commissions are making little difference in the patterns of selection. Certainly it has done little to increase the number of women and blacks in that field. The Judicial Selection Project, a group promoting the recruitment of women and minorities, noted that of the seventy-seven nominees thus far—competing for fifty-four slots—there have been only three black men, three Hispanic men, three white women, and two black women. Further, as Attorney General Bell told the Senate Judiciary Committee, the merit commissions established in the twenty-four states were as likely as individual Senators to nominate only white males to judgeships. In fact, two of the states without such commissions, Texas and Maryland, accounted for half of the women/minority nominations. Common Cause, which first attacked Carter for going slow on the campaign promise to create such commissions, later accused the Carter Administration for not being vigorous in recruiting women and minorities and for not limiting senatorial prerogatives.)

# TWENTY-TWO

## Bargaining Style

IN HIS DECEMBER, 1976, strategy memo to Carter, Patrick Caddell had pinpointed where Carter's initial problems might lie. Possible challengers to Carter's policy and his presidency included Democratic leaders—Ted Kennedy, George McGovern, Morris Udall, and Jerry Brown. Labor, metropolitan political machines, and Congress were also seen as potential political threats. When this opposition did appear, it was partly Carter's doing.

### Mixed Signals

In dealing with Congress, Carter employed much the same strategy as with the Georgia legislature, and once again faced the same problems. His staff members showed some insensitivity in their early contacts with congressional leaders. In the summer of 1976 Carter had told Democrats that Frank Moore would be his congressional liaison person. By early November a number of Democrats were complaining about Moore's arrogance and unavailability. Once, when some House Democrats were to meet with him to give campaign suggestions for key states—Pennsylvania, Ohio, Illinois—Moore canceled the meeting on short notice, saying he "just remembered an important engagement." Later, Representative Al Ullman (House Ways and Means Committee Chairman) prepared papers on key legislative issues at Moore's request, but Moore was absent at the follow-up meeting. The House, at Carter's request, had passed a post card voter registration bill, but when it was stopped in committee in the Senate and Senator Majority Leader Mike Mansfield indicated he'd bring the bill to the floor on a go-ahead from Carter or Moore, none was forthcoming. Then there were small insults. Speaker "Tip" O'Neill's request for extra seats at the inaugural festivities were rejected by Jordan. (It was then he began calling Jordan "Hannibal Jerkin.") The relationships between O'Neill and Jordan, Powell, and Rafshoon would never be warm.

Carter himself gave out mixed signals. On one hand he consulted with congressional leaders. Two weeks after the election he met with fifteen Democratic Senators and Representatives in Lovejoy, Georgia, the home of Senator Herman Talmadge. (That setting was chosen instead of Plains as a convenience for Congressmen—Lovejoy was closer to the Atlanta airport.) In his first trip to Washington as President-elect, Carter again met with leaders of the Senate and House—and this time Republicans were included. From them he solicited nominations for his Cabinet and staff, offered his unlisted phone number and his private address. In January he once more met with selected members of Congress to discuss foreign policy issues. In one four-and-one-half-hour session at Lillian's Pond House, he worked with them on an economic package—compromising his original package to increase the amount allocated for public works.

Yet in his first weeks in office Carter moved out on specific matters without doing his political advance work. His initial choice of Theodore Sorensen for CIA director showed this clearly. Sorensen had requested draft exempt status earlier in his career and had given depositions opposing the overclassification of national security documents in the Pentagon Papers (1971) and Daniel Ellsberg (1973) cases. If Carter was serious about this nomination, he was the victim of poor advance work. In any event, he did not communicate with Senate Majority Leader Robert Byrd or other Senators on the Senate committee that would have to approve Sorensen, to gain their feedback on this potentially controversial nomination. When Sorensen's affidavits in the above-mentioned cases were circulated before the hearings, he came under wide attack.

Conservatives wanted the withdrawal of his nomination and Byrd noted that there would be "serious difficulty" with it. Carter took an ambiguous stand. While publicly standing by Sorensen, he failed to lobby the cause with Byrd and other important people. Consequently, on January 17, 1977, the first day of his Senate confirmation hearings, Sorensen announced his withdrawal as nominee.

Carter also showed a disregard for the sensitivities of the Democratic leadership by not giving them the courtesy of consulting them on appointments from their states. Republican John Ellis of Ohio was named as Carter's choice for deputy commissioner of education without first telling Ohio Democrat John Glenn, one of Carter's staunchest supporters. Glenn complained that the Ohio people signed on by the Administration were not active Democrats and that he found out about the appointments only from the press. More damaging was Carter's political rudeness to House Speaker O'Neill. In early February, 1977, Nixon's Attorney General, Elliot L. Richardson, a Republican from O'Neill's home state (Massachusetts), was named as U.S. representative to the Law of the Sea Conference. Richardson was expected to run for governor of Massachusetts against O'Neill's oldest son, and O'Neill was understandably upset that he had not been consulted before the appointment. Further, Carter appointed Massachusetts Republican Evan Dobelle as U.S. chief of protocol, while rejecting O'Neill's suggestion that Lieutenant General James Gavin (a more realistic possibility than Sorensen) be named to head the CIA. (As a gesture to O'Neill, Carter subsequently named O'Neill's close friend Robert T. Griffin as deputy administrator of the General Services Administration. Later in the year he went with another O'Neill suggestion, naming Republican Monroe McKay as federal judge in Utah.)

Aside from these confrontations Carter failed to touch bases with congressional leaders on policy matters of special concern to them. When the Administration proposed a major revamping of HEW, it failed to consult House Whip John Brademas (Indiana), who had designed many of the programs affected by the reorganization. Republicans had their complaints, too. Republican John Rhodes of Arizona, who helped Carter get his original reorganization proposal through the House, stated that Carter did not consult with Republican leaders at all.

Carter's early legislative initiatives further disturbed his relations with Congress. On February 21, in his 1978 budget revision proposals. Carter axed nineteen water projects. Not only was he threatening projects of special interest to several Congressmen, he surprised them with his move. Carter's people had been assuring the Congress that there was no plan to get rid of these projects, though they had been targeted as "questionable" by members of the transition staff. Once the decision to eliminate the projects was made, phone calls and memos were sent out to the affected Congressmen, but they came so late in the week that several had already gone home for the weekend where they learned about the cuts from local newspapers. (Jody Powell explained that the affected Congressmen had been "basically informed. Of course, on a budget, the Congress has its authority to dispose in its wisdom with [sic] the President's recommendations. I don't think it is general practice to involve them in the budget decisions before the budget is presented.")

The Congressional reaction was fury. Representative Butler Derrick (D-South Carolina), whose district was directly affected by the cuts, said: "I found out about it from the newspapers, and I was so mad and embarrassed I couldn't see straight." (Although Derrick later supported Carter's hit list, he felt Carter should have shown "simple political courtesy" in handling the budget cuts.) Representative Morris Udall, whose own state (Arizona) would be affected, said: "I seem to remember some speeches . . . about openness and consulting with Congress . . ." When Cecil Andrus, the Interior Secretary, backpedaled, saying that no final decision had been made, Representative Lloyd Meeds (D-Washington) replied that all the projects had been subject to thorough congressional review. Carter's decision was "presumptuous" and "arrogant." Colorado Senator Gary Hart said: "I don't think we were dealt candidly with . . . It's known as being blind-sided."

The Senate as a whole reacted by voting 65-24 to halt Carter's cut of the projects. Senator J. Bennett Johnston, Jr., who sponsored the legislation, labeled Carter's act "government by executive." Had Carter talked with the Senators, Robert Byrd commented, they might have felt differently: "At least the members would have felt that they had been consulted and heard." Frank Moore lamely claimed that he never knew it was the tradition to tell people what's going to be in the budget "before it was being released."

Later Carter was forced to compromise somewhat and to continue some of the projects. But he still threatened to use his veto if the funding of the projects was considerably more than he recommended. Tip O'Neill warned that such a veto would cause serious confrontation between Congress and Carter. In July both chambers approved a compromise measure that restored funding for several of the projects.

Carter's bill authorizing him to reorganize the national government also brought him into conflict with Jack Brooks, the Democrat who would ordinarily have provided the leadership in the House for the measure. Brooks was concerned about the legality of the reverse veto arrangement—which, like Carter's earlier Georgia proposal, would have the chief Executive's proposals automatically take effect (after sixty days in this instance) unless a congressional majority voted against them. Brooks proposed, instead, a positive vote by the Congress as a whole on any reorganization matters. Carter had to resort to Republicans in the House—Minority Leader John Rhodes and two other Republican Representatives—to sponsor his measure. (When Representative Brooks realized that he didn't have enough support for his alternate bill, he ended up supporting an amended Carter bill for governmental reorganization.)

As in Georgia, Carter was often saved by the leaders in the House and Senate. Common Cause's Fred Wertheimer would later suggest that "Carter would be in terrible shape" had it not been for the efforts of Byrd and O'Neill in pushing his legislation.

House Speaker O'Neill was an old-style Democratic politician whose basic rule of action was that he should help a Democratic President. O'Neill warned Carter about his approach to Congress in one of their first conversations. Carter was telling him "how he handled the Georgia legislature, by going over their heads directly to the people." O'Neill said, "Hey, wait a minute. You have 289 guys up there [the House Democrats] who know their districts pretty well. They ran against the Administration, and they wouldn't hesitate to run against you." Carter said, " 'Oh, really?' "* Later, in the middle of June, O'Neill called a gripe session of fifty House members and Ham Jordan, Frank Moore, and Jim King (Carter's aide in charge of personnel). The Representatives complained of patronage requests ignored, of form letters from Cabinet officers, of Republican holdovers administering programs in their districts. "I busted my butt for Carter," said Representative Walter Flowers of Alabama," and there's nobody I know who got an appointment. I call up and I'm talking to the same people I

* Once, in a three-hour discussion with Frank Moore and Jack Watson (Carter's transition planning chief), Lawrence O'Brien, who had been involved in the Kennedy transition to the White House, had given similar advice: "A President can't whip members of Congress into line." He should try to keep "the lines of communication open." O'Brien also mentioned that little things (phone calls, meetings, publicity help) count, and the Administration shouldn't try to go over the heads of Congress to get things done.

talked to under Nixon and Ford." O'Neill said: "We won the election, but you'd never know it."

Besides giving advice, O'Neill used all his authority and political skill to push the Administration's omnibus energy bill through the House. Carter had said that energy was his number-one priority in a television address on April 18 and in a speech to Congress on April 20, 1977. The package he presented, however, did not meet the simplicity test he had declared he favored. Rather, it was a potpourri including everything from phased deregulation of the price of new oil, an increase in natural gas prices, and a tax on new "gas guzzlers," with benefits going to small-car buyers and homeowners who undertake energy-saving efforts. Several of these provisions were not warmly received. In a meeting with congressional leaders on May 19, 1977, Senate Majority Leader Byrd and Majority Whip Alan Cranston criticized the gas-guzzler tax, which would finance rebates to small-car owners. Byrd suggested the funds go for mass transit and roads. Nevertheless, O'Neill managed to get the package to the House floor virtually intact (except for the rebate measure), which resulted in the House passage of a bill close to Carter's original proposal. The vote was 244-177.

Byrd, too, put his personal prestige on the line to save Carter from defeat—on his amnesty and Korean policies, auto pollution, the Clinch River breeder reactor, and several other issues. For example, in June, Senator Howard Baker (R-Tennessee) proposed an amendment that would delete from one bill Carter's commitment to a phased withdrawal of American troops from Korea. Byrd, not wanting Carter embarrassed by the likely passage of Baker's amendment, used his parliamentary skills to avoid a direct test of support for Carter's policy. Congress postponed consideration of the issue until 1978.

The Democratic leaders' work was made more difficult by Carter's tendency to depreciate those outside his camp. His labeling of an early congressional recess as "what they call a district work period" was not much appreciated. Despite the advance warnings of O'Brien and O'Neill, Carter was soon blasting the entire Congress (just as he had blasted the Georgia legislators). When the House Ways and Means Committee voted down the gasoline tax with rebates to buyers of small cars, Carter told O'Neill of his intention to take his case to the people. (Despite Carter's threats, the House overwhelmingly voted, 339-82, against the proposal.) In one meeting with a Senate commerce subcommittee, Carter said that deregulation of natural gas prices would be "obscene and immoral." And when he lost the committee vote 12 to 10, he was publicly outraged.

Carter also had a tendency to back off from parts of programs about which he had earlier been adamant, leaving his backers politically stranded. His 1977 economic stimulus package, for example, included an across-the-board fifty-dollar tax rebate to individual tax payers. The measure was generally unpopular. (Democrats saw it as requiring too much of a budget cut and Republicans saw it as too lean a tax cut.) But Al Ullman backed the President against his "better judgment" and managed to get it through the House (defeating a Republican proposal for a permanent tax cut). In the Senate, Ed Muskie, who headed the Budget Committee, worked on revisions of the entire budget to allow for the rebates. Suddenly, Carter dropped the plan after Senator Byrd convinced him in a private meeting that he wouldn't have the votes. The ultimate result: the Senate voted 74 to 20 to eliminate the tax rebate, but it kept the tax cuts for businesses, which Carter said he did not want. When Congress finally approved an overall tax plan, the package was very different from Carter's original proposal. Democratic congressional leaders claimed that the gutting of Carter's tax plan was due to "administration meddling." They received too many mixed signals.

Nor did Carter's staff communicate well with Speaker O'Neill, who thought he was backing the Administration when he pushed hard for the B-1 bomber when it was being debated in the House. Two days after the debate began, Carter publicly stated his opposition to the bomber. O'Neill was informed of Carter's decision only ten minutes before the public announcement.

On the deregulation of natural gas prices Carter confused some of his "supporters." Carter had backed deregulation during the 1976 campaign, probably as a part of his effort to secure the support of persons such as Governor David Boren of Oklahoma. (His letter to Boren promising such deregulation was published in the House of Representatives publications of the 1976 campaign documents.) During his first months in office, Carter made several statements that, if one reads the bottom line, indicated he was for phased deregulation of natural gas prices. Though his actual policy choices were close to what the natural gas companies wanted, this was obscured by his heavy attacks on the "special interests" and their desire for immediate and complete deregulation. In Norfolk, Virginia, on September 24, 1977, for example, he attacked the gas companies as "very powerful in Washington as you well know," and said: "I hate to veto a bill that a Democratic Congress passes, but you can depend upon it; I'll protect your interest when the bill crosses my desk." Given statements such as these, Senator Howard Metzenbaum (D-Ohio) and James Abourezk (D-South Dakota) thought the Administration would at least remain neutral as they filibustered for several days in the fall of 1977, hoping to pick up votes against deregulation. They were shocked when Vice-President Mondale came down to the Hill to preside over the Senate and—in accord with a strategy worked out with Senators Byrd, Cranston, Baker, Hansen, and Long—ruled them out of order and ended the filibuster. The Senate agreed to natural gas price deregulation on October 4 by a close vote of 50 to 46. It was close enough that the Administration's lobbying might have made the difference. Senator Abourezk wrote in the Sunday New York Times on October 9, "The puzzle went beyond the display of raw power exercised by Vice President Mondale and majority leader Robert C. Byrd of Virginia. It included a startling reversal of position by the Administration on the issue—a shock to nearly everyone involved."

Eventually Carter had a moderately successful first year. His proposals for the creation of a Department of Energy, for authority to reorganize the government, and for the building of a natural gas pipeline from Alaska were approved, as was his economic stimulus package, which included an income tax cut and a major public works job-funding measure. According to *Congressional Quarterly's* count, his legislative success was 75.4 percent, lower than either Kennedy's or Johnson's first year scores (81 and 88 percent respectively). Carter did have a better batting average than Ford, Nixon, or Eisenhower, the consequence of having his party in control of both houses of Congress. Nixon scored only slightly lower than Carter in his first year, with 74.0 percent.

## Adaptation

Publicly Carter denied having problems with Congress, saying reports of such problems were "generated by the news media." But in 1978 the Administration showed it had learned something from its first year's experiences. In mid-April Carter and his aides met at Camp David to set legislative priorities and to consider how to improve their relations with Congress and Democratic leaders. As a consequence, the Congressional liaison staff added three new members (increasing its size from four to seven), including experienced Washington insiders. The clerical staff was doubled. And the number of priority bills was cut from sixty to thirty. Tim Kraft was shifted from handling presidential appointments to become patronage dispenser. Anne Wexler was appointed to organize special-interest groups in favor of Carter legislation and get them to pressure Congress for its passage. On the advice of Mondale and other aides, Carter had already begun campaigning for Democratic Congressmen running in 1978. In mid-February he flew to New England and helped Senators Claiborne Pell of Rhode Island, Thomas McIntyre of New Hampshire, and William Hathaway of Maine.

In 1978 Carter's personal lobbying led to some important successes. The Panama Canal treaties (guaranteeing the neutrality of the canal and its full transfer to Panama by 1999), signed in September, 1977, had been postponed for Senate ratification on Senator Byrd's advice. This time Frank Moore actively worked with Mondale, Byrd, Frank Church (floor manager), and others to win votes for their passage. And Senator Howard Baker, minority leader, played a key part in creating support for the treaties, even traveling to Panama to visit President Omar Torrijos. Carter personally lobbied every Senator, offering small favors: "I'll stand by the door and if you would like to come and have a picture made, fine." With some of the undecideds, such as Democrats Dennis DeConcini of Arizona and Ed Zorinsky of Nebraska, he conferred by phone or in person several times. He even worked on sixteen Senators who were firmly opposed to the treaties in a three-hour session one day and won over Howard Cannon of Nevada. His strategy paid off. In June of 1977, only twenty-seven Senators had supported the treaties, but in February, 1978, sixty-two were either in favor of or leaning toward supporting them. The first treaty, which assures the canal's neutrality, passed the Senate in March, 68–32. The second, which transfers the canal to Panama, had an identical vote a month later.

Carter lobbied hard also for the arms sales package to Saudi Arabia, Israel, and Egypt. He sent every Senator a letter saying that rejecting plans for Egypt would be a "breach of trust" with Sadat, who had put his faith in the United States, and he phoned Senators before the vote. The package received Senate support. Carter's efforts led to the lifting of the Turkish arms embargo was in August, 1978; and the President and his aides lobbied effectively for the withdrawal of funds for the B-1 bomber, again calling several Congressmen personally and sending "a letter to each Democratic member of the Appropriations Committee." Even the Cabinet departments were instructed to contact the House members wavering on the issue. The House also upheld a Carter veto of a $37 billion defense bill funding; Carter vetoed it partly because of a $2 billion allotment for a nuclear aircraft carrier, which Carter saw as a relatively ineffective weapon for the money.

## Pattern Maintenance

But certain tendencies in the Administration seemed too deeply ingrained to be overcome. In the summer of 1978 the White House fired Tip O'Neill's close friend Robert Griffin, deputy administrator of the General Service Administration. O'Neill learned the news from the paper and he publicly proclaimed that both he and Griffin had been "treated in a shabby manner." He forbade Frank Moore to enter his office. However, O'Neill added that he was still a loyal Democrat and that he was not seeking a confrontation. True to his word, O'Neill stuck to his commitment to push Carter's civil service reform bill through the House in August. Later he tried to repair his bruised relations with the White House. Though openly admitting resentment of the White House staff, he said: "I'm not mad at Frank [Moore]. Out of all the damned crowd down there, he's the only one who's ever been very friendly to me. . . . I don't know, maybe they don't understand my style. Maybe they [Jordan, Powell, Rafshoon] don't want to."

Carter again showed that he sometimes did not know (or care) how to time his compromises to achieve what he seemed to want. In 1978 when it first appeared that his tax bill was in trouble, he refused to make any concession. On June 22 three Democrats from the House Ways and Means Committee (Al Ullman of Oregon, Dan Rostenkowski of Illinois, and Joe Waggonner of Louisiana) met with Carter to urge a compromise, but Carter refused. As a result Ullman was unable to unite the Democrats to stand firm against an amendment proposed by Representative William Steiger (R-Wisconsin) that would slash the capital gains tax. After stands had been taken, the bargains made, the Administration belatedly came forth with its own amendment. O'Neill, who had earlier warned Secretary of the Treasury Blumenthal against such late action, was able to get the Carter amendment through the House Rules Committee and to a floor vote. With the lines already hardened, however, Carter's last-minute tax amendment failed (225-193), and the tax bill that passed (362-49) had the reduced capital gains tax in it and generally bore little resemblance to Carter's original plan. O'Neill maintained in floor debate that if Carter's tax amendment had been proposed five months earlier, it would have been accepted by the Ways and Means Committee and passed. (The Senate devastated the tax bill even more, and Carter, in a late October meeting with Senator Russell Long and Representative Al Ullman, threatened to veto the whole bill.)

House leaders were upset at the Administration's belated action and Representative John Brademas (D-Indiana) suggested that if Carter had put as much effort into getting support for his tax proposals as he had into getting the Turkish arms embargo lifted, his tax plan might have passed.

Carter's congressional support score improved, from 75.4 percent in 1977 to 78.3 percent in 1978, but it was relatively low when compared to Kennedy's (85.4 percent) and Johnson's (93 percent) second years. And in the domestic arena he had lost the big ones. His tax bills and domestic energy programs had been shredded beyond recognition. His proposal for the creation of a Consumer Protection Agency died in the House (227 to 189). And he received a public works bill he felt he had to veto. (On October 5 the House sustained the veto.)

Ironically, Carter's significant successes in 1978 were in the area of foreign policy, and Republicans were crucial to them: the Panama Canal treaties, Mideast planes sales, lifting of the arms embargo against Turkey, and a continued moderate policy toward Rhodesia. His Civil Service Reform Act, the phased deregulation of the airline industry (a measure long supported by Senate liberals such as Ted Kennedy), legislation requiring barge users of the national waterways to pay fees were relatively noncontroversial measures that attracted strong support from both Republicans and Democrats.

Even after these successes, Carter was soon back to lambasting Congress as the representative of the special interests. When that body was temporarily immobilized in April of 1979 by conflict between those who were opposed to the president's policies from both ends of the political spectrum (i.e. those who opposed price decontrol and those who wanted decontrol with a minimal excess profits tax) Carter gave congressional leaders a stern lecture. Congress was afraid to confront the energy crisis, he said. He would decontrol oil prices and let Congress worry about the consequences. "I'd rather do that," he said, "and accept the political blame than spend another two years arguing with you about what ought to be done—when you *know* what ought to be done." He noted that it was not politically popular to decontrol prices with inflation such a problem and with public opinion against oil companies, but he had no other choice. Later at an Academy of Science meeting in New Hampshire, he linked profit-hungry oil companies with congressional allies who wanted to lighten his excess profits tax. "Their new strategy seems to be to try to hoodwink the American

people by passing a windfall-profits tax that is in fact a charade." In a press conference held during the Cabinet shake-up of 1979, Carter again criticized
Congress for its concessions to big oil companies and for its manipulation of his
windfall profits tax.

Carter's problems with the Congress, as this account suggests, were not
simply based on any disinclination to lobby individual Congressmen for legislation he favored. The problems he had with the Congress were in part residues
of the insensitivity with which he and his aides had first encountered the legislature. The continued tendency to lambast Congress and to ignore or undermine supporters on the domestic measures he proposed reinforced that initial
impression.

The result was a resentment of Carter that even influenced his backers. In
February, 1977, Byrd had complained publicly about Carter's ineptness at lobbying Democratic leaders when he planned his emergency energy legislation.
Byrd suggested that Carter should seek and accept their help—"it's not a matter of being vindictive but of smoothing things for him." Later, when Carter
blamed special interests and lobbies in Congress for the problems with his
energy legislation, Byrd countered that Carter's ineffective lobbying and his insensitivity to the legislative process were responsible for the failure. Of the
House Ways and Means Committee's rejection of Carter's proposed measure
for a tax on gasoline and rebates to people buying economical cars, Byrd suggested that the proposals were "ill-conceived and likely to be ineffective in con-
serving energy." Though he valiantly fought for the President's programs, Tip
O'Neill also let show his resentment at the cavalier treatment he had received
from Carter's top staff people. The result: Carter had little personal popularity
to draw upon when he was in trouble. Carter's failure on the Consumer Protection Agency in 1978 was described by one House leader as a backlash against
the Administration. The White House people "still think we're just a pack of
crooked whores."

Aside from these strategic errors, Carter was also alienating his strongest
and most consistent support in the House and Senate by his growing conserva-
tivism on domestic policies and his apparent lack of concern for those measures
he did back. For example, the Administration's 1978 urban legislation was
drafted hastily by inexperienced officials and submitted late in the session.
Despite his attacks on the oil industry and the other special interests, he had
moved further in their direction than many Democrats in the Congress. Liberals were opposed to his suggestion that gasoline prices gradually be decon-
trolled. Indeed, the Democratic caucus voted against decontrol, and the Congressional Budget Office claimed that higher fuel prices would "increase
United States oil production by 405,000 barrels a day by 1985, far less than the
742,000 barrels the President had projected." Further, Carter's plan to hinge
implementation and funding of a national health insurance plan on the state of
the budget and the economy had caused an open break with Ted Kennedy. In
July the Senator charged that Carter's step-by-step phasing in of the plan would

destroy its effectiveness by making it a victim of special-interest groups and lobbies.

His proposed social security cuts caused a general reaction among party leaders. Representative Brademas (D-Indiana), House Majority Whip, anticipating the move, proclaimed: "They're going to run into a buzzsaw if an effort is made to eliminate major benefits in the social security system." Representative Al Ullman also publicly opposed the social security cuts, and speaker O'Neill said, "I didn't become Speaker to dismantle programs I've fought for all my life." Senator Ted Kennedy said on January 22, 1979: "The fact is that the Administration's budget asks the poor, the black, the sick, the young, the cities and the unemployed to bear a disproportionate share of the billions of dollars of reductions." Carter even had problems with the ordinarily conservative Democrat Patrick Moynihan of New York. The proposed welfare cuts would hurt New York and other cities with high welfare costs, Moynihan complained. When Moynihan, in a meeting with Carter, insisted that his interests be met, Carter was said to have "stared icily" at him and responded: "Pat, I hope you realize this is something where you and I are going to have to continue to disagree."

In all fairness to Carter, it must be stated that Congress itself, though mainly Democratic, was composed of independent types determined not to be a rubber stamp for any Administration. As Representative Dan Rostenkowski (D-Chicago) said: "I don't see this Congress rolling over and playing dead now. . . . Carter is going to set up his priorities, and we are going to set up ours. We'll see where we go from there."

### Russia, the Middle East, and China

Carter, fresh from his victory over Ford and apparently desiring the establishment of a new foreign policy that would distinguish his presidency from that of his predecessor had rushed forward with an aggressive human rights campaign. In his inaugural address he said:

The world itself is now dominated by a new spirit. Peoples more numerous and more politically aware are craving and now demanding their place in the sun—not just for the benefit of their own physical concern, but for basic human rights. . . . The passion for freedom is on the rise. Tapping this new spirit, there can be no nobler nor more ambitious task for America to undertake on this day of a new beginning than to help shape a just and peaceful world that is truly humane.

The first object of this campaign was the U.S.S.R. On January 27 the State Department warned the Soviet government that if it tried to silence Soviet physicist Dr. Andrei D. Sakharov, it would be violating "accepted international standards of human rights." (The Soviet Ambassador, Anatoly F. Dobrynin telephoned Secretary of State Cyrus Vance and protested such interference in Soviet internal affairs.) On February 11, 1977, the United States announced it was canvassing members of the United Nations for information on the recent arrest of dissidents in the Soviet Union. In mid-February, Sakharov unveiled a remarkable letter he had received from Carter pledging that the issue of human rights was "a central concern of my administration."

Some State Department officers privately warned Carter that he could not press the Russians so boldly on the treatment of their dissidents without endangering future arms control talks. But Carter brushed aside such qualms, while White House officials insisted that all the moves had been meticulously weighed. On March 22 Carter announced that he wanted to spend $45 million on twenty-eight new transmitters for Radio Free Europe and Radio Liberty in order to increase their range. In his speech to the United Nations in March, Carter spelled out for the first time all the main themes of his foreign policy. The stress was heavy on human rights. Pointedly Carter declared that "no member of the United Nations can claim that mistreatment of its citizens is solely its own business. The basic thrust of human affairs points toward a more universal demand for fundamental human rights. The United States has a historical birthright to be associated with this process."

These stances were taken prior to the Administration's first meeting with the Russians over the SALT II agreements—which had been temporarily suspended during the 1976 presidential campaign. There was some talk at home that the aggressive and public stance by Carter as head of state might jeopardize the forthcoming talks. But Carter pressed ahead, while Hamilton Jordan gave assurances that Carter would press Moscow on the subject even if there was a risk that the action would jeopardize our relationships with the Soviet Union on other matters like nuclear proliferation and the reduction of arms.

Cyrus Vance took the more traditional diplomatic stance when he arrived in Moscow in late March to open the SALT talks. He announced the day before the talks were to begin, that he would not meet Soviet dissidents who had requested such a meeting. He would have problems enough with the arms reduction proposal he had to offer. He had two plans. One was a contingency proposal that differed little from the old Ford-Kissinger package, which had seemed close to approval before the 1976 elections. The other was a comprehensive program for substantial reduction of missile launchers and war heads, with a freeze on the development of new weapons systems, including the Soviet backfire bomber. Carter seems to have insisted personally on the second package. It certainly opened up all kinds of problems that had been laboriously worked over since 1972. And it was presented to the Russians without any advance warning—something they detest.

Two days later the talks were over, with an outright Soviet refusal to deal with the President's proposal. Soviet Foreign Minister Andrei Gromyko called a press conference (unusual for him) to criticize the American proposal and procedure. The Carter Administration, he said, presented the disarmament plans in public, knowing they would not be accepted, and then blamed Moscow for impeding the negotiations. The proposed plan was unacceptable because "the Soviet Union would be put into a worse position than the United States."

Some Americans voiced their concern. According to Hedrick Smith of *The New York Times*, Soviet specialists in Washington were describing the "blowup" with the Kremlin as "the worst public turn in Soviet-American relations in five years of detente." Though one congressional observer and some senior Administration officials said they had predicted the negative Soviet response to the proposals, the intensity of the attack was said to catch the White House by surprise. As Christopher Wren pointed out, the Soviets found it awkward to thrash out the issues publicly and were embarrassed by Carter's running commentary on the negotiations, which forced the Soviets to respond via Gromoyko.

After the collapse of the Moscow talks, Carter showed no public signs of backing down. When asked, in a press conference, if he would modify his human rights stands if it were necessary to achieve progress, he said no. And he threatened: "If we feel at the conclusion of next month's discussion that the Soviets are not acting in good faith with us and . . . an agreement is unlikely then I would be forced to consider a much more deep commitment to the development and deployment of additional weapons." He told 800 high-school students in the White House Rose Garden, "The people of our nation think we ought to be a beacon light [on human rights] to the rest of the world . . . even if it means suffering temporarily a disturbance in our relationship with a few countries around the world."

Nevertheless, Carter did shift. Some time later at the Geneva SALT talks in May, Vance and Gromyko were working on a compromise, and this time the talks were held in secrecy and without fanfare. There were no presidential pronouncements on human rights, no preliminary public statements about the United States proposals. The new bargaining terms showed that the President had backed away from the earlier take-it-or-leave-it attitude. This time he seemed willing to tailor his long-range aspirations to short-term realities. Thus, Vance and Gromyko agreed to a three-part framework for a SALT II treaty. The treaty itself would last until 1985; in essence, it reconfirmed the Vladivostok agreement reached between Leonid Brezhnev and Gerald Ford in 1974; both sides, however, indicated that they would consider paring their strategic arsenals, perhaps by as much as 10 percent. A protocol to the treaty, which would last three years, would include restraints on the use of two weapons—the United States' cruise missile and the Soviet's backfire bomber. General principles would be discussed as possible ground rules for negotiations leading to SALT III.

No formal agreement was reached at this time. Still, Gromyko and Vance had managed to restore some measure of order and good will to the process of SALT negotiations, which had been badly shaken at the Moscow meeting. A high Administration official said: "I think we're on a sound negotiation track now. We accomplished more than we expected."

For the purpose of making this meeting run smoothly, both sides ignored the human rights issue. And it was clear, from demands made by the Soviets for the next scheduled meeting, in October, that they wanted to keep it that way. The Soviet negotiators asked that the October meeting be kept short, with a fixed termination date before Christmas, obviously to limit discussions on their violations of human rights. They insisted that the next meeting stress "positive criticism," which would focus on future goals, rather than human rights.

In the fall when Vance met with Gromyko, the Russian suddenly asked for a meeting with Carter. So Carter and Gromyko met in the Oval Office on September 27 with seven of Carter's advisers. Gromyko later told reporters that both countries had "a firm intention to work toward conclusion of this second agreement—as you Americans say, to finalize it." And the United States decided to take a lower-key stand on human rights in the Helsinki treaty review meetings in Belgrade later in October. Arthur Goldberg, before departing for the conference, was given orders to defend human rights but not to antagonize the Russians.

The next spring the tension levels were up once again, as Soviet activities in Africa led Carter to harsh attacks on Soviet adventurism in two speeches, one at Wake Forest University in North Carolina and another at Annapolis. In the latter, after reiterating his commitments to SALT II and détente, the President very scornfully commented on the Soviet economy. (The Soviet Union's growth rate is "slowing greatly and its standard of living does not compare favorably with that of other nations at the same equivalent stage of economic development.") The following summer, when the United States learned that Soviet dissident Anatoly Schcharansky was actually going to undergo trial despite Carter's statements on his behalf, the tension level climbed again. Vance had to decide whether or not to cancel a meeting already scheduled with Gromyko, as a gesture of displeasure by the United States. After meeting with aides, Vance made calls to Brzezinski and President Carter. His decision: to have Marshall Shulman, his chief adviser, make a statement to the Soviet Union expressing America's "deep concern" over the trial. According to aides, Vance never really considered scrubbing the talks, as he believed in "keeping the line open" to Russia.*

Not until June 18, 1979, after many ups and downs, were Carter and Brezhnev to sign the SALT treaty. Binding until January 1985, the treaty would limit both sides to 2,400 (and later 2,250) bombers and missile launchers, with each side limited to one new type of missile. But it did permit expansion in numbers of war heads and continuation of programs for improving existing weapons.

---

*Several other actions were taken, however. Two missions by the United States government leaders were canceled. Carter personally expressed his dismay in a letter to Brezhnev. A decision was made to examine other U.S.-U.S.S.R. relationships (such as trade and technology) to see if they could be scaled down. Arthur Goldberg issued a statement intimating that "future US-Soviet relations" could be jeopardized by the trial.

Back in Washington, Carter told a joint session of Congress that the treaty was not a gift to the Russians; it was in our interests—to prevent "uncontrolled and pointed nuclear arms race that would damage security of all countries including our own." Anticipating significant opposition to the agreement, he warned of "grave consequences" should the United States Senate fail to ratify it. This time, however, the Republican leadership would defect from the President and several Democrats would challenge the agreement for being disadvantageous to the United States. By the end of the year, the treaty would be in major trouble.

Carter would have more success in the Middle East. He started out here, as in his dealings with the Russians, distinguishing his position from that of the Ford-Kissinger team. Throughout 1977 he insisted he would settle for nothing less than a comprehensive peace in the Middle East. But his various suggestions for reaching such a settlement brought strong reactions from American Jews and Israelis, forcing hasty retreats from time to time.

An altogether new possibility for peace was presented with Egyptian President Anwar Sadat's historic trip to Jerusalem in November, 1977, which suggested he had determined to secure a settlement. By the summer of 1978, however, it seemed that the Egyptian-Israeli negotiations on a Middle Eastern treaty had reached a stalemate. On one occasion Sadat vowed that he would not engage in any further negotiations with the Israelis, describing Prime Minister Menachen Begin's attitude as "negative and backward." Not only that, he was threatening to abrogate the United Nations peacekeeping mandate in the Sinai, an action that would heighten instability in the region. Saudi Arabia was exerting additional pressure on Sadat to reconcile his differences with Syria's Hafez Assad, a hardliner in the Middle East conflict. Such reconcilation could bring Sadat back into the radical Arab bloc, thereby enhancing the likelihood of another round of Middle East war, a resurgence of Soviet influence in the area, and a possible oil embargo against the United States.

Against this background Carter decided to take a big chance. On August 5, 1978, he sent Secretary of State Cyrus Vance to the Middle East with an invitation to Sadat and Begin to meet with him at his presidential retreat in the Catoctin Mountains in Maryland to work on the Middle Eastern situation. They immediately accepted.

Abandoning his earlier "populist" commitments to open diplomacy, Carter now would rely on secret diplomacy—and the force of his own personality—to bring about the desired results. Explaining his new philosophy to newsmen just prior to boarding the helicopter to Camp David, he said: "We will be almost uniquely isolated from the press and the outside world." He went on: "My hope is that this degree of personal interchange, without the necessity for political posturing or defense of transient stand or belief, will be constructive."

The 143-acre presidential hideaway, sealed off from the world, offered an ideal setting for the realization of such a hoped-for objective. During the next thirteen days the secrecy Carter promised was rigidly maintained with a near-total news blackout. The White House canceled all press interviews and not even senior State Department officials were informed of the deliberations to prevent inadvertent news leaks. Such was the determination to shield the talks from the outside world that when Menachem Begin invited two senior Israeli officials in Washington to have a Sabbath supper with him during the first weekend of the summit, the White House quickly "disinvited" them. Indeed, the only clues the world had about the thirteen-day summit were Jody Powell's daily briefings to newsmen stationed six miles away in Thurmont, Maryland, and these consisted of generalities rather than diplomatic substance.

Carter held his first one-on-one chat with Begin on the evening of September 5. The following morning he repeated the exercise for two hours with Sadat on the patio behind Aspen Lodge. Later that day all three met for a joint session, a format that proved ineffective. The third day the three leaders held what would be their last trilateral session until the final day of the summit. This session turned into a shouting match between Sadat and Begin more than anything else. After this stormy meeting Carter's guests were kept apart. Carter began a mini-shuttle diplomacy, going between Sadat and Begin, while Secretary of State Vance, National Security adviser Brzezinski, and Defense Secretary Brown were left to conduct lower-level negotiations with other officials of the two conference parties. By the first weekend of negotiations the Americans were making their compromise proposals, incorporating the Israeli and Egyptian positions.

By the eighth day a settlement was still elusive. At this point Carter abandoned his commitment to a comprehensive peace. A crucial decision was made to separate the Sinai issue from the Gaza Strip and West Bank issues. Carter personally took charge of the Sinai issue, which had the greatest chance for success, and tirelessly shuttled between Begin and Sadat with his suggestions; Cyrus Vance headed the United States negotiating team that concentrated its attention on the problems of the West Bank and the Gaza Strip.

Yet even the negotiations over the Sinai did not proceed very smoothly. On the evening of the tenth day, Sadat secluded himself at his Dogwood Lodge, dropping some ominous hints that he wished to return home. Badly shaken and disappointed, Carter quickly instructed Vance and Brzezinski to make sure that Sadat did not board a helicopter out of Camp David without his prior written authorization. The President met with Sadat the following morning to plead with his guest to remain. Failure at the summit, Carter indicated, would damage him (Carter) politically. Sadat was deeply touched by Carter's personal intervention and decided to stay. The Egyptian President later confessed that he had "a soft spot in my heart for President Carter."

As soon as he was able to persuade Sadat to remain, Carter took one more big chance—he gave Walter Mondale a handwritten note to deliver to Begin and Sadat, setting a Sunday deadline for the conclusion of the talks. Carter clearly wanted to pressure the two leaders into an agreement. In the meantime he had been trying to formulate workable compromises for each position. Only the previous day, the President had succeeded in getting the Israelis to drop their insistence on retaining control over their three airfields in the Sinai by promising to build them two new ones in the Negev Desert. But that still left the question of civilian settlements in Sinai unresolved. Happily, Begin put this issue out of the way when he promised to leave final decision on the matter to the Israeli Knesset. The summit ended, finally, on September 17, 1978.

For all his talk of his stubbornness, at Camp David, Carter showed his flexibility in the bargaining process. In his first months as President, he had expressed his preference for a comprehensive Middle East settlement, and he had envisaged a Geneva Confence that included Russia. At Camp David, under the pressure of a potentially serious blowup, he settled for less: a separate peace between Israel and Egypt and an important settlement of the Sinai issue, while the thorniest issues of all, the status of Jerusalem and "interests" of Palestinians in the West Bank, were left for future negotiations. All in all, the summit outcome represented the "step-by-step" approach that Henry Kissinger had long favored.

Carter's ability to dramatize his success was evident in the celebration that followed, before a special joint session of Congress. Begin, Sadat, and Rosalynn Carter moved ahead of Carter into the House of Representatives; when, moments later, the President himself strolled into the crowded chamber, the House was literally brought down by wild applause. In his twenty-five-minute address (punctuated fourteen times by applause), Carter began by noting that it had been 2,000 years since "there was peace between Egypt and a free Jewish nation," and that such a peace might be secured "this year." The agreement was "a chance for one of the bright moments in history." At one point he turned to the two Middle Eastern leaders and quoted Jesus' words in the New Testament: "Blessed are the peacemakers for they shall be called the children of God."

Camp David did miracles for the Carter presidency. Prior to the summit, he had suffered a steady decline in the polls, and many people, including members of his own party, were beginning to question the effectiveness of his leadership. There was even talk that he might very well be a one-term President. Suddenly his former critics, both within and outside his party, were hailing him as a hero and statesman. Even former Secretary of State Henry Kissinger was effusive in his praise, saying that the President deserved the "gratitude of the American People and the whole world." In the Senate, William Roth (R-Delaware) went so far as to sponsor a resolution that Carter be recommended for the Nobel Peace Prize for his effort. A CBS survey showed that popular approval of Carter's Administration climbed from 38 percent in June to 51 percent the week of September 25, while it rose in a Gallup Poll from 39 percent in August to 56 percent. When Carter himself took a post–Camp David tour of the country, cheering crowds greeted him for his historic success.

Carter had accomplished a great deal at Camp David in substantive foreign policy terms, but the drama obscured the fact that a peace treaty had not been signed at Camp David—only a long-term framework for a general peace and a shorter-term framework for a treaty. There were still hard negotiations ahead, and from time to time it looked as if they might fail. Despite the euphoria of Camp David, Egypt and Israel remained deadlocked over several points; and in a desperate effort to resolve these problems, Cyrus Vance shuttled between the two countries from December tenth to the fifteenth—in an attempt to meet the December 17 deadline Carter had set for an agreement.

Few noticed that the agreement was not forthcoming as that deadline approached, since Carter had something altogether new to offer. On Friday, December 15, Carter announced on national television that members of his Administration were in the process of finalizing a "normalization" agreement between the United States and China. Full diplomatic relations with the People's Republic would be established on January 1.

While the "normalization" of diplomatic relations between the United States and China was a surprise to most Americans and the world at large, the process had been a year and a half in the making. Secretary of State Cyrus Vance had visited the People's Republic in September, 1977; he told Communist Party Chairman Hua Kuo-feng that their rigidity on Taiwan was a block to normalization, and reaffirmed the American commitment to human rights. (He did not mention, publicly at least, China's own less than perfect record on that score.) Carter had called this initial foray "a major step" toward normalization. Yet in an interview with newspaper editors that was released over the Labor Day weekend, Carter renewed the United States' "longstanding commitment to Taiwan" and added that "I don't feel under any constraint in this instance to act precipitously just to get an agreement. . . . I feel like I have got time." At that time *Newsweek* called the results of Vance's trip a "diplomatic stalemate." Indeed, it was. Both nations were willing to test the waters, but neither was ready to make any major concessions.

Now it appeared that the United States had done most of the backing down. Contrary to long-standing American policy, the United States agreed to recognize the government of the People's Republic of China as the sole legal government of China, including Taiwan. Formal diplomatic relations with Taiwan would be ended, the mutual defense treaty abrogated, and American forces withdrawn from that island. Mainland China would offer no formal pledge that the Nationalist Chinese would be safe from military attack.

Yet Carter apparently expected wide public approbation of this new breakthrough. After concluding his brief speech, Carter leaned back on his chair and, unaware that a microphone was still on, said, "Massive applause . . . throughout the nation."

He overestimated the positive response to his "breakthrough." Senator Barry Goldwater dismissed the Carter Administration's actions as "cowardly" and said that it "stabs in the back the nation of Taiwan." New York's moderate Republican Senator Jacob Javits refused to endorse the idea fully. *Newsweek* reported that Carter's mail was running four to one against the normalization process—with Taiwan cited as the main reason for opposition to it. In New York's Chinatown, police mediated between 2,000 Peking supporters and about 6,000 Taiwanese sympathizers. (One placard read: CARTER SELLS PEANUTS AND FRIENDS.)

Carter held to his normalization agenda, and full relations with the People's Republic of China commenced on January 1, 1979. At the United States Liaison Office in Peking, Ambassador Leonard Woodcock clinked champagne glasses with Deputy Prime Minister Teng Hsaio-ping. In Washington more than 500 guests munched egg rolls and sipped mao-tai at the Chinese Liaison Office.

On January 29 Deputy Prime Minister Teng Hsaio-ping, third-ranking official in China, began his visit to the United States. Carter and Teng toasted each other at a White House state dinner that included Richard Nixon as a guest. After concluding talks with Teng in the White House Cabinet Room, Carter called the discussions "one of the most historic events in our nation's history." The conversations were "very cordial and harmonious." Teng replied: "I agree with every word that the President just said." At a ceremony in the East Wing of the White House, he and Carter signed agreements on cooperation in science, technology, space, and cultural exchange. The Administration also agreed to sign a joint communiqué that condemned efforts by any country "to establish hegemony [a favorite Chinese word used to describe Russia's efforts] or domination over others."

The Soviets' views on the new relationship between the United States and China were predictable: Soviet President Leonid Brezhnev accused the Chinese of "attempting to gain the support of the military forces of imperialism . . . which should then serve their broad ambitions to gain hegemony and great-power status." The Soviet government also requested a clarification on what was said and agreed upon in Washington.

On February 17, shortly after Teng's visit, China invaded Vietnam—striking four provinces along the 480-mile border. (Peking said it was a counterattack on the Vietnamese aggressors.) Suddenly China's friendship was a problem for the United States. The Russians had signed a military alliance with Vietnam—to "take immediate and effective measures to safeguard peace and the security of the countries"—back on November 3, 1978.

As if this were not problem enough for the Carter Administration, the peace talks between Israel and Egypt were now near collapse. Sadat announced on February 25, 1979, that he would not attend a proposed second meeting at Camp David, sending instead Egyptian Premier Mustafa Khalil. This caused the Israel Knesset to instruct Begin also to refuse participation in the conference.

Carter invited Begin to Washington to meet with him alone. In the ensuing three days of talks, Begin agreed to compromise on several issues—moving closer to the Egyptian position. Shortly after that Carter once again put his own reputation on the line. On March 5 he announced that he would personally travel to the Middle East to try to conclude the negotiations. He then flew to Jerusalem on March 10. There, in an address to the Knesset, he chided both countries for not taking a chance for peace. His mission an apparent failure, Carter made a stopover at the Cairo airport on the way home. There Sadat accepted the final Israeli proposal and Carter called Begin to tell him the news. At this Begin put his own reputation on the line—he would submit the proposals to the Knesset and resign from the government if they failed to be approved.

The Knesset approved the pact 95 to 18 on March 12, 1979. And on March 26 Carter capped his effort with a triumphant signing ceremony in Washington—before 1,600 invited guests on the White House lawn.

Overall, Carter showed himself to be a risk taker in his bargaining style. Whether with the United States Congress or the Russians or the Egyptians and the Israelis, he was prone to move out, to try big things. Sometimes he did this without testing the political ground beforehand, embracing grand projects and afterward doing the political leg work. But when unexpectedly checked or thwarted on a matter of great concern to him, he could compromise, try a new approach, and get down to the details that would save the deal he wanted. His flair for the dramatic enabled him to attract widespread publicity for what he had done, and general acceptance of it as a grand accomplishment.

# TWENTY-THREE

# Roller Coaster:
# The Political Front

CARTER HAD PROBLEMS from the beginning of his Administration with important groups usually considered the backbone of the Democratic Party. His off-the-cuff remarks calling for a "Palestinian homeland" during his town meeting in Clinton, Massachusetts, and after his meeting with Syrian President Hafez Assad in May, 1977, created problems for him in the Jewish community. And Mark Siegel, the White House aide in charge of liaison with Jewish groups, found himself increasingly alienated from others in the White House and without adequate information on relevant Administration policy. When he learned about the sale of F-16s to Saudi Arabia in the spring of 1978—not from the White House, but from an angry audience he was addressing—he resigned, saying his role had become a "deception and a sham."

Organized labor, despite its efforts on behalf of Carter's candidacy in 1976, did not reap any large return in 1977. The Administration disappointed labor with its initial proposal that the minimum wage be increased to $2.50 an hour rather than the $3.00 labor wanted. Moreover, the Administration never backed labor's common situs picketing bill. And only after months of delays did labor finally secure Administration support for a new law intended to facilitate union organizing. In addition, Carter broke all precedent with his refusal to address the AFL-CIO at its biennial meeting in 1977. AFL-CIO President George Meany told the convention that the working person was no better off under Carter than he had been under the Republican Gerald Ford.

Blacks, who had poured out to vote for Carter in 1976, were also disappointed by the Administration's failure to address urban problems or minority unemployment. For a short time in the summer of 1977 there was even some concern that the government might back Allan Bakke in his challenge to the principle of affirmative action, upon which minority groups relied to make up for years of discrimination. When Carter addressed the Urban League in July that year, Vernon Jordan accused him of having failed to keep his campaign promises to the poor of the cities.

Feminist groups were concerned about the cutback in social welfare programs—as well as HEW Secretary Califano's opposition to any government payment (through Medicaid) for abortions for low-income women. Members of the President's National Advisory Committee for women, which had been organized after the Houston Women's Conference in 1977) canceled their first scheduled meeting with the President in November, 1978, because he had allotted them only fifteen minutes. Later some of the committee members issued a press release attacking Carter's austerity budget for its cutback on social programs and its "military extravagance." Shortly after that the President, in a meeting with the committee, accused the women of confronting him with tactics that "sap our joint strength." Cochair Bella Abzug retorted that not enough attention had been paid to what they said. After the meeting Abzug told reporters the President had been "very anxious that we present our beefs and gripes." A few minutes later she was fired. She was asked to report to Hamilton Jordan; he and Lipshutz gave her the news. Twenty-one of the forty women on the committee resigned to protest Abzug's treatment.

Then the mayors were upset. On December 10, 1978, the National Conference of Democratic Mayors sharply attacked the Administration for its plans to reduce aid to the cities. Indeed, at the midterm Democratic Party convention in Memphis, the Administration had to stack the rules and the committees and make compromises to forestall the liberals' criticism of the budget and secure endorsement of the President's proposed austerity program.

Several state party organizations were also disaffected because of Carter's neglect during his first two years in office. In July, 1977, he refused to address Cook County Democrats, an invitation a Democratic President would not usually ignore.* In 1978, when it seemed that an alternative invitation might go to Jerry Brown he did accept. After two years in office and considerable pressure from Wisconsin Democrats, he made an appearance in that early primary state for a January, 1979, fundraiser for local Congressmen. By early 1979 Californians were feeling neglected and notably lukewarm in their attitudes toward Carter. Even experienced Democratic politicians with no love for Brown— State Treasurer Jesse Unruh, State Comptroller Ken Covy, State Assembly Speaker Leo McCarthy—had not been approached.

These problems—with Congress, labor leaders, blacks, feminists, and party leaders—did not create broader political problems for Carter in the early months of his presidency. His standing in the polls remained relatively high throughout the spring of 1977. When his ratings among the general public did

*When he did come to one of their dinners, George Dunne, the chairman of the Cook County Democrats, told a pointed joke about some illiterate Georgians who came to Washington to get a job. Carter retorted: "We may not know how to spell so good. But there is one word I do know how to spell: the word Dunne: D-O-N-E.

decline, it was probably more related to incongruities in his self-presentation and persistent questions about his competence.

The big drop in public support first showed itself after weeks of headlines about Bert Lance's personal finance and banking practices and his political ties to Carter. The Administration opened this Pandora's Box in July, 1977, when it requested that the Senate Governmental Affairs Committee release Lance from a pledge to sell his bank stocks on the grounds it would cause an unnecessary economic hardship for him. (The pledge, necessitated by Carter's new ethical standards for avoiding conflict of interest, would have required Lance to dispose of his stocks within a year after assuming office.) Later, the Senate Government Affairs Committee, headed by Abraham Ribicoff, asked Lance to explain the circumstances of a $3.4 million loan from a Chicago bank, but after Lance's testimony, they dropped their investigation with the conclusion that there was nothing improper there. The national media, however, had begun to look more closely at Lance's banking practices, and further congressional inquiries took place. It appeared there were substantial problems in terms of overdrafts by Lance and his friends at his own banks, as well as questions of whether or not he had proper collateral for some of his big loans at other banks. Eventually the Justice Department, the Securities and Exchange Commission, and the Comptroller of the Currency looked into the matter. On August 18, more than a month after the Administration's initial request, the Comptroller of the Currency made his first report: though there were serious questions about Lance's banking practices, there was no evidence of indictable criminal conduct.

During the Senate hearing Jody Powell attempted to discredit Senator Charles Percy of Illinois, who had questioned Lance closely. He called the Chicago *Sun-Times* Washington bureau chief to say that Percy had taken free rides on a Bell and Howell company plane. (Bell and Howell didn't even have a company plane.) Carter himself stood by Lance for several weeks of the inquiry. When the Comptroller found no indictable criminal conduct, Carter reaffirmed his faith in Lance's "character and competence." "Bert, I'm proud of you," he said.

However, the Comptroller's report contained other information that raised serious questions concerning the propriety, if not the legality, of Bert Lance's banking practices. The press did not let Carter divert public attention from those problems. The result was an Administration slide in the public opinion polls. According to Gallup, 42 percent of the public had strongly approved of Carter's performance in March, 1977, but only 24 percent did so in October, 1977. The Louis Harris poll registered a drastic loss of public approval during Carter's defense of Lance: from 59 percent in July to 48 percent in October.*

The Lance affair challenged the claim to moral superiority of the Carter Ad-

---

* After the Lance affair Carter made a special attempt to downplay the outsider/regional theme in order to avoid the image of the White House staff as a Georgia mafia. He stressed Vice-President Mondale's influence at the White House in a thirty-minute phone call to Jack Nelson, bureau chief

ministration. Other events raised questions about Carter's competence. By the fall of 1977 it was clear that his top legislative priority—the energy bill—was bogged down in conference committee. And if it ever came out, it was clear that it would differ considerably from what Carter had proposed. Other measures dealing with tax and welfare reform were in trouble in Congress. Beyond that, there had been no apparent progress on the SALT talks, the vote on the Panama Canal treaties had been put off until the next year, and there was little apparent progress in the Middle East peace talks.

Carter had arranged for a grand tour of the world for several overseas meetings in November of 1977, but he delayed the trip to lobby for his energy bill, to no avail. When he finally went abroad, from December 29, 1977, to January 6, 1978, Carter suffered other embarrassments, which reinforced questions about his competence. The tour, which would take him to Poland, Iran, India, Saudi Arabia, Egypt, France, and Belgium, started under a cloud of press speculation that he, like other Presidents before him, was using foreign trips to draw attention away from his failures to deal with domestic problems. Actually, Carter used the trip to announce certain important foreign policy decisions and to meet with foreign leaders.

The press, however, concentrated on the more interesting trivia—in this case the several gaffes of the Carter party. In Poland, Carter had an incredibly poor State Department translator, whose Polish suggested that the President had referred to Polish "lusts" and that Carter had abandoned the United States for good. The translator's replacement the next day seemed to be stumped completely by Carter statements and withdrew for yet another. In India a side comment to the Secretary of State in which Carter suggested a "get tough" stance with India's government was picked up by a microphone and broadcast to the world.

As if that were not enough, Carter did not seem to be in control of his own administrative house his first fifteen months in office. Andrew Young traveled around the world making impolitic statements—in May, 1977, he told reporters on a trip to London that the "old colonial mentality" is still strong in Britain and that the Russians and Swedes are racists. Aides Jody Powell, Midge Costanza, and Hamilton Jordan got themselves into public imbroglios that raised questions about their discretion, if nothing else. (Jordan purportedly insulted the wife of the Egyptian ambassador at a dinner party and spit out his drink at a young woman in a singles bar; and Costanza had held a fund raiser to pay off an old Congressional campaign debt, without reporting it to the FEC.) Further, as Congress ripped apart the Administration's tax bill and hospital cost containment bill, stories appeared in the press to the effect that the White House congressional liaison operation was in shambles and that the official line on policy was often not clear, with Cabinet officers endorsing positions inde-

---

of the L. A. *Times* in early October, 1977, after Hamilton Jordan had tried to convince skeptical reporters of that influence.

pendently of the White House. It was not clear, for example, if Carter and his people totally agreed with Califano's policies at HEW: his guideline for funding women's sports, his push for integration in North Carolina universities and Chicago public schools, and his very visible and aggressive campaign against smoking. (Indeed, Carter, on one of his visits to North Carolina, seemed to be countering him with a statement saying that smoking was not all that dangerous, thereby shoring up his position in that tobacco-growing state.)

In the spring of 1978 Carter took some remedial action. Hamilton Jordan collected White House staff gripes against the Cabinet, while Charles Kirbo, again in his role as informal political adviser, polled the Cabinet members for their complaints about the White House staff. The weekend of April 13, Carter assembled both groups for a showdown at Camp David. Charles Kirbo ("Mr. Kirbo" as Jordan called him) flew down for the occasion—he had a room of his own in Aspen Lodge, the presidential guest house. Rosalynn was also there, sitting on the side, taking notes. From one account, Kirbo read the complaints he had gathered to staff aides, stressing their failure to coordinate and follow through. Carter himself rode herd on his aides in at least one meeting and laid down the law to his Cabinet members at another—reading from Jordan's records the complaints that they were undercutting his policies. Dissent before a decision was made, he said, is one thing, but after-the-fact quarrels would no longer be tolerated. Further, Cabinet members should be active on the Hill in his support and treat Frank Moore as if they were speaking to Carter himself. Then Carter met both groups together, to warn them against the leaks about policy differences that had been filling the press. To begin with, he did not want to read anything about what had happened at this meeting in the press. "Only Jody Powell is to do the talking on this meeting."

In addition to these attempts at dampening policy differences with the Cabinet, more concrete steps were taken to compensate for the weaknesses of the Georgia staff and improve the Administration liaison with Congress and interest groups. The ensuing changes in the legislative liaison operation have already been discussed. In other staff changes, Jack Watson was put in charge of urban planning, and Stuart Eizenstat instituted a new system to keep tabs on interagency domestic issues. Midge Costanza, who had shown a great deal of independence, was downgraded, losing her staff and most of her responsibilities. A decision was made, at Rosalynn Carter's suggestion, to bring Gerald Rafshoon into the White House to improve their public-relations efforts, though he would not join the Administration until July 1, after putting his Atlanta and Washington business offices into trust.

But Carter would not personally bring his Cabinet and staff into harmony for some time. One of the complaints registered against Carter at the meeting was that he had not provided the sense of direction, the list of priorities, the framework within which Cabinet members could operate. Further, it was clear from external events that Carter failed to consult with Cabinet members on items that were within their professional domain. The original energy program had been drawn up by Carter and Energy Secretary James Schlesinger without consulting Treasury Secretary Michael Blumenthal, even though the program required new taxes and subsidies. As a consequence, the Treasury Department had to send out corrections for two months after the original proposal had gone to the Hill. Although Secretary of Commerce Juanita Kreps, a professional economist, was responsible for foreign trade policies, she was not admitted into any of the economic discussions.

There was no easy answer, no routine way of dealing with these problems. Certainly the President could not rely on others to provide unity. The economists consulted on his economic programs were already giving him conflicting advice on how to deal with inflation. (Blumenthal favored cutting back on spending, while Labor Secretary Ray Marshall and Charles Schultze, the chief of the Council of Economic Advisers, were not so predisposed.) Essentially it is the President's responsibility to choose between alternatives and then exercise his authority to see that they are given a fair try.

Carter, however, brought in yet another person, an old pro noted for his ability at rubbing heads together, to bring about some unity: Bob Strauss, the former head of the Democratic National Committee, who had been pinch-hitting for Carter in a variety of fields, from energy to the coal strike to the Panama Canal treaties, was asked to lead the fight against inflation. (Eizenstat had broached the idea earlier, but it had been checked by Treasury Secretary Blumenthal.)

Appointment of a new person to create order did not, however, solve the problem. Strauss's responsibilities overlapped Blumenthal's; and after the appointment Blumenthal went first to the President to register his complaints and then to the Vice-President. The press heard about his dissatisfaction.

In addition, Carter intimates such as Andrew Young continued to speak out in ways that embarrassed the President. In July, 1978, Young said that there were hundreds, perhaps thousands, of political prisoners in the United States. That same month Dr. Peter Bourne, the President's old friend and Assistant for Health Affairs was caught in a situation that ultimately led him to admit that he had written a prescription (for Quaalude, a controlled drug) for an assistant, using a false name. Bourne had passed a professional boundary; having no constituency to protect him, and his resignation was submitted to the White House and accepted the next day. *The New York Times* quoted him as saying, on his way out, that there was a high incidence of marijuana and occasional cocaine use by White House aides. Though he would later say he had not made the statement, the charge did further tarnish the reputations of the Georgia staff.

In early 1979 the inflation rate was increasing and America was still confronted with a serious energy problem for which the Administration had found no appropriate remedy. Indeed, even the new Department of Energy seemed to be "sinking into a bureaucratic stupor," as *Time* magazine noted on June 19, 1979. To further the leadership problem, questions were raised about the ability of the Administration to pick the best and most disinterested persons for the job. Energy Secretary James Schlesinger's problems were not completely of his own doing, as he was preoccupied with getting the energy program through Congress. But Schlesinger had a tendency to gather decisions into the hands of himself and a small circle of principal aides, which did not inspire confidence in the new department. There was also delay in the approval of early appointees because of potential conflicts of interest; Lynn Coleman's appointment as general counsel was held up eight months by a Senate committee because of suspicion of his connections with John Connally's Houston law firm (which had oil industry clients). Robert Thorne, who was slated to become assistant secretary for energy technology, was opposed by some as having a record too pro–nuclear energy for the post. And it was not clear if Omi Walden, formerly Director of the Georgia Office of Energy Resources, had the necessary credentials for the post of assistant secretary for conservation and solar applications.

## Polls

More than most Presidents', Carter's popularity waxed and waned with public reporting of the events delineated here. In July, 1977, a *New York Times*-CBS poll showed the nation generally approving of Carter, though there was increasing doubt about his ability to achieve his objectives. Between July and October, however, when the Lance problems dominated the headlines, Carter suffered a major loss. An October Harris poll showed he had sunk to a 48 percent approval rating. Although Presidents usually suffer losses, these were both serious and greater than normal. When the Lance story died down, Carter's popularity went up again—to a 57 percent approval rating in Harris's December, 1977, poll; Gallup showed a 56 percent approval rating.

Yet by the summer of 1978, Carter was in deep trouble again. A Harris survey showed a 61 percent negative rating on the President's ability to inspire confidence in the White House—a turnaround from the 65 percent positive rating in June 1977. Indeed, Gallup showed Carter's overall popularity had sunk to its lowest to date, with only 11 percent registering "strong approval."

Carter's popularity surged after his Middle East successes. Immediately after the Camp David meeting, Carter's rating went from 39 percent approval to 59 percent. The popularity created by the Mideast summit did not maintain itself, however. As the peace failed to materialize, some of the glow wore off. By the last week of March, 1979, Carter had once again declined to 39 percent approval, 50 percent disapproval. By May, with inflation rising, no energy solution in sight, and Carter's government in disarray, only 26 percent would give a "good" or "excellent" rating for the overall job done by Carter; 52 percent would rate him only "fair." A CBS-*New York Times* poll of June 5 showed Carter's popularity had dropped to a low of 30 percent support. It looked as if Carter was indeed heading for the end of his presidency.

## *Retrenchment at Camp David*

Carter was in Tokyo for a summit conference with leaders from Japan and Western Europe in late June, 1979, at the time gas lines were forming throughout the United States. Initially he had planned on a short vacation in Hawaii on his way back to the States. Now, however, he canceled that stopover and went to Camp David to prepare a speech that might finally push his energy program through the Congress. He spent several days looking at various speech drafts and hearing the conflicting advice of his advisers. Then, July 4, a bare twenty-four hours before he was to appear on national television, he requested that Jordan and Rafshoon cancel the speech. They urged him to give the public an explanation, but he gave none.

Rumors that something might be wrong with Carter spread rapidly around Washington and the capitals of Europe. The dollar plunged dramatically. Blumenthal put in a call to Camp David—he learned Carter was out walking with the dog. Finally, he obtained a general statement from the President that he would take some decisive action on energy and got it on the wire services in time to stop the run on the dollar. On Thursday, July 5, Mondale, Jordan, Powell, Rafshoon, and Caddell—Carter's political advisers, not his policy makers—were lifted off the White House lawn for a trip to Camp David. There they compiled a list of national leaders and began telephoning them to invite them to Camp David. Beginning Friday, July 6, and continuing for ten days, people from politics, the media, business, unions, ethnic, religious, and civil rights groups flew into Camp David to meet with the President. Among the 134 guests were twenty governors, ten academics, Congressmen, and interest group leaders like John W. Gardner of Common Cause, PUSH leader Jesse Jackson, Lane Kirkland of the AFL-CIO, and Clark Clifford, a pillar of the Democratic establishment. Most of the people who eventually came had close ties to Carter or previous Democratic Administrations. There were no Republicans—nor any Kennedys or Browns.

Carter met his visitors in groups at breakfast, lunch, or dinner and engaged in long dialogues with them after the meal. They found him serene and ready to discuss in an open atmosphere what was wrong with the country and his Administration. Mostly he opened the various sessions with a commentary on the forces in national life that made national leadership impossible. Pat Caddell, he said, had been warning him for some time about his findings that a majority of Americans believe for the first time that their children's lives might be worse than their own. He spoke of how he had decided to cancel his early speech after consultation only with Rosalynn. He had already addressed the subject in televised addresses, with dwindling audiences—80 million had watched the first, 30 million the fourth speech. So he decided he didn't want to make another speech to which no one listened. His feelings of doubt about whether the country was prepared to make the necessary sacrifices had weighed on him during his recent travel to Vienna and Tokyo—bringing him to a kind of spiritual exhaustion. Now he decided he had been too bogged down in details, that he had not stayed close enough to the people. His role, he felt, should be one of moral leadership. (He also complained of how he had trouble finding movies his daughter could watch without being embarrassed, and he described the pop culture of *People* magazine.) At a more specific level he explored points of consequence for an energy program.

There were reports of how Carter invited criticism even of himself, earnestly taking notes on a yellow sheet with a felt pen. Some visitors pressed upon him the need to shake up his own governing apparatus—targets included Carter favorites such as Jordan and Schlesinger. Someone even complained about Jody Powell's increasing defensiveness regarding the press, including his recent call to a television station that had been critical of Carter, for a personal dressing down.

Carter not only brought leaders to Camp David, he also took some dramatic forays out to meet the people. Toward the end of his stay, as aides worked on drafts of the energy speech, he came down from the mountain to nearby Carnegie, Pennsylvania for a ninety-minute back-porch visit with machinist William Fisher, his wife, Bette, and their friends. (The Fishers were told beforehand that a national pollster and a Washington "VIP" wanted to interview them and their neighbors.) The next morning he went to West Virginia for a call on Marvin Porterfield, a retired Marine major and disabled veteran of World War II, his wife, Ginny, and seventeen friends and neighbors. His purpose was to renew his contact with the American people and to show them that their leaders were concerned about them. "There has been a lost sense of trust," he told aides, "a loss of confidence in the future."

One Camp David visitor, *Newsweek* columnist Meg Greenfield, perceived the talisman quality of the entire affair. The President prefers to lead by "dealing directly with individuals, engaging personally, one on one . . . circumventing or fleeing or ignoring the machinery of government itself." She continued:

> It is a highly personal anti-institutional method, and it combines in some odd proportions humbleness and notions almost of royalty. Carter is the plain fellow asking your opinion and submitting himself to your criticism. But he is, in addition, somehow the benevolent Shakespearean duke, the ruler figure in whom all authority reposes, along with all capacity to bring peace and blessing to the duchy—the majestic leader who goes freely and willingly among his people. . . .

There were signs, too, that Carter was making political capital out of the invitation list. The guest list was not a cross section of America but was mainly composed of persons close to this or past Democratic Administrations (excluding potential rivals). There was even a little horse trading over the invitations. Colorado's Governor Richard Lamm, a sharp critic of Carter, was offered an invitation on the condition that he would join other Democratic governors in a resolution endorsing the President for renomination. (Lamm would not agree to this and so did not receive an invitation.) Further, Mondale and Rosalynn left Camp David to round up endorsements at the Democratic governors' meeting. (Carter no longer spurned the importance of political endorsements as he had done early in his '76 campaign.) Now he sought them early—in a clear attempt to preempt challenges from others in the party.

Whatever his original motivations for canceling the speech and going into retreat, it turned out to be good politics—in a way. The meeting at Camp David became high theater. The affair created an aura of crisis and renewal and turned eyes toward Carter and his doings or nondoings. Most of the guests went away singing his praises. Syndicated columnist David Broder later talked of Carter's openness, wondering if future psychohistorians could tell us what enables a man to have the strength to learn and correct his own course as Carter seemed to be doing.

But it was a high-risk venture. The dollar had dropped. Speculation had run rife about the President's possible emotional or physical breakdown. And the anticipation he caused by the subsequent drama put a burden on him—when he emerged he had to give a stunning performance, or else. As economist Walter Heller noted after his session at Camp David: "That speech is going to have to be a stem-winder, and Carter unfortunately is not a stem-winding speaker."

Carter came down from the Catoctins on Saturday night. On Sunday he practiced his speech several times—something he had often been reluctant to admit publicly in the past. (He even practiced clenching his fist as a gesture of his determination to lead.) That same night he gave the thirty-two-minute speech that could make or break his presidency.

It was the quintessential Jimmy Carter. He opened by talking of his own faults, quoting one leader at Camp David who had told him, "You're not leading this nation, you're just managing the government." His more detailed diagnosis of the problem, however, placed the problem elsewhere. The leader who criticized him had also noted that his *"disciples"* (italics mine) were not following his lead. Carter harked back to his old anti-Washington theme, separating himself from the government, which he described as a system that seems incapable of action marked by "paralysis and stagnation and drift." Indeed, "Washington D.C. had become an island. The gap between our citizens and our Government has never been so wide." His mistake, Carter suggested, was that he had been too influenced by the Washington scene. Now he would go back to the people. But for the first time he found some fault in the people. They were too concerned with self, too filled with despair. He would provide the kind of moral leadership that the people needed.*

When he came to the specifics of his new energy policy (his third), Carter

---

*Later that fall, in another one of his call-in shows (on PBS October 13), when asked about his statements concerning the public malaise, Carter said that he saw a healing process already under way, though he did not say what had caused such a turnaround. When asked about his own lack of popularity, he noted that Congress, the news media, and the churches all stood lower in the polls than he.

announced a program that seemed to meet the standards he had set for Schlesinger earlier—it was "bold and forceful and highly acceptable." There would be no rationing, no price control. Neither would there be an exclusive return to the private market. What he proposed was price decontrol, which, it had been argued, would give the incentive to increase production, accompanied by an excess profits tax, which would raise billions that the government could funnel back to the private companies for the development of new energy sources.

Once the huzzas for his new energy program were over, Carter moved to tighten his control over his Administration. On July 17, at a meeting following the Camp David retreat, he told the members of his Cabinet that their performances had been unsatisfactory. When one Cabinet member suggested that Carter might like their resignations, he did not demur. So on July 17 all the Cabinet members (except CIA head Stan Turner) plus the senior White House aides offered Carter their resignations. It was a reminder that they owed their positions to him and had better shape up, but it was also an unusual way of dealing with a problem—precedented in recent history only by Nixon's request for resignation of all his Cabinet members after his sweep in the 1972 elections.

Carter had already chosen Hamilton Jordan as his new Chief of Staff, and had told his aides that Jordan's "orders were to be obeyed as if they were the President's. . . . He's got the power to fire you or any of your subordinates without any appeal or review." Jordan promptly distributed a hastily drawn-up competence and loyalty questionnaire to be filled out for every White House or other executive branch employee making $25,000 or more. It asked for such things as arrival time at work, political "savy" [sic], and attitude and loyalty to Carter. Transportation Secretary Brock Adams later threw his questionnaires into the wastebasket.

By Friday resignations were accepted from Califano, Schlesinger, Adams, Blumenthal, and Griffin Bell (who had already made plans to resign). New appointments were quickly made (completed on July 27), indicating that Carter was tightening his control over the Cabinet and looking forward to the 1980 election. Patricia Harris, who had never gone public with her conflicts, was moved from HUD to HEW. G. William Miller, who had essentially the same philosophy as Blumenthal but was more of a team player, was placed in the Treasury. Charles Duncan, Jr., formerly a high official with Coca-Cola in Atlanta, went to the Energy Department (despite having oil industry ties); Benjamin Civiletti, the Deputy Attorney General, an Italian Catholic with no political base of his own, was named to head the Justice Department.

Two of the new appointments had obvious value for the 1980 campaign. For HUD, Carter chose Moon Landrieu, past mayor of New Orleans. Landrieu brought with him a large base of support both as a prestigious Southern politician and as past president of the U.S. Conference of Mayors. In addition, New Orleans had favored Ford in 1976, as had several other large Southern cities, and would possibly lean toward Reagan in 1980. Thus, Carter was shoring up his backing with Southern leadership and possibly urban mayors as well. A

Catholic, Landrieu also made up for the recent loss of Califano at the national level. The second appointment also carried a double play for 1980. Neil Goldschmidt, the new Secretary of Transportation, had worked in Oregon for Carter in 1976; thus, the appointment paid an old debt. Carter had lost Oregon by a narrow margin and the appointment of Goldschmidt could possibly bring the state into the Carter camp. Goldschmidt is also Jewish, so with Blumenthal gone, his appointment allowed Carter to retain an ethnic balance in the Cabinet.

There was an immediate disadvantage to the purge, however. Carter's tightening of control over the Administration showed his tendency to take a good thing too far. It might have been more appropriate had he singled out only the Cabinet officers he wished to resign and asked for their resignations. And the competence and loyalty questionnaire (complete with misspelled words) made the entire operation look amateurish. Indeed, the question about loyalty suggested that the whole exercise had been one of circling the wagons, rather than creating a team of effective and cooperative managers. Further, Carter seemed to have fired some of his strongest players. One economic official was quoted as saying: "It looks like Carter is promoting his problems and firing his solutions." Symbolically, the openness that had seemed to characterize the Camp David talks was now contradicted by signals suggesting that Carter could not stand criticism and was subject to emotional whims and overkill. There was also a feeling that ". . . his house cleaning instead gutted his domestic policy team of some of its strongest players, signaled to survivors that political loyalty has priority over professional competence and sent a seism of anxiety around the world about the stability of his reign."

Certainly those he fired suggested this, as they went out shooting. Blumenthal told the press that the President cited "incompatibility with my staff" as the only reason for his firing. Later he would criticize the Administration for having no consistent economic philosophy. Califano, often praised by Carter for his performance at HEW, told reporters that Carter thought the very drive and independence that had made him the best HEW head ever had also brought him into collision with the White House. Brock Adams was perhaps the most vocal of those fired. A few weeks after he left the Cabinet he said: "I think one of the problems is . . . there's a difference between campaigning and governing. Governing takes a different kind of person. You can't govern being against government."

At the time of his big Cabinet shuffle, Carter left Andrew Young alone—even though Young had come to epitomize Carter's inability to control his own people. Over the thirty-one months Young served as ambassador to the United Nations, he increasingly embarrassed the Administration by his comments on American "political prisoners," British and Swedish "racism," and Cuba's role as a stabilizing force in Africa. But Young was the symbol of black support for Carter, and to fire Young would have been to risk losing that support completely. But finally Young went too far. On August 14 Secretary of State Vance reprimanded him for having held an unauthorized meeting with the PLO and for giving the State Department inaccurate reports of the meeting. The next day Young resigned, saying that he could not stay out of controversies that would be politically embarrassing to the President. Carter accepted the resignation "reluctantly" and two weeks later chose another black, career diplomat and Young's deputy at the United Nations, Donald F. McHenry, to succeed him.

The negative reaction to his Cabinet reshuffling led Carter to summon thirty-five reporters to the White House for a dressing down. He had no regrets at what he had done—only that he had waited so long. He claimed that the "Eastern Press" had given too much attention to personalities and gossip and not enough to those persons who had been chosen as replacements. Moving back to an old theme, Carter said that those "outside" the capital better understood him and so he would return to them. He implied that the press was a distorting influence—a charge made before by him and his people—and that he would hold fewer press conferences; instead he could get around the country to meet the people directly to gain from them a more accurate picture of the reaction to his policies.

Shortly thereafter Carter returned to the people—much as he had done when he had found himself in trouble in Georgia back in 1973 and 1974. This time he would visit the heartland of America, taking the paddle steamboat, the *Delta Queen*, down the Mississippi River from St. Paul, Minnesota to St. Louis, Missouri, with forty-seven stops in between. Initially Jody Powell put down for the press on that trip some of the "most restrictive ground rules in recent memory," as *Newsweek* noted. Coverage was limited to specific times and journalists were not to interview passengers who had talked with the President. However, when UPI, AP, *Time*, and *Newsweek* threatened to send no photographers on the trip, Powell was confronted with the Administration's dependence on the very media they wished to avoid for portraying the President's people-to-people image, so he backed down—returning to the usual ground rules.

For the occasion Carter portrayed himself as the leader of the nation, above partisan politics and controversy, simply trying to sell the nation as a whole on his energy program. But at a town meeting in Burlington, Iowa, on August 22, he told the assembled crowd that Iowa farmers would have sufficient diesel fuel to harvest their crops. Once again people responded favorably to this demonstration of power coming to the people. Amiable, but not emotional, crowds greeted him at most of his forty-seven stops, and people cheered him from the banks of the river as the *Delta Queen* chugged by. At St. Louis, about 10,000 people showed up, but the crowds lacked the enthusiasm they had shown at the smaller towns where he had stopped earlier.

The trip did show that Carter could attract friendly crowds and won him some good publicity. It did not turn the polls around. By early September a *Time* survey showed that few had faith in Carter's leadership ability or in his approach to the nation's problems. Sixty-two percent of the Democrats said they preferred Senator Kennedy as the party's nominee (compared to 24 percent for Carter). In the leadership category, Kennedy led all the candidates. Fifty-eight percent felt he was "very strong." Carter, with 12 percent, ranked last, below even Crane, Dole, and Bush.

Stu Eizenstat, however, insisted that Carter was getting a "bum rap," predicting Kennedy's strength would be weakened when issues were raised. What Eizenstat could not have predicted was that Carter would be able to shore up his national home base as he had once done in Georgia, by "proving" himself in a broader political arena, linking his own political fortunes with the restitution of feelings of worth in a polity feeling diminished by outside forces.

# TWENTY-FOUR

# The Campaigner as President as Campaigner

CARTER'S increasingly conservative domestic policies and his neglect of many party leaders had created a restiveness among Democrats. On top of this, his dramatic decline in the polls in the summer of 1979 promoted open challenges to his renomination. Most of his opponents looked to Ted Kennedy to carry their banner in 1980. Though Kennedy would not formally announce his candidacy until November, the expectation that he would run haunted Carter throughout 1979. The Senator had openly broken with Carter over his refusal to offer a comprehensive medical care program in 1978, and at the midterm Democratic conference in Memphis, he had presented his plan in a speech that evoked spontaneous emotional response of the sort Carter could not elicit.

On May 14, 1979, Kennedy introduced his own competing health care program in Congress. On June 24 the Americans for Democratic Action started a dump-Carter movement, voting to endorse Kennedy for the presidency instead. Several leaders of unions associated with the liberal coalition in 1976 were pressing Kennedy to challenge the President in the Democratic primaries. The National Organization of Women voted in early December not to endorse any candidate, a slap at the President. Earlier, in late 1978, the National Conference of Democratic Mayors had assailed Carter on the budget cuts he planned for urban areas. And George Meany had told reporters that Carter was "the most conservative president I have seen in my lifetime." The President, he charged, was trying to curb inflation by encouraging unemployment.

Congressional leaders, too, were backing off. In an August, 1979, poll two thirds of the members of Congress rated Carter's performance below average. Lack of leadership was considered his greatest weakness. (Sixty-four percent ranked him below average; 47.5 percent said his greatest ability is in foreign policy.) By September, 1979, Carter's support in Congress was so low that Tip O'Neill told reporters he didn't think Kennedy "could be denied the nomination if he were to run." Several leaders of Congress said they would support the Democratic nominee in 1980, leaving their allegiance open. Included in this category were O'Neill, James Wright (House Majority Leader), John Brademas (House Majority Whip), and Alan Cranston (Senate Majority Whip).

Carter is not one to give up, in any circumstance. In early 1979 he had authorized Democratic National Committee Treasurer Evan Dobelle to establish committees to raise money for his 1980 campaign. The day after Kennedy introduced his own health care program in Congress, Carter warned Kennedy he would "whip his ass" should he enter the race. And in the fall of 1979 he moved to put together his campaign organization. No amateurs were found at the top this time. Bob Strauss would manage the campaign and Bob Keefe, Scoop Jackson's campaign manager in 1976, would play a key role.

Hamilton Jordan had told a reporter in 1978 that the theme in 1980 would be Carter as the "experienced outsider": one who is still with the people but has gained the inside access and experience needed to govern effectively. There were elements of that mixed theme at Carter's domestic Camp David meetings, as well as in Carter's reduced interactions with the national media—with the explanation that he had to relate more directly with the people.

Actually Carter had been acting as a Washington insider from the beginning of his term. Like other Presidents before him, he had used appointments to position his own people in key spots and win support from new groups. But he went beyond most other Presidents in the volume and variety of intangible rewards—those little signs that suggest to "average people" that they, too, have a moment in history and a chance to influence policy. He worked the country as if it were a smaller district—sending out volumes of invitations to White House affairs and making other forms of personal contact with people from all sectors of the population. At Christmastime in 1978, for example, there was a ball at the White House for members of Congress; and nearly 5,000 individuals—White House staff members and volunteers, Secret Service people, congressional aides, journalists, senior citizens, and mentally handicapped children—were invited to parties and tours at the executive mansion. A long list of performers entertained the crowds, including the Smothers Brothers and newscaster Walter Cronkite, who read "The Night Before Christmas." Additionally, over 100,000 Christmas cards were sent out, addressed by volunteers solicited through the Democratic National Committee.

Carter said: "I think anybody would say that we've used the White House for receptions and so forth more than any previous President." Then he listed the kinds of groups that visited: "Every two weeks, I have a meeting with about 35 editors from outside the Washington news corps. They ask me questions, and I can derive benefit from that. We have TV and radio executives come in as well." Early campaign supporters, he commented, from Iowa, Florida, New Hampshire, and other states had been in the White House. "Immediately after

I was inaugurated, we had 800 people with whom we had spent the night during the campaign in for a White House reception. . . . And every week I call a few old friends. Rosalynn does the same thing. Fritz Mondale does the same thing. My son Chip does the same thing." He was quite aware of how those visits affected people.

And sometimes it only takes a 2-minute visit in the Oval Office from a person to let them feel that we really have a close relationship with them and that we really appreciate what they've done—that they can come in and bring their family, shake hands, see the Oval Office, have a photograph taken. I never saw the Oval Office till after I was elected President. I had never met a Democratic President. And so this is a way to let them know we care about them.

By the fall of 1979 invitations from the White House were flooding the country, as Carter entertained groups from SCLC, the Mayors Conference, stock car racers, the Country and Western Music Association (headlined by Dolly Parton); and the Gospel Music Association. Carter began holding White House briefings on policy matters for the public. "One bewildered legislator [Florida]—a black woman—found herself on the manifests both for the Mountbatten funeral and for a SALT II briefing in the White House."

The visit of Pope John Paul II in October, 1979, provided the opportunity for broadly scattered rewards and favors, since the Administration was in charge of the Pope's itinerary and invitations to several functions in Washington, D.C. The President arranged, for example, for the Pope to make a short foray to Iowa to visit a very small but politically supportive group of Catholics. The political highlight of the trip was the reception in Washington itself. Being a Catholic was not the most relevant consideration. The largest group of invitations went to government officials; another 6,000 invitations went to mayors, governors, and average people. "To get one of the coveted invitations, it also helped to be an early Carter supporter, . . . or a potential supporter next year."

Rosalynn Carter from the very beginning had aided Carter in these activities. A cumulative list of her activities during her first two years in the White House included the following: 400 White House official and social functions, 248 major speeches and remarks, 154 press interviews, 68 appearances at political events, 641 briefings attended, 36 countries visited, 152 United States cities visited. By the summer of 1979, she was campaigning almost full time for her husband. In June she was raising money for the 1980 campaign. By late fall she had visited twenty-nine cities and towns and collected $700,000. She also took to the hustings, flying in an Air Force DC-9 jet called the "Executive One" to Florida, Illinois, New Hampshire, Iowa, and other early caucus or primary states (expenses paid by the Carter-Mondale Committee), bringing her personal blessings from Jimmy and defending his programs.*

* With all these activities the size of the first lady's White House staff had expanded to an all-time high of twenty persons. Forty years earlier, Eleanor Roosevelt had done her work with three aides—an administrative secretary, a social secretary, and a messenger.

Mrs. Carter was joined in these trips by Cabinet members, White House staff aides, and other top political appointees. Her two-day fundraising trip to Florida in late September was followed by a visit by three of the top presidential advisers the next week. Vice-President Mondale was sent on a five-day, eleven-city blitz. One observer commented: "If Carter would only work Congress or the Russians over like he's working Florida, he would have less to worry about."

Carter had made it clear that he expected Democratic leaders to work for him, and they would be rewarded or punished accordingly. When legislation implementing the Panama Canal treaties failed in the House, Carter angrily warned that the Congressmen who constantly voted against his bills would not receive favors such as "invitations to White House dinners, help in their campaigns, appointments for filling patronage jobs, etc." At a political dinner for the Cabinet and other political appointees on November 6, 1979, he said that he expected all his appointees to be "actively engaged" in the campaign. The implicit message, according to one guest, was that those not wishing to do so could resign. Cabinet members should coordinate their travels with the campaign staff so that political appearances could be worked into their schedules. Carter covered himself, however, adding that appointees covered by the Hatch Act—and thus legally unable to campaign—would not be subject to these directives.

In preparation for Campaign '80, Carter also began distributing programmatic favors to various Democratic areas and persons. Before the elections for the state convention delegates in Florida in October, there were presents galore. The White House instructed government agencies to expedite grants earmarked for the state, and they were announced by Mondale and the Cabinet members while they campaigned there. (According to one Democratic Congressman from Florida: "I've never seen anything like it. We're getting money for highways, for housing, for hospitals. One more grant and the state will sink under the weight of these projects." For New Hampshire, Carter had instructed the Department of Energy to see that heating oil supplies were on hand for the winter of 1979–80.)

Carter announced some of the important favors himself. Earlier Carter had ignored and irritated the Cook County Democratic organization in Illinois by his reluctance to address their annual meeting. But Illinois would be crucial in the 1980 camapign—the first head-to-head contest between Carter and Kennedy in a big industrial state, the kind of state Democrats have to win in presidential elections. So in mid-October he came courting Mayor Jane Byrne and the Democratic organization there. HEW had been trying to promote racial integration in the Chicago schools. Carter now said that the school integration question should be answered by the federal courts, which took the pressure off himself and the mayor. Carter also pledged early clearance for plans and funds to add to the O'Hare Airport complex. Byrne, in this meeting, said that if she was making a decision at the time, she would support the President.

When Byrne decided in late October to switch her support to Senator Kennedy, the Administration openly resorted to threats.* New Transportation Secretary Neil Goldschmidt told reporters in late November that Chicago would receive less federal aid for transportation as a consequence of her shift. "My confidence in her has gone down a great deal," he said. "I've got a lot of pink slips [telephone messages] stacked up on my desk. Hers would not be the first one I'd answer." This kind of statement buttressed Byrne's charge that the Administration was engaging in "dirty politics." But as *Newsweek* noted on December 3, "the message would not be lost on other local officials." Capitol Hill sources were quoted as saying that real danger to Chicago could be expected in long-term projects the President could block, for example, O'Hare Airport expansion and snow removal aid.

Finally, Carter courted new supporters in early primary states with the federal jobs in his pocket. Reubin Askew, who had been neutral when Carter campaigned in Florida in the 1976 primaries, was appointed chief trade negotiator in 1979. In the summer of 1979 William Dunfrey, a leading New Hampshire politician-businessman, was named a member of the United States delegation to the United Nations General Assembly, the third Dunfrey to receive an appointment. Jean Hennesy, a member of the Democratic National Committee and an ally of Governor Hugh Gallen of New Hampshire (a Carter supporter), received a year's job as a member of the United States-Canadian International Joint Commission. Earlier, the same job had been discussed with Dudley W. Dudley, a former Carter supporter, who decided instead to lead the Draft Kennedy Movement in New Hampshire. A former Kennedy aide, Mary Louise Hanock, was offered a $32,442-a-year job as special assistant to a regional administrator of HUD. As David Broder noted, the actions seemed to be an attempt to pick off past and prospective Kennedy supporters, despite White House denials.†

Carter also used a loophole in his new Civil Service Reform Law to keep presidential patronage alive in the hiring of 275,000 temporary workers needed to conduct the 1980 census. In March, 1979, in accordance with a provision allowing the President under exceptional circumstances to waive the prohibition against patronage hiring, Carter directed the Census Bureau to hire census employees as much as possible from the neighborhood in which they would work. As Robert L. Hagan, the bureau's acting director, noted, "the political

---

* Michael Sneed, speaking for Byrne, said her decision was based on an Illinois poll showing Carter doing poorly against both Kennedy and a number of Republicans, and on her talks with local party leaders who thought he was unlikely to win in Illinois. County Chairman George Dunne suggested that the backtracking was also due to personal resentment against Carter, based on his earlier neglect. The President, he said, "hasn't shown the kind of respect 'for the people of Cook County' that they deserve. He failed to consider us for any possible appointments in his administration."

† Carter made his political awards, however, on the basis of future political service, not past contributions. Joe Timilty, who had run Carter's Pennsylvania campaign, had hoped for a sub-Cabinet post, but received instead a part-time slot on an obscure commission. When he decided to contest Mayor Kevin White of Boston, Carter aides came forth with only token assistance. It was a waste to fight Kennedy in his home state no doubt.

parties provide an ideal network for recruiting temporary employees such as these." By the fall Carter aides were making it clear that he would not simply accept the recommendation of local Democrats on these matters. They would have to support him actively in order to receive this bounty.

To mobilize support from blacks and Latinos, White House staff aides distributed lists of minorities appointed to high-level positions by the Administration. Rick Hernandez, one of Tim Kraft's two deputies in the Office of the Assistant to the President for Political Affairs and Personnel, organized a coalition of Mexicans, Cubans, and Puerto Ricans called the Hispanic American Democrats, ostensibly to increase their political awareness while helping them and the party. He began distributing information in early 1979, pointing out that the Carter Administration had appointed 131 Hispanics to super-grade, non-career (i.e., political) positions.

In January, 1980, White House aide Louis Martin mailed to black leaders around the country a fact sheet that listed all the blacks in the government, from Patricia Roberts Harris and Donald McHenry in the Cabinet through 12 black ambassadors, 30 federal judges, 25 generals, admirals, and other military officers, 6 United States Attorneys, 118 sub-Cabinet officials, 110 members of advisory boards and commissions, and 25 White House aides. Carter's flair for the politics of trying—i.e., his intentions to aid the poor and the unemployed in the future—were also advertised in this fact sheet. In January, it noted, he asked Congress for $2 billion in federal funds by the fiscal year 1982, for the "most comprehensive youth employment and training program ever accomplished or envisioned in our nation."

Carter also tried to preempt the Kennedy challenge by collecting political endorsements from Democratic movers and shakers across the country. In late October, 1979, he invited Democratic leaders from across the nation to a dinner in Washington to mark the unofficial opening of his campaign. Those invited were informed that their attendance would be construed as an endorsement of the President. It was an attempt to tip the undecideds over into the President's camp—threatening them with political isolation if they did not. Overall, 500 party influentials showed up—including 109 Congressmen, 12 senators, several governors (including Ella Grasso of Connecticut, Brendan Byrne of New Jersey, Julian Carroll of Kentucky, Bruce King of New Mexico) and Mayors Edward Koch of New York City, Thomas Bradley of Los Angeles, Coleman Young of Detroit, and Maynard Jackson of Atlanta. (Still, there were notable absences. None of the Democratic leaders in the Senate were there.) After this meeting Coleman Young, a long-time Carter supporter, made public noises to the effect that other mayors better get on board while the getting is good. Finally, even the reluctant black leadership of Washington, D.C., began to support Carter. And by late November, 1979, Carter had won the endorsement of the National Education Association—the day after Congress approved that group's most important legislative goal, the new Department of Education. With other unions Carter and Kennedy were in a battle for endorsements. Carter had the appeal and clout of incumbency, while Kennedy had a near-perfect record on labor issues.

Overall, by the fall of 1979 Carter was engaged in an extraordinary public show of the insider's muscle. In the flush of his 1976 victory, which he had evidently seen as primarily his own doing, Carter had neglected the traditional groupings in the Democratic Party and their legislative interests as formulated by their leaders. As he prepared for 1980, he tried to make up for that by inverting what he had done in 1976: the leaders would be worked on first so that the public would come around. Endorsements were necessary to check the expectation that he was finished politically; the leaders' assistance was essential to pull out victories—symbolic or otherwise—in the early straw polls, caucuses and primaries.

This strategy worked in the election of delegates to the Florida state Democratic convention. Carter assured himself of victory in the straw poll at the November convention by winning 518 to Kennedy's 292. Yet Carter still had a long way to go. Practically every public opinion poll taken in October showed the Senator leading among Democrats and independents by a 2 to 1 margin. Basically, there was a feeling that Carter was not a good leader. A Harris poll published in mid-November showed only 23 percent of Democrats polled had high confidence in Carter's abilities to lead the country, with only 11 percent of independents and 9 percent of Republicans agreeing. In another poll at the same time, only 16 percent of the public at large expressed "a great deal" of confidence in Carter. Further, the public was not buying the idea presented earlier that summer at Camp David that the malaise was in the country. Harris's polls, for example, showed that 72 percent of Democrats had high confidence in the country, and they showed 65 percent of the public expressing "a great deal" of confidence in the American people. As the pollster noted, "It is the perceived belief that he [Carter] just doesn't know how to do the job he had been elected to do."

On Wednesday, November 7, Edward M. Kennedy finally announced his candidacy for the Democratic presidential nomination. In Boston's historic Faneuil Hall, surrounded by his family, including wife, Joan, and sister-in-law Jackie Onassis, Kennedy introduced what was intended as the cornerstone theme of his campaign—Carter's lack of leadership: "Did we change so much in these three years? Or is it because our present leadership does not understand that we are willing, even anxious, to be on the march again? . . . The only thing that paralyzes us today is the myth that we cannot move."

However, despite his standings in the polls and the public support of his theme, Kennedy was vulnerable. A few days earlier, in an interview for CBS, Roger Mudd (competing with *Jaws* on another network), chewed away at Kennedy with questions about the legitimacy of his challenging a President of his own party, about Chappaquiddick and rumors of other women in his life (an area normally considered off limits by the respectable press—no other candidates, even those considered vulnerable on that score, were ever asked such questions). At his announcement celebration another reporter asked Kennedy whether his wife, from whom he had been living apart for some time, planned to campaign. The fragile Joan Kennedy stepped forward to handle that one herself, saying she would. Later *Reader's Digest* and *The New York Times* would raise other questions about what Kennedy had really done that night at Chappaquiddick. There was an even more crucial political liability, however, that Kennedy could not have anticipated. The President would be aided in his campaign by the Ayatollah Khomeini, by Leonid Brezhnev, and by the press and evening news television shows.

## Second Chance: Iran

On Sunday morning, November 4, three days before Kennedy announced his candidacy, hundreds of militant Iranians, followers of the Ayatollah Khomeini, gathered in downtown Teheran outside the United States embassy to protest the admission of the former Shah of Iran into the United States. At the same time, eighty miles away, the Ayatollah Khomeini was telling a student that foreign enemies were plotting against the Iranian revolution; he called the American embassy a "nest of spies." At 11:00 A.M. the militants broke open the gate at the American compound. By 4:00 P.M. the entire compound was in the militants' hands and the embassy staff were being bound, and blindfolded. The militants issued a communiqué saying that the takeover was a protest against the United States' offering asylum to the "criminal Shah," and Khomeini himself backed the action, calling the United States government (the *dolat*, as contrasted to the *mellat*, "the people") the "Great Satan."

The American decision to admit the Shah into the United States had been taken against a background suggesting that just such an attack might occur. American Embassy officials had been the object of takeovers earlier in the year. The previous February, days after Khomeini had returned to Iran, leftist guerrillas had invaded the U.S. embassy and held Ambassador William Sullivan and 100 embassy personnel hostage for two hours. That same month the American Ambassador to Afghanistan, Adolph Dubs, had been kidnapped by Moslem extremists in Kabul, Afghanistan, held prisoner in a hotel room, and killed, either by his abductors or in cross fire, when security men representing the Afghan government stormed the hotel. Most important, there had been explicit warnings from the members of the Iranian Revolutionary Council, as well as the Iranian embassy in Washington, that admission of the Shah could lead to attacks on the embassy. The American Chargé d'Affaires in Iran and Iranian specialists in the State Department (including Undersecretary of State for Political Affairs, David Newsom) had warned against admitting the Shah.

The taking of hostages, however, was a form of political blackmail, and the refusal of the Iranian government to provide protection for the embassy personnel was a blatant violation of one of the most honored rules of international law.

Carter, who had been spending a quiet weekend at Camp David at the time of the takeover, arrived grim-faced, at the White House at 8:15 Monday morning. The National Security Council went into almost continuous session for the next few days, evolving the broadline outlines of the Administration's policy.

The Administration's first responses were restrained. A mission headed by former Attorney General Ramsey Clark was sent to Iran to negotiate. He was stopped in Istanbul, Turkey, however, when Khomeini refused to meet him. At another level there was an attempt to mobilize world opinion against the Iranian actions. On November 9 the United Nations Security Council unanimously (the U.S.S.R. included) voted in favor of a resolution calling for the release of the hostages. And on November 29 the United States took its case against Iran to the International Court of Justice at The Hague. Two weeks later, in a unanimous decision, the fifteen members of the court called on Iran to release the hostages and restore the United States embassy to American control.

While these avenues were being pursued there was an effort to get the Shah out of the United States. It would clearly change the bargaining situation—the United States would no longer be in a position to return him to Iran. On December 2 the Shah officially went under government protection as he was taken to Lackland Air Force Base in Texas, pending other arrangements. On December 15 the former monarch flew from Texas to Contadora Island off the coast of Panama.*

The Administration also took two preemptive steps just in time to avoid further embarrassment at the hands of Iran. On November 12 Carter announced an indefinite halt to U.S. oil imports from Iran, a week after the Teheran militants called for a cutoff of oil to the United States and just before the Iranian government moved to institute the oil boycott on its own. On November 14 Carter signed an order to freeze all Iranian assets in the United States—after receiving reports that Iran planned to withdraw all assets here. Finally, on December 25 the Administration asked the United Nations Security Council to recommend an economic boycott of Iran to the nations of the world. (Another deal was worked out, however. Secretary General Kurt Waldheim would fly to Teheran to negotiate release of the hostages. If no agreement could be reached, the economic sanctions resolution would be introduced.)

There were signs of vacillation. On December 12, more than a month after the embassy takeover, the State Department ordered all but 35 of the 218 Iranian diplomats accredited to the United States to leave the country in less than a week. Not for four months would diplomats actually be expelled. The military option, publicly rejected by the President at first (a foolish signal, removing as it did that element of uncertainty for the Iranians), was followed by hints in late November and December that it might be used after all. On No-

---

*Ironically, in the middle of this very delicate negotiating period the Shah's memoirs were published in Paris—and in them he blamed the United States for his downfall, claiming a NATO official had instructed the Iranian military to stand back and allow the revolution to take place.

vember 20 President Carter sent out the message that "other remedies available to the United States existed under the charter of the United Nations." Subsequently, the Navy ordered the aircraft carrier *Kitty Hawk* and several escort vessels to the Indian Ocean. Carter warned that Iran would face "extremely grave" consequences if any hostages were harmed, that freeing the hostages would not "wipe the slate clean." In December the White House warned that the United States might take punitive measures if the hostages were placed on trial as spies. And Secretary of State Vance refused to rule out the possibility of a naval blockade against Iran.

The escalating rhetoric covered what appears to have become a stalemate. There was no viable military option that would actually rescue the hostages. The United States had not found any political or economic levers to move the militants or Khomeini from their positions. After two months of pressure and exchange Carter seemed to have few options. The United States could only hope that the Iranian elections, scheduled for January 25, might bring a more responsible government to power.*

## Afghanistan

On December 28, just at the point when Americans were becoming restive over the stalemate in Iran, Russian tanks and troops moved across the border into Afghanistan to support Babrak Karmal in a bloody coup, the third in two years.

The extent of the Soviets' ambition was not completely clear at the outset. Initially some officials in Washington saw the move as an attempt to preserve Soviet influence there, against the disintegration of the Afghan government and army. The number of Soviet troops and tanks that rolled in, however, combined with the chaotic situation in Iran, opened up the possibility that the Russians might be positioning themselves for a drive through Iran or Pakistan to the Persian Gulf and valuable oil fields as well.

President Carter, right after the invasion, told reporters at the White House that the Soviet intervention was a "grave threat to peace." On January 3 he recalled from Moscow the American ambassador, Thomas J. Watson (the first political appointee to have held the post since World War II)—going beyond the United States' response to the Russian invasion of Czechoslovakia in 1968, when the ambassador had stayed in Moscow. The next day on national television, Carter announced an embargo of economic and cultural exchanges with the U.S.S.R. which included a partial embargo on the shipment of American grains to Russia, as well as a deferral of most Soviet-American cultural and

---

* It still might have helped, earlier, if Carter had attempted to take the spotlight off the hostages, rather than vowing that his attention would not be diverted from them. Carter's publicly making their release his top priority and going along with daily press coverage of the scene in Teheran, the militants were reinforced in their idea that they had considerable leverage vis-à-vis the United States.

exchange programs, including plans to open new consular offices in New York and Kiev. After several trial balloons Carter announced on "Face the Nation" his plans to pursue a boycott of the 1980 Olympic games in Moscow, should Soviet troops not be fully out of Afghanistan by mid-February. He asked Congress to suspend a ban on nuclear trade with Pakistan (imposed earlier because that country seemed to be working on nuclear weapons) and offered Pakistan's President Mohammad Zia $400 million in aid (Zia said that he had not been consulted before the public offer of aid had been made, that it was only "peanuts," that military assistance had to be coupled with long-term economic aid. Eventually his request for "billions" led the Administration to put aside its plans to ask Congress for the aid).

Within the month Carter had inflated a serious problem into the "most serious threat to peace since World War Two" (as he said in his State of the Union Address). He also had outlined a new doctrine, hinted at earlier in the month, that was reminiscent of John Foster Dulles's attitude toward the Mideast back in the 1950s. Any attempt by an outside force "to gain control of the Persian Gulf Region," he declared, "will be regarded as an assault on the vital interests of the United States. It will be repelled by use of any means necessary, including military force." He looked forward to the establishment of a "cooperative security framework in the area" and pledged assistance to Pakistan against outside aggression. Beyond that, he called for the revitalized Selective Service System (with the institution of military registration), an increase in American defense expenditures, and approval of a new CIA charter. In the space of a month, "détente" had been laid low and a new cold war was in the making.

There were second thoughts about some of the United States' responses as time wore on. Carter himself backed down from a tentative decision to cut the number of American diplomats in the U.S.S.R. when Ambassador Watson opposed it. (It was foolish to consider cutting down just at a time when the United States needed all the information it could get on what was happening there.) Further, some of United States Western European allies saw the economic and cultural boycott as going too far. Deputy Secretary of State Warren Christopher, in mid-January, was able to get several European nations to agree not to increase their own exports to undermine the American embargo; but they would not cut back on their own trade. (In the meantime Brazil and Argentina were stepping up their grain exports to the U.S.S.R.) The Olympic boycott brought similar results. The initial trial balloons over the boycott won the support of the United States Congress as well as editorial support in *The New York Times* and the Washington *Post*. But the United States Olympic Committee, the American athletes on the Olympic teams (according to an AP poll) and the International Olympic Committee were opposed to such action. The head of the United States Olympic Committee when first approached called the idea "inappropriate and gauche." Lord Killanin, president of the International Olympic Committee, said: "I deplore athletes being used as pawns in political problems that politicians cannot solve themselves." Secretary of State Vance's plea to the International Olympic Committee just before the winter games opened at Lake Placid, New York, was met coolly and unanimously rejected by that body.

Carter led a public, frustrated over the apparent inability of the United States to find quick solutions to these two crises, into symbolic displays of commitment and strength. The Christmas tree lighting ceremony at the White House in 1979 showed the quintessential Jimmy Carter. The tree had been lit each year since Calvin Coolidge started the ceremony in 1923. But when Carter pulled the switch, only the white star on its top came on, while blue lights, set off by Amy, sparkled on fifty smaller trees. To the astonished onlookers Carter explained that there was one small tree for each hostage: "We will turn on the rest of the lights when the hostages come home." In his call for American support of economic and cultural sanctions against Russia, Carter called upon Americans to make patriotic sacrifices for the country—while assuring them they would not be hurt. Except for the Olympic boycott, the bottom line in every case was that there would be no real costs. The grain exporters would receive government economic supports, the women who might be registered for the draft would never have to serve in combat. The high point of this reassurance came on February 15, when 200 student body presidents from across the nation met with Carter in the East Room of the White House. He assured them that his call earlier in the week for draft registration was only "symbolic." It did not mean that they would actually have to come up for service.

## Oval Office Strategy

Carter and his Administration forestalled public discussion of alternative ways of dealing with the Teheran impasse with the suggestion that discussion would be a sign of disunity that would hurt the hostages. Right after the hostages were taken in Iran he asked members of Congress and the other presidential candidates to refrain from criticism. It would enable him to keep his options open and present a unified front to Khomeini and the militants in Teheran. When Republican presidential hopefuls John Connally and Ronald Reagan nevertheless commented on the President's handling of the situation, Howard Baker, the Republican leader in the Senate and a contender in presidential lottery himself, rebuked them. Senator Henry Jackson of Washington declared after a briefing session at the White House, "Restraint is the order of the day." The result: throughout November and early December the presidential challengers in both parties checked potential criticisms of the President.

When Ted Kennedy, after weeks of silence on the Iranian matter, publicly criticized the Shah, saying he had run "one of the most violent regimes in the history of mankind" and had stolen "umpteen billion dollars," the media and the Administration hit him hard. (Kennedy's remarks were in response to a question suggesting that the United States owed the Shah a permanent home here because of his long friendship with this country.) The New York *Post* ran the headline "Teddy Is The Toast of Teheran." The State Department suggested that Kennedy might have jeopardized the delicate negotiations for the hostages. And Carter himself fed the "stab in the back" interpretation. "I don't give a damn whether you like or do not like the Shah," he told a bipartisan group from Congress in an off-the-record briefing. "The issue is that American hostages, 50 of them, are being held by kidnappers—radical and irresponsible kidnappers. They're trying to blackmail this country. *Anytime we try to* interrelate the two issues, even we hurt the prospect for the release of the hostages (emphasis added)."

Carter also withdrew, on December 28, from the Iowa debate with Kennedy and Jerry Brown on grounds of patriotic duty. (He had agreed to the debate after the hostages had been taken.) In an appearance on NBC's "Meet the Press" the Sunday night before the Iowa caucuses, Carter himself said, "In a time of crisis for our country, I believe it is very important for the President not to assume in a public way the role of a partisan campaigner in a political contest." (After the Iowa caucuses campaign manager Robert Strauss, conceded that Carter did have some time to campaign in primary states; but Carter would not risk damaging the *unity* behind the President.) Later, in a phone call to leaders of the American Olympic hockey team, after they had won their medal at Lake Placid, Carter again implied that he and his aides were so busy working on Iran and the economy that they could not even give the games their undivided attention on TV.

Rosalynn, campaigning in Iowa, had explained that she and others had "begged" the President to stay in the debate, but he had felt that national unity during the Iran crisis would be jeopardized by participation in a partisan event. He would do what was good for the country, even if it was bad for him politically. Actually, the Oval Office strategy was to Carter's political advantage, as it had been to other Presidents before him (Nixon in 1972, Ford in 1976). The President has ways of politicking that a challenger does not, and Carter used them to the hilt.

While Carter refrained from personally taking to the hustings, his family and Cabinet members and other political associates continued to do it for him. Vice-President Walter Mondale worked Iowa. Calling for the grain embargo against Russia, he said the President "put the country first"; Kennedy (who opposed the grain embargo) was playing "the politics of the moment." Secretary of Agriculture Robert Bergland spent his Christmas vacation flying about the country. In Iowa he gave the call to colors. "We're being tested by the Russians to see what we're made of," he said. But the farmers could be patriotic without getting hurt. Bergland promised the farmers emergency economic relief. And in an unusual weekend action shortly before the voting, Stuart Eizenstat told the press that the Commodity Credit Corporation would pay local market prices for corn and soya products in states that had surpluses. (Eizenstat denied that Carter did this for political reasons.)

Carter, himself, freed from the need for personal appearances, had time to use one of his trump cards—direct people-to-people contact. This time he did it via telephone in a "Reach out and touch someone," strategy. Every night he made twenty to forty phone calls (many more on weekends) to political leaders and backers in Iowa, Maine, and New Hampshire. In New Hampshire, according to Evans and Novak, Kennedy's precinct workers were finding some blocks where nearly every Democratic household had received a presidential phone call. "More people were called by the President than at any time since we had phones," complained Maine's governor, Joseph E. Brennan, in early February.

Nor did the Oval Office strategy end Carter's policy of bringing groups through the White House. On Monday, February 4, 1980, Carter entertained 205 guests, including members of Congress, Cabinet officers, business types (the chairmen of Aetna Life Insurance and Braniff Airways), the head of the American Legion, and campaign supporters—for example, a Chicago couple whose invitation was a reward for the volunteer work on an earlier fundraising dinner, and the cochairs of the Carter-Mondale artist and athletes committee. (When asked who was paying for the affair, Powell said it was not really a campaign event—just a social to which you could invite anyone you want. That meant it was paid for out of the White House entertainment budget.) The conference with the student body leaders has already been noted. Aside from their meeting with Carter, the students had been briefed earlier in the day by National Security Adviser Zbigniew Brzezinski and Domestic Affairs Administrator Stuart Eizenstat. (The effect of such invitations: University of Illinois Senate Student Association President Matt Bettenhausen, upon receiving the invitation, said, "At first I thought it was a joke . . . I'm going to believe it when I leave." The trip, he said, is a "once in a lifetime opportunity.") That same day Carter also met with editors of several national magazines. He told them that a review of relations with Iran before the ouster of the Shah would not be appropriate at this time, but that he was looking forward to establishing "normal relationships" with Teheran. On February 19 Carter spoke to 500 American Legion members. He appreciated "the firmness, patience, the unity and the will" extended by "almost all" Americans during the crises in Afghanistan and Iran.

The strategy also removed Carter from certain temptations of the campaign trail. His tendency to take swipes at his opponents undermined the "presidential" look. Earlier, in September, 1979, at a town meeting at Queens College, New York City, he had said that at least he doesn't panic in a crisis. Which caused him and Powell to spend a day denying that he was making any reference to Kennedy and Chappaquiddick. (Powell said that Carter was referring to his own composure during 1977 when U.S. helicopters in North Korea were shot down, during the fall of the Shah, and in September, 1979, when Soviet combat troops were discovered in Cuba.) Later, at his dinner for party supporters in late October, Carter openly mocked Kennedy and his earlier statement that the attitude of his mother and wife would influence his decision about running for President. Carter said: "I asked my mama . . . She said it was OK. My wife, Rosalynn, said she'd be willing to live in the White House for four more years." One Carter operative said the point was to see if Kennedy "has the stomach to go through the humiliating, deflating experience of fighting for the nomination." Another added, "He's going to get clawed. He's going to bleed, and then he's going to start dropping in the polls." To which Carter himself added: "Kennedy has no idea what he's in for."

Carter's Oval Office strategy and his call for unity worked for almost two months, as both Republicans and contenders within his own party held their fire. On January 1, however, Bill Brock, the Republican National Chairman, broke ranks, assailing Carter for using the Iranian crisis to divert attention from his foreign policy weaknesses. "It's time to take the gloves off." After Carter had canceled his appearance in the Iowa debate, Kennedy and Brown had accused him of using the hostage situation to help himself politically. On learning that Carter would not debate as scheduled, Brown charged that Carter was "ducking the debate and using Iran as his excuse. The hostages will not get home any sooner by Jimmy Carter hiding in the White House." And Kennedy struck out at Carter's foreign policy for the first time in two months. The Administration, he charged, has been "lurching from crisis to crisis" in international affairs.

After his defeat in the Iowa caucuses, Kennedy threw off the remaining constraints. (Aside from avoiding foreign policy criticism he had been downplaying his traditional liberalism with a guarded approach to domestic issues his aides were calling "pragmatism.") His most slashing attack was at Georgetown University on January 28. Kennedy suggested that the President had exaggerated the foreign policy crisis in Afghanistan. The Soviet occupation of Afghanistan was brutal, he admitted, but was it really the gravest threat to peace since World War II as Carter claimed? He recalled the Berlin blockade, the Korean war, and the Cuban missile crisis. This country, he warned, should not "rush into a helter-skelter militarism." Moreover, he suggested, the President may have "invited the Soviet invasion of Afghanistan" by doing nothing when that country first came under Soviet influence in 1978 and ignoring warning signals thereafter. Indeed, the President had little credibility with the Russians, having first said that Russian troops in Cuba were unacceptable and then later accepting them. Kennedy's own view: that it is more important for the United States to keep up its conventional forces than to rush to the development of new nuclear weapons. As for the hostages in Iran, he proposed the establishment of a United Nations Commission to investigate Iran's charges against the Shah, with the condition that the hostages be released before the investigation began. Later, in an interview with CBS News in Boston, Kennedy said there is "a war hysteria in this country now. It's diverting."

Kennedy also staged a mock debate with Carter before the Consumer Federation of America. Carter addressed the group first, complete with "Hail to the Chief" (reinstated several months earlier) and the Presidential seal on the podium. He quickly left the hall after his speech. Kennedy came up afterward; joking about the removal of the seal and how Carter had to rush back to the White House "to read a vital national security document—the Portland, Maine, telephone directory." Kennedy held up a tape recorder, pressed a button, and out came Carter's statement at a 1978 news conference that a projected 9 percent inflation was "a temporary aberration." (The 1979 inflation rate exceeded 13 percent.) Launching into a stinging attack on Carter, Kennedy pointed to his economic policies and his refusal to come out and campaign: "We do not pick a president for eight years, but for four-year terms. The referendum we are holding in 1980 is not a secondary side show, it is a primary element of our freedom."

A week later, buoyed by his near victory in Maine, Kennedy accused Carter of seeking "blank-check" approval of a "failed foreign policy." In a speech at Harvard University, Kennedy blamed Carter's policies for helping create the crises facing the nation. Claiming that Carter had ignored "months of signals" about the Soviet move into Afghanistan, Kennedy said another President "would have raised the issue in advance, instead of drawing a line after it was already crossed." And if the Administration had not "parlayed the SALT treaty into nearly certain Senate defeat," he said, "the Soviets would have had something to gain by restraining their aggression." Had he been President, Kennedy suggested, "The crisis might have ended with nothing more than Soviet military maneuvers near the Afghan border. . . . No president should be reelected because he happened to be standing there when his foreign policy collapsed around him." The Senator repeated his earlier charge that the hostage situation was the "predictable" result of the decision to admit the exiled Shah of Iran to the United States. In addition, the Administration had delayed the release of the hostages by first threatening and then withdrawing economic sanctions against Iran, by rejecting and then moving to accept a "commission of Iranian grievances." Kennedy said: "We are now in the 101st day of a crisis that never should have happened . . . The last gasp of a failed policy is war."

Carter aides, in their regular meeting with the President the following morning, were angry. Later that day they lashed out at Kennedy on several fronts. By noon Jody Powell had summoned reporters to his office, where he characterized Kennedy's speech as "offensive, inaccurate, and obnoxious." Later, Secretary of State Vance issued a statement saying that, "Contrary to the Senator's charge, and as he knows, we have been working with the United Nations Secretary General for months on the possibility of creating an international commission that could lead to the release of the hostages." That same night, when asked about these comments in his televised press conference, Carter said the Kennedy statements on Iran have not been "true" or "responsible," and "they have not helped our country." Carter also interpreted Kennedy's attack on him as an attack on America: "Somehow the Soviets [in Kennedy's view] were not the culpable party, but somehow the U.S. was responsible."*

Later in the campaign, when Ronald Reagan similarly charged that Carter's vacillation and weakness were a cause of the disasters in Iran and Afghanistan, Carter again identified his own fortunes with the nation's. That "ridiculous claim . . . could only damage our own nation's prestige," he said. "I think the people in the Kremlin would agree completely with what Mr. Reagan said."

Overall, this call for unity and Carter's projecting himself as above "partisan politics" made good sense in terms of his own political fortunes. Americans, regardless of their partisan or ideological orientation, traditionally support their President when he acts as head of state. In foreign policy crises, this tendency to rally around the President and the flag is particularly strong. (A Harris poll in 1966, for example, showed that popular support for the bombing of the Hanoi-Haiphong area in North Vietnam increased from 50 to 80 percent after the bombing of those targets had begun. According to Gallup's poll, Johnson's decision to halt the bombing of North Vietnam in the spring of 1968 dramatically cut the number of people opposed to such a halt by 51 to 24 percent. These followers "were found disproportionately among the affluent, the better educated and the young.")

In Carter's case, the rhetoric from Iran—Khomeini's calling the American government Satanic and Carter a Hitler—when combined with Carter's "tough" but modest stances on TV, no doubt reinforced the tendency to support the President. In any event, Carter experienced a dramatic reversal of his standing in the polls. Gallup showed public approval for the Carter presidency jumping from 30 to 61 percent in the first weeks after the U.S. embassy was taken. Gallup called it the greatest positive upturn in presidential support since national polling began. In Iowa, Carter easily retook the lead—the Des Moines *Register* poll showed Carter rising from a 40-to-40 deadlock to a 57 to 25 percent lead over Kennedy in the space of a month. In early February, after the Iowa caucuses, the Washington *Post*, reporting on its own national survey, noted how Carter in three months had "undergone one of the most stunning transformations imaginable: Carter is trusted, his character admired, his policy decisions supported. Huge majorities think that no one around can do a better job of handling the nation's most excruciating problem: obtaining the return of American hostages in Iran." The poll showed Carter with a lead of more than 2 to 1 over Kennedy for the Democratic nomination and with similar leads over the chief Republican contender.

Even Kennedy's attempts in February to make clear the differences between himself and the President did not pay off. A *New York Times-CBS* poll

* The sensitivity of the Carter staff may have been compounded by the fact that they had apparently agreed to the establishment of a commission to look into the Shah's "crimes" and American "complicity" in them without first securing the release of the hostages, a condition Kennedy had placed on his proposal. By February 24 Khomeini would state that the hostages would not be released until the new Iranian assembly was elected, an indication that the commission was proceeding without a guarantee even of simultaneous release of the hostages.

taken in mid-February, after Kennedy's Harvard speech and the President's counterblast on national television, showed twice as many people were finding fault with Kennedy for "trying to capitalize politically on current international tensions" as were finding fault with the President on the same grounds. A majority of those polled did not see the President's decision to remain in Washington as a political tactic. Most did not want the policy on Iran debated. Even Kennedy's advocacy of wage and price controls and gasoline rationing had not won him support. Seventy percent of the respondents did not even properly perceive his stand on those issues. Carter maintained a 58 percent lead among Democrats, compared with 23 percent for Kennedy, 7 percent for Brown, with 12 percent undecided. The Iran and Afghanistan crises, then, and Carter's initial responses to them, had given him a political rebirth his reassessment at Camp David had not.

It was not clear how a show of unity to the Iranians would get them to change their minds, or how economic or Olympic boycott threats would get the Russians to leave Afghanistan. Carter had gotten himself on a slippery slope diplomatically speaking and might have to pay the political costs as these American displays came to naught. Further, the economy was heating up. By early March the inflation rate would be running near the 18 percent mark, interest rates nearing 17 percent, and the unemployment rate threatening to climb. Maybe the voters would start voting their pocketbooks, as the traditional wisdom says they do.

In late January there were signs that the moratorium on criticism was breaking down. Tom Shale, television critic for the Washington *Post*, wrote on January 30: "And all the while TV has been beating up on Kennedy, there's been almost benign neglect of Carter. Here you have a guy who is really a disaster, but the networks have gone right along with his Rose Garden strategy. There is absolutely no innovation in their coverage." Anthony Lewis, in *The New York Times* on February 4, noted a "creeping deification of Jimmy. Portions of the American press, both print and television, are treating him with a hushed reverence." James Reston on February 6 queried: "Having cheered President Carter's . . . warning to the Russians to stay out of the Persian Gulf . . . or else, Washington is now beginning to ask: 'or else what?' "

On February 20 Reston further shared with the nation his "Doubts in the Night": "The allies from the start, and lately the American press, have begun to question Mr. Carter's judgment that Afghanistan was the most serious foreign policy crisis since the last World War; and most recently, Mr. Carter has begun to agree with them and withhold sanctions against Iran and his opposition to a U.N. commission to investigate the charges against the Shah before the American hostages are released." Moreover, Carter's talk about "more sacrifices to come, about the possibility of war in the Persian Gulf, higher defense budgets, higher unemployment, new mobile combat units and new missile and conscription systems" ran contrary to the traditional orientation of the Democrats "as the party of the young, the old and the poor; of low prices and interest rates, and cooperation with the allies." The party, he suggested, "is divided and troubled because many of its leaders fear that its political success for the moment rests on a false premise—an exaggerated and maybe even a contrived fear of war—and that this will become clear during the long Presidential campaign—especially when the major threat of the domestic economy finally becomes the central issue for debate." According to Reston, Carter's "natural political supporters are beginning to wonder where it's all going."

The irony of the 1980 primary campaign was that Carter's party never required him to account for departing from its traditional domestic concerns, as Reston thought it might. Nor did his increasingly obvious use of the foreign policy crises for his own political advantage, his failures to secure the return of the hostages from Iran, or to get the Russians out of Afghanistan ever catch up with him in the primary returns.

There were, it is true, serious setbacks. He "lost" several industrial states to Kennedy—New York, Pennsylvania, and Michigan. And midway through the season, in April and early May, the Gallup polls showed a drop in Carter's popularity relative to his opponent in the party—down from 59 and 60 percent in March to 53 and 51 percent in April and early May.

There was also a steady decline in Carter's standing relative to Reagan —from a 58 to 33 percent lead in the Gallup poll at the end of February to a 6 percent lag behind Reagan in an ABC-Lou Harris poll in mid-May. Further, many voters were dissatisfied with the Carter and Reagan alternative by April. A New York Times-CBS poll showed both had been running in a dead heat, but half of those polled were dissatisfied with the two candidates. Even as the primary season came to an end there were indications that the support for Carter was lukewarm at best. In the May 3 Texas primary almost 20 percent of the Democrats voted for neither Carter nor Kennedy. And an Associated Press-NBC exit poll in Indiana showed that 50 percent of those who voted for Carter were voting more for the presidency or against Kennedy than for Carter. Then on May 5, Governor Hugh Carey of New York noted that events since the New Hampshire primary might have changed the minds of the delegates, and suggested that the best way to unite the Democratic Party would be for both Carter and Kennedy to release their delegates.

Despite these problems, and except for that dip in April and early May, Carter sustained an almost two to one edge over Kennedy throughout the primary season, with the rest of the voters favoring Brown or undecided. He was able to prevent a more serious defection from his candidacy for several reasons. Partly it was his ability as an incumbent to win over local leaders through the use of spoils. Partly it was that the "character" issue played to his advantage. Kennedy had been seriously wounded by press questions about his role at Chappaquiddick and his relationships with his wife and other women—while his political character went virtually ignored. Carter, by way of contrast, was still perceived as a highly moral man—a theme played upon, indirectly, in his advertisements used in Illinois and Pennsylvania. One advertisement emphasized Carter as "father, husband, President. He does each job with distinction." Another featured men and women on the street, saying that they could not trust Kennedy, that he was too big a spender.

In addition, Carter was successful in convincing many Americans that his problems in governing were not of his doing. He had long blamed his legislative failures on the "selfish interests" that controlled Congress, and at his domestic Camp David meeting he had ever so subtly suggested that his problems also resided in the people, who were not inclined to sacrifice for the greatest good. Aides elaborated on these themes in their exchanges with the press. Ignoring the Great Depression, World War II and the near collapse of Europe after it, and the development of the atomic bomb, they claimed that the great unprecedented complexity of the problems Carter had to deal with made it impossible for any man to do better. Many Americans bought this view.

Carter and his aides also showed their extraordinary ability at "damage limitation," even when they made mistakes during the campaign season and when the Carter foreign and economic policies failed to accomplish their objectives. U.S. backing of the United Nations Security Council resolution condemning Israel for the establishment of settlements in occupied Arab territories was repudiated by the President within seventy-two hours, as Israeli and Jewish-American leaders expressed their outrage. The Administration explained that there had been a communications failure, and Cyrus Vance took full responsibility for the mistake. The potential losses from this fiasco were limited to the New York and Connecticut primaries. A possible slide away from Carter was checked the following Tuesday, the day of the Wisconsin and Kansas primaries. Carter, in an unusual 7:18 A.M. television announcement, informed the American public that there were indications that the Iranian militants would soon hand over the hostages to the Iranian government. The announcement was clearly premature, but it had a positive effect on Carter's showing in the Wisconsin race. Carter beat Kennedy there by a margin of 56 to 30 percent (with Jerry Brown taking 12 percent). Of those who made up their minds in the last two days before the election, Carter gained 47 percent of the vote (as contrasted to Kennedy's 35 percent)—reversing the tendency of last-minute deciders in New York and Connecticut.

When the hostages were not transferred to the Iranian government, Carter resorted to a new tough line, making public his threat that the United States might have to use force should America's allies not gather around his economic and Olympic boycotts. With this new show of toughness, America's allies began to fall behind his policies and Carter regained some of the authority he had been losing at home.

Even the ill-fated hostage rescue operation on April 24 worked to his advantage. There was a potential for real political damage, for not only did the operation fail, it seemed to have been conducted in an amateurish way. It was undertaken without advance consultation with any members of Congress, which gave rise, for a moment, to the concern that the President might have violated the

War Powers Act. Moreover, American allies, who had reluctantly followed the American lead on sanctions as a means of blocking further use of force, were privately distressed at not having been informed in advance and let American journalists know about it. Then, two days after the rescue mission, Secretary of State Vance announced his resignation. He indicated that he had made his decision even before the operation had been undertaken because he could not support it. This could have raised questions about the wisdom of the operation.

The Administration, however, said and did all the right things thereafter. Like John Kennedy after the Bay of Pigs, Carter took public responsibility for the failure. But subsequent information released by the Administration suggested, without going into detail, that the operation had been a feasible one, and had failed because of unanticipated accidents. The dangerous part of the mission was the first part, the Administration claimed, and to substantiate this claim they had to tell the public that they would have had considerable help from people on the ground in Iran. A possible Congressional investigation of the whole affair was cut short when Carter named Edmund Muskie, one of the Senate's own stars, his new Secretary of State, the day after Vance resigned.

Most important, Carter showed once again that he had done his best. "A deeper failure," he said, in a press conference shortly after the rescue attempt would have been "the failure to try." And the voters seemed to agree with him. An ABC exit poll of Indiana voters in May showed that Democrats approved of his handling of the Iranian situation by a two to one margin.

With the failure of the rescue mission and the apparent dispersal of the hostages in Iran, there seemed nothing else that the United States government could do. When Senator Byrd and others asked him to resume campaigning Carter decided to do so, for the Oval Office strategy was becoming a liability. On April 30 he announced that foreign crises had become "manageable enough" to allow him to resume a limited travel and campaign schedule. Shortly thereafter, he made it clear that he would not debate Kennedy, however, and he further said he had no intention of sharing a platform with Anderson in the fall. Carter had been for "open government" but he would not debate his policies with two of his potentially strong adversaries, proposing major policy alternatives.

The consequences of the Carter economic policies came too late in the primary season to change the outcome. The lifting of controls on oil prices earlier in his Administration had contributed to the inflationary spiral which showed in the spring. The President's refusal to deal with the inflation through mandatory wage and price controls, as Kennedy had urged, meant that higher interest rates and credit controls were the only dampeners that could be used. The ultimate consequence of this approach—a drain on the budget due to increased payments for unemployment compensation and a potentially serious recession, had been anticipated by a few professional economists. But it received little public attention until just before the final primary round. On May 30 the government released a report showing that twelve economic indicators were foreshadowing a serious recession. Carter, who had earlier said that any recession would be short and mild, had to concede the next day that it would be much "steeper than we've anticipated."

By that time, however, Carter was but twenty-eight votes short of having the majority of delegates needed for nomination, and the final primary round could bring him embarrassment at the worst.

Carter had won, once again, by a combination of luck, a skillful political strategy, and an almost uncanny ability to influence how people interpreted him. From the earlier expectation he had raised that he might be great, he had managed to convince many people that greatness was impossible—that the best America could hope for was a man who said he was honest and showed he was trying. The man who asked "Why not the best?" in his 1976 campaign autobiography now argued for reelection on the theme that things could be worse.

# VI

# Interpretations

# TWENTY-FIVE

# Thought: Substance and Process

*Stylistic Populism*

CARTER'S POPULISM is unique in American politics. In the 1976 campaign he offered what one observer called an insurgency of the middle. Or, as James W. Caesar noted, Carter managed to "pit virtually the entire population against no one." Rhetorically, he tapped resentments against the "big shots," a privileged few whom he portrayed as wheeling and dealing with each other; yet the specific reforms he backed reflected mostly the good government values associated with middle-class reform movements. Public business should be conducted in the open and leaders should be available to the people. Policies should be based on reason and offices awarded on the basis of excellence, not political contributions. The bureaucracies should be organized in accord with the businesslike principles of efficiency that govern private enterprise. These changes would be accomplished simply by selecting an outsider like himself, a man who was from the people, who could represent them because he was more in tune with their needs and wishes than those he would oust. Unlike the populists of the 1890s, he called for no trust busting, no major policy shifts, no development of countervailing political groups to oppose the politically or economically entrenched.

In power, Carter was neither as "populistic" nor as naïve as his campaign rhetoric suggested. As governor, he had worked comfortably with big business, and as a presidential candidate in 1976 , he had indicated that a similar arrangement would exist during his presidency. In the governorship and the presidency he would function politically as an "insider" once he had obtained the office he sought. In his various "people-to-people" techniques he showed a keen sensitivity to the magnetic pull that association with power has for all kinds of people. And for all his talk of the merit system in choosing officeholders, in practice Carter has had the traditional politician's bent for putting his own people in key governmental positions and channeling discretionary resources at his command to build his own political base.

Given his centrist views and his practical knowledge of how to win and exercise power, as President, Carter might have turned out to be an effective consolidator, a middle-of-the-road leader who could restore faith in government by his manifest personal honesty and make government more efficient through his management skills.

He has his failings, however, even as a mainstream politician. He lacks, it seems, a well-thought-out conceptual framework to guide his concrete political choices. He immerses himself in the technical details of programs that interest him, testing various strategies and rhetorical appeals. Yet he fails to bring the components together in an integrated approach that would give him a sense of direction and set up priorities for his various programs.

## Power

At the most basic level, Carter fails to address directly the relevance of power to the political process. Although his "populism" is based on the premise that the people should have a larger voice in government, it projects no clear vision of the institutional mechanisms for guaranteeing wider participation; nor does Carter seem to be aware of the possibility that even leaders brought into office through popular acclaim may misuse their power or use it to reinforce the status quo.

Rather, Carter's whole approach is based on the assumptions that good will and connection with the people are sufficient guarantees that political power will be used for the good. A good person need not have any institutional checks on his behavior. To deal with the misdeeds of the CIA, Carter promised during the 1976 campaign to tell the people if the CIA did something wrong and punish those responsible. As President, he told the country the United States could safely develop the neutron bomb because he would never use it for a first strike. The magical quality of this transformation he seeks was portrayed in a commercial used in the 1976 campaign (rather appropriately called "Dreams"). The camera showed vignettes of typically American people and places, then a shot of the presidential greats chiseled in stone at Mount Rushmore, then a panoramic view of the White House. As the announcer asked if the people have felt shut off from government, the camera panned to a close-up of the White House, which dissolved into a portrait of Jimmy Carter, earlier identified with a collage of faces representing the melting pot of America.

Nor does Carter appear to have a clear view of the historical process by which the people are to assume power. Mainly he seems to embrace the old American notion that progress is inevitable. In his earlier career as a businessman and farmer, and in his reorganization efforts as governor, he had embraced the concept of planning as the primary tool for improvement, a manifestation of an increasing rationality that is central to the historical progress. As governor, he added to that notion: the people are demanding and will inevitably receive a greater voice in their own government. In *Why Not the Best?* Carter interprets Tolstoy's *War and Peace* as a populistic saga. Ignoring the table of contents (which lists princes, princesses, counts, and generals as the main characters), he interprets the book, not as being about the Emperor or the Czar, "but mostly about the students, farmers, barbers, housewives, and common soldiers." The purpose of the book is "to show that the course of human events—even the greatest historical events—is determined ultimately not by the leaders, but by the common, ordinary people."

### *Virtue*

Carter's political views rest on a simplistic moralism. We should honor the same high moral standards "in our home, our office or our government," he told a group of Southern Baptists in 1974.

In *Why Not the Best?* he made a similar point:

Our personal problems are magnified when we assume different standards of morality and ethics in our own lives as we shift from one responsibility or milieu to another. Should elected officials assume different levels of concern, compassion, or love toward their own family or loved ones? Should a businessman like me have a lower standard of honesty and integrity in dealing with my customers than I assume as a Sunday School teacher or a church deacon? Of course not. But we do.

He advocated purity for all government officials, even for those who must engage in covert operations.

Public officials, the President, the Vice-President, Members of Congress, Attorneys General, federal judges, the head of the CIA, the head of the FBI and otherwise, ought to set a standard that is absolutely exemplary. We ought to be like Caesar's wife. We ought to be free of any criticism or allegation. We ought to be open about mistakes that we make, not try to hide from the public what is done. It's erroneous. In that way, mistakes can be more quickly corrected.

His international human rights campaign is based on a missionary assumption that we must not permit violations of the American Bill of Rights in the world at large and that it is our duty to take the lead.

Private virtues, then, become civic virtues. Self-sacrifice and abnegation, which Carter views as the highest goal for an individual (one should love God and his neighbor before himself), is also a value for the citizen in his relations with the government. He told one group during the 1976 campaign: "If you think I'd be the best President, support me in a sacrificial way." Conversely, placing one's interests first is a vice. Both as governor and President, Carter has inveighed against the "special interests"—i.e., those who put their own goals above the public good. Moreover, intimacy and love—values in small and permanent groups—may connect a political leader to the people. (As Carter told

Bill Moyers in 1976, he can relate, on a personal level, to people he meets on the campaign trail.) Helping and caring for others—an important and healing virtue in small hometowns like Plains—can be applied directly to the country's relations with other nations. As governor, Carter had embraced the "people-to-people" exchange as a way of building international good will. As candidate, he argued that such volunteer efforts could have a positive effect on international relations. So, too, frugality and hard work, virtues in managing a household or small business, are virtues in the management of the affairs of larger, more complex political enterprises. Indeed, political leadership should provide the same kind of moral stewardship that is relevant in the church. And virtue and adherence to duty will be rewarded by responsibility: political office is a kind of prize to be awarded to the one who works hardest and is "the best"—even the presidency of the United States.

True, he recognizes that both nations and individuals fall short of the perfectionist standard. Reform—salvation—is apt to flow out of a renewed commitment to the higher standard, and in public life reform will often take the form of wider popular participation in government. This is what he means in his frequent quote from Reinhold Niebuhr, "The sad duty of politics is to establish justice in a sinful world."

But the seamlessness of this morality covers potential conflicts between religious and political values. Carter could not foresee a situation in which he would have to choose between his religion and political necessity. He didn't see any conflict between religion and politics, he told a black audience early in 1976. "The purposes are the same—to establish justice in a sinful world." As President, Carter told the Southern Baptist Brotherhood Commission that he has "never detected nor experienced any conflict between God's will and my political duty. It's obvious that when I violate one, I . . . violate the other."

To the contrary, Carter has suggested that religious faith is the source of political virtue. His own faith allows him to be more serene and confident in facing problems. "I know the reassurance I get from my own religion, and it helps me to take a more objective viewpoint and a calmer approach to crisis. I have a great deal of peace with myself and with other people because of my religious convictions. I think that sort of personal attitude—environment—within which I live helps me to do a better job in dealing with the transient and quite often controversial decisions that have to be made in political life, or in business life, or in a family life."

Most important, his religion provides moral vision. In his speech before the African Methodist Episcopal conference in Atlanta in 1976, Carter said: "I believe there's an eagerness among our people to search for a higher standard of ethics, morality, excellence, greatness that can be derived from those who have a knowledge of that higher standard. We Christians have that knowledge; we have a perfect example [Jesus] of what a person ought to be. We can't meet that example, measure up to those standards, but we know what it is." Indeed, political leadership is a special form of moral stewardship. In an interview with religious broadcasters Carter said, "I cling to the principles of the Judeo-Christian ethic. Honesty, integrity, compassion, love, hope, charity, humility are integral parts of any person's life, no matter what his position in life may be. But when someone is elected and trusted by others to help determine one's own life quality, it puts an additional responsibility on the pastor or the schoolteacher or someone who has a public life. So, the Christian or the religious commitment is one that's especially useful to me."

Beyond this, Carter overlooks the possibility that religion might be diluted by making it so public. In 1976, for example, Carter watchers discussed the following: Did the candidate believe in a literal hell or not? What are his views on the literal interpretation of the Bible? Did he and Rosalynn kneel down to pray when they had conflicts? (She said she first heard about that in the newspapers). His answers to such questions could lose him votes from fundamentalists if he gave one answer, and from liberals if he gave another.

But by submitting his religious life to such public scrutiny in an election campaign, a candidate subjects it to the same pressures for hedging and bland stances that influence his specifically political commitments. Thus, Carter did not say whether he believes in a literal heaven and hell. (Even one former minister did not know Carter's stance on this for sure.) The statement in the *Playboy* interview that he was guilty of lust in his heart was in response to a question about his views about the legal rights of homosexuals, which question he never did answer. When pushed on his notion of women's roles, in view of Biblical accounts of creation, he said that he believed in the literal interpretation of Genesis but did not say what he understood that to mean. And after the election, when the Plains Baptist Church split in two and Carter's neighbors and friends had to choose one group or another, Carter backed off again. He avoided Plains on Sundays for a while. (His mother went to a third church in Americus.) When he finally did return to Plains on a Sunday, he compromised by attending the services at both the old and the new church.

These beliefs—that the same values are relevant to private and public life and that moral rejuvenation in one area automatically spills over into the other—are deeply ingrained in the American political tradition. Indeed, the melding of the private and public virtues, of the sacred with the secular, has been the source of what sociologist Robert Bellah has called the American civic religion—a "set of religious beliefs, symbols, and rituals growing out of the historical American experience interpreted in the dimension of transcendence." It assumes that the American people, because of their piety, are special people with a special moral mission.*

This particular "gestalt," however, does not provide a very good map of the

* Carter's recent predecessors in the presidency were in this tradition. Lyndon Johnson, as Doris Kearns pointed out, embraced a faith in the relevance of American values to the world as a whole as he tried to bring the war on poverty to Southeast Asia. Richard Nixon, as Reinhold Niebuhr pointed out, used religious services in the White House for his own political power and made claims for American moral leadership in the world based, in part, on our spiritual and technological superiority.

political world and it suggests, at its base, a superficial understanding of the human situation. Certainly it is antithetical to the tragic perceptions of the existential theologians Carter has so often quoted. It tends to obscure the fact that different virtues are applicable to different realms. Killing a neighbor is generally forbidden—yet men are expected to kill enemies in times of war. An individual may sacrifice his own virtues for a higher good—but it is not considered legitimate for a statesman to sacrifice the national security for some higher goal. One may depend on individual compassion for the care of the weak and sick in the family, but organized supports (jobs, health insurance, retirement programs) are necessary to give substance to compassion in the public realm.

Aside from obscuring such moral dilemmas, the tendency to equate private and public virtues may also mask aspects of power relationships. As Niebuhr has pointed out, love is not the relevant virtue in the political realm. Indeed, to speak of love at the political level is to mask power relationships central to the political process. Justice, Niebuhr argues, is the relevant virtue for the political order, and justice requires that power be confronted and somehow constrained. Further, in international affairs moral reductionism can provide a rationalization of attempts by one nation to extend its influence abroad in the guise of moral salvation. Indeed, the introduction of religious symbols into the public sector, Niebuhr argues, tends to provide support for power. In giving power a dimension of the sacred, one limits the searching inquiry into what government does. To question may become sacrilegious and unpatriotic.

### Humility and Pride

Such a perspective on the world is apt to be accompanied by a sanguine personal philosophy, a tendency to gloss over personal vulnerabilities as well as any ultimate ironies or tragedies.

Take, for example, Carter's handling of the problem of Christian humility. Pride had been his chief failing before his born again experiences. But during the 1976 campaign he suggested he had mostly overcome these tendencies. He often said he thought himself no better than others. Like all persons, he is subject to the temptations of the flesh. As President, he vowed, he would do his best to remain humble. Thus, in an interview with religious broadcasters in October, 1976, he said: "I would always remember the admonitions of Christ on humility and absence of pride, a prohibition against judging other people. I would try not to consider myself better than others." In another setting he said: "Christ in many ways admonishes us against self-pride, against the condemnation of others, when we have within ourselves sinfulness as well. This is the kind of attitude that I would try to adopt as President."

Yet, Carter does not admit to many politically relevant failings. His confidence in his capacity to resist the temptations of power is manifest in his *Playboy* interview. His religion and his character, he suggested, would keep him from "lying, cheating and distorting the truth," the way Johnson or Nixon did. Earlier he had assured Bill Moyers that he had no unhealthy power drives, no "unpleasant sense of being driven." And when Moyers asked, "Do you need power?" Carter responded, "Well, I think so," in what may have been a slip of the tongue. Then he went on to say that he had no "all-obsessive hunger" for power, that he only wanted to correct social inequities and protect those who are not strong. At another point in the interview he indicated he would not be too upset should he lose the race. "I don't feel that I've got to win, or that I, you know, that I'll be terribly disappointed if I don't win. I feel a sense of equanimity about it." The presidency, he said, would only give him "a chance to serve."

Not only did Carter gloss over the possibility that, like others, he might be motivated by self-regarding as well as altruistic concerns in the pursuit of position and power, he found it difficult to admit that he had personal failings which could obtrude on his performance in office. His tendency to lash out at his critics, he explained while he was still governor, is simply a legitimate use of his office to defend the programs he considers important. His stubbornness is a political asset, an aide in bargaining and a sign he will be tenacious in pursuit of the good.

Moreover, the failings he admits to stop short of full admissions. In the *Playboy* interview, he agreed that he could have spoken out earlier on the Vietnam war and the issues of racial integration. But there were good reasons for his reticence. He did not deal with the Vietnam issue until March, 1971, because "it was the first time anybody had asked me about it. I was a farmer before then and wasn't asked about the war until I took office as governor of Georgia." (His recollections are wrong, here. See above.) "It is easy to say in hindsight what you would have done if you had had the information you now have." Finally: "If there are issues I'm avoiding because of a lack of courage, either I don't recognize them or I can't make myself recognize them." Even Carter's admission, in the last campaign debate in 1976, that he made a "mistake" by being interviewed by *Playboy* has the appearance of a strategic retreat. He had only been unwise in his choice of a format. About the same time he pointed out to a religious group that in his *Playboy* interview he had been engaged in Christian witnessing.

His admissions, as President, that he lacked some expertise when he first came to Washington can also be viewed as strategic retreats. He clearly had drastic losses in his public and congressional support in his first eighteen months in office. It was clearly more preferable to credit that to inexperience rather than more deeply ingrained faults. One confession of error is particularly puzzling. A few days after the Russian invasion of Afghanistan, Carter told Frank Reynolds on ABC that "the action of the Soviets had made a more dramatic change in my opinion of what the Soviets' ultimate goals are than anything they've done in the previous time that I've been in office." Yet from the earliest draft of his speech announcing his candidacy for the presidency, through campaign commercials in 1976, to his Wake Forest University and Annapolis speeches in

1978, Carter had never talked as if he thought the Soviet Union was a peace-loving, moderate state. Perhaps he was trying to dramatize, in the Reynolds interview, the uniqueness of this particular Soviet challenge and justify an increase in defense spending, contrary to his earlier commitments.

Most of Carter's confessions to faults, then, are to private or minor ones (or hidden virtues) or they are face-saving explanations of why he has been doing poorly. His prevailing motif, as Robert Scheer wrote in *Playboy*, is that he has always been virtuous. "Despite Carter's acts of courage [during the earlier civil rights struggle in the South], he didn't always act courageously. He was caught in a terrible time and he was only human—which means often he didn't do the right thing. *But Jimmy Carter won't admit it!* The real heroes of the era were less than ten miles up the road in either direction from his home all his life, taking the most terrible punishment, and he won't admit that he shunned them like everyone else. Like all of us."

Pride can also be manifested in claims to emotional invulnerability—and Carter has shown these tendencies. During the 1976 campaign he indicated, as we have seen, that he had no social insecurity, no ultimate doubts about God or life or his faith. The idea of being President scared him not at all. Indeed he has never been afraid—not even of death.

This kind of self-assurance, on the face of it, is apt to be based on a repression of complex feelings. It certainly reflects a perspective on life that radically differentiates Carter from the existentialist philosopher, Sören Kierkegaard, whom he often quotes. As Ernest Becker has pointed out, Kierkegaard's most basic insight was that peace can only come once one has confronted the ultimate anxiety. "This is the terror: to have emerged from nothing, to have a name, consciousness of self, deep inner feeling, an excruciating inner yearning for life and self-expression and with all this yet to die." It is only by the confronting of this truth that human beings can find self-transcendence and a deeper contact with reality. That is the ultimate education.

## *Creativity*

A person who lives on the surface of things is not likely to have high creative ability, i.e., "the capacity to find new and unexpected connections . . . to find new relationships in time and space, and thus new meanings." Lawrence Kubie, who has given this definition, notes that creativity flows from the preconscious processes, as evident in free association, and that it is impeded when a person insists on complete rationality and control. As he says:

. . . free associations are the most natural and spontaneously creative process of which the mind is capable. . . . There are individuals for whom the process is impossible, except where they are entirely off guard, . . . These are individuals for whom this mental leap-in-the-dark is so fraught with guilt or terror that they can no more allow their thoughts to roam freely than they could run down a flight of stairs with closed eyes. Such individuals have to stretch out their mental toes to feel carefully for each next step before they can trust themselves to express a next word. Logical and chronological sequences are the hand-rail to which they always cling.

Jimmy Carter seems like a man who insists on such control. According to his sister Ruth, he is "a very logical, methodical, punctual, well-programmed man with a mind like a steel trap. I would not say that he's particularly creative or innovative." There is other evidence that Carter has a mechanical approach to problem solving. He makes lists. On one occasion (the *Playboy* interview) he explained how he had derived his program as governor of Georgia: "I remember keeping a check list and every time I made a promise during the campaign I wrote it down in a notebook. I believe I carried out every promise I made." The same procedure was used during the 1976 presidential campaign. Working with Stu Eizenstat on his issues stances, Carter moved through the alphabet from Abortion to Zero-based budgeting, discussing the issues, not on the basis of their importance, but in their alphabetical order. As President, he had a list of his campaign promises made up to provide guidance to his policy-making team. He uses a similar method for composing speeches. He says: "I list the points that I want to make, just like an engineer. In a non-sequential way. I just turn 30 or 35 different items in my mind and then try to drive them into four or five themes. I go down the list and put A, B, C, D, and E by each one of those 35 or so points. I rearrange those and then write individual paragraphs in the structure." (His Annapolis speech, according to James Fallows, was written this way. Carter just spliced together the often contradictory viewpoints of his advisers Cyrus Vance and Zbigniew Brzezinski.)

To understand poetry he works in a similar fashion. When *New York Times Book Review* writer Harvey Shapiro asked how he came to understand Dylan Thomas's "A Refusal to Mourn the Death, by Fire, of a Child in London," Carter replied, "I didn't understand the poem when I read it, but the last line said, 'After the first death there is no other.' And I thought about it for a while and I went back and read the poem again. I couldn't understand it still, so then I went back up to my little desk in the front [of the warehouse in Plains] and I diagrammed all the sentences and I finally understood what Dylan Thomas was saying." A Carter friend, Anne Robbins of Rockville, Maryland, observes how Carter explained the poem to her: "I kept questioning him about it. So he would recite it again and again."

There are other cues that Carter does not deeply understand many of the philosophers and poets he quotes. When asked about their views, he usually elaborates on certain external facts of their lives or how he came to know their work, but does not engage in reflection on the meaning of what they say. When Norman Mailer offered a passionate soliloquy on Kierkegaard during his interview with Carter in August, 1976, he drew only a smile, and Mailer realized that "Carter was not necessarily one of America's leading authorities on Kierkegaard. How foolish of Mailer to expect it of him—as if Norman in his turn had never quoted an author he had not lived with thoroughly." When asked in

May, 1977, whether the quotations from Niebuhr, Bob Dylan, and Dylan Thomas used as epigraphs in *Why Not the Best?* "describe a mental landscape for you?" Carter responded: "I don't know. I think in some ways you can tell the interrelationship between Dylan Thomas' poems that I cherish and the Reinhold Niebuhr quote." What the connection might be he did not specify, but went on to say that he had always wanted to meet Niebuhr.

But if Carter lacks high creativity, how does one then explain the rhetorical genius of his 1976 presidential campaign? Carter seems to have used a kind of trial-and-error approach—he tested a wide variety of themes, and when they worked, he incorporated them into his repertoire. Richard Reeves, in August, 1979, noted this:

Carter did not know what he was doing and did not understand the emotions he had tapped. He had just taken advantage of the unique opportunity of trying out a presidential campaign on the road. No one covered him in the beginning and he had memorized and tested a script that he had figured out worked with crowds—the words weren't the product of inspiration, but of trial and error. Still, it was a pretty good show and some of us bought it: a government as good and decent . . . I'll never lie . . . cut the bureaucracy . . . put the big shots in jail . . .

These themes were already in the air prior to his election. The love-and-intimacy theme had been tried, tested, and found useful early by Joseph Biden in his winning campaign for the Senate from Delaware in 1972. And Biden, who was cochairman of the Carter National Steering Committee in 1974, had discussed the potency of this approach with Carter at the governor's mansion in Georgia. Fletcher Knebel's 1972 novel *Dark Horse* has an interesting parallel to Carter's own campaign. The protagonist of the novel is an unknown New Jersey highway commissioner who nearly wins the presidency with an anti-Washington, anti–big shot campaign in which he promises, "I'll never tell a lie." And Carter's "roots" theme was anticipated by Robert Altman's 1975 film *Nashville*. The presidential candidate in that film (Hal Phillip Walker) and his Replacement Party campaigned on the theme "New Roots for America," complete with tributes to the superiority of the people and the value of their common sense over the machinations of the politicians and the lawyers.

Supporting this interpretation is Carter's tendency to go on automatic when using some of his themes. He acted, at times, as if he had a formula, using a theme whether it was suited to a particular situation or not. He took his search for a common ground with audiences sometimes to absurd extremes: While campaigning in Idaho in 1976, he told one audience that he identified with them because the major products of Idaho and Georgia were raised underground—Idaho potatoes and Georgia peanuts. Later he noted that both Oregon and Georgia have important lumber industries. To a West Virginia crowd Carter said: "You have tremendous coal deposits under your surface lands. As you know peanuts grow under the ground also, so I have a lot in common with you there." (Norman Mailer, who was in the audience, thought he was telling a bad joke.) During a visit to the West Coast in August, 1976, Carter observed that even Hollywood reminded him of Plains. When a startled listener asked him "Why?" Carter explained that both towns had trees. And in September at Brooklyn College, Carter found himself "much at home," observing that "both a neighborhood and a small town have their own special character, their own distinctive life. I don't come from Americus, or Vienna, or Cordele. I come from Plains. You come from Flatbush—and not Sunnyside or Bay Ridge or Brooklyn Heights. We feel most at home where our roots run deep."

Similarly, at times Carter took his intimacy theme to points that were potentially embarrassing—for himself or others. As governor, he had addressed a conference of psychiatrists, saying: "There were a few months when I was deathly afraid that I was going to get sick and would have to go out of state or come to one of you for treatment. I was hoping that if I did get sick it would be some emotional problem and not some physical problem, because I doubt that I could have found a doctor in Georgia who would have treated me with love and compassion . . ." Later, writing about his childhood desire to attend Annapolis, Carter confessed his anxieties about a disability called "retention of urine." He wrote: "I was always ashamed to ask whether the last clinging drop would block my entire naval career?" (This last admission provided the reporters who were traveling with Carter with much material for in-group jokes.) His response in February, 1979, to some Yankee baiting by President José López Portillo in Mexico—a recollection that he had first taken up running years ago, between Mexico City's Palace of Fine Arts and the Majestic Hotel where he was staying, only to find that he was afflicted with "Montezuma's Revenge"—created a nervous embarrassment in his audience on the spot and won him stories around the world. His offer of sympathy to Baltimore Orioles manager Earl Weaver on the death of Weaver's mother (he spoke of how upset he and his family were about it) was misplaced because Weaver's mother had not died; Pirates' manager Chuck Tanner was the one who had been bereaved.

Overall, Carter's thought possesses a surface quality, and he lacks both creative ability and a basic philosophy to guide him in his political choices. James Fallows, who has worked with Carter as a speechwriter, has made a detailed analysis of his intellectual characteristics and their ramification for Carter's leadership.

. . . Carter has not given us an *idea* to follow. The central idea of the Carter Administration is Jimmy Carter himself, his own mixture of traits, since the only thing that finally gives coherence to the items of his creed is that he happens to believe them all. . . . I came to think that Carter believes fifty things, but no one thing. He holds explicit, thorough positions on every issue under the sun, but he has no large view of the relations between them, no line indicating which goals (reducing unemployment? human rights?) will take precedence over which (inflation control? a SALT treaty?) when the goals conflict. Spelling out those choices makes the difference between a position and a philosophy, but it is an act foreign to Carter's mind. He is a smart man, but not an intellectual, in the sense of liking the play of ideas, of pushing concepts to their limits to examine their implications. Values that others would find contradictory complement one another in his mind.

In an ordinary leadership position, this deficiency might not be of any particular consequence. As President of the United States, however, coming to the office with the promises he made, these intellectual characteristics were almost bound to create problems for him in setting his political agenda and to make him disappointing to those who expected some special moral and political creativity from him. Moreover, these characteristics cannot be changed by admonitions to do better—which is what Fallows attempts to do in his critique of Carter's approach to problems. They are ordinarily too deeply rooted in the personality structure for that.

# TWENTY–SIX

# Personality

ARTER HAD PREDICTED in February, 1975, that his personality would be the central issue in the 1976 presidential campaign. In a speech before the New Hampshire Senate he said: "If I can personify in my personal life the aspirations of the American people, I will be elected President. If I cannot, I will not."

Moreover, Carter knew what signs the psychobiographers would look for to determine if a candidate was of good presidential timber. As noted earlier, Bert Lance had given him a copy of James David Barber's book, *The Presidential Character*, and Carter studied it carefully. On one occasion, at the governor's mansion, Jimmy Carter outlined Barber's basic categories for his sister Ruth, challenging her to match specific Presidents with Barber's personality types. Ruth recalls their exchange as follows:

> He would say, "How about Kennedy?" And I would say, "He was probably active-positive." And he said, "Yeah, that's right." Then he asked about Nixon, and I said he was "active-negative." And he said, "Yeah, you're right. How do you know so much about psychology?" I said, "Oh, you know. It's just that I'm smart.

After this exchange, Ruth recalls, Carter strove to be more "positive-active" (the personality type Barber describes as best suited to effective performance in the presidency—i.e., the leader is active in the exercise of power and positive in his affect toward himself in that role). Carter invited Barber and his wife to visit the governor's mansion, and in February, 1974, they all spent a pleasant evening together. Later, during the early primaries, Carter would call attention to Barber's work as the "best book I've ever read" on the analysis of Presidents.

During the 1976 campaign, Barber made no public judgments about the character of any of the presidential contenders. But Carter himself used Barber's terminology. "I would be active and positive in approach as president," he told a reporter at one point. "I don't feel ill at ease. I don't feel afraid of the job. I think I would be able to admit a mistake in public when one was made." In July, 1976, Carter told David Broder and several other reporters that he had been "heavily influenced by James David Barber's writings and I think a lot of my ideas come from there." Was he "positive-active?" "That's what I would like to be," Carter responded. "That's what I hope to prove to be."

Carter associates reached similar conclusions, drawing on the data that Carter had presented in *Why Not the Best?* (written in 1975, after Carter had read the Barber book). Dr. Peter Bourne said that "Carter's immense inner security means that he can be a bold leader, confident enough to run the kind of open administration he promises." Ruth Carter Stapleton, in an interview during the early primaries, pointed to Carter's mother and father to confirm that Carter combined the best traits of each parent: "Jimmy's got the perfect combination of the strong male image and the warm compassionate love of mother. If she hadn't been there, Jimmy could have been probably a tyrant."

Given Carter's motivation to win, his decision to make his personality a central issue in the campaign, and his knowledge of the traits psychobiographers might note, one cannot simply accept his self-presentations or his summary judgments about what he is like as the full truth. Yet the capacity for self-censorship is limited for anyone. Much can be learned about Carter from the overall tone of his self-presentations, the implicit as well as the explicit themes. When these characteristics are checked against his behavior, as documented here, general patterns in his personality structure can be seen.

### Surface Traits

There is a grandiose, a perfect quality to the claims Carter makes for himself. He claims to be able to love individuals he meets on assembly lines. He would never tell a lie. He has never experienced fear; death has no terror for him. He is not awed by the presidency, and he knew all along that he was going to make the White House.

Beyond that, Carter seems convinced, at one psychological level, that he has obtained the perfection he seeks. The warmth, calm, and ease he showed on the campaign trail, and later in his "people-to-people" contacts and his dealings with small groups, suggest confidence. His going heavily into debt to finance a long-shot campaign suggests that he did believe he would win. The facility with which he explains his apparent past failures as mistakes due to lack of information or simple lapses in judgment, suggests that he is not often conscious of falling short. He even finds it difficult, as one friend reports, to admit he gets ideas from other people. It's as if he thinks of everything good himself.

The quality of his ambition suggests that he early saw himself as a man of destiny. While still a student in southwest Georgia, he confided to a friend that he would one day be governor of Georgia. While at Annapolis, he expected to become Chief of Naval Operations. As a young naval officer, he applied for a Rhodes scholarship. He seems to have been thinking of the presidency even as he fought his losing gubernatorial campaign in 1966. He set his sights high, given his background. He had no naval commanders or Presidents or Cabinet officers in his family tree to make that goal seem attainable. Moreover, during his formative years he did not exhibit extraordinary leadership qualities that would mark him as a star and indicate that he was on the road toward his goal.

Once he was on the political track, Carter proved to be in an unusual hurry to move on. After only four years in the Georgia State Senate, and with no substantial statewide political base, he bypassed a sure congressional seat for a long-shot try at the governorship. Immediately following that defeat, he organized a second campaign for the same office, sure that he would win the next time around. There was even some talk at that time that he had his eye on the presidency. Before his inauguration as governor, it is clear, he was seeking national ties and shortly thereafter was making his first moves to win national attention. After eighteen months as governor, he was actively seeking the vice-presidential nomination at the 1972 Democratic convention. After that unsuccessful bid, and with problems of political support even in his own state, Carter began, nonetheless, the race for the presidency.

Carter's ability to reach his goals were enhanced by several key personal traits. His intelligence, for one. In his early life as a student and in his early career (from the Navy through the governorship), he showed a capacity for mastering the technical aspects of a job that earned him the respect of influential others. As a presidential candidate in 1976, his skill in handling technical issues and discussing policy options was an important ingredient in winning over the national elites, including the very important press. Further, he could see opportunities where others did not and fashion novel strategies and rhetorical appeals that maximized his own political situation. And whatever his problems as President, no one has questioned his ability to master a wide variety of facts.

Carter's charm has also been a crucial factor in his political advance. Pleasant and self-confident (most of the time), from his first entry into politics he could inspire close friends to work for him. And as he gained experience and power, his self-confidence blossomed, coming to a peak in the summer of 1976, when he could weave a spell on all kinds of people, from folks of Plains and blacks, to representatives of the national media and the "establishment" as well. And at the beginning of his presidency he showed the same kind of magic.

Perhaps even more important is Carter's capacity, once he has decided upon a goal, to concentrate all of his energy on its pursuit. From his first campaign for the Georgia State Senate in 1962 (where he refused to be counted out despite the first negative tally of the vote), through his unsuccessful 1966 gubernatorial bid, to the subsequent victorious campaigns for the governorship and the presidency, he showed an absolute commitment to his goal, a willingness to put in twelve- to sixteen-hour days in its pursuit, and a relish for the conflict such battles entailed.

Finally, Carter has shown an almost Protean flexibility in the selection of strategies and rhetorical appeals. Going beyond the "down home" shrewdness he might have come by naturally as Earl Carter's son, Carter has demonstrated an extraordinary capacity for tailoring his alliances, his problems, his campaign rhetoric, and his own image to meet the changing political currents. From the beginning of his public career, Carter avoided taking stands on controversial issues—either on the campaign trail or in office—that would hinder his upward climb. Ever since his first state senate race, Carter made his own personality and skills and his dedication to good government the central focus of his campaigns. In office, he distinguished himself by promoting important, but basically noncontroversial, programs that challenged no fundamental values. Thus, in the Georgia Senate he concentrated on improving educational standards in Georgia. As governor, he made reorganization of the state government structure his top priority—a project that turned out to be controversial, not because of disagreements over values, but because it sparked fights over political territories. As President he has chosen a central course, pursuing substantive policies not too different from those of his Republican predecessors.

Moreover, like many other politicians', Carter's alliances could shift as new opportunities opened up. He had gone all out to beat Homer Moore in his first race for the state senate in 1962, but welcomed Moore's support in his first bid for the governorship in 1966. He campaigned for Garland Byrd for Congress in 1964, yet ran against him for governor in 1966. And though he ran as a racial moderate in the 1966 primary election and would later talk of how depressed he was at Maddox's ultimate victory, he refused to endorse Maddox's competitor, Ellis Arnall, in the run-off primary, as many other "good government" people and even some of his fellow downstate politicians were doing. As President, he brought the aides of his former denouncers and opponents into his Administration, and after a shaky start, established a working relationship with the Democratic leaders of the House and Senate.

Sometimes, however, he did not pay his political debts. As a state senator Carter had had a close working relationship with Governor Carl Sanders, but that was transformed, at Carter's initiation, into a no-holds-barred competition in the 1970 gubernatorial primaries, in which Carter impugned Sander's integrity. He sought the endorsements of influential segregationists such as former Governor Marvin Griffin and newspaper publisher Roy Harris, but once in office, forgot the segregationists, and ultimately learned how to work with Sanders's allies in the General Assembly. As President, he has not done much for the traditional blocs in the party—the blacks, other minorities, and women activists who aided him in his 1976 campaign.

Carter is able to take both the low and the high road in his dealings with political opponents—depending on the circumstances and phase of the campaign. In opening his 1970 campaign, for example, he suggested that former Governor Sanders had used his office for private gain. But after Carter became the front runner in the run-off primary, he became statesmanlike, above the fray, while a frustrated and angry Sanders thrashed about. In the early phases of his 1976 presidential campaign, he took occasional swipes at his opponents, suggesting they were weak, or contemptible, or part of a conspiracy to stop him. But as he approached the Democratic nomination in the summer and then became the all-but-certain winner in the general election, Carter took the high road—acting presidential, the great unifier. In 1979 he took on Kennedy, beginning his open conflict with the Senator on a low note, stating he would "whip" Kennedy's "ass" and indirectly reminding Americans of Chappaquiddick. With the seizure of the Teheran embassy, Carter was in a less vulnerable position and again assumed the statesman's role. When Kennedy and Reagan questioned his policy, he could thus imply they were being unfair, even helping our enemies in Iran or the U.S.S.R.

There was subtlety in his attacks, a veiled aggression that differentiates Carter's campaign from the more open and direct exchange of political charge and countercharge. Listen to his hints in 1976 about Morris Udall's health: "He's [Udall] a better candidate than the others I have mentioned [Jackson, Bentsen, and Bayh]. . . . I think that because of his campaign in the rest of the nation he has suffered to some degree. He has had a problem with his health. He has missed three or four engagements because he became nauseated or because he had a backache." His reminders about Hubert Humphrey's age were similarly subtle, as were his allusions to Kennedy's character in 1979. This same quality was evident in his swipes at Cyrus Vance shortly after the latter's resignation as Secretary of State in the late spring of 1980. When asked about his new Secretary of State, Carter retorted that Ed Muskie would be a "much stronger and more statesmanlike senior citizen figure," and a more "evocative spokesman," while less likely to get "bogged down in details." (As Jon Margolis noted in his report of this episode in the Chicago *Tribune* on May 23, the problem was not that Carter criticized Vance, but how he did it. "Carter could have forthrightly said, 'Actually Vance wasn't such a good secretary of state . . .' and gone on from there.")

These attacks on others were sometimes made with a surprising disregard for the facts. Carter's initial proof that Sanders was really interested in the 1972 Senate race was based on the "fact" that the registration number on his private plane showed this intent, in code form. This "fact" was quickly shot down but Carter did not acknowledge the error. Similarly, his charge in the spring of 1976, that Udall had used Carter's religion against him in the New Hampshire primary, could not even be substantiated by Carter's own campaign manager in the state. And when Jody Powell took a swipe at Senator Charles Percy, falsely suggesting that Percy had used Bell and Howell planes as a Senator, Carter did not discipline Powell. Indeed, he seems to have completely forgotten the affair when, several weeks later, he said he would fire Powell if he ever caught him lying.

Carter felt free to attack others even in areas where he himself was vulnerable. His problems in arranging meetings with heads of state during his 1973 trip to Europe and the Middle East did not stop him from commenting negatively on Wallace's similar lack of success in 1975. Thus Carter trips as governor at the expense of Lockheed, Coca-Cola, and Georgia lumber companies did not deter him from portraying Ford's golfing holidays and trips, also hosted by prominent businesses, as a sign that Ford was beholden to special interests. (At the same time he failed to note that in his own recent primary campaign Bert Lance had provided the Carter organization with at least four free trips on the Bank of Georgia plane.)*

His capacity to operate comfortably on discordant levels was evident in 1976, as in 1970, when he mobilized public support by running as an "outsider," while simultaneously soliciting the support of "insiders." He lambasted his Washington opponents for being politicians (i.e., for making deals with each other and placing of their friends in political offices), while incurring debts and rewarding friends himself—as governor of Georgia and as president. (In 1979 Gerald Rafshoon took this to the extreme with his suggestion that Carter run as the "experienced outsider" in 1980.)

Carter would evoke his family and his past in different ways, depending upon the effect desired. To foster a Horatio Alger image, he sometimes overemphasized the poverty of his youth and the hard work required of him as a small farm boy. (No doctors or nurses lived in his home county, he claimed. His mother had to work twelve- and sixteen-hour days during the Depression. He rose very early in the morning to put in long and grueling hours on the farm, and, as a small boy of six, took his peanuts to town to sell.) His own educational accomplishments were dramatized by his recollections that he was the first male of his father's family to graduate from high school. At other times he attributed to his family a prestige and status higher than they had. While in the Navy, he discussed his "plantation" with at least one friend and implied that Plains would fall apart without his father's hand at the helm. In *Why Not the Best?* he gives his maternal grandfather credit for having sold Tom Watson the idea for his single greatest legislative accomplishment, the R.F.D.

Carter tended to exaggerate his own past record. Academically, he was sixtieth in his class at Annapolis, and he stood ninety-ninth in his overall leadership score, but he talks as if his record justified a Rhodes scholarship. And he certainly was not a finalist in the competition, as he told columnist Jack

---

*When confronted about the nature of these attacks, Carter has several different techniques to avoid admitting he uses them. He may simply provide another, benign interpretation. Thus, when Jack Nelson asked him in 1976 about his Humphrey stories (which, while ostensibly friendly, suggested that Humphrey was senile), Carter blandly responded that Amy had smeared Humphrey's face with cookies because she liked him and that he and Rosalynn had been telling the same story, in an affectionate way, for the past four years. On other occasions Carter has disarmed criticism of attacks on others by saying that his staff had acted without his knowledge. And when these denials do not work, he has a fallback position, in which he promises to take corrective action and then forgets to follow through. As Tom Ottenad has pointed out, in New Hampshire, Carter denied that he was using a tough commercial blaming his presidential rivals for the country's tax problems. When it turned out that the commercial carried Carter's own voice, he indignantly told reporters that he might kill the announcement. It remained on the air until the election, however, and a similar spot was used in the Florida campaign two weeks later.

Anderson he had been. His military experience was less relevant to the presidency than he implied: his claims to being a nuclear scientist were based on twelve months in the nuclear submarine program and one semester of noncredit courses in basic nuclear physics at Union College. He appropriated literary figures and theologians of whom he had a superficial understanding: Sören Kierkegaard, Reinhold Niebuhr, Dylan Thomas, and others. Prior to his presidency Carter also suggested friendships with powerful or glamorous figures with whom his contact had been cursory. While running for governor and serving in that post, he suggested he was closer to Senator Russell and Admiral Rickover than he seems to have been. (In one of his speeches Carter implied that he was in almost daily contact with Rickover; the protégé relationship contact suggested is not sustained by his own correspondence.) He peppered his speeches with the names of important figures he had met and suggested he was on intimate terms with foreign heads of state and other such leaders. On the campaign trail in early 1976, Carter hinted at friendships with Golda Meir, Helmut Schmidt, and Bob Dylan (all people he'd met only once). George Ball and Wilbur Cohen were listed as advisers, though they had not yet been consulted.

Sometimes during the 1976 campaign there were indications that the line between fact and wish had become blurred in his mind. Certain slips of the tongue suggested an unconscious tendency toward upgrading himself. "I think they still feel that I'm a good President," he said nine months before the election. In one exchange with the press in August, 1976, he casually recalled his role as chairman of the Democratic National Committee (when in fact he had been a cochairman of the campaign committee from 1972 to 1974, a moderately prestigious service committee of the DNC).

In short, though Carter was unwavering in his drive for position, he could be very flexible while pursuing it. He showed unusual freedom from internal constraints—of personal loyalties, strong political commitments, or concern for the egos of his opponents—and he seemed slow to experience shame or guilt.

## A Guide . . .

When Carter burst upon the national consciousness, members of the press and Carter observers picked up on these various traits: his claim to perfection, the height of his ambition, the tenacity, single-mindedness, and tactical flexibility with which he pursued it. Several interpreted these qualities as signs of future greatness—others were worried about the contradiction between what he said and did. Many gave up, as Eleanor Randolph has noted, and settled for calling him an enigma.

We do not have to settle for any of these options. Karen Horney's description of the expansionistic (subtype: narcissistic) personality provides a model that makes sense (i.e., provides congruency between Carter's self-presentation and behavior patterns as outlined here).

Briefly, Horney's theory may be summarized as follows. Some individuals have developed highly idealized images of themselves with which they identify and which they love—" . . . the person is his idealized self and seems to adore it."

This basic attitude gives him the buoyancy or the resiliency entirely lacking in the other groups. It gives him a seeming abundance of self-confidence which appears enviable to all those chafing under self-doubts. He has (consciously) no doubts; he *is* the anointed, the man of destiny, the prophet, the great giver, the benefactor of mankind. All of this contains a grain of truth. He often is gifted beyond average, early and easily won distinctions, and sometimes was the favored and admired child.

This unquestioned belief in his greatness and uniqueness is the key to understanding him. His buoyancy and perennial youthfulness stem from this source. So does his often-fascinating charm. . . . His feeling of mastery lies in his conviction that there is nothing he cannot do and no one he cannot win. He is often charming indeed, particularly when new people come into his orbit. Regardless of their factual importance for him, he *must* impress them. He gives the impression to himself and others that he "loves" people. And he can be generous, with a scintillating display of feeling, with flattery, with favors and help—in anticipation of admiration or in return for devotion received. He endows his family and his friends, as well as his work and plans, with glowing attributes. He can be quite tolerant, does not expect others to be perfect; he can even stand jokes about himself, so long as these merely highlight an amiable peculiarity of his; but he must never be questioned seriously.

For all the positive attributes such an individual may have and all the success he may obtain, problems arise in his adaptation. His ideal self is so omniscient, so omnipotent that it is beyond the possibility of human realization. And his feeling that he is actually meeting that ideal leads him simply to dismiss, as if "by the use of a magic wand," his own shortcomings and failures. "His capacity to overlook flaws, or to turn them into virtues, seems unlimited. A sober onlooker would often call him unscrupulous, or at least unreliable. . . . He is not, however, a scheming exploiter. He feels rather that his needs or his tasks are so important that they entitle him to every privilege."

This apparent self-confidence, however, is less great than it seems. As in all neurosis, his ideal self is, in many respects, a fiction created in early life as a defense against underlying feelings of vulnerability. Ordinarily it grows out of a situation in which the child does not receive the genuine warmth and interest that make him feel loved for what he is. As a consequence, he feels lonely, isolated, vulnerable. Sometimes even "adoring" parents may create this problem.

He may feel wanted, liked, and appreciated not for what he is but merely for satisfying his parents' needs for adoration, prestige, or power. A rigid regime of perfectionist standards may evoke in him a feeling of inferiority for not measuring up to such demands. Misdemeanors or bad marks at school may be severely reprimanded, while good behavior or good marks are taken for granted. . . . All these factors, in addition to a general lack of genuine warmth and interest, give him the feeling of being unloved and unworthy—or at any rate of not being worth anything unless he is something he is not.

Adapting to this reality, the individual participates in a kind of "devil's pact." The creation of an idealized self (he is what he would like to be) provides for a surface self-esteem and escape from painful feelings, but it also alienates the individual from his own vulnerable and complex actual self—and inhibits the possible strengthening of the true self through coming to terms with his own deeper feelings. At base, he retains his feelings of being unlovable, unworthy.

The adaptation is based on a certain detachment from his inner life—that is, the repression of thoughts and feelings that do not accord with what the individual thinks he *should* think and feel. It also creates a barrier between him and others and some kinds of external reality. His need for superiority, perfection, invulnerability give rise to *claims* that the world *must* recognize the perfection he claims for himself. Overall, the result of this *pride system* is a basic *self-centeredness*, not always in the sense of an explicit selfishness, but in the fact of being "wrapped up" in himself. As Horney says:

This need not be apparent on the surface—he may be a lone wolf or live for and through others. Nevertheless he lives in any case by his private religion (his idealized image), abides by his own laws (his shoulds), within the barbed-wire fence of his own pride and with his own guards to protect him against dangers from within and without. As a result he not only becomes more isolated emotionally but it also becomes more difficult for him to see other people as individuals in their own right, different from himself. They are subordinate to his prime concern: himself.

The development of this whole pride system (i.e., of an idealized self with an inability to admit any internal or external questioning) is a feature of all neurosis. The expenditure of effort to win high position or accomplish great things is a feature of one type of neurotic adaptation (a defining characteristic of the expansionistic subtype). The compulsive nature of the drive is what differentiates it from mature ambition, and that compulsiveness is manifest in three qualities. First, its indiscriminate component is evident in a tendency to seek the limelight in a variety of situations: "Since the person's real interest in a pursuit does not matter, he *must* be the center of attention, *must* be the most attractive, the most intelligent, the most original—whether or not the situation calls for it; whether or not, with his given attributes, he *can* be the first. He *must* come out victorious in any argument, regardless of where the truth lies." Second, the drive has the quality of insatiability: "It must operate as long as the unknown (to himself) forces are driving him. There may be a glow of elation over the favorable reception of some work done, over a victory won, over any sign of recognition or admiration—but it does not last." Third, the strong negative reactions to failure or frustration in his upward drive suggest that he has a deep psychological need to win.

Although this is not always plainly visible, the search for glory is a most powerful drive. . . . And so the reactions to frustration must be severe. They are indicated by the terror of doom and disgrace that for many people is spelled in the idea of failure. Reactions of panic, depression, despair, rage at self and others to what is conceived as "failure" are frequent, and entirely out of proportion to the actual importance of the occasion.

## . . . Toward Understanding Carter

Looking at Carter with this guide in hand, we may go past the surface complexities to the underlying personality patterns. His self-presentation has the perfectionist features one might see as characteristic of the idealized self described by Horney. He projects, as we have seen, a somewhat grandiose self—claiming a near perfection in some traits, exaggerating his past accomplishments, glossing over his own darker side. The ease with which he makes these claims and his willingness to undertake great endeavors suggest he may be unaware of the tension between his ideal and real selves. His resistance to inner questioning, abstract statements about his humility to the contrary, suggests he does not want to confront these discrepancies.

Nor does he take kindly to external questioning. The complaint in the 1976 campaign that he was fuzzy on the issues reflected the observer's failure to penetrate Carter's complexity; people thought him fuzzy because he was not a "knee-jerk liberal." Early in his presidency he reacted strongly to a memorandum from women aides urging him to reconsider his stand on abortion funding by telling his whole Cabinet: after I have made a decision, don't pressure me to reverse it. When Vernon Jordan criticized the Administration for being insensitive to the needs of the poor, Carter took him aside for a personal warning that "erroneous or demagogic statements" would remove "the last hope of the poor" that government might help them in some way. In one meeting with George Meany, Carter did not like it when the labor leader wanted to talk back to him. Carter walked into a conference room in the Executive Office Building, smiled, gave a little speech on how good it was that he could count on the voluntary cooperation of labor for his wage-deceleration plan, then stood as if to leave. Meany stopped him. "Wait a minute, Mr. President, I want you to hear our response." Carter listened, his face expressionless, as Meany explained how Labor could not go along with wage deceleration. When he was finished, Carter said: "If you can't support me, I'd rather not talk," and he walked out of the room. His scolding of the press, for its attention to his Cabinet shakeup in July 1979, has been noted.

There are some indications that he claims (possibly at the unconscious level) external recognition as his right. Opposition, he assumes, is unfair, motivated by some hidden desire to hurt him. His attitude is perhaps clearest in his characterization in 1976 of the reasons for the Atlanta *Constitution*'s critical stories on him in 1970: "Since the newspaper strongly supported Governor Sanders, I presume that the editors recognized me as his major potential opponent and wanted to destroy me early in the campaign." Even his political opponents are badly motivated. Early in the spring of 1976, Carter hinted that his opponents were forming a cabal to stop him. Their goal, he suggested before the Massachusetts primary, was to subvert the public interest or, as he said in his late spring speech to the Ohio AFL-CIO, to stop the reforms he would institute. The Washington establishment's opposition to him was an insider's objection to an outsider; they were "upset that some one unknown to them could be a success without their knowing it." (Carter's oldest son, Jack, articulated the underlying attitude fostered by his father. Appearing on a New York talk show he said, "You learn to ignore it or consider them [the critics] just not very good people.")

Support for an opponent may be dealt with as if it were illegitimate. During his 1966 gubernatorial campaign, for example, he angrily sought out Eugene Patterson, then editor of the Atlanta *Constitution*, to complain about some favorable coverage of Bo Callaway, who was seeking the Republican nomination for governor. Later Carter was furious that the paper backed Ellis Arnall, Carter's opponent in the Democratic primary. After the election was over, Patterson received word that Carter was " 'really beating up on you down there: bad mouthing you down there: he never forgets.' " During the 1970 gubernatorial race he acted as if Sanders's "support" of Arnall in 1966 had been illegitimate.

Even doubters bother him. The night he won the presidency, on the plane from Atlanta to Plains, he had gone back to meet his press retinue. As William Miller reports, "Carter came back to the press seats exulting, chortling, rubbing it in: you were *wrong*. I *won*. His need to score that point, and nail it repeatedly, emotionally, caused her [Dewar of the Washington *Post*] to be stunned when in Plains the exultant victor suddenly admitted that he had made mistakes—that the closeness of the election was the *candidate's* fault. Three weeks after the election Carter phoned Vernon Jordan, who had advised Carter against running for President back in 1974: "You remember that conversation we had in the governor's mansion? Guess what. You were wrong as hell."

There are other indications that Carter has that detachment—both from his own deeper feelings and from meaningful connection with *others* (i.e. with people whom he perceives as different from, rather than extensions of himself)—that is a feature of this development. The surface quality of his thought, and the ease with which he shifts his interpretations of his past and self seem to be manifestations of the former. Associates have given testimony that suggests the latter.

Carter's warmth toward others can be turned on and off like a spigot—sometimes without apparent reason. One April morning in Detroit in 1976, he stopped Kandy Stroud in the middle of her note taking, placing both his hands on her shoulders and staring soulfully into her eyes, not saying a word, for five or six seconds. He repeated this gesture on another occasion when she interviewed him at his home in Plains. Later, Stroud recalls, when she returned to the Carter press corps after several weeks' absence, Carter "seemed aware" of her presence but did not acknowledge it: "Not that one expects formal salutations or personal greetings from a candidate, but normally they were forthcoming from Carter." After about five days of this treatment, Stroud was tailing Carter at a campaign breakfast in Des Moines while he was shaking hands. "I was within three or four inches of him, taking notes, but each time Carter turned in my direction to move on to another table, it was as though I were invisible." Even personal friends and campaign aides found they could be cut off this way. As one friend from his early days told me: "It's an observation that I've made of Jimmy and I've heard of many others who felt or thought they were close to Jimmy only to find out they were out in the cold somewhere." Another friend from southwest Georgia noted that "you can drop out of favor like this [snapping her fingers] with Carter. And maybe never really know why."

This detachment shows itself in another way. Even close associates note Carter's guardedness. Charles Kirbo admitted during the campaign, "I'm not sure what, politically, he cares about." Another friend, Elliott Levitas, Democratic Congressman from Georgia, noted that Carter "is an unusually complex person and an unusually private person. He's a person with great control over his emotional self and psychic self," who reveals only that aspect of himself that is directly relevant to the person he is with. One acquaintance has talked of the "disappointing experience" that some people have when their relationship with Carter turns out to be less of a "two-way relationship" than they thought it had been.

Such detachment was already evident when Carter was a young naval officer—as we have seen. He often held himself apart. When he was governor, he was never "one of the boys" at the various governors' conferences—avoiding most of the behind-the-scenes socializing and interpersonal exchanges that accompanied membership in this group. As Martin Schram noted, some of the governors had privately confided to him (Schram) that they resented Carter because they felt his main interest seemed to be getting the major share of the publicity. Early in his 1976 presidential campaign, as Wendell Ford remarked, Carter had not contacted any governors or former governors for support. Carter himself insisted that he is indebted to no one for his accomplishments. During the spring of 1976 Carter was reported to have said of the political bosses and power elite, "I don't need them. And they know it." His reluctance that fall to court and deal with his fellow politicians suggests that he was not inclined to ask for help from his equals even when it would be to his advantage to do so. (By 1980 he could seek their help—partly because he was operating from a superior position, partly because he had no choice, given his standing in the polls and his commitment to his reelection.)

Carter, moreover, shows a touch of the self-centeredness that flows out of this detachment. In his speeches Carter has been unusually self-referent, interlacing his discussions of issues with personal recollections about his boyhood and interpretations of his own personality. At times he suggests that he was, before it became true, the center of attention of the powerful. As governor, he suggested that his old boss, Admiral Rickover, was vitally interested in everything he did in that office. Indeed Rickover was a kind of guardian angel looking over Carter's shoulder daily to praise or blame him for what he had done. On occasion—for example, when nominating Henry Jackson for President in 1972 or when upstaging Ted Kennedy at the University of Georgia Law Day celebration in 1974—he pulled the spotlight toward himself when it belonged to someone else.

At a 1976 memorial service for Congressman Jerry Litton of Missouri (Litton and his family had been killed in a plane crash en route to celebrating his winning the Democratic nomination for Senator), Carter gave a speech in which he talked almost as much about himself as about the man being memorialized. He recalled how special Litton had been and noted the "kind of mutuality" he and Litton had found in their first brief meeting at one of the campaign "Dialogues with Litton." After returning home from that meeting, Carter recalled, "I told my wife, Rosalynn, 'I have just met a young man who shocked me and who startled me and who inspired me. And I believe that some day he has a good chance to be President of the United States. Because there is something about him that is unique.' " A bit later in the speech he made his identification with Litton more explicit:

Jerry Litton and his family—three generations at least—provided an inspiration to us, and an inspiration to him. He was born, like I was, on an isolated farm—before the Roosevelt-Truman era—without electricity, without indoor plumbing. But it didn't hurt us. And he became, at a very early age, a young man who made the best of his opportunities. There was not a handicap or an obstacle that caused him to be discouraged or to withdraw from the competition of an increasingly adult world. He went to high school, he was a president of a National Honor Society. He joined the FFA like I did as a high school boy. And he not only succeeded at his own high school—I was secretary of the Plains High School FFA—but he went on beyond that and became president of all the Future Farmers of Missouri. And he wasn't satisfied with that. He went on and became a national officer.

Indeed, as presidential speechwriter James Fallows has noted, Carter's speeches take fire on those occasions when he talks about the subject that most inspires him—"not what he proposed to *do*, but what he *was*."

On occasion that self-absorption can lead Carter to give inappropriate advice. Back in 1974 he advised Jerry Brown, who was then running for governor of California, to go out and shake hands, as he, Carter, had done in Georgia. Brown wryly noted that all he had to do was call in the chits due his father—for all the appointments he had made when he was governor. Brown apparently did not tell Carter—and Carter did not know—that just a week earlier his opponent had said that Brown's shaking hands was one of the best things he could do to hurt his (Brown's) cause.

At other times this self-absorption led to embarrassing situations. In 1979, after the last game of the World Series, Carter became the first President to visit the winning team's locker room after the game, apparently without prior invitation. During the presentation of the trophy by the baseball commissioner to the captain of the winning Pittsburgh Pirates, Carter stood center stage on a very small platform, forcing them to pass the trophy over his head.

The high point of this self-centeredness was manifest in Carter's reactions to his meeting with the wives and parents of the eight young men killed in the hostage rescue operation in Iran. On his first trip out of the Oval Office in May 1980, Carter confided to a Philadelphia audience that he had had some trepidations about visiting these relatives. "But in every instance," he said, "they reached their arms out for me and we embraced each other, and I could feel that their concern was about me, not about them." (In his report of this episode in the Chicago *Tribune* on May 23, Jon Margolis saw Carter as not too different from those young wandering poets who see "all the world as reflections of their own egos.")

Carter's ambition also follows the pattern typical of the expansionistic-narcissistic personality. He has the ability and the self-confidence (at one level) to seek external success, thereby winning external support for his idealized self. And he enjoys it. Speaking of a visit with schoolchildren in New Hampshire in 1975, Carter said, "They just mobbed me. They ran up and grabbed my legs, my hands—they wanted to touch me. It really makes me feel good." On another occasion he talked about his feelings in controlling an adult audience:

I could have left them in such a state they'd still be applauding. It's easy to do. You pause at just the right points, end a sentence on an upbeat note. But I don't do that. . . . I like to see the audience's intensity of concentration, their lack of movement and coughing. It doesn't matter to me whether they applaud hysterically. That kind of enthusiasm can evaporate right after the speech.

His feats have won him adoration from those in his immediate circle. Lillian, Billy, Ruth testify to Jimmy Carter's special qualities, as we have seen—as do staff aides and close friends. Theodore Sorensen, a former Kennedy aide who advised Carter's 1976 campaign, called Carter "the smartest man I've met in politics since JFK." Even former Carter speechwriter James Fallows, in his critical 1979 article, was extravagant in his assessment of the core man.

With his moral virtues and his intellectual skills, he is perhaps as admirable a human being as has ever held the job. He is probably smarter, in the College Board sense, than any other President in this century. He grasps issues quickly. He made me feel confident that, except in economics, he would resolve technical questions quickly, without distortions imposed by cant or imperfect comprehension.

Rosalynn Carter is his greatest admirer and supporter. Unlike Eleanor Roosevelt, to whom she is sometimes compared, she does not appear to serve as her husband's conscience—the friend in the court who reminds him of the moral concerns he might be forgetting in the stress of political pressures. In private she gives him advice and is considered one of his closest confidants. Carter himself has said that his wife is "*an extension of myself*" (italics mine) But to one friend, at least, her role is as a kind of political gate-keeper for her husband. "I think Rosalynn, personally, has an instinct for who is going to be true-blue to the bitter end. . . . it was either 'for' or 'against,' all or nothing. And she has the ability to zero in on somebody that adored Jimmy. And then if they did, they were trusted. This is where Jimmy takes her advice."

In public she admits to none of Jimmy's vulnerabilities. In the fall of 1976, when the power failed during the first debate between Carter and Ford, she told Ed Rabel that Jimmy had been "in complete command of the whole situation . . ." And no, he was not nervous when the debate began. "I came over here with him and I was the nervous one."

This desire for external recognition and the ability to win a strong personal following is not *by itself* a feature of neurotic ambition. It is a problem when the drive shows compulsive features outlined by Horney. The roots of Carter's ambition, as we have seen, suggest he was propelled by a desire for recognition in *some* field, rather than a strong, burning interest in political goals. Even as he won political power, he continued to manifest a need to win recognition for other accomplishments. He has sought recognition of himself as a scientist, intellectual, and moral leader.

Aside from this indiscriminate feature of his drive to excel, Carter's reactions to losses are revealing. His depression after failing to receive a Rhodes scholarship in the 1940s and the governorship of Georgia in 1966 indicate that winning is very important to him, psychologically speaking. On the tennis courts at the governor's mansion he had to win. One journalist told me Carter would serve toward a rose bush near the line, making it difficult for his opponent to make a good return without landing in the bush, and that Carter showed satisfaction when the ploy worked. On the softball diamond of Plains, Carter showed similarly fierce determination. As President, he persisted in a foot race, up and down the hills in the Catoctin Mountains to the point where he collapsed and had to be carried off the course. Though he risked health and authority in the process, he later boasted, "They had to drag me off . . . I didn't want to stop."

His opposition to criticism similarly suggests a need to be right, a need never to lose a point. On occasion, Carter's reactions to criticism even suggest rage at being questioned. When pressed hard, his eyes and face freeze and sometimes a vein on his forehead or temple visibly throbs as he reaches for defenses.

I saw this reaction and an interesting diversionary tactic at a press conference in Plains on August 17, 1976. After energy briefing at the Pond House, a wire service reporter asked Carter about Secretary of Transportation William Coleman's charge that when Coleman had been bailing civil rights workers out of jail in Plains ten, fifteen years earlier, Carter was nowhere to be found. Carter's face went blank, his eyes iced over. Then he provided an answer—quietly, slowly: ten or fifteen years ago he had not even been living in Plains. He hesitated for a moment, then continued. Plains does not even have a jail. The conversation went back to energy for a while, then another wire service reporter asked Carter where he had been living ten or fifteen years ago, if not in Plains. He froze again. Out in the county, he responded. He had no authority over the Plains government. In an aside he recalled that they may have a small lockup in Plains to hold prisoners temporarily until they can be transported elsewhere. But there had been no civil rights disturbances in Plains. Coleman, he implied, is a political hack. "He works for President Ford."

His statement that there was no "jail" in Plains was obviously accurate. But during the period Coleman spoke of, Carter had never lived more than two miles from the center of Plains, and from 1963 to 1966 he represented the area in the state legislature. During the sixties, civil rights activists were jailed in the Sumter County jail in Americus and in other nearby towns—and there had been one small civil rights disturbance in Plains over a voting rights demonstration. The fact is, Jimmy Carter did not stand up to be counted with the civil rights movement, but rather than conceding as much, he chose to belittle Coleman and befog the issue.

Such strong reactions to criticism and potential failure suggest that underneath Carter's self-confidence he suffers, as many human beings do, from some fear of not being worthwhile. Other signs, which Horney does not categorize or delineate in *Neurosis and Human Growth*, indicate that Carter's self-confidence is less perfect than it seems. His ease, his warmth, his calm can dissipate when he is threatened with a "loss" in a public situation. In his speech nominating Jackson for President in 1972, there were clear signs of nervousness as he failed to attract the delegates' attention. (His voice was high-pitched, his face taut, and he licked his lips.) He showed similar indications of tension when he was booed during his "amnesty/pardon" speech to the American Legion Convention. And his publicized complacency before the first debate with Ford was displaced, as he met the President, with a stiffness and nervousness apparent to all watching. As President, certainly his formal addresses to Congress and to the people have shown a stiff quality. Indeed, Carter has two speaking styles. With blacks, children, the "people"—the powerless?—Carter is at the height of his emotional spontaneity and warmth. But before larger, more prestigious audiences, such as the American Bar Association and the Chicago Council on Foreign Relations, or in situations where he might lose, Carter is likely to hide behind facts and figures and a monotone.

Carter's memories of his interaction with important authorities in his past give further proof that his anxiety is based on the assumption that being less than perfect is terrible indeed. In his Rickover stories Carter shows us that he accepts punishment as the legitimate response to falling short. His recollections of his screening interview with Rickover show him sweating as he is tested by the great man, forced in the end to back down from his proud boast that he was fifty-ninth in his class at Annapolis to an admission that he had not done his best. His accounts of his relationship with Rickover on the job make it quite clear that he accepted public humiliation as the legitimate response to not being perfect. Even as governor, Carter said, he broke into a cold sweat when Rickover telephoned him, not sure whether he would receive blame or praise from that great man.

What we know of Carter's childhood lends credence to this interpretation of his personality. Carter's memories of his father and mother and the descriptions of them made earlier in this book suggest that young Jimmy was offered a kind of conditional love. Earl, who seems to have been the main emotional provider, simply seemed to expect the best of Jimmy, punishing him if he fell short, but not rewarding him when he did live up to his father's standards. Even when Jimmy accomplished something worthwhile (e.g., shooting his first quail), his joy and spontaneity could be cut short by a reminder from Earl that his performance had not been perfect (that he had dropped his gun in the excitement of the situation).

Carter seems to have had a more distant relationship with his mother. For all the abstract admiration Carter proclaims for her in *Why Not the Best?* and his talk of her compassion for others, he shows only one interaction between the two of them and his own ambivalent response. Lillian offers him cookies with love, but he hesitates for fifteen or twenty seconds because to receive it he would have to put down the stones for his slingshot that filled his hands and pockets. Moreover, the portrait of Lillian gleaned from her interviews and recollections of friends indirectly suggests that she did not provide the kind of nurturance that would have balanced her husband's demands. Indeed, her speech and behavior suggest that she has some of the same personality traits we now see in her son—for all her obvious virtues, she also projects an idealized self-portrait of giving and receiving perfect love and is sensitive to criticism. Neither parent, for one reason or another, seems to have given him that warm, simple acceptance of him as himself which is the ultimate condition of being comfortable with one's real feelings, one's real self.

## Political Relevance

The kind of personality type outlined here has certain characteristic strengths and weaknesses. Of all the neurotic adaptations, the expansionistic-narcissistic personality, as Horney has pointed out, is most apt to be successful in the affairs of the world—especially if blessed with superior intelligence and/or special talents.

To Horney's observation I would add another. Identification with an exalted self-image is of particular value to persons in careers that require gaining the confidence of many other people. Certainly this characteristic is attractive to all the ordinary, uncertain human beings who stumble around not knowing for sure where they are going. Moreover, the detachment that typically accompanies this personality type, with the desire for mastery, is a condition for a kind of manipulative skill.

Yet these very strengths are also a source of weakness. First, as Horney points out, expansionistic types tend to overrate their capacities, their special gifts, and the quality of their work. Conversely, their self-centeredness causes them to underestimate others. In addition, the defensive response to criticism minimizes the possibility of learning from it. "Any criticism, no matter how seriously or conscientiously given, is *eo ipso* felt as a hostile attack." In the end, as in all neurosis, an underlying self-centeredness causes expansionistic-narcissistic types to be more concerned with the appearances of doing well, rather than with the actual quality of the work done. "Questions as to how he made out or how he should perform are of greater concern to him than the work itself."

The extent to which Carter's own political style has been influenced by tendencies such as these has been outlined in the course of this work. His drive for mastery and the feeling he could win were essential ingredients in his ability to take on long-shot political campaigns and to carry through with them. This same quality has been apparent in his decisions in office to take on one or two difficult tasks—the reorganization of state government as governor of Georgia, the tackling of the Middle East settlement as President of the United States—and to dramatize the results. Moreover, his self-confidence, his certainty, was clearly a central part of his earliest appeal, as Carter himself knew and as the reactions of some of the journalists around him proved. His ability to detach himself from both internal and external ties seems to have been a condition of his manipulative skills—of his Protean capacity to adapt his strategies and rhetoric to shifting political currents.

Yet he also has shown some of the political weaknesses that accompany these traits. His propensity to overrate his power relative to others' best explains his tendency to move out on political matters for which he has not done his homework—as manifest in his early dealings with the Georgia legislature, the U.S. Congress, and the Russians.

His negative reactions to opposition and criticism suggest that he may have trouble learning from his mistakes. Most of his projected learning experiences as President (for example, his domestic Camp David consultations and his reassessment of Russian motives after the Afghanistan invasion) have the appearance of face-saving retreats rather than of occasions when new and broader perspectives were developed. Certainly his defensiveness has undermined his authority both on the campaign trail and in office. As governor, he got pulled into name-calling exchanges with his opponents, an exercise that diminished his general political authority and made it more difficult to secure support for later political measures. As President, he has done less of this, but the tendency to belittle his opponents remains—and detracts from his claim to moral authority.

At a more basic level, Carter's problems stem from his concern for appearances over substance. As governor of Georgia, he backed down on many matters to save his final reorganization program—something any good politician might have done—but he denied the compromises and overvalued the positive results flowing from the reorganization. The zero-based budgeting technique was blown up into a magic device for bringing the federal government under control. Even his troubled relations with Georgia's General Assembly were glossed over at the end, as Carter claimed to have secured from that body most of what he had gone after.

In the presidency, Carter's early emphasis on the symbols of open and rational government seem never to have been taken seriously. In his first legislative offerings (energy and tax programs), as well as in his approach to the Russians, he came out with dramatic proposals but then did not really carry through on most of them. He hid the nature of his problems with Congress, as well as his own compromises, behind rhetorical flourishes about the special interests and their cohorts on Capitol Hill. In the handling of the Iran and Afghanistan crises he choreographed a series of dramatic responses, mobilized national sentiment behind them, and created a demand for results that his policies could not satisfy. His resort to a high-risk commando raid aimed at rescuing the hostages in Iran led one long-time President watcher, Hugh Sidey, to wonder about the nature of Carter's commitments. "The French," Sidey wrote, "have an expression that gets to the heart of the issue. 'Un homme serieux' is a person of maturity and dedication, someone who grasps through experience and intelligence the larger realities of the events around him. He then," according to Sidey, "addresses the substance of the issues, intent not on image or adulation but on results. Being a SERIOUS man does not have much to do with one's manner or disposition or even whether he wants to be serious or not. It has to do with his nature."

As for Carter, Sidey says that in making the hostages "an integral and sustaining" part of his reelection campaign; in calling the Soviet invasion of Afghanistan "the most serious threat to world peace since the Second World War," then failing to develop new strategies and doctrines and the military might to meet the threat; in ruling out wage and price controls as inflation soars and the economy falters—in all these ways the President has not come to terms with what is going on around him. "It is a difficult concept to assimilate, but it may be yet another of the bizarre turns in today's politics that the . . . Jimmy Carter of these hours is not a serious man."

### System Impact

Carter's problems, as this work suggests, are not simply that he has fallen short of an ideal he presented in 1976—or even a consequence of an unmanageable drift in the political system. His difficulties, to a great extent, are of his own making.

Yet, in some respects, his career is a reflection of aspects of the American political system and culture. Certain trends in American politics were a condition of his rise to power. Most important has been the diminution of the role of party leaders in choosing presidential candidates. Access to the media (whether through incumbency, money, or a fresh and novel presentation) and the ability to look like a winner (as evident in the early primary "wins" and the judgments of political votes, as caught in the early public opinion polls) are prime ingredients in establishing a candidate's credibility. And the absence of strong ideological differences among the candidates or in the minds of the electorate, when combined with the demise of winner-take-all primaries, makes it likely that these early factors will determine the final outcomes. Carter recognized this, using his particular situation—as an outsider in 1976 and an insider in 1980—to secure those important early victories. The party in both instances was reduced to a vehicle for guaranteeing his election. In Jody Powell's terms, the function of the Democratic Party has indeed become one of "winning."

Carter's career is a reflection of our political culture in other ways. He expertly played upon certain deeply embedded strains in the American consciousness in his rise to power, magnifying them in the process. At the most basic level, he has reinforced the illusion that power politics can somehow be transcended by good people. Projecting the idea that political leaders can and should make up their minds on their own as to what is best for the country, that they can and should choose their aides on the basis of merit rather than political reward, that they and their followers are motivated only by the desire to serve—he embraced a perspective on the political process adhered to by good government reform leaders throughout the twentieth century. But no one, including Jimmy Carter, has been able to win political power by acting in accord with that perspective. Indeed, insofar as the people believe that this model has been achieved, they cannot deal with the realities of who has power and how it can be checked and curtailed in some approximation of a "general interest."

Carter has also played on a related, latent distrust of mediating groups, their leaders, and brokerage politics in general. In 1976 he worked through group leaders—blacks, women, labor. But when leaders—George Meany, Vernon Jordan, and Bella Abzug—made claims on him later, he treated their claims as somehow illicit. He was the one who would interpret what was good for those groups. Indeed, even the members of Congress were doing something wrong when they attempted to protect constituent interests or bargained to secure outcomes which would compromise their varied interests.

With this perspective on the political system, the President with a mystic tie to the people, becomes the central actor in the political system—the sole spokesman for the public interest. It is an old idea and politically dangerous in some ways. Those with access to the media and a superior ability to touch the right psychological button can create a following. This is what the "Imperial Presidency" is about—not fancy uniforms or "hails to the Chief" as the discussion during the 1976 campaign suggested it was.

Whatever the dangers in such a political process, it is clear that Carter has not performed well even in accord with its assumptions. Rather than acting as the moral and political leader of the nation, he has used his position and his ability to command attention to promote a further trivialization of political dialogue in America and an obfuscation of the political alternatives before the nation.

From the beginning of his presidency, Carter has used his public relations skill to focus on his own person rather than on these political alternatives. The agenda for the nation has been compiled out of a random list of promises he had made on the campaign trail and his *ad hoc* reaction to events in terms of his political interests. The national debate has focused not on the wisdom of his policies, but on whether or not he is tough enough for the job, whether or not he has learned while in office, and whether or not his authority has waxed or waned as the result of his handling of the latest crises. When he does participate in general political discussion, he often offers political slogans that do not really explain what is going on. He has hidden the extent to which he has departed from the liberal tradition in his own party, on matters such as energy pricing and the budget, by lambasting conservatives to the right of him as the representatives of special interests. His swing toward a "harder line" toward the USSR—explained in terms of his growing understanding of their aggressive intent—belied other indications that earlier he had been just as suspicious as he later claimed he had become. He took to the Oval Office to devote his full attention to the Iranian hostage situation and remove it from partisan politics, then proceeded to use it to his own political advantage. For those who hesitate in the face of his policy failures, he holds out reassurances, based on a historically false generalization, that a President normally does better his second term than his first, removed as he is from the concerns about running again.

Despite all his political maneuvering, Carter probably does aspire to be a great President. He clearly has been influenced by James MacGregor Burns' idea, presented in his book *Leadership*, that the great political leader is at base a moral leader. Carter told Burns in the fall of 1978 that he had read the book, and in his address to the nation after his domestic Camp David meetings Carter attempted to provide that moral leadership with his call to selfless action by the people. Admonitions to be unselfish, however, are not what Burns has in mind when he talks of moral leadership. The moral direction that great leaders provide is based on some deeper appreciation of the requirements of justice in their time, along with an ability to tap the emotions and the interest of their people to win their support for this larger vision. The sad thing for Jimmy Carter, and maybe for America as a whole, is that for all his high ambition, he does not understand this.

# ABBREVIATIONS USED THROUGHOUT THESE NOTES

## Books

*Addresses*   *Addresses of James Earl Carter*. Atlanta: The Stein Printing Company, 1975.

*Campaign 1976*   *The Presidential Campaign 1976*. Volume 1, Parts 1 and 2. Washington: United States Government Printing Office, 1978.

*Campaign Commercials*   The television and radio campaign commercials of Jimmy Carter in 1970 campaign for governor and 1976 campaign for President. University of Georgia.

*Ga. Archives*   Georgia Archives, Atlanta, Georgia.

*Ga. HJ*   *Journal of the House of Representatives of the State of Georgia*. Atlanta: State of Georgia, published annually.

*Ga. SJ*   *Journal of the Senate of the State of Georgia*. Atlanta: State of Georgia, published annually.

*Ga. Manual*   *Manual of the General Assembly of the State of Georgia*. Compiled by Ben W. Fortson, Jr., Secretary of State. Atlanta: State of Georgia, 1962, published annually thereafter.

*Ga. Register*   *Georgia Official and Statistical Register*. Atlanta: HML&P, Inc., published annually.

*Government As Good*   Jimmy Carter. *A Government As Good As Its People*. New York: Simon and Schuster, 1977.

*Pool Report*   A report prepared by a small group of journalists for distribution to everyone in Carter's press retinue. Done whenever press space was limited during 1976 campaign.

*RCS, Brother Billy*   Ruth Carter Stapleton. *Brother Billy*. New York: Harper and Row, Inc., 1978.

*RCS, Inner Healing*   Ruth Carter Stapleton. *The Gift of Inner Healing*. Waco: Word, Inc., 1976.

*WNB*   Jimmy Carter. *Why Not the Best?* New York: Bantam Press, 1976.

*TV News*   Television News Archives, Vanderbilt University, Nashville, Tennessee.

## Newspapers and Magazines

| | | | |
|---|---|---|---|
| ATR | Americus (Ga.) *Times-Recorder* | CT | Chicago *Tribune* |
| AC | Atlanta *Constitution* | CSM | *Christian Science Monitor* |
| AH | Albany (Ga.) *Herald* | LAT | Los Angeles *Times* |
| AJ | Atlanta *Journal* | NW | *Newsweek* |
| AJC | Atlanta *Journal-Constitution* (Sunday edition) | NYT | *New York Times* |
| | | USN | *U.S. News and World Report* |
| BG | Boston *Globe* | WSJ | *Wall Street Journal* |
| CST | Chicago *Sun-Times* | WP | Washington *Post* |

## Others

| | | | |
|---|---|---|---|
| ai | interview with author | BC | Billy Carter |
| al | letter to author | GC or GCS | Gloria Carter Spann |
| aq | questionnaire returned to author | JC | Jimmy Carter |
| CQ | Congressional Quarterly | LC | Lillian Carter |
| CR | Congressional Record | RC | Rosalynn Carter |
| EC | James Earl Carter, Sr. | RCS | Ruth Carter Stapleton |

# Source Notes

## PROLOGUE

Carter quote on capitol dome: Janet Merritt/ai. 1966 gossip, JC presidential ambitions: Joseph A. Bacon to Janet Merritt, 16 January 1967, as shown to author. LC's 1966 views on JC goals: Prof. McKim Marriot/ai. In 1976, however, LC told interviewers that JC told her in 1972 that he was running for President, and she said, "President of what?" Bill Schemmel, "My Son Jimmy," *Ladies' Home Journal,* August 1976, p. 73. JC's scorn for politicians: Bobby Logan/ai. Rachael Clark on Plains and Carter: ai.

## 1.  ROOTS

Details on the Gordy and Carter ancestry drawn primarily from original records of Kenneth H. Thomas, Jr., "Georgia Families—Carter-Gordy," *Georgia Life* 3 (Winter 1976), p. 40; and James M. Black, Research Specialist, Genealogical Department, the Church of Jesus Christ of Latter Day Saints (charts sent to author on September 15, 1977). Derivative accounts are found in Saul Friedman, "Settlers and Skeletons Rattle in the Carter Family Closet," *Chicago Tribune,* February 8, 1977; Margaret Shannon, "A President in the Family," *Atlanta Journal and Constitution Magazine,* January 16, 1977; "Presidential Roots," *The New Yorker,* March 14, 1977, p. 31; National *Enquirer,* March 15, 1977.

I have checked materials in these accounts against several county histories. Most useful was "Families' Histories" by A. J. Clark and M. Clark, in *History of Stewart County,* Sarah Robertson Dixon, ed., (A. H. Clark: Waycross, Georgia, 1975); bible and cemetery records for various Carter families are in Vol. II, pp. 332–33, 467, 703–709. For the Gordy's: Vol. II, pp. 795–796. Vital statistics on Earl and Lillian Carter—marriage, Earl's will, births and marriages of their children—have all been checked in the Sumter County Courthouse.

In addition, I have visited and taken notes on the Carter, Gordy, Murray, and Smith families and prominent families in the area from cemeteries located at Quebec in Schley County (Wiley Carter's family), Harmony Cemetery in Richlands (the Gordy family), in Americus (a related Carter family), the Botsford Church south of Plains, and the New Lebanon cemetery on the Old Preston Road outside of Plains (where the present Carter, Smith, Murray families, as well as other whites from the Plains area, have their burial plots). For background on the black community I visited two black cemeteries near the New Lebanon cemetery on that Old Preston Road (where the Bishop Johnson and his wife are buried). The *ATR* has been checked for the period 1915 to 1976 for obituaries on all these families, and the Columbus *Inquirer* for details on the Gordys.

The newspapers and county histories noted above have also provided background information on the cultural, economic, and social history of the area. The specific background material on Plains is from *History of Plains* (Gammage Print Shop, Americus, Georgia; compiled under the auspices of the churches of Plains, 1976). I also took, in the summer of '76, David Ewing's "Tour of Plains." It had been in Bob Arnebeck's, "A Shnook's Tour of Plains," Washington *Post/Potomac* July 10, 1977. Statistics on population, voters, and offices held by Alton, Earl, and Jimmy Carter from *Ga. Register,* survey from 1924–70.

Background information on culture and politics in the South: Neal R. Peirce, *The Deep South States of America* (New York: W. W. Norton & Co., 1974), pp. 306–376, and V. O. Key, Jr., *Southern Politics* (New York: Vintage Books, 1949); William Anderson, *Wild Man from Sugar Creek* (Baton Rouge, La.: Louisiana State University Press, 1975); John Dollard, *Class and Caste in a Southern Town,* 3rd ed. (Garden City, NY: Doubleday Anchor Books, 1957).

### The Carters

William Archibald Carter's death: *Early County Times,* 3 September 1903; Alton Carter/ai. Move to Plains, Alton Carter's early life there: Alton Carter/ai, and RCS, *Brother Billy,* pp. 12–14. EC as good investor: Alton Carter/ai. For EC's military service, *ATR* 20 July, 13 August, 1 October 1917; also, Americus cafe owner/ai. There were a few days missing from the *ATR* for the wartime period. It is possible that information about EC came out on those days. LC meets, dates EC: quoted in Tom Collins, *The Search for Jimmy Carter* (Waco, Tex.: Word, Inc., 1976), pp. 35–36. EC "fine catch," "drifts": Orde Coombs, "The Hand That Rocked the Cradle," *New York,* 14 June 1976, p. 42. For different version of first meeting: Richard Hyatt, "Jimmy's Father, Earl, Had That Magic Touch," Columbus (Ga.) *Ledger-Enquirer,* nd. LC to finish nursing: James Neyland, "The Carter Family Scrapbook," *Good Housekeeping,* July 1977, p. 100.

There is, however, no record of LC at Grady Hospital, but according to Delmar Yoder, who is doing a history of the hospital, she could have attended a summer session without its being on record: Delmar Yoder/ai. Gordy-Carter wedding: *ATR,* 28 September 1923.

### The Gordys

LC as politician: Alton Carter/ai, and Henry Allen, "Just Plains Folks," Washington *Post/Potomac,* 15 August 1976, p. 28. JC on JJ Gordy as politician: *WNB,* p. 85. LC quoted on thirteen at dinner table: Orde Coombs, *op. cit.,* p. 42. LC and younger children: Mary Elizabeth Gordy Braunstein/ai. Mary Ida Gordy, "fine lady": M. Lorene Gordy/ai. LC close to her father: Henry Allen, *op. cit.,* p. 28. LC on father as "biggest politician": Nanette Rainone et al., "Lillian Carter Talks About Racism, the Kennedys and 'Jimmy's Reign,' " *Ms.,* October 1976, p. 51. Gordy wrote a letter to Watson (Letter to editor column, *Watson Magazine,* Volume 4, number 2 [April 1906], p. 260) which does not suggest any special closeness: Kenneth H. Thomas, Jr./ai. On Gordy's relationship to Watson: Kenneth H. Thomas, Jr./ai. Gordy's letters to Watson, according to Thomas, were only formally acknowledged by Watson. Watson's biographer, C. Vann Woodward, says that John M. Stahl, an Illinois editor, originated the idea: *Tom Watson, Agrarian Rebel.* (New York: The Macmillan Company, 1938), pp. 244–245. LC on her father's compassion: Coombs, *op. cit.,* p. 42. Gordy's offices: Mary Elizabeth Gordy Braunstein and local farmer/ais. Obituaries: *ATR* 16 June 1948; Columbus *Enquirer* 17 June 1948. Gordy as guard: Mary Elizabeth Gordy Braunstein/ai. JC says that Gordy, in late life, was a "doorkeeper" at the state capitol (*WNB,* p. 88). The *Ga. Register,* which lists all officeholders in the state, including doorkeepers, does not include Gordy's name. He may have been an aide to the doorkeeper.

### Archery

EC buying farm on credit: James Neyland, *op. cit.,* p. 100. Descriptions of Archery: author, and Ivy "Ruby" Watson Lamb, Billy Wise, Joseph Bacon, Annie Mae Kitchens/ais. Carter home and farm routine: *WNB,* pp. 14–20. JC's studies come first: *WNB,* p. 19. Blacks help Lillian: Annie Mae Kitchens and Rachael Clark/ais; Orde Coombs, *op. cit.,* p. 42. JC on the commissary: *WNB,* pp. 15–16. EC provides recreation: Ivy "Ruby" Watson Lamb, local farmer, Richard Salter/ais; *WNB,* p. 9. EC builds Pond House: GCS in John Osborne, "Carter Talk," *New Republic,* 25 September 1976, p. 17. Reading at the table: RCS, "Christmas with the Carters," *Ladies' Home Journal,* December 1977, p. 76. EC "matter of fact": Bobby Logan/ai; EC and games: Ivy "Ruby" Watson Lamb/ai. EC controls Lillian: LeRoy Young/ai. LC on EC as "strong one": Paul Elovitz, "Three Days in Plains," *The Journal of Psychohistory,* Fall 1977, p. 177. EC working with blacks: Alton Carter/ai; EC regrets time away from home: local farmer/ai. Impact of Depression: Miriam Timmerman Saylor and Richard Salter/ais; William Baily Williford, *Americus Through the Years,* (Atlanta: Cherokee Publishing Co., 1977), pp. 291–293, 296–298. LC on EC's buying and selling properties: Beth Tartan and Rudy Hayes, *Miss Lillian and Friends* (New York: The New American Library, 1977), p. 7. EC businesses: LeRoy Young, Ernest Turner/Nellie Walters/ais. EC anti-New Deal: LeRoy Young, Joseph Bacon, local farmer/ais. EC's meadowland: local farmer/ai. EC and REA: Ivy "Ruby" Watson Lamb/ai. LC must have forgotten her husband when she said, "Everybody thought FDR was wonderful, and we never heard any criticism of the President. Now that's all you hear. Every election it's just the bad

things and not the good." LC in GCS "Miss Lillian: My Two Sons," *Ladies' Home Journal,* August 1977, pp. 36–37. Earl on school bus: Ivy "Ruby" Watson Lamb/ai. EC threatens foreclosure: local farmer/ai. EC's generosity: Miriam Timmerman Saylor/ai. EC and girl graduate: Ida Lee Timmerman/ai. EC remembers Nellie Walters: Nellie Walters/ai; copy of EC's will in Sumter County courthouse. EC's recreations: R. E. Sullivan, C. J. Vaughn, and local farmer/ais. LC "swinger": LeRoy Young/ai; LC "interesting": Bobby Logan/ai. LC as maverick: GCS quoted in John Osborne, *op. cit.,* p. 17. Also Miriam Timmerman Saylor/ai. This quality was evident in my interviews with her. EC "tight as a tick": LeRoy Young/ai; GC's purse: Ida "Ruby" Watson Lamb/ai. LC helps friends in need: Ivy "Ruby" Watson Lamb, Ida Lee Timmerman, Allie Murray Smith/ais; also *WNB,* p. 13. LC on lack of close friends: Coombs, *op. cit.,* p. 40; see also Allen, *op. cit.,* p. 30. LC on loving everybody: GCS, "Miss Lilliam: My Two Sons," p. 120. LC "most liberal": Allen, *op. cit.,* pp. 27, 30. LC on Annie B. and Ida Lee Timmerman: Allen, *op. cit.,* p. 30; see also Elovitz, *op. cit.,* p. 185. LC on criticism from JC: Claire Safran, "The Women in Jimmy Carter's Life," *Redbook,* October 1976, p. 84. LC on local critics: Allen, *op. cit.,* p. 38. LC on "white lies": Interview with LC, "My Son, the President," *USN,* 7 March 1977, p. 54. LC on JC's colitis: Bruce Mazlish and Edwin Diamond, "Thrice-Born," *New York,* August 30, 1976, p. 30. JC's pacifier and goat: Emily "Sissy" Dolvin, Miss G. Abrams/ quoted in Elovitz, *op. cit.,* p. 196. LC returns to nursing, blacks help, discipline children: LC/ai; Annie May Holly Jones, quoted in Elovitz, *op. cit.,* pp. 194–195; Rachael Clark, Annie Mae Kitchens/ais. JC as tease: Annie Mae Harvey Lester, quoted in *AC,* 17 July 1976. Children not talking back to LC: Elovitz, *op. cit.,* p. 185. LC not spank children: Ivy "Ruby" Watson Lamb, Rachael Clark, and Bobby Logan/ais; LC on reading: Elovitz, *op. cit.,* p. 185. JC on LC as extrovert: *WNB,* p. 80. JC and cookies: *WNB,* pp. 38–39. JC does mention his high-school teacher as one of the important influences in his life: *WNB,* pp. 29–31. EC nurturing: author from Bobby Logan, Rachael Clark/ais. Carter used to follow his father around, according to Mazlish and Diamond. JC is quoted as having said, "We were very close. . . . During the times when I was very young, when my mother was out nursing, I would come and get into bed with my father and sleep with him.": Mazlish and Diamond, *op. cit.,* p. 81. JC on EC virtues: *WNB,* pp. 8–9, 12–13, 25. JC on whipping: *WNB,* pp. 9, 12. JC, wide open, quail story: Richard Hyatt, *op. cit.* JC on BC like EC: *WNB,* p. 79. Others on how he differs: Rachael Clark, Ray Blanton/ais.

### In The Mold

JC as little entrepreneur: *WNB,* p. 21; and Hugh Carter/ai. But Ivy "Ruby" Watson Lamb/ai, does not recall JC selling peanuts at age 6. She says she asked LC about some of the stories in *WNB* and LC admitted they had to "flower up" some things for the campaign. JC's desire to win: Davis quoted in Tartan and Hayes, *op. cit.,* pp. 31–32; LC in "My Son the President," p. 52. RCS makes same point in "Christmas with the Carters," p. 76. GCS a "tomboy": Ivy "Ruby" Watson Lamb/ai. Also JC, interview, 14 June 1976. GC and "money" tree: GCS as quoted in Elovitz, *op. cit.,* p. 189. JC and B.B. gun: *WNB,* p. 12. LC on JC and the barn: "My Son, The President" idealized by EC: Tartan and Hayes, *op. cit.,* p. 5; RCS agrees: *Inner Healing,* pp. 15–18; JC agrees RCS was favorite: airborne interview, 14 June 1976, transcript in author's files. RCS "queen of universe," shock when goes away to college, father as "perfect human being": *Inner Healing,* pp. 15–18. EC teaches JC to swim and hunt:

Richard Hyatt, *op. cit.* LC saves JC's schoolwork: Elovitz, *op. cit.*, p. 177.

### Plains

Background detail on Plains mainly from *History of Plains*, pp. 4, 6; author's interviews with Alton Carter, Bobby Logan, Miriam Timmerman Saylor, Richard Salter, H. H. Sutherland, Ida Lee Timmerman, LeRoy Young, Billy Wise, Bill Murray. JC on Plains: *WNB*, pp. 8, 15. EC's business: Ernest Turner and Nellie Walters/ais. Political, civic offices of EC and Alton Carter: *Ga. Register*, 1922–53. EC and LC church activities: GCS, in John Osborne, *op. cit.*, p. 17. Also Miriam Timmerman Saylor, Bobby Logan/ais.

### Social Setting

Remarks on culture, politics and race from Neal R. Peirce, *The Deep South States of America* (New York: W. W. Norton & Co., 1974), pp. 306–376; V. O. Key, Jr., *Southern Politics;* (New York: Vintage Books, 1949); William Anderson, *Wild Man from Sugar Creek* (Baton Rouge, Louisiana Press 1975). On the subtleties of interactions in the caste system, John Dollard, *Class and Caste in a Southern Town. Population and voting statistics from Ga. Register*, 1920–1953. Background on local black culture: Rachael and Tyler Clark, Rev. John Henry Holley, Alma Soloman, Bowman Wiley, local white/ais. JC as "rural royalty": RCS, "Christmas with the Carters," p. 74. Courthouse "gangs": Anderson, *op. cit.*, pp.

17–18. On law, mob as buttress of system: *ATR*, 22 September 1920, 28 September 1922, 24 October 1933, 20 December 1933. For an ambiguous situation revolving around the pursuit of a black who accidentally killed Alice Ruth Timmerman, one of Plains's beautiful and free-spirited women, see *ATR*, 3, 5, 6, 9 April 1926. Blacks and whites playing together: Billy Wise/ai; JC, *WNB*, p. 14; Tartan and Hayes, *op. cit.*, pp. 31–32, 55. LC's warmth to blacks: Annie Mae Kitchens/ai; Orde Coombs, *op. cit.*, p. 42; and Paul Elovitz, *op. cit.*, p. 185; LC on EC and blacks: Tartan and Hayes, *op. cit.*, p. 21. See also LC in Coombs, *op. cit.*, p. 42; and LC interview, "My Son, the President," *USN*, 7 March 1977, p. 53. Earl working with blacks: Alton Carter, Rev. J. H. Holley/ais. "Black/white etiquette:" Billy Wise/ai. Bishop Johnson in car: Tartan and Hayes, *op. cit.*, p. 21. RCS on games: *Inner Healing*, p. 17. JC on Johnson visits: *WNB*, p. 33. LC and Alvin Johnson on his visit: Tartan and Hayes, *op. cit.*, pp. 21–22. John Dollard on system: Dollard, *op. cit.*, p. 62. The underlying ambivalence in some of these relationships can be seen in extreme form in the following remarks of an Americus policeman speaking in 1957: "There's a nigger I grew up with on the farm. . . . He was my friend; we used to do everything. He loves me. Today he's the superintendent in the plywood mill and if he came in here right now he'd put his arm around me. But the minute he stopped in that door, he'd take his hat off. If he didn't, I'd pull my gun and shoot him dead." André Fontaine, "The Conflict of a Southern Town," *Redbook*, October 1957, p. 51.

## 2. EDUCATION

JC's mental habits: Paul Elovitz, "Three Days in Plains," *The Journal of Psychohistory*, Fall 1977, p. 186. White House replica: AH, 17 April 1977.

### Country School

Background details on Plains school: *History of Plains*, and author's interviews, former students: almost every living member of Carter's high-school class was contacted and most consented to an interview. Lists of teachers, pay scales, and minutes of Sumter County Board of Education are in Plains High School Materials Storage Center, south of Plains. A report found at the storage center," Georgia Education Survey of Sumter County Public Schools ( January 1928 through March 1929)," gives a portrait of the educational deficiencies of the school. Background on Julia Coleman *WNB*, pp. 29–30; *History of Plains*, pp. 44, 52–3. Coleman's use of corporal punishment: Robert M. Logan, Jr., Roy Thompson, Richard Salter/ais; Coleman's teaching techniques: Roy Thompson, Miriam Timmerman Saylor, Al Seckinger, Lottie Tanner/ais. Lottie Tanner kindly showed me copies of her scrapbooks. They were clearly proudly and carefully done. Students were encouraged to make lists (a trait Carter carried into adult life)—of their favorite Georgia poets or paintings—and to illustrate them. JC's on Gloria's talk: GCS in "He Has a Schedule," *Newsweek*, 19 July 1976, p. 26. Reputations of older neighbors and relatives: author's deductions from interview with Ivy "Ruby" Watson Lamb, Miriam Timmerman Saylor. Retarded cousin: Plains farmer/ai. JC as a smart boy: Eleanor Forest (teacher) and students Robert M. Logan, Lottie Tanner, Thomas Lowery, Rebekah Williams Karr, Grace Wiggins McCoy/ais. Diamond ring story: teacher Eleanor Forest in *People* magazine, 19 July 1976. JC's nice grin: Grace Wiggins McCoy/ai. JC's recreations with Plains schoolmates: Robert M. Logan, Thomas Lowery, Richard Salter/ais. JC's dates: Ivy "Ruby" Watson Lamb, Richard Salter, June Davis

Andrews/ais. On sodas and prom parties: Ivy "Ruby" Watson Lamb, William Wise, Al Seckinger/ais; On flashier Americus boys: local socialite/ai. JC's in extracurricular activities: Richard Salter, June Davis Andrews/ais; school photo display, Earl Carter Library, Georgia Southwestern College. On making noise at chapel: Al Seckinger/ai. On playing hooky: Richard Salter, Grace Wiggins McCoy, June Davis Andrews/ais. JC, according to one classmate, also had one of his first fights at this time—beating up another boy and gloating over it: classmate/ai. On lack of class rankings: Richard Salter/ai. *ATR*, 31 May 1941, also gives no class rankings. Graduation celebrations, '41: *ATR*, 15, 28 May 1941: William Wise, Grace Wiggins McCoy/ais. Graduation ceremony, JC's speech: *ATR*, 31 May 1941; Lottie Wise Tanner, William Wise/ais and correspondence. JC on being governor some day: B. T. Wishard/ais.

### Higher Education

Generalizations about student life in this section and Carter's involvement in it (or lack thereof) at the colleges he attended are from the following yearbooks: The *Gale* for Georgia Southwestern; the *Blueprint* for Georgia Tech. (ed. S. C. McLandon, 1943); *The Lucky Bag* for Annapolis. Also useful were: The *Sou'wester; A Friendly College Newspaper*, Americus, Georgia: Georgia Southwestern College, February 17, 1942; *The Log*, the Annapolis humor magazine; *Reef Points* (a student handbook), (Annapolis: U.S. Naval Academy, 1943), ed. by James C. Mason, pp. 18–19. For curricular details: Georgia School of Technology, *Bulletin*, Vol. XL, No. 4, August 1973, Atlanta; U.S. Navy, Bureau of Navigation, *Catalog of Course Instruction of the United States Naval Academy* (Washington, D.C.: U.S. Government Printing Office, 1943, 1944, 1945); United States Naval Academy, Department of English, History and Government, *The Course in After-Dinner Speaking* (pamphlet). For class standing: The Georgia Tech Bulletin mentioned above and *Annual Register of the United States Naval Academy* (Washington, D.C., U.S. Government Printing Office). Published materials giving physical appearances, histories of the three colleges Carter attended are: Mary Bishop Gray, *Through the Years: A Brief Informal Record of Georgia Southwestern College 1908–1957*, (Americus Printing Co., 1957). Robert B. Wallace, Jr., *Dress Her in White and Gold*, revised edition, (Atlanta: Georgia Technical Foundation, Inc., 1969). Kendall Banning, *Annapolis Today* (New York: Funk and Wagnalls, 1945); Writer's Program of the Works Progress Administration of the State of Maryland, *A Guide to the United States Naval Academy*, (map), (New York: Devin-Adoir Company, 1941); Leland P. Lovette, *School of the Sea*, (Frederick A. Stokes Company, New York, 1941); Louis H. Bolander, "The Naval Academy in Five Wars," *Proceedings of the U.S. Naval Institute*, Vol. 72, No. 4 (April 1946), p. 44; Captain W. L. Puleston, *Annapolis: Gangway to the Quarterdeck*, (D. Appleton-Century Company, New York, 1942); Earl W. Thompson, "The Naval Academy as an Undergraduate College," *Proceedings of the United States Naval Institute*, Vol. 74, No. 3 (March 1948). For the Academy as a culture: Arthur Heise, *The Brass Factories* (Washington, D.C.: Public Affairs Press, 1969), Morris Janowitz, *The Professional Soldier*, (Glencoe, Illinois: The Free Press, 1960); John P. Lovells, *Growth and Change at the Service Academies: Some Organization Consequences*, delivered at the 1976 Regional Meeting of the International University Seminar on Armed Forces and Society, Air Command and Staff College, Maxwell AFB, Alabama, October 22–23, 1976. In addition, questionnaires were sent (based on accessibility of addresses) to Carter's Georgia Southwestern classmates and most members of his company at Annapolis. Instructors at Georgia Tech and Annapolis who might have known JC were sent questionnaires; most responded. JC's early interest in Annapolis: *WNB*, pp. 41–43. For diseases the Annapolis candidate must not have: Kendall Banning, *op cit*. pp. 6–9, and U.S. Navy, *Regulations Governing the Admission of Candidates*, 1941, p. 16. Science curriculum at Plains High School: Robert Logan/ai. Cousins' success at Georgia Southwestern: *The Gale*, 1936, 1939. Tuition at Georgia Southwestern: Mary Bishop Gray, *op. cit.*, p. 24. JC commuting to college: Frank and Virginia Williams/ai. Curriculum at Georgia Southwestern: Gray op. cit., pp. 24–25; Carolyn Hess/al, Helen Ashworth, Edward Brooks/aqs. While Carter was at Georgia Southwestern, the college was disaccredited by the Southern Association of College and Secondary Schools for "undue political activity in the University System." Students and faculty lobbied and were able to lift the disaccreditation before it was to go into effect in the fall of 1942. (Gray, *op. cit.*, pp. 24–25.) JC courses and basketball: *The Gale*, 1942, p. 58, and Helen Ashworth, Edward Brooks/aqs. On JC's shyness, fraternity hazing: Robert Logan/ai. On sophisticated Americus insiders: local socialite/ai. Membership in the "Investors": *The Sou'wester*, 17 February 1942; Helen Ashworth, Edward Brooks/aqs. Party at Pond House: *The Sou'wester*, 17 February 1942. JC writing in contest: *The Sou'wester*, 19 April 1977. JC not big on campus: deduction from Lambuth R. Towson (fraternity brother)/al; Robert Logan/ai; *The Gale*, 19–42, club lists, photos. JC on class politicians: Robert Logan/ai. JC's eye on governorship: B. T. Wishard/ai. The role of the Academy in educating rural Southern boys: Morris Janowitz, *op. cit.*, pp. 87, 89, 107. Service academy graduates in Carter's circle of acquaintances were to include Howard Callaway, Judge Tom Marshall, and Philip Alston/ais. On Georgia Tech roommate and regimen: Professor R. Kenneth Jacobs, Lawrence Gellerstedt/ais. JC on honor roll: Georgia

School of Technology, *Bulletin*, April 1942, p. 126. On JC's company: James H. Forbes/al; C. H. Shaddeau/aq; Quotations on hazing in general: James H. Forbes, Blu Middleton, Albert Rusher/ais. Leland Lovette (*op. cit.*, pp. 3–32, 148) and Kendall Banning, (*op. cit.*, pp. 50–64) give general portrait of hazing. JC on not taking hazing seriously: WNB, pp. 43–44. JC as cruise box champion: Blu Middleton/ai. JC's diary entry on hazing: Paul Elovitz, *op. cit.*, p. 186. Paddling episode: classmate/aq. Regimen at Annapolis: W. D. Puleston, *op. cit.*, pp. 150–51. Classroom practices and curriculum: Professor James Abbott/al. Carter's contacts with his professors were slight. Of 12 professors I contacted, only two (Ellery Clark and George Starnes/als) remember having had Carter in any of their classes. JC's recreation: cross-country track experiences: Ellery Clark, track coach/als. JC reads and listens to records: Blu Middleton, Thomas B. Brenner/ais. The company as a natural fraternity: James Forbes/al. JC's closest friends: Al Rusher/ai; James H. Forbes/al. Death of Bob Siddons: James Forbes/al. JC not a "slash": James Forbes/al; "blends into woodwork": classmate/ai. Yearbook entry about JC: *The Lucky Bag*, 1947, p. 176. JC's academic standing: *Annual Register*, 1944–45, p. 90; 1946–47, p. 33; cf. *WNB*, p. 64. JC's conduct and aptitude scores: *Annual Register*, 1944–45, p. 90; 1945–46, p. 81; 1946–47, p. 54. For details on evaluation system, see Banning, *op. cit.*, pp. 105–6, 116–28. JC not a class leader: two classmates/al, aq. Selection procedures for class leaders: James H. Forbes, Blu Middleton/ais. Classmates amazed at JC's later success, Turner the standard: company member/ai. RC, LC pin on boards: Al Rusher/ai; photo at Earl Carter Library, Georgia Southwestern.

### Courtship

Ideal Girl chart: adapted from chart in Banning, *op. cit.*, pp. 196–97. Allie Smith and Edgar Smith background, RC as an obedient child: Allie Smith/ai. Edgar Smith's illness: Allie Smith/ai Edgar Smith's deathbed testament: Gail Sheehy, "Ladies and Gentlemen, the Second President—Sister Rosalynn," *New York*, 22 November 1976, p. 54. Also Kandy Stroud, "Growing Up with Rosalynn Carter," *Good Housekeeping*, August 1977, p. 174. Smith money for children's education; Allie goes to work; "Captain Murray" sells land to JC: Allie Smith/ai. RC's worship of her dad: *CT*, 13 August 1976 see also Gail Sheehy, *op. cit.*, p. 54. Murray Smith on life without their father: *Ibid*. On Allie Smith's financial situation: Allie Smith/ai. RC works for pin money, subject to strict discipline, an "excellent student," doesn't pay for her education: Allie Smith/ai. RC's worst subject social studies: Trude B. Feldman, "Rosalynn Carter at 50," *McCall's*, August 1977, p. 198. RC's interest in JC: Gail Sheehy, *op. cit.*, p. 54; and Charlotte Curtis, "What Kind of First Lady Will She Be?" *McCall's*, January 1977, p. 26. JC asks RC for first date: Charlotte Curtis, *op. cit.*, p. 26. JC tells mother he wants to marry RC: *WNB*, pp. 67–68. Lillian has another account of their first date: "Well, one night, on one of his trips home from the Academy, Jimmy and some of his friends decided to give a dance over here at the Pond House. . . . It just happened that Ruth and Rosalynn were spending that weekend here with us. I don't know what it was that gave them the idea—maybe there was a temporary shortage of girls, or something—but the boys saw Ruth and Rosalynn here at the house and they said, in a sort of offhand way: 'Why don't you girls get somebody to bring you, and come and join the party.' " The girls were thrilled at the idea of going to a "college boy's party" and found dates. At the party, "Jimmy danced first with Ruth and then with her —Rosalynn. And while he was dancing with her,

Jimmy said to Rosalynn, 'Don't you think the date I brought is pretty?' And Rosalynn said she snapped right back at Jimmy: 'She's not half as pretty as I am!' " Howard Norton, *Rosalynn* (Plainsfield, N.J.: Logos Press, 1977), pp. 31–32. LC on RC as not sophisticated: Gail Sheehy, *op. cit.*, p. 54. RC responds to JC proposals: *WNB*, p. 68. RC's wedding, honeymoon: *ATR*, 8 July 1946.

## 3. NAVAL CAREER

JC recalls *Wyoming* and *Missouri: WNB*, pp. 50–51. Carter's billets are documented in a short biography sent to me by the Department of Defense in 1976/author's files. JC friendships in Virginia: Al Rusher/ai. JC depressed about Rhodes scholarship: JC quoted by Jack Anderson, *Parade*, 27 November 1976; friends don't see effect on him: T. R. Reid, *WP*, 27 November 1976. JC on other Rhodes finalist: Bruce Mazlish and Edwin Diamond, *Jimmy Carter* (New York: Simon and Schuster, 1979), p. 102. JC on "best opportunity": *WNB*, p. 51. Quote about submarine training: Roth E. Ledderick/al. On informal entertainment, JC's and RC's shyness: Roth E. Leddick/al. JC on *Pomfret*: Warren Colegrove, *AJ*, 25 March 1976. JC being washed overboard: *WNB*, pp. 52–53. Lifelines normally used: Colegrove/ai. Colegrove does not recall JC's being washed overboard. However, if a wave hit when the watch had just been changed, it could easily catch a man before he had strapped himself in. On officers as clique: Roy C. Smallwood/ai. Other officer on close-knit crew: Lowell F. Fitch/ai. JC recalls closeness: T. R. Reid, *WP*, 27 November 1976. JC as person apart: Roy C. Smallwood, Lowell F. Fitch/ais; Warren Colegrove, Sam Colston in T. R. Reid, *WP*, 27 November 1976. JC on their married life: *WNB*, p. 69. Details on Hawaiian social life, RC's style, Carters' desire for girl: Albert and Ruby Trottier/ais. RC in San Diego: *WNB*, pp. 69–70, 55. JC on K-1: *WNB*, p. 55. JC command thesis: *WNB*, p. 57. The theory and original write-up for the thesis were done by Francis Callahan and Lt. C. E. Woods, who were operators of the fire-control system. They suggested that JC use it as a command thesis. Francis Callahan/al. JC an effective officer: quote from sailor (Sam Colston), "People and Politics [on JC]," *Campaign 1976*, I, 1, p. 13. Smallwood and Colegrove quotes: ais. Yet JC was not the star of the K-1. Frank Andrews, a Yale Ph.D., had been third in his class at Annapolis; Francis Callahan had done graduate work at MIT, earning a 4.89 average on a 5.00 system; Charles Woods received his Masters in Operations Research. "Jimmy did not stand out in this group," according to Francis Callahan/al. Charles E. Woods and Roy B. Cowdrey quotes in T. R. Reid, *WP*, 27 November 1976; Frank Andrews/ai. Bill Lalor on JC humor: "People and Politics [on JC]," *Campaign 1976*, I, 1, p. 14. "He was interested . . ." Warren Colegrove, "People and Politics [on JC]," p. 13. JC's lack of political affiliation: Lowell F. Fitch, Roy C. Smallwood/ais; Frank Andrews, "People and Politics [on JC]," p. 13. JC's "finest billet," interview

with Rickover: *WNB*, pp. 58, 63–64. Carter was not ordered back to Schenectady as the "senior officer," as he says in *WNB*, p. 55. In training as an engineering officer, he was the only officer around for a while, working with the precommissioning crew. Certainly he never commanded a nuclear submarine, as observers during the 1976 campaign often assumed; indeed, he never even rode on a nuclear submarine, in all probability, until he became President. JC tutoring: *WNB*, p. 59. JC quote on radiation: *WNB*, p. 60. Specifics of nuclear physics course: Harold E. Way/al. Quotes on JC as nuclear engineer: Kenneth Baker and Joel Snow in Nicholas Wade, "Carter As Scientist or Engineer: What Are His Credentials?" *Science*, 6 August 1976, pp. 462–63. JC quotes on Rickover: *WNB*, pp. 60–62; also in "People and Politics [on JC]," p. 15. JC on Rickover's critical style: Speech to National Wildlife Federation, 15 March 1975, *Campaign 1976*, I, 1, p. 65. Details on Rickover's two roles, promotion: Clay Blair, Jr., *The Atomic Submarine and Admiral Rickover* (New York: Henry Holt and Company, 1954), pp. 119–20, 173–269. Page footnote and details on organizational style, promotion: Elmo Zumwalt, Jr., *On Watch* (New York: Quadrangle, 1976), pp. 85–122. Rickover subordinates collaborate: unidentified colleague, "People and Politics [on JC]," p. 15. JC "adverse reaction" to Rickover: *Ibid*. On JC's painting: Paul Elovitz, "Three Days in Plains," *Journal of Psychohistory*, Fall 1977, p. 188. JC detachment, not seeing EC: "People and Politics [on JC]," p. 15. Details on visits, EC and JC: "Plains" news section, *ATR*, 1946 through 1953. JC on parents' visits, San Diego: *WNB*, p. 70 Observations on lack of decorations on EC grave on Memorial Day (and day after) 1977, by author on visit there, May-June 1977. Role reversal, JC and Russell: JC interview, Richard Russell Oral History Project; ex-Russell aides/ais. 17 JC 1 November 1970. Frank Andrews on JC's "plantation": T. R. Reid, *WP*, 27 November 1976. JC talks with father: *WNB*, p. 64. GCS on JC & EC's death: *NW*, 19 July 1976. JC on significance of father's life: *WNB*, p. 64. JC on father's responsibility for Plains: unidentified man (probably Bill Lalor), "People and Politics [on JC]," p. 16. Also Bill Lalor/ai. JC on RC and Plains: *WNB*, pp. 66, 70. RC on return to Plains: *WP*, 2 February 1976. JC ambition to be CNO: Interview with Bill Moyers, 6 May '76; *Campaign 1976*, I, 1, p. 164. Annapolis classmates leave service: James H. Forbes/ai, and Moss, quoted in *WP*, 1 August 1976. Statistics on classmates' careers from *Shipmate*, October 1975.

## 4. RETURN TO PLAINS

Factual details on political, social, and economic happenings in Sumter County and the activities and places of residence of the Carter family in the fifties and sixties are drawn mainly from the Americus Times-Recorder, 1953 through 1970. (The "Plains" news section lists everything done by middle-class people in town.) These newspaper reports have been checked against William Bailey Williford, *Americus Through the Years: The Story of a Georgia Town and Its People, 1832–1975* (Atlanta, Georgia: Cherokee Publishing Company, 1975), which gives a detailed social and economic history of Americus from the "years of the rebellion" through the 1960s. Specific materials on Plains community and school are from *History of Plains*, and the school yearbook, *The Buffalo*, volumes

1950–51 through 1969–70 (the volumes are stored in the school library). Earl Carter's will and the Carter family land holdings in Sumter County are recorded in the Sumter County Courthouse records. For farming conditions in the fifties and sixties, I have used Charles Floyd, *The Georgia Regional Economies: The Challenge of Growth* (Athens: University of Georgia Press, 1974), p. 14–15; 22–23; Atlanta Journal, 16 September 1970; also local farmer, Mary Anne Thomas, Agnes McRainey/ais. Data on economic and political trends in south Georgia: Neal R. Peirce, *The Deep South States of America* (New York: W. W. Norton & Co., Inc., 1974), pp. 306–377.

Merging Earl Carter's estate: LC/ai; EC's will in Sumter County Courthouse. JC 1953 trips home: Gail

Sheehy, "Ladies and Gentlemen, The Second President—Sister Rosalynn," *New York*, 22 November 1976, p. 54. Problems in collecting loans: *WNB*, p. 71, and LC/ai. Rally, contact with Thompson and Griffin: *ATR*, 28 August 1954. LC quote, "no house big enough . . ." Gail Sheehy, *op. cit.*, p. 55. The Atlanta Constitution, 16 October 1975, carried a human interest story of the "haunted" Wise house and the Carters, as its former tenants. LC worries about the boys: Agnes McRainey/ai. LC on RC as "partner"; RC accounting course: Sheehy, *op. cit.*, p. 55. RC felt important: Kandy Stroud, *How Jimmy Won* (New York: William Morrow and Company, 1977), pp. 113–14. BC's "testament": *The Buffalo*, 1955. BC schooling, wedding, and military service: *ATR*, 15, 23 August, 1955; RCS, *Brother Billy* pp. 59–74. BC restlessness: John Osborne, "Carter Talk," *New Republic*, 25 September 1976, p. 15. RCS on same: *Brother Billy*, p. 73–74. LC quotes: Nanette Rainone et al., "Lillian Carter Talks About Racism, the Kennedys and 'Jimmy's Reign,'" *Ms.*, October 1976, pp. 51, 52. White Cadillac: Henry Allen, "Just Plains Folk," Washington *Post/Potomac*, 15 August 1976, p. 37. Earl Carter and Agricultural Extension Station: local farmer/ai. Jack Carter's activities: *ATR*, 26 May, 24 September 1964; 16 March 1965. Carters into self-improvement: Mary Anne Thomas/ai, Alexander Palamiotis/ai. For speed-reading course: Howard Norton, *Rosalynn, A Portrait* (Plainfield, N.J.: Logos International, 1977), p. 110. Plains and Americus circles: author from interviews with B. T. Wishard, L. C. Godwin, Georgia friend, John Pope, Mary Anne Thomas. RC quote: "I've never had time for friends . . ." "Kandy Stroud, *op. cit.*, p. 112. JC as "seductive": Georgia friend/ai. JC discusses religion: Georgia friend/ai. "I remember . . . he read a lot of books," Mary Anne Thomas/ai. The Carters, Americus social structure: Mary Anne Thomas, local socialite, Allie Smith/ais. There is other indirect evidence that initially the Carters were not socially prominent: several other local families—the Laniers, the Marshalls, the Crups, the Thomases, the Sheffields—rated multicolumn spreads in the *ATR* when members married or died. The Carters did not. See also William Williford, *op. cit.*

### Black and White

Date on blacks in Plains from *History of Plains*, the Americus *Times-Recorder* for the 1950s and 1960s, and my interviews with several blacks: Rachael and Tyler Clark, Charles and Peggy Hicks; Rev. Holley; Annie Mae Kitchens; Bowman Wiley; Alma and Walter Soloman. General background on the origins of the sharecrop system, the concentration of Negroes in shantytowns in sections of urban areas, the segregation system: Allan Comish, *The Reconstruction of Georgia* (Minneapolis: University of Minnesota Press, 1966); and John Dittner, *Black Georgia in the Progressive Era* (Champaign, Ill.: University of Illinois Press, 1977). For subtleties of caste system as observed in 1930s: John Dollard, *Caste and Class in a Southern Town*, 3rd ed. (Garden City, N.Y.: Doubleday Anchor Books, 1957). Blacks at Carter farms: see discussion in Chapter 7, "Winning." Black medical facilities: *ATR*, 26 October, 1953. Black agricultural agent: *ATR*, 14 October, 1952. LC, on hands' funerals: Nanette Rainone et al., *op. cit.*, p. 86. "He was all right"; details on Floyd funeral: young Plains black/ai. Employers bail out "darkies": William Williford, *op. cit.* Lundy story: Beth Tartan and Rudy Hayes, *Miss Lillian and Friends* (New York: The New American Library, 1977), p. 34. John Dollard's quotes on affection and system: Dollard, *op. cit.*, pp. 81, 386. Asymmetry in black and white relations: author's interpretations from: Billy Wise, Bobby Logan, Frank and Virginia Williams/ais. Brooks Hays, a moderate Southerner from

Arkansas, for example, recalls it as a conscious break with tradition when he asked church officials to let Negroes sit where they liked at his mother's funeral in 1955. Brooks Hays, *A Southern Moderate Speaks* (Chapel Hill, N.C.: The University of North Carolina Press, 1959.) p. 221. JC's policies on Sumter County School Board: board minutes, 7 February 1956 through 8 January 1963. (Minutes on file, Sumter County Courthouse). JC's library policies for board of the Americus Carnegie Library Association, January, 1962 through February, 1963: minutes (on file, Lake Blackshear Library). Minutes of Sumter County Hospital Board are closed. But from other evidence, it is clear that there was no effort to integrate the hospitals until 1964–65: Americus man/ai; JC quote, "It seems hard to believe . . ." *WNB*, pp. 72–73. JC favors school consolidation: *ATR*, 12, 14 July 1961. Hugh Carter opposes it: *ATR*, 17 July 1961. JC on "stinging disappointment" and reason for opposition: *WNB*, p. 88. Opponents to consolidation: L. C. Godwin, Mayor Blanton/ais. "As a State Senator . . ." and second consolidation attempt. *ATR*, 20 March 1964; and subsequent issues in 1964.

### Challenge and Response

Background on legal challenges: *Race Relations Law Reporter*, 1957 through 1966. On the KKK, State's Rights Council, and resistance by Georgia politicians: Numm V. Bartley, *Rise of Massive Resistance* (Baton Rouge, La.: Louisiana State University Press, 1969). On Koininia: Williford, *op. cit.*, pp. 335–339; André Fontaine, "The Conflict of a Southern Town," *Redbook*, October 1957, pp. 39ff. On adaptation of Americus to integration: Marshall Frady, "Discovering Another in a Georgia Town," *Life*, 12 February 1971. On the Albany Movement: Howard Zinn, *Albany, A Study in National Responsibility* (Atlanta: Southern Regional Council 1962), pp. 3–27; also Howard Zinn, *SNCC* (Boston: Beacon Press, 1965), passim. On civil rights confrontations in Americus and integration of Sumter County schools: Williford, *op. cit.* All data has been checked against the Americus *Times-Recorder*, 1962–70, and most of the material on the integration of the Americus and Sumter County schools has been derived from it, plus HEW orders on file in the Plains Materials Storage Center. Interviews especially helpful on racial conflict and change in Plains and Americus include: Rev. R. L. Freeman, C. B. King, local farmer, local woman, Warren Fortson, and Frank Meyers. Americus chapter of States Rights Council: *ATR*, 12 January 1956. Other chapters were formed in Webster County: *ATR*, 21 January 1956; Sumter County: *ATR*, 3 February 1956. There was a KKK cross burning on Friendship Road: *ATR*, 15 November 1957. Pressures on Jack Singletary: local farmer, "Jimmy, We Hardly Know Y'All," *Playboy*, November 1976, p. 189. Dr. King quote "Don't stop now . . . ": Zinn, *SNCC*, p. 131. King was called "boy" by the Americus sheriff: Williford, *op. cit.*, pp. 365–66. Black churches burned down: Zinn, *SNCC*, p. 139, *NYT*, 16 August 1962; *NYT* 10, 14, 18, 21 September 1962. Actions of Americus City Council to calm situation: Williford, *op. cit.*, p. 356. White civic leaders behind scenes: Warren Fortson/ai. Roberta Freeman: Rev. Freeman and C. B. King/ais. Whatley murder: *ATR*, 5 August, 1965, and Williford, *op. cit.*, p. 337. Carl Sanders on "outside influences": *ATR*, 2 August 1965. Attempts at biracial committee: Warren Fortson/ai. Hugh Carter addresses protest meeting: Williford, *op. cit.*, p. 377.

### Avoiding the Issue of Race

JC refuses to join States Rights Council, *WNB*, p. 73–74. JC on blacks at church: Billy Wise and Frank Williams/ais. JC and RC concerned for Jack Singletary: Robert Sheer, *op. cit.*, p. 189. JC speaks up for Warren

Fortson: Fortson/ai. Florence Jordan on JC visit: Robert Scheer, *op. cit.*, p. 186. The civil rights demonstration in Plains was met with bricks, and one of the demonstrators apparently was beaten up. No person could be found to testify against the man or men who attacked the demonstrators: Americus lawyer, Plains black/ais. On standing up: Warren Fortson/ai member of a long-prominent Georgia family, he was not seeking confrontation and was shocked that his attempt to form a biracial committee raised such a storm. For other local

whites who stood up in the mid-1960s (including the head of Georgia Southwestern), see William Williford, *op. cit.* Earlier, at the state level, Ellis Arnall, Georgia's governor from 1942 to 1946, had eliminated the poll tax and substantially increased black voter registration in the state. And former mayor Ivan Allen of Atlanta by 1963 was testifying in Washington, D.C., for a public accommodations act, which eventually became part of the 1964 Civil Rights Act.

## 5. ENTRY INTO POLITICS

Background details on the traditional political system in Georgia are from V. O. Key, *Southern Politics* (New York, Vintage Books, 1949), pp. 106–107, 108–117, 117–130. Recent political trends from Neal R. Peirce, *The Deep South States of America*, (New York: W. W. Norton & Co., Inc., 1974), p. 311–23.

Details on Carter's first senate campaign, in addition to my interviews, are primarily from the Americus *Times-Recorder*, July through November, 1962, as supplemented by congruent accounts in the Atlanta *Constitution* and Atlanta *Journal* for the same period. Descriptions of Carter's political career as a state senator are based on stories in the *Times-Recorder*, 1962 through 1966, and Georgia Journals of the Georgia Senate, 1963 through 1966. For Carter's participation in the 1964 general election and his short congressional campaign in 1966 I have relied primarily on the Americus *Times-Recorder* and the Columbus *Enquirer* for that period. For the gubernatorial campaign 1966 I have drawn from congruent accounts in the *Times-Recorder*, Columbus *Enquirer*, Atlanta *Constitution*, and Atlanta *Journal*. Biographical details on political figures mentioned here, the offices they held, and election statistics are drawn from the *Ga. Register* for 1962–63 through 1970–71. Also: Richard B. Russell Memorial Library, University of Georgia.

"I just never figured . . .": Bobby Logan/ai. JC's "transient and superficial" political involvement: *WNB*, p. 87. Naval colleagues on JC political interests: see notes to Chapter 3. As governor, however, Carter told a reporter that he had been intensely interested in politics since the age of eight, though he had had no ambitions for the governorship as a youth: Beau Cutts, *AJC*, 3 October 1971. Coleman on Roosevelt commission: Richard Salter/ai. EC as conservative: Joseph Bacon, other Plains farmers/ais. EC's and Frank Meyers's 1962 campaign styles: Frank Meyers/ai. EC entertains Talmadge: *ATR*, 4 June 1953. JC's friends suggest he run for office: Warren Fortson/ai. LC on JC's motives for entering politics: "My Son, the President," *USN*, 7 March 1977, p. 53; Mary Anne Thomas/ai. "We were somewhat upset . . ." and details on Americus good government groups: Warren Fortson/ai. JC emphasizes personal qualities: campaign brochure, JC file, University of Georgia, Athens, Ga. JC's campaign "amateurish": *WNB*, p. 89. *ATR* endorses JC: *ATR*, 13 October 1962. "Collapsible voting booths . . .": Tom Collins, *The Search for Jimmy Carter* (Waco, Texas: Word Books, 1976), p. 58. JC on hurst "reached into box": *WNB*, pp. 90, 92. Exchange between Pope and Hurst: Collins, *op. cit.*, p. 59, and Pope/ai. Hurst threatens Pope: *WNB*, p. 91. Other quotes and details of Hurst's interference in Georgetown election: *WNB*, p. 91–93, JC says Georgetown interviews went well: *ATR*, 17 October 1962; *AJ*, 22 October 1962; later recalls difficulties: *WNB*, p. 91. JC, on "nearby Columbus newspapers": *WNB*, p. 91. JC approaches Pennington: H Carter/ai. Pennington story: *AJ*, 22 October 1962. JC's case to State Democratic Committee: John Pope/ai. Kirbo helps Carter: Kirbo, Fortson/ais. JC, "the officials

seemed mystified": *WNB*, p. 94. Tom Gray's testimony on Hurst: *ATR*, 2 November 1962; see also *AJ*, 1 November 1962. Judge Crow throws out vote: *ATR*, 3 November 1962. Party secretary on "long weekend vacation": *WNB*, p. 94. Ben Fortson intervenes: *AJ*, 5 November 1962, and *ATR*, 5 November 1963. Friends put JC's name on ballot: John Pope/ai. Ordinaries can't get names off ballot: *AJ*, 4 November 1962. See also *ATR*, 6 November 1962. Two ordinaries won't strike JC's name: *AJ*, 6 November 1962; also ATR, 6 November 1962. Judge Marshall's "Any further action . . .": *ATR*, 7 November 1962; see *ATR*, 29 November 1962. *FBI* "wanted to get Joe Hurst": Pope/ai. See also *AC*, 27 January 1965, for other details. JC quote on "only on request" and details on help to Balkcom: *AJ*, 5 March 1964.

### State Senate

Carl Sanders's state senate address: *Ga. SJ*, 16 January 1963. Reg Murphy on new senate men: *AC*, 15 January 1963. JC's friends in legislature: Robert Rowan, Brooks Pennington/aq; Robert Smalley, Billy Blair, and Janet Merritt/ais. JC hotels, regimen: William Blair/ai; Tom Collins, *op. cit.*, p. 61. JC reads bills: *WNB*, p. 98. Senators "would fall all over . . .": Stephen Ball, "Politics South," *AJC*, 8 November 1970. Reg Murphy quote: *AC*, 16 January 1964. JC, "I spoke . . .": *Addresses*, pp. 260–61. JC on proposed bill of rights: *WNB*, p. 101. "Questions" passed: *Ga. SJ*, special session 1964. LC, 1964 campaign: *ATR*, 21 August, 5 October 1964. In 1976 the suggestion was made that the Carter women suffered from helping Johnson. Mary Anne Thomas (ai) says that their action was looked at as "liberal crazy" and was "sort of overlooked by the nice people. But nobody wanted to hurt them." JC vs. Callaway: *ATR* 9, 14 October 1964, *WNB*, pp. 108–09. On reading bills: *ATR* 6 July 1963; JC, Sheffield: *ATR* 21 January 1966, *ATR* 4 February 1966. Reg Murphy, JC: *NW*, 19 July 1976. Influential lawmaker: *ATR* 9 May 1965.

### First Gubernatorial Race

Surprises friends: Mary Ann Thomas, John Pope/ais. On Callaway: *WNB*, pp. 110–11. Draft JC: Macon *News* 24 May 1966; *ATR* 2 June 1966. JC, Russell conservative: *AJ*, 18 April 1966. JC quotes on labels: *ATR*, 13 June 1966. See also: *AJ*, 12 June 1966. Hugh Carter keeps distance, "conservative": Americus civic leader/ai; ads: *ATR*, 2 November 1966. John Pope, Warren Fortson in campaigns/ais. Broad support: *ATR* 24 August 1966. Smith background: *ATR*, 4 February 1956. Friends help: Brooks Pennington/al; Frank Moore/ai. Atlanta people help: Phil Alston, Robert Lipshutz, Charles Kirbo/ais. JC staff: Columbus *Ledger-Enquirer*, 15 May 1966; *AC*, 24 June 1966; *AJ*, 18 June 1966; Mary Anne Thomas/ai. Russell, Talmadge post card: attached to letter from A. L. Barron to W. H. Jordan, 13 September 1966, in R. B. Russell Library. Gillis post cards: JC's 1966 campaign file, University of Georgia, Athens, Ga. Also see *AC*, 5 July 1966. Russell has no connection to cards: Barron to Jordan, 13 September 1966, in R. B. Russell Library.

Gillis denounces post cards: *AC*, 13 September 1966. Russell has no choices in race: W. H. Jordan to A. L. Barron, 16 September 1966, R. B. Russell papers. JC compared to Kennedy: Columbus *Ledger-Enquirer*, 28 November 1965; Wynn, Columbus *Enquirer*, 15 May, 1966; Galphin, *AC* 2 July 1966. "If I ever let you down," *AJ* 15 July 1966. Letter, children: *AJ* 15 July 1966. Wade in: *AC* 6 September 1966. "I've investigated charge," *AC* 10 September 1966. "No longer can voters," *ATR* 9 July 1966. Avoid crowds: *AC* 28 July 1966. Handshaking: *AJ* 1 September 1966, *AC* 6 September 1966. Opposes "home guards": *ATR* 22 September 1966. Negro educators: *ATR* 24 August 1966. Vs "rebel rousing;" Macon *Telegraph*, 3 September 1966. Trailing, polls: Macon *News* 29 July 1966. Attacks opponents: *ATR* 21 July, 11 August, 1966; *AC* 27 July, 2 September 1966; Columbus *Ledger* 11 August 1966. JC's family helps out: *ATR*, 30 August 1966; *AJ*, 15 September 1966. LC joins Peace Corps: Nanette Rainone et al, "Lillian Carter Talks About Racism, the Kennedys and 'Jimmy's Reign,' " *Ms.*, October 1976, pp. 51–52. LC, "My boy gets what he wants.": McKim Marriot/ai. Public note about LC's decision to join Peace Corps: *ATR*, 9, 16 December 1966 (in latter story, from AP, LC shown meeting snake charmers in India). *AC*, 12 December 1966. JC refuses to endorse Arnall: *AC*, 19 September 1966; AP in Valdosta *Daily Times*, 19 September 1966. JC says Maddox wins because of Republican crossover: *WNB*, p. 111.

## 6. BORN AGAIN

The best single source on the Plains church and Carter's specific religious activities is in James Hefley and Marti Hefley, *The Church That Produced a President* (New York: Wyden Books, 1977). William Lee Miller has some interesting insights in *Yankee from Georgia* (New York: Times Books, 1978) but has done less research than Hefley and Hefley, and I think he is mistaken in seeing Carter as a "puritan." James T. Baker, *A Southern Baptist in the White House* (Philadelphia: Westminster Press, 1977) pretty much takes Carter's own accounts at face value. General works describing the organization, ethics, and salvation theology of the Southern Baptists are: George D. Kelsey, *Social Ethics Among Southern Baptists, 1917–1969* (Metuchen, N.J.: The Scarecrow Press and the American Theological Library Association, 1973); Robert A. Baker, *The Southern Baptist Convention and Its People, 1607–1972* (Nashville: The Broadman Press, 1974); Norman H. Maring, *American Baptists* (Valley Forge, Pa.: The Judson Press, 1968). For comparison with the Methodist church, see Nolan H. Harmon, *The Organization of the Methodist Church* (Nashville: The Methodist Publishing House, 1962). For background on charismatic movement and baptism by fire: Prudencio Damboriena, S.J., *Tongues As of Fire* (Washington: Corpus Books, 1969).

JC's depression: *WNB*, p. 112; on "stage of life": interview with Bill Moyers (6 May 1976), *Campaign 1976*, I, 1, p. 176. RCS, JC on walk in woods: *WP*, 21 March 1976; Jules Witcover, *Marathon* (New York: Viking Press, 1977), pp. 287–88. "More intimate relationship . . .": Interview with Bill Moyers, *Campaign 1976*, I, 1, p. 176. JC on "wonderful work," "a pharisee": *WNB*, pp. 152–53. Toccoa retreat: Hoyt Robinson/ai. Details on missionary work, Lock Haven: Milo Pennington and Hoyt Robinson/ais. JC on persons saved, describes Pennington: Bruce Mazlish and Edwin Diamond, "Thrice Born," *New York*, 30 August 1976, p. 28. Pennington, "Jesus is knocking . . .": Hoyt Robinson/ai. JC with Farewells: Farewells/ais. JC, "almost a miracle": Mazlish and Diamond, *op. cit.*, p. 28. JC on politics and religion: Robinson/ai. JC letter to the Farewells: *ATR*, 11 August 1976. Springfield missionary trip: Robinson/ai (unless otherwise noted). Eloy Cruz: *WNB*, pp. 149–50. JC to Newton: Jim Newton, *World Misson Journal*, in Vertical File on JC, Lake Blackshear Library, Americus, Georgia. Billy Graham crusade: *ATR*, 11 December 1968. JC later incorrectly recalled the sequence of these events, placing the crusade before his missionary trips: speech to South Carolina Baptist Convention, 14 November 1973, transcript in *Ga. Archives*.

### Church Christian

Carter as church Christian: *WNB*, p. 151; interview with Bill Moyers, *Campaign 1976*, I, 1, p. 176.

Details on his ministers and church offices from Hefley and Hefley, *op. cit.*, pp. 193–94, 199–200, and ai with Ida Lee Timmerman. Visiting (and other) ministers on politics: *WNB*, p. 88. "Visiting minister" helps JC in 1966 campaign: Hefley and Hefley, *op. cit.*, p. 199. JC vs. "state religion": *WNB*, p. 101. JC vs. banning blacks, Plains church: *WNB*, p. 75; also, John Pope/ai. LC on vote: Beth Tartan and Rudy Hayes, *Miss Lillian and Friends* (New York: The New American Library, 1977), p. 199; Bill Schemmel, "My Son Jimmy," *Ladies' Home Journal*, August 1976, p. 142. JC takes no radical stance: Billy Wise, Frank and Virginia Williams/ais.

### Family Healing

RCS's religious evolution: Myra MacPherson, "Jimmy Carter's 'Inner Healing' Sister," *WP*, 21 March 1876; RCS, *Inner Healing*, pp. 13–14, 17–19. RCS interview with Michael Dixon, Chicago *Daily News*, 2–3 April 1977. Data on William Hardy, Gloria Carter: *ATR*, 1945. Hardy background: Brown Hodges, other Americus resident/ais. GCS's religious evolution: GCS, "Heartache of a Son Gone Wrong," *Good Housekeeping*, January 1977, pp. 56–58, 60, 63. LC's salvation experience: Lloyd Shearer, "Miz Lillian Carter: Lady of Courage and Christianity," *Parade*, 5 June 1977, p. 8. Nature of salvation experiences: Rev. Glenn Spivey, Brooks Hays, Rev. Fred Collins/ais. "To all who patiently wait . . .": James T. Baker, "Jimmy Carter's Religion," *Commonweal*, Vol. CIII, 14, 2 July 1976, p. 431. On sanctification: M. Pearlman, *Knowing the Doctrines of the Bible* (Springfield, Mo., 1937) quoted in Prudencio Damboriena, *op. cit.*, pp. 90–91. RCS's interest in charismatic movement: RCS, *Inner Healing*, pp. 84–90; GCS's: Mary Anne Thomas/ai; (there was, for a period of time, an interest in "signs" in "respectable" churches in Americus: Mary Anne Thomas, Brown Hodges/ais. RCS collapses ideal and real: "A Message for Easter," *Ladies Home Journal*, April 1977; GCS's equanimity: GCS/ai. LC on religious commitment: Lloyd Shearer, *op. cit.*, p. 8; also Claire Safran, "The Women in Jimmy Carter's Life," *Redbook*, October 1976, p. 84; Tartan and Hayes, *op. cit.*, pp. 9–10. JC's "passing interest": he lent Mary Anne Thomas a book of GCS's on speaking in tongues. Mary Anne Thomas/ai. JC prays frequently: interview with Bill Moyers, *Campaign 76*, I, p. 165. JC on Christian vulnerability: Interview with Jim Newton, *World Mission Journal*, n.d., in Lake Blackshear Library, Americus, Georgia. JC on "search": speech before United Methodist Conference, Atlanta, 1974, *Ga. Archives*. JC on good politician: interview with Jim Newton, *op. cit.* JC on loser: *WNB*, p. 112.

## 7.  WINNING

Decision to run: Philip Alston/ai. JC Appreciation Dinner: *AJ*, 5 November 1966. Charles Kirbo on JC: ai. JC on building contacts: *WNB*, p. 112–13. JC on Democratic Party: 9 September 1968. JC on conservatism: *AC*, 8 March 1969. JC on merit, other stands: *AC*, 21 November 1969. JC supports Nixon: *AC*, 18 October 1969. Pou on JC: Charles Pou, *AC*, 14 April 1969. Jordan and Powell: biographies in *Ga. Register*, 1971–72; *AJ*, 7 April 1970; *AJ*, 28 July 1970; and Kandy Stroud, *How Jimmy Won* (New York: William Morrow, 1977), pp. 181–84, 233–35. JC's polls: *WNB*, p. 114. Atlanta influentials: Philip Alston, Robert Lipshutz, John Pope/ais. Political cast: Brooks Pennington, J. Frank Meyers, John Pope, Hugh Carter, L. C. Godwin/ais. JC campaigns: Hoyt Robinson and Joe Andrews/ais. JCs 1970 plan: Bill Shipp's report in *AC* 8 November 1970.

### Primary Battle: the Low Road

JC announcement speech: *ATR*, 3 April 1970; *AC*, 4 April 1970. Plains rally: *ATR*, 6 April 1970. JC strategy: Steve Ball, *AJ*, 7 April 1970, see also *ATR*, 26 March 1970. TV attack on Sanders: *AJ*, 8 May 1970. JC's financial statement: *AJ*, 18 June 1970. Sanders plane number: *AJC*, 28 June 1970. Sanders on "smear," FAA: *AC*, 30 June 1970. JC's quote on Sanders and Fuqua in 1966: *AC*, 10 July 1970. Sanders "I told him . . .": *AC*, 10 July 1970. JC letter: *AC*, 16 July 1970. Sanders's expenditures: *AC*, 26 June 1971; *AJ*, 25 June 1971. JC TV spots: Bill Shipp, *AC*, 21 July 1970. JC on Wallace: *AC*, 26 August 1970. JC "proof package": *AC*, 27 August 1970. JC on contributors: *AJC*, 30 August, 1970. Sanders, JC "penny antiest" politician: *AC*, 27 August 1970. JC, "I've been accused . . .: Macon *Telegraph*, 28 August 1970. JC on Atlanta papers' bias: *AJ*, 18 June 1970; *AJC*, 28 June 1970; *AC*, 17 August, 3 September 1970. JC threat, Reg Murphy: Reg Murphy/al. JC's debt to Anne Cox Chambers: from contributors' list, published 1976; *AC*, 18 October 1976; JC to Anne Cox Chambers, 10 May 1973, *Ga. Archives*. Carter platform: *AJC*, 29 July 1970. JC on national guard: *AC*, 14 July 1970. In the fall he said he might give "shoot to kill" orders: Selby McCash, Macon *News*, 26, 29 October 1970. JC on drugs: *AC*, 29 July 1970. JC progressive stands: *AJ*, 5 August 1970; *AC*, 14 July 1970; *AC*, 26, 28 August 1970. JC at South River: *AJ*, 5 August 1970. JC on schools: *AJ*, 27 July 1970; *AC*, 28 August 1970. Advertisement against "black" vote: *Campaign Commercials*. JC to appoint black leaders: *AC*, 3 September 1970. Sanders platform: Selby McCash, Macon *Telegraph*, 2 August 1970. JC on Russell: *AC*, 8 July 1970. Russell denial: *AC*, 8 July 1970. JC claims "misquote," "off the record": Beau Cutts/al. JC endorsed by Vandiver, Griffin: *AJ*, 16 August 1970; *AC*, 4 September 1970. "Dirty tricks," cuff links ad: Bill Shipp, *AC*, 27 July 1970. Abernathy, Wood stories: ais; Phil Stanford, "Carter," *Citizen's Guide to the 1976 Presidential Primaries* (Washington, D.C.: Capitol Hill News Service, 1976), pp. 21–23. Pederson

story: *AC*, 15 October 1976. C. B. King (ai) told me he was out of funds at the time those radio advertisements appeared and has no idea who paid for them. Jody Powell later denied all these dirty tricks in a memorandum rebutting charges raised by Steven Brill: *BG*, 6 February 1976. Some of his proofs were ingenuous —for example, Carter could not have distributed copies of a picture showing Hubert Humphrey and Carl Sanders together because that day Carter was on vacation; there was no commercial showing money changing hands the way Brill described it. (But there were two commercials that Powell briefly describes that could well have had components of the exchange.) For an analysis of the Brill charges, Powell's response, and a discussion of other research that suggests the Carter organization's responsibility for such "dirty tricks," see Phil Stanford, "The Most Remarkable Piece of Fiction Jimmy Carter Ever Read," *Columbia Journalism Review*, July/August 1976. Steve Ball on Carter: *AJC*, 18 July 1970. JC's victory over the establishment: AJ, 10 September 1970.

### Run-Off: the High Road

Sanders attack: AC, 12, 13 September 1970; *AJ*, 14 September 1970. JC responds: *AJ*, 16 September 1970. JC, "I am a Christian . . .": *AJC*, 20 September 1970; JC also accused Sanders of moving his campaign "to the gutter,": *AC*, 21 September 1970. Carter on debate: *AJ*, 19 September 1970; also Macon *Telegraph*, 13 September 1970. "Sick man," then retraction: *AC*, 18 September 1970. Competitive leafletting: *AJC*, 20 September 1970; *AC*, 21 September 1970. For a discussion of the competitive leafletting, Carter's subtle, double-edged use of the race issue in the 1970 campaign, see Reg Murphy and Hal Gulliver, "Jimmy Who?" in *The Southern Strategy* (New York: Charles Scribner's Sons, 1971), pp. 173–197. JC "buddy system": *AJ*, 14 September 1970. Election results: *AC*, 21 September 1970.

### General Election

Carter debates Suit, for capital punishment: AC, 24 September 1970. Gillis, Fuqua support, quotes: Macon *News*, 7 October 1970. Corporate contributions: *AC*, 18 October 1976; *NYT*, 18 October 1976. JC on Andrew Young: *AJ*, 21 October 1970. JC on Lester Maddox: *AJ*, 7 October 1970; *AC*, 21 October 1970. JC: Harris out: 16 October 1970. JC meets Roy Harris: Roy Harris/ai; *AC*, 15 September 1970; *AJ*, 16 October 1970. Harris to vote for JC: *AC*, 15 September 1970. JC defends Harris before Atlanta Hungry Club: *AJ*, 22 October 1970; *AC*, 26 October 1970. JC vacillations on Harris: Duane Riner, *AC*, 20 October 1970. JC identifies with political establishment: *AJC*, 1 November 1970. JC on media: *AJC*, 1 November 1970. Populism: C. Vann Woodward, *Tom Watson, Agrarian Rebel* (New York: Rinehart and Co., Inc. 1938), pp. 216–20. Talmage-style populism: V. O. Key, *Southern Politics* (New York: Vintage Books, 1949), pp. 116–17.

## 8.  THE COMPLEAT POLITICIAN

Details on Carter's routine as governor and the responsibilities of his aides are drawn mainly from Bill Beazley, with extra details from Bill Pope, Duane Riner, Rita Samuels, and Frank Moore/ais., as checked against Carter's calendars, and interoffice memos, which are in the governor's papers in the Georgia Archives in Atlanta. (There is a good index to the governor's papers in the archives, so I shall simply identify items used here by author and/or recipient, subject matter, and date, where given.) Materials on the background and responsibilities of Carter aides are

from these same sources, plus biographies in the *Ga. Register*. The background and roles of Atlanta influentials in his administration come from Phil Alston, Charles Kirbo, Peter Gambrell, Joseph Andrews/ais; and William Gunter/aq. Carter's management of the Democratic Party is derived from Charles Kirbo, Joseph Andrews, and Marge Thurman/ais; and lists of party officials found in *Ga. Register*, 1971–72, 1972–73.

For Carter's resort to spoils politics, I have checked the annual *Ga. Register* and the *Ga. SJ and*

Ga. Manual (both of which carry lists of state officers) against a list of political friends compiled from my interviews and questionnaires. Beyond that, there are extensive memoranda and correspondence in the governor's papers that show that Carter and his aides were explicitly concerned with rewarding friends. I have cited here only the items most directly relevant.

Carter's relationship with business has been reconstructed mainly from his desk calendars (which show his trip arrangements) and his correspondence with leaders from several major firms based in Atlanta.

Inaugural descriptions and quotes: Celestine Sibley, AC, 13 January 1971. JC's inaugural remarks on race: AJ, 13 January 1971; Addresses, p. 79. Yolande Gwinn on sunshine halo: AJ, 18 January 1971.

## Supports

JC on swimming pool, etc.: Bill Shipp, AC, 6, 28 May 1971. The executive suite and thirteen other offices at the state capitol also were refurbished. Among the changes were installation of royal blue plush carpet and hanging of works by various Georgia artists, including Lamar Dodd. The press release on the remodeling suggested JC was being very frugal, comparing original estimates for the job of $75,000, to the final cost of $15,244.61, with much of the work being done by the staff of the Georgia Building Authority: AJ, 6 April 1971. On Rosalynn's gatekeeper role: Americus friend/ai: ATR, 29 May 1970; AC, 23 June 1973; Rabhan, Jeff Carter: NYT, 5 December 1976. See also: William Gunter to JC: 23 February 1973, Ga. Archives. On Amy AJ, 14 March 1971; Irene Horne/ai. Staff aides: See introduction to this chapter's notes. Powell's popularity: wire service reporter, Atlanta/ai. Powell letter to constituents: AC, 16 March 1972. Powell on JC speech drafts: quotes here from penciled notes on draft of JC's presidential announcement speech, Ga. Archives. Powell quotes that "there are still numerous . . . ," "I hope you have not . . .": Jody Powell to JC, 25 April 1973. Ga. Archives. Bill Hamilton on "bigwigs": Hamilton to JC, 15 April 1971, Ga. Archives. Rafshoon on JC tour: Rafshoon to JC, 11 September 1973, Ga. Archives. Rafshoon offers advice: e.g., penciled notes on drafts of JC presidential announcement speech, Ga. Archives. Other contracts: NYT, 4 April 1976; AC, 4 April 1976. On Kirbo: The "unprecedented" move of giving a nonofficer an office, Powell explained, was not important; Powell said Kirbo would not be using it a great deal and it would be available as a small conference room for the executive department as when Kirbo was not there: AC, 13 April 1971.

## Routine

Handling of mail: Betty Rainwater to JC, n.d., and D. Rogers to JC, 12 March 1972, GA. Archives. Jordan to JC on handwritten notes: 15 November 1972, Ga. Archives, JC to Johnson, 18 December 1972, Ga. Archives. JC on his handwritten notes: AJ, 30 September 1971. "Speak Up Day": AC, 7 April 1971; AC 7 October 1971. JC social rounds: AC, 30 September 1971. JC at local events: AC, 11 March 1971. Sunday night group: John Pope/ai; AC, 10 April 1971. JC out-of-state trips: aside from desk calendars, see also AC, 8 September 1973. Gift of bird-hunting clothes: Jack Crockford to JC, 9 November 1972, Ga. Archives. "He doesn't spend any time . . .": quote from Phil Stanford, "Jimmy Carter," Citizen's Guide to the Presidential Candidates, 1976 (Washington, D.C.: Capitol Hill News Service, 1976), p. 27. JC "lax on attire": AC, 5 February 1971. JC delegates authority: Mary Beazley/ai. Jordan chairs meeting: AC, 24 November 1971.

## Spoils

JC on office resources: AC, 11 September 1974, JC changes party leaders Thurman and Trotter: Joseph Andrews, David Gambrell, Marjorie Thurman/ais; AJ, 11 May 1972; and party officers listed in Ga. Register for 1971–72, as of 1970–71. Senate appointment: David Gambrell/ai; and Hugh Carter and Frances Spatz, Cousin Beedie and Cousin Hot (Englewood Cliffs, N.J.: Prentice-Hall, 1978). pp. 141–42. Campaign funds to JC: Jimmy Deriso to JC, 19 July 1972; JC to Jimmy Deriso, 27 July 1972, Ga. Archives. New jobs to fill: T. McNeill Simpson, "Georgia State Administration: Jimmy Carter's Contribution," paper presented at Southern Political Science Association, Atlanta, 1973, pp. 3, 4. JC appoints Robinson: Hoyt Robinson/ai. JC appoints other friends: this date derived through checking JC's 1970 contributor list (AJ, 18 September 1976) against new appointees listed in Ga. Register, 1971–72, 1972–73, 1973–74. Aided by Kirbo, "of those persons . . .": Charles Kirbo to Bruce Kirbo, 8 April 1971, Ga. Archives; and Hugh Carter's memorandum, "Supporters Wanting Appointments," n.d., Ga. Archives. Tickets for family and friends: Frank Moore to Hugh Carter, 16 May 1973; LC to JC, March, n.d., 1972, Ga. Archives. JC told "Ham" on mother's request, "This is very important" (JC's underline), n.d., Ga. Archives.

## Symbols

Reunions for family and friends: desk calendars, Ga. Archives; Lottie Tanner/ai. Stock car drivers at mansion: AC, 2, 3 April 1971. JC on Dylan: Law Day Speech, U. of Ga., Athens, Ga., May 4, 1974, Addresses, p. 257. Acquainted with Otis Redding: "Playboy Interview," November 1976, in Campaign 1976, p. 957. "State Capital for a Day": AJC, 31 October 1971, and AC, 15 December 1971. Powell on TV coverage: J. Powell to JC, n.d., Ga. Archives. JC woos blacks, appointment of Jenkins: AJ, 13 January 1971. Morris Brown College degree: AC, 2 June 1971. Idea for King portrait: R. J. Samuels to JC, 13 March 1973, Ga. Archives. Selection committee, appointment, process, results: Haynes Walton, Jr./al; also AH, 17 October 1973. Mandus offers to paint portraits: minutes of the portrait selection committee, Friday, 9 November 1973, Ga. Archives. Hiding the canvas: George Mandus/ai. Fear JC called a "King lover": Rita Samuels and Jody Powell to JC, 14 November 1973, Ga. Archives. Unveiling ceremony: AC, 18 February, 1974.

## Self-Presentation

Could make money, "criticism never bothered . . ." "What It's Like To Be Governor," AJC Sunday Magazine, 18 August 1974: Addresses, pp. 51–52. Carter was critical of the press for its coverage of reorganization: Beau Cutts, AC, 2 October 1971. Retarded cousins: Speech to Georgia Psychiatrists, 9 September 1972, Addresses, pp. 149. "My nature . . ." Speech at Governors Education Conference, 10 May 1974, Addresses, p. 268. "I still am heavily influenced . . .": Speech to Georgia Association of Broadcasters, 13 June 1972, Addresses, p. 136. JC also implied at times a protégé relationship with Russell: Bill Shipp, AC, 23 January 1971. Rides Bull Sluice rapids: National Enquirer 4 January 1977. Anticipates jail: AJ, 5 January 1973.

## Business Connections

Big business model for reorganization: Speech to Chartered Property, Casualty Underwriters, 12 September 1974, Addresses, p. 277; government officials "icing on a cake": Speech to Atlanta District Export Council, 17 September 1974, AC, 18 September 1974.

Promotes Lockheed; Dan Haughton Day: *AJ*, 23 June 1971, *AC*, 29 July 1971: trip to Brazil: JC desk calendars, *Ga. Archives; WP* and *AC*, 4 April 1972. On C-130 Hercules: JC to R. Roche, 5 May 1972, *Ga. Archives*. Europe and Israel trip: Carter trip schedule in *Ga. Archives;* planning failure *AJ*, 17 May 1973; other details of trip: *AJ*, 17, 23, 29, 31 May 1973; *AC*, 25, 31 May 1973. Anwar Sadat and Coca-Cola: JC to R. J. McCloskey, 15 August 1976, *Ga. Archives;* a vice-president of the Coca-Cola company suggested the invitation: Ovid Davis to Frank Moore, 7 August 1974, *Ga. Archives*. Georgia offered for filming of "Hec Ramsey": JC to J. Wells, 9 January 1974, *Ga. Archives;* aids *Longest Yard:* Al Ruddy to JC, 14 November 1973, *Ga. Archives*. Backs legislation on tape-pirating bill: *New Times*, 3 September 1976, *Rolling Stone*, 9 September 1976. Peanut rot: Gary Miller/ai. Hodgson appointment: *AC*, 24 January 1976. JC on Coca-Cola State Department: Speech, Commission on Foreign Relations, 12 November 1964, *Addresses*, pp. 281–82; Lockheed trips: Desk Calendars, *Ga. Archives*. Coca-Cola transportation to Southern Governors' Conference, Ovid Davis to Frank Moore, 4 September 1974. (See also JC entries on his desk calendar for 1 February 1979: "Mary contact Earl Leonard of Coca-Cola . . . for limousine service from Airport to Hilton.") *Ga. Archives*. Lumber companies: Desk Calendars, *Ga. Archives*. Campaign favors: On bank deposits: J. B. Dodd, Jr. (complaint) to "Ham" (n.d.,

circa 1 April 1971); and J. B. Dodd (thank you) to Hamilton Jordan, 6 April 1971, *Ga. Archives*. JC lashes out at Georgia Power: *AC*, 5 March 1971. Commends them for green belts: *AC*, 2 July 1971; receives Palisades donation: Edwin I. Hatch to JC, 17 May 1972 (JC made note on Hatch letter, to an aide: "Write profuse thanks—Let me sign.") *Ga. Archives*. Subsequent disputes with Georgia Power: over proposed rate increases: *AC* 5 December 1974; over energy usage: JC to E. I. Hatch, 10 December 1973, *Ga. Archives*. Corporate contributions, narcotics program, donors list; JC executive correspondence, Box 58, *Ga. Archives;* JC accepts personal donations: 1970 campaign contributions: JC to Anne and Bobby Chambers, 10 May 1973, *Ga. Archives*. Rabhan relationships: *NYT*, 5 December 1976.

### Alliances

Hugh Carter doesn't receive Senate job: Hugh Carter and Frances Spatz, *op. cit.*, pp. 140–44. Nunn incident: *AC*, 20 May and 30 August 1972. JC supports Nunn: *AC*, 30 August 1972. JC proud of Nunn: JC to Nunn, *Ga. Archives*. "Piggyback poll": *AJ*, 5 December 1973, *AC*, 7 November 1973, and 1, 4 December 1973. Copy of poll in author's possession. Lance praise of JC: Bert Lance to JC, 20 July 1972, *Ga. Archives*. JC praise of Lance: JC to Bert Lance, 2 March 1973, *Ga. Archives*.

## 9. MAKING A RECORD

Reorganization study teams: *AJ* 4 February 1971. Business lobbyists on study teams: *AC*, 29 April 1971. JC on value of business participation: *WNB*, p. 131. JC on tax savings through business donations; JC asks Moore for labor names: *AJ*, 3 June 1971. Make-up of executive committee: *AJ*, 6 April 1971. Quote, JC "working just as hard": James Wooten, *NYT*, 17 May 1976. JC sells reorganization to public: *AJ*, 15 February 1971; Bell and Stanton: *AC*, 29 May 1971. Rafshoon on citizen involvement: G. Rafshoon to JC, Reported in *AC*, 9 June 1971. JC travels, Goals for Georgia project: *AJ*, 12 August 1971. JC, "We spelled out . . .": *WNB*, p. 130–131. JC on reaction of public: *AC*, 16 August 1971. Bill Harper plans "spontaneous reaction": Memo to JC 24 November 1971, *Ga. Archives*. "Citizens Committee for Reorganization": *AC*, 28 December 1971. JC assures department heads: *AC*, 2 April 1971. JC instructions to study groups: *AC*, 15 June 1971. Negative reaction to plan: *AJ*, 29 July 1971; *AC*, 9 September 1971. Departmental vetoes and rejection by JC: *AC*, 21 December 1971, 23 February 1972. Legal challenge by Caldwell: *AJ*, 31 December 1971. Court delays action: *AC*, 8 January 1972. JC not to implement reverse veto: *AC*, 8 January 1972. Harper on advantage of legal delay: *AJ*, 8 January 1972. Ben Fortson at EREG Committee: *AC*, 14 December 1971. Busbee and Smith support reorganization: *AJ*, 19 January 1972. JC compromises, wins GOP support: *AC*, 12 January 1972. Maddox on senate role: *AJ*, 15 January 1972. Holley quote: *AJ*, 12 January 1972. JC conciliatory: *AJ*, 12 January 1972. JC condemns Gillis: *AJ*, 21 January 1972. Rewrite of sections of bill: *AJ*, 21 January 1972. JC assurance on reverse veto: *AC*, 26 January 1972. Further senate problems: *AC*, 26 January 1972; *AJ*, 17 February 1972. Omnibus bill passes: *AJC*, 2 April 1972. JC, "I had to browbeat . . ." Harry Murphy, *AJ*, 26 December 1971. JC, "I intend to fight . . .": *AJ*, 28 July 1971. JC labels opponents selfish: *AJ*, 11 December 1971. JC crusade: *AC*, 11 December 1971. Riner on JC: *AC*, 11 December 1971. JC in Macon on EREG: *AJ*, 17 December 1971. JC on "inquisitorial" committee: *AJ*, 30 December 1971. Footnote on selfish opposi-

tion: *WNB*, p. 130. JC compromises to secure reorganization: T. McNeill Simpson, "Georgia State Administration: Jimmy Carter's Contribution," paper presented at Southern Political Science Association, Atlanta, 1973; and Simpson, "One Appraisal of the Carter Administration: 1971–1974," *Georgia Political Science Association Journal*, Vol. IV, No. 2, Fall 1976. Others on JC compromises: Robert Shaw/al; Carl Sanders/ai; Tom Murphy/al, ai. JC on reorganization: *WNB*, p 128.

### Proving Ground

Jordan on DHR: *AJC*, 7 May 1972. Composition of DHR: *Georgia, Reorganization and Management Improvement Study*, 1970, pp. 109–120. MAG objections to DHR: *AC*, 2 April 1972. Dowda on MAG position: *AC*, 7 April 1972. Jordan to get around MAG: Jordan to JC. Memo, undated, *Ga. Archives*. Background on MAG and how to deal with it: Stan Jones to JC: memo, 15 March 1972, *Ga. Archives*. JC appointments to board: *AC*, 7 April 1972. MAG/JC formula: *AC*, 16 April 1972. JC's medical nominees, Watson, and Lipshutz: *AC*, 12 May 1972. Jim Parham and J. Battle Hall in DHR: *AC*, 10 March 1972. Parham, de facto head of DHR: *AC*, 14 April 1972 and *AC*, 7 April 1972. Selection of Richard Harden: Gary Miller/al; Richard Harden/ai. Harden's Division of Community Services: press release, DHR, 24 October 1972. Backs uniform statewide system: Harden memo to Jack Watson, and Watson to all employees: 20 October 1972, *Ga. Archives*. "Service area" concept developed: Harden memo to McIntyre, 20 July 1973; Harden to all employees, 25 May 1973; *Watson to Harden*, 13 July 1973, *Ga. Archives*. Funding difficulties: Steven Chandler to JC, 3 October 1973, *Ga. Archives*. Internal bickering in DHR: Simpson, "Georgia State" and "One Appraisal." Miller's past work: Joseph A. Hertell, M.D., to Gary Miller, 29 May 1977, provided author by Dr. Miller. Miller plans for DHR: Miller/al. Special award from Georgia Psychological Association: Jim Parham letter, 21 May 1976, *Ga. Archives*, Miller's problems with Harden, Watson, General Assembly: *AC*, 27 May, 25 August 1972, Battle Hall to

Gary Miller, 16 June 1972, *Ga. Archives*. Miller controversy with Ga. Psychiatric Association: Turner to Miller, 16 November 1973; Miller Memo to Parham, 11 August 1972, *Ga. Archives*. Kidd to Texas, attacks Miller: *AJ*, 9 August 1973. Background on Miller conflict with Kidd: Beverly Long to James A. Mackay, 23 October 1973, *Ga. Archives;* Culver Kidd to Richard Harden, 15 January 1973. *Ga. Archives*. Mrs. H. E. Butt (on Miller) to JC, 14 September 1973, *Ga. Archives*. Kidd attacks "open door policy": *AC*, 19 October 1973. JC backs Miller: *AC*, 29 October 1973. Miller-Harden relations: B. Long to J. Watson, 15 June 1973, *Ga. Archives;* see also memo R. D. Gay to R. Harden, 17 October 1973, *Ga. Archives*. (Miller saw his own relationship as better than that: Miller/al.) House inquiry into DHR: Thomas B. Murphy to Lester Maddox 21 March 1974, *Ga. Archives*. Miller et al. at Jekyll Island: Miller/al. Miller background, call to JC: Miller/ai; also general summary Miller to his attorneys, 16 October 1975 (provided author by Miller). JC, "Gary tells me . . .": JC to Jack Watson, 6 April 1974, *Ga. Archives*. Watson on Miller dismissal: Watson to JC, 6 April 1974, *Ga. Archives*. JC with Miller after dismissal: Miller/ai. JC, no politics in dismissal: JC to B. Long, 6 May 1974, *Ga. Archives*. JC assures Bond: JC to Julian Bond, 10 June 1974, *Ga. Archives*. JC press conference: *AC*, 9 April 1974. Miller legal action: Miller/ai. Extra Miller payment: JC to Frank Moore, 16 May 1974, *Ga. Archives*. Final pay arrangement: G. Miller/al. Skelton appointment: Savannah News, 19 April 1974. DHR audit by Ernest Davis: *AC*, 8 January 1974. Later audit: *AC*, 8 January 1974; *AJ*, 26 January 1974. JC meets house leaders: reported, *AC*, 28 April 1974. Harden meets JC often: Harden/ai. JC compliments: JC to R. Harden and R. Watson, 19 July 1973, *Ga. Archives;* JC to Harden: 24 July 1974. Criticism: JC to R. Harden, *AC*, 10 July 1974. Harden resignation: *AJ*, 19 September 1974. Basic problems of DHR: Jim Parham (draft for discussion), "The Basic Problems of DHR", 9 September 1974, *Ga. Archives*. Busbee changes DHR: *AC*, 12 May 1975.

### Reorganization: The Results

JC on special interests: Harry Murphy, *AJ*, 27 December 1971. Reorganization increased governor's authority: T. McNeill Simpson "One Appraisal," pp. 96–98. Footnote on education, personnel: *AJ*, 5 July 1972. Reorganization and state merit system: Simpson, "One Appraisal," p. 97. Reduction of agencies: *AJC*, 7 April 1971; 2 April 1972. Problems of centralization: Simpson, "Georgia State Administration," p. 11. Caldwell on centralized computer system: George Lardner, *WP*, 28 February 1976. JC on reorganization savings: *AJC*, 7 November 1971; *AC*, 21 July 1972. JC on percentage decrease, administration costs: 28 June 1973, *Ga. Archives*. Capital costs in motor pool: Culver Kidd to JC, 28 February 1973, *Ga. Archives*. Savings, job cuts: Nixon/ai. JC quote on rate of increase in jobs: JC memo, 28 June 1973, *Ga. Archives;* see also *AC*, 29 July 1972.

### Zero-Based Budgeting

Overview of zero-based budgeting in Georgia: George S. Minmier and Roger H. Hermanson, "A Look at Zero-Base Budgeting—The Georgia Experience," *Atlantic Economic Review*, July-August 1976, pp. 5–12. Zero-based budgeting in State of State address: 11 January 1972. *Addresses*, p. 125. JC, zero-based budgeting "extremely valuable": quoted in Minmier and Hermanson, *op. cit.*, p. 6. Governor not review all decision packages: Robert N. Anthony, "Zero-Based Budgeting Is a Fraud," *WSJ*, 27 April

1977. "Only cursory examination" of spending: *Ibid*. Zero-based budgeting and change in availability of funds: Minmier and Hermanson, *op. cit.*, p. 9. Only two department heads see allocation change: *Ibid.*, p. 7.

### Protecting the Environment

JC on natural resources: *WNB*, p. 133. Increased spending on national resources: Furman Smith, "Environmental Law—The Carter Years," *Georgia State Bar Journal*, Vol. 13, No. 3, 1977, p. 110. Strengthening enforcement: Neal Peirce, *The Deep South States of America* (New York: W.W. Norton, 1974), p. 334. Promotes land use planning: Smith, *op. cit.*, p. 111. JC withholds permits, etc.: *AC*, 22 July 1971; *AJ*, 9 July 1971. JC establishes Georgia Heritage and Trust Commission: *WNB*, p. 135. JC and I-485: *AC*, 20 October 1972. Editorial on JC's I-495 poll: *AJ*, 7 November 1973. Deadlock on I-75: *AJ*, 6 July 1971; quote from *Village Voice*, 18 October 1976.

### System of Justice

Ellis MacDougall reforms corrections system: *AJ*, 21 May 1971; *AC*, 2 July 1971. JC urges probation: *AC*, 28 December 1974. Judicial reactions: *AJ*, 5 March 1974. JC may refuse inmates: *AJ*, 16 October 1974. JC attempts to reform GBI: *AJ*, 7 January 1972; *AJ*, 19 November 1971, and *AJ*, 22 October 1974. Civil Disorders Unit: T. McNeill Simpson, unpublished manuscript, Ch. 6, p.5. JC on prison riots: *AJ*, 16 September 1971; electronic surveillance: Phil Stanford, "Carter," *Citizen's Guide to the 1976 Presidential Candidates* (Washington, D.C.: Capitol Hill News Service, 1976), p. 13; death penalty: *WP*, 29 March 1973; rape advertisement and Powell comment to JC on "vocal" women: *AJ*, 21 November 1973. JC on organized crime: *AC*, 5 October 1974; on gun registration: *AJ*, 4 October 1974; on drug legislation, on judicial reforms: Judge Hall/ai; T. McNeill Simpson, "Restyling Georgia Courts," *Judicature*, Vol. 59, No. 6, January 1976.

### Affirmative and Nonaffirmative Action

JC to anti-ERA group: *AC*, 17 January 1972. RC demonstrates for ERA: *AJ*, 18 January 1972. NAACP and Atlanta busing plan: Julian Bond/ai. Blockbusting law: HB 1615, *Ga. HJ*. Andrew Young to JC: 26 May 1971, *Ga. Archives*. JC asks chairman of Real Estate Commission to step down: JC to E. A. Isakson, 6 January 1972, *Ga. Archives*. Enforcement of blockbusting law: H. Jordan to JC, undated memo, *Ga. Archives;* Bill Harper to JC, 21 June 1971, *Ga. Archives*. Statement of JC: 28 February 1972, *Ga. Archives*. JC appoints commission members: *AC*, 24 June 1972. Nothing changes: Report of Atlanta Community Relations Commission on Real Estate Commission: April 1976, *Ga. Archives*. Rev. Hope on black employment: *AC*, 9 October 1972. JC to SCLC on minority appointments: 20 February 1973, *Ga. Archives; AJ*, 31 October 1971, *AC*, 9 August 1976. Figures on black, female employment: Governor's Commission on Human Relations: 1973, *Ga. Archives*. JC, "indefensible situation": letter from JC, 16 February 1973, *Ga. Archives*. Harden incident: July 1973, *Ga. Archives*. JC against quotas: Office release, 11 July 1973, *Ga. Archives*. JC record on employing minorities: John Martin and David Fox to JC, 18 February 1974, *Ga. Archives*. Bill Hamilton, "stylistic populist": *WP*, 7 May 1976. JC inaugural quote: *Addresses*, p. 81. John Crown on JC: *AJ*, 22 January 1973. Piggyback poll: *AJ*, 5 December 1973.

## 10.  LEGISLATIVE FRONT

Materials in this section are drawn mainly from the Georgia Archives in the Atlanta *Journal*, the Atlanta *Constitution*, and the Georgia Senate and House Journals. The following persons, all of whom have served in the General Assembly, provided useful background information on Carter's political style (some have differing perspectives from mine): Julian Bond, Hugh Carter, J. Battle Hall, Al Holloway, Pete McDuffey, Janet Merritt, Brooks Pennington, Robert Smalley, Hoyt Robinson, Bobby Rowan, Andrew Young. The following journalists and/or public-relations persons were also helpful: Beau Cutts, Roy V. Harris, Reg Murphy, David Nordan, Duane Riner, Bill Pope, and Bill Shipp.

Carter's on combative governorship: *WNB*, p. 126. Jordan on Carter not making deals: *AC*, 27 November 1971; and "Carter on the Rise," *NW*, 8 March 1976, p. 29. Duane Riner, JC own worst enemy: AJC, 9 January 1972. Carter fight over Smalley: *AJC*, 8 November 1970; *AC*, 6 November 1970. Carter on Maddox's anger: *AJC*, 8 November 1970. Maddox, "if I crossed him . . .": "Jekyll and Hyde," *NW*, 17 July 1976, p. 25. Composition of EREG Committee: *Ga. Register*, 1971–1972, p. 437. Marcus, "Most people have . . .": *AJC*, 9 January 1972. Aides' insensitivity: *AC*, 28 February 1971. Carter signals he will bargain: *AJ*, 11 and 13 March 1971. JC threatens to go to the people: *AC*, 19 December 1971. Carter woos legislators: *AJ*, 20 January 1972. Jody Powell on proposed busing amendment: routing sheet on letter of John T. Bowman to Jimmy Carter, 8 October 1971, *Ga. Archives*. Busing resolution passes and footnote, Johnson speech: *Ga SJ*, 1972, pp. 428–431. Also *Ga. HJ*, 1972, pp. 1661–3. Sutton's liaison duties: *AJC*, 9 January 1972. Road resurfacing: JC to Lance, 16 May 1972, *Ga. Archives*. Road projects, Sumter County: Robert L. Pitts to Ray Baldwin, 11 September 1971, *Ga. Archives*. Funds for emergencies only: Jimmy Carter to Dr. Jim Hinson, 28 November 1972, *Ga. Archives*. JC, "Let him ask me": JC note on Frank Moore to JC, 19 November 1973, *Ga. Archives*. "Full political advantage": Jordan to Spinks and Riner, 14 June 1972, *Ga. Archives*. Help for Bert Hamilton: Hamilton Jordan memo to JC, 12 September 1972, *Ga. Archives*. List of allotments: Emergency Fund, FY, 1973, *Ga. Archives*. Carter appoints friends: Hamilton Jordan to Jimmy Carter, 12 September 1972, *Ga. Archives*; and *Ga. Register*, 1971–1972, 1973–1974. JC punishes Hugh Gillis's brother: *AJ*, 18 May 1973. JC threatens Senator Dean: *AC*, 12 January 1974. JC criticizes Bagby: *AC*, 19 July 1974. JC tries to pack Democratic caucus, Johnson is "his own man": *AC*, 16 November 1972; See also *Ga. SJ*, 1973, pp. 9–24. Efforts to reorganize the Senate: *Ga. SJ*, 1973. JC-Smith conflict on budget: *AJ*, 2 January 1974, *AJ*, 12 January 1973; and *Ga. HJ*, 1973. Carter attacks house budget: *Addresses*, p. 177; response to speech: *AJ*, 11 January 1972. Battle over appropriations bill: *AJ*, 20 February 1973; *AJ*, 20 February 1973; *AJ*, 27 March 1973. Consumer protection bills: *AC*, 27 September 1972. Details on credit code law: *AC*, 26 January 1973; 9 and 16 February 1973, *AC*, 3 March 1973: *Ga. HJ*, 1973, pp. 1585–1604, 1826–1843. David Nordan on "rupture": *AJ*, 14 February 1974; also *AC*, 3 March 1974. JC to cut budget: *AC*, 4, 18 January 1974. Legislature line-itemizes budget: *AJ*, 11 January 1974. JC compliments legislature: *AC*, 23 January 1974. JC responds to line-

item budget: *AJC*, 27 January 1974 and *AC*, 24 January 1974. JC backs down: *AJC*, 27 January 1974. Carter and Floyd meet: *AJ*, 30 January 1974. Carter supports cost-of-living increases; *AC* 9 February 1974. Carter vetoes tax relief: *AC*, 29 March 1974. Carter signs budget: *AJ*, 3 April 1974. JC bills don't pass in the form he recommends: *AC*, 4 January 1974. JC's "greatest disappointment": Phil Stanford, "Carter," *Citizen's Guide to the 1976 Presidential Candidates* (Washington, D.C.: Capitol Hill News Service, 1976), p. 11. Consumer protection effort too late: *AJ*, 21 March 1974. Consumer protection bill fails: Stanford, *op. cit.*, p. 11. Interest rates too high: *AC*, 14 February 1974. Howell Raines maintains that in 1974 Carter and his staff made no coordinated effort to get administration bills through The General Assembly showed a strange "indifference to the consumer protection legislation which he had been talking about all year.": *AC*, 3 March 1974. JC's ethics bill: *AJ*, 26 October 1973; *AC*, 12 January 1974; Howell Raines, "Georgia: The Politics of Campaign Reform," in *Campaign Money: Reform and Reality in the States*, Herbert E. Alexander, ed., (New York: Free Press, 1976). JC, "no major defects . . .": Raines, *op. cit.*, p. 189. General Assembly overrides JC vetoes: *AC*, 4 January 1974. Tax relief for elderly: *AJ*, 10 January 1974; on its constitutionality: *AC*, 24 January 1974, and *Ga. SJ*, 1974. Dam project: *AC*, 2 October 1973; *AJ*, 3 October 1973, and *AJ*, 15 February 1974. Checked against *Ga. SJ*, 1974. For general background: Furman Smith, Jr, "Fundamental Law—The Carter Years," *Georgia State Bar Journal*, February 1977, pp. 110–111. JC blasts legislative leaders: *AJ*, 14 February 1974. Groover responds: *AJ*, 14 February 1974. House debating mood: *AC*, 15 February 1974. Senate fight: *AJ*, 4 March 1974 and *Ga. SJ*, 1974, p. 2511. Holloway on JC: *AH*, 7 March 1976. Like many Georgians, Al Holloway, then vice-chairman of the Georgia Democratic Party, later supported his party's candidate for President. *AH*, 29 October 1976. JC, "intense lobbying efforts . . .": *AJ*, 4 March 1974. "Parole mill" controversy: *AC* and *AJ*, August through October, 1972. Franklin on evidence: *AC*, 14 October 1972. Kidd suggests a trade-off: *AJ*, 12 September 1973; JC rejects trade-off: *AJ*, 12 September 1973; Murphy's criticism of JC: *AC*, 13 November 1974, 7 November 1976, 22 November 1974. Carter attacks Maddox: Bill Shipp, *AC*, 4 July 1973. Memos in the governor's papers show JC's interest in tracking Maddox's use of state planes: Prentice Palmer, *AJ*, 23 July 1973. Dean McBee's questions JC: McBee/al. JC on Commission of the Status on Women: *AC*, 18 May 1972. JC conflict with Georgia Association of Educators: *ATR*, 25 January 1973. JC, "year for the teacher": *AJ*, 23 January 1973; JC continues attack on GAE: *AC*, 23 January 1973. Mrs. Lacy calls JC S.O.B.: *AC*, 30 March 1973; JC, "educational anemics": *AJ*, 3 August 1973. JC exchange with Bobby Pafford: Harry Murphy, *AC*, 21 September 1971. Piggyback poll: *AJ*, 7 November 1973; *AJ*, 29 November 1973; *AJ*, 5 December, 1973; *AC* 22 December 1973. Busbee on poll: *AJ*, 5 December 1973. GOP chairman asks for investigation: *AC*, 22 December 1973. JC, poll "political mistake": *AC*, 22 December 1973. Gambrell disavows JC: *AC*, 21 July 1974. Smith on JC: *AC*, 21 July 1974. Busbee criticizes JC: *AC*, 4 July 1974. David Nordan on Bert Lance: *AJC*, 9 December, 1973.

## 11.  AIMING HIGH

Kirbo on JC's presidential potential: Kirbo/ai. Moore's 1970 message: Frank Moore/ai. Hamilton on

polls: William Hamilton to JC, 15 April 1971, *Ga. Archives*. RC on JC's presidential qualities: Howard

Norton and Bob Slosser, *The Miracle of Jimmy Carter* (Plainfield, N.J.: Logos, 1976), p. 54. JC on same: *WNB*, pp. 158–9.

## New South

Herman Talmadge on blacks: Neal Peirce, *The Deep South States of America* (New York: W. W. Norton, 1974), pp. 336–37. VFW on Calley, JC response: *AC*, 2 April 1971; *AJ*, 1 April 1971. JC later comments on Calley: *WP*, 10 December 1975. JC on Muskie: *AC*, 21 May 1971. JC on "being singled out": *NYT*, 21 April 1971. JC antibusing resolution at National Governors' Conference: *AC*, 15, 16 September 1971; at Southern Governors' Conference: *WP*, 21 November 1971. JC antibusing amendment, school boycott: *AJ*, 22 February 1972. JC hails Wallace: *AC*, 21 May 1971. JC on Nixon *vs.* Wallace: *AC*, 6 August 1971. JC at Wallace "appreciation" day, *AJ*, 9 June 1972. JC on Wallace for vice-president: *AC*, 2 June 1972. JC on other Southern vice-presidential possibilities: *WP*, 1 September 1971. JC to Larry O'Brien: 31 January 1972, Response: *Ga. Archives. Larry O'Brien to JC:* 4 February 1972 *Ga. Archives.* JC on McGovern: *AC*, 14 March 1971. JC and Vietnam as campaign issue: *AC*, 22 June 1971. JC in ABM movement: *AC*, 2 June 1971. Little support for ABM at Houston: *AC*, 6 June 1972. JC meets McGovern: *AC*, 13 June 1972. JC to Platform Committee: 9 June 1972, *Addresses* p. 69.

## . . . And Beyond

JC barely elected delegate: *AC*, 12 March 1972. Wallace on JC commitment: Elizabeth Drew, *American Journal* (New York: Vintage, 1976), pp. 122–23. Wallace asks support: Wallace to JC, 21 June 1972, *Ga. Archives.* JC responds to Wallace: 26 June 1972, *Ga. Archives.* JC backs Jackson: *AJ*, 11 July 1972. For speech nominating Jackson, 12 July 1972: videotape, CBS, *TV News.* And for audience response, see David Nordan, *AJ*, 12 July 1972. The speech was not delivered late at night, as aides were to say later. It simply did not attract audience response and thus national attention. JC compares self to John Kennedy: *AJ*, 14 April 1972. Maynard Jackson on JC: *AJ*, 11 July 1972. Contacting Caddell: Jules Witcover (New York: New American Library, 1977), pp. 114–115. JC calls Andrew Young: Jules Witcover, *WP*, 23 April 1976. Footnote on Julian Bond: Julian Bond/ai.

## The Plan

Carter aides plan for 1976: Carter aide/ai; and Witcover, *Marathon*, pp. 109, 116–117. JC won't campaign for McGovern: *AJ*, 15 July 1972. JC meets Wallace: *AC*, 24 August 1972. JC backs Wallace at Southern Governors' Conference: *AC*, 24 August 1972. "Out of family pictures": Jody Powell note, on Eleanor McGovern to RC, 28 September, 1972, *Ga. Archives.* Jordan memo on 1976 strategy: Kandy Stroud, *How Jimmy Won* (New York: William Morrow, 1977), pp. 186–87. JC's Sunday night group: John Pope/ai. JC meets Strauss: Witcover, *Marathon*, p. 126. JC co-chair of Committee to Elect Democrats: *CT*, 1 May 1973. Jordan at DNC: *AJ*, 26 May 1973; and Robert Keefe/ai. JC tries to keep others off trail: JC to Walter Mondale, 7 August 1973, *Ga. Archives.* JC meets Democratic groups: *WNB*, p. 163. JC campaigns for Howell: *AC*, 3 November 1973. JC initiates Rockefeller meeting: Christopher Lydon, "Jimmy Carter Revealed," *Atlantic Monthly*, July 1977, p. 51. Even before JC had taken the oath of office as governor, he was in New York City (on December 14, 1970) with several state officers to meet with William E. Simon (a partner in the prestigious Salomon Brothers firm) and several other financiers. The guest list for the luncheon is in the Fulton County file, *Ga. Archives.* Alston plows for JC: Philip Alston to JC, 4 January 1974. *Ga. Archives; see*

also *AC*, 4 January 1974. Young supports JC: Andrew Young/ai. Peter Bourne and Mary King: Carter aide/ai.

## Speaking Out

Powell advice to JC: 26 February 1973, *Ga. Archives.* JC on Nixon as *AC* 19 January 1973. JC on Nixon: *Addresses*, pp. 187–88. Nixon and JC exchange snubs: Rowland Evans and Robert Novak, *WP*, 14 February 1973; *AJ*, 1 March 1973. Caspar Weinberger, Nixon's domestic aide, wrote JC (22 February 1973) that his office had no record of a JC phone or mail request for an interview. JC responded (3 March 1973) that they may have been "ineffective" in their approach. *Ga. Archives.* Nixon invited to Georgia: Referred to in Nixon aide's response (David Parker to JC, 12 March 1973). Powell comments on Parker letter suggest they were not serious in their invitation. *Ga. Archives.* JC attacks Nixon programs: *AJ*, 12, 19 July 1973. JC to Democrats on Watergate: *CT*, 13 May 1973. JC not call for Nixon's resignation: *AJ*, 5 June 1973. JC to Democrats, "to win fairly": *Addresses*, pp. 70–111. John Crown on JC: *AJ*, 29 August 1973. JC on Watergate and personal honor: JC commends Nixon on press conference: *AJ*, 24 August 1973. *Addresses*, p. 67. JC, Agnew not guilty: *AC*, 10 August 1973. JC calls Agnew: *AJ*, 21 September 1973. JC surprised at Agnew resignation: *AJ*, 11 October 1973. JC, Nixon "paranoic": *AJ*, 22 October 1973. Georgia GOP on JC: *AC*, 23 October 1973. Bush on JC: *AC*, 31 October 1973. JC retreat on "paranoic": *AC*, 21 November 1973. JC compliments Ford: *AC*, 10 August 1974. JC attacks Ford: *AC*, 24 October 1974.

## The Credibility Problem

JC on "What's My Line?": *WP*, 15 July 1976. JC on people met: *AJC*, 1 August 1974 (Schirra was JC's classmate at Annapolis). On being treated almost as a head of state: Speech, Commission on Foreign Relations, 12 November 1974, *Addresses*, p. 281. JC meets Garry Wills: Wills, "The Plains Truth," *Atlantic Monthly*, June 1976, p. 41. JC meets Sulzberger, Phillips: JC desk calendars, *Ga. Archives. Reader's Digest* story, 1974. JC tries to meet foreign statesmen: Philip Alston to JC, 12 February 1973, *Ga. Archives.* JC on VIPs he met: Speech, Commission on Foreign Relations, 12 November 1974, *Addresses*, p. 281. JC solicits Rickover advice: JC to H. Rickover, 19 October 1973, *Ga. Archives.* Background, Trilateral Commission: Peter White to JC, 20 April 1973, and attachments. JC presents Trilateral concept to governors, Democrats: Gerard C. Smith to JC, 15 January and 10 June, 1974, *Ga. Archives.* Jordan warns JC about competitors: Stroud, *op. cit.*, p. 186; Witcover, *Marathon*, pp. 119–20. JC, Wallace no longer able to deliver vote: *AJ*, 8 March 1974. JC, Wallace "wasting his time": *AJ*, 3 June 1974. Kennedy and Nordan: *AJ:* 5 May 1974. Details on Kennedy visit, Law Day Speech: Hunter Thompson, *Rolling Stone*, 3 June 1976. For JC's planning regarding this meeting: Ralph Beard, 23 April 1974, *Ga. Archives.* Though JC had a formal speech prepared for the celebration, his actual presentation seems to have come from scribbled notes. JC regrets Kennedy not running: JC to Edward Kennedy, 25 September 1974, *Ga. Archives.*

## Mending Fences at Home

Slippage in Georgia: *AC*, 2 June 1973 and Mary Anne Thomas/ai. Griffin on JC: David Nordan, *AJC*, 2 April 1973. Funds for Lake Blackshear: F. Moore to JC, 11 June 1973, *Ga. Archives.* Funds for pool in Plains: H. Carter to JC, 6 August 1973, *Ga. Archives.* Other allocations to district: Moore to JC: 11 June 1973, *Ga. Archives.* People tours: *AC*, 13, 14 August 1973. Hugh Carter on "tourist town": *AC*, 15 August 1973. Cordele fish fry: *AC*, 15 August 1973; *AH*, 17 August

1973. Purpose of trip: *AC*, 27 July 1973. JC on filming trip: JC memo to Rafshoon, 30 August 1973, *Ga. Archives*. JC's effect on people: David Nordan, *AC*, 18 August 1973. Footnote on JC tours: *AC*, 12 March 1974; *AH*, 14 March 1974.

### Surfacing

JC feints as Talmadge competitor in D.C.: *AC*, 10 February 1973; and at Yale, *AJ*, 19 April 1973. Shaw accepts feints: *AC*, 1 December 1973. Busbee on JC's aid to Lance: *AC*, 4 July 1974. JC at George Press Association: *AC*, 22 July 1973. JC suggests no 1974 or 1976 ambitions: *AC*, 19 July 1973. JC on Kirbo's float of JC name: *AH*, 14 March 1974. JC in New Hampshire on 1976 plans: Margaret Shannon, *AC*, 28 April 1974.

JC, "I'm not running . . .": Address at Shoal Creek Music Park, 10 July 1974, *Addresses*, pp. 272–73. On JC national ambitions: *AJ*, 12 September 1973; Shipp, *AJC*, 18 April 1973; Nordan, *AJC*, 18 April 1973. JC leaks 1976 plans: *AC*, 3 October 1974. Jordan and "Committee for JC": *AJ*, 20 November 1974. JC admits candidacy: *AC*, 26 October 1974. Kansas City brochure: *AC*, 6 December 1974; JC speaking at Kansas City: *AC*, 11 December 1974; at cocktail parties: *CT*, 12 December 1974. JC's formal announcement: 12 December 1974, *Addresses*, p. 286–293. Journalists comment on speech: *AC*, 13 December 1974. Atlanta announcement: *AC*, 13 December 1974. Text, *Addresses*, pp. 293–295. JC saves fund for Busbee: *AC*, 23 December 1974. Reporters' certificates: reporter/ai. Farewell note to Busbee: *AH*, July 1976.

## PART III • CAMPAIGN STRATEGY

Some of the data in this section and in Part Four are based on my own observations of Carter and the campaign as a member of the press corps in Plains in August 1976. I have also gone through all the Carter campaign commercials on file at the University of Georgia and done a spot check of the ABC, NBC, and CBS evening news programs, which are on file at the Television News Archives at Vanderbilt University. In addition to these, I have relied upon the following published sources for Carter's own statements: *Addresses, Government As Good*, Wesley Pippert's *The Spiritual Journey of Jimmy Carter* (New York: Macmillan Publishing Co., 1978), Committee on House Administration, U.S. House of Representatives, comp., *The Presidential Campaign 1976*, Vols. I and II, and *Jimmy Carter* (Washington, D.C.: U.S. Government Printing Office, 1978). Campaign position papers and press handouts not found in these sources are either in my possession or in the Democratic National Committee library, which has a two-volume collection of most of Carter's campaign statements.

The narrative of the campaign has been drawn primarily from the national media: the network news and the Washington *Post, New York Times, Wall Street Journal; Time* and *Newsweek;* regional leaders such as the Atlanta *Constitution* and *Journal,* Boston *Globe,* Chicago *Tribune,* Chicago *Sun-Times,* Los Angeles *Times;* and statewide newspapers for the period immediately before the relevant primary election or caucus. The votes in the various primary and caucus states and for the general election are from *C.Q., Guide to the 1976 Election* (a supplement to *C.Q. Guide to U.S. Elections,* C.Q.: Washington, D.C., July 1977). Delegate counts are from the *U.S. News and World Report:*.

The behind-the-scenes planning details are from draft memos and letters in Carter's papers in the

Georgia Archives, interviews with Carter associates and other campaign managers, and the recollections of the campaign managers as reported in Jonathan Moore and Janet Fraser, eds., *Campaign for President: Managers Look at '76* (Cambridge, Mass.: The Ballinger Publishing Co., 1977). For the Republican campaign in the fall I have used Ron Nessen's *It Sure Looks Different from the Inside* (Chicago, Ill.: Playboy Press, 1978) and Malcolm MacDougall, *We Almost Made It* (New York: Crown, 1977).

Additional inside material, as well as press response to the campaign, is drawn from the writing of the following reporters who covered it: Jules Witcover, *Marathon: The Pursuit of the Presidency 1972–1976* (New York: The New American Library Inc., 1977); Martin Schram, *Running for President: A Journal of the Carter Campaign* (New York: Simon and Schuster, 1977); Elizabeth Drew, *American Journal: The Events of 1976* (New York: Vintage Books 1978). A cross-section of the religious, liberal, youth, labor, ethnic, and special interest press who also surveyed to obtain reactions to the Carter candidacy. Those materials are cited where relevant in the notes.

Poll results cited throughout this section were drawn, initially, from published sources: the CBS, ABC, and NBC polls as reported on the evening news; and the CBS polls, which were done with the *NYT* and also reported in that paper. The Yankelovich polls are reported in *Time*. The Gallup polls are summarized in annual reports for 1975 and 1976. Dareden polls are from newspaper accounts in the Atlanta *Constitution* and Atlanta *Journal;* and the Harris polls are from the *AC*, ABC news, and a variety of newspaper sources. For JC's campaign finances, I have relied upon preliminary and final FEC reports on file in Washington.

## 12. EARLY PRIMARIES

### Beating the Bushes

JC's first campaign trip: Tom Ottenad, St Louis *Post-Dispatch,* 26, 27 January 1975; Jack Germond, *AC*, 25 January 1975. See also, *CT*, 26 January 1975; *WP*, 28 January 1975. In Santa Fe: *AC*, 24 January 1975. Bourne on McGovern: Peter Bourne to JC, 24 October 1973, *Ga. Archives*. JC on "Meet the Press," NBC, 15 December 1974, transcript. Campaign formula: Tom Ottenad, St. Louis *Post-Dispatch,* 2 February 1976. JC on Wallace, Louisiana legislature: *AJ*, 21 January 1975; *AC*, 1 March 1975; *AC* 12 September 1945. JC would accept conditional commitments: *AC*, 22 January 1976. Jordan memo; Witcover, *Marathon* (New York: New American Library, 1977), p. 144. Campaign in Florida: Andrew Young, Julian Bond/ais; Tom Ottenad, St. Louis *Post-Dispatch,* 14 December

1975, 2 February 1976; *AC*, 15 and 20 November 1975. Reston quote: *NYT*, 6 June 1976. Jahn dinner in Iowa: *WP*, 27 December 1976. "Brutal" travel schedule: *AC*, 23 June 1975. At Grand Ole Opry: *AC*, 23 June 1975. National publicity dearth: *AC*, 17 February 1975. Aides on good local publicity: *AC*, 15 February 1975. Actual local publicity: *LeMars Sentinel, WP* 27 December 1975; JC complaint; *AJ*, 24 October 1975. JC fundraising problems: *AJC*, 15 February 1976. Aides work without pay: *AC*, 20 November 1975. Income, 1975: FEC report: copy in author's files. Rock stars' aid: Robert Anson, "The Capricorn Connection," *New Times,* 3 September 1976. JC qualifies: *WP*, 30 September 1975. Iowa poll: Martin Schram, *Running for President* (New York: Simon and Schuster, 1977), p. 20; Witcover, *op. cit.,* p. 214.

Apple on poll, *NYT,* 27 October 1975; Goldman, Duncan follow suit; David Barber, *Race for the Presidency,* (Englewood Cliffs, N.J.: prentice-Hall, 1978), p. 39–40; Wicker, *AC,* 8 November 1975. Florida poll: *CT,* 11 November 1975; *AC,* 17 November 1975. Positive press: Marquis Childs, *WP,* 16 December 1975; Frank Starr, *CT,* 5 December 1975; Patrick Anderson, "Peanut Farmer for President," *NYT Magazine,* 14 December 1975, and Patrick Anderson/ai. JC in polls: see *Gallup Poll* Index, November-December 1975, p. 39; Northeast, *WP,* 29 September 1975; Waterloo, *AJ,* 24 November 1975, *AC,* 26 November and 8 December 1975. Jimmy the Greek odds: *WP,* 24 November 1975.

### Moving Out Front

Apple ranks candidates: *NYT,* 19 January 1976. Udall on "silly" poll: Schram, *op. cit.,* p. 19. Press descends on Iowa: Witcover, *op. cit.,* pp. 215, 288; *NW,* 2 February 1976. Press and McGovern in 1972: Donald R. Matthews, " 'Winnowing': The News Media and the 1976 Presidential Nominations," in Barber, *op. cit.,* p. 58. JC people working in Iowa: *AJC,* 18 January 1976. Bayh, Udall in Iowa: Fraser and Moore, eds., *Campaign for President* (Cambridge, Mass.: Ballinger, 1977), pp. 83–85. TV press guidelines: William E. Bicker, "Network Television News and the 1976 Presidential Primaries: A Look from the Networks' Side of the Camera," in Barber, *op. cit.,* p. 95. JC gets Iowa news from Powell: Witcover, *op. cit.,* p. 228. Press response: F. Christopher Arterton, "Campaign Organizations Confront the Media-Political Environment," in Barber, *op. cit.,* pp. 21–22. R. W. Apple: *NYT,* 22 January 1976. JC on Mississippi results: Witcover, *op. cit.,* pp. 229–230. JC conservative in New Hampshire: Moore and Fraser, *op. cit.,* pp. 88–89. Loeb editorial: Manchester *Union Leader,* 10 December 1975. JC at N.H. dinner: *NYT,* 25 January 1976. Powell on N.H. strategy: Moore and Fraser, *op. cit.,* pp. 87, 91. Organization in N.H.: Witcover, *op. cit.,* pp. 243–246. Lance, Alston help: Manchester *Union Leader,* 7 February 1976. Peanut Brigade: *AJ,* 7 January 1976. John Pope on Peanut Brigade: John Pope/ai. Betty Pope on Brigade: Kandy Stroud, *How Jimmy Won* (New York: William Morrow, 1977), pp. 427–28. JC's N.H. victory celebration: *Ibid.,* p. 249. "Being from the South . . ." Miami *Herald,* 25 February 1976. Decision to campaign in Mass.: Schram, *op.*

*cit.,* pp. 32–3; *USN,* 7 February 1976. JC on taxes: Position paper, *Campaign 1976,* I, 1, p. 632. Reaction: Miami *Herald,* 3 March 1976; *Manchester Union Leader,* 27 February 1976; Jackson quote: Witcover, *op. cit.,* p. 261. JC aide on "high road": Witcover, *op. cit.,* p. 262. JC at Faneuil Hall: Steven H. Chapman, *Harvard Crimson,* 28 February 1976. JC at Salem factory, Powell on bus: Timothy Carlson, *Harvard Crimson,* 28 February 1976. Jackson's Mass. campaign: Miami *Herald,* 4 March 1976. Wattenberg on media, Jackson: Moore and Fraser, *op. cit.,* pp. 92–93. JC shaken by Mass. loss: Witcover, *op. cit.,* pp. 264–67. Proving JC up North: Moore and Fraser, *op. cit.,* p. 88. Lou Harris on Florida: *AC,* 12 January 1976. Floridians on JC: Miami *Herald,* 4 March 1976. Jackson in Florida: *AC,* 18 February 1976; attacks JC: Miami *Herald,* 7 March 1976. JC attacks Jackson: Miami *Herald,* 5, 6 March 1976. Caddell on black votes: Schram, *op. cit.,* p. 86. Wallace campaign problems: *AC,* 16 March 1976. Problem due to wheelchair: quoted in Witcover, *op. cit.,* p. 289. Florida result, analysis: Miami *Herald,* 11 March 1976; St. Louis *Post-Dispatch,* 2 February 1976; NBC news poll, 9 March 1976. Joel McCleary on post-Florida organizations: F. Christopher Arterton, "Campaign Organization," in Barber, *op. cit.,* pp. 6–7. Caddell on media: Moore and Fraser, *op. cit.,* p. 97. JC courts Mayor Daley: *CT,* 16 March 1976; Witcover, *op. cit.,* p. 371; Schram, *op. cit.,* p. 97. Jim Wall reassures Daley: Schram, *op. cit.,* p. 98. Illinois primary result: Downstate: *CT,* 17 March 1975; Daley quotes: Schram, *op. cit.,* p. 101. JC not first choice of Illinois voters: *AC,* 17 March 1976. Pollster on results: *USN,* 29 March 1976. Wallace, "warmed over McGovern": Witcover, *op. cit.,* p. 381; Wallace at Winston-Salem: Elizabeth Drew, *American Journal* (New York: Vintage, 1978), pp. 123–24. JC responds: *AC;* 21 March 1976. Jordan, Caddell on strategy: Schram, *op. cit.,* p. 113. Wattenberg on press: Moore and Fraser, *op. cit.,* p. 97. Patrick Caddell on Pennsylvania strategy: Schram, *op. cit.,* p. 113. JC's Pennsylvania campaign: Witcover, *op. cit.,* p. 318; Schram, *op. cit.,* p. 138; Drew, *op. cit.,* p. 158. JC media blitz in Pennsylvania: *WP,* 19 April 1976. Jackson in early polls: Witcover *op. cit.,* pp. 315–17. ABC movement: *WSJ,* 29 April 1975; *AC,* 28 April 1976; Drew, *op. cit.,* p. 164. Pennsylvania exit poll: *WP,* 28 April 1976 JC's broad appeal: NBC, CBS exit polls, April 1976.

## 13. BANDWAGON

JC's outsider theme: Miami Herald, 2 February 1976, and *AC,* 28 February 1976. Speech at Berlin rally: Andrew Glass, *AC,* 19 February 1976; TV advertisements; "And I think my victory in Iowa . . ." *Campaign Commercials.* Reactions to anti-Washington stance: Morris Udall: *WP,* 20 February 1976; Terry Sanford: *NW,* 2 February 1976; politicians' uneasiness: Elizabeth Drew, *American Journal* (New York: Vintage, 1978), p. 15. JC thrives on opposition; on "potshots": *AC,* 21 January 1976; being "an obstacle": *WP,* 20 February 1976; "when you have Udall . . .": *AC,* 28 January 1976; on New York political bosses: *AJC,* 14 March 1976. JC on Humphrey: *WP,* 26 March 1976. JC on "stop Carter": *WP,* 1 April 1976. JC on "machinations": *WP,* 1 April 1976; Jules Witcover, *Marathon* (New York: New American Library, 1977), p. 16. Humphrey's shadow candidacy: Jonathan Moore and Janet Fraser, *Campaign for President* (Cambridge, Mass.: Ballinger, 1977), p. 79; also Drew, *op. cit.,* p. 152; Martin Schram, *Running for President* (New York: Simon and Schuster, 1977), p. 111; *WP,* 1 April 1976. No help for Udall in Wisconsin: Schram, *op. cit.,* p. 111; *WP,* 1 April 1976; see also R. W. Apple,

*NYT,* 31 March 1976. JC on "Stop-Carter Alliance in Pennsylvania": Philadelphia *Bulletin,* 14 April 1976.

### Bandwagon

Humphrey won't campaign: *NW,* 10 May 1976. McGovern fires aides: *WP,* 1 June 1976; also CBS News, 30 May 1976. Dugan N. J. Effort: *WP,* 1 May 1976. Yankelovich poll results: *Time,* 10 May 1976. Darden polls, Wallace ahead: *AC,* 9 July 1974. Georgia endorsements slow: *AC,* 13 December 1974; *WP,* 13 December 1974; Bill Shipp in *AC,* 18 March 1976. Georgia election date: Rex Granum, *AC,* 19 September 1975. Busbee, Jackson endorsements: *AC,* 23 April 1976; for Talmadge and Nunn endorsements, which came right after that, see *AC,* 30 April 1976; earlier story on Georgia bandwagon: *AC,* 26 March 1976. Georgia vote: *AC,* 6 May 1976 (an *AJC* poll, taken the week before, showed Carter preferred over Wallace by a vote of 63.7 percent to 21.3, the rest going to the others: *AC,* 6 May 1976). Mickey Kantor on Brown's campaign strategy: Moore and Fraser, *op. cit.,* p. 107. JC not worried by Church, Brown: *WP,* 19 May 1976. Carl Albert on Brown: ABC Evening News, 6 May

1976. Brown on JC: Witcover, *op. cit.*, p. 357. On JC setbacks: Ken Bode, "Broken Spoke in the Bandwagon," *New Republic*, 29 May 1976, p. 10. Hiding results of a poll: Schram, *op. cit.*, pp. 192–93. JC claims 1,000 delegates: *AC*, 26 May 1976. JC on Brown and delegates: *AC*, 3 June 1976. Hal Gulliver on delegates: *AC*, 27 May 1976. Draft-Humphrey meetings: Moore and Fraser, *op. cit.*, pp. 100–01; Schram, *op. cit.*, p. 169–70; *NW*, 31 May 1976; *WP*, 20 May 1976. Kennedy on JC vagueness: *AC*, 26 May 1976; *Time*, 7 June 1976, p. 10. Kennedy not run or push Humphrey: *WP*, 27 May 1976; ABC-TV, 26 May 1976. Humphrey on not entering race: ABC Evening News, 4 June 1976.

### Home Stretch

California poll: Witcover, *op. cit.*, p. 366. JC California effort minimized: Schram, *op. cit.*, p. 196. Humphrey, Brown in New Jersey: *Ibid.*, pp. 206–07. JC and Ohio: *AC*, 4 June 1976; Church in Ohio: Kandy Stroud, *How Jimmy Won* (New York: William Morrow, 1977), pp. 305–06. JC problems on June 8: Albert Hunt, *WSJ*, 3 June 1976. JC stresses Ohio: Jim Merriner, *AC*, 5 June 1976. JC-Daley relationship: Witcover, *op. cit.*, pp. 370–72. JC phones opponents: *AC*, 10 June 1976. Competitors' actions after June 8: ABC, CBS, and NBC Evening News, 9–14 June 1976. Brown concedes: *AC*, 26 June 1976.

### How He Did It

"Bandwagon": *Campaign Commercials*. JC meets Wurf: *AJ*, 19 March 1976. Troy on boat leaving: *AC*, 14 May 1976. Van Den Heuvel on train leaving: *NW*, 31 May 1976. JC woos competitors: Birch Bayh: Drew, *op. cit.*, p. 174; George Wallace: New York *Daily News*, 26 May 1976; Udall: *AC*, 14 June 1976. Jackson efforts weakened: Witcover, *op. cit.*, pp. 316–18. Humphrey backs off: "Sleeping with Hubert," *New Times*, 11 June 1976. Possible combined efforts after Pennsylvania: Moore and Fraser, *op. cit.*, pp. 1000ff. Church wants Udall to drop out: Schram, *op. cit.*, p. 195; see also Witcover, *op. cit.*, p. 349. Snider on Wallace support of JC; Keefe on Jackson delegates: Moore and Fraser, *op. cit.*, p. 109–10. No "critical mass": Ken Bode, "Is He Stoppable?" *New Republic*, 5 May 1976. Peter Hart, "The one thing . . .": Moore and Fraser, *op. cit.*, p. 86.

### Campaign Finance

Early fundraisers in Tennessee, D.C., Annapolis, Georgia: *AC*, 23 June 1975; *AC*, 19 October 1975; 15 August 1975. Peanut Brigade contributions: John Pope/al. Rock concerts: *AC* 15 October 1975; *AC* 22 October 1975. JC at Nashville concert: *AH*, 18 May 1976. Direct mail solicitations: *AJC*, 8 December 1974;

*AJ*, 11 March 1976. Press's travel expenses: *AC*, 15 September 1976. Bandwagon effect on contributions: FEC Disclosure Series, No. 7: 1976 Presidential Campaign Receipts and Expenditures, p. 13, Monthly Adjusted Primary Receipts. Matching funds payments: FEC Disclosure Series, No. 7, p. 11. Effect of freeze on Jackson, Udall: John Gabrusi and Robert Keefe/ais. See also *CT*, 14 April 1976. Caddell on JC cash advantage: Schram, *op. cit.*, p. 149. JC loans: Amendment to FEC Report of Committee for Jimmy Carter, filed 8 November 1976. Rafshoon helps out; JC private debt: *AC*, 17 June 1976. JC exonerated: *WP*, 12 December 1978. Example of public-relations aspect of finances: *AC*, 23 February 1976. Charles Kirbo to JC: memo, 26 November 1974, *Ga. Archives*. JC accuses Jackson, Bentsen: *AC*, 17 December 1974. JC, Jackson, and Bentsen on "Meet the Press": NBC, 15 December 1974, transcript in author's files. Press reports JC in the black: *AC*, 3 February 1976. Lipshutz withholds funds in Pennsylvania: Schram: *op. cit.*, p. 140. "Grassroots" rhetoric: Lipshutz, final report to FEC. JC and small contributors: FEC report. Letter, Lipshutz to Orlando B. Potter, Staff Director, FEC, 6 November 1976. Amended FEC report shows debt pattern: FEC Disclosure Series, No. 7, pp. 45–56. Conflicts in financial organization: Ohio: James Kittleman/ai; California: Herbert Hafif/ai. JC on payments to California ministers: *CT*, 9 August 1976. Funds for "travel advances"; Lipshutz admits mistake: *AC*, 15 December 1976; *FEC* absolves JC campaign: *CT*, 14 October 1978. FEC finds other violations: *WP*, 10 September 1977; *CT*, 14 October 1978.

### Outsider, Insider

Wall Street Committee for JC: "Wall Street Rallies 'Round Jimmy Carter," *Business Week*, 12 April 1976. Wooing Democratic "fat cats": *AJ*, 16 March 1976. Bourne's work: Carter aide/ai. JC visits Brookings: Steve Hess/ai. JC meets former McGovernites: *AJ*, 2 February 1976. JC meets "power structure": *Time*, 29 March 1976; *NW*, 29 March 1976; Smith Bagley fundraiser, *AJ*, 17 March 1976. JC wins "biographical register . . .": *WP*, 8 May 1976. JC visits O'Neill: Schram, *op. cit.*, p. 70–71. JC, "It had been . . .": Interview with Jack Nelson, *LAT*, 1 June 1976; *WP*, 25 January 1976. Fellow governors' attitudes: Witcover, *op. cit.*, p. 125; Drew, *op. cit.*, p. 459. JC, "not anti-Washington": *AC*, 12 May 1976; Witcover, *op. cit.*, p. 357. Frank Moore liaison officer: *AC*, 5 June 1976. JC staff meets congressional staff: *WP*, 11 June 1976. JC mends fences: *NW*, 4 July 1976; *AC*, 25 June 1976. Young on anti-Washington theme: CBS, 24 June 1976; *AC*, 25 June 1976. JC with mayors, governors: *Campaign 1976*, I, 1, pp. 276, 283; JC with governors: *ATR*, 6 July 1976. "I am not running . . .": *WP*, 17 March 1976.

## 14.  SECURING THE NOMINATION

### Heir Apparent

Background details on JC's vice-presidential search: *NW*, 21 June and 12 July 1976; *Time*, 28 January and 12 July 1976; Elizabeth Drew, *American Journal*, (New York: Vintage, 1978); Jules Witcover, *Marathon*, (New York: New American Library, 1977). Description of convention procedures and floor behavior in this chapter from Frederick K. Hatt, Maura A. McKenna, and Ruth Rose, eds., *The Official Proceedings of the Democratic National Convention*, and network news coverage, as available in the TV News Archives. Richard Reeves, in *Convention* (New York: Harcourt Brace Jovanovich, 1977) provides additional behind-the-scenes information. JC considers black woman for VP: *ATR*, 24 June 1976. JC seeks compati-

ble VP: Jules Witcover, *WP*, 25 June 1976. Atlanta press check candidates: Witcover, *Marathon*, p. 385. JC aides on "demeaning" trips: *NW*, 12 July 1976. Muskies travel to Plains: *NW*, 12 July 1976. JC quote on Muskie: Witcover, *Marathon*, p. 387. Mondale at airport: JC meets Mondale and Glenn: Martin Schram, *Running for President*, p. 225. *Ibid.*, pp. 223–226; Witcover, *Marathon*, pp. 387–88. JC aides want unity platform: Witcover, *Marathon*, p. 379; Elizabeth Drew, *op. cit.*, p. 257; *CSM*, 12 July 1976. Women's 50 percent proposal; meeting with JC; compromise, feeling like insiders: Jo Freeman, "Something Did Happen at the Democratic National Convention," *Ms.*, October 1976, p. 74–76, 113–115. Friedan quoted: Kandy Stroud, *How Jimmy Won* (New York: William

Morrow, 1977), pp. 426–27. JC meets black caucus: *WP*, 13 July 1976. "Sleep with me now . . .": Nora Sayre, "The Democrats: Winning Is the Only Thing," *Progressive*, September 1976, p. 15. Background on Strauss-Carter control of convention: *WP*, 18 July 1976; *AC* 19 July 1976. Harrington TV offer: Michael Harrington/ai. Kennedy friend: ai; Kennedy on perimiter pass: Reeves, *op. cit.*, p. 132. Kennedy-Cronkite interview: Reeves, *op. cit.*, p. 166. Strauss, "Let's just wait . . .": *Ibid.*, p. 34. Fight over Rules Committee minority report: Frank Mankiewicz and Joel Swerdlow, "Chinese Boxes," *Harper's* (October 1976), p. 102. "loser night": Reeves, *op. cit.*, p. 118; see also *WP*, 14 July 1976. JC staffers celebrate roll call victory: Stroud, *op. cit.*, p. 321. JC aides discuss VP candidates; Jane O'Reilly on Caddell's "secrets": Reeves, *op. cit.*, p. 138. On Church, Jackson, Glenn, Muskie:

*Ibid.; NW*, 12 July 1976; Schram, *op. cit.*, pp. 230–33; Stroud, *op. cit.*, p. 324. On Stevenson: Mike Royko, *CST* 11 February 1979. *Children's Express* picks Mondale: *NYT*, 16 July 1976. JC announces VP choice: Drew, *op. cit.*, p. 309–10. Mondale on *WNB: Ibid.* p. 311. RC upstages Joan Mondale: Reeves, *op. cit.*, p. 193. JC in hotel during convention: *Ibid.*, p. 181; For atmosphere in convention hall: Reeves, *op. cit.*, p. 206. Mondale acceptance speech: *Official Convention Proceedings*, pp. 397–400. JC enters hall: CBS, NBC, ABC Convention Coverage, TV News Archives, Nashville. JC's original plan scratched: Reeves, *op. cit.*, pp. 204–06. JC's acceptance speech: *Campaign 1976*, I, 2, pp. 401–06. People to podium, King benediction: *Official Convention* Proceedings, pp. 406–09.

## 15. MEDIA

In addition to the sources cited at the beginning of Part III, background on the media and its campaign coverage in 1976 is mainly drawn from James David Barber, ed., *Race for the Presidency: The Media and the Nominating Process* (Englewood Cliffs, N.J.: Prentice-Hall, Inc., 1978); Doris Graber's unpublished manuscript given to the author in 1978; Timothy Crouse, *The Boys on the Bus: Riding with the Campaign Press Corps* (New York: Random House, Inc., 1973); and Thomas E. Patterson and Robert D. McClure, *The Unseeing Eye: The Myth of Television Power in National Politics* (New York: G. P. Putnam's Sons, 1976). The following articles provided additional background: Joseph Lelyveld, "The Selling of a Candidate," *New York Times Magazine*, 23 March 1976, pp. 16 ff. Paul Weaver, "Captives of Melodrama," *New York Times Magazine*, 29 August 1976, pp. 6, 47–57; Robert Shrum, "No Private Smiles," *New Times*, 11 June 1976, pp. 23–42; Phil Stanford, Most Remarkable Piece of Fiction Jimmy Carter Ever Read," *Columbia Journalism Review*, July-August 1976, pp. 13–17; Steven Brill, "Jimmy Carter's Pathetic Lies," *Harper's*, March 1976, pp. 77–88; Richard Reeves, "Richard Reeves on Political Books," *Washington Monthly*, December 1977, pp. 57–58; Eleanor Randolph, "The Carter Complex," *Esquire*, November 1977, pp. 166–184; Leon D. Epstein, "Political Science and Presidential Nominations," *Political Science Quarterly*, vol. 93, 2 (summer 1978), pp. 177–195; and the following articles from *Annals of the American Academy*, 427 (September 1976): John P. Robinson, "The Press and the Voter," pp. 95–103; Dan Nimmo, "Political Image Makers and the Mass Media," pp. 33–43; Albert H. Cantril, "The Press and the Pollster," pp. 45–52, and Elmer E. Cornwell, Jr., "Mass Media in American Politics," pp. 83–94.

### Strategy

Stroud on Jordan memo: Kandy Stroud, *How Jimmy Won* (New York: William Morrow, 1977) p. 185. Witcover and map: Jules Witcover, *Marathon* (New York: New American Library, 1977), p. 561. Germond on JC campaign: *AC*, 17 March 1976. Decision to base JC in Plains: John Pope/ai; author's observations. Powell on ballroom, Rafshoon on journalists' access: Arterton in Barber, *op. cit.*, p. 42. Footnote on Jay Pike: *WP*, 1 May 1976. Kandy Stroud on interview: Stroud, *op. cit.*, pp. 219–21. Scheer's access to JC: Robert Scheer, *"Playboy* interview," Campaign 1976, I, 1, p. 940.

### Providing Good Copy

Interviewers to read *WNB:* Elizabeth Drew, *American Journal* (New York: Vintage, 1978), p. 97–98. JC questions image choice: Witcover, *op. cit.*, p. 117.

Rafshoon memo on phases: Martin Schram, *Running for President,* (New York: Simon and Schuster, 1977), pp. 59–60. JC's Kennedy image: *AC*, 10 November 1976. JC hairstyle: Tom Petit, NBC, 1 June 1976, TV News Archives, Nashville. JC "best-dressed": *AC*, 12 February 1976. Eizenstat's, Kirbo's comments on JC announcement speech and JC's reactions to them: Notes on various drafts of speech in Speech File, Executive Branch *Ga. Archives*. JC's "A" to "C" performances: Joseph Lelyveld, *op. cit.*, pp. 16 ff. JC uses TV well: David Halberstam, *NW*, 19 July 1976. JC upstages Udall: John T. Farmer, Philadelphia *Bulletin*, 26 April 1976. Peanut as symbol: Drew, *op. cit.*, p. 145.

### Coverage

Publicity orgy after N.H.: Thomas E. Patterson "Press Coverage . . . in Presidential Primaries: the 1976 Democratic Race," American Political Science Association paper, 1977. Udall on New Hampshire *WP*, 17 April 1976. Quotes on JC's front-runner status: *AJ*, 11 February 1976; Paul Weaver, "Captive of Melodrama," *New York Times Magazine*, 29 August 1976; *Time* and *NW*, 19 April 1976. Polls: Darden; *AC*, 20 January 1975; Harris, Yankelovich polls: *Time*. The CBS, NBC exit polls are from the network news programs at the time indicated in the text. Delegate counts: Donald R. Matthews, "Winnowing: The News Media and the 1976 Presidential Nominations," in Barber, *op. cit.*, p. 72.

### Banana Peels

Romney and Muskie slips: Timothy Crouse, *op. cit.*, pp. 64–65, 196; and Theodore White, *The Making of the President 1972*, (New York: Atheneum, 1973), pp. 104–107. Publication details on Brill article: Lewis Lapham, "Card Tricks: Dealing Jimmy Carter from the Bottom of the Deck," *Harper's*, May 1976, pp. 12–17. See also: Phil Stanford, *op. cit.*, pp. 13–17. Powell refutation of Brill: text in *BG*, 6 February 1976. JC on Brill story: James Wooten, *NYT*, 3 February 1976. See also Miami *Herald*, 23 February 1976. Powell's personal attacks on Brill: Lapham, *op. cit.*, pp. 12, 16–17. Press attacks on Brill: Germond in Washington Star, 4 February 1976; "Doing a Job on Jimmy'',*Time*, 6 February 1976; Hal Gulliver, "How Only *Harper's* Saw the Truth," *AC*, 24 April 1976; see also David Nordan, *AJ*, 6 February 1976. AP on reorganization in Georgia: *NYT*, 18 February 1976. Details on ethnic purity flap: *WP*, 11 April 1976. JC quotes on ethnic purity: Robert Turner, *"I'll Never Lie To You;" Jimmy Carter in His Own Words* (New York: Ballantine Books, 1976) pp. 109–13. Journalists replay tapes: Witcover, *op. cit.*, p. 322; Stroud, *op. cit.*, pp. 277–78. Carter-Lydon exchange on press bus: quoted by Stroud, *op. cit.*, pp. 278–80. Blacks react: Mayor Jackson, Jesse Jackson:

*Time,* 19 April 1976; Julian Bond: Orde Coombs, "Blacks and Rednecks: The Holy Alliance of '76," *New York,* 19 July 1976, p. 60. Hosea Williams: *AC,* 13 April 1976. Andrew Young: Witcover, *op. cit.,* p. 324. Aides urge JC to lay off: Schram, *op. cit.,* pp. 135–36. JC at Philadelphia press conference: Chicago *Daily Defender,* 10 April 1976; also *WP,* 9 April 1976. Udall on JC's word choice: *WP,* 9 April 1976. Powell, Scott on press rituals: Barber, *op. cit.,* pp. 49–50. Bond contacts reporters: Julian Bond/ai. (Witcover in *Marathon* gives this item one footnote.) "You have arrived": Robert Sam Anson, in introduction to Robert Shrum's "No Private Smiles," *New Times,* 11 June 1976, p. 23. Shrum on joining and leaving JC campaign: Shrum, *op. cit.,* p. 24; also Jules Witcover, *WP,* 3 May 1976. JC's reaction to Shrum's resignation: Witcover, *Marathon,* pp. 345–46. JC, "Shrum dreamed up . . .": Robert Scheer, "Playboy interview," *Campaign 1976,* I, 2, pp. 944. Powell attacks Shrum: *AC,* 5 May 1976. "Darker stories": Robert Sam Anson, *op. cit.,* p. 23. Media coverage of Shrum resignation: *NW,* 17 May 1976; *WP,* 3 May 1976; and *Time,* 17 May 1976. Incongruent JC stories surface: See Chapter 20, "Victory."

### The Boys (and Girls) on the Bus

Early network critiques: ABC Evening News, 10 June 1976. Reporters probe JC: Witcover, Broder, Turner stories from Witcover, *Marathon,* p. 260. Wes Pippert: author's observations. Tom Ottenad, "Jimmy Carter: A Smile and a Shoeshine," *The Progressive,* May 1976, pp. 24–27. Eleanor Randolph on JC: Randolph, *op. cit.,* pp. 166–68, 178–184.

### The Reasons Why

Zone to candidate coverage: Arterton in Barber, *op. cit.,* pp. 31–36; also *AC,* 6 June 1976. Jones on "cocoon": Arterton in Barber, *op. cit.,* pp. 35–36. Reeves, Wilkie on their relationship to JC: Richard Reeves, *op. cit.,* p. 57. (The professional rivalry of one young journalist is evident in the Tom Bethell's "Anybody But Broder: Our Stop-the-Columnists Movement," *Washington Monthly,* July–August 1976. Bethell savages established columnists such as Broder and Kraft and Wicker for being out of touch with the people, not sensing the anti-Washington trend in the country.

### Ambivalence

JC charming press people: Witcover, *op. cit.,* p. 124. JC, fall, on press coverage: Robert Y. Youman and Neil Hickey, "Interview with Jimmy Carter," 9 October 1976, in *Campaign 1976,* I, 2, pp. 920 on "concentrated attention": Witcover, *op. cit.,* p. 240. JC confronts reporters: Wilkie, Lydon and Weisman, Wooten: Stroud, *op. cit.,* pp. 131–32, 276, 279–80; Mohr: Witcover, *op. cit.,* p. 345. JC complaint against Gray: *AC,* 11 February 1976. Goes to Graham of *WP,* Stroud, *op. cit.,* p. 276. JC with Gloria and Walter Spann: Robert Scheer, "Jimmy, We Hardly Know Y'All," *Playboy,* November 1976, p. 96. JC, "Washington political figures . . .": Drew, *op. cit.,* p. 98. JC on press's "zero interest" in issues: Scheer, "Playboy Interview," *Campaign, 1976,* I, 2, p. 944. Weaver on journalists: Paul H. Weaver, *op. cit.,* pp. 6, 48, 54–57, 61. Mohr on JC press critique: Bill Neikirk: *CT,* 25 October 1976.

## 16.  PROMISES PROMISES

Issues not important quotes: Jody Powell to JC, 26 February 1973, Peter Bourne to JC, 24 October 1973, *Ga. Archives.* JC on McGovern and issues: Steven Brill, "Jimmy Carter's Pathetic Lies," *Harper's,* March 1976, p. 77; JC to network VIPs: William E. Bicker, "Network Television News and the 1976 Presidential Primaries: A Look from the Network's Side of the Camera," in James David Barber, ed. *Race for the Presidency: the Media and the Nominating Process,* (Englewood Cliffs N.J.: Prentice-Hall Inc., 1978), p. 104. Evolving issue stands: Stuart Eizenstat/ai: and "Eizenstat Aids Carter with Campaign Issues," *National Journal,* 21 August 1976, p. 1167. JC on taking cues from public: *WNB,* p. 167; *NYT,* 12 July 1976. JC on "worst bureaucracy": *AJ,* 16 December 1975. Promises to reduce bureaucracy: *NYT,* 11 February 1976. On breaking up HEW: *USN,* 26 July 1976. On zero-based budgeting: *AC,* 4 December 1975. Announcement of Candidacy, December 12, 1974, *Addresses,* p. 286–293. JC positions summarized: *WNB,* 167–179. JC on effects of waste, inflation, "Inflation Bills," TV ad: *Campaign Commercials.* JC on "No. 1" responsibility: Interview with John Mashek *USN,* 24 May 1976, *Campaign 1976¿* I, 1, p. 202. JC says reorganization will cost no federal jobs: *NYT,* 11 February 1976. Bureaucrats may increase: *USN,* 26 July 1976, p. 34. "If we had some tough, . . .": TV ad, *Campaign Commercials.* JC on cutting defense spending: *The Progressive,* October 1976, pp. 506. JC for "truly progressive" tax rates: *WSJ,* 2 April 1976; equal tax treatment for businesses, individuals: *Business Week,* 3 May 1976; *USN,* 26 July 1976; *BG,* 26 February 1976. JC on cutting welfare rolls: *AC,* 2 August 1975. JC to lower unemployment and inflation: Interview with *Fortune* editors. May 1976, *Campaign 1976,* I, 1, p. 149. JC on health insurance, "Health Care" 21 January 1976 *Campaign Commercials.* JC on full employment, "An Economic Position Paper for Now and Tomorrow," 22 April 1976, *Campaigns 1976* I, 1, p. 142. JC on ERA: *Campaign 1976,* I, 1, p. 221. See also JC response to questionnaire, *Women Today,* 15 March 1976, *Campaign 1976,* I, 1, pp. 93–94. Nordan on JC technique: *AJ,* 7 March 1976. JC on Taft-Hartley and busing: "Meet the Press," 11 July 1976, *Campaign 1976,* I, 1, pp. 303–04; *AJ,* 2 December 1975; *AC,* 19 December 1975. JC on grain embargoes, *WP,* 27 August 1976. JC on Panama Canal, withdrawal from South Korea: *AC,* 14 February 1976. JC in Florida on South Korea: *Time,* 31 May 1976, p. 15. JC on Korea: Interview with Bill Moyers, 6 May 1976. *Campaign 1976* I, 1, p. 171. Iowa abortion issue and JC's ambiguous position: Jules Witcover, *Marathon* (New York: New American Library, 1977), pp. 220–221; Rowland Evans and Robert Novak, *WP,* 3 September 1976. JC meets Catholic bishops, speaks of "embryonic start": Martin Schram, *Running for President* (New York: Simon and Schuster, 1977), pp. 251–252; See also William Willoughby, *AC,* 3 September 1976, and *CT,* 3 September 1976. JC fails to get photos with bishops: *National Catholic Reporter,* 1 October 1976. Archbishop Bernadin against JC position: *AC,* 1 September 1976. Footnote on JC's earlier abortion stands: *AJ,* 6 October 1971. JC American Legion address, 24 August 1976, *Campaign 1976,* I, 1, pp. 510–518. Legion reaction to speech: Kandy Stroud, *How Jimmy Won* (New York: William Morrow, 1974), pp. 343–344. "2000 years ago" quote: *WNB,* p. 7. JC as missionary with non-English speakers: Witcover, *op. cit.,* p. 288. JC on Allman Brothers: Joe Klein and Dave Marsh, "Rock and Politics," *Rolling Stone,* 9 September 1976, p. 32. JC on Bob Dylan: Robert Scheer, "Playboy Interview," *Campaign 1976,* I, 2, p. 957; and Law Day Speech, University of Georgia, May 4, 1974, in *Addresses,* p. 257. T. D. Archer on JC: *USN,* 5 July 1976. JC on nuclear power: *AJ,* 11 July 1975; *AC,* 11 July 1975. JC, no need for B-1 bomber:

AC, 14 February 1976. Favors B-1 in Omaha: NYT, 11 June 1976. JC reads presidential biographies: WNB, p. 162. JC religious id., advise of aides, drafts of speech, Speech files, Governor Papers, Ga. Archives. Survey of literature on apathy: Ira Carmen, Power and Balance (New York: Harcourt Brace Jovanovich, 1978), pp. 465–70. JC in N.H. on employment, balancing budget: "Employment for New Hamsphire, "Management," TV ads, Campaign Commercials. JC criticizing Ford: "Ford Against": 6 October; 1976, Campaign Commercials. JC criticizing Republicans, "Reality 60": 19 October, 1976, Campaign Commercials File. JC, "I never characterize myself . . .": LAT, 21 January 1976. JC, "I'm a farmer . . .": NYT, 26 January 1976. JC on voters' trust: Interview "Face the Nation," 14 ¹, pp. 99.

### Populism: New Style

JC as populist: AC, 15 July 1976. JC, "I think so.": Time, 26 July 1976. JC not define populism: AC, 15 July 1976. Kirbo on JC as populist: NW, 19 July 1976, p. 24. JC on open government and Cabinet: WNB, p. 170; interview with Bill Moyers, 6 May 1976, Campaign 1976, I, 1, pp. 169–170j. JC for disclosure laws: AC, 2 July 1975. JC for sunshine laws: "Formal Announcement," at National Press Club, Washington, D.C., 12 December 1974, Campaign 1976, I, 1, pp. 4–5. JC, "we must never again . . .": Speech before American Chamber of Commerce, Tokyo, 28 May 1975, Campaign 1976, I 1, p. 67. JC "almost everytime . . .": National Issues Conference at Louisville, Ky., 23 November 1975. Campaign 1976, I, 1, p. 77. JC on government secrecy: Scheer, Campaign 1976, I, 2, p. 950. JC on U.S. intervention abroad: AJ, 28 May 1975. JC on Kissinger: Address to Chicago Council on Foreign Relations, 15 March 1976, Campaign 1976, I, 1, p. 116. JC on Kissinger: Scheer, op. cit., p. 953. JC on "fat, bloated" ambassadors: National Democratic Issues Conference, 23 November 1975, Campaign 1976, I, 1, pp. 78–79. JC on merit basis in ambassador appointments: Chicago Council on Foreign Relations, 15 March 1976, Campaign 1976, I, 1, p. 119. JC supports national secrets act: AC, 28 May 1976. Mondale on need for intelligence apparatus: NW, 26 July 1976, p. 26. JC, "I'll be the one . . .": Daily Illini, 23 February 1976. JC on national policy and morality: WNB, p. 141. JC, "I don't ever want . . .": Sheer, op. cit., p. 952. JC to treat foreigners as individuals: WSJ 2 April, 1976. JC on U.S. as moral leader of world: WNB, p. 141. JC resentment of poor: "Acceptance of

the Democratic Nomination," 15 July 1976, Campaign 1976, I, 1, p. 349. JC on Ford's tax plan: AC, 8 October 1975. JC on Ford's gas rationing, tax hike proposals: AC, 22 February, 1975. Ford's proposed oil tariff: AC, 4 June, 1975. Ford's lack of leadership: AJ, 11 July, 1975. JC, "The fundamental question . . .": ad described by Witcover, op. cit., p. 357. Television ad, Carter in White House: "Dreams," Campaign Commercials. JC friendly to Lockheed, Coca-Cola: see Chapter 8, "The Compleat Politician." JC on business and world peace: Address to Atlanta District Export Council, 17 September 1974. JC on government corrupting business: AC, 5 May 1971. JC energy program: speech before National Press Club, 11 July 1975, Campaign 1976, I, 1, pp. 71–76. JC, "economic declaration of war": AC, 11 December 1975. Supports gas deregulation: NYT, 11 February 1976. Five-year trial period: USN, 26 July 1976. JC not worried about energy monopolies: energy briefing, 17 August 1976, Campaign 1976, I, 1, pp. 386–93. JC on taxes at 21 Club: WP, 23 July 1976; see also Fortune, September 1976, pp. 96. Phil Alston assures business people: Alston/ai. Lance works to win over business: AC, 21 October 1976. Carter no threat to established order: editorial, Fortune, September 1976, p. 95.

### The Fuzziness Charge

Udall on JC's fudging: AC, 29 January 1976. Bayh on JC's being against government: AJ, 23 February 1976. Udall trying to pin JC down: AC, 17 May 1976. Udall ads about JC: Schram, op. cit., p. 164; Witcover, op. cit., p. 359. Eberhard on "issues" issue: Alan Eberhard, WP, 25 April 1976. Nation on JC's fuzziness; editorial, The Nation, 15 May 1976, pp. 578–9. Fuzziness jokes: Time, 31 May 1976, p. 10. Polls about "fuzziness" WP, 26 April 1976. Revising JC's primary commercials: Janet Fraser and Jonathan Moore, eds., Campaign for President (Cambridge: Ballinger, 1977), p. 99. (see also WP, 26 April 1976.) JC speech on national health policy, 16 April 1976, Campaign 1976, I, 1, pp. 128–135. JC Position Paper on Economy, 27 April 1976, Campaign 1976, I, 1, pp. 141–162. JC overwhelms Oregon audience with issues: Elizabeth Drew, American Journal (New York: Vintage, 1978), p. 187–88. JC on Udall "knee jerk" reaction: Interview in Capitol Times (Madison, Wisc.), 29 March 1976. JC on looking for "shallow, easy answers": CSM, 16 June 1976. JC quote on rhetorical levels: Stroud, op. cit., p. 342. Jody Powell quote, "I think people draw an artificial . . .": Fraser and Moore, op. cit., p. 90.

### 17. RACE, RELIGION, REGION

Woodcock endorses JC: WP, 8 May 1976. "Three R's": Tom Ottenad/ai. JC, close friends with blacks: WNB, pp. 73–75; JC as governor, with blacks: Time, 8 March 1976, p. 18. Mississippi ad: Campaign Commercials. New York radio ad: Campaign Commercials. JC rapport with blacks: Kandy Stroud, How Jimmy Won, (New York: William Morrow, 1977), pp. 173–74. JC's Chicago address. Elizabeth Drew, American Journal, (New York: Vintage, 1978), pp. 99–100. JC to AME conference, 18 June 1976: Wesley Pippert, ed., Spiritual Journey of Jimmy Carter (New York: Macmillan, 1978), pp. 225–42; with audience response for latter from William Cotterell, Pool Report, 26 June 1976. Footnote, Howard Norton, Rosalynn (Plainfield, N.J.: Logos, 1977), p. 61. JC quote on South and segregation: AJ, 14 July 1976. Andrew Young on JC: AC, 4 July 1976; Elizabeth Drew, op. cit., p. 100. JC on black infrastructure: Kandy Stroud, op. cit., pp. 175–76. Young, "He grew up . . .": Interview, UPI, 3 July 1976; also Kenneth Bode, "Why Carter's Big with

Blacks," New Republic, 10 April 1976, p. 14. JC eating chitlins: Time, 8 March 1976. King's endorsement of JC: AC, 14 February 1976; cuts audiotape, "Jimmy Carter, JCR: Martin L. King, Sr.," Campaign Commercials. For usage in newspaper ads, see Chicago Daily Defender, 15 March 1976. Young works for JC, getting deeper into the campaign: Robert Shrum, "Andy Young Takes on the World," New Times, 8 July 1977, p. 29; works liberal, black networks: Young/ai. Young with labor leaders: AC, 4 May 1976. Bond on Young, King endorsements: Stroud op. cit., p. 170. JC asks Bond's support: AC, 9 August 1976. Bond shifts to Udall after Florida: Julian Bond/ai. Hosea Williams against JC: AJ, 31 March 1975. JC response to Williams: AJ, 20 March 1975. JC black endorsements: New York Amsterdam News, 17 July 1976; Chicago Daily Defender, 6 November 1976; AC, 9 August 1976. Rev. King, others in Atlanta park: Jules Witcover, WP, 14 April 1976; William Cotterell, Chicago Daily Defender, 15 April 1976. JC ad on housing: Audiotape, "Housing, JCR," *Campaign Commercials*. Black vote in South: *Time*, 5 April 1976, and Bode, *op. cit.*, p. 13; in Michigan, Witcover, *Marathon*, p. 337. Bond on black support for JC: Bode, *op. cit.*, p. 14; Orde Coombs, "Blacks and Rednecks: the Holy Alliance of '76," *New York*, 19 July 1976, pp. 61–62. JC response to Bond: *AC*, 9 August 1976. Black Democrats meet JC: *Time*, 17 May 1976. JC includes blacks, women on VP list: Chicago *Daily Defender*, 28 June 1976. JC appeals for minority delegates: *AC*, 11 September 1976. Black voting trends: Matthew C. Quinn, Chicago *Daily Defender*, 11 September 1976.

## Religion

JC on St. Paul, on Amy: Andrew Glass in *AC*, 19 February 1976. Carter speech to children: Witcover, *Marathon*, pp. 247–48. Volunteer, "the last time . . .": Glass, *AC*, 19 February 1976. Tom Whitney on JC: Martin Schram, *Running for President*, (New York: Simon and Schuster, 1977), pp. 12–13. Footnote on Billy Graham: Chicago *Daily News*, 26 September 1977. JC, "one of the things . . .": Interview with Bill Moyers, 6 May 1976, *Campaign 1976*, I, 1, p. 178–179. "genuine interest . . .": Bruce Mazlish and Edwin Diamond, "Thrice-Born: A Psychohistory of Jimmy Carter's Rebirth," *New York*, 30 August 1976, p. 28. JC outlines religious history: *WNB*, p. 147–57. RCS, JC on JC walk in woods: *WP*, 21 March 1976; also Witcover, *Marathon*, p. 287–288. JC "witnessing" on veranda: Witcover, *Marathon*, p. 288–289; Schram, *op. cit.*, p. 104. JC, "It wasn't mysterious . . . ." Schram, *op. cit.*, p. 105; *AC*, 25 March 1976. JC on religion in Kenosha: *AC*, 2 April 1976. JC at Marquette University: *WSJ*, 12 April 1976. JC at men's bible class, 28 March 1976: Pippert, *op. cit.*, pp. 155–56. JC on prayer life: Interview with John Hart, NBC News, 28 March 1976; Pippert, *op. cit.*, p. 43; also *Time*, 12 April 1976, p. 14. JC with visiting minister: *WNB*, p. 88–89; Interview with Bill Moyers, 6 May 1976, *Campaign 1976*, I, 1, pp. 178–179, 165. JC does not impose lifestyle: *Time*, 10 May 1976, p. 20. JC as existential Christian: E. Brooks Holifield, "The Three Strands of Jimmy Carter's Religion," *New Republic*, 5 June 1976, p. 17. JC on press attention to his religion: *Georgia Baptist Convention News Magazine*, 27 May 1976. JC addresses the Disciples of Christ: Pippert, *op. cit.*, pp. 226–37. JC addresses AME ministers 18 June 1976: *Ibid.*, p. 242. JC, "America is learning . . .": *AC*, 21 June 1976. JC Sunday school lesson: William Cotterell, *Pool Report*, 17 June 1976. JC at Plains church service: *WP*, 19 July 1976. Men's Bible class crowded: William Cotterell, *Pool Report*, 20 June 1976. JC on purpose of Sunday school: *AC*, 19 July 1976; aides on "his concern . . .": *WP*, 19 July 1976. Footnote on women reporters: author's observations. RCS letters for JC: Schram, *op. cit.*, pp. 98–99. RCS predicts JC win: *ATR*, 16 April 1976; on need for man of faith: *ATR*, 18 June 1976. RC church appearance: Howard Norton, *op. cit.*, pp. 55–70; Aunt "Sissy" quote, *AC*, 16 May 1976. Chip Carter on father: *Christianity Today*, 18 June 1976. LC on political value of Christianity: Magda Palacai *op. cit.*/ai. Coleman Young-Morris Udall dispute: Witcover, *Marathon*, pp. 359–360. Ad on JC: *CT*, 31 July 1976. Wallace on JC's religion: Drew, *op. cit.*, p. 124. Jackson on JC's religiosity: quoted in Albany *Herald*, 22 April 1976. Schlesinger on JC's trust theme: *WSJ*, 28 April 1976; Charles P. Henderson, "The Politics of Love: Religion or Justice?" *Nation*, 8 May 1976, p. 556. "Yet the candidacy . . .": Roger Rosenblatt, "The Carter Congregation," *New Republic*, 7 August 1976, p. 42. Interview with Sally Quinn: *AJC*, 28 March 1976; cf. Schram, *op. cit.*, p. 105. JC on religion and politics: *WSJ*, 12 April 1976. No politics in JC's missionary

work: *WP*, 21 March 1976. JC aide, "It may not go over . . .": Drew, *op. cit.*, p. 271. Georgia farmer on JC's religion: *AJC*, 21 March 1976. Michael Novak on hidden power base: *WP*, 4 April 1976; footnote on power base: *WP*, 4 April and 22 August 1976; *WSJ*, 8 September 1976. JC wins over conservatives: CBS-NYT Poll, Reported on CBS, 4 June 1976, *TV News*. JC weak with Catholics and Jews: *AC*, 27 July 1976; *WSJ*, 8 July 1976. "Why do they hate him? . . .": Howard Norton and Bob Slosser, *The Miracle of Jimmy Carter* (Plainfield, N.J.: Logos International, 1976), p. 104–105. Bias against JC's religion: Gannon in *WSJ*, 12 April 1976; Puckett and Baptist editor in *Christianity Today*, 18 June 1976; Apple in *Florida Times-Union*, 11 November 1976. "Carter makes people nervous . . ." and "there is nothing tougher . . .": *Brooklyn Tablet*, 17 June 1976. Anti-Defamation League study cited in *Commentary*, August 1976, p. 45. Quote on morality and politics, *Florida Times-Union*, 11 October 1976. Account of JC, Jews, Samuels in New York: *AC*, 25 July 1976; see also *Commentary*, August 1976, p. 45. JC meets Jewish leaders in L.A., footnote on Meier: Schram, *op. cit.*, pp. 203–04.

## Region

JC as "good" Southern alternative: *AC*, 22 January 1976. JC on rise of South: *AJ*, 12 July 1974; JC TV ad, "I'm proud of our heritage . . .": *Campaign Commercials*. JC, "I sometimes mean . . .": Speech, 1 June 1976; *A Government As Good*, pp. 109–10. JC on Amy: TV commercial, 29 March 1976, *Campaign Commercials*. JC on bias against Russell: Speech at Jefferson-Jackson Day Dinner, 2 March 1971, *Addresses*, p. 98. JC anticipates anti-South prejudice in fundraising letter: *AC*, 22 January 1976; in TV ads in New Hampshire and Massachusetts: *Campaign Commercials*. JC, "the ones who cheered me . . .": Robert Coles "Jimmy Carter: Agrarian Rebel?" *New Republic*, 26 June 1976, p. 18. JC on tendency to stereotype: Interview with Robert Scheer, *Playboy*, November, 1976, pp. 69, 77. Quotes from radio ads on prejudice against South: *Campaign Commercials*. Larry L. King, "We Ain't Trash No More!" *Esquire*, November 1976, p. 156. Powell quote: *Newsweek*, 19 July 1976; Lew Grizzard quote: *CST*, 14 November 1976. On prejudice as basis of opposition to JC: Derian, Morgan quotes: *NYT*, 12 March 1976; Coles quote, Coles, *op. cit.*, p. 18; Merriner, *AC*, 21 July 1976. "There's no one quite so bitter . . .", *AC*, 28 April 1976; Abbot quoted in Laura Foreman, Knight News Wire Service story, n.d./author's files. Northerners on JC as an object of prejudice: TRB, *New Republic*, 7 February 1976; David Broder, *WP*, 14 April 1976. JC equates movement in South with national trends: Speech at Jefferson-Jackson Day Dinner, 2 March 1971, *Addresses*, p. 98. "He won, and underdog . . .": Coles, *op. cit.*, p. 16. On hicks vs. sophisticates: King, *op. cit.*, p. 152. Eastern elite "bites dust": David Nordan, *AJ*, 1 August 1976. JC, "That's where I come from . . .": *Campaign Commercials*. JC on lack of personal security: James Reston, *AC*, 5 August 1976. JC on idyllic youth: *WNB*, p. 31; "When I grew up on the farms . . .", quoted in Robert W. Turner, *"I'll Never Lie to You"—Jimmy Carter in His Own Words* (New York: Ballantine Books, 1976), p. 22. JC on stability in childhood: Interview with Bill Moyers, 6 May 1976, *Campaign 1976*, p. 181; in Plains after winning nomination, *WP*, 19 July 1976; in Sunday school class, *AJC*, 6 September 1976. JC on Plains as reflection of nation: *WNB*, p. 160. JC invites people to join his family, remarks at old folks house, Manchester, N.H., 10 February 1976, quoted in Turner *op. cit.*, p. 25.

## 18. THE EXTRAORDINARY, ORDINARY MAN

JC on the President as moral leader: Interview with Bill Moyers, 6 May 1976, *Campaign 1976*, I, 1, p. 175. JC "did not intend to lose": Mike Barnicle, "The Outsider With a Smile," *BG*, 1 March 1976. "We were confident . . .": Elizabeth Drew, *American Journal* (New York: Vintage, 1978), p. 99. JC on self-assurance: Vermont Royster, *AC*, 12 September 1976. RCS on JC's stability: RCS interview with Wes Pippert, UPI, 15 July 1976, author's transcript. JC would not be pushed around: James Wooten, "Excerpts from a Conversation with Jimmy Carter," *NYT*, 16 June 1976. Hamilton Jordan on JC toughness: Helen Dewar, "Jimmy Carter Has Good Teeth and Is Always on Time," *Esquire*, April 1976, p. 125. Firing people in Georgia: Charles Kirbo, *NW*, 12 July 1976. Quote on Carl Sanders: Hamilton Jordan interview, *NW*, 12 July 1976. JC on unwillingness to compromise: *WNB*, p. 161; *Parade*, 31 October 1976. Kirbo on JC's stubbornness: Interview, *USN*, 20 December 1976. JC's strenuous campaign: Elizabeth Drew, *op. cit., p.* 148; Kandy Stroud, *How Jimmy Won* (New York: William Morrow, 1977), p. 70. Compared to Jackson as campaigner: Stroud, *op. cit.,* p. 265. Iowa snowstorm: *AC*, 10 December 1975. JC softball games, Secret Service agents: Helen Dewar, "Carter Tough on Field," *WP*, 2 August 1976; JC throws out umpire: Eleanor Randolph, "Can the Bionic Peanut Befome a Regular Guy?" *CT*, 8 August 1976. JC's childhood, campaign reading: *WNB*, pp. 29, 30, 162. First meeting with Rickover: *WNB*, pp. 63—64. As "scientist": Announcement Speech, *Addresses*, p. 286; requests CIA briefings: *AC*, 26 June 1976. JC's diverse musical tastes: Stroud, *op. cit.,* p. 148. JC on Dylan Thomas, other authors: Interview, (Madison, Wisc.) *Capital Times*, 29 March 1976. JC on love of nature: *WNB*, p. 120. Stock car

racing fan: Interview with Sally Quinn, *WP*, 28 March 1976. RC on their intellectual, cultural pursuits: Phyllis Battelle, "The Jimmy Carters' Untold Love Story," *Good Housekeeping*, October 1976, p. 186. BC on JC's intelligence: Interview with John Osborne, *New Republic*, 25 November 1976. JC compassion, concern for poor: Law Day Speech, 4 May 1974, *Addresses*, p. 262; Announcement of Candidacy, 12 December 1974, *Campaign 1976*, Vol. I, p. 8; *WNB*, pp. 149–51, 154–55; Robert Scheer, Playboy Interview, *Campaign 1976*, I, 2, p. 957; Kandy Stroud, *op. cit.*, p. 142; and interview with Bill Moyers, 6 May 1976, *Campaign 1976*, I, 1, p. 165. No doubts, ultimate goals, loves people on assembly lines: Interview with Bill Moyers, 6 May 1976, Campaign 1976, I, 1, p. 168. Never experienced fear: Interview with Mike Barnicle, *BG*, 1 March 1976. JC's affinity with diverse groups: *AJC*, 21 March 1976; comparison with Lyndon Johnson: Airborne interview with Mike Barnicle, 14 June 1976. E. G. Marshall commercial: *Campaign Commercials*. JC on combining virtues of previous Presidents: Interview, *Time*, 19 July 1976. JC "never claimed to be better . . ."; "could roll up his sleeves . . .": Stroud, *op. cit.*, p. 425. Page footnote, JC staff has no interest in personal gain: quotes of Patrick Caddell, Stuart Eizenstat, Charles Kirbo from Stroud, *op. cit.*, p. 197, 216, 205; Andrew Young, *AC*, 4 July 1976, and "Carter owes me nothing personally": *New Yorker*, 19 July 1976. Carter's promise to tell the truth: Phil Stanford, "Jimmy Carter," *Citizen's Guide to the Presidential Candidates, 1976* (Washington, D.C.: Capitol Hill News Service, 1976), p. 29; interview with Bill Moyers, 6 May 1976, *Campaign 1976*, I, 1, p. 171. JC on media catching him if he lied: *AC*, 15 September 1976.

## 19. FANTASIES

JC meets Ralph Nader: Helen Dewar, "Carter Consumer Stance 'Admirable' Says Nader," *WP*, 8 August 1976. James Fallows impressed: "The Passionless Presidency," *Atlantic Monthly*, May 1979, pp. 35–36. JC as "angry agrarian populist": Hunter Thompson, "Third-Rate Romance, Low Rent Rendezvous," *Rolling Stone*, 3 June 1976, p. 64. Commentators on JC's "populism": Anthony Lewis, *AC*, 15 June 1976; Simon Lazarus and Harry Huge, "Looking Forward to Carter," *New Republic*, 5 June 1976 p. 13. Neal Peirce, "A Preview of a Carter Presidency," *Current*, September 1976, p. 42; Tom Wicker, "Class and Carter," *NYT*, 31 October 1976. Others see JC as deeply religious: Wesley Pippert, "The Moral Dimension of the News," *HIS*, February 1978, p. 30; Garry Wills, "The Plains Truth," *Atlantic Monthly*, June 1976, p. 54. On JC as Southerner and military man: Garry Wills, "Love and Profit," *New York Review of Books*, 5 August 1976, p. 19. On JC's intellect: Peirce, *op. cit.*, p. 40 (Pierce, in *The Deep South States* [N.Y.: Norton, 1974], described JC as "wealthy" and "tall," with a toothy smile like Kennedy, p. 320); Robert Pierpoint quoted in Lloyd Shearer, "Twenty Years at the White House," *Parade*, 27 November 1977; Fallows, *op. cit.*, p. 34. Lazarus and Huge, JC not fuzzy: Lazarus and Huge, *op. cit.*, p. 13. James Reston JC "answer more questions . . .": Quoted in *Ibid*. Norman Mailer on JC: Norman Mailer, "The Search for Carter," *NYT Magazine*, 26 September 1976, p. 92. Robert Scheer on JC: "Playboy Interview," *Campaign 1976* I, 2, p. 941. Neal Peirce on JC's cruel side: "A Preview of the Carter Presidency," p. 42. Carl Albert predicts JC landslide: NBC News, 24 June 1976. Mike Mansfield sees JC unifying party: ABC News, 24 June 1976. Clarence

Dodson compares JC to St. Paul: *AJC* 6 September 1976. On JC aides: Robert Scheer, "Jimmy, We Hardly Know Y'all," *Playboy*, November 1976, pp. 91–92; and Margaret Shannon, *AC*, April, 1976. On RC and JC: Gail Sheehy, "Ladies and Gentlemen, the Second President—Sister Rosalynn," *New York*, 22 November 1976, p. 50. RC as another Eleanor Roosevelt: Lillian Hellman, "Plain Speaking with Mrs. Carter," *Rolling Stone*, 18 November 1976, p. 45. Norman Mailer on RC as archetypical American woman: Mailer, *op. cit.*, pp. 19–21, 69–92. Orde Coombs on LC: Coombs, "The Hand That Rocked the Cradle," *New York*, 14 June 1976, pp. 40–43. Henry Allen on LC: Allen, "Just Plain Folks," *Potomac*, 15 August 1976. On Carter family: James Neyland, *The Carter Family Scrapbook* (New York: Grosset and Dunlap, 1977), p. 84. On JC as healer of nation, Plains as Camelot: Mailer, *op. cit.*, pp. 19–21, 69–92. Reynolds Price on Plains: Quoted in *Time*, 3 January 1977. Patrick Caddell on JC anonymity: quoted in Lloyd Demause, "Jimmy Carter and American Fantasy," *The Journal of Psychohistory*, Vol. 5, Fall 1977, pp. 167–68. JC "was a genius . . .": Fallows, *op. cit.*, p. 35. JC more liberal than supposed: Stanley Cloud in "TRB," (Richard Strout) *New Republic*, 26 June 1976; Scheer, *"Playboy Interview," Campaign 1976* I, 2, pp. 942–43. Voters see JC like themselves: poll reported *NYT*, 11 June 1976; Robert M. Teeter as quoted in Jonathan Moore and Janet Fraser, eds., *Campaign for President* (Cambridge, Mass.: Batlinger, 1977), pp. 119–21. For Roper polls see also *AC*, 4 June 1976. JC a spellbinder: Tom Wicker, *NYT*, 31 October 1976; Helen Dewar, "Jimmy Carter Has Good Teeth and Is Always on Time," *Esquire*, April 1976, pp. 71;

Fallow, *op. cit.*, p. 35. Page footnote: Fallows, *op. cit.*, p. 35. JC with Georgia sheriffs: Garry Wills, "Plains Truth," *op. cit.* p. 50. JC's daring, impudence: Hunter Thompson, *op. cit.*, p. 64; TRB (Richard Strout), "What Carter's Not," *New Republic*, 19 June 1976, p. 2; Sam Donaldson, as quoted by Nancy Lewis, *AC*, 4 July 1976. On JC's darker side: Curtis Wilkie/ai; Larry King, "We Ain't Trash No More," *Esquire*, 7 November 1979 pp. 90, 155; "Distrust is precisely . . .": Harold Eggers as quoted in Bill Raspberry, *CST*, 23 October 1976. "Audiences yearn . . .": TRB, *New Republic*, 7 February 1976.

On fate of President as fate of the nation: Fred Greenstein, "The Psychological Functions of the Presidency for Citizens," in Thomas Cronin, *The American Presidency;* this article and the following references to survey data on trust cited in James A. Nathan and James K. Oliver, *United States Foreign Policy and World Order* (Boston : Little, Brown, 1976). Polls show President among "most admired men": John E. Mueller, *War, Presidents, and Public Opinion*, (New York: John Wiley and Sons, 1973), p. 185. Public's reactions to John Kennedy's death: Shearsley and Feldman, "The Assassination of President Kennedy: A Preliminary Report on Public Reaction and Behavior," *Public Opinion Quarterly*, XXVIII (1964), pp. 189–215. Children idealizing President: David Easton and Jack Dennis, *Children and the Political System: Origins of Political Legitimacy*, (New York: McGraw

Hill) pp. 134, 171, 178, 206. Textbooks idealize President: Thomas Cronin, "Our Textbook Presidents," *Washington Monthly*, June 1970, pp. 46, 48–49. Diminishing satisfaction with Presidents: Polls cited in Hazel Erskine, "The Polls: Government Information Policy," *Public Opinion Quarterly*, 35, #4, pp. 636–651. Children's disillusionment: Harold M. Barger, "Images of the President and Policemen Among Black, Mexican/American and Anglo School Children: Considerations of Watergate," Paper prepared for delivery, American Political Science Association, Chicago, Ill., 29 August–2 September 1974, pp. 11–12. Stanley Hoffman on lack of trust: Robert J. Tucker and William Watts, eds., *U.S. Foreign Policy in Transition*, p. 119. JC on voters' search for trust: Robert Turner, *I'll Never Lie to You* (New York: Ballantine, 1976), p. 66; *NYT*, 21 October 1976. "Who else had done that?": Charles Morgan in *AC*, 15 September 1976. On themes of charismatic leader: Irvine Schiffer, *Charisma: A Psychoanalytic Look at Mass Society*, (Toronto: University of Toronto Press, 1973), pp. 9, 25, 30, 34, 38, 41–43, 49. On fragility of popular tie to JC: Patrick Caddell in Moore and Fraser, *op. cit.*, pp. 134–34; Robert Teeter in *Ibid.*, pp. 121–25. Reporters' ambivalence to JC: Kandy Stroud, *op. cit.*, p. 130; Sam Donaldson in Nancy Lewis, *AC*, 4 July 1976; Scheer, "Jimmy, We Hardly Know Y'all," p. 91; Royko, "Oh Jimmy be for real!" Chicago *News*, 16 July 1976.

## 20.  VICTORY

### Summer Solstice

JC appearances and press conferences in Plains and descriptions of the mood of the town, unless otherwise noted, are from author's own notes or transcripts while in Plains, August 1976.Joke about Brigadoon: Eleanor Randolph, *CT*, 29 June 1976. Primary nights in Plains, street celebration on JC's nomination: *ATR*, 19 May, 16 July 1976. Peanut Brigade fish fry: Helen Dewar, *WP*, 27 June 1976; also *CT*, 29 February 1976. Women's clubs, townspeople prepare food, help JC: Betty Godwin/ai. Descriptions of Bush, Brown visits to Plains, as well as energy and domestic policy briefings: author's observations; see also *WP*, 8 August 1976; Macon (Georgia) *Telegraph*, 13 August 1976; *AC*, 16 and 24 July 1976; *Time*, 9 August 1976. Softball games: Eleanor Randolph, *CT*, 8 August 1976. JC talks as if President: "Face the Nation," 14 March 1976, *Campaign 1976*, I, 1, pp. 99–100. JC to N.J. delegates: Richard Reeves, *Convention* (New York: Harcourt Brace Jovanovich, 1977). Trip to Johnson City, Blanton on tourists: *NW*, 19 July 1976; *AC*, 2 July 1976. Plains High plans White House reunion: *WP*, 2 August 1976. Theodore White on winning 50 states: *ATR*, 15 August 1976.

### Small Flags

Sale of souvenir land titles, eviction of Pittmans: Eleanor Randolph, *CT*, 29 July 1976; *Time*, 17 May 1976. JC critiques Ford in N.H.: Helen Dewar, *WP*, 4 August 1976. JC in Hollywood, JC quotes: Helen Dewar, *WP*, 24 August 1976. On JC campaign strategy: Thomas W. Ottenad, St. Louis *Post-Dispatch*, 10 July 1976; Powell quote: Jonathan Moore and Janet Fraser, eds., *Campaign for President* (Cambridge, Mass.: Ballinger, 1977) p. 131.

### Planning

Data on JC campaign staff : Moore and Fraser, *op. cit.*, p. 130; *AC*, 21 August 1976; Tom Ottenad, St. Louis *Post-Dispatch*, 5 September 1976; Lawrence Stern, *WP*, 12 August 1976. Field organizers: Tim Kraft press briefing and press handout, August

1976/author's notes. On issues task forces and transition committees: *WP*, 29 July 1976 and 12 August 1976; *National Journal*, 21 August 1976; *AJC*, 28 November 1976; *AC*, 14 August 1976 and 23 July 1976. "Z" on envelope: Stephen Hess/ai. TalentBank letters/author's files. Jordan planning memos: Witcover, *Marathon*, (New York: New American Library, 1977), pp. 550–54. Jordan on strategy: Moore and Fraser, *op. cit.*, p. 129. Point system for family members' visits: Tom Ottenad, St. Louis *Post-Dispatch*, 5 September 1976; Witcover, *op. cit.*, p. 552.

### The Fall

Caddell's predictions: Plains press conference, 14 August 1976/author's note. Also, Macon *News* and *Telegraph*, 15 August 1976. Final polls before election: from Gallup Opinion Poll, December 1976, p. 13; Harris polls: *NYT*, 30 October 1976. On JC's shallow support: Julian Bond, "Why I Don't Support Jimmy Carter," *Nation*, 17 April 1976. Caddell polls, including quotes: Martin Schram, *Running for President*, (New York: Simon and Schuster, 1977), pp. 245–47. Teeter's polls and Ford strategy: Robert Teeter in Moore and Fraser, *op. cit.*, pp. 119–21; on "weak perceptions" of JC: Malcolm MacDougall, *We Almost Made It* (New York: Crown, 1977), pp. 49–50. JC Labor Day speech: 6 September 1976, *Campaign 1976*, I, 2, pp. 701–03, and *AC*, 7 September 1976. JC upstages Dole: Schram, *op. cit.*, pp. 304–05. Invites drivers to White House: *AC*, 7 September 1976. See also Kandy Stroud, *How Jimmy Won* (New York: William Morrow, 1977), p. 346. Foul-ups in Manhattan, Brooklyn, Scranton, Milwaukee: Ken Auletta, *Village Voice*, 20 September 1976. JC on Kelley: Witcover, *op. cit.*, pp. 583–84. Problems in Pennsylvania: *AC*, 12, 18 September 1976. JC's childhood diseases: *CT*, 10 September 1976; David Broder, *WP*, 11 August 1976. Exchange on Kelley: transcript of press conference in author's files. JC's DNC whistle stop tour: *CT*, 22 September 1976. Press questions JC on train: Stroud, *op. cit.*, pp. 354–55; Witcover, *op. cit.*, pp. 604–05. Evening headlines: *NW*, 4 October 1976. Robert Scheer, Playboy Interview, *Campaign 1976*, I, 2, p. 964. JC's defenders: Joseph Duffey, *WP*, 21 September 1976; James Wall, *CT*, 23 September 1976; Dr. Barnhart, *AC*, 13 October 1976. JC's religious critics: Harold Lindsell, *AC*, 12 October 1976; Atlanta preachers: *AC*, 12 October 1976; Beverly Smith: *WP*, 27 September 1976. Reaction to *Playboy* interview: Stroud, *op. cit.*, pp. 350, 354. Jordan on "weirdo factor": Witcover, *op. cit.*, p. 608. Page footnote: Norman Mailer, "The Search for Carter," *NYT Magazine*, 26 September 1976, pp. 19–21, 69–92. On first debate: *NW*, 6 September 1976, *Time* September 1976, Stroud, *op. cit.*, pp. 363–69, Drew, *op. cit.*, *NYT* 23 September 1976. JC in Texas, San Diego meet, Witcover, *op. cit.* pp. 619–20; Powell, press plane, reporter on "you see we really care": Barbara Howar, "Patching Up the Carter Balloon," *New York*, 11 October 1976, pp. 48, 52–53. On prospect, JC defeat: Robert Scheer, "Jimmy, We Hardly Know Ya'll," *Playboy*, November, 1976, p. 91.

### Counterattack

JC relations with press worsen: Stroud, *op. cit.*, pp. 371–372. JC on "bloated mess" in Washington: Rally, 27 September 1976, *Campaign 1976*, I, 2, pp. 833–34. On Ford as leader: *NYT*, 29 September 1976. JC drained, later revitalized: Gary Regar's notes/ author's files; Plains, 28–29 September 1976/ author files. JC on Ford trips: *NYT*, 30 September 1976. JC on his trips: *CT*. 3 October 1976. Marine union supports JC: *WSJ*, 13 October 1976. Lance plane used by JC campaign: *CT*, 3 October 1976. JC attacks special interests:CBS News, 1 October 1976; AP story on Cabin Bluff trips: *WP*, 2 Oct. 1976 and *NYT*, 2 October 1976. JC compares his trips to Ford's: *CT*, 3 October 1976. JC on Butz affair: *CST*, 3 October 1976; Catholics and Italians: *NYT*, 3 October 1976; Ford's handling of affair: *WP*, 5 October 1976; savors Ford's discomfort: Walter Cronkite, CBS News, 4 October 1976. Quotes from Ford-Carter, debate: *Campaign 1976*, Vol. III, p. 112; Salt II, p. 108. Teeter on post-debate polls: in Moore and Fraser, *op. cit.*, p. 142. JC assails Ford in Salt Lake City, Albuquerque: *WP*, 8, 9 October 1976; in Cleveland; Witcover, *op. cit.*, p. 647. Ford accuses JC of double talk: *CT*, 10 October 1976, *WP*, 10 October 1976; Ford response to JC: Ron Nessen, *It Sure Looks Different from the Inside* (Chicago: Playboy Press, 1978), p. 299. Ford on JC "hide and seek,"; Charles Mohr, *NYT*, 13 October 1976; on whistle stop train: *CT*, 17 October 1976.

### High-Low Roads

Caddell on JC loss of support, change of tactics: Schram, *op. cit.*, p. 365, 371, 366. JC not to attack Ford personally: *ABC*, 18 October 1976. Quotes from third debate: *Campaign 1976*, III, p. 130. Reactions to debate: *Gallup Opinion Poll*, December 1976, p. 1. JC says Ford, "decent": *NYT*, 24 October 1976; JC in Dallas, crowd response, *NYT*, 1 November 1976; quotes from *Campaign 1976*, I, 2, pp. 1104–08. ads in order of appearance in text: "Southern," "New Southerner," "Conscientious," "Europe," "Detente," "Foreign Policy," "V. P. Mondale," "Ask Jimmy Carter," (shown election eve), from *Campaign Commercials*. See also Moore and Fraser, *op. cit.*, p. 141.

### Final Hurdles

Ford TV ads: Nessen, *op. cit.*, p. 307; MacDougall, *op. cit.*, pp. 143, 173–74, 201–03, 221–22. Ford print media ads: Nessen, *op. cit.*, p. 302. JC campaign manual: *CT*, 11 October 1976; *AJ*, 11 October 1976; *AC*, 10 October 1976. JC orders manual revised: *AC*, 12 October 1976. JC organizational problems: *AC*, 6 October 1976; Stroud, *op. cit.*, p. 371, 388. Siegel on DNC and campaign: Moore and Fraser, *op. cit.*, p. 149. Hafif's ad: *CT*, 1 November 1976. Though a CBS reporter did a long interview with Hafif, it never was shown/ai. For Cronkite report on ad: CBS News, *AC*, 31 October 1976. Ron Nessen on ad; Republicans circulate ad: Nessen, *op. cit.*, pp. 308–309. Clennon King at Plains Baptist Church: *NYT*, 1 November 1976; Rev. Edwards, Hugh Carter quotes: *WP*, 1 November 1976. Plains church, tourists' pressures: James Hefley and Marti Hefley, *The Church That Produced a President* (New York: Wyden, 1978), p. 5. Helen Thomas questions, account of church meetings in week preceding confrontation: *Ibid.*, pp. 212–13. Powell confronts reporter: Schram, *op. cit.*, p. 386. JC first statements on church action: Witcover, *op. cit.*, p. 675. Powell contacts JC: *Ibid.*, p. 676; press conference in Sacramento, Calif., 1 November 1976, *Campaign 1976*, I, 2, pp. 1109–10. JC aide on incident: *CT*, 2 November 1976. Blacks rally around JC: Coretta King, NBC Evening News, 1 November 1976; others: Witcover, *op. cit.*, p. 676–77. Ford telegram to black ministers, Rainwater contacts networks: *AC*, 2 November 1976; *NYT*, 2 November 1976; *WP*, 2 November 1976. Campaign disappoints journalists: Apple *NYT*, 20 October 1976; Kondracke, *CST*, 17 October 1976; terHorst, *CT*, 27 October 1976.

### The Prize

Predictions on election: Bob Smalley/ai. JC claims victory: *AC*, 4 November 1976; slightly different version in *Campaign 1976*, II, i, p. 1121–2. JC greets followers in Plains: *WP*, 4 November 1976.

### The Reasons Why

Final vote tallies and electoral votes data in this section are from *CQ*, *President Carter*, p. 68–69, and *CQ Guide to 1976 Election*, p. 23. All Gallup Poll information is from *The Gallup Opinion Poll*, December 1976, pp. 2, 10–11. Additional information on the Jewish vote is from a CBS-*NYT* poll in the *CT*, 7 November 1976. Information on blacks, union voters from *NYT*, 26 November 1976. Turnout in key states from *WP*, 4 November 1976. On DNC registration drive and results: Moore and Fraser, *op. cit.*, p. 149; Witcover, *op.cit.*, p. 678; see also *CT*, 4 November 1976; *WP*, 5 November 1976; *NW*, 25 October 1976. Organized labor's vote drive: *NYT*, 26 October 1976; *WP*, 31 October 1976. Protestant, professional, noncity voters contribute to JC win: *CT*, 6 November 1976. Polls show JC support soft: Late September CBS–*NYT* poll, reported in *NYT*, 27 September 1976; NBC *postelection poll, reported on NBC News*, 3 November 1976. Intelligentsia uneasy about JC: Robert Kaiser, *WP*, 23 October 1976. Caddell memo on JC's problems: *WP*, 7 August 1977. Powell on voter concerns about JC: Moore and Fraser, *op cit.*, pp. 125, 131.

## 21. SYMBOLS AND SPOILS

The narrative for the presidency is taken primarily from national news sources: *New York Times, Washington Post, Wall Street Journal, Time*, and *Newsweek*. Presidential statements and news conferences are mainly from texts reproduced in *The Presidency, 1977* (Washington: Congressional Quarterly, Inc., 1978), *President Carter 1978* (Washington: Congressional

Quarterly, Inc., 1979). My interviews with Carter aides are cited in the relevant notes.

George Le Grange, Shirim Jamasb, and Percy Osime did papers on Carter's bargaining style for a graduate seminar that provided useful background for the chapter on bargaining style. Frederic Neikirk shared with me the results of his extensive survey of Congressional aides on Congressional-Executive liasion under the Carter Administration. His results are similar to mine, except he reports a greater improvement in Administration liasion with the House leadership sine the spring of 1978. My colleague, Gary Orfield suggested the title for chapter 24.

JC, "First official and completely open Ceremony": *WP,* 1 February 1977. Rex Granum on Cabinet meeting: Chicago *Daily News,* 9 February 1977. First fireside chat: Text, *The Presidency, 1977,* pp. 68a–71a. Call-in show: Text, *The Presidency, 1977,* p. 70a; *NW,* 14 March 1977; *WP,* 5 March 1977. Average citizens invited to White House: *NW,* 1 March 1977. Town meeting, Clinton, Mass.: Text, *NYT,* 17 March 1977. Town meeting, Yazoo, Miss.: Text, *NYT,* 22 July 1977. JC on press conferences: Chicago *Daily News,* 9 February 1972. Jody Powell on spokes of wheel: cited in *National Journal,* 16 April 1977. Hamilton Jordan on chief of staff: "Face the Nation," November, 1977/author's transcript. JC, White House staff not dominate Cabinet, JC, "The place to start . . ." *The Presidency, 1977,* pp. 68a–71a; *WP,* 5 February 1977. Staff organization: *National Journal,* 12 February 1977. JC pardons draft evaders; proposes Energy Department: Texts, *The Presidency, 1977,* pp. 5a, 11a. Press conference on domestic problems and foreign policy: Text, *Ibid.,* pp. 128a and 132a. JC adjusts campaign pledges on welfare, defense: *WP,* 30 December

1976. Patrick Caddell on winning over public: James Wooten, *NYT,* 4 May 1977. Early polls on JC: *CT,* 6 December 1977; *CT,* 20 January 1977; *NYT,* 29 April 1977; Gallup Public Opinion Poll, annual report, 1977. See also *NYT,* 29 April 1977. Journalists react to JC style: David Broder, *WP,* 9 February 1977; Tom Wicker, *NYT,* 13 March 1977; William Safire, *NYT,* 7 February 1977; Joseph Kraft, *WP,* 17 February 1977. Powell's response: *CST,* 18 February 1977; *WP,* 17 February 1977.

### Early Spoils

JC appointments: *The Presidency, 1977,* p. 39–52; *National Journal,* 30 December 1977, p. 2085. Diplomatic spoils: Robert Morris, *Harper's,* November, 1978. Traditional elites: Dom Bonafede, *National Journal,* 18 November 1978. "Past eight years" a "dream" and other quotes from Hugh Sidey: *Time,* 17 January 1977. Political activists: *NW,* 22 January 1979. TIP questionnaires stored: Dom Bonafede, *National Journal,* 18 November 1978. Cabinet appointees choose own aides: *WP,* 6 June 1977. Campaignworkers neglected: *AJC,* 6 April 1977. Judicial commission results: *President Carter 1978,* p. 57. Common Cause on JC's judicial appointments: *WP,* 11 May 1977. Civil Service Reform, census spoils: "Patronage Is Alive," *National Journal,* 7 April 1979.

## 22. BARGAINING STYLE

Potential challengers to JC: Caddell memo cited in James Wooten, *NYT,* 4 May 1977. Moore cancels meeting with congressional leaders: *AC,* 20 November 1976. Postcard registration; JC calls Mansfield: *AC,* 1 August 1976; *WP,* 5 November 1976. JC meets congressional leaders: *NW,* 29 November 1976. Sorensen's nomination, withdrawal: *The Presidency, 1977,* p. 40; *NYT,* 18 January 1977. JC disregards Democratic leaders in his appointments: John Glenn, *WSJ,* 25 March 1977; Tip O'Neill, *CT,* 20 February 1977; *NYT,* 24 January 1977. Robert T. Griffin appointed: *NYT,* 18 February 1977. JC fails to consult leaders on their policy concerns: HEW: *WSJ,* 25 March 1977; reorganization: *CT,* 20 February 1977; water projects: *NW,* 7 March 1977; Jody Powell on consultations: *New Republic,* 5 March 1977. JC to cut budget/water projects: *The Presidency, 1977, p.* 14. Water projects axed: Transmittal of purposed cuts to Congress, 21 February 1977, *CR,* 95th Cong. 1st Sess., Vol. 123, pp. 5742–5743. Congressional leaders react to JC's cuts: Morris Udall: Champaign (Ill.) *News-Gazette,* 24 February 1977; Lloyd Meeds: *News-Gazette,* 24 February 1977; Gary Hart: *NW,* 7 March 1977. Senate rejects cuts, Bennett Johnston's response: *NYT,* 12 March 1977; Frank Moore's excuse: *WSJ,* 25 March 1977. Bennett Johnston, "government by executive": Remarks in Senate, 10 March 1977, *CR,* Vol. 123, part 6, p. 7127. House blocks water projects cuts: 10 March 1977, Ibid., p. 7138. Republicans help JC on reorganization and Jack Brooks's role: John Osborne, *New Republic,* 5 March 1977; Reorganization: Act as amended, passed in Senate, S626, 3 March 1977, *CR,* Vol. 123, p. 6153. Wertheimer, JC "in terrible shape": *WP,* 7 August 1977. O'Neill warns JC: *WP,* 24 November 1976. Lawrence O'Brien on President and Congress: *WP,* 24 November 1976. Representatives, JC staff, Flowers, O'Neill: M. Tolchin, *NYT Magazine,* 24 July 1977. Energy bill: *NW,* 2 May 1977. National Energy Act: JC speech before Congress, 20 April 1977, *CR,* Vol. 123, pp. H8826–H8827. Byrd and Baker help JC: *The Presidency, 1977,* p. 16. Korean commitment, Byrd maneuvers: *U.S. Defense Policy: Weapons, Strategy and Commitments* (Washington, D.C.: Congressional Quarterly, 1978),

p. 43. JC depreciates Congress: on Congressional recess, *NW,* 7 March 1977; JC will go to people: *NYT Magazine,* 24 July 1977; Senator reacts to JC accusations: *CST,* 30 September 1977. JC strands supporters: Ullmann: *Presidency 1977,* p. 9; Muskie supports rebate; JC withdraws support: 19 April 1977, *CR,* Vol. 123, part 9, pp. 11254–11255. Senate passage with amendments: 29 April 1977, Ibid., pp. 12958–12959. House debate and passage: 8 March 1977, Ibid., 6582–6635, 6635–6636. O'Neill on B-1 bomber: *NYT Magazine,* 24 July 1977. Page note on JC tax plan: Chicago, *Daily News,* 28 April 1977. JC to Boren on deregulation: 19 October 1976, *Campaign 1976,* I, 2, pp. 1060–61. JC encourages filibuster: *CT,* 1 October 1977; Schlesinger promises no interference: *WP,* 5 October 1977; Mondale ends filibuster: *WP,* 5 October 1977; Abourezk, "The puzzle . . .": *NYT,* 9 October 1977. Natural gas deregulation: Mondale: 3 October 1977, *CR,* Vol. 123, pp. S16152–S16170, S16323–S16325, JC legis. record: *The Presidency, 1977,* pp. 12–13, 31–32.

### Adaptation

JC accuses news media: *CT,* 25 May 1977. JC and aides at Camp David: *National Journal,* 13 January 1979. JC lobbies on canal treaty: Frank Moore/ai and author observation. Moore let me sit in his office for about two hours while he and aides dealt favors on the phone. See also *NW,* 27 March 1978. Panama Canal Treaty: White House lobby efforts: *U.S. Defense, op. cit.,* p. 109; details of treaty passage: Ibid., pp. 99–116. JC on arms: *President Carter 1978,* pp. 3, 39.

### Pattern Maintenance

JC's conflict with O'Neill: firing of Robert Griffin: *CT,* 29 July 1978; O'Neill still for civil service reform: *WP,* 2 August 1978; tries to repair relations with White House: *WP,* 11 August 1978. Footnote on Griffin, Strauss: *CT,* 4 August 1978. Confrontation on energy: "accept the political blame": *NW,* 16 April 1979; Congress trying to "hoodwink the American people": *NW,* 7 May 1979; Congress manipulating windfall profits tax: *NW,* 6 August 1979. Bad timing on tax bill: *WP,* 11 August 1978; Brademas on bill: *CST,* 15 August

1978. JC's congressional support: *President Carter 1978*, p. 13. JC offers favors for support: *NW*, 16 October 1978. JC's support in foreign policy: *President Carter 1978*, p. 38. Byrd complains about JC: *CT*, 20 February 1977; JC's ineffective lobbying: *CT*, 19 June 1977: JC's proposals "ill conceived": *WP*, 12 June 1977. O'Neill lets resentment show: *NW*, 20 February 1978. ". . . pack of crooked whores": *NW*, 20 February 1978. Congressional Budget Office on oil production: *NW*, 4 June 1978. Kennedy attacks JC's health plan: *WP*, 29 July 1978. JC's social security cuts: *National Journal*, 27 January 1979. JC to Moynihan on cuts: *NYT*, 1 April 1979. Congress independent: Dan Rostenkowski quoted, *CT*, 14 November 1976.

*Russia, the Middle East, and China*

JC on human rights: Inaugural address, text, *The Presidency, 1977*, pp. 4a, 5a. State Department warns Soviet on Sakharov: *NW*, 28 February 1977. U.S. canvassing UN Human Rights Commission: *WP*, 12 February 1977. Sakharov gets JC letter: *CT*, 20 February 1977. State Department warns JC: *NW*, 8 February 1977. JC at UN: *NYT* 18 March 1977; Jordan on JC, human rights, *Time*, 7 March 1977. Vance's package for Soviets: *NYT*, 3 April 1977. Gromyko's press conference: *NYT*, 1 April 1977; Christopher Wren,

*NYT*, 1 April 1977. JC won't back down: JC press conference, 30 March 1977, *The Presidency, 1977*, p. 73a. JC to high-school students: *NW*, 30 May 1977. Vance and Gromyko reach SALT II framework: *WP*, 22 May 1977. Human rights ignored in June meeting: *Time*, 27 June 1977. Gromyko, "a firm intention . . .": *NW*, 10 October 1977. JC addresses Congress on SALT II: *WP*, 19 June 1978. Sadat says Begin "negative and backward": *WP*, 20 July 1978. Sadat and Saudi Arabia: Joseph Kraft, *WP*, 10 August 1978. Camp David "uniquely isolated": *NW*, 18 September 1978. Background and details of Camp David summit: *Time*, 11, 25 September and 2 October 1978. Sadat's "soft spot" for JC: *NW*, 2 October 1978. Begin leaves settlement issue to Knesset: *WP*, 23 September 1978. Camp David "step-by-step" approach: *Time*, 2 October 1978. Kissinger praises JC: *NYT*, 19 September 1978. CBS, Gallup polls: *Time*, 2 October 1978. JC announces China "normalization": Text, *President Carter 1978*, p. 161a. Early Vance trip to China: *NW*, 5 September 1977. "Massive applause . . .": JC TV address, 15 December 1978, CBS Special/author's notes. Response to China moves: *NW*, 15 January 1979. Celebration of "normalization": *NW*, 15 January 1979. Teng's tour of U.S.: *Time*, 12 February 1979. Sadat not attend second Camp David: *WP*, 26 February 1979. Begin refuses: *WP*, 28 February 1979. JC publicly invites Sadat: *WP*, 28 February 1979.

## 23.  ROLLER COASTER: THE POLITICAL FRONT

JC remarks on Palestinian homeland: *NYT*, 17 March 1977. Siegel's resignation: *NW*, 20 March 1978. Labor problems: *The Presidency, 1977* (Washington, D.C.: Congressional Quarterly, 1978), pp. 6–7. Bakke case: *CST*, 22 August 1977. Vernon Jordan charges indifference, JC says remarks demagogic: *CST*, 26 July 1977; Tom Wicker, *NYT*, 29 July 1977. Abzug fired: *NW*, 22 January 1979. Mayors Conference: *NYT*, 12 December 1978. JC, Cook County Democrats: *CT*, 29 March 1978. JC, California Democrats: Champaign (Ill.) *News-Gazette*, 20 February 1979. JC and polls: Harris Survey, *CT*, 10 October 1977; CBS–NYT, 30 January 1979. Bert Lance affair: *The Presidency, 1977*, pp. 1–2; *USN*, 19 September 1977; *CST*, 28 August 1977. Powell and Percy: AP, Champaign (Ill.) *News Gazette*, 14 September 1977. "Bert, I'm proud of you": *WP*, 19 August 1977. Comptroller Report: Inquiry into Certain Matters Relating to T. Bertram Lance and Various Financial Institutions, Comptroller of the Currency, Washington, D.C., 3 volumes, 1977. JC slides in polls: *WP*, 10 October 1977. JC tour abroad: *WP*, 6 January 1978; *NYT*, 8 January 1978. Young on Angola: *NW*, 3 January 1977. Young on "colonialism": *NYT*, oo May 1977. Jordan's insults: *USN*, 27 February 1978. JC vs. Califano: *WP*, 12 January 1978. JC, staff, and Cabinet at Camp David: *WP*, 18 April 1978; *NW*, 2 April 1978. Reorganization of JC staff: *WP*, 19 April 1978. Midge Costanza: *USN*, 24 April, 1978. Rafshoon on board: *NYT*, 9 September 1978. Staff-Cabinet conflicts: *WP*, 18 April 1978. Young on political prisoners: *NW*, 27 August 1979. Energy Dept. problems: *Time*, 19 June 1979.

*Polls*

JC in polls: CBS-*NYT*, polls reported in *NYT;* Harris poll: *CT*, 10 October 1977; Summer, 1978, in *WP*, 5 June 1978. Mideast summit impact: *CST*, 8 October 1978 and *CST*, 8 April 1979; Summer, 1979: *CST*, 8 May 1979, and *NYT*, 7 June 1979.

*Retrenchment at Camp David*

JC cancels energy speech: *CT*, 5 July 1979. Details on JC "Domestic Summit" at Camp David: *NW*, 16 July 1979, 23 July 1979, and 30 July 1979; *WP*, 14 July 1979; *Time*, 23 July 1979. "Lost sense of trust": *CT*, 15 July 1979. Meg Greenfield on Camp David meeting: "A Government in Exile," *NW*, 23 July 1979. Democratic governors endorse JC: *CST*, 10 July 1979. Guest reactions: *WP*, 9 September 1979. Broder on JC openness: *CST*, 18 July 1979. Speculation on JC's health: *CT*, 15 July 1979. Heller on JC speech: *Time*, 23 July 1979. JC energy speech: 15 July 1979, *Vital Speeches of the Day*, 15 August 1979. Details on Cabinet and staff reorganization: *NW*, 30 July 1979, 6 August 1979; *Time*, 30 July 1979. JC second call-in show: PBS, 30 October 1979. JC "promoting his problems . . ."; "gutted his domestic policy team": *NW*, 30 July 1979. Blumenthal and Califano on departure: *NW*, 30 July 1979. Adams on "campaigning and governing": *WP*, 26 September 1979. Young resignation: *NW*, 27 August 1979. JC summons press: *NW*, 30 July 1979. JC on *Delta Queen: NYT*, 17–24 August 1979, press ground rules: *NW*, 27 August 1979. Post–Camp David polls: *Time*, 10 September 1979; Eizenstat on "bum rap": *CST*, 17 September 1979.

## 24.  THE CAMPAIGNER AS PRESIDENT AS CAMPAIGNER

George Meany on "the most conservative president": *WP*, 10 November 1978. Congressional poll on JC: *CT*, 6 August 1979. O'Neill on Kennedy: *WP*, 11 September 1979. Leaders of Congress leave allegiances open: *CT*, 16 September 1979. JC would "whip his ass": *NYT*, 13 June 1979. JC as "experienced outsider": *CSM*, 8 November 1978. White House invitations: Interview with JC, *USN*, 28 August 1978. Florida black woman: *NW*, 6 October 1979. Invitations to see Pope: *WP*, 6 October 1979. RC trips: *USN*, 5

November 1979. "If Carter would only . . .": quoted in Evans and Novak, *CST*, 6 October 1979. JC warns Congress on White House favors: *CST*, 22 September 1979. JC expects Cabinet to be "actively engaged": *NYT*, 7 November 1979. "I've never seen . . .": Basil Talbott, *CST*, 17 November 1979. JC on N.H. heating oil: David Broder, *WP*, 12 September 1979. Jane Byrne at dinner for mayors: *Time*, 5 November 1979. Neil Goldschmidt on aid to Chicago: *Time*, 3 December 1979. JC appointments pick off potential Kennedy supporters: David Broder, *WP*, 12 September 1979. Census patronage: "Patronage Is Still Alive," *National Journal*, 7 April 1979. JC mobilizes Hispanics: *National Journal*, 10 March 1979. JC's black appointments: Louis Martin, *Fact Sheet 108*, Washington: The White House, January 1980. JC collecting endorsements: *Time*, 5 November 1979. NEA endorses JC: *CST*, 14 October 1979. Kennedy lead in polls: *CT*, 12 November 1979. Kennedy announces candidacy: *WP*, 8 November 1979. Mudd interview: CBS Report, 4 November 1979.

### Second Chance: Iran and Afghanistan

Background and details of American embassy takeover: *USN*, 19 November 1979; *Time*, 19 November 1979; *NW*, 26 November 1979. State Department concedes Iranian officials have not left U.S.: *CST*, 25 December 1979. Background details on Russian invasion of Afghanistan and the American response from *NYT*, *WP*, *NW*, December, January, and February 1980. JC's "new strategic doctrine": Text, *NYT*, 24 January 1980. Watson, American diplomats in USSR: *WP*, 8 January 1980. JC and the Christmas trees: *Time*, 24 December 1979.

### Oval Office Strategy

Kennedy criticizes Shah: *NW*, 17 December 1979. JC accuses Kennedy of hurting hostages: *NW*, 17 December 1979. JC will not campaign during crisis:

"Meet the Press," NBC News, 20 January 1980/author's notes. Strauss concedes JC has time to campaign: Strauss Interview, CBS Evening News, 12 February 1980/author's notes. JC phones Olympic hockey team: "Winter Olympics," ABC, 24 February 1980/author's notes. Mondale, Bergland work Iowa: *NYT*, 2 January 1980. JC uses phone to campaign: Evans and Novak, *CST*, 7 February 1980. White House socials: participants/ai. JC tells students draft registration "symbolic": *NYT*, 16 February 1980. Student on JC invite: Champaign *Daily Illini*, 14 February 1980. "Normal relationship with Teheran": *WP*, 16 February 1980. JC to Legionnaires: *NYT*, 20 February 1980. JC aides allude to Kennedy: *Time*, 5 November 1979. Brock, "time to take the gloves off": *NYT*, 2 January 1980. Kennedy criticizes JC foreign policy: Speech at Georgetown University, 28 January 1980/author's notes. Kennedy, "war hysteria": *WP*, 2 February 1980. Kennedy's mock debate: *WP*, 8 February 1980. Kennedy says JC seeking "blank check": Speech at Harvard University/transcript. Carter, aides accuse Kennedy of being self-serving: *CST*, 14 February 1980. Accuse Reagan of hurting nation: Mary McGrory, *CT*, 16 April 1980. Poll on Johnson, bombing in North Vietnam: John Mueller, cited in James Nathan and James Oliver, *United States Foreign Policy and World Order* (Boston: Little, Brown, 1976), pp. 559–60. Criticism of TV treatment of Ted Kennedy: Tom Shale, *WP*, 30 January 1980. On JC problems: James Reston, "Doubts in the Night," *NYT*, 20 February 1980.

## 25. THOUGHT: SUBSTANCE AND PROCESS

### Stylistic Populism

JC's "insurgency of the middle": William Schneider as cited in James W. Caeser, *Presidential Selection: Theory and Development*. (Princeton: University Press, 1979), p. 252; "pits . . . entire nation,": *Ibid*.

### Power

JC TV ad: "Dreams": *Campaign Commercials*. JC on Tolstoy: *WNB*, p. 31.

### Virtue

JC on "domestic and foreign policy action" and "our personal problems . . .; *WNB*, p. 141, 156. On public officials setting standard: speech, National Religious Broadcaster, 9 October 1976, *Campaign 1976*, I, 2, p. 972: For similar statements to CIA employees; speech August 16, 1978 in *Weekly Compilation of Presidential Documents*, August 21, 1978, Vol. 14, No. 33, (Washington D.C.: Federal Register, National Archives, Records Services, GSA), p. 1436. He said: "You have to be even more clean, more decent and more honest than almost any persons who serve in government, because the slightest mistake on your part is highly publicized . . . whereas your great achievements . . . quite often are not publicized and are not recognized, and they certainly are never exaggerated." National and international standards: speech, United Nations, 13 May 1976, *Campaign 1976*, I, 1, p. 194. JC asks "sacrificial support": quoted in *LAT*, 3 May 1976. JC cares about people on assembly lines: Interview with Bill Moyers, 6 May 1976, *Campaign 1976*, I, 1, pp. 178–79. JC volunteer effort as governor: W. L. Miller, *Yankee from Georgia: The Emergence of Jimmy Carter*. (New York: New York Times Books, 1978), p. 179; as candidate, speech at Notre Dame, 10 October 1976, *Campaign 1976*, I, 2, pp. 996–97. Political, moral stewardship: He didn't see any conflict: Speech 21 March 1976, Wes Pippert *Spiritual Journey of Jimmy Carter* (New York: Macmillan, 1978), p. 115; and "never detected": Southern Baptist Brotherhood Commission, 16 June 1978, Wes Pippert, *op. cit.*, p.

115. Religious virtue: "I know the reassurance . . .": Interview with Ralph Blodgett, *Liberty Magazine*, October 1975, in *Campaign 1976*, I, 2, p. 975; "I believe there is . . .": Pippert, *op. cit.*, p. 243. "I cling to the principle . . .": Interview with religious broadcasters, 9 October 1976, *Campaign 1976*, I, 2, p. 967. Religion, campaign: On JC and hell: John Osborne, *New Republic*, 20, 27 August 1977, p. 12; RC and JC praying: *CT*, 22 September 1976. JC on hell: Reverend Collins/ai; hedging on homosexuals: Robert Scheer, "Playboy Interview: *Campaign 1976* I, 2. p. 946–47, 964. JC on women and Bible: *AC*, 25 October 1976; straddles split in Plains Baptist Church: James Hefley and Marti Hefley, *The Church That Produced a President* (New York: Wyden Books, 1977), p. 234. Robert Bellah quote and other background: Barnard F. Donahue "The Political Use of Religious Symbols," *Review of Politics*, January 1974, pp. 48–59. On conflicting public, religious values. Reinhold Niebuhr, *Moral Man: Immoral Society* (New York: Charles Scribner's Sons, 1936), pp. 90–95, 257ff. Page footnote: Doris Kearns, *Lyndon Johnson and the American Dream* (New York; Harper and Row, 1976). Reinhold Niebuhr (on Nixon): "The King's Chapel and the King's Court," *Christianity and Crisis*, 4 August 1969.

### Humility and Pride

"I would always remember . . ." Interview with Ralph Blodgett, October 1976, *Campaign 1976*, I, 2, p. 981. Not like Johnson: "Playboy Interview," *Campaign 1976*, I, 2, p. 964. "Christ admonishes": Interview with religious broadcasters, *Campaign 1976*, I, 2, p. 969. No unhealthy power drives: Interview with Bill Moyers, *Campaign 1976*, I, 1, pp. 165, 178. Reasons for not speaking out on Vietnam: Robert Scheer, "Playboy Interview," *Campaign 1976*, I, 2, pp. 948–49. Playboy interview as christian witnessing: Interview with religious broadcasters, 9 October 1976, *Campaign 1976*, I, 2, p. 973. Learning, Russians: Interview with Frank Reynolds, 31 December 1979, ABC, transcript, author's files. Virtue motif: Robert Sheer, "Jimmy We Hardly Know Y'All," *Playboy*,

November 1976, p. 190. Kierkegaard summarized: Ernest Becker, *The Denial of Death*, (New York: The Free Press, 1973), pp. 87–88.

### Creativity

Lawrence Kubie on creativity: *Neurotic Distortion of the Creative Process* (Lawrence, Kan.: University of Kansas Press, 1958), pp. 58, 141; RCS on JC: in Miller, *op. cit.*, p. 31. JC uses lists: as Robert Scheer, "Playboy Interview," *Campaign 1976*, I, 2, p. 943; Stuart Eizenstat/ai; for speeches: Harvey Shapiro, "A conversation with Jimmy Carter, *The New York Times Book Review*, 19 June 1977. For his use of lists for decision making, see Hedrick Smith, Problems of a Problem Solver," *NYT Magazine*, 8 January 1978. Diagrams poetry: Shapiro, *op. cit.* Recites Thomas: Kandy Stroud, *How Jimmy Won* (New York: William Morrow, 1977), pp. 142–43. Mailer, JC on Kier-

kegaard: Norman Mailer, "The Search for Carter," *NYT Magazine*, 26 September 1976. JC on Thomas, Niebuhr: Shapiro, *op. cit.* JC themes, trial and error: Richard Reeves. "Trial-and-Error Presidency of Jimmy Carter," *CST*, 23 July 1977. Campaign themes, Biden on love: Allen Eberhard, *WP*, 25 April 1976; Fletcher Knebel, *Dark Horse* (Garden City, New York: Doubleday, 1972). Common ground themes: Elizabeth Drew, *American Journal* (New York: Vintage, 1978), pp. 193, 212: Mailer, *op. cit.*, p. 72; on Hollywood party: *AC*, 23 August 1976; Brooklyn neighborhoods: *Campaign 1976*, I, 2, p. 705. Intimacy themes: fear of sickness: Speech to Georgia Psychiatrists Association, 9 September 1972, *Addresses*, pp. 149–50; urine retention, *WNB*, p. 43; Montezuma's revenge: *NW*, 26 February 1979, p. 41; baseball manager: NBC 17 October 1979/author's notes. "Carter had not given us an idea": James Fallows, "The Passionless Presidency," *Atlantic Monthly*, May 1979, p. 42.

### 26. PERSONALITY

Most of the data used to illuminate the personality of Jimmy Carter in this chapter is taken from previous chapters, where the specific references are given. Only data cited for the first time in this chapter will be noted. The analysis of the personality of Jimmy Carter is based on the theories of Karen Horney, *Neurosis and Human Growth* (New York: W. W. Norton, 1950). Other personality theorists or psychobiographers consulted were Heinz Kohut, *The Analysis of Self* (New York: International Universities Press, Inc., 1971), Otto Kernberg, *Borderline Conditions and Pathological Narcissism* (New York: Jacob Aronson, 1975), and James David Barber, *The Presidential Character* (Englewood Cliffs, N.J.: Prentice-Hall, 1977). For my methodology in interpreting the personalities of public figures see "Psychobiography: Contributions to Political Science," J. Knutson, ed., *Handbook of Political Psychology* (San Francisco: Jossey-Bass Publishers, 1973, pp. 296–321.

JC sees personality as key to campaign: *AC*, 13 February 1975. RCS recalls conversation on Barber's types: Interview with Michael Dixon, Chicago *News*, 2–3 April 1977. Barber visits JC: The *Presidential Character*, pp. 497–498; calls it "best book": Madison (Wisc.) *Capital Times*, 29 April 1976. JC on being "positive-active"; *AC*, 13 September 1976; to reporters, (in later edition) James David Barber, *op. cit.*, pp. 498–499. In *WNB*, (pp. 27, 49, 126, 149, 162) Carter talks of how hard he worked at various jobs and how much he liked them—indications that he is in Barber's "positive-active" category. Peter Bourne on JC's "inner security": Chicago *News*, 31 July and 1 August 1976. RCS on JC is ideal combination: Interview with Myra McPherson, *WP*, 21 March 1976. Also RCS, interview with Wes Pippert, UPI, 15 July 1976.

### Surface Traits

JC thinks of everything himself: Americus friend/ai. JC on Morris Udall: quoted by Bill Shipp, *AC*, 4 August 1975. JC would fire aide who lied: *CST*, 23 October 1977. On Meir, Schmidt, Ball, and Cohen: *WNB*, p. 143; *NW* 18 October 1976; Martin Schram, *Running for President* (New York: Simon and Schuster, 1977), p. 174. Upgrades self: *Campaign 1976*. Plains press conference, 13 August 1976/author's transcript.

### A Guide . . .

JC an enigma: Eleanor Randolph, "The Carter Complex," *Esquire Magazine*, November, 1977, pp. 166, 184. Attributes of the idealized self, "This basic attitude . . .": grandiose tendencies: Karen Horney, *op. cit.* pp. 194–95. As Horney notes (p. 191) typologies are not perfect: people differ in their gifts

and there may be intermediate types. Origins, vulnerabilities of idealized self: pp. 23–24, 35, 86–87; underlying isolation: pp. 48, 155–65, 292; the search for glory: pp. 34–38; self-centeredness: 291–92; drive for success: 25–31.

### . . . Toward Understanding Carter

External questioning: on Vernon Jordan: *WP*, 29 July 1977; George Meany: Nicholas Lemann, *Washington Monthly*, September 1978, p. 22. Attacks Atlanta *Constitution*: 00 February 1976. On the Washington establishment: Elizabeth Drew, *American Journal*, (New York: Vintage, 1978) Jack Carter on critics: *AC*, 12 October 1976. Reacts to Patterson support, Callaway: William Lee Miller, *Yankee from Georgia* (New York: New York Times Books, 1978), pp. 104–106; *NW*, 19 July 1976. On press plane, to Vernon Jordan: Miller, *op. cit.*, pp. 101–102. On JC's blowing hot and cold: Kandy Stroud, *How Jimmy Won*, (New York: William Morrow, 1977), p. 133. Friends on JC detachment: Warren Fortson, Georgia friend/ais. Charles Kirbo and Elliot Levitas quotes: *NW*, Spring 1976. JC lacks governor's support: Jules Witcover, *Marathon*, (New York: New American Library, 1977), p. 117; Martin Schram, *op. cit.*, p. 94; also *NW*, 26 July 1976. JC on Litton: Address at Jerry Litton Memorial, 15 October 1976, *Campaign 1976*, I, 2, pp. 1031–33. JC advises Jerry Brown: Robert Keefe/ai. JC with schoolchildren: Interview, 21 February 1976, Robert Turner, *I'll Never Lie to You* (New York: Ballantine, 1976), pp. 5–6. JC, "I could have left them . . .": Michael Pousner, New York *Daily News*, 26 May 1976. On RC as adviser: Georgia friend/ai; CBS tape of Ed Rabel. Other admirers on JC virtues: Theodore Sorensen, AP interview, 16 July 1976; Robert Fallows, "The Passionless Presidency," *Atlantic Monthly*, May 1976. JC, tennis: Atlanta journalist/ai. Foot race, quote: *CST*, 18 September 1979. JC's response to Coleman charge: Press conference, Pond House, 17 August 1976/author's notes.

### Political Relevance

Expansionist-narcissistic personality and success: Horney, *op. cit.*, p. 312; overconfidence, self-centeredness, defensiveness: pp. 321, 310–16; On the serious man: Hugh Sidey, *CST*, 27 April, 1980.

### System Impact

JC on incumbency: James Reston, *NYT* 21 May 1980. Carter influenced by Burns: James MacGregor Burns/ai. Burns received a call from Patrick Caddell on Sunday, July 15; he was calling for the President whose speech that night would carry an emphasis similar to Burn's own in his book, *Leadership*.

# Interviews, Letters, Questionnaires

## Interviews

Philip H. Alston, Jr., 14 October 1976; Patrick Anderson, 15 August 1976; Frank Andrews, 5 October 1976 (GRt); Joe Andrews, 9 July 1977 (t); June Davis Andrews, 18 October 1977 (DRt); Charles E. Bacon, 30 May 1977; Joseph Bacon, 26 May 1977; Mary Beazley, 1 September 1977; William E. Blair, 29 October 1976 (GR), 20 September 1977 (GRt); A. L. Blanton, 30 May 1977; Julian Bond, 20 August 1976; Peter G. Bourne, 31 August 1977; Mary Elizabeth Gordy Braunstein, 20 October 1977 (JFt); Thomas B. Brenner, 12 Nov. 1977 (CSt); Tom Brophy, 25 October 1976; Gayle Broussard, 12 November 1977 (CSt); Bryan Brown, 3 December 1977 (CSt); Moody B. Brown, 13 November 1977 (CSt); James MacGregor Burns, 3 June 1980 (t); Charles E. Campbell, 15 September 1977 (GRt); Alton Carter, 19 August 1976; Hugh Carter, 15 August 1976, 29 September 1976 (GR); Hugh Carter, Jr., August 1979; Lillian Carter, August 1976, 28 September 1976 (GR); Lynda Charleston, 13 August 1976; Arthur A. Cheokas, 2 June 1979; Rachael and Tyler Clark, 27 May 1977; B. A. Clendinning, 29 October 1976 (GRt); Warren Colegrove, 4 December 1977 (CSt); Rev. Fred Collins, 31 October 1977 (DDt); Capt. Roy B. Cowdrey, 19 November 1977 (CSt); Rev. Elroy Cruz, 27 September 1977 (GRt); Beau Cutts, 15 September 1977 (GRt); Helen Dewar, 13 August 1976; Stuart Eizenstat, 31 August 1979; Thelma Farewell, 27 September 1977 (GRt); Lowell Fitch, 19 November 1977 (CSt); Joseph P. Flanagan, 13 November 1977 (CSt); Dr. H. F. Folsom, Fall 1977 (JFt); Rembert Forrest, 20 October 1977 (DRt); Rosalind L. Forrest, 28 May 1977; Ben W. Fortson, Jr., 16 September 1977 (GRt); Warren Fortson, 30 September 1976 (GR), 14 October 1976 (BG); Rev. R. L. Freeman, 12 October 1976; John Gabusi, 24 May 1979; David Gambrell, 27 September 1976 (GRt); Doris Wiggins Garrett, 20 October 1977 (DRt); Laurence Gellerstedt, Jr., 29 April 1977 (GRt); Betty Godwin, 27 May 1977; L. E. Godwin, Jr., 13 June 1977; Fannie Surasky Gordy, 39 October 1977 (JFt); M. Lorene Gordy, 20 October, 1977 (JFt); Seli Groves, 16 September 1977 (GRt); Robert Hadden, 3 December 1977 CSt); Herbert Hafif, May 1977 (t); Justice Robert H. Hall, 15 June 1978 (DRt); Richard Harden, 26 August 1977 (t), 7 September 1977 (GRt); William L. Harper, 18 August 1978 (NCD); Roy V. Harris, 25 October 1976 (GR); Brooks Hays, 31 December 1976; Rev. Tom Henry, 26 September 1977 (GRt); Louise Herrington, 15 October 1977 (DRt); Steven Hess, May 1979; Charles Hicks, 15 August 1976; Peggy Hicks, 19 August 1976; Brown Creighton Hodges, 25 August 1978; Rev. John Henry Holley, 3 June 1977; Al Holloway, October 1978 (NCD); Irene Horne, 2 June 1977; Evelyn Lewis Hudson, 5 October 1977 (DRt); Rev. Theodore Jackson, 29 October 1976 (JRt); Richard Johnson, 31 October 1977 (DRt); Rebekah Williams Karr, 15 October 1977 (DRt); Robert Keefe, 25 May 1979; C. B. King, 12 October 1976; Annie Mae Kitchens, 3 June 1977; Charles H. Kirbo, 30 September 1976 (GR); James M. Kittelman, 18 July 1977 (t); William Lalor, 15 October 1976 (GRt); Ruby Watson Lamb, 25 May 1977; W. C. Lamb, Sr., 29 September 1976 (GR); Richard Laning, 5 October 1976 (GRt); Robert J. Lipshutz, 30 September 1976 (GR); Robert M. Logan, Jr., 11 October 1976; Thomas Lowery, 15 October 1977 (DRt); M. Louise McBee, 9 July 1977 (t); Grace Wiggins McCoy, 19 October 1977 (DRt); Pete McDuffey, 4 October 1977 (NCD); Agnes McRainey, July 1977 (LC); George Mandus, 20 July 1978 (DCt); McKim Marriot, 7 November 1977 (JFt); Thomas O. Marshall, 21 September 1977 (GRt); Janet S. Merritt, 21 September 1977 (GR); Austin ("Blu") Middleton, 6 October 1976 (CSt); Gary E. Miller, 17 June 1977 (t), 5 September 1977 (t); Frank Moore, 1 September 1977; Kaye Morris, 30 May 1977; Mr. & Mrs. L. K. Moss, August 1978 (DC); Bill Murray, 15 August 1976; J. Frank Myers, 16 September 1977 (GRt); William M. Nixon, 27 September 1976 (GR); Doris Cosby Osborne, 20 October 1977 (DRt); Tom Ottenad, 1 September 1977; Carl Ostertag, 19 November 1977 (CSt); Randy Oven, 13 April 1978 (DCt); Magda Palacai, 17 August 1976; Alexandra Palamiotis, 27 September 1977 (GRt), 1 June 1977 (BG); Daniel Patillo, 19 September 1977 (GRt); Milo Pennington, 27 September 1977 (GRt); S. Thomas Peterson, 24 May 1977; Richard Pettys, 28 August 1978; Wes Pippert, 15 August 1976 (BG), 6 February 1979 (DR); William Pope, 6 September 1978 (NCD); John Pope, 1 June 1977; Olivia Preston, 14 August 1976; Eleanor Randolph, 13 August 1976; Kenneth Reich, 14 August 1976; John Riley, 29 December 1977 (CSt); Duane Riner, 1 September 1978 (NCD); Hoyt Robinson, 28 September 1977 (GRt); William H. Roper, 18 August 1978 (NCD); Robert Rowan, 28 October 1976 (GRt); Albert H. Rusher, 5 October 1976 (GRt); George Saliba, 12 June 1980 (SWt); Richard Salter, 28 September 1977 (GRt); Rita Samuels, 26 October 1976 (GRt); Carl Sanders, 30 October 1976 (GRt); Miriam Timmerman Saylor, 21 July 1977, 8 December 1976; Robert Scott, 5 October 1976 (GRt); Al H. Seckinger, 18 October 1977 (DRt); Elaine Shannon, 13 August 1976; William A. Shipp, 21 August 1978 (NCD);

---

Interviews were done by author in person, except as otherwise noted. Initials are those of research assistants; "T" is for a telephone interview.

Paul Simon, May 1979; Roy Smallwood, 12 November 1977 (CSt); Allie M. Smith, 3 June 1977; Alma Solomon, 27 May 1977; Walter Solomon, 27 May 1977; Gloria Carter Spann, 27 May 1977; Rev. Glen Spivey, 1 June 1977; John H. Stembler, 14 October 1976 (GRt); R. E. Sullivan, 19 September 1977 (GRt); A. H. Sutherland, June 1977; Lottie Wise Tanner, 16 August 1976, 13 October 1976; Kenneth H. Thomas, Jr., 29 October 1977 (JF); Mary Anne Thomas, 31 May 1977, 2 June 1977; Fletcher Thompson, 20 July 1978 (DCt); 21 August 1978 (NCDt); Kathleen Green Thompson, 15 October 1977 (DRt); Roy Thompson, 1 June 1977; Russell Thorton, 27 October 1976 (GRt); Ida Lee Timmerman, 26 May 1977; Albert Trottier, 23 September 1977 (GRt); Ruby Trottier, 23 September 1977 (GRt); Ernest Turner, 28 September 1976 (GR); Norman L. Underwood, 16 September 1977 (t); Mrs. C. J. Vaughn, 19 August 1976; DeDe Voigt, March 1979 (DR); Martin Wagner, 21 September 1977 (GRt); Nelle Walters, 18 August 1976; Hanes Walton, Jr., 26 May 1977 (t); Bowman Wiley, 1 June 1977; Curtis Wilkie, 31 August 1976; Frank Williams, 28 September 1976 (GR); Virginia Williams, 28 September 1976 (GRt); Betty Wise, 29 September 1976 (GR); William E. Wise, 29 September 1976 (GR); B. T. Wishard, June 1977; Dot Wood, 19 October 1978 (NCD); Leonard Wright, 29 October 1976 (GR); Delmar Yoder, 20 September 1977 (GRt); Andrew Young, 11 October 1976; W. Leroy Young, 29 May 1977

## Letters

James Abbott, 25 April 1977; Joe Andrews, 16 May 1977, 22 August 1978; Steve Ball, 16 June 1977; Arthur K. Bolton, 24 May 1977, 6 July 1977; Julian Bond, 3 June 1977; J. W. Bowen, 2 May 1977; Moody B. Brown, 10 April 1978; Harold Bush-Brown, 7 June 1977; Sam Caldwell, 23 June 1977, 11 April 1978; Francis J. Callahan, 20 January 1978; Howard H. Callaway, 31 May 1977, 26 July 1977; Charles E. Campbell, 7 April 1978; Ellery Clark, 16 April 1977, 6 May 1977, 7 May 1977, 8 May 1977; Rev. Fred Collins, 4 November 1977; Beau Cutts, 5 September 1978; H. E. Dennison, 21 April 1977; E. D. Dunn, 17 May 1977; Henry L. Edwards, April 1977; James H. Forbes, 25 November 1977; Herbert Hafif, 29 April 1977, 15 September 1977; Robert H. Hall, 27 June 1978; J. Robin Harris, 19 May 1977; Roy V. Harris, 20 September 1977, 13 December 1978; James E. Hendrix, 21 June 1977; Carolyn D. Hess, 20 June 1977; R. Kenneth Jacobs, 25 May 1977; James M. Kittelman, 30 June 1977; Frederick A. Klemm, 31 May 1977; Reba B. Lacy, 16 May 1977; Roth S. Leddick, 8 June 1977, 9 May 1977; C. P. Lemieux, 18 April 1977; J. H. Lucas, 23 April 1977, 19 May 1977; M. Louise McBee, 23 May 1977; Gary E. Miller, 11 September 1978, 30 October 1978; Frances Morrow, 25 April 1977; Reg Murphy, 8 June 1977; David Nordan, 17 May 1977; Howard Norton, 28 October 1977; Brooks Pennington, 20 May 1977; W. Donald Pennington, 24 May 1977, 25 April 1977; Earl R. Pinkston, 18 April 1977; John Pope, 30 August 1978; E. B. Potter, 15 July 1977; Robert J. Shaw, 25 May 1977; D. Wayne Smith, 18 May 1977; William M. Spicer, 19 April 1977, 26 April 1977; Lottie Wise Tanner, 21 October 1977 (ND); Hanes Walton, Jr. 26 May 1977; Harold E. Way, 19 June 1977; Betty Brimson Whittier, 20 July 1977.

## Questionnaires

Helen L. Ashworth; Arthur K. Bolton; Edward C. Brooks; Sam Caldwell; Francis J. Callahan; H. E. Dennison; E. D. Dunn; J. Battle Hall; James E. Hendrix; Carolyn D. Hess; Wayne R. Lippert; Joseph E. Loggins; Brooks Pennington; Guy W. Rutland, Jr.; Foster R. Schulz; C. H. Shaddeau; M. O. Strickler; Harold E. Way.

# Index